The Americans: A Brief History
Third Edition

Third Edition

The Americans
A Brief History

Henry F. Bedford
Phillips Exeter Academy

Trevor Colbourn
University of Central Florida

Under the General Editorship of John Morton Blum,
Yale University

Harcourt Brace Jovanovich, Inc.
New York/San Diego/Chicago/San Francisco/Atlanta
London/Sydney/Toronto

Picture Credits continued on page A-31.

Cover photograph: Cupola of Faneuil Hall, Boston, Massachusetts.
Erik Leigh Simmons from the Image Bank.

ISBN: 0-15-502613-5

Library of Congress Catalog Card Number: 79-88850

Printed in the United States of America

Preface

The most casual observer of the American scene cannot fail to notice the enormous number of historical books, periodicals, and monographs that come from the nation's presses. No other nation boasts such a profusion of textbooks that attempt to describe, analyze, and synthesize its history. The abundance of such publications suggests that people continue to search for history's relevance, an inference that encourages historians to keep publishing new scholarship and new editions.

In this third edition of *The Americans: A Brief History* we have attempted again to achieve brevity without serious omission, to offer interpretation without idiosyncratic distortion, and to interest and inform our readers. To these ends, we have set out themes in the Introduction that seem to unify a study of the American past. Four times, as the book proceeds, we draw back from our chronological narrative to review and reflect on those themes. These brief introductions are designed to complement the interpretations contained in the chapters that follow them.

As we prepared this edition, there were signs of diminished national confidence. Americans began to doubt that the economic graphs would continue to climb from lower left to upper right, to wonder about America's image around the world, to challenge the effectiveness of American political institutions, and to question whether the values that once seemed eternal still unified the American people. It is our belief that this book suggests a historical perspective that will improve Americans' insight into their national character and national institutions. In addition, we hope that our book provides a basis for understanding the nation's past and that it nurtures determination without bluster or arrogance, compassion without condescension, unity without conformity.

Any text must derive substantially from the learning and judgment of others. We are especially grateful to historians who have provided the scholarship that permits us to give more attention to America's ethnic minorities and female majority—attention that deserves a wider audience. For specific suggestions and for general editorial guidance, we are particularly indebted to John M. Blum, Yale University. We wish also to thank the members of the College Department of Harcourt Brace Jovanovich, particularly William J. Wisneski and Paula F. Lewis for their encouragement and patience, and Helen Faye, Arlene Kosarin, Nina Ackerman Indig, and Jenny Peters-Jenks for their excellent contributions to the book. We are grateful for the suggestions and criticisms of Richard D. Schubart and Albert C. Ganley, Phillips Exeter Academy. Andrew W. Hertig, Phillips Exeter Academy, and his students have made conscientious recommendations as a result of their classroom use of the text. For the third edition we are grateful for the suggestions and criticisms of Carol R. Berkin, Baruch College, Robert M. Calhoon, The University of North Carolina at Greensboro, and John M. Murrin, Princeton University. The lists of suggested readings at the end of each chapter are rather arbitrary selections from the available scholarship; we have excluded all journal articles from these lists as well as many important monographs. But every historian cited at the end of each chapter is our unacknowledged collaborator, as are scores of others in the historical fraternity.

HENRY F. BEDFORD
TREVOR COLBOURN

Contents

Chapter 18
Cultural Collision in the 1920s   **409**

Chapter 19
Depression   **433**

Chapter 20
Isolation and Intervention   **457**

1945 — 1980: An Introduction

482

Introduction
What Is an American?

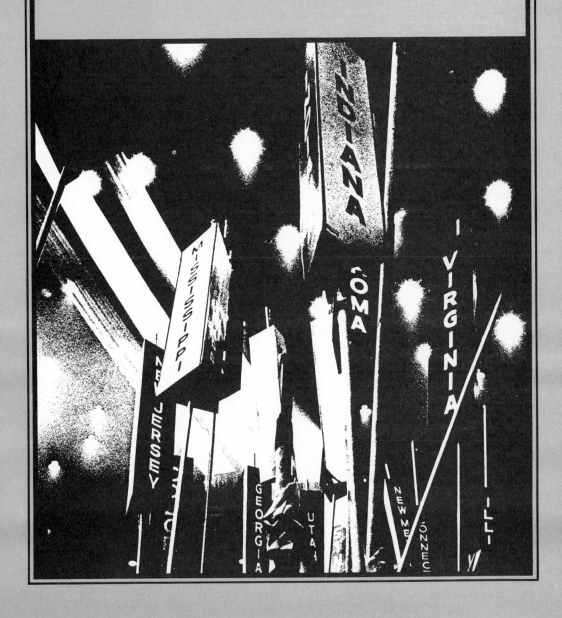

In 1492 Christopher Columbus sailed from southern Spain and landed, after a trying voyage, on San Salvador. Most of the facts about that epic journey are clear, but their interpretation produces questions. Should Columbus be credited with the discovery of a new world? Or should Norse sailors from centuries before? Or Indians before that? Does hoisting a flag and putting foot to sand complete the act of discovery? Or must one also be aware of what has been found, as Columbus was not?

Questions about the meaning of American history have multiplied in the years since the voyages of discovery. All Americans can agree, for instance, that the period between 1861 and 1865 was extraordinary. But not all Americans refer to events of those years as a civil war, nor do they concur on the causes or the results of that conflict. Interpretive disputes about that war fill more than history books; these debates filled the lives of subsequent generations and shaped the history that we, in turn, have inherited from them.

Semantic confusion compounds interpretive difficulty. Even the word "American" is used imprecisely. Citizens of the United States typically rule out all other inhabitants of the Western Hemisphere and assume an exclusive right to be "Americans"; they then argue with one another about what the word means. Before 1900 most people who considered themselves Americans would never have included Indians, whose claim to be 100 percent Americans had obvious merit. Modifiers produce a deceptive precision: German American, Afro-American, patriotic American, deprived American, and, to define who is left out, un-American.

Moreover, the word "American" sounds singular, but the phenomena it describes are plural. The American woman, the black American, the American student, and even the American tourist, are mythical creatures; there are women and blacks and students in America, and wandering tourists abroad, and all resist definitive categorization. Americans come in two sexes, several colors, and all ages, shapes, and sizes. They come from all sections of a country that stretches from Maine to mid-Pacific. They work at various occupations, for which they receive various incomes, which they spend in various ways. They worship various gods, not all of which are religious, and some worship no god at all. They raise children who differ from all the other children in their suburb, block, apartment house, town, or ghetto, and who surely differ from those of any other environment. And, since they raise their children differently from the way their parents did, generations also differ.

Yet Americans know that there is "an American," that there is "an American way of life," that, within the diversity, there is a common bond that unites them. For the word "American" connotes more than citizenship, residence, rights, and identification with the nation or state; "American" also describes a state of mind. Whatever their individual peculiarities, Americans differ less from one another than they do from Russians, Turks, Japanese, or even the English. In the mind of every

American is a set of values, attitudes, habits, customs, morals, traditions, prejudices, and manners that prescribes and limits behavior. An American may reject some or even all of these cultural limitations, but to do so risks ostracism. Even when an individual decides to discard part of his cultural legacy, he usually expects other Americans to be true to their heritage and to play by the old rules.

That heritage and those rules establish an American behavioral perimeter, a boundary that divides the legal from the illegal, the orthodox from the heretical, the normal from the abnormal, the acceptable from what "just isn't done." Some of those limits are described in books of statutes or canon law; others are internal inhibitions that curb the instincts of individuals and restrict the choices from which the nation selects policies. The lives of Americans are regulated by a bewildering variety of political agencies—nation, state, county, municipality, school board, zoning board, and sewer district. In addition, most Americans are subject to family control and voluntarily accept the norms of a host of organizations, such as the Rotary Club, the Knights of Columbus, the American Federation of Musicians, the Urban League, and Delta Kappa Epsilon.

These groups have different objectives and different behavioral limits. Yet, those differences seem details when compared with the important ideals and assumptions that most Americans agree on. Management and employees may differ profoundly or even deadlock during the negotiation of their contract, but both accept most of the clichés Americans use to describe free-enterprise capitalism. Equal opportunity has different meanings in rural Georgia, suburban Illinois, and official Washington, but most Americans concede that equal opportunity is part of a citizen's birthright.

Continuity and Change

The persistence of such ideals as free enterprise and equal opportunity illustrates the continuity of American history; evolving definitions of those phrases illustrate change. Whatever "free enterprise" means in an age of billion-dollar corporations, the union shop, and the Occupational Safety and Health Act, Americans are as dedicated to the concept as they were in the days of small businesses and laissez faire. Likewise, we argue more often about quotas and the details of affirmative action than about the principle of equal opportunity. Change occurs, and conflict ordinarily takes place, at the edge of the behavioral circle, not at the center.

But not always. If Americans share a behavioral perimeter with their contemporaries, it is not precisely the same one that limited their ancestors. Small changes, over time, have gradually altered national character and conduct; major developments—industrialization, emancipation, an explosion of technology—have forced perceptible shifts within a single generation. For most of the nation's history, for instance, Americans believed that the future would inevitably be better than the past. But events in the later twentieth century mock that complacent faith in progress, and the optimism that once sustained expansion, investment, and reform may in consequence be waning, with results we cannot yet calculate.

A corollary to the certainty of automatic progress was the belief of earlier Americans in their collective mission. Whether granted by God, nature, fate, or destiny, Americans had a dispensation from rules that governed others of the world's peoples. Americans thought they had a right to preempt the lands of those who had adopted less advanced means of cultivation, less democratic political institutions, or less Protestant prayers. As the first European settlers had a call to establish "a city on a hill" to be an example for the rest of the world, so their descendants had a manifest destiny to enlarge the country's territory, a duty to uplift less fortunate people on the other side of the world, and a commitment to save humanity from Communism and other political perils.

This sense of national mission was rooted in religious conviction. For most Americans, until relatively recently, God was near at hand; worship, prayer, and alertness to divine purpose were no mere Sunday activities. The sectarian diversity that characterized American religious observance from the outset was less significant than the nearly universal acceptance of Christianity—initially Protestant Christianity. Dispute about doctrinal details prevented the establishment of a national church, but agreement on broad religious principles substituted an unofficial Protestant establishment that shaped the nation's outlook on moral questions for more than two centuries. The United States was born and raised in the Protestant faith, and that upbringing still shows.

Similarly, we were born and raised on the farm, where experience confirmed the moral homilies delivered from Protestant pulpits. Sloth and extravagance were not only sinful but stupid, for hard work and temperance were essential to produce and preserve the harvest. Life on the farm was the godly life, and the self-sufficient farmer, who with God's help brought wealth from the earth, personified virtue. The family farm has provided the model for the family business, and agrarian aspirations, values, and habits have outlasted the farms themselves. Americans still go to school by the agrarian calendar, protect farmers from a competitive market, and subsidize them through crop supports and in several more subtle ways. The nation's agrarian past has, in retrospect, seemed the nation's paradise lost.

The city, by contrast, was imagined as the center of sin, where thieves, "slickers," gamblers, and worse waited to debauch unwary country folk. City people did not produce things; they shuffled papers and manipulated money and otherwise exploited simple, diligent rural residents. This image of the city as the corrupting serpent belies the republic's origins, for the first settlers lived in towns as well as on farms. While a few mavericks sought the woods, most colonists tried to cut them down; the frontier was no sylvan utopia, but a hardship to be endured. Most settlers wanted to move with other people; they preferred an inhabited frontier. Neither the Puritans of Massachusetts nor the first families of Virginia were backwoods hicks.

Yet, paradoxically, as the nation's cities grew, Americans clung to the notion that farming was the good life. This rural outlook, together with faith in progress, Protestant Christianity, and a sense of national mission, have helped differentiate Americans from residents of other lands and from domestic misfits. But the later twentieth century may one day seem one of those times when the behavioral perimeter shifted rather abruptly. The rural past has become for most Americans a nostalgic fantasy rather than a personal experience. Cultural pluralism has undermined Protestant morality. A series of shocks—genocide in Germany, the collapse of civility in American cities, the triumph of totalitarianism abroad—created doubt about uninterrupted progress. And the nation's shiny mission seemed tarnished by manifestations of arrogance and injustice and corruption that could not be explained away as exceptions.

One consequence of a modified behavioral perimeter is difficulty achieving a sympathetic understanding of the society's past. Without a grasp of the importance of Protestant Christianity, for instance, the actions of early white immigrants or early black civil rights activists do not make much sense. Unless the confirmed city-dweller can imagine the hold that rural life had on nineteenth-century Americans, their behavior will seem inexplicable or at best quaint. And those who have given up on progress in the face of intractable present problems will not sense the urgency that inspired abolitionists and New Dealers.

Cultural Checks and Balances

Of course, contemporary Americans have not entirely lost touch with the past, though change may momentarily seem more important than continuity. The nation must constantly redefine liberty, justice, individualism, and the other ideals that guide society. Decisions may produce psychic conflict for the individual and social conflict for the nation, for our ideals often conflict. We are, as historian Michael Kammen has remarked, a people of paradox, conceived in revolution, yet insistent on constitutional procedure. We believe in the peaceful settlement of disputes as well as in the shoot-out, vigilantes, and unconditional surrender. We cheer for Billy the Kid and Bonnie and Clyde as loudly as for Matt Dillon and the G-men. We proclaim a classless society and invent institutions to foster a social hierarchy. We work hard at our

Farming: a way of life

leisure and loaf at our work. For almost four centuries, while we preached thrift, we wasted the continent and lived on the installment plan.

It is tempting, fashionable, and wrong to dismiss these contradictions as hypocrisy. Nor must they be resolved, for they are the cultural equivalents of political checks and balances. As the Founders checked tyranny with conflicting grants of political power, so, through conflicting ideals, society maintains an equilibrium among the competing interests that make up a disparate nation.

From the start, for instance, Americans have held that human equality required no proof; equality was, in Thomas Jefferson's noble phrase, self-evident. But even Jefferson himself did not adhere fully to the ideal he had stated, and neither he nor his contemporaries meant that all individuals were equal in all respects to all other individuals. Forty years after the Declaration of Independence, John Adams wrote Jefferson a letter that sounds like a clarifying footnote: "That all men are born to equal rights is true," Adams began. But, he continued,

to teach that all men are born with equal powers and faculties, to equal influence in society, to equal property and advantages through life, is as gross a fraud, as glaring an imposition on the credulity of the people, as ever was practiced . . . by the self-styled philosophers of the French Revolution.

Those who established the nation's traditions and institutions did not intend to found an equalitarian utopia. Full equality, as they saw it, would have unjustly abridged individual liberty, the right of every American to run up the score in the game of life. In the competition we take to be universal, some individuals best others and inequality results. Tension between the belief in human equality and the desire for individual liberty underlies much of American history. And each individual, each day, must deal with a comparable tension between self and society. The nation's mood at some times emphasizes equality and at others individualism, just as individuals are now self-centered and later socially aware. The tension in society may be creative or crippling, and in individuals productive or paralyzing. But it is always there.

Few Americans spend much energy worrying about the conflict between equality and individual liberty. Both are taken for granted as ideals; if they are incompatible, we live comfortably with the contradiction. We aspire to equality with the Joneses and assume that the Smiths can take care of themselves. We advocate individual initiative when we have achieved equality, and we ask society for equality when we cannot achieve it ourselves.

Like most ideals, human equality has a definition that varies with time, place, and personality. The effort to bring the ideal closer to reality moved Eugene Debs to spread the socialist message and Walter Rauschenbusch to preach the social gospel, Franklin Roosevelt to remember "the forgotten man" and feminists to brand his phrase sexist. Those who have resisted the equalitarian thrust of American society have, for the most part, done so obliquely by emphasizing the monotony of an imaginary society in which everyone would be just like everyone else, or by pointing out that individual liberty would have to be curbed in order to achieve equality.

In fact, equality sometimes comes at the expense of someone's liberty. Should the interest of society in integrated schools displace the right of parents to choose the school their child attends? Does equality of opportunity imply equality of result? Must an equal place at the starting line result in a tie at the finishing tape? She was none too subtle, but a black woman from Georgia answered all the questions with a crisp working definition of equality: "We want," she said, "what you got."

Few Americans would be willing to say aloud that the woman probably had about what she deserved. Yet most of them believe that individual liberty means that one is the master of one's fate, that each person makes his own way in the world in competition with everyone else. The theoretical result of individual liberty is a bustling society dominated by an aristocracy of merit—wise, independent, and enterprising citizens, who have earned their wealth, power, and prestige. "Deserve" and "earn" are two of the most important verbs in the nation's vocabulary. They provide the moral link between people and consequences. An individual must deserve success; an employee must earn his wage; a reward must be related to effort—or the nation's ethic collapses.

The conflict between human equality and individual liberty, or between other opposing ideals, is not a recent development. Americans today, troubled by racial injustice, share with their white ancestors both the equalitarian ideal and the prejudice that has postponed racial harmony. The movement to preserve the environment meets the same economic obstacles conservationists met decades ago. The imperialism that critics have discerned in recent American foreign policy also brought on the war with Mexico, fought by a restless, aggressive, enterprising, grasping generation of Americans more than a century ago.

Henry David Thoreau, who opposed the Mexican war and was something of a misfit in nineteenth-century Massachusetts, once protested that he did "not wish to be regarded as a member of any incorporated society" that he had not formally joined. Thoreau complained that he could not resign from all the societies he had not joined because he could never compile a complete list. He discovered that some of these organizations, such as the Commonwealth of Massachusetts, did not accept resignations. Contemporary American nonconformists will rediscover Thoreau's dilemma. One can renounce American citizenship and find refuge in Canada or Sweden; one can reject the trappings of an American upbringing; one can refuse to study the American past and scorn its relevance. But the burdens of nationality turn out to be deeper than an accent or a craving for hamburger. The American past lingers in the behavioral perimeter, which some present Americans reluctantly inherit and which will profoundly influence the American future.

The Law and the Profits

Modern America does not preserve the infinite variety of the American past. The fact that Swedes once settled along the mid-Atlantic shore, for instance, is now of less significance than the fact that the English and their institutions prevailed along most of the rest of the coastline. Even those settlers who were not English by nationality or inclination became English subjects. English laws and political principles, English currency and economic theory, English Protestantism and its ethic, English customs and English prejudices shaped the society to which newcomers had to adapt. Americans are the cultural heirs of England, even if individual genealogies show Irish, Mexican, or African ancestors.

England governed the colonies for nearly two centuries, and political institutions in the new territory and the political assumptions of its people derive from the British experience. A civil war, a bloodless revolution, and a great deal of constitutional debate in seventeenth-century England had curbed royal power. Three thousand miles of ocean diluted that power still further. Authorities in the colonies, representing the Crown, a proprietor, or a colonizing corporation, permitted delegates of the settlers to join in political decision-making. The House of Burgesses first met in Virginia in 1619; the Fundamental Orders of Connecticut established the representative General Court in 1639; in 1701 William Penn gave in to the demands of Pennsylvanians for a representative assembly. Although governors and representatives wrangled endlessly about prerogatives, the English principle that some regulations require the consent of the governed prevailed.

As colonial assemblies were modeled on Parliament, so institutions of local government resembled those in England. Counties (in Virginia and Maryland) and towns (in New England) enforced local regulations, built roads, and licensed businesses. County clerks recorded wills and the contracts of indentured servants. Sheriffs collected taxes and carried out the decisions of justices of the peace and of the county courts. None of these officials behaved precisely like his counterpart in England, but every colonial bureaucrat drew on the British experience.

That experience was explicitly relevant in the courts. Legal questions tend to reflect the complexity of the society from which they arise. Early cases in the colonies, for instance, stemmed from relatively simple disagreements over wills and property lines. To such disputes colonial courts applied the English common law, which assured familiarity with local circumstance through a local jury and yet established common legal principles throughout the entire realm. Common law was traditional, not legislated, and it existed in the form of decisions, not statutes. Judges applied the wisdom of other judges or abstracted from earlier cases rules that seemed appropriate. The importance of precedent, the insistence on a jury, and above all, the requirement that all citizens of whatever rank bow to the supremacy of law are among the legacies of English justice.

Yet, for all the similarities, Americans are not imitation Englishmen; parts of the heritage have been discarded. Unlike members of Parliament, for instance, American legislators must live in the regions they represent and renew their mandate frequently. American political parties— amorphous, inconsistent, undisciplined—are unlike the political parties of any other nation. American judges have abandoned some of the common-law precepts of their colonial predecessors. So the English heritage has only influenced, not determined, American political and legal assumptions.

Until recently the respect of most Americans for their political institutions bordered on reverence. Washington has become the destination of demonstrators because it is the nation's secular shrine; what appears to be a protest is also a solemn pilgrimage. Even if Americans distrust a particular politician, even if they are cynical about politics in general, they continue to express their aspirations in legislation, to translate their needs into political programs, and to believe that all problems are susceptible to political solutions. Americans respond to injustice with the remark that "there ought to be a law."

Underlying the American faith in political institutions are several assumptions. Most Americans believe, for instance, that the ideal form of political organization is a stable government responsible to its electorate. Although the twentieth century has conclusively demonstrated that unrepresentative governments can achieve mass support, Americans nevertheless tend to regard these examples as temporary and somehow improper. Yet, for many people, even for many Americans, political stability is patently undesirable. Discontented people and ambitious

August 1963: "I have a dream. . . ."

nations want change, perhaps even chaos, rather than order. Stability, after all, is the maxim of those who are satisfied.

The American impulse to use political action is not a universal method of solving problems. Instead of governments and politicians, many societies rely on a body of religious or secular doctrine to supply answers to social questions. Many of the peoples of Asia, including the Chinese, have no tradition of regular political procedure; philosophies and faiths furnish methods of meeting life's problems and provide punishments for those who err. Confronted with a challenge, a Communist refers to the theories of Karl Marx or Vladimir Lenin; an American calls on his lawyer for advice and his senator for action.

Laws and governments, Americans have always believed, should promote the welfare of the citizenry. Americans find baffling the idea that a state might have different interests from those of its citizens; the very distinction between state and citizens is strange. But for generations Europeans understood that "reasons of state," dynastic connections, or the whims of the nobility dictated policy that harmed the state's citizens. There is little evidence that today's Russian peasants want to overthrow the Communist regime, although in many ways it does not meet their needs. Russians do not expect their government to be responsive in the same way Americans do.

So it has been since that November day in 1620 when the men of the *Mayflower* solemnly assembled "in the presence of God and one another," to form a "civil body politick, for our better ordering and preservation." Order was ever a concern of the English and a "civil body politick" was the tested means to the end. English settlers brought their political prejudices, institutions, and ideals to the colonies. The settlers found it convenient first to claim the rights of Englishmen and then to add some that native Englishmen had yet to secure.

One of the undoubted rights of an Englishman was the right to enjoy his property. "The great end of men's entering into society," wrote John Locke in 1690, was "the enjoyment of their properties in peace and safety." Locke makes sense even to those Americans who know nothing of the English political philosopher, for Americans have outdone their English forebears in defense of property rights. Often, as was the case during more than two centuries of slavery, property rights have taken precedence over human rights. With the exception of the emancipation movement, the occasional assaults on property rights seem in retrospect rather feeble, partly because property has been so widely distributed that no challenge has had a popular base.

Those who at one moment have no property expect to get some the next. Americans have always been speculators, betting on the future. Sir Walter Raleigh, the stockholders of the London and Virginia companies, and every settler who came to the New World expected to turn a profit. Early immigrants staked whatever they had on their belief that the New World held more for them than the Old. Some, with only their labor to pledge, shipped as indentured servants; others started with a plot of land and a few tools. Americans ever since have retained their appetite for profit and their faith in the American economy. If it falters, "Prosperity is just around the corner." Booms are a matter of course. "Don't sell America short" has been more than a slogan; it has been a secular creed.

Property in America has been the measure of accomplishment and the reward for effort. The accumulation of property, whether land or money, has always been a proper goal of life. America has been the land of opportunity, and Americans have come to think of economic growth as a permanent condition. We have assumed wealth to be unlimited, and that those who obtain it do so, not at the expense of others, but from the earth or from some other natural source of riches. Thus, any addition to one person's fortune was a net gain for the whole society. Economic individualism—or, less tactfully, greed—was supposed to produce social progress as well as a personal fortune. Whether the example be the indentured servant who accumulated a sizeable estate, the immigrant who rose from bobbin boy to industrial magnate, or the executive of Irish parentage who made a fortune in the stock market, Americans have been proud, not resentful, of those who succeeded.

The first immigrants, like those who came later, were simple people with simple tastes. Dukes, after all, do not usually emigrate, and paupers can rarely afford to. Most of the first arrivals were English yeomen— sturdy, hard-working farmers of the English countryside, whose agricultural skills and frugal habits were proverbial. The more prosperous settlers were gentry, people who in England had operated farms or occasionally businesses of moderate size, which brought them enough income for comfort but not enough for indolence. Although the companies and proprietors that established early settlements found their investments disappointing, the colonists themselves, whose expectations were more modest, discovered economic opportunity in land. And of land there was plenty. To own land in America became much more common than in England and carried fewer privileges. But the American landowner was as jealous of the rights of property as was the English squire.

The essential elements of what Americans call free-enterprise capitalism came with the earliest settlers. The terms are not precise, but Americans have always believed they knew what "free market," "fair competition," "individual enterprise," and "equal opportunity" meant. And they have been equally sure that monopoly, socialism, and special privilege were beyond the bounds of acceptable economic behavior. The Puritans knew what was proper; central to their code of conduct was the notion that hard work was morally uplifting. Other Puritan virtues, such as thrift, perseverance, honesty, sobriety, punctuality, and initiative, conveniently brought profits as well as clean consciences. Anyone can develop these virtues; capacity, aptitude, and genes are less important than character, which alone limits a person's horizon.

To be sure, Americans have not always practiced the economic theory they have preached. A monopoly, for example, even if unfair, has been enviously regarded as "good business." But while the economy has evolved from agricultural simplicity to the complexity of modern industry, the old economic vocabulary and many of the Puritan attitudes have endured.

Moving

Restlessness has been a national characteristic since the first Americans left Europe and discovered that Jamestown was not just right either. Americans today lament their lack of roots even as they pack and fill out change-of-address forms; the mobile home could serve as the national symbol. This refusal to stay in one place means that large American communities are full of people who were born and educated elsewhere. "Where are you from?" is a standard conversational opening, because all Americans, it is assumed, are from someplace else. So a suburb of Spokane is quite like a suburb of Cincinnati; both are inhabited by people from Arkansas.

Partly because they cannot stay long in one spot, Americans tend to form tentative attachments to people and places. Life for many is a blurred recollection of half-remembered neighbors, who do not live there any more. We make friends easily and forget them without much regret. Our casual use of first names indicates the quickened pace of social life, since friendships must be made immediately or not at all.

Communities are no more stable than friendships. Shopping centers, oil fields, and housing developments spring up on the ancestral farm; the old Jewish neighborhood gives way to office buildings. And population changes with the landscape. When Americans use the name of a place—San Diego, San Antonio, Sheboygan—they refer to the people as well as the city. But perhaps a third of those people did not live in that city three years before, and another third is already anxious to leave. Because cities themselves do not move, the word "city" connotes a continuity that has misled generations of urban planners, politicians, and historians, who have too often overlooked the transient population.

Moving on is supposed to mean moving up; geographic mobility presumably leads to social mobility. The frontier or the city, California or Chicago, has been for Americans the promised land where opportunity beckoned and a stale career would revive or be changed. Every road sign points to another chance, and the freedom to move helps sustain the nation's faith both in equality, which will surely be available in another location, and in individualism, which will surely be rewarded there. In fact, however, social mobility is more easily believed than achieved. For every Benjamin Franklin or Andrew Carnegie, there have been millions of Americans who began in rags and were buried in them.

Yet enough have progressed in skill, status, and property to keep our national face turned toward the future, our collective back to the past. Our history has become a civil religion, used to reinforce moral homilies, marked by occasional rituals, and otherwise neglected. Both as individuals and as a nation, Americans think of themselves as emancipated from the past—from the roots that might inhibit change and from the traditions that might guide it.

But that is self-delusion. Even the willingness to change has itself hardened into a tradition that Americans can no more ignore than they can rid themselves of their English political heritage, the Puritan ethic, or their ambitious restlessness. All these characteristics tend to reduce the regional and ethnic differences among Americans and to promote the homogeneous society that has long been an American ideal. As an article of national faith, Americans believe that the "melting pot," the frontier, and the schools have fused diverse nationalities (but not different races) into one unique people. Evidence of the inaccuracy of this belief is as near as the closest urban neighborhood. Italian, Jewish, and Polish areas still exist in American cities, to say nothing of black, Puerto Rican, and Mexican enclaves. Many immigrants never reached the frontier; some who did preserved their European culture in the American wilderness.

If the melting pot has not functioned perfectly, the goal—one people—is a worthy goal. Many idealistic Americans are striving to remove geographic, racial, religious, and sexual distinctions that still divide the United States. Regardless of local peculiarities, schools teach the same skills, and for most Americans, education is still the ladder to success. All churches reprove immorality, which they define in almost the same way. Most lodges and clubs begin their meetings by saluting the American flag. Whatever the differences between Fort Worth and Fort Lauderdale, both have a chamber of commerce that exaggerates the city's virtues and solicits settlement. *E pluribus unum* is probably an unattainable ideal, but the United States has progressed in its self-imposed task of making one people from many.

The Exception to Every Rule

Since the day in August 1619 when a Dutch trader unloaded twenty Africans in Jamestown, the black population has been the unacknowledged exception to most of the generalizations about Americans. Every American, according to the nation's faith, has an equal chance in the land of opportunity—except black Americans. Every American is the equal of every other American before the law—except

The exception to the rule

black Americans. The history of American race relations points directly to the contradiction between human equality and individual liberty, a contradiction that white Americans for too long resolved by regarding people who were not white as less than human.

The habit began with slavery and did not end with emancipation. Seventeenth-century legislation distinguished between white indentured servants, who served a stated term, and black slaves, whose permanent bondage passed to their descendants. The indentured servant might look beyond the present to a limitless future, but unskilled hard labor was both the present and the future of the slave. And of most black Americans since. As the black slave replaced the white indentured servant on southern plantations in the seventeenth and eighteenth centuries, so the unskilled black laborer has replaced white immigrants in northern cities in the twentieth century. As planters exploited black slaves and sharecroppers, so urban whites have exploited black cooks and maids, black doormen and delivery boys. Southern legislatures decreed the ignorance of slaves by prohibiting their instruction; northern legislatures have provided black children with inferior schools in deteriorating slums. Post-emancipation discrimination has been less overtly degrading than slavery, but the result too often remains an unskilled black population available to do the bidding of whites. Emancipation only confirmed the belief of white Americans in their own supremacy.

That belief persists. A comparison of the condition of black and white Americans may be taken as evidence of white superiority, if one assumes that all Americans have equal opportunities. But while the white worker complains about unemployed black social parasites he keeps black craftsmen out of his union. The middle-class white attributes the deterioration of an urban ghetto to black slovenliness, while his zoning regulations keep blacks out of the suburbs. Faith in human equality and individual liberty makes whites believe that blacks can prosper if only they will try. Their relative lack of prosperity often reinforces the belief in white supremacy instead of prodding whites to a greater effort to make equality real.

"What then," asked Hector St. John de Crèvecoeur in 1782, "is the American, this new man?" Well might Crèvecoeur have asked, for he had guessed wrong on the American Revolution and wound up an exile. But his writing glowed with admiration for Americans, whose uniqueness he believed lay in their expanse of unsettled land, their mixture of nationalities, and their unparalleled chance to improve themselves. Every subsequent foreign visitor has repeated Crèvecoeur's question, and if so inclined, published his answer, as did Alexis de Tocqueville, James Bryce, and a host of other, less perceptive, tourists. Americans, too, continue their search for national identity. In their continuing effort to discover the precise dimension of their behavioral perimeter, Americans are polled, prodded, and poked, and their psyche is bared in countless books and articles each month.

This is one of those books.

American Origins: An Introduction

America's history is largely one of settlement, first from Asia by those so-called Native Americans (or First Americans, perhaps), misnamed Indians by Christopher Columbus. Their civilizations were the first in the New World and they were the victims of the subsequent European invasions that began in the fifteenth century and continued into the twentieth.

The Native Americans' fate and the fate of their diverse cultures has received belated recognition and concern, but this attention does not obscure the essentially European origins of which the Founding Fathers were so acutely aware. To understand fully the American experience, one must consider the factors that permitted colonization on the one hand and the motives that stimulated it on the other. The decline of feudalism in western Europe, the accelerated growth of commercial capitalism, the contributions of the Renaissance, the rise of the nation-state, and the religious climate that led to the Protestant Reformation—all contributed to the expansion of the Old World into the New.

The first century of American colonization was dominated by Spain, whose main interest was treasure. The second and third centuries belonged to England and France. Both were interested in gold, but the English rapidly turned their attention to agricultural settlement. The French directed their energies to trade. But both England and France knew domestic distractions that delayed and ultimately affected the character of later and more serious colonization endeavors.

Religion was, of course, one of those distractions, one that not only played its part in stimulating national rivalries in the sixteenth and seventeenth centuries but was also a significant force in creating and shaping colonial settlement. Each settlement had a specific religious identity: the Spanish and French colonies were citadels of Roman Catholicism; the English, Dutch, and Swedish colonies were as stoutly Protestant (with the brief exception of Maryland). The impulse towards colonization was at least partly fed by the desire to propagate the Christian faith or one particular sect or denomination. This was still an age of faith, when men and women were engrossed in their relationship to God and the fulfillment of His purpose. If religion could contribute to the execution of one English monarch and to the exile of another, it is hardly surprising that doctrinal differences crossed the Atlantic and resulted in a persistent concern with the relations of church and state—only to reach a conclusion in the separation of one from the other with the emergence of the United States as an independent nation.

That emergence was infinitely more gradual and less predictable than its celebrants sometimes suggest. Many colonists persistently saw themselves as transplants rather than as potential founders of a new nation. Their concern for education, for example, stemmed at least partly from anxiety to maintain the traditions and culture brought to the New World from the Old, but their implementation reflected local needs and saw educational arrangements marked by a dispersion of educational opportunity beyond anything to be found at that time in England. Such dispersion in turn spoke to problems of geography and distance—it was often easier to journey to London than from one colonial town to another. And geography helps explain the enduring spirit of separatism that was a commonplace of early American history.

Intercolonial rivalries were often matched by intracolonial divisions and uprisings. The fact that colonial history was one of continual change, with constant infusions of immigrants and continuous expansion of the economy, made social, religious, ethnic, and class friction inevitable. The wonder is not that there was a Bacon's Rebellion in Virginia, a Leisler Rebellion in New York, Regulator movements in the Carolinas, and widespread persecution of Quakers, Roman Catholics, Native Americans, and blacks, but that there were not more such upheavals, more discrimination and savagery reflecting an age and an environment known for its extremes and its insecurity.

The miracle that some historians have discerned in the successful creation of a new nation may well be the American capacity to reconcile divisions and diversity and, better yet, reach towards the accommodation of both. Suffice to note that the accommodation remains incomplete, that it was singularly deficient throughout the first two centuries of American history. It is more than ironic that, as Gary Nash has observed, many blacks and red Americans concluded that their revolutionary goals could best be achieved through fighting against the side that proclaimed the equality of all men (not women) and with the side that white Americans accused of trampling on their natural irreducible rights. But this was no failure of judgment: their later history confirms they would have fared no better had they sided with Jefferson and Adams in their quest for life, liberty, and the pursuit of happiness.

Chapter 1
New World Origins

Chronology

28,000 B.C. First migrations to the New World •

1492 Columbus discovers "an Other World" •

1517 Luther initiates the Protestant Reformation •

1585 Raleigh's Roanoke Island settlement •

1607 Jamestown settlement •

1620 Plymouth settlement •

1733 Georgia settlement—the thirteenth colony •

Humans were not indigenous to the Western Hemisphere. The people of the Old World became the people of the New some 30,000 years ago, when the first immigrants crossed the land bridge from Siberia to Alaska. Slowly they fanned out southward, into the plains of the Southwest, then south again through Mexico into Central and South America. They may have been joined about 3000 B.C. by voyagers from Asia who scattered along the western coasts of the Americas. Archeological discoveries indicate that these first migrants reached the Atlantic coast of North America by 10,000 B.C.

These Native Americans not only discovered the Americas but explored and settled both continents before white colonists arrived. Those who marveled at the courage of European explorers rarely noted that Indians had blazed the trails. The Indians made no maps and kept no written records, but they knew their land; they traveled routes extending a thousand miles inland when the first white settlers were struggling to establish themselves on the coasts.

The European settlers—of whatever nation or faith—were more alike than the natives, who spoke more than a thousand different languages. More than two hundred distinct tribes lived in California alone. The variety of cultures testifies to the Indians' remarkable capacity to adapt to and live in harmony with the environment, and to their ability to develop new customs and new tools for new places. Some Indian groups established urban societies with complex political and social hierarchies, well-established trade routes, elaborate religions, and intricate art. Stone Age Mayans in Guatemala and Honduras built monumental palaces and temples. Aztecs in Mexico and Incas in Peru domesticated animals, irrigated crops, devised an accurate calendar, and wove fabrics. For a millennium after A.D. 500, a highly developed Indian society flourished in the southwestern part of what became the United States.

But, generally, most North American tribes were culturally less sophisticated. They gathered and ground wild grains—primitive grinding tools found in Utah date from 8500 B.C.—and relied on game and fish, rather than agriculture. The Indians encountered by white settlers along the Atlantic coast lacked plows and lived in scattered villages. Although the Algonquians and the Five Nations of the Iroquois had developed sophisticated political institutions, among other tribes the authority of chiefs and village councils varied with custom and the need for central direction. Retributive justice—an eye for an eye—furnished enough law for most tribes, as had been true, indeed, for medieval Europeans.

Indians had their own values and did not know the need for the elaborate law codes the Europeans had developed by the seventeenth century. A hunting society shares its game; it uses, but does not possess, land. (Only with settled agriculture did land ownership become crucial.) Feathers and other decorations, not property, were the signs of rank and status among the Indians, whose society, in material terms, was roughly egalitarian.

Indian tribes traded and fought with one another. Salt was the crucial commercial commodity, but copper from along the shores of Lake Superior has been found in the weapons of eastern tribes, and the teeth of alligators and sharks have turned up in burial mounds in the Ohio Valley. Although hospitality toward strangers was the usual practice among hunting people, intertribal conflict certainly hindered the Indians' ability to resist the demands of grasping white intruders.

At first, Indians were sympathetic to white requests for refuge from the rigors of ocean travel and the oppression of established religion and government. But the Spanish custom of enslaving the natives, and the English custom of cheating them, soon gave whites a bad reputation that the more benign French settlers were unable to erase. Even more dangerous to Indians than white men's laws about property and their firearms were white men's diseases, for which Indians had no natural immunity. Smallpox, technology, and the encroachment of white settlement eventually brought about what Wilbur Jacobs has called "a demographic disaster with no known parallel in world history." Whites displaced the Indian culture they found, but absorbed little of it.

The geography of the Americas had a greater impact than Indians on European colonization. The indented coastline made for widely dispersed settlements—and considerable separatism. The Appalachians slowed westward expansion and forced a concentration of population in the East during the seventeenth and eighteenth centuries. The arid climate and lack of good harbors slowed settlement on the Pacific coast; the first significant Spanish settlements in California were not established until the 1770s. And the flow of America's rivers proved particularly influential: in the East the rivers provided highways westward as far as the mountains; but in the trans-Appalachian West, the rivers ran from north to south, drastically affecting the pattern of migration. The Midwest was linked more closely to the South than to the Northeast until the railroads appeared; then sectional sympathies began to shift.

The European Context

Pre-Columbian settlements by Europeans did not last. The first European visitors to the New World were probably the Vikings, who established settlements on Iceland, then Greenland, and perhaps Labrador and Newfoundland by A.D. 1000. None were on hand to welcome Christopher Columbus or John Smith. The transformation of the Old World of the Middle Ages made their success possible. This transformation can be seen, for instance, in the disappearance of the feudal manor and its static agricultural economy. These were supplanted by commercial capitalism, with its reliance on money rather than service. Nation-states emerged as a result of merchants' alliances with erstwhile feudal monarchs. Merchants helped finance the standing armies that the Crown used to suppress rebellious feudal vassals; as a reward the King granted new chartered privileges to his friendly creditors. Order and security were the desire of both merchant and monarch. They worked together for new secular laws, applicable on a countrywide basis. And they cooperated in de-emphasizing canon law and the international (and supranational) influence of the Roman Catholic Church.

The Church, centered in Rome and long supreme in western Europe, found its religious assumptions and temporal influence increasingly challenged. Critics, particularly those in northern Europe, charged that the Church failed to live up to the ascetic ideals it preached. This criticism reached a climax in 1517, when Martin Luther nailed on the Wittenberg church door ninety-five theses denouncing papal abuses and deceptions. Essentially a conservative reformer, Luther insisted on salvation through faith (rather than through what the Church called "good works") and argued for direct communication with God through the Bible (rather than through the Church).

In 1536, some fifteen years after Luther was excommunicated, John Calvin presented a radically different theology in his *Institutes of the Christian Religion.* Calvin saw humans as sinners always tempted; the death of Christ redeemed but a select few, who were predestined for salvation. Even though a life of good works might not guarantee redemption, each person had a duty to live piously in the hope of being one of the elect. Calvin believed that government should glorify God; thus, the state had an obligation to educate the people in the true faith. He saw the production of wealth and its enjoyment as part of the godly life. God would reward only the pious: poverty was a badge of sin and often the result of it. Some merchants may have found the Calvinist ideology more hospitable to commercial activity than the Catholic doctrine, which considered trade a necessary evil at best. However, it is doubtful that either Catholicism or Protestantism favored—or hurt—the growth of capitalism.

Commercial capitalism began before the twelfth and thirteenth century

Crusades, which immensely stimulated mercantile activity. Ships built to transport the crusaders to the East were later used for trade; profits were to be made from furnishing supplies to the armies; and the European invaders discovered eastern luxuries, particularly spices, silks, drugs, and perfumes, which the crusaders determined to continue to enjoy after they went home. (Spices were especially appreciated for their value in preserving foodstuffs.) Thus arose a demand for new commodities, which were compact and easily shipped. Merchants and consumers along the Atlantic coasts of Europe, who profited less than those in Italy, gave serious thought to alternative trade routes to the oriental sources of the spices and silks in such demand.

But mercantile ambition was not enough; logistical and technical support was vital. With the fourteenth century came the Renaissance, a rebirth of learning and a fresh enthusiasm for scholarship. Out of the Renaissance came a reacquaintance with the past, and with the achievements of the ancient Greeks and Romans. And from this reaffirmation of human potential came a new view of one's abilities to fashion one's own earthly fate, in part with the aid of recent scientific knowledge. The magnifying lens, gunpowder, the printing press with movable type (1450), clocks, new navigational aids, such as the compass and the astrolabe, all contributed to the sense of capability and opportunity and reduced both ignorance and superstition.

Early Exploration

Western Europeans resented the cost of importing eastern goods through Mediterranean merchants. The new nation-states found their dependence on Italian merchants humiliating. The unfavorable trade balance led to a serious currency shortage, followed in some instances by efforts to prohibit the outflow of gold and silver. The solution seemed simple: western European nations must deploy national resources to seek another sea route to the East, a route that new science and ancient geography suggested must exist.

The first in the national procession was Portugal, unified under King John I in 1383. Unable to expand eastward against the Castilians, the Portuguese looked to the sea for opportunity. John's third son, the famed Prince Henry the Navigator, who lived from 1394 to 1460, never went to sea himself, but he did promote exploration of the African coast, first in a search for new trade, then in quest of Asia and the Indies. When Bartholomeu Dias rounded the Cape of Good Hope in 1488, he pointed the way for Vasco da Gama's voyage to India in 1498. Portugal thus broke the mercantile supremacy of the Italian commercial cities, and the Atlantic ports of Lisbon and Antwerp became new trade centers for western Europe. Portugal subsequently laid claim to Brazil when, in 1500,

Pedro Cabral visited the eastern shores of South America when he was blown off course on a voyage to India via the South African Cape.

Spain was also a newly unified nation (Ferdinand of Aragon married Isabella of Castile in 1469). Ironically, it was a seaman from Genoa, Italy, who, in an unsuccessful search for another route to Asia, gave Spain early leadership in the New World. Christopher Columbus (1451–1506) was hardly original in his conviction that the earth was round, that sailing due west would bring him to the Indies. His distinction was his comforting underestimation of the distance from Spain to Asia along with his tenacity in seeking Isabella's support. The fame he earned for reaching the Bahamas on October 12, 1492, after a scant six weeks at sea, has obscured his own sense of failure in not reaching the Indies. As a colonizer and administrator Columbus probably deserved his self-criticism. His three subsequent voyages were anticlimactic, futile attempts to reach the Asian mainland. Columbus died a deeply disappointed man. He never fully realized his accomplishment; he never understood that an entire continent barred his way to the East. Spain's monarchs, however, saw the immediate wealth available to them in what Columbus vaguely termed "an Other World," and in 1494, with the aid of a Spanish-born Pope, they divided the New World with their rival nation, Portugal, in the Treaty of Tordesillas. Neither nation knew yet the extent of its pretension. Nor were others ready to offer effective challenge.

France, for instance, found too many domestic distractions at that time to allow serious attention to overseas adventures. Until the mid-fifteenth century France was engrossed in expelling the tenacious English from French soil; France then spent nearly a century squabbling with the Pope

Columbus

and dissipating resources in fruitless wars in Italy. Nor were the British in a much better position: Henry VII, who wore the crown from 1485 to 1509, was by nature parsimonious and in any case preferred to secure his dynasty at home rather than engage in expensive foreign adventures. His son, the much-married Henry VIII, who ruled from 1509 to 1547, was less closefisted but not less involved with domestic difficulties, which were due partly to his extravagance and partly to his dedicated quest for a legitimate male heir. Thus, for more than fifteen years after Columbus's first voyage, the Spanish settlement on Hispaniola, or Haiti, was the only European colony in America. But from this affluent base Spanish explorers soon embarked on an extraordinary sequence of conquests.

The achievements of the conquistadors, the Spanish military adventurers and explorers of the sixteenth century, are as astonishing as they are controversial. By 1508 Alonzo de Ojeda had established a settlement in the region of Panama; five years later Vasco Núñez de Balboa reached the Pacific, and Ponce de León discovered Florida (which he thought an island). Between 1540 and 1542 Francisco Coronado clanked his way in heavy armor through Arizona and New Mexico into Kansas. In the same period Hernando de Soto moved westward through Florida to discover the Mississippi River, and Juan Cabrillo sailed up the California coast beyond Monterey to San Francisco Bay. More spectacular were the conquest of the Aztecs by Hernando Cortés in 1521 and Francisco Pizarro's subjugation of the Peruvian Incas a decade later.

The ruthlessness of the conquistadors has shadowed their extraordinary achievement. These Spanish conquerors lived in an age of cruelty and intolerance, and their actions reflected the temper of their times. Harsh enslavement and European diseases sharply reduced the native population, which was partly replaced by black slaves from Africa. Still, there was more to the Spanish empire than a brutalizing quest for wealth and the destruction of ancient civilizations. In less than a century, more than 160,000 settlers were scattered over vast territories, governing some 5 million natives and introducing Spanish language, learning, and agriculture. With the sword of the conquistadors came the cross of the Spanish priests. Cathedrals and universities testified to a new civilization in the New World, an empire that, for all the inflexibility of its commercial policy and its centralized government, outlasted the dominions of the British and French.

Both England and France approached the New World with much initial hesitation. England advanced its first tenuous claim to North America on the basis of John Cabot's voyage along the Atlantic coast between Newfoundland and Chesapeake Bay (1497—98). Modestly funded by Henry VII, Cabot sought the western sea route to the Asian mainland. Twenty-six years later, Francis I of France sponsored the voyage of Giovanni de Verrazano, who had no more luck than Cabot in the same quest. But unlike Henry VII, Francis I did not give up. In 1534 he supported further voyages by Jacques Cartier, who sailed up the St.

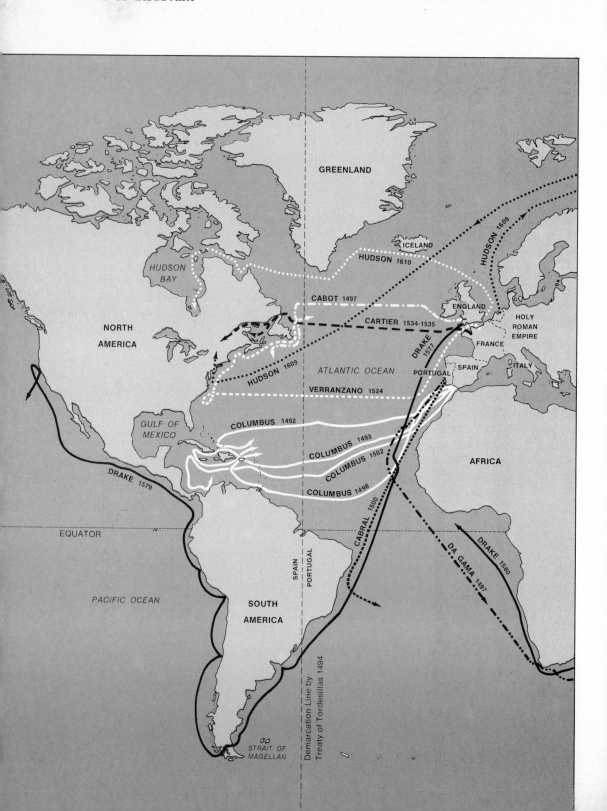

Lawrence River to the future sites of Quebec and Montreal. Not until the reign of Elizabeth I (1558–1603) did the English again take up their interest in North America. The first effort came under the leadership of Sir Humphrey Gilbert, whose settlement in Newfoundland in 1583 failed. This was followed closely by Sir Walter Raleigh's colony on North Carolina's Roanoke Island. But the colony was unsuccessful and disappeared without a trace before 1591. For all England's envy of and hostility to Spain, no English colony remained in the New World when the Elizabethan age concluded. And yet, a few years later there were major new settlements planned, and a new age of English colonization began.

Origins of English Colonization

Although English colonization was essentially a seventeenth-century phenomenon, its origins derive partly from the theological controversies of the preceding century. The ideas of Luther and Calvin bitterly divided western Europe. In England, the Protestant revolt gained unexpected encouragement from Henry VIII. Henry separated from Rome and made himself head of the Church of England, primarily to secure a divorce from Catherine of Aragon. His sickly son and heir, Edward, who ruled between 1547 and 1553, embraced a more serious form of Protestantism, but Mary, who succeeded her half-brother Edward, tried to restore Roman Catholicism. When Elizabeth I, Mary's half-sister, ascended the throne in 1558 she knew she depended on her Protestant subjects for survival. The Pope regarded Elizabeth as illegitimate and formally excommunicated her in 1570. An astute politician, Elizabeth embraced a theological compromise—a Protestant creed with many Roman Catholic forms. But her Anglican Church, which helped solidify England as a nation-state, was unacceptable to Roman Catholics and Calvinists alike, and Elizabeth harassed both with increasing zeal and fine impartiality.

Her Anglicanism probably made conflict with Catholic Spain un-avoidable; indeed, she provoked hostility. Elizabeth aided the Protestant Dutch in their rebellion against Spain, and she quietly encouraged such "sea dogges" as Francis Drake to raid Spanish treasure-fleets in the New World. Elizabeth even knighted Drake in 1580 after he circumnavigated the world and returned with £600,000 in Spanish bullion—the Queen's share was £263,000. Philip II of Spain sought revenge with his Armada in 1588, but the combination of poor Spanish strategy, miserable English weather, and superior English seamanship ensured Elizabeth's survival. English sea power, an essential ingredient for colonization, was confirmed and available.

There were other vital ingredients for colonization besides religion and sea power. The sixteenth century was a period of rapid economic growth for England. The middle class grew in size and wealth and perfected its business structure and organization. Joint-stock companies, such as the Muscovy Company, the Levant Company, and, the most famous, the British East India Company, reduced individual risks and increased national resources. The English population grew from three million in 1485 to four million by the end of the sixteenth century. The wool trade flourished, aided by refugees from European wars and religious persecution. Profits from sheep raising stimulated the enclosure movement, which saw common lands fenced off by private acts of Parliament for the benefit of sheep owners. But, for large numbers of English people, the consequence of this movement was economic distress, which constituted another ingredient for colonization. With the reduction of land for cultivation (a form of technological unemployment) came a sharp increase in the landless poor. Food prices rose far beyond the reach of the lower classes, partly because food production failed to keep pace with population growth and partly as a result of the European price revolution, brought on by the great flow of gold and silver from Spanish America. Prices rose 250 percent between 1500 and 1650. Most affected were workers, whose real income declined nearly 50 percent, and the old aristocracy, dependent on a fixed income. By 1600, one in every three in England was on poor relief. Conditions did not improve rapidly. In the early seventeenth century, disastrous harvests drove food prices still higher, and the Thirty Years' War closed off England's European markets, contributing to a severe depression. There was, in short, no lack of incentive for the English to consider leaving home.

English Colonization: The South

The death of Elizabeth I in 1603 brought to the throne the inept and unpopular Stuart dynasty. Elizabeth's death also precipitated new religious and political dissension that provided further impetus for England's colonization of North America. In 1606, less than two years after making peace with Spain, James I granted a charter creating two branches of one Virginia Company of London. One branch was authorized to settle in America between the thirty-fourth and forty-first parallels; the other, known as the Virginia Company of Plymouth, was authorized to settle between the thirty-eighth and forty-fifth parallels. Although the grants clearly overlapped, the companies were warned to keep at least one hundred miles apart in their actual settlements. The Plymouth Company made the first move, establishing a short-lived colony in southern Maine, but it was the London Company that established the first successful English settlement at Jamestown, Virginia, in April 1607.

Both Virginia companies had similar motives: a quest for gold and for the long-sought passage to Asia, and a pious interest in converting what they called pagan Indians to Christianity. Such aspirations induced the London Company stockholders to fund three ships that sailed from England in December 1606 with more than one hundred would-be settlers. Captain Christopher Newport selected the peninsula of Jamestown as his base, in spite of the hazard of malaria; his main concern was defense, not physical comfort.

Weak initial leadership and futile efforts to find gold produced disaster in the colony's early years; fewer than half the original colonizers survived the first year. But John Smith eventually provided leadership, and John Rolfe found in tobacco an economic base for future growth and prosperity. In 1616, 2,500 pounds of tobacco were exported; by 1618 the total had climbed to 30,000 pounds, and by 1627 tobacco exports had reached 500,000 pounds. A tobacco rush supplanted the hunger for gold: the settlers neglected food cultivation as they planted tobacco seeds everywhere—in graveyards and even in Jamestown streets. In 1619 a Dutch trader stopped by and sold some twenty black slaves, and the future of the Virginia economy seemed assured.

Actually, there were relatively few slaves in Virginia until the end of the century. The London Company resolved to add to the labor supply by establishing the "head right" system, whereby settlers arranged their own transportation and that of dependents in return for fifty acres per "head" transported. Once established, settlers favored the use of white indentured servants, who sold their labor for a period of years to pay for their passage. But black slaves arrived in larger numbers in the 1680s, when the British Royal African Company made its efficient presence known; slave prices declined just as new regulations in Britain made bondservants more difficult to acquire.

Politically, Virginia afforded an unsteady example for later colonies to follow. Beginning in 1609, the Company undertook various experiments in authoritarian government until 1619 when white, male freemen assembled in the first representative assembly in the New World and announced that Virginia would live "by those free lawes" that prevailed in the mother country. Three years later, an Indian onslaught reduced the colony's population by some 250, furnishing James I with a handy excuse to revoke the London Company's charter in 1624.

Bankruptcy actually preceded revocation. In its eighteen years the Company invested—and lost—some £250,000 and sent over some 6,000 settlers, of whom only 1,200 survived. The Company's leadership had sometimes demonstrated a capacity for business sagacity and sometimes for administrative wisdom, but it failed to combine such essential virtues. A succession of Crown-appointed governors administered Virginia as a royal colony; the representative assembly met annually without royal sanction until 1639, when the King finally appointed a governor with instructions to convene the House of Burgesses at least once a year.

Maryland was Virginia's first neighbor, the brainchild and possession of a former stockholder in the London Company, and the first proprietary

A Brief DESCRIPTION
OF
The Province
OF
CAROLINA
On the COASTS *of* FLOREDA.
AND

More perticularly of a *New-Plantation*
begun by the *ENGLISH* at *Cape-Feare*,
on that River now by them called *Charles-River*,
the 29th of *May*. 1664.

Wherein is set forth
The *Healthfulness* of the *Air*; the *Fertility* of
the *Earth*, and *Waters*; and the great *Pleasure* and
Profit will accrue to those that shall go thither to enjoy
the same.

Also,
Directions and advice to such as shall go thither whether
on their own accompts, or to serve under another.

Together with
A most accurate MAP of the whole *PROVINCE*.

London, Printed for *Robert Horne* in the first Court of *Gresham-
Colledge* neer *Bishopsgate street*. 1666.

colony. Sir George Calvert, later made Lord Baltimore, wanted his own colony for the personal advantage of his family and for the benefit of fellow Roman Catholics who were encouraged to settle there. His son inherited the royal charter granted by Charles I in 1632 and began settlement on the northern bank of the Potomac in 1634. As a later settlement, Maryland had several advantages over its uneasy neighbor: the Calverts pursued a conciliatory policy with the Indians, selected a healthy settlement site at St. Mary's, and enjoyed provisions imported from Virginia and New England. Like Virginia, Maryland had a form of representative government, subject in this case to the approval of the proprietor and the governor he appointed.

The Calverts were less successful in realizing their hope for a Catholic refuge. From the outset Protestants were in the majority, which explains in part Maryland's famous "Act Concerning Toleration" (1649) that granted religious freedom to all Christians who believed in the Trinity.* Five years later the Protestant majority in a rebellious assembly briefly repealed the measure. Political and religious conditions in the mother country affected the Calverts' control. In 1691 William and Mary extended their rule to the colony and established the Church of England there. Not until the fourth Lord Baltimore renounced his Catholic faith in 1715 did the Calverts regain proprietary rights, which they exercised until the American Revolution.

Just as Maryland owed much to the benevolence of Charles I, the Carolinas derived their proprietary status from Charles II's wish to pay his political debts to eight court favorites who helped him regain his throne in 1660. He conferred on these gentlemen title to all land between the thirty-first and thirty-sixth parallels. The 1663 charter gave the Lords Proprietors essentially the same rights enjoyed by the Calverts in Maryland, with the stipulation that the Carolinas' laws were to be agreeable "to the laws and customs of England." In a bid for settlers the proprietors promised a representative assembly and religious toleration for Protestants. In practice the owners did little for their province beyond outfitting a modest expedition in 1670 that located at Charleston. Huguenot refugees from Catholic repression in France and a constant influx of West Indian planters swelled the settlement; the latter group was primarily responsible for the swift popularity of slavery in the southern portion of the province. Early in the eighteenth century the population totaled some 5,000 persons, half of whom were black slaves working on rice plantations.

To the north, in the Albermarle Sound area, a very different and less aristocratic society emerged. Scattered settlers, many from Virginia, pursued diversified agriculture and earned for their region the label of "a vale of humility between two mountains of conceit." But nowhere was proprietary rule particularly effective or rewarding. By 1712 North Carolina had its own governor, and seventeen years later the Crown bought out the surviving Lords Proprietors and the Carolinas became two separate royal colonies.

The last of the southern settlements, Georgia was established 125 years after the first. The philanthropy, paternalism, and imperialism that produced Georgia illustrated the changing attitudes of England toward colonization and even suggested problems that would contribute to the

---

* Nonbelief in the Trinity was declared a capital offense, which placed Jews and atheists in some danger.

American quest for independence. The philanthropists were the twenty-one paternalistic proprietors of Georgia: best known was General James Edward Oglethorpe, a tough-minded military man who looked on Georgia as a vital buffer between the Spanish in Florida and the English in South Carolina and also as an alternative to debtors' prison for England's poor. But, during the proprietors' trusteeship, Parliament's grants of some £130,000 to Georgia went for imperial defense, not to aid debtors. The 1732 charter guaranteed religious freedom to Protestants and fifty acres to each settler; but it lacked a provision for a representative assembly. Actually, few debtors ever reached Georgia. They rarely passed the careful scrutiny of trustees, who also sought to embargo slavery and "Rum, Brandies, Spirits or Strong Waters." Settlers' resentment of such restrictions matched the trustees' rapid disillusionment with their noble experiment. By 1752 the trustees were ready to surrender their colonial ward to the English state, and Georgia joined the ranks of royal colonies, complete with a Crown-appointed governor and an elected general assembly.

English Colonization: New England

Sir John Popham and Sir Ferdinando Gorges, leading figures in the Virginia Company of Plymouth, shared some of the humane and expansionist impulses later exemplified by Oglethorpe in Georgia. But the Plymouth Company's Sagadahoc settlement on the lower Kennebec foundered barely a year after its establishment in 1607. When the company reorganized as the Council for New England in 1620, it functioned largely as a landholding group with sea-to-sea title between the fortieth and forty-eighth parallels. John Mason, an associate of Gorges, joined with him in taking a grant in 1622 from the council for the area between the Merrimac and Kennebec rivers, a grant they later divided but did little to develop. Mason eventually gained formal title to New Hampshire and Gorges secured Maine, both confirmed by royal charter in 1629.* But the council had lapsed into inactivity by 1623 and surrendered its charter to Charles I in 1635, partly to aid the Crown in its conflict with the Puritans who settled in Massachusetts Bay.

One of the more successful New England settlements was that established at Plymouth, the first of the religious commonwealths that came to dominate New England. Plymouth had its origins in the sustained discontent of radical English Protestants with the moderation and compromise of the Elizabethan Church of England. The Puritans wanted to "purify" the English Church of much of its ritual (which they

---

* Migration from Massachusetts Bay led to the annexation of New Hampshire in 1643; in 1679 Charles II separated New Hampshire from the Bay Colony. Massachusetts purchased Maine from Gorges's heirs in 1677.

saw as popish); they wished to abolish the Anglican Book of Common Prayer, elevate the Bible as a source of divine truth, and preach the Calvinist doctrines of predestination, original sin, and "covenant theology," whereby God pledged salvation in return for the faith of His chosen few. They extended this covenant concept to the secular realm, arguing that a contract (or social compact) bound the governing and the governed. The Puritans believed that James I and his son Charles were increasingly ignoring those obligations. The "good community" would be one that combined church and state; it would be, ideally, a "godly commonwealth."

Puritans found it hard to agree on the best way to achieve their goals—or even on the precise form of those goals. Most supported a Presbyterian, or conciliar, form of church governance, as practiced in Scotland, Holland, and parts of Germany. Others favored independent parishes in which each congregation would choose its minister and church officials. Within this faction there was further division: those who wanted to maintain independent churches within the Church of England and those who wanted to separate from it. Separatists founded their own congregational church in Nottinghamshire in 1606. Faced with mounting persecution, they settled at Leyden in Holland three years later. But the economic and political disadvantages there induced some Separatists, led by William Bradford, to migrate to Virginia.

This group of emigrants, as an unincorporated joint-stock company, first secured permission for their settlement and then money from the London Company; they chartered the *Mayflower* late in the summer of 1620. But the Pilgrims did not, of course, reach Virginia. After a stormy voyage they sighted Cape Cod and finally disembarked at Plymouth on December 26, 1620. Before landing they drafted the Mayflower Compact, a preliminary form of government based on majority rule.

Lacking supplies and unprepared for the rigors of the New England climate, the Plymouth settlers suffered severely in the first year: less than half of them lived through the winter, and at one time only seven were well enough to care for the sick and to bury the dead. Without Indian assistance, the leadership of William Bradford, and religious dedication, the Pilgrims might not have survived. The colony was never especially prosperous or populous. The settlers had pledged to work for seven years, to place the fruits of their labor into a common store, and to assign all profits to the London investors. But this exercise in economic cooperation failed: no profits appeared, and the London merchants withdrew their support. The Pilgrims negotiated a financial settlement, whereby they paid £1,800 in modest installments to secure title to their land. By 1630, the colony numbered 300 settlers; in 1691, when William and Mary incorporated the settlement into Massachusetts Bay Colony, Plymouth could count a population of only 7,000.

On a small scale Plymouth illustrated the pattern of expansion encountered by other colonies. At the conclusion of its independent existence (1620—91) Plymouth contained some twenty-one townships as well as numerous smaller communities. Settlers scattered rapidly in their quest for land and wealth. As historian John Demos has observed, those who moved were usually young; often one man settled in a new community and then brought members of his family. The rapid turnover in land ownership suggests that acquisition was often more important than land use. Occasionally a parent used a gift of land to persuade a son to remain in the neighborhood, or as an inducement to "better behavior."

Substantive differences divided Plymouth from its northern neighbor, Massachusetts Bay. To be sure, Calvinists settled both, but unlike Plymouth, Massachusetts Bay was not an ill-planned, underfinanced, meagerly populated Separatist settlement. Rather, Massachusetts Bay must be counted among the most coherent of colonization ventures—well funded, well conceived, and well executed. The Bay Colony began in 1623 as a small fishing post at Cape Ann, financed by Dorchester businessmen. That venture failed and some settlers returned to England, while others moved south to Salem. The Salem settlement attracted the attention of John White, an Anglican minister with Puritan sympathies, who saw a chance for missionary work among the Indians. He helped organize the New England Company and secured a patent from the Council for New England; in 1629 Charles I granted the company a new charter as the Massachusetts Bay Company.

The Crown authorized a conventional trading company but failed to stipulate that the colony should be administered from the mother country. This oversight gave the company its unique opportunity: when economic depression and religious persecution increased in England, John Winthrop and eleven other Puritans joined in the Cambridge Agreement in 1629 and pledged to take themselves and the company to Massachusetts. Thus began the so-called Great Migration: seventeen ships and some 2,000 settlers crossed to the Bay Colony in 1630; by 1642 about 16,000 had migrated and founded a score of towns radiating from the principal settlement at Boston.

The economic and religious origins of Massachusetts Bay affected its political history. The Cambridge Agreement transformed what began as a trading venture into a corporate act of colonization. When the company moved to Boston it lost its profit-making identity; most of the later capitalization of the Bay Colony came from wealthy Puritans who sold their English property and funded their own migration to Massachusetts. The corporate origin of the colony had an important and unique political consequence when the company governor, deputy governor, and council of assistants (elected by stockholders) became the first governmental structure of the province itself. In effect, the colony was self-governing. Although the percentage of those good Puritans who qualified as freemen fell rapidly after the late 1640s, they remained a majority in this Bible Commonwealth.

Predictably, the Bay Colony's form of self-government and its preoccupation with its own version of the true religion did not satisfy everyone. Charles I, for instance, thought he had been tricked and instituted legal action to nullify the 1629 charter, but the English Civil War erupted before he could complete his design. It was not until 1691 that Massachusetts Bay became a royal colony.

Independent spirits, such as Anne Hutchinson and Roger Williams, also issued an early challenge to the religious oligarchy. Anne Hutchinson had arrived with her husband and children (eventually fourteen in number) in 1634; she joined the Boston church but soon questioned its teachings. An early feminist, she suggested others were gifted with deeper spiritual insight than Pastor John Wilson and contended that Christianity was less a matter of good works than of the spirit within, which led to communion with the Lord. She and her assistants were denounced for their theological presumptions and for having stepped outside their proper sphere as women. A lengthy controversy concluded with her banishment from the colony in 1638. With her family and friends Hutchinson left for Rhode Island and settled in Portsmouth; later they moved to what is now New York State, where they were butchered by Indians, an atrocity John Winthrop thought clear evidence of the hand of God.

Roger Williams was more fortunate. A Cambridge scholar who championed the rights of Indians, he questioned the land title of the Bay Colony and insisted the power of civil magistrates did not extend to matters of conscience or religion. Williams too was banished. He fled to Narragansett Bay, where he founded Providence in 1636. Other dissenters settled in Rhode Island, or "Rogues' Island," as stalwart Puritans termed the predominantly Baptist settlements. Williams secured a parliamentary patent for the colony in 1644 and a royal charter from Charles II in 1663.

Although never really reconciled to the Rhode Island "latrina of New England," Massachusetts Bay entertained more cordial views toward other neighbors. The Connecticut settlements largely derived from Puritan migration from Massachusetts Bay, such as that led by the Reverend Thomas Hooker in 1636 into the Connecticut River valley. In 1639 the newly established towns of Hartford, Wethersfield, and Windsor united in the Fundamental Orders of Connecticut, which copied faithfully the governmental arrangements of the Bay Colony. In an effort to establish religious uniformity, Connecticut provided a death penalty for atheists and persecuted dissenters from congregational Puritanism. Other Connecticut settlements, such as Saybrook and New Haven, were joined to the main colony under the royal charter of 1662.

The Middle Colonies

English expansion into the Connecticut River valley preempted a Dutch claim to the territory between Maryland and Massachusetts. For Holland the seventeenth century was a golden age when, liberated from Spain, it achieved preeminence as a commercial and maritime nation and collided with England in three major naval wars. Dutch interest in the New World stemmed from Henry Hudson's voyages of exploration—in 1609 he looked for the Northwest Passage to India along the river now bearing his name. Holland established a trading post on Manhattan Island as early as 1612 and chartered the Dutch West India Company in 1621. The first major settlement came in 1623, soon followed by the famous purchase of Manhattan from Indians for goods worth twenty-four dollars. The Dutch built a fort and founded New Amsterdam as capital of their colony of New Netherland. But the settlement grew grudgingly and British, not Dutch, settlers soon moved in. The Dutch lacked the incentives that drove the English to migration. By the 1640s the population in New Netherland was actually declining, so Governor Peter Stuyvesant welcomed New England migrants. By 1645 the Dutch West India Company was bankrupt, and its colony became prey to English ambition.

The Dutch presence became intolerable to England when Charles II found that New Netherland stood in the way of his policy of commercial regulation in the colonies. In 1664 the King granted the territory between the Connecticut and Delaware rivers to his brother and heir, James, Duke of York. When James dispatched an expedition to New Amsterdam, Stuyvesant promptly surrendered, and New Netherland became the proprietary colony of New York. James was virtually absolute monarch of his province. He ruled—from England—as duke until 1685 and without a representative assembly until 1683.

James did not exercise his authority over the entire area granted him:* Massachusetts and Connecticut successfully withstood his claims, and the duke assigned the region from the Hudson to the Delaware to Sir George Carteret and Lord Berkeley. Berkeley sold west New Jersey to a Quaker group in 1674; Carteret's heir followed suit with the eastern part in 1681. For a time New Jersey was united as a part of New York, but in 1738 the Crown constituted New Jersey a separate royal colony. Delaware, which had been the scene of the only Swedish settlement (1638–55), was granted to William Penn to be part of his proprietary province in 1682; the three "lower counties" of Delaware were allowed their own assembly in 1704 but remained subject to Pennsylvania's governor until the Revolution.

Pennsylvania itself was not part of James's original grant, but owed its separate existence to Charles II and William Penn, after whose father, Sir William Penn, the colony was named. Penn's father had been a distinguished admiral to whom the Crown owed some £16,000. The debt alone does not explain Charles II's agreement to grant Sir William's son the area between the fortieth and the forty-second parallels. Penn's

---

* Charles II granted his brother all of Maine between the St. Croix and Kennebec rivers and from the coast to the St. Lawrence River, all islands between Cape Cod and the Narrows, and all land from the west bank of the Connecticut River to the eastern shore of Delaware Bay.

NOVUM AMSTERODAMUM

proprietary charter was also testimony to his ability to win royal support in spite of his notorious Quaker faith.

The Quaker sect was established by George Fox, who preached that worldliness had undermined true Christianity. Success had even corrupted the Reformation. Quakers believed in the innate divinity of human beings, who could achieve salvation by true repentance and faith; they rejected ritual, oaths, war, and a tax-supported church. Many fled persecution in England only to find worse treatment in America. In Dedham, Massachusetts, for being a Quaker preacher, Christopher Holder was sentenced to thirty lashes with a three-corded whip, three days and nights in a bare cell without bedding or food and drink, and nine wintry weeks in jail without a fire but with a whipping twice a week. (Holder recuperated in Barbados, then returned to Dedham and was brought to Boston to have an ear lopped off.)

Many early fanatical Quakers sought and found martyrdom, but Penn preferred to establish a colony in which the Quaker views on religious and political toleration might be practically applied. He made his request to Charles II in 1680; the King responded the next year. The result was a

COLONIZATION: Sequence of Settlement[1]

1585 Roanoke Island (Sir Walter Raleigh)
1607 Sagadahoc (Plymouth Company)
1607 Jamestown (London Company)
1620 Plymouth (Pilgrims)
1623 New Netherland (Dutch West India Company)
1630 Massachusetts Bay
1634 Maryland (Cecilius Calvert, 2nd Lord Baltimore)
1636 Connecticut (Thomas Hooker)
     Rhode Island (Roger Williams)
1637 New Haven (John Davenport and Theophilus Eaton)
1638 Swedish Delaware
1663 Carolinas
1681 Pennsylvania (William Penn)
1732 Georgia

[1] Omitted are scattered piecemeal settlements (Maine, New Hampshire) and colonies that changed ownership or shared government (New Jersey, New York).

proprietary colony under royal surveillance: Penn was required to maintain an agent in London; he was enjoined to comply with English mercantile regulations and to submit Pennsylvania's legislative actions to the Crown's Privy Council for review. His charter secured, Penn undertook a tremendous publicity campaign, distributing pamphlets in Dutch, French, and German. He proclaimed his commitment to a liberal land policy and to freedom to worship (but political officeholding was denied to Catholics and Jews). The Indians posed no threat, thanks to the Iroquois domination of the weak Delawares and Penn's careful negotiations for their land. Philadelphia was founded in 1682; in 1683 some 3,000 settlers arrived in the province. Pennsylvania grew more in three years than New Netherland had in forty.

But for Penn the cost was high. There were constant boundary controversies with New York and Maryland, and he was always embroiled with contentious settlers. Because Penn was identified with the exiled James II, whose professed enthusiasm for religious toleration Penn took seriously, William and Mary deprived Penn of both charter and colony from 1692 to 1694. Frequently in debt, Penn found his proprietary revenues hard to collect; at one time he unsuccessfully attempted to sell his province back to the Crown for £12,000. But Penn's heirs eventually found economic as well as spiritual rewards in this last but most successful of England's proprietary colonies. Within about 125 years England had established its sovereignty—in an uneven fashion—along the length of North America, from Maine to Georgia. But the exceptions to the English monopoly of North America's Atlantic seaboard were significant: the Spanish presence in Florida and the French thrust into the St. Lawrence River valley were to create major problems in the eighteenth century as well as occasional difficulties in the seventeenth. But the extent of England's influence in North America was impressive, especially to European rivals. It remains a source of astonishment that so small an island should have exerted such influence and should have commanded so vast a continental domain.

The English empire was diverse. Its economy shifted sharply from colony to colony. Religious purpose and identity were no less varied. There were divisions within colonies as well as between them. Settlers came from many nations and spoke many languages. Some came in search of a better life, a farm of their own; some sought, and infrequently found, religious toleration; some looked for, and often did discover, religious freedom; and some came involuntarily, to discharge an obligation to an Old World society in the New World. There were royal colonies, proprietary colonies, corporate colonies, but each colony enjoyed a measure of self-government, a measure of economic, religious, and political opportunity. And each knew an association with a small island 3,000 miles distant, a mother country whose concept of their purpose and role proved increasingly at variance with their own.

Suggested Reading

The best treatment of the European context for discovery and colonization is furnished by J. H. Parry, *The Age of Reconnaissance* (1963); for new insights to the pre-Columbian Americas, see William Denevan, *The Native Population of the Americas in 1492* (1976), and a fresh approach to colonization presented by Francis Jennings, *The Invasion of America* (1975); for the English scene, see Wallace Notestein, *The English People on the Eve of Colonization** (1954); and for a more recent account of social conditions see Carl Bridenbaugh, *Vexed and Troubled Englishmen, 1590–1642* (1969).

Samuel Eliot Morison is still probably best known for his *Christopher Columbus Mariner** (1955), which first appeared in a two-volume version, *Admiral of the Ocean Sea* (1942); Morison's *The European Discovery of America: The Northern Voyages* (1971) is a thoroughly engaging and superbly illustrated treatment of all known voyages across the North Atlantic to the New World prior to 1600. A companion volume, *The Southern Voyages* (1974), is no less attractive. David B. Quinn has described England's early efforts at empire in a collection of excellent essays, *England and the Discovery of America, 1481–1620* (1974).

Early Spanish colonization is admirably presented in Charles Gibson's *Spain in America** (1966) and Paul Horgan's *The Spanish Conquistadores* (1963). Of the several excellent studies of the first Americans, the best are Alvin M. Josephy, Jr., *The Indian Heritage of America* (1968), and Wilcomb E. Washburn, *The Indian in America* (1975). C. W. Ceram's *The First*

American (1971) is an unusually readable review of archeological discovery in the New World. For British colonization, see Wesley Frank Craven's *The Southern Colonies in the Seventeenth Century* (1949), Edmund S. Morgan's *American Slavery, American Freedom: The Ordeal of Colonial Virginia* (1975), Richard S. Dunn's *Puritans and Yankees, The Winthrop Dynasty of New England 1630–1717* (1962), and John E. Pomfret's (with Floyd M. Shumway) *Founding the American Colonies, 1583–1660** (1970).

For an excellent introduction to New England Puritanism, see Alan Simpson, *Puritanism in Old and New England** (1955), and Darrett B. Rutman, *American Puritanism: Faith and Practice** (1970).

* Available in paperback edition

Chapter 2
Colonial America

The British have never been noted for their capacity for imperial planning and organization. Nor did they show particular foresight or understanding for their tasks as colonizers. Their social, economic, and political experiences at home did little to prepare them for the demands imposed by their new circumstances. The history of the British colonization of North America is characterized by the colonists' struggle to reconcile their previous experiences and traditions with an environment for which few of them were prepared.

The Colonial Economy

Although the colonists arrived unprepared for future political battles, they were well equipped to pursue their professions and to develop a healthy economy in the new land. About 90 percent of the American colonists engaged in agriculture. They adopted some Indian crops—maize (or Indian corn), tobacco, sweet potatoes, pumpkin, squash, wild rice, white potatoes—and brought others from the Old World—small grains, clover, forage grass, citrus fruit, farm animals. Draft animals enabled European immigrants to improve significantly on the cultivation techniques of the Indians, but the very abundance of land argued against scientific agriculture. Colonists rarely rotated or fertilized their crops; after they depleted the soil in one area, they left it to recover, cleared another and reduced that too. Equipment was primitive, labor scarce, and abandoned farms commonplace in the eighteenth century in America.

Throughout the colonial period, settlers clustered along the Atlantic seaboard, where they found the greatest opportunities and the fewest obstacles since, for generations, Indians had been clearing the coastal plain for their own farms. The Narragansetts, for instance, had cleared land up to ten miles inland; just a few miles upriver from the starving Jamestown settlers were hundreds of acres of cleared land ready for colonists' crops.

The southern "plantation" colonies were properly known for the cash crops they raised for export. The wide coastal plain, with its rich soil and long growing season, favored the cultivation of tobacco in the northern tier (Virginia and Maryland) and of rice and indigo in the two southernmost colonies (South Carolina and Georgia). Tobacco cultivation depleted the soil especially rapidly and tied its producers to a one-crop economy that was highly vulnerable to price fluctuations. Initially, tobacco was remarkably profitable—three shillings a pound in 1619—but within a decade it had dropped to one-twelfth of that sum. Over the next century and a half, the price hovered around two pence a pound and sometimes dropped to as low as one penny, causing plant-cutting riots in Virginia in the 1680s. But production seemed to rise regardless of price—to twenty million pounds per year by 1690 and to one hundred million by the time of the Revolution. Declining prices forced tobacco farmers into large-scale, plantation-style production and into heavy dependence on slave labor. Much the same was true for the South Carolina rice-growers, whose production rose from 90,000 barrels in 1740 to 155,724 barrels in 1771. Indigo, a vital textile dye, was introduced to the southern mainland in the 1740s and encouraged, actually supported, by British subsidies of six pence a pound; by the 1770s over one million pounds of indigo were raised annually. Subsidies—and thus the production of this cash crop—ended with the Revolution.

Grain was the basis of colonial agriculture. In the South, Indian corn, raised primarily for livestock, was probably more valuable than tobacco. Wheat, oats, barley, and rye were grown in the backcountry. From the Potomac to the Connecticut rivers, with some exceptions in New York, small farmers raised wheat and other cereal crops as well as fruits and vegetables. With ample wheat for export, milling became an important industry in New York.

Yet most American farmers produced, not for the market, but for themselves. New England's farms were mainly devoted to Indian corn, followed by oats, rye, barley, and flax. Dairy farming was popular in Connecticut and Rhode Island, where a few slave traders practiced a plantation-style agriculture. There was some sheep raising, particularly on the offshore islands, where the threat of wolves could be controlled.

Throughout the British colonies the agricultural economy and landholding opportunities interacted. Although many settlers came to America to escape surviving vestiges of feudalism, a feudal farm system did endure in isolated instances. In Maryland and New York, for example, large landowners (called patroons by the Dutch) had authority to hold their own manorial courts; such courts sustained the lord's feudal privileges and regulated his tenants' lives. South Carolina's Lords Proprietor attempted to establish a feudal class-structure. More significant was the quitrent, first a feudal payment to the local lord for protection and then a form of annual land tax. It was rarely invoked in New England but was commonplace elsewhere. Local forms of feudal tribute varied, often according to who the renter was. Usually the quitrent was paid at a rate of two to four shillings per hundred acres, but in New York one landowner paid one beaver skin annually for a million-acre tract; in Pennsylvania another magnate contributed one red rose annually. In the royal colonies the income went to the Crown; in the proprietary provinces a few patient and conscientious proprietors collected a sizable revenue from quitrents. Even in the eighteenth century, a few of the largest proprietors received feudal revenues that rivaled those of the great English landholders.

Occasional feudal survivals hardly explained all the economic inequality that prevailed in colonial America. In the middle and southern colonies, protected estates, inherited only by the firstborn son, nourished the growth of large landholdings and encouraged a new aristocracy. The head-right system, introduced in early Virginia, enabled wealthy landowners to acquire more land by funding additional immigrants. In the eighteenth century the head-right system fell into disfavor, but it was still easy to have a county surveyor (particularly in the southern colonies) lay aside an unappropriated area to which title might be secured from the governor.

Land hunger was real, and it was gratified: in Virginia, William Byrd II inherited 26,000 acres from his father and left 180,000 to his profligate heir in 1744; Robert Carter, also of Virginia, left an estate of 300,000 acres, 1,000 slaves, and £10,000 in cash; Benjamin Fletcher, governor of New York from 1692 to 1698, is estimated to have given his friends about 75 percent of the land then available in the colony. Landholding arrangements were usually different in New England, where geography combined with tradition to favor villages in which each family received a small lot in the township and perhaps 100 acres in surrounding tracts. Frequently, it was ministers and magistrates who acquired the best land. The result was provincialism and clannishness; newcomers were unwelcome. Denied a free share in communal land, these new settlers were often forced to attempt a purchase or, more likely, to move to the frontier.

But for all the inequality of its distribution, land was available, and as a partial consequence, labor was not since colonists preferred to farm their own land rather than someone else's. In an attempt to solve the persistent labor shortage, colonists produced large families and used servants, both white and black. White bondsmen, or indentured servants, were often free immigrants who pledged three to seven years of their

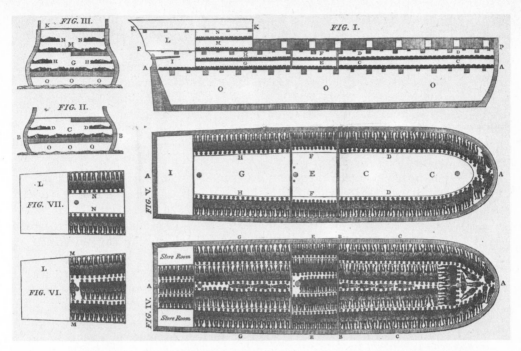

Conditions on the slave ships. The sketch below is the only known drawing executed on a slave vessel.

labor in return for a transatlantic passage. A significant number—possibly 50,000 or more—came involuntarily in discharge of court sentences for major crimes. British courts equated fourteen years of servitude in America with capital punishment in the mother country; seven-year terms were assigned for less serious crimes. Benjamin Franklin once suggested that, at the very least, Americans should return England's favor by shipping rattlesnakes to the mother country. Yet there never seemed enough white bondservants; moreover, they were costly, and their servitude was temporary. For many Americans the answer was the black slave.

The eighteenth century was the true age of colonial slavery. In fact, more black Africans than white Europeans had come to the New World by the end of that century. Ninety percent of all slaves going to the Americas ended up in the Caribbean islands or in Iberian America, where slave shipments kept pace with a horrifying death rate. Only in British North America was slave birth-rate substantially higher than slave death-rate. Virginia had 16,400 slaves in 1700; by 1760, with 140,600 slaves, almost half the Virginia population was black. By 1776 one-fifth of the total colonial population were slaves. Even a few of Philadelphia's Quakers owned blacks and supported savagely repressive legislation designed to sustain slavery. Some of the few instances of private manumission of slaves seem to have been prompted by a desire to avoid the cost of keeping a slave in his old age rather than by any concern about the morality of owning slaves. Protest, while grudging and slow, did come: in Pennsylvania in 1765 the Society of Friends disowned Quakers who imported slaves; three years later the Quakers' Yearly Meeting urged general manumission in Pennsylvania—but with limited results. Before the Revolution, only a few critics, like John Woolman, seriously addressed the moral issue of slavery.

Colonial Commerce and Manufacturing

British goods cost about twice as much in America as in Britain, and the colonial trade imbalance—colonies spending more on imports than their exports earned—created a serious shortage of currency for exchange with the mother country. These facts of colonial economic life led virtually every farmer and planter to undertake small-scale manufacturing to produce cloth, soap, candles, furniture, and crude tools and utensils. Iron smelteries, some subsidized by colonial legislatures, sprang up throughout the colonies. Domestic bounties, granted by colonial legislatures, encouraged distilleries and cloth mills.

The strongest encouragement came from England. Beginning in 1705 the mother country launched a program designed to foster the production of needed naval stores—tar, pitch, turpentine. The British

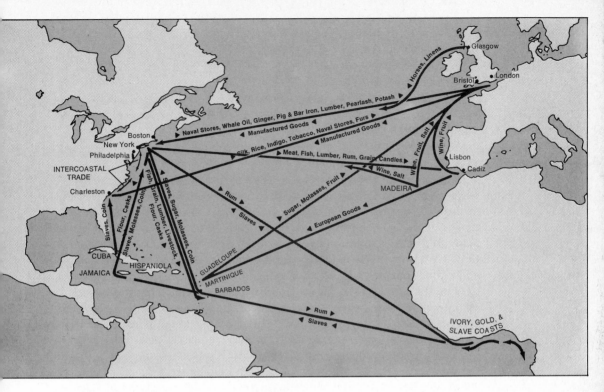

COLONIAL OVERSEAS COMMERCE

also purchased colonial ships and ship timber. (Perhaps 75 percent of American commerce was carried in colonial-built ships by 1775.) But the English viewed other colonial manufacturing activity less favorably, particularly if it competed with an English industry. The Hat Act of 1732 tolerated the colonial hat industry only to the extent that no hats could be exported from the colony of manufacture; the Iron Act of 1750 encouraged the colonial iron industry only in its production of bar and pig iron, which had then to be manufactured into finished goods in England.

By the mid-eighteenth century the American colonists were able to meet an astonishing number of their own economic needs. Massachusetts produced shoes; Pennsylvania manufactured wool stockings; paper production and publishing were widespread, and breweries and distilleries even more so. Timber and furs contributed to the economy of all the colonies. The fishing industry was a mainstay of New England's economy from the beginning. A major whaling industry, with a fleet of 360 ships operating out of northern ports, produced some 45,000 barrels of sperm oil by the 1770s. This growing sophistication of the colonial economy brought America into increasing commercial conflict with the mother country.

By the seventeenth century, England, in company with most European nation-states, had come to believe that power (and possibly survival) depended on wealth. Since riches meant national security, England took steps to promote and regulate its economic life. This view of national economic purpose, known as mercantilism, powerfully affected the English perception of the American colonies. The English considered the colonies to be vital sources of raw materials and important markets for English manufactured goods. A favorable trade balance and the husbanding of bullion were the mercantilist goals of English statesmen throughout the history of the first British Empire.

England began to regulate colonial commerce as early as the 1620s, when the Crown decreed that Virginia's tobacco had to be shipped exclusively to the mother country in British vessels. At the same time tobacco growing was forbidden in England, and very high import duties were imposed on foreign-grown tobacco. While England was caught up in its Civil War in the 1640s, the Dutch increased their commercial activity and threatened to monopolize the colonial trade. But once Cromwell had triumphed over Charles I, England was able to address the Dutch commercial threat. The result was the interregnum navigation laws that required foreign ships trading with the English colonies be licensed by the British government; goods from Asia, Africa, or America be shipped in English ships; and intercolonial trade be conducted in English ships, including of course, the vessels of English colonists.

But this was merely a beginning. In 1660 Charles II catered to English mercantile interests with another Navigation Act that restated the earlier legislation and enumerated a list of items—initially, sugar, tobacco, and cotton—that the colonies could send only to England or to another English colony. Three years later the Staple Act required most European goods destined for America to be shipped via England. And a decade later Charles supported the Plantation Duty Act, which imposed duties on enumerated articles to be paid by colonial shippers at the port of export. New England's infractions of the Navigation Acts provoked this legislation, which in turn occasioned the dispatch of British customs officials to the colonies. William and Mary codified earlier legislation in 1696 and provided for enforcement through vice-admiralty courts, which did not require a jury trial. Colonial laws contrary to these Navigation Acts were declared automatically void.

In the eighteenth century, England progressively lengthened the enumerated list to the point that most colonial exports were covered. Forced to sell to—and buy from—England, even tobacco planters and rice planters found themselves earning less and paying more in a noncompetitive market. The major beneficiaries seemed to be English middlemen whose charges for freight, handling, insurance, and distribution cut deeply into colonists' profits. Northern colonies, lacking the staples that England wished to import, were driven to complex trade patterns to earn currency with which to buy English goods. New

Englanders shipped fish and lumber to Spain and Portugal in return for wines, fruits, and coin, which they then took to the mother country for English goods. Or they shipped northern wheat, fish, and other provisions to the Caribbean in return for currency, sugar, molasses, and rum, much of which in turn was again exchanged for English goods.

Such trade rarely followed the so-called triangular routes; recent scholarship shows that colonial ships mainly shuttled directly from port to market. Although colonial merchants apparently preferred this simpler pattern, occasional multilateral voyages were necessary: some New England rum was shipped to Africa for black slaves who were in turn sold to the West Indies for coin and for molasses used to manufacture more rum. The British pretended to regulate trade in molasses with the Molasses Act of 1733, a measure that imposed a duty of sixpence per gallon on colonial imports of foreign molasses. Since the British West Indies alone could not meet mainland colonists' needs, this regulation could have been particularly burdensome. But the measure went unenforced, and the British Treasury never budgeted income from its duties.

Northern colonies probably fared better than those to the south. In addition to the currency earned from their trade patterns, English support of New England shipbuilding fostered a major currency-earning industry, one that enabled Boston to emerge as an important distributor of goods to other colonies.

But currency was still hard to come by. The colonies always lacked enough gold and silver to conduct domestic and foreign trade. They attempted various expedients, such as commodity money: tobacco was designated legal tender in Virginia and Maryland, as were beaver skins and wampum in New York.* But this currency was cumbersome and subject to debasement by spoilage. Promissory notes and bills of exchange helped, but the favored devices were illegal mints and printing presses. Massachusetts set up a mint in 1652 and issued coins until 1684, when Charles II stepped in. Between 1730 and 1750 the colonies resorted to paper money, often unsecured and, in New England and the Carolinas, rapid in its depreciation: New York, Virginia, and Pennsylvania managed their currency with considerable success.

British regulation of the colonial economy occasioned inconvenience and irritation, but it was hardly tyrannical or exploitive. Indeed, British merchants often tolerated large indebtedness, and in effect permitted credit that eased commercial friction until the 1760s. England was the natural financial and distribution center for colonial commerce and a logical source of capital. Colonial shipping benefited from protective features of the navigation laws, as did colonial recipients of British subsidies for indigo and naval stores. In any case, British enforcement of

---

* Wampum: small beads made of shells and used by North American Indians as money and for ornament.

those measures to which colonists objected was remarkably lax. Smuggling was commonplace, and customs officials were easily bribed. Although the mother country placed its own interests above those of the colonies, England did practice an early form of imperial preference that gave Americans a protected marketplace, often at the expense of the English consumer.

Colonial Society

Obviously, any reference to "English" colonies must be qualified. Large numbers of non-English immigrants made their contributions to what Hector St. John Crèvecoeur called "this promiscuous breed, that race now called Americans." The largest non-English white group was the Ulster Scots, who settled in western Pennsylvania in large numbers; there were a few English refugees from unsuccessful uprisings against the first two Hanoverian monarchs (in 1715 and 1745), but most came from the ill-fated settlement of northern Ireland. Germans, many of whom were refugees from the Thirty Years War (1618 – 48) and its bitter aftermath, received a warm welcome from William Penn. They kept to themselves and retained their own language and customs. (The Amish, still abundant in Lancaster County, are the best-known of the German Pietist survivors.) In addition, there were numbers of Dutch (in New York), Huguenot refugees from France (prominent in South Carolina), some Jews (first admitted to New Amsterdam), and Welsh, Swedes, Irish, and Swiss. All could acquire British citizenship after 1740, when Parliament stipulated a seven-year residence prerequisite. Of the fifty-six signers of the Declaration of Independence eighteen were of non-English ancestry and another eight were born outside the colonies.

The most populous colonies were in the South, where by 1763 more than a third of the 700,000 inhabitants were black. But rapid demographic growth characterized almost every colony, and, throughout the colonies, the population nearly doubled every twenty-five years after 1700: the 200,000 Americans of 1688 had become more than 600,000 in 1730, more than 1 million in 1750, and more than 2 million on the eve of independence. A high birthrate and a long life span were more responsible for population growth than immigration. If the vital statistics of one Massachusetts town are representative, one out of four American-born males survived to age 21; at that age, however, he could expect to live to be 70. The life expectancy of women was somewhat shorter, for one out of thirty births led to maternal death. The average couple produced about eight children, with two- or three-year intervals between births.

The nuclear family—father, mother, children—was the basic social unit: "Ruin families and you ruin all" was a widely repeated warning. Within the family, lines between generations blurred when fifteen or twenty years separated brothers and sisters. Apprentices and servants often added to the range of ages in a single family circle. A child's contact with other children was ordinarily less frequent than in contemporary America, but other social contacts were more varied.

Although most American women in the seventeenth and eighteenth centuries tended family and hearth, a few kept taverns or inns and others managed farms or plantations. American law contained fewer sex-related inequities than European law, fewer double standards, and more legal protection. A woman might assume legal responsibility—with or without her husband—for her children, and she was usually entitled to inherit at least a third of her husband's estate. She could sign contracts, own property, hold licenses, legally complain of her husband's abuse, and in very rare instances obtain a separation and divorce.

Protestant Christianity influenced every aspect of colonial life. Most Americans belonged to Calvinist denominations, such as the New England Congregational, the Presbyterian, and the Dutch and German Reformed churches. The Church of England prospered only in Virginia and Maryland. The balance of the colonial population was composed of Baptists, Quakers, Lutherans, Pietists, Methodists, Roman Catholics, and Jews.

The Congregationalists emerged as a bulwark of conservatism in New England. In seventeenth-century Massachusetts, attendance of the Congregational Church was required by law, and Sunday, with its two sermons, was the emotional and intellectual climax of the Puritan week. According to Calvinist doctrine, people's instincts were naturally evil, to be suppressed for the good of the soul. On Sunday, Congregationalists were forbidden to "make mince pies, dance, play cards, or any musical instrument, save the drum, trumpet and Jew's harp." But with the passage of time came concessions; in 1662 the Half-Way Covenant permitted baptism to children of "half-way" members—persons in good standing with the church but who had not testified to their experience of God's grace. By the end of the century it was possible to take communion without a prior public confession to faith.

Even so, there were resurgences of religious fanaticism, of which the best known and most lamentable was the witchcraft delusion in Salem. In 1692 the two young daughters of the local minister began to behave eccentrically, and they blamed their conduct on neighbors whom they identified as witches. A special court soon found its docket filled as the witchcraft mania infected the entire community. By the time Governor Phips was persuaded to abolish the court it had legally murdered 20 persons, including 14 women and a Congregational minister. Fifty who had confessed to being witches survived—the prosecution contended the Devil would not permit his genuine servants to admit their identity—and another 150 still awaited trial as the panic passed. But events of the times—the bloody King Philip's War (1675—76), which cost the lives of 1 in every 20 New Englanders and was viewed as God's judgment on His errant children, a smallpox epidemic, outbreaks of major fires, Cotton Mather's books on witchcraft—were all part of the context for tragedy.

In the 1720s, a new wave of evangelism threatened the Puritan oligarchy as well as the unity of other sects. The Great Awakening was a spontaneous interdenominational revival movement that began in the 1730s with the vigorous preaching of Theodore Frelinghuysen and Gilbert Tennent, followed by Jonathan Edwards and George Whitefield. In Northampton, Massachusetts, Edwards sought to communicate to his congregation the intensity of his own religious convictions, to demonstrate anew the omnipotence and splendor of Calvin's God. Whitefield, a traveling English evangelist and the herald of American Methodism, made seven trips to the American colonies from England to urge the spiritual regeneration of his vast audiences and to argue for a return to Christ and an end to sectarianism. But a reaction against such emotional fervor followed. Edwards's relentless exhortation led to his dismissal from the Northampton parish in 1750. Whitefield's crowds diminished in size. Schisms appeared: some conservative Puritans preferred the quiet comfort of Anglicanism; revivalist "New Side" Presbyterians separated from "Old Side" conservatives until 1758. The

Princeton: colleges for men only

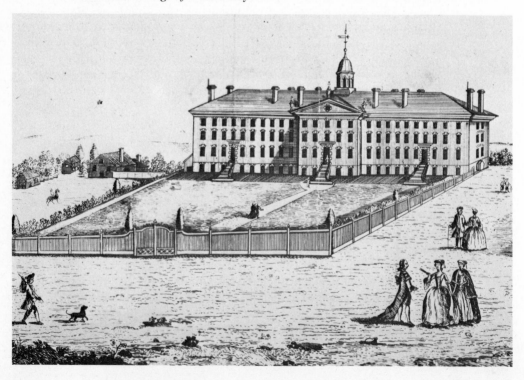

Great Awakening left the colonies with more religious sects, and these were less dominated by their ministers than other sects had been. By emphasizing the individual's relationship with God, rather than with the clergy, the revival had challenged all authority and undermined easy acceptance of the existing social order.

Although America's Old World heritage favored formal education only for the aristocratic few, many Protestants who settled in the colonies sought to make all society at least literate. The Puritans, in particular, argued that all should be able to read the Bible in order to study the source of divine truth, and that ministers should be scholars of Greek and Latin in order to read the original records of the Christian faith. The concept of public education was imperfectly grasped and infrequently practiced, but, in 1647, Massachusetts required towns of more than fifty families to provide a schoolmaster, and communities of more than one hundred families to establish a Latin grammar school. The fine for noncompliance was only £5, however. Other New England colonies passed similar legislation, with the exception of Rhode Island, where there was concern that public schools might lead to coercion in matters of private conscience.

Religious division unquestionably inhibited the growth of public education. Anglicans in New York opposed the school system established by the Dutch; Roman Catholics in Maryland resented Anglican efforts on behalf of public education in that colony; Quakers quoted George Fox, who said, "God stood in no need of human learning," and who termed Greek and Latin "the unsanctified work of pagans." And in the South, planters grouped together to hire a schoolmaster for the private tutoring of their children. Southerners generally saw public education as a badge of poverty and an act of charity, although this view still did not allow education for slaves.

Higher education fared better. A majority of the colonies had colleges by 1770, usually supported by the locally dominant church. Harvard was founded in 1636, but no degrees were conferred until 1642, and no charter was granted until 1650.* The College of William and Mary was founded in 1693 and Yale College in 1701. "The College Enthusiasm," as Ezra Stiles of Yale termed the wave of new colleges after 1746, was a consequence of the Great Awakening and the renewed colonial concern for denominational education. Twice as many colleges were founded between 1746 and 1769 as in the preceding century, and the number of new colleges doubled again between 1769 and 1789. Many of the new colleges sought to reduce costly denominational conflicts: King's College (Columbia) included representatives from four denominations in addition to its Anglican members; Rhode Island College (Brown) tolerantly named

---

* It was issued by the General Court, but with doubtful authority. Issuance of college charters was the prerogative of the Crown; the monarchy was in an uncertain condition during the Civil War, and Charles I was beheaded in 1649.

Baptists, Quakers, Congregationalists, and Anglicans as trustees. "There is so much defect in all [of us]," commented Stiles, "that we all need forbearance and mutual condescension."

These institutions—for men only—offered a similar range of programs, which usually included logic, rhetoric, philosophy, grammar, ancient history, Greek, Latin, and Hebrew. Some interest in science and modern languages developed at King's College and at Benjamin Franklin's Philadelphia Academy. Complaints about the relevance of college programs were common, as were charges of lax academic standards. "Ignorance wanders unmolested," and "after four years dozing there, no one is ever refused the honours of a degree." One real test was financial, for the fees were only within the reach of the wealthy.

But the colonists did not depend exclusively on formal education for their learning. They were an astonishingly bookish people. John Adams spoke for many when he asked in his diary, "How can any man judge, unless his mind has been opened and enlarged by reading?" Book collecting was popular, and collections ranged from the 40 volumes Peter Jefferson left his son Thomas to the 3,500 volumes amassed by William Byrd II. Even a Baltimore County ironmaster, Joseph Smith, left a modest estate comprising clothing, a penknife, two razors, an ink pot, and Rapin's *History of England.* For those less fortunate there were subscription libraries; Franklin founded the first in 1731 in Philadelphia,* and others quickly followed in Charleston, Newport, New York, and Lancaster. By 1776 there were sixty such libraries. The bookshelves were crowded with volumes on theology, geography, law, and particularly on history and politics. Most were imported from England, but many were printed in America, often as a sideline to newspaper publishing.

The first colonial newspaper, the *Boston News-Letter,* had appeared in 1704. Between 1713 and 1745 some twenty-two newspapers were launched, and by 1765 every colony except New Jersey and Delaware could boast of its own paper. At first the press, modest in size and ambition, focused on advertisements, shipping news, and local items of interest. Soon its attention extended to the larger world of colonial and international politics.

Historians have exaggerated the degree to which the famous case of John Peter Zenger's *New-York Weekly Journal* provided freedom for the colonial press. Zenger's acquittal after his indictment for seditious libel meant freedom for Zenger, not for the press. As late as 1804 New York courts were rejecting truth as a defense against charges of criminal libel, and throughout the period of the Revolution, Patriots intimidated editors.

To some extent, the proliferation of American colleges, libraries, and newspapers was a reflection of the growing urbanization of the colonies. Such cultural amenities prospered in the towns and cities. With the

* The Library Company of Philadelphia still survives; in 1773 it was located in Carpenter's Hall and served effectively as the first Library of Congress.

growth of commerce and the increasing sophistication of the economy, primitive trade centers became urban centers. Philadelphia, the largest colonial city, had a population of some 30,000 by 1770; New York was close behind, followed by Boston, Newport, Charleston, Salem, New Haven, Baltimore, Norfolk, and Wilmington. Annapolis and Williamsburg were political centers of seasonal importance. The towns and cities contained only 10 percent of the total population, but they exerted a cultural and political influence far beyond mere numbers. Colonial cities were commercial centers, not industrial sites. Even so, their polluted surface wells, open sewers (until the 1740s), and uncollected garbage would have disturbed any thoughtful ecologist. Obviously, urban problems were not unknown in colonial America.

Colonial Politics

From the outset, white, male English settlers expected representative self-government patterned after that of the mother country. As a result, companies, proprietors, and the Crown alike found themselves obliged to broaden the colonists' political involvement in the affairs of their province. Every North American English colony steadily increased the authority of its own political institutions. Politics soon became an avenue to power, wealth, and reputation in the New World as well as in the Old. Although the British Crown ruled the colonists, the English in America soon sought to define legislative power so that its center of gravity would be in the colonies.

The titular head of government in all colonies was the governor. In Connecticut and Rhode Island, he was elected by the voters, and in Maryland, Delaware, and Pennsylvania, he was named by the proprietor. In the royal colonies the Crown appointed the governor. These royal governors were representative of the British governing class. There were those like Queen Anne's cousin, Lord Cornbury, a drunkard and an embezzler given to wearing women's clothes; there were others like Alexander Spotswood of Virginia or William Shirley of Massachusetts, who governed with skill and intelligence. The governor of a royal colony held office at the King's pleasure; sometimes that pleasure was of brief duration, but tenure usually averaged five years. Each governor's authority was more apparent than real: his approval of colonial legislation was essential but could be overridden by the Crown; he could summon and dissolve the colonial assembly, and sometimes he could control his council, the upper house, but his influence over the lower house steadily diminished.

Colonial legislatures were ordinarily bicameral; the council (the upper house) was effectively selected by the governor, sometimes from a listing furnished by the assembly (the lower house). Initially prestigious, the council was a colonial version of England's Privy Council, which combined judicial, executive, and legislative functions. Although gubernatorial acts required the approval of council members, the fact that these council members could be suspended from office at the governor's pleasure restrained their independence. The lower house clearly had greater independence: elected by qualified property-owners and usually weighted in favor of the tidewater gentry, the colonial assembly saw itself as equivalent to England's House of Commons, particularly in regard to personal privilege, freedom of debate, and control over appropriations, including the governor's salary. In the colonies north of Maryland, the governor could anticipate financial harassment if he displeased the assembly: as New Yorkers noted in 1741, they would "starve him into compliance." Just as in England Parliament used its power of the purse to bring the Stuarts to heel, so did the colonial assembly extend its power at the governor's expense.

Throughout the colonial experience there was division and dissension, particularism and separatism, both within and among the colonies. The causes of internal division—and the open insurrection they sometimes produced—varied from colony to colony. Frequently, economic and political frustration were factors; powerful and prosperous early settlers dominated provincial political life, provoking the resentment and anger of recent immigrants, who were excluded from the inner circle of influence. Immigration and the expansion of the economy aggravated social, class, and political friction. Bacon's Rebellion in Virginia, the Leisler Rebellion in New York, and the Regulator movements in the Carolinas were all manifestations of this discontent.

Indian attacks on the Virginia frontier occasioned the uprising led by Nathaniel Bacon, but charges of political privilege and discriminatory taxes aroused public support for him. The precise motives for Bacon's angry march against the governor, Sir William Berkeley, in 1676 are unclear, owing to Bacon's sudden death from dysentery ("the flux") and the vigorous retribution taken by Berkeley against the rebels. In the Leisler revolt (1689–91), Jacob Leisler, a contentious German merchant in Manhattan, led a city mob against the entrenched oligarchy; he subsequently summoned a representative assembly that broke the trading monopoly of New York merchants. Leisler's was an ethnic struggle against the ruling Anglicans, one that the honest but hot-tempered German mismanaged; charged with treason by Governor Henry Sloughter, Leisler and his son-in-law were hanged in May 1691.[*] The Carolina Regulators are less easily categorized. In South Carolina in the 1760s and 1770s there was relatively little hostility among the tidewater, frontier, and backcountry sections. The Regulation movement there took the form of a vigilante group acting against lawlessness on the frontier, an effort toward more, not less, government. In North Carolina, however, the

[*] In 1695 Parliament reversed the verdict and returned Leisler's property to his family; Leisler's personal resurrection was clearly more difficult.

Regulators were western debtors protesting extortion and corruption on the part of the eastern establishment headed by Governor William Tryon. Government forces triumphed over the Regulators in a bizarre battle in 1771, and Tryon promptly executed seven rebel leaders. Many Regulators subsequently sided with the Loyalists in the Revolution, because they identified Patriot leadership with the ruling aristocracy.

If Americans had difficulty maintaining unity in a single colony, they found an even greater challenge in their periodic experiments with intercolonial union. Of all such efforts before 1774, the Confederation of New England was most nearly autonomous. Created in 1643 when the mother country was diverted by domestic divisions between Crown and Parliament, the confederation was a conscious colonial effort to meet common dangers from the Dutch, French, and Indians. Massachusetts Bay, Plymouth, Connecticut, and New Haven constituted the membership of this Puritan confederacy, which appointed eight commissioners to deal with Indian problems, foreign threats, and internal differences. These so-called United Colonies had limited effectiveness since the commissioners had only an advisory role, and Massachusetts clearly dominated the smaller member colonies. The commissioners did assist with several boundary disputes and brought some coordination to the New England effort against King Philip of the Wampanoags and his allies in the bloody Indian war of 1675 – 76.

By 1680 the British government—which never recognized the Confederation of New England—had developed its own reasons for intercolonial union. Charles II established the Lords of Trade and Plantations (a new committee of his Privy Council) and sent Edward Randolph to investigate New England's notorious noncompliance with the new Navigation laws. Randolph's reports led directly to the revocation of the Massachusetts Bay Charter in 1684 and the decision to establish the Dominion of New England. In 1685 James II appointed Sir Edmund Andros as governor-general of the dominion, which was made up of New York, New Jersey, and the New England colonies. Colonial legislatures were abolished, their power transferred to Andros, and a council named by the Crown. Andros's efforts to levy new quitrents, impose Anglicanism, and challenge earlier land titles brought an immediate outcry from the colonists. The occasion for the downfall of the dominion was soon forthcoming: in England Protestant alarm over the birth of a Roman Catholic heir to James II brought about the Glorious Revolution in 1688 and the invitation to William and Mary to assume the throne; news of the overthrow of James reached New England in March 1689 and stimulated a spontaneous and successful uprising against Andros. In 1691 William and Mary granted Massachusetts a new charter, which substituted a property qualification for the earlier religious test for suffrage. The new royal province incorporated Plymouth and Maine; the other colonies involved in the dominion resumed their former style of government.

Interest in intercolonial union did not end with this ill-fated dominion. English enthusiasm for more efficient imperial administration persisted, as did colonists' concern for greater defensive capacity against the growing French and Indian menace. The British Board of Trade gave serious consideration to a defensive union of the colonies in 1754 but rejected the proposal for domestic political reasons. At the same time, England called for a meeting of representatives from the northern colonies to assemble in Albany in 1754 to improve American relations with the Iroquois. Colonial delegates made modest progress with their Indian diplomacy, then discussed the need for some form of confederation for "general Safety and Interest." The result was a Plan of Union (the Albany Plan) comprising a President-General, appointed (and paid) by the Crown, and a Grand Council, elected by the colonial assemblies. This new intercolonial legislature would administer western lands and Indian affairs, levy taxes, and direct general defense, subject to the approval of the President-General. Despite mounting fear of the French, not one colony approved the Albany Plan. Some feared it would open the door to stricter British rule; others resented the reduction of their sovereignty. In any case, colonial approval was irrelevant since the British government had already decided colonial union was neither timely nor wise; the arrival of copies of the Albany Plan in London provoked neither comment nor action.

The Contest for Empire

The defensive needs of the English colonies reflected the international crisis that marked the mid-eighteenth century. Although this crisis was largely European, North America now shared the Old World's difficulty in living peacefully with itself. Anglo-French rivalry in the New World occasioned the outbreak of the French and Indian War, or the Great War for the Empire, which lasted from 1754 to 1763.

French power in North America began with Samuel de Champlain. This soldier-explorer led a trading expedition up the St. Lawrence to the falls above Montreal in 1603, later explored the coast northward from Cape Cod, journeyed inland to the lake that bears his name, and founded a settlement in Quebec in 1608. He allied with the Algonquin Indians against their Iroquois enemies, an impolitic error and one the Iroquois never forgot or forgave. Quebec grew almost grudgingly, partly because Champlain saw it only as a Jesuit missionary outpost, partly because of its checkered history of company rule before the absolutist Louis XIV took over and ruled from 1643 to 1715.

Jean Talon, the first deputy of Louis XIV, brought a thousand troops and the stability needed for French colonization in North America. Talon's objective was the extension of French influence to the west and south. He sponsored the expeditions of Louis Joliet and Father Marquette, who in 1673 descended the Wisconsin River to the Mississippi. In 1682, Sieur de La Salle explored the Mississippi to the Gulf of Mexico, naming the region Louisiana for his sovereign. A decade later France sponsored an agricultural settlement in the Illinois area, which was later assigned to Louisiana for administration. The major population growth on the lower Mississippi took place early in the eighteenth century: by 1730 Mobile and New Orleans were firmly established, with a total settlement of some 5,000 whites and 2,000 slaves. Yet, by 1750 the combined population of French settlements was only 60,000.

French settlements were widely scattered, exclusively Roman Catholic in religion, autocratic in government, and feudal in design. French colonists were much more victimized by their mercantilist mother country and were much less agrarian in their economy than the English colonists. This absence of a firm agricultural base and the lack of diversified industry combined to render New France economically vulnerable.

French emphasis on the fur trade and the fishing industry aroused the jealousy and resentment of English competitors. And neither politics nor religion endeared the French colonists to their English neighbors. But conflict did not surface immediately, partly because the nature of each group's colonization was so different. The English colonial presence was open and conspicuous, from Maine's rock-bound coast to Georgia's low-lying shores. French colonization was slow, feebly supported, and handicapped by the physical geography and the feudalism of New France. It required events in Europe to set conflict in motion.

Colonial America was never an entity separate from its European source. Nowhere is this fact more evident than in the Anglo-French wars of the colonial period. Between 1620 and 1680 the Stuarts were (with Cromwell's interruption) on the English throne; the Stuarts tended to ally with their Catholic friends in France. But the arrival of William and Mary after the Glorious Revolution of 1688 altered this cozy relationship overnight: Louis XIV recognized James II as the legitimate ruler of England and thus precipitated King William's War (1689–97, known in Europe as the War of the League of Augsburg). This was followed by Queen Anne's War (1702–13). In both instances, England and France paid little attention to the American theater.

The occasion for Queen Anne's War, called the War of the Spanish Succession in Europe, was Louis XIV's support for his grandson to succeed to the Spanish throne, coupled with French insistence on recognizing the son of the deceased James II as rightful monarch of England. Significantly, the new (French) King of Spain, Philip V, assigned the valued *Asiento*—the exclusive right to supply slaves to Spanish colonies—to a French company, which infuriated the envious English. An Anglo-American expedition to Port Royal, Acadia (Nova Scotia), succeeded because the French garrison was outnumbered by at least eight to one.

In the ensuing peace settlement at Utrecht in 1713, British gains reflected the scale of the Franco-Spanish defeats: France ceded Newfoundland, the Hudson Bay area, and all of Acadia except Cape Breton Island, and acknowledged British suzerainty over the Iroquois; the British finally accepted Philip V as King of Spain and received a thirty-year grant of the coveted *Asiento*.

Anglo-French relations did not improve in the twenty-six years of peace that followed Utrecht. Each power prepared for the next encounter in colonial America: the French strengthened Fort Louisburg on Cape Breton Island, making it an invaluable base from which privateers preyed on New England fishing and shipping; border disputes abounded; rivalry for the fur trade persisted as both sides constructed forts on Lake Ontario. There were growing commercial difficulties with Spain. It was in this context that an English sea captain, Robert Jenkins, claimed that his ear was sliced off by a Spanish naval officer. His tale, along with the news that Spain had revoked the *Asiento*, aroused sufficient emotion in England to bring about what was initially called the War of Jenkin's Ear in 1739. This colonial war with Spain soon grew into a major war in Europe (the War of the Austrian Succession) aimed at France. In America (where it was known as King George's War), Georgia managed a stalemate with Spanish Florida, but the major event was an Anglo-American attack on Fort Louisburg, which fell after a forty-nine-day siege. Under the Treaty of Aix-la-Chapelle (1748), a new six-year truce was declared: England returned Fort Louisburg to France, to the lasting disgust of New England, in order to regain Madras in India. But nothing—in Europe or America—was really settled.

Both sides used the brief period of peace to prepare for the next reckoning. The British strengthened their hold on Nova Scotia while the French expanded their influence above Lake George and Lake Champlain. But the most crucial area of conflict was the Ohio Valley, where the French linked their Louisiana settlements with New France to the north; a strong link would prevent English expansion into the trans-Appalachian west. It was near the Monongahela River that young George Washington met his first defeat when he had to surrender to the French at Fort Necessity on July 4, 1754.

The undeclared French and Indian War had been thus underway for two years before it became the Seven Years' War in Europe (1756—63). This long struggle between Prussia (allied with England) and Austria (allied with France and Russia) for control of central Europe drained France, distracted England, and served neither nation. Spain at first remained neutral but eventually entered the war—just in time to lose Florida to Britain.

In America the British continued to demonstrate incompetent leadership. Defeat followed defeat: the French took Fort Oswego in 1756, repulsed a British attack on Fort Louisburg in 1757, and even captured Fort William Henry, on Lake George, that August. The West was visited

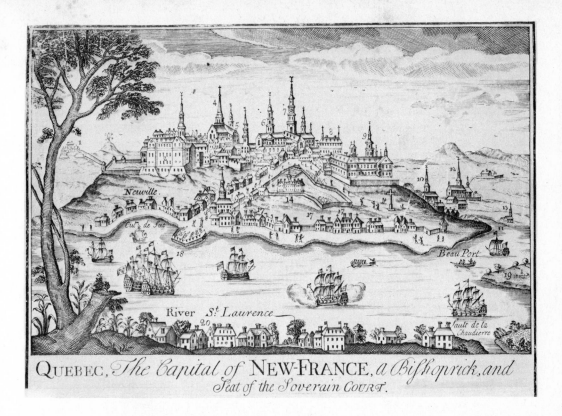

QUEBEC, *The Capital of* NEW-FRANCE, *a Bifhoprick, and Seat of the Soverain* COURT.

with fire and pillage, the French seeming to do what they pleased. Not until William Pitt came to power did the direction of England's fortunes improve. A superb orator, incredible egotist ("I am sure I can save this country and that no one else can"), and excellent strategist, Pitt infused new vigor into the national war effort and put new leaders in command of its forces. In 1758 Jeffrey Amherst and James Wolfe captured Fort Louisburg, and later that year John Forbes (with Washington on his staff) reached the smoldering ruins of Fort Duquesne in the Ohio Valley. Deserted by their Indian allies, the French were in retreat. The next year was decisive. Wolfe landed nearly five thousand men on the Plains of Abraham outside Quebec; both Wolfe and the French commander, the Marquis de Montcalm, fell in the ensuing battle, but Quebec was taken. A year later the remaining French army surrendered Montreal, and the war was essentially over in America.

But making the peace was almost as difficult as winning the war. Pitt was maneuvered out of office because he seemed too eager to widen the war rather than to end it. A new King, the young George III, wanted his former tutor, Lord Bute, in the government and had his way. Eager to end the costly conflict, Bute made major concessions to France. The resultant Treaty of Paris (1763) was so unpopular that Bute gained parliamentary approval only through ruthless use of patronage. By the

ANGLO-FRENCH WARS, 1689—1763

1689—97 King William's War (War of the League of Augsburg)[1]
1702—13 Queen Anne's War (War of the Spanish Succession)
1739—42 War of Jenkins' Ear
1744—48 King George's War (War of the Austrian Succession)
1754—63 French and Indian War, or Great War for the Empire (Seven
Years' War, 1756—63)

[1] Names in parentheses refer to terms used in Europe.

treaty, England acquired New France and all of North America east of the Mississippi. Spain assigned Florida to England and as a compensation, France ceded to Spain the Louisiana territory west of the Mississippi by a separate secret treaty. England returned to France the captured West Indian islands of Guadeloupe and Martinique, and France retained fishing rights on the Newfoundland banks.

Perhaps the most difficult problem for England had been the decision to retain Canada rather than the islands of Guadeloupe and Martinique. France had made clear its determination to resume the war rather than part with all three possessions. It was noted that the islands' exports to England in 1761 were forty times those of Canada, that as islands they were more easily controlled, and that they would meet New England's economic need. Those advocating Canada argued that control of the North American fur trade was vital, that Canadian markets would expand and be receptive to British trade, that only the expulsion of the French would bring stability and peace to British America. Of course, the acquisition of Canada made for a tidier map and happier sugar planters in the British West Indies, who did not care to compete with Guadeloupe and Martinique.

The series of wars thus concluded explain more of the colonial condition than the campaigns and peace treaties immediately suggest. Clearly, colonial life was persistently shaped by decisions made in Europe rather than in America. Military power belonged to the nations that colonized America. Clearly, the contest for empire rarely reflected the real value of the territories in dispute; the colonists' interests were subservient to the larger political struggle between European adversaries. Of course, it was no less clear that the Treaty of Paris was hardly definitive; the defeated French looked for revenge; and the English observers predicted that the removal of the French threat to the English mainland colonies could well lead these colonies into independence. After all, the colonies would no longer need their mother country for protection.

Benjamin Franklin, for one, could not take this prospect seriously: the colonies had been unable to support union against the hated French in 1754, so what chance could there be for union against the mother country?

Suggested Reading

One of the most readable and illuminating surveys of colonial America is Clarence L. Ver Steeg's *The Formative Years, 1607–1763* * (1963), which can be most profitably accompanied by Daniel J. Boorstin, *The Americans: The Colonial Experience* * (1958), and Louis B. Wright, *The Cultural Life of the American Colonies* * (1957).

Carl Bridenbaugh has made vast contributions to our understanding of the American as colonist; his studies of colonial cities—*Cities in the Wilderness* * (1938) and *Cities in Revolt* * (1955)—are very informative. Bridenbaugh's *Myths and Realities: Societies of the Colonial South* * (1952) is readable and provocative. Several new monographs have added to our understanding of New England colonial society, notably John Demos's *A Little Commonwealth: Family Life in Plymouth Colony* * (1970); Richard L. Bushman's *From Puritan to Yankee: Character and the Social Order of Connecticut, 1690–1765* * (1967); Kenneth A. Lockridge's *A New England Town: The First Hundred Years, Dedham, Massachusetts, 1636–1736* * (1970) and *Literacy in Colonial New England* (1974).

Richard B. Morris's *Government and Labor in Early America* * (1946) retains its value, particularly when read with Jack P. Greene's *The Quest for Power* (1963) and Charles Sydnor's charming study of *Gentlemen Freeholders* * (1952). Michael Kammen's *Empire and Interest: The American Colonies and the Politics of Mercantilism* * (1969) includes a useful introduction to Anglo-American commercial and economic difficulties. Lawrence A. Harper's *The English Navigation Laws* (1939) remains the reference volume on that subject. Gary M. Walton and James F. Shepherd, in *Shipping, Maritime Trade, and the Economic Development of Colonial North America* (1972), provide an excellent review of colonial trade patterns. Joseph A. Ernst's *Money and Politics in America, 1755–1775* (1973) reminds us of the economic realities that confronted colonists in the eighteenth century.

In *White over Black* (1968), Winthrop D. Jordan has furnished an outstanding study of the black experience in early America. Jordan's study can now be supplemented with Peter H. Wood's *Black Majority* (1974), an excellent account of blacks in South Carolina from 1670 to 1739.

For further reading on colonial religion, see Edwin S. Gaustad, *The Great Awakening in New England* * (1957), and Alan Heimert, *Religion and the American Mind from the Great Awakening to the Revolution* (1966); Marion L. Starkey's *The Devil in Massachusetts* * (1952) is less demanding but very good reading. Colonial education is admirably treated in Bernard Bailyn's brief essay *Education in the Forming of American Society* * (1960), in Robert Middlekauff's *Ancients and Axioms* (1963), and in Lawrence A. Cremin's *American Education: The Colonial Experience, 1607–1783* (1970).

The history of France in America is still poorly recorded, but Lawrence Henry Gipson gave a fine summation in the fifth volume of his massive

The British Empire Before the American Revolution (1942). G. M. Wrong's *The Rise and Fall of New France* (1928) is still a good survey, and Howard H. Peckham supplies a fine military history in *The Colonial Wars, 1689–1782** (1964), which can be usefully consulted in conjunction with Douglas Leach, *Arms for Empire: A Military History of the British Colonies in North America, 1607–1763* (1973).

* Available in paperback edition

Chapter 3
The Real Revolution,
1763 — 1776

Chronology

1760 George III ascends throne •

1761 Britain invokes writs of assistance; challenged by James Otis •

1763 Pontiac uprising • Proclamation of 1763 grants western lands to Indians •

1764 Currency Act • Sugar Act •

1765 Stamp Act •

1766 Stamp Act repealed • Declaratory Act •

1767 Townshend Acts • John Dickinson's *Letters from a Farmer in Pennsylvania* published •

1770 Townshend Acts repealed • Boston Massacre •

1773 Tea Act • Boston Tea Party •

1774 Coercive Acts; Quebec Act • Thomas Jefferson's *Summary View* • First Continental Congress meets in Philadelphia •

1775 Battles at Lexington and Concord • Second Continental Congress meets •

1776 Thomas Paine's *Common Sense* issued • *July 2:* Lee's resolution on independence approved 12–0 • *July 4:* Jefferson's Declaration of Independence approved 12–0 • *July 9:* New York endorses Declaration •

Thirty-five years after the official conclusion of the American War for Independence John Adams was still pondering, "What do we mean by the revolution?" It was not the war—"That was not part of the revolution. It was only an Effect and consequence of it." He was convinced that "the real American Revolution" was the "radical change in the principles, opinions, sentiments, and affections of the people." Adams, significantly, did not contend that the change extended to religious, economic, or social assumptions. But the Revolution illustrated the American habit of seeking and sometimes stumbling on political solutions to urgent problems. Although we are still charting the dimensions of Adams's "radical change" as applied to the Revolution as a whole, there was indeed significant change between the conclusion of the war for empire in 1763 and the proclamation of independence in 1776.

At first glance, Anglo-American relations appear to have been unusually harmonious in the early 1760s. British arms and British ships, with some colonial support, had destroyed French power on the North American mainland. The acquisition of Canada opened up vast new economic opportunities for both the colonies and the mother country. Americans basked in the reflected glory of their membership in the greatest empire ever known. As Benjamin Franklin remarked, the colonies felt closer to their mother country than to one another.

But gratitude is poor political currency, and the British soon discovered that their American colonists were conveniently forgetful of the expenditure of British blood and treasure that had brought them security. Colonists rapidly realized that their safety and welfare no longer depended on Britain; indeed, they soon found their interests threatened and frustrated by their mother country. For the British attitude toward America had also shifted: whereas periods of "benign neglect" had marked the course of British conduct early in the eighteenth century, the 1760s reflected larger expectations in regard to colonial regulation and revenue. The young king who ascended to the throne in 1760 was mentally and emotionally immature, but George III was deadly serious about politics. His complacent conservatism led him to view American disaffection as a wanton attack on an ideal kingdom. As England and America continued on a collision course, Americans came increasingly to believe that it was British policy to deny them the fruits of the victory of 1763.

In a decade and a half American colonists found a surprising degree of unity in war against the very nation that had made them secure. Few American revolutionaries either calculated or anticipated the consequences of their insistence upon rights and privileges. War with the mother country was unsought; independence was announced with a widespread misgiving and hesitation, and not a few colonists declined this ultimate step and joined the ranks of those loyal to Britain.

Conflicting Interests in the West

Anglo-American misunderstanding was first exposed by conflicting interests in western lands so recently wrested from French control. Before 1760 Britain and the colonies had a common objective—to encourage western population growth in order to frustrate French expansion. But after 1763, settlement could no longer be considered a defensive measure. Southern planters, discouraged by diminishing profits, and northern merchants, dismayed by British commercial restrictions, looked westward for speculative opportunities and profits. Britain feared that rapid expansion westward would reduce the value of British investment in the eastern section of America. Moreover, British fur-trading merchants did not want hordes of settlers destroying the animals and disturbing the Indians. After 1760, the British and the Americans differed sharply on the appropriate treatment of Indians: the British preferred to leave them alone and thus avoid conflict, but the Americans began a systematic occupation of Indian lands, driving the Indians away and stirring up trouble.

George III
(1760 – 1820)

When, in 1760, Lord Jeffrey Amherst, the British commander in chief, stopped distributing gifts to the Indians as a measure of economy, unscrupulous colonial traders moved in, debauched the Indians with liquor, and swindled them with ease. When the news reached the Indians that France had ceded their land to Britain in the Treaty of Paris, they were persuaded to attempt to block further white settlement. Ably led by Pontiac, an Ottawa chief, Indians swept over seven of the nine British garrisons in the Upper Ohio Valley by June 1763. Pontiac's brief success owed something to the poor judgment of General Amherst, who discounted the threat and left his forts undermanned, but it owed more to surprise. An early example of bacterial warfare—distribution of smallpox-infected blankets to the Indians—and two major military expeditions in 1764 eroded Indian power; Pontiac held out until 1765.

The British government did not wait to subdue Pontiac before addressing problems in the West. Even before news reached London of Pontiac's attacks, Lord Shelburne had planned to close to settlement lands west of the headwaters of the rivers flowing into the Atlantic— and not yet secured by purchase or Indian grant. In October 1763, Shelburne's plan, known as the Proclamation of 1763, was approved and issued without the provisional character Shelburne had intended. George Washington, an avid speculator in western lands, spoke for many when he remarked "I can never look upon that proclamation in any other light . . . than as a temporary expedient to quiet the minds of the Indians." Although the proclamation had a brief effective life, many colonists saw it as impossibly restrictive; their irritation abated only slightly when Britain negotiated treaties that opened more land to settlement.

Commerce and Currency

Commerce and currency had long caused quarrels with the mother country. Colonial merchants invariably succumbed to the easy lines of credit extended by British factors—who then imposed stringent controls (and high interest rates) on their imprudent clients. Trade became less free, even within the confines of the imperial regulation of colonial commerce; debtor-merchants sought every possible avenue of escape from the frequently severe liquidity crises brought on by periodic efforts to collect colonists' debts. The war with France created both opportunities and new problems. Many colonial merchants were unable to resist the windfalls to be made from selling provisions to the enemy. The British government used writs of assistance, or general search warrants, to enforce the claim to full control of American commerce. Long in use in the mother country, such writs were not customary in America. When the writs came up for renewal on the occasion of the coronation of George III, Boston merchants retained James Otis to challenge the legality of the writs in 1761. The writs, Otis charged, violated the fundamental rights of British subjects as confirmed by the Magna Carta. "An act against the Constitution," Otis insisted, "is void." John Adams, present at court, was enthralled: "Otis was a flame of fire," Adams recalled later, "American independence was then and there born." The judge found Otis less persuasive and referred the question to London, where the government promptly declared the writs constitutional.

The currency impasse provoked similar rhetoric based on similar constitutional arguments. Constantly confronted by a shortage of bullion, the colonists had acquired a history of monetary experimentation, to which the war with France added another chapter. For many colonists, especially in the South, the only way to meet the war's fiscal demands was to issue paper money or to establish commodities as currency. They used paper currency to finance local military efforts and to pay off British creditors. And even before the war Virginians had used tobacco for local transactions.

The Anglican clergy in Virginia, whose annual salary had been pegged at 16,000 pounds of tobacco since 1696, might have benefited from this arrangement. When tobacco prices rose sharply in 1755 and 1758 the Virginia Assembly passed a law pegging clergy salaries at a third of the market price. The clergy, outraged over losing a 300 percent salary increase, persuaded the British Privy Council to disallow this legislation and then brought suit for the balance due. But Patrick Henry attacked the council's action as unconstitutional. Virginia's charters, thundered Henry, guaranteed Virginians their rights, "as if they had been abiding and born within the Realm of England." As a result of young Henry's oratory, the plaintiff in the case, the Reverend James Maury, received the most nominal compensation, precisely one penny in damages. The impunity with which Henry could attack the king (he had "degenerated into a tyrant," Henry claimed, and should forfeit "all rights to his subjects' obedience") and the attention colonists gave such remarks made the costs for Britain far greater.

Virginia's creditors strongly supported the British postwar drive against colonial paper money. This campaign reached a successful conclusion in 1764, when Britain passed a new Currency Act that extended to all colonies the prohibition on paper money, which had been applied to New England in 1751. A postwar depression made such legislation disastrous for Americans: the British action denied the colonists their most convenient and available medium of exchange. Most modern economists argue that currency in circulation should be expanded, not reduced, in time of depression. Britain, however innocently and justifiably, did contribute to the economic difficulties of its American colonies—and was readily blamed by them.

Taxation

The friction provoked by the regulation of commerce and currency appeared minor compared with the colonists' reaction to Britain's revenue-raising efforts. A staggering national debt and heavy domestic taxes convinced Britain's chancellor of the exchequer, George Grenville, to require the colonists to share the cost of the new military establishment that was to be stationed in America. Grenville hoped to raise from the colonies one-third to one-half of the £350,000 needed for 10,000 troops. To this end he tightened the administration of the customs service and then, in 1764, introduced the American Revenue Act (more popularly

Americans throwing the Cargoes of the Tea Ships into the River, at Boston

known as the Sugar Act). The Sugar Act was the first serious effort to tax for revenue rather than for imperial regulation. In order to defray "the expenses of defending, protecting and securing the said colonies," the new measure reduced the duty on foreign molasses from sixpence to threepence per gallon, increased the duty on sugar, prohibited the importation of foreign rum (which was negligible), imposed high duties on wines, and then made provisions for rigorous enforcement.

Since the anticipated annual net income would probably be only £20,000, the economic advantage seemed hardly worth the substantial political price. The Massachusetts General Court protested the infringement of "the most essential rights of Britons." New York's Assembly flatly opposed parliamentary taxation, and John Dickinson warned fellow Pennsylvanians against efforts "to tax them into obedience." The Sugar Act sensitized Americans to taxation as an issue. Consequently, they reacted with greater hostility to Grenville's next revenue effort, the Stamp Act of 1765, which proposed to raise between £60,000 and £100,000 a year. The act levied internal taxes on the colonies through duties on a wide range of legal and commercial documents, including customs papers, playing cards, newspapers (and advertisements therein), pamphlets, and almanacs; rates could reach 200 percent. The stamp agents would be American, and the revenue was to be spent in the colonies. Offenders were to be tried without a jury, which, colonists believed, was another breach of their rights.

Opposition to the Stamp Act was swift and widespread, particularly since Grenville had now alienated three powerful political groups: lawyers, publishers, and merchants. In Virginia, Patrick Henry insisted that only the House of Burgesses had the right to levy taxes and warned that anyone who disagreed would "be deemed an enemy to his Majesty's Colony." By August 1765, riots had erupted in Boston, followed swiftly by others in Newport, New York, Annapolis, and Charleston. Patriots, often organized as Sons of Liberty, persuaded (frequently by intimidation) most stamp agents to resign their posts. Rioters all but destroyed Chief Justice Thomas Hutchinson's home in Boston.* In October, nine colonies sent delegates to a Stamp Act Congress in New York. Walking a constitutional tightrope, the congress acknowledged Parliament's imperial authority but denied it any right to levy internal or external taxes on the colonies.

The Stamp Act was enforced only in Quebec, Nova Scotia, the Floridas, and the British West Indies. American newspapers appeared without stamps (sometimes omitting the publisher's name from the masthead); cargoes, lacking stamped papers, gained clearance without duties; college presidents awarded degrees by letter rather than with stamped diplomas. Many courts suspended proceedings, to the general pleasure of debtors, and merchants and consumers agreed to boycott British goods until the law was repealed.

Domestic politics in Britain helped bring about a face-saving repeal of the Stamp Act. In June 1765, George III dismissed Grenville because of what the king imagined to be an insult to his mother (Grenville had omitted her from the Regency Commission). Grenville's successor, Lord Rockingham, lacked enthusiasm for such controversial legislation. Then Pitt, in a major parliamentary speech, urged outright repeal of the Stamp Act, and British merchants, who were inconvenienced by the disruption of their American trade, supported him. During the debate Benjamin Franklin, colonial agent for Pennsylvania, warned Parliament that any distinction between internal and external taxation (if, in fact, it existed) would soon disappear if the Stamp Act did not.† And so, largely for reasons of expediency, Parliament voted to repeal in March 1766. But simultaneously Parliament passed the Declaratory Act, which boldly asserted Parliament's authority over the colonies "in all cases whatsoever." Anti-American feeling was high in Britain, and as long as fiscal problems remained, there would be further efforts to raise revenue through taxes in the colonies.

---

* Ironically, Hutchinson opposed the Stamp Act, but because he believed in the sovereignty of Parliament, he was identified with the hated tax measure. Isaac Barre's much-praised denunciation of the Stamp Act probably derived from Hutchinson's private memorandum condemning the measure.

†At this time, colonists generally accepted Parliament's right to impose external (regulatory) taxes.

The Rockingham ministry did not long survive the demise of the Stamp Act. By the summer of 1766 an oddly assorted coalition, led nominally by an ailing Pitt, now in the House of Lords as Lord Chatham, and his friend the unimpressive Duke of Grafton, had taken office. The new chancellor of the exchequer, Charles ("Champagne Charlie") Townshend, was by default the effective head of government. Long interested in colonial affairs, Townshend had for years urged effective revenue taxes to defray the costs of imperial administration and defense. His hand was somewhat forced by a British taxpayer's revolt that cut the land tax by £500,000 a year. New colonial taxes were necessary—and just—in Townshend's view.

In November 1766 Townshend modified the Sugar Act in a realistic fashion by imposing a penny tax on all molasses entering colonial ports—a profitable measure that brought £12,000 in revenue by 1768 and £20,000 by 1772. More substantial, and therefore more controversial, were the Townshend Acts passed in 1767. The Townshend duties were external taxes to appease those Americans whose case against the stamp duties rested on opposition to internal taxes. These new duties, expected to produce some £40,000 a year, were levied on glass, painter's colors, paper, and tea. The revenue was to defray customs-administration costs and pay the salaries of colonial governors and judges, who might thereby achieve a degree of fiscal and political independence they had rarely experienced when the colonial legislatures voted such funds. A new enforcement program reaffirmed the legality of writs of assistance, set up four more vice-admiralty courts to try breaches of the Navigation laws, and established a new Board of Customs in Boston to more closely supervise collection of duties. Finally, Townshend proposed the suspension of the New York Assembly until it complied with the Quartering Act passed two years earlier; under that measure colonies had been obliged to supply provisions and barracks for troops based within their borders. New York, as a major colonial highway, found the Quartering Act an onerous as well as a devious tax, but finally bought relief from the threatened suspension of its legislature by voting an unrestricted sum for the troops.

The Townshend Acts passed with large parliamentary majorities. Although Townshend did not live to see the results of his legislation, his ministerial associates watched with dismay as the anger of the colonists mounted. Bostonians urged a selective boycott of imports. In Philadelphia, John Dickinson began the publication of his famous *Letters from a Farmer in Pennsylvania*, the first carefully dated November 5, to commemorate the anniversary of the day William III had landed in England to rescue England's liberties in 1688. Dickinson's tone was one of patient, sweet reason, reflecting a lawyer's concern for history, custom, precedent, and justice. He found evidence of an advancing parliamentary program of tyranny aimed at the destruction of the constitutional liberties of the English in America. Parliament was, he charged, practicing a dubious double standard by attempting to deny American legislatures the very rights for which Parliament had long fought in England. The Townshend duties, Dickinson concluded, were only superficially regulatory; in reality they were a form of taxation as unconstitutional as the Stamp Act. Nearly every colonial newspaper reprinted Dickinson's *Letters*, and by 1769 seven editions had appeared in book form.

As the *Pennsylvania Chronicle* went to press in February 1768 with Dickinson's final installment, Samuel Adams voiced the political opposition to Townshend's legislation that was stirring in Massachusetts. In its Circular Letter to the other colonies, Massachusetts urged unity against taxation without representation. Although the language of the letter was moderate, the newly appointed secretary of state for colonial affairs, Lord Hillsborough, denounced Massachusetts for attempting to disturb "the public peace." When the Massachusetts legislature refused to rescind the Circular Letter, Hillsborough had Governor Bernard dissolve the assembly. Meanwhile Boston merchants moved forward with their proposals for a boycott against the mother country. By August 1769 New Yorkers also had joined in a nonimportation agreement, followed by Philadelphians the next spring. Even conservative Virginians passed vigorous resolutions insisting on their exclusive right to tax themselves. When Governor Botetourt responded to the Virginia Resolves by dissolving the assembly, its members moved down the street to the Raleigh Tavern and voted their own nonimportation agreement.*

These agreements were not completely effective since some colonists found it profitable to ignore the boycotts; others subscribed because they had excessive inventories of British goods. The vigor with which patriot vigilante groups, such as the Sons of Liberty, terrorized violators of nonimportation and nonconsumption agreements suggested that colonial unity was grudging. Mobs, often well controlled and organized, had long been an important aspect of the colonial political scene.

Samuel Adams's effective direction of a Boston mob provoked Lord Hillsborough into sending several regiments of troops to that city in June 1768. Their presence brought an uneasy peace, which was increasingly disturbed by clashes between soldiers and mocking citizens. On March 5, 1770, a mob attacked a customs-house sentry. Alarmed, Captain Thomas Preston mustered a small detachment to protect the customs treasure; an unidentified voice shouted "Fire!" and the troops did just that.† Five Bostonians lay dead or dying in the snow, including Crispus Attucks, an itinerant seaman and the first black casualty of the American Revolution. Momentarily stunned, the mob angrily prepared to attack the troops, who discreetly retired to a nearby guardhouse. Lieutenant Governor Thomas Hutchinson restored peace by moving the troops out of the city.

---

* By 1769 most of the assemblies in the royal colonies were dissolved for expressing support for the Massachusetts Circular Letter.

† Preston was accused of murder, but it is unlikely that he ordered the fatal volley since he was directly in the line of fire.

Paul Revere's view of the Boston Massacre

When Captain Preston and his troops were brought to trial for murder,
John Adams and Josiah Quincy, Jr., skillfully and courageously defended
them. All were acquitted except two who, allowed the medieval custom
of pleading "benefit of clergy," were branded on the hand and freed.* A
form of justice may have been served, but so was patriot argument:
Massachusetts had its martyrs, and the memory was kept fresh by annual
public orations, such as Joseph Warren's eloquent injunction in 1775 to
"take heed, ye orphan babes, lest, whilst your streaming eyes are fixed
upon the ghastly corpse, *your feet slide on the stones bespattered with
your father's brains.*" The British were rapidly losing the contest for the
"affections of the people."

* "Benefit of clergy" derived from the Middle Ages, when the Church claimed clerical
transgressors for its ecclesiastical courts; the vital qualification was literacy, demonstrated
by a recital of the twenty-third (or "hanging") psalm.

Ironically, on the very day of the Boston Massacre, Townshend's successor was presiding over the repeal of the duties that had indirectly occasioned these tragic events. Others in the cabinet had been ready to urge repeal as early as 1768, so alarmed were they over the economic and political portents; but Lord North, the new chancellor of the exchequer, had objected. In 1769 he finally agreed to repeal, largely because British merchants were restive as their business losses mounted, and only nominal revenues were being collected. And so, on March 5, 1770, Parliament voted to repeal all the controversial duties except the one that had brought in revenue—that on tea. Since tea was not grown in England, English producers would not be injured, and at the same time Parliament's authority would once again be confirmed and a significant source of income would be maintained.

North's concessions were modest, and the colonists knew it. But the urge for peace and prosperity was powerful. Trade with Britain had declined to £1.6 million in 1769; in 1771 it climbed up to £4.2 million. The ensuing three years were superficially tranquil; but, in reality, nagging questions remained, and patriot agitation continued. Samuel Adams helped organize committees of correspondence that spread as far as South Carolina and whose purpose was to keep patriots informed about British transgressions. Friction between merchants and customs officials persisted. In 1772 Rhode Islanders successfully attacked and burned the British revenue cutter *Gaspee*. A Boston mob tarred and feathered a customs official and then carted him through the streets. Peace often seemed possible only so long as royal officials declined to enforce Parliament's wishes.

Even so, radicals despaired of maintaining any colonial unity of purpose and resolve without further British provocation. Parliament came to their rescue. In 1773 Lord North rushed through the Tea Act in a desperate effort to enable the British East India Company to compete against smuggled Dutch tea in the colonial market. The Tea Act permitted the company to export up to seven million pounds of tea free of the tax usually paid on its entry into Britain; further, such exports, while still subject to the Townshend duty, could be sold directly in the colonies through the company's own agents. Thus the company would enjoy a comfortable monopoly of the American market, bypassing both English and colonial middlemen in the process. Colonial tea merchants and smugglers were equally outraged as they calculated the lower price at which the superior British tea could now be sold. Some, more altruistic, attacked the measure as an insidious device to raise revenue by making a hated external duty more tolerable. Still others suddenly discovered in tea the source of all sorts of threats to American health; partisan allegations were circulated claiming that tea caused cancer, impotence, and premature senility. Presumably, smuggled Dutch tea held no such terrors.

Colonial tempers rose with charges of monopoly and unfair taxation. Radicals determined no British tea would be landed. Those merchants selected by the company to handle its tea were intimidated and persuaded to resign; ship captains were warned of their personal peril. In Boston, Governor Hutchinson forced a confrontation with the colonists by refusing permission for three tea ships to leave port without unloading their cargoes. Patriots feared the tea might be seized for nonpayment of duties, then landed and auctioned—thus gaining the market they wished to deny it. So, in December 1773, radicals, poorly disguised as Indians, boarded the vessels and dumped forty-five tons of prime tea into the harbor. In Charleston the tea was in fact landed and seized for nonpayment of duties, but it remained in a warehouse for three years before being auctioned for the treasury of the newly sovereign state of South Carolina. New Yorkers preferred to emulate the Boston example. The remaining tea ships turned around and sailed back to England, their cargoes intact. The Boston Tea Party was, for John Adams, "an Epoch in History," for Lord North, the work of "New England fanatics." But John Adams was correct in one respect: it did have, as he said, "important consequences."

Coercive Acts

The alarming destruction of property in Boston Harbor dismayed many Americans, but England's immediate and vigorous response drove hesitant colonials further toward the radical camp. When such pro-Americans as Pitt—now Lord Chatham—found the Boston action "criminal," Lord North knew he had plenty of support in Parliament. In March 1774 he summoned Parliament to discuss the American disturbances and determine appropriate punitive measures.

As author of both the Tea Act and the coercive legislation that followed the Boston Tea Party, Lord North has long been blamed almost personally for the Revolution that ensued. This view oversimplifies the Revolution and the politics of the period preceding it. Frederick North, second Earl of Guilford, was no simple anti-American puppet of George III. To be sure, North was fiercely loyal to his monarch, but he had another loyalty as well: he had profound constitutional convictions that Parliament was the supreme legislature in the British Empire. He would make necessary concessions for the sake of peace, but he would allow little questioning of Parliament's authority. North had dominated the Pitt-Grafton ministry upon the death of Townshend in September 1767; in January 1770 he headed a new government that held power until the total collapse of its American policies in 1782. He had the unreserved support of his king; without it neither North nor his policies could have survived for those twelve critical years. The king and his first minister were complementary forces; they understood each other, and politically they thought alike. In particular, they agreed on the wisdom of the Coercive Acts of 1774.

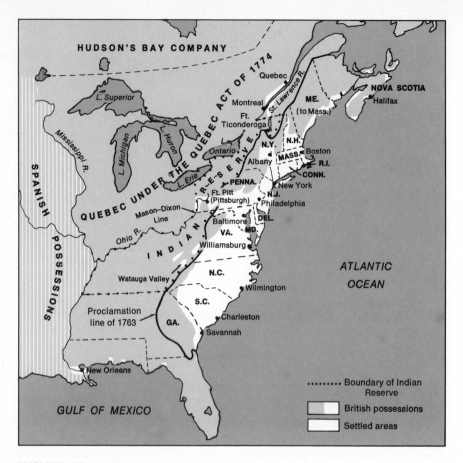

ENGLISH COLONIES, 1776

Lord North's first response to the Tea Party was the Boston Port Act in March 1774. It called for closing Boston to all shipping until the East India Company was recompensed for the destroyed tea. In May and June further measures stirred additional controversy. Under the Massachusetts Government Act, the royal governor, rather than the legislature, would select members of the council. The governor would also select most judges and other officials; even town meetings were to require the governor's consent. The Administration of Justice Act provided that a royal official charged with a capital offense committed in the course of his duties could be tried in another colonial court or in Britain if the governor doubted the likelihood of a fair trial in the local court. A new Quartering Act made local authorities responsible for finding billets for troops who had to be stationed in troublesome areas.

Finally, in June 1774, came the Quebec Act, not one of the Coercive Acts, but one visited with bad timing and an unfortunate association in the colonists' minds: this measure filled a decade-old promise of autonomy and religious privileges for French residents of the province. Specifically, the act extended Quebec's borders to the Mississippi River in the west, the Ohio River in the south, and Hudson Bay in the north. French residents were permitted French civil law (which did not include trial by jury) and "the free Exercise of the Religion of the (Roman Catholic) Church, subject to the King's supremacy"; government would be continued with a royal governor and appointed council, but with no representative legislature.

Many Americans considered the Quebec Act the worst, the most intolerable, of all North's measures. The land hungry—particularly Virginians—felt shut out of their Northwest; fur traders felt the competition of British traders operating from Montreal; and many Protestants felt encircled by the popery they had fled the Old World to escape. Quebec, in short, seemed to illustrate everything that was so desperately wrong with British rule: it offered precedents for an alien religion and legal system and for government without consent of the governed. The news that General Thomas Gage was not only to continue in command of the troops in Massachusetts but was also to replace Hutchinson as governor confirmed the colonists' worst fears. Resistance was essential.

The Intellectual Origins of the Revolution

The Boston Port Act provoked particularly vigorous denunciations of parliamentary tyranny. Many argued that if Boston's very life could be destroyed, so could that of New York or Philadelphia. From Boston, from New York, from Williamsburg, Virginia, came calls for an intercolonial congress to discuss a common effort for redress of grievances. Philadelphia was to be the meeting place; September 1774 was the date. During the hot summer of 1774 the colonists named their delegates, discussed their instructions, debated proposals for resistance and their justification.

Disagreements were inevitable: in fact some who supported the call for a congress did so with the hope that delay and moderation might prevail; others looked for agreement on an immediate embargo of British trade as an appropriate response to the Coercive Acts. Revolution was not yet a serious proposition, although the colonists' frame of reference did not render such a possibility particularly repugnant. The colonists saw revolution in the context of the transfer of political power that took place in the mother country (and the colonies) in 1688–89, an eminently respectable exercise undertaken "to preserve our ancient indisputable laws and liberties." Even Joseph Galloway, best known as an unhappy and unsuccessful Loyalist, was at one time able to remark that "nothing would save us but a revolution" because it seemed an unexceptional constitutional development.

The colonists' concept of their constitutional rights had enormous relevance to their political debates and final decisions. They expounded these concepts in an ever increasing torrent of pamphlets and oratory, clarifying their own thinking as well as that of their readers and listeners. They confirmed their awareness of their God-given power to reason, their God-given ability to use their intelligence to understand their world and improve it. Locke's *Essay on Human Understanding* was in fact much more familiar than his *Second Treatise on Civil Government.* As students of politics on the other hand, colonists were very aware of Algernon Sidney's *Discourses on Government* (1698) and his curious blend of history and philosophy. Sidney not only argued that man should not be deprived of property and liberty without consent, that a people could overthrow a government that betrayed its obligations to the governed, but he demonstrated that throughout history this had happened—particularly in England. It was Sidney who insisted that tyranny should be blocked at the first opportunity, lest despotism fasten too tight a yoke upon a misgoverned people.

Sidney was one of the Commonwealthmen identified by Caroline Robbins as a libertarian group originating in the seventeenth century but coming into full flower in eighteenth-century England. The English Commonwealthmen spoke for ancient liberties endangered by modern corruption. They criticized a Parliament they saw as unrepresentative and thus offered American readers and admirers views that were singularly acceptable in the 1760s and 1770s. Thomas Jefferson was only one of their many disciples, but his *Summary View of the Rights of British America* constituted one of the ablest of the many briefs offered for the colonial case against the mother country.* Written in the form of instructions to the Virginia delegates to the first Continental Congress, this eighteen-page pamphlet was addressed to George III as "chief magistrate of the British Empire." Jefferson reminded his monarch of the ancestral rights of all English subjects, rights to be traced to the noble Saxons who migrated from German forests without owing any residual allegiance to the land of their origin. He noted the long struggle for freedom in England, its near success in the seventeenth century, and its seeming eclipse in the eighteenth. William the Norman had brought feudal tyranny to the British Isles; George III should not inflict the same experience on British America. Parliament, corrupt and unrepresentative, appeared to have extended the despotism of Charles I and James II; the king must now intervene to end parliamentary usurpation in America. "Let not the name of George III be a blot on the page of history," Jefferson enjoined.

* Illness reportedly prevented Jefferson from attending the special Virginia convention, which met in August 1774; he thoughtfully sent two copies to Williamsburg where they were published to wide acclaim, but it is unlikely the *Summary View* alone earned him his later assignment to draft the Declaration of Independence.

The First Continental Congress

In this ideological context the first Continental Congress convened on September 5, 1774. Fifty-six delegates—representing all colonies except a divided Georgia—packed into Philadelphia's Carpenter's Hall to discuss what action was to be taken. The delegates remained far from united: there were cautious moderates, anxious conservatives, and a few impatient radicals. They were predominantly men of social, intellectual, and political distinction. About one-third were college graduates; thirty were lawyers (twelve had studied in the mother country); nine were planters, joined by a like number of merchants. As Garry Wills has noted, in his book *Inventing America*, "This was no ragtag band of revolutionaries."

Joseph Galloway of Pennsylvania argued for a new plan of union, replete with a legislative council (elected by the colonial legislatures), presided over by a president general (named by the king) with veto authority. The core of his proposal was the provision that parliamentary legislation affecting the colonies would require the council's approval, and council legislation would require parliamentary concurrence. Thus further Coercive Acts would be prevented. But Galloway's plan was defeated by one vote, perhaps because of the personal unpopularity of the author. In any case, it is unlikely that Lord North would have shared imperial sovereignty in such a fashion.

Instead of Galloway's plan, at the suggestion of delegates from Massachusetts, the Congress adopted the Suffolk Resolves, which denounced the Coercive Acts as unconstitutional, proposed a militia for defense of the colonies, and demanded immediate economic sanctions against Britain. The Congress then voted a Declaration of Rights and Grievances, which conceded Britain's right to regulate external commerce—and little else. Finally, and ominously, the Congress approved a Continental Association under which importation of British goods and the slave trade would cease as of December 1, 1774, to be closely followed by an embargo on exports to Britain in September 1775. By assigning enforcement of the Continental Association to local committees, the Congress helped create the very structure of a public rebellion. By determining that the Congress would reconvene the following May, it also determined that it would be an ongoing body. True, some delegates spoke to their hopes and beliefs that economic pressure would once again persuade British merchants to work for the rapid repeal of the detested Coercive Acts and thus rescue the empire. But others gloomily expressed doubt that such sanity would prevail and forecast new challenges for the next meeting. Thus, when the Congress concluded its lengthy sessions and adjourned on October 26, 1774, its members departed with very mixed feelings.

The Road to Rebellion

Colonial hopes rested more on the record of the past than on the reality of the present. Britain had indeed retreated when faced with resistance to the Stamp Act and then to the Townshend duties; but retreat was no longer likely. Anti-American sentiment had steadily risen in Parliament; Edmund Burke's voice had been almost alone in opposition to the Boston Port Bill in 1774. British mercantile interests had become less susceptible to American boycotts because they had found markets elsewhere. Lord North had wide political support for his American policies; it was actually his inability to execute them that eventually brought his political downfall.

"The dye is now cast," commented George III in September 1774, "we must not retreat." And his new Parliament agreed. Chatham pleaded in vain for compromise; his suggestion that troops withdraw from Boston and that Parliament pledge no future taxes without colonial consent lost by a vote of nearly four to one. In February 1775, Parliament declared Massachusetts in a state of rebellion, a rebellion that the king might suppress with up to 10,000 troops if needed. Lord North then offered his own plan for reconciliation: Parliament would not tax a colony that itself raised the necessary revenues requested by the mother country. He did not abandon the right to tax. Nor did he abandon his inclination to repression: in March he secured passage of the New England Restraining Act, which forbade fishing off the Grand Banks and restricted New England's international trade to Great Britain and the British West Indies. Before a nearly empty House of Commons Burke fruitlessly sought concessions, reminding his few listeners that the spirit of liberty was "stronger in the English colonies probably than in any other people on earth." But, despite such efforts, the drift to war continued unimpeded.

Americans were even more divided, uneasy over the course of events, often reluctant to acknowledge the inexorable logic of their own arguments. Patrick Henry might wax emotional and paraphrase Addison's *Cato* with remarks on "liberty or death," but even John Adams found this fatal alternative "cold comfort." As action resolved thought, so military developments would help resolve the political dilemma. In April 1775, General Gage received orders from the secretary of war to seize military stores that were reported to be in nearby Concord. His seven or eight hundred troops met seventy Americans on the Lexington village green and left eight of them dead and ten wounded.

Incredible though it seemed to many colonists, the second Continental Congress (convened in May 1775) continued to make conciliatory gestures in spite of such events. John Dickinson's Olive Branch Petition blamed the North government for all Britain's difficulties in America, begged the Crown to prevent further parliamentary tyranny, pending efforts at reconciliation, and requested the repeal of the Coercive Acts and the Declaratory Act. John Adams denounced Dickinson's suppliant tone, but unjustly, for the Olive Branch was intended to show Americans—and the world—how patient and how wronged they were. Dickinson's tone became more belligerent in the Declaration of the Causes and Necessity of Taking Up Arms, voted by the Congress the next day, July 6, 1775. Here Americans announced their readiness to die to prevent their own bondage. "Our cause is just. Our union is perfect. Our internal resources are great, and if necessary, foreign assistance is undoubtedly attainable." The Congress raised armies not for independence but "for the preservation of our liberties." Two weeks later the Congress ordered a total of $3 million in paper money to finance its struggle, established a postal system, and then, on July 31, formally rejected North's plan for conciliation. The exhausted delegates to the Congress adjourned for a month's rest on August 2.

After the Congress reconvened (this time joined by delegates from Georgia), it awaited Britain's response to its humble petition of July. The answer came early in November: the king refused to receive the Olive Branch; the House of Commons, less proud, formally rejected it as a basis for reconciliation by a vote of 83 to 33. At the same time the Congress learned of the royal proclamation of August 23, which declared the colonies in open rebellion. Even so, in December, the delegates reaffirmed their allegiance to the Crown—while once more denying the authority of Parliament. In the same month, that esteemed body was passing the Prohibitory Act, which forbade all commerce with the rebellious colonies and proclaimed a blockade of their ports.

Independence Declared

Clearly, the prospects for reconciliation had dimmed. By the end of 1775 the Crown was the sole surviving connection between the angry colonists and their mother country. Yet how could Americans be loyal to a monarch who denounced his colonial subjects as traitors and rebels? How could Americans think they were still loyal subjects when their representatives were at war with Britain and negotiating for assistance from the French? Tom Paine, a recent arrival from the mother country, had no time for such sophistry, as he made plain in his widely read pamphlet *Common Sense,* which was issued in January 1776. Paine's success stemmed from both his timing and his rhetoric. He said what more and more were now thinking: Britain was corrupt, had forgotten its own legacy of liberty, and would soon corrupt America as well. It was not enough to oppose tyranny, one should oppose the tyrant too: "The blood of the slain, the weeping voice of nature cries, TIS TIME TO PART."

Common Sense contributed powerfully to the general colonial movement toward total separation from the mother country. By early

Jefferson's rough draft of the Declaration of Independence

April, the Congress was ready to open all colonial ports to all
nations—except Britain. Within a week North Carolina had authorized its
congressional delegation to vote for independence and foreign alliances.
Rhode Island followed in a slightly more cautious fashion. Then came
Massachusetts and Virginia. The stage was set for the final debates in

Philadelphia when, on June 7, 1776, Richard Henry Lee of Virginia rose to move

that these United Colonies are, and of right ought to be, free and independent states, that they are absolved from all allegiance to the British Crown, and that all political connection between them and the State of Great Britain is, and ought to be, totally dissolved.

The opening speeches revealed strong reservations on the part of representatives from some of the middle colonies. As John Dickinson observed, while ripening rapidly they were not yet ready to part from Britain. Accordingly, the delegates postponed further debate for three weeks while they consulted their constituents, and congressional committees labored over the various sections of Lee's resolution. When discussions resumed on July 1, an initial ballot showed South Carolina and Pennsylvania opposed, Delaware divided, and New York still without instructions (New York's Provincial Congress did not vote to endorse the Declaration until July 9). On July 2 South Carolina's delegation came out for independence; Caesar Rodney's arrival swung the Delaware vote; and Dickinson joined with Robert Morris in staying away, thereby creating a Pennsylvania majority for Lee's resolution.

Lee's resolution thus passed unanimously on July 2—the date that John Adams confidently predicted would hereafter be celebrated as the new nation's birthday. Actually, some thought the July 2 vote something of an anticlimax: eight days earlier the Congress had passed resolutions defining treason as furnishing aid to Great Britain, a vote that was unquestionably a *de facto* declaration of independence.

But the formal Declaration had yet to be approved. Jefferson believed the object of the Declaration was to rally its colonial readers, to set down for all to see the justification for the momentous step the Congress was taking. For this purpose, the famous and felicitous opening paragraphs were perhaps the least important part of the document, although Jefferson's identification of the rights of Englishmen with the rights of man was superbly, succinctly phrased. Whether the Declaration was a total commitment to freedom and equality for all Americans remains debatable: Jefferson did not insist that all men were equal—he believed otherwise—but he did claim equal legal and political rights for all free white men. Not for black slaves. He did blame George III for forcing African slavery on the colonies, an indictment the Congress tactfully deleted from the final version.

Most of the document was devoted to a summary of British iniquities. Jefferson and his colleagues had earlier attacked Parliament, but now they focused on the king, a tyrant "unfit to be the ruler of a people who mean to be free." Jefferson also pointed out that some of the responsibility belonged to the British people as well, because they had constantly ignored colonial complaints about the tyranny visited on the colonies. The English had been warned "that submission to their

Parliament was no part of our constitution." And now came "the last stab to agonizing affection," the dispatch of "foreign mercenaries to invade and deluge us in blood." Jefferson's long, detailed list of causes for revolution demonstrated more than the colonists' clear right to rebel. It also showed the colonists' reluctance to claim the right of revolution and thereby reflected the intrinsic conservatism of many Patriot leaders.

Independence emerged as a philosophical, legal, and historical imperative. On July 4, after a final two days' debate, the Congress approved the Declaration. It was now the task of the American people to translate this moral mandate into political reality.

Suggested Reading

Lawrence H. Gipson's *The Coming of the Revolution, 1763 – 1775** (1954) is one of the most succinct and attractive studies of the origins of the American Revolution; also recommended are John R. Alden, *A History of the American Revolution* (1969), Merrill Jensen, *The Founding of a Nation* (1968), and John C. Miller, *The Origins of the American Revolution* (1943). The latter is not to be confused with Bernhard Knollenberg's *Origin of the American Revolution** (1960), which focuses on the period 1759 to 1766 and examines the British political context; see also Knollenberg's final volume, *Growth of the American Revolution, 1766 – 1775* (1975). John Brooke's sympathetic biography, *George III* (1972), adds a useful biographical dimension. Edmund and Helen Morgan's *The Stamp Act Crisis** (1953) establishes that event as the turning point in Anglo-American relations.

Clinton Rossiter supplied a pathfinding account of the colonists' concern for political liberty in *Seedtime of the Republic** (1953). Bernard Bailyn's *The Ideological Origins of the American Revolution* (1967) is the best and most coherent treatment of the political ideas of eighteenth-century colonists. Trevor Colbourn's *The Lamp of Experience* (1965) examines the colonists' sense and use of the past and also suggests that their history enabled conservative colonists to take their revolutionary posture. Pauline Maier finds conservatism even among the so-called radicals in *From Resistance to Revolution: Colonial Radicals and the Development of American Opposition to Britain, 1765 – 1776* (1972). For British policy making after 1763, see John Shy's excellent *Toward Lexington* (1965), complemented by David Ammerman's *In the Common Cause: American Response to the Coercive Acts of 1774* (1974).

The decision for independence—and its form—is well treated by Carl L. Becker in *The Declaration of Independence** (1922) and, more recently, by David Hawke in *A Transaction of Free Men* (1964). But neither should be read at the expense of Garry Wills's *Inventing America: Jefferson's Declaration of Independence* (1978), which is remarkable for its insight into the intellectual dimensions of the Revolution and its leaders. Benjamin Quarles has an excellent chapter on "The Negro and the Rights of Man" in *The Negro in the American Revolution** (1961). S. G. Kurtz and J. H. Hutson, in *Essays on the American Revolution** (1973), furnish a useful survey of recent and ongoing scholarship.

* Available in paperback edition

Chapter 4
The New Nation,
1776—1789

Chronology

1776—81 Revolutionary War: *March 1776:* British evacuate Boston • *September 1776:* Howe occupies New York • *December 1776:* Washington surprises British at Trenton and Princeton (*January 1777*) • *September 1777:* Howe takes Philadelphia • *October 1777:* Burgoyne surrenders at Saratoga • *June 1778:* France enters war as ally of America • *June 1779:* Spain enters war as ally of France • *October 1781:* Cornwallis surrenders at Yorktown •

1777 Congress votes Articles of Confederation •

1781 Articles of Confederation ratified •

1782 Preliminary treaty of peace (effective 1783) •

1785 Land Ordinance •

1785—86 Jay-Gardoqui negotiations •

1786 Virginia disestablishes Anglican Church • Annapolis convention • *Trevett* v. *Weeden* case •

1786—87 Shays' Rebellion •

1787 Constitutional convention opens in Philadelphia • Northwest Ordinance •

1787—88 All state conventions but North Carolina and Rhode Island ratify Constitution •

1789—90 North Carolina and Rhode Island ratify Constitution •

In establishing American independence," remarked David Ramsey in 1789, "the pen and press had merit equal to that of the sword." But the sword was essential to the survival of the nation proclaimed by Jefferson and his colleagues during the hot, hopeful summer of 1776. Their handiwork drew open contempt on both sides of the Atlantic: they were, after all, calling for victory over the greatest European empire, over the nation that had recently humiliated France. Patriot and Loyalist alike wondered at American temerity and pondered prospects for military success. Muskets and artillery had to sustain Jefferson's provocative words.

More than military matters perplexed the colonists in 1776. There were immediate political problems. How were erstwhile colonies to become self-governing states? What would be their new constitutional structure? How would they relate to one another? How would independence affect the American economy, the social order? Would there be, in fact, a real revolution, a social change beyond mere political separation from Great Britain? Could Americans overcome the deep divisions within the colonies created by the quest for independence itself? There was no lack of questions for thoughtful colonists who were concerned about their country's future. The thirteen years that followed the French and Indian War had determined the verdict for independence; the succeeding thirteen years would decide how—and whether—America would successfully emerge as a nation.

The Context for Conflict

The immediate task facing rebellious Americans in 1776 was national survival. Their frequent self-doubts lengthened the discouraging odds. They remained a divided people, in spite of their leaders' patient, cautious approach toward independence. They lacked arms, armies, military traditions. They were without money and effective government. And the quality of their military leadership was as untested as their ability to attract the foreign alliances that many considered essential to victory.

The War for Independence was also a civil war since thousands of Americans remained loyal to the mother country. In contrast to what has been often believed, Tories, or Loyalists, were not all rich property-owners fearful of losing status and political power. Some just loved England. Others, convinced of British military superiority, would not risk support for an unsuccessful rebellion. Still others were simply allergic to being labeled rebels, which was perhaps one reason so many Patriots argued that theirs was not in fact a revolution, that *Britain* was rebelling against acknowledged *American* rights. Local politics often interfered with colonial unity: some New Yorkers supported the British out of distaste for the aristocratic Livingston family, which was firmly in the Patriot camp. For Samuel Seabury, loyalty to the Crown was more a matter of style: "If I must be enslaved," he said, "let it be by a *King* at least, and not by a parcel of upstart lawless Committeemen. If I must be devoured, let me be devoured by the jaws of a lion, and not gnawed to death by rats and vermin."

There were Loyalists of every station, occupation, race, and religion. They comprised about 20 percent of the white American population; possibly as many as 20,000 took up arms for Britain; certainly about 8,000 appeared on British army rolls in 1780. Had the British made effective use of this support, the war might have taken a very different course. Instead, many Loyalists found their offer of help spurned by British generals. The Patriots, on the other hand, sometimes practiced brutal intimidation: known Loyalists faced imprisonment and confiscation of estates; some were tarred and feathered, but few were hanged. There was no reign of terror in this revolution but rather a wide reverence for order, for law. And in any case, many Loyalists wisely removed themselves from Patriot reach; perhaps 80,000 ultimately fled to Canada, where they nurtured an enduring dislike for the United States.

The sad condition of the British forces more than compensated for internal American division. Britain's was a gentlemen's army in many ways: officers bought their commissions rather than being awarded them for meritorious service; wives and mistresses of troops of all ranks burdened logistics by traveling with the army. Some 2,000 women accompanied General "Gentleman Johnny" Burgoyne's 7,000-man army to its fateful rendezvous at Saratoga. The principal weapon of the British soldier was still the 14-pound Brown Bess musket, inaccurate and limited in range. (There was no order to aim in the army manual.) Many regarded the musket as merely a device to carry a bayonet. Britain had not abandoned its tradition of unpreparedness: in 1775 the army's total strength was less than 50,000, of which only 8,500 were in North America. American privateers and 3,000 miles of ocean intensified problems of supply and transportation; the nearly total lack of cooperation from the Royal Navy hardly reduced these difficulties. Finally, the British had a dangerous contempt for their American enemy. Since it was said that "the flower of Mr. Washington's army" was made up of "the Gleanings of

A British view of the American soldier (1776)

British prisons," it seemed humiliating to risk death at the hands of riffraff—in fact, it was considered so demeaning that some disdained to fight in America. Still others refused out of sympathy for the American cause. Faced with such limited enthusiasm, North's ministry was forced to look to continental Europe for troops and hired some 30,000 Germans (of whom only 1,200 were the notorious Hessians).

In some ways, American military prospects seemed little better. Washington's greatest achievement as commander in chief may well have been keeping an army in the field, even if it rarely exceeded 8,000 in number. The heavy reliance on local militia reflected the American fear of standing armies and the widespread unwillingness of most men to enlist for the long term. Up to the rank of captain, officers were elected by their men, usually winning on popularity rather than competence. Few had significant military experience, which enhanced the value of such European volunteers as the Marquis de Lafayette, Baron von Steuben, and Count Pulaski. The large incidence of desertion provoked Washington to remark that he would "have to detach one half of the army to bring back the other." Poor clothing, equipment, and pay brought on mutinies in 1780, 1781, and 1783. No wonder Washington despaired, criticizing his troops as "an exceedingly dirty and nasty people."

But to Washington's and his soldiers' advantage, they were fighting on home ground. Washington knew his terrain and he could pick his battleground. He had short internal lines of communication and supply. And he had the inestimable assistance of British military and political mismanagement on a scale that dwarfed even the tribulations caused by the American Congress. In short, the War for Independence was like most wars: it produced dissension, disaffection, and disorganization, a few heroes, and fewer effective leaders—on both sides. The ultimate American victory was in some respects miraculous.

The War for Independence

Although Washington forced the British to withdraw from Boston in March 1776, he failed to dislodge them from New York later that summer. He even had the inadvertent help of the cautious and indolent General William Howe, whose ineffectiveness was so notorious it produced widespread rumors that he was secretly in the pay of the Americans. Washington's subsequent winter forays at Trenton and Princeton helped raise American morale and demonstrated the limited control of the countryside that had been secured by British garrisons.

In contrast, the grotesque miscarriage of General Burgoyne's plan to slice through New York and New England was of major military and political moment. Burgoyne had conceived of three British armies converging in New York, but one army, under St. Leger, was stopped at

REVOLUTIONARY WAR, 1775—1778

1775—1777

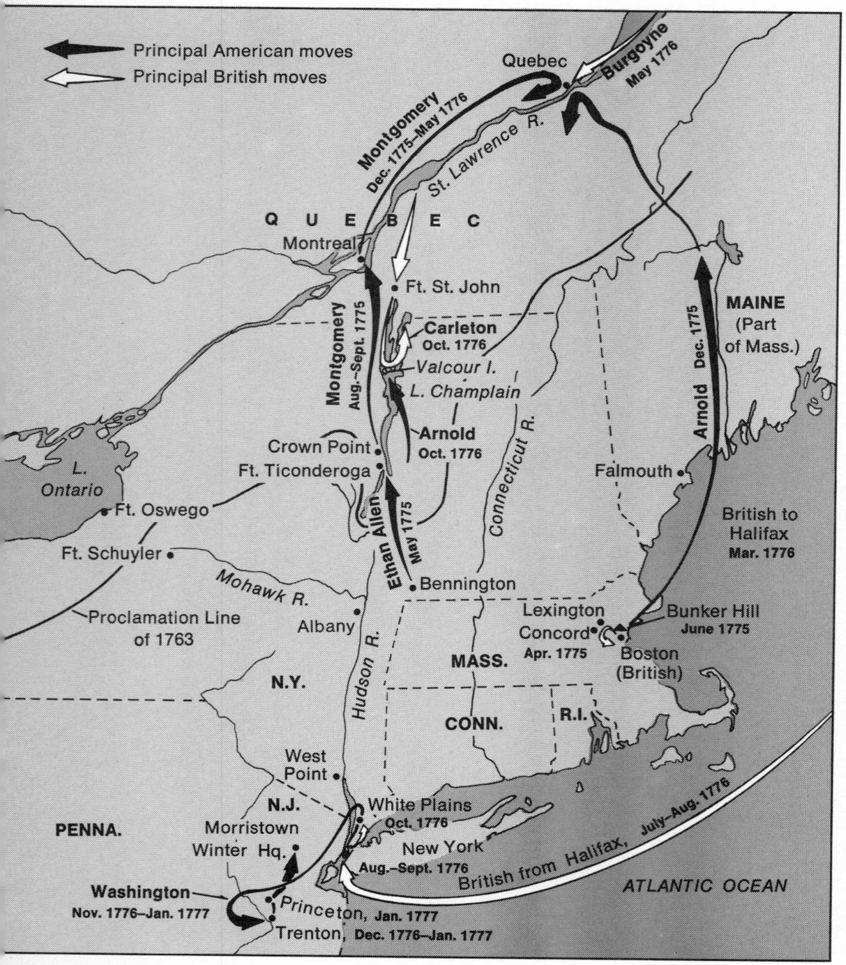

1777—1778

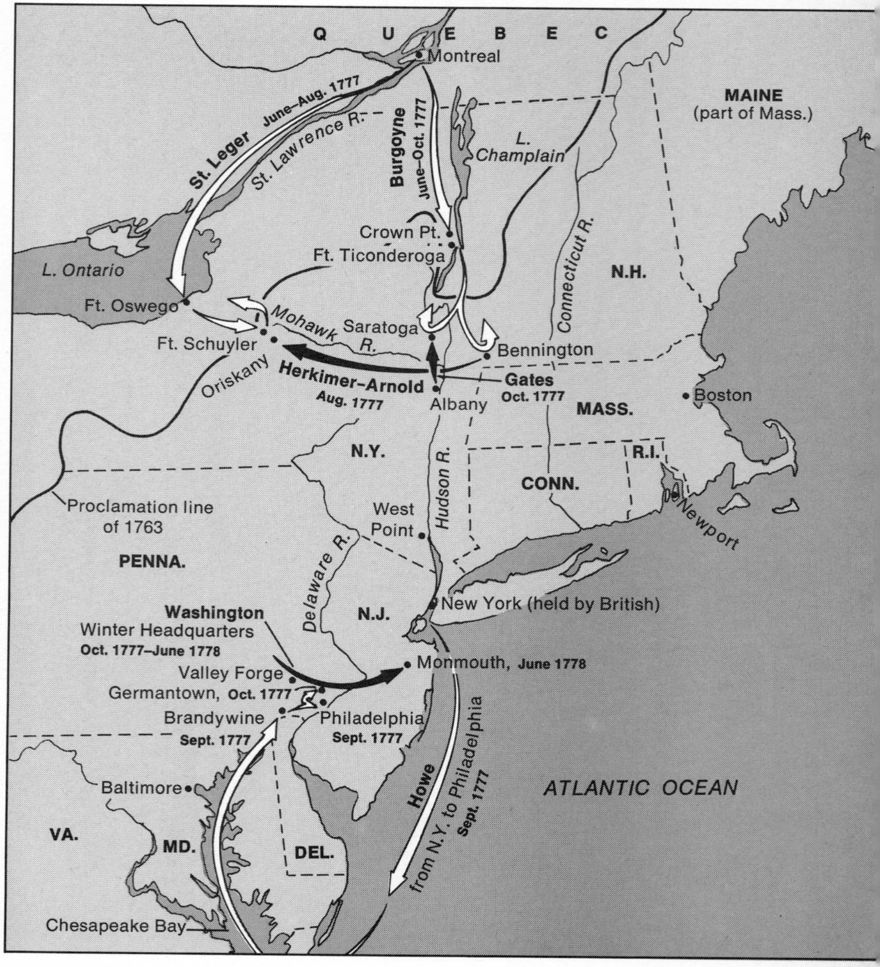

Legend

→ Principal American moves
⇨ Principal British moves

Map 1 (1775—1777):

L. Ontario
Ft. Oswego
Ft. Schuyler
Proclamation Line of 1763
Mohawk R.
Albany
N.Y.
West Point
Hudson R.
Bennington
Connecticut R.
CONN.
R.I.
MASS.
Lexington
Concord Apr. 1775
Boston (British)
Bunker Hill June 1775
British to Halifax Mar. 1776
Faulmouth
MAINE (Part of Mass.)
Arnold Dec. 1775
Quebec
Burgoyne May 1776
QUEBEC
Montreal
Montgomery Dec. 1775–May 1776
St. Lawrence R.
Ft. St. John
Carleton Oct. 1776
Valcour I.
Arnold Oct. 1776
L. Champlain
Crown Point
Ft. Ticonderoga
Ethan Allen May 1775
Montgomery Aug.–Sept. 1775
White Plains Oct. 1776
New York Aug.–Sept. 1776
British from Halifax
British from Halifax, May–Aug. 1776
ATLANTIC OCEAN
West Point
N.J.
Morristown Winter Hq.
Princeton, Jan. 1777
Trenton, Dec. 1776–Jan. 1777
Washington Nov. 1776–Jan. 1777
PENNA.

Map 2 (1777—1778):

MAINE (part of Mass.)
QUEBEC
Montreal
St. Lawrence R.
St. Leger June–Aug. 1777
L. Ontario
Ft. Oswego
Ft. Schuyler
Oriskany
Herkimer–Arnold Aug. 1777
Mohawk R.
Saratoga
Crown Pt.
Ft. Ticonderoga
Burgoyne June–Oct. 1777
Bennington
Gates Oct. 1777
Albany
N.H.
Connecticut R.
MASS.
Boston
Newport
R.I.
CONN.
Hudson R.
West Point
New York (held by British)
N.J.
Monmouth, June 1778
Howe from N.Y. to Philadelphia Sept. 1777
Philadelphia Sept. 1777
Germantown, Oct. 1777
Brandywine Sept. 1777
Valley Forge Winter Headquarters Oct. 1777–June 1778
Washington
PENNA.
Proclamation line of 1763
Delaware R.
DEL.
MD.
Baltimore
Chesapeake Bay
VA.
ATLANTIC OCEAN

Fort Stanwix and the other, under Howe, moved south into Philadelphia instead of north up the Hudson River. Unaware of this lack of support, Burgoyne pushed southward from Canada, finally to be surrounded at Saratoga by an American force three times the size of his own. On October 17, 1777, Burgoyne and his surviving 5,700 men surrendered their arms to General Horatio Gates.

In the long run, the British defeat at Saratoga had more diplomatic than military importance. (Burgoyne's men failed to keep their pledge not to serve again in the war against America and reappeared in the Virginia Campaign.) Two months after Saratoga, France formally recognized American independence, while Lord North vainly sought a settlement that might preclude this Franco-American alliance. Congress denounced the British overtures and in May 1778 ratified the treaty concluded in Paris by Silas Deane and Benjamin Franklin. The American struggle became a theater in a new world war as first the French, then the Spanish and the Dutch entered the conflict.* In 1780, Russia headed a European coalition known as the League of Armed Neutrality whose purpose was to defy the British navy. By then, Britain's resources were seriously strained—and American opportunity for victory increased.

The strategic importance of Saratoga was not immediately apparent to Washington and his weakened forces as they wintered at Valley Forge while Howe and his army enjoyed the warmth and hospitality of Philadelphia. But Washington retained his command and the support of the Congress while Howe was replaced by Henry Clinton, who withdrew from Philadelphia to New York in June 1778.

It became increasingly apparent that the French alliance provided only the opportunity for victory, not a guarantee of victory. George Rogers Clark's victory at Vincennes in the West furnished the only notable American success in the year 1778. Washington was inactive, and his troops again suffered when they spent the winter of 1778–79 in New Jersey. The defection of the able but ill-used Benedict Arnold and agitation against Washington as commander in chief demonstrated widespread disaffection, which lasted into 1780.

But 1780 saw the beginning of the end for the British, who demonstrated their ability to snatch defeat from the jaws of victory. General Clinton, in company with Lord Cornwallis, achieved a major victory over General Gates at Camden, South Carolina, in August. But Cornwallis could not prevail against Daniel Morgan in North Carolina and so moved north into unprotected Virginia. Here Cornwallis made a major miscalculation: he marched his 7,000 men to Yorktown, expecting to be met by the British navy. Instead, he discovered the French fleet of the Comte de Grasse and Washington's and the Comte de Rochambeau's combined armies (about 15,000 men), which had moved south from New

---

* Spain did not enter as an American ally but in support of France, which promised to force the British to return Gibraltar, and, later, Florida; Britain declared war on Holland to close off their commercial traffic with the Americans.

REVOLUTIONARY WAR, 1778 – 1781

New York
(held by British)

N.J.

DEL.

Graves from N.Y.

Repulse of British fleet
Sept. 5–9, 1781

Yorktown Surrender, Oct. 19, 1781

De Barras, R.I.
from Newport, R.I.

De Grasse
from West Indies

ATLANTIC OCEAN

PENNA.

Philadelphia

Baltimore

MD.

Washington, Rochambeau, Sept. 1781

Lafayette
June–Sept. 1781

VA.

Richmond

Williamsburg
July 1781

Cornwallis
Apr.–May 1781

Wilmington

Ft. Pitt

Redstone

Charlottesville
June 1781

James R.

Guilford C.H.
Mar. 1781

Cheraw

N.C.

Greene
Jan.–Mar. 1781

Proclamation line of 1763

Charlotte

Cornwallis
Jan.–Mar. 1781

Winnsboro

Camden

S.C.

Ninety-Six

Charleston

Cowpens
Jan. 1781

George Rogers Clark
1778–1779

Ohio R.

Boonesborough

KY.

Harrodsburg

Watauga
Settlements

Savannah R.

Augusta

GA.

Hamilton 1778

Wabash R.

Vincennes
Feb. 1779

Mississippi R.

St. Louis
Cahokia

Kaskaskia

Cornwallis
Mar.–May 1780

N.C.

Cheraw
Aug. 1780

from Watauga

Kings Mt.
Oct. 1780

Charlotte

Gates Aug. 1780

Camden, Aug. 1780

Winnsboro

Cornwallis

S.C.

Ninety-Six

Charleston

Savannah R.

Augusta

GA.

British
Dec. 1778

Savannah

York and Rhode Island. As early as September 23, 1780, Cornwallis advised Clinton, "If you cannot relieve me very soon, you must be prepared to hear the worst." The worst occurred on October 17, when Cornwallis surrendered and so, in effect, ended the war.

Peace

"Oh, God! it is all over," cried Lord North when he heard of the humiliation at Yorktown. Actually, Britain was defeated only in America; elsewhere Britain maintained its power, as Admiral George Rodney's destruction of the French fleet in 1782 confirmed. Gibraltar survived the Franco-Spanish onslaught, and British armies remained in New York as well as in the Northwest. But Yorktown had a major impact on the British political scene. North's parliamentary majority steadily shrank: his margin of one hundred in 1780 was down to nineteen early in 1782. Finally, on March 20, 1782, North resigned. George III contemplated abdication, but the prospect of the son he hated becoming king forced him to accept his new ministry. Sir Guy Carleton, who replaced Clinton, had orders to conciliate, not fight. Meanwhile, Lord Shelburne initiated peace negotiations.

Victory at Yorktown: American and French forces accept the surrender of Cornwallis

In spite of the British eagerness for an end to hostilities, accomplishing a peace was no simple task. Neither France nor Spain cared to see the British presence in North America replaced with a powerful new United States of America; indeed the Spanish regarded colonial rebellions with the natural distaste of a nation with colonies of its own in the New World. Nor were the British any more eager to see a strong, independent United States; but they were determined to cut their losses and woo Americans away from the French embrace. The American peace commissioners, Benjamin Franklin, John Jay, and John Adams, made the most of their opportunities; they opened negotiations with extravagant demands, including the cession of Canada, and then settled for the boundaries of the Mississippi River on the west (which Spain opposed), the thirty-first parallel to the south, and the Great Lakes in the north. In return the Americans agreed to allow British creditors to sue for prewar debts and recommended that states restore Loyalist property. The French foreign minister, the Comte de Vergennes, was dismayed by Britain's generosity and the speed of independent American diplomacy, but Franklin's tact not only overcame the French alarm but won from them another large loan for the United States. Final agreement, in the form of the Treaty of Paris, took place on September 3, 1783, when the treaty was signed by Britain and the United States.

The Articles of Confederation and State Constitutions

The Revolution was much more than a war for independence. Thirteen colonies had to shape new governments to replace their British structures. The former colonists also had to decide how much hard-won sovereignty to surrender to a federal government that had fought the war. Progress was unsteady and judgments sometimes flawed.

Aware of the political risks of infringing on the sovereignty of proud, new states, the Congress, unauthorized, had undertaken to create a form of national union that would at least permit national survival. In June 1776, a committee under John Dickinson began to draft a new national constitution. In 1777, the Congress approved the plan and recommended its ratification by the states, in spite of bickering over slavery, conflicting claims to western land, and the small states' nervousness over the power of their larger associates. Well might the Congress approve, for Dickinson's proposed Articles of Confederation merely described on paper what was already being practiced. It was, wrote Dickinson, "a firm league of friendship"; certainly it was not much more.

Dickinson recognized a league of sovereign states, which would permit the Congress to control external affairs. Each state, regardless of size or wealth, had an equal voice, and the states elected and paid their own delegates to the single-chamber national legislature. Lacking an executive, the Congress operated through committees. Major questions required the support of nine of the thirteen states; constitutional amendments required unanimity. Congressional authority was confined to foreign policy (war and peace), the army, interstate and border disputes, the post office, Indian affairs, coinage, and loans. Authority to levy taxes or to regulate interstate commerce was conspicuously missing.

But these limitations and omissions reflected political reality. Americans had declared their independence because they feared the potential tyranny of a strong, centralized government. They were not about to replace one such administration with another—not even one of their own making. Even so, the Articles of Confederation waited four years for ratification. Those states with fixed western boundaries, such as Maryland, insisted that unsettled lands west of the mountains should be assigned to the new national government. Not until 1780 did New York finally relinquish its western land claims to the Congress, a lead that was soon followed by Connecticut and Virginia. The way was then clear for ratification; Maryland formally accepted the Articles of Confederation in February 1781, and Congress proclaimed that the new government of the United States of America was in effect as of March 1.

Each state had to devise its own form of government too. As early as 1774 all the colonies except Georgia had elected delegates to the first Continental Congress through extralegal conventions. Many states then used these conventions as a first step in responding to Congress's recommendation in May 1776 to "adopt such government as shall best conduce to the happiness and safety of their constituents."

Most of the constitution-making that ensued was more conservative than might have been expected in a revolutionary era. New state constitutions were often slightly revised versions of the old colonial form of government. A major reduction in the power of the governor was the usual change. Most states denied the governor the veto power and limited him to a one-year term; usually he was to be elected by the state legislature, which now wielded most of the constitutional power. The assemblies were bicameral from the outset (except those of Vermont, New Hampshire, Pennsylvania, and Georgia), with the (often enlarged) lower house frequently modeled after Britain's powerful House of Commons. Particularly significant was Virginia's precaution of incorporating George Mason's widely copied Bill of Rights, which was intended to protect citizens even from their own legislators. As Jefferson remarked in his *Notes on Virginia*, "An elective despotism was not the government we fought for"; he recalled that the time to guard "against corruption and tyranny is before they shall have gotten hold of us." The frequency of legislative elections was also significant: in careful contrast to Britain's septennial arrangement, most American states called for elections every year or two in order to insure legislators would stay in close contact with voters.

Historians have argued about the measure of democracy introduced by these new state constitutions. In fact, the constitution-makers were not consciously seeking democratic government; they were more concerned with stability and security. No state gave the vote to all, not even to all white men; all required property ownership for suffrage, and in some instances (as in New York) the requirement increased after separation from Britain, as did the property qualification for officeholding. Furthermore, eastern sections of the states sometimes still dominated both the process of constitution-making and the allocation of political representation that resulted. For example, the more populous western section of South Carolina received only half the number of legislators assigned the eastern Tidewater region. Although each state constitution cited the people as sovereign, the sovereign people had not yet achieved full control and there was no thought of including women or blacks in the political process.

The Internal Revolution

If there was not absolute democracy, there was reform. As increased economic and political opportunity brought new faces into legislative halls the influence and power of the aristocracy diminished. The war created opportunities for new entrepreneurs in trade and commerce. Confiscation and sale of Loyalist estates brought some measure of redistribution of landed wealth; in New York, for instance, Roger Morris's 5,000 acres went to 250 new landowners and James DeLancey's vast estate emerged as some 275 new farms. But in Somerset County, New Jersey, Patriots who had adjoining property divided, rather than redistributed, the confiscated land and thereby added to their propertied power.

Many saw the Revolution as an admirable opportunity to sweep aside the last remnants of New World feudalism. Quitrents, the annual payments denoting obligations for ownership of land, were soon abolished, despite conservatives who thought to assign such revenues to the state governments. Entail, which prohibited the portioning of an inheritance, was ended by 1786, but primogeniture, which assured descent of property to the first-born male heir, lingered in some states until the turn of the century. Even the rights of women received some attention: most states began to give daughters equal inheritance rights with sons. Although the democratizing effect of these changes has been exaggerated, such reforms did help divide large estates. Jefferson, for one, was delighted: "Are we not the better," he asked a friend, "for what we have hitherto abolished of the feudal system?" For him such land reform was fully justified as a return to the prefeudal, pre-Norman era of "our wise British ancestors."

Land reform advanced equality of opportunity for white men, but not

The first cotton gin, drawn by William L. Sheppard

for black slaves. Yet many Americans took seriously the philosophy underlying the Revolution. In fact, the founding of the Quaker Anti-Slavery Society took place a year before the Declaration of Independence was written. The implications of the Patriots' argument for the natural rights of men were substantial. Did such rights know a color line? Could a struggle for freedom be waged for white men only? Crispus Attucks was one of the earliest casualties in the war, and he had company from among 5,000 other blacks who joined the revolutionary struggle. Beginning with Rhode Island and Pennsylvania, all states north of Maryland provided for emancipation by 1804. And the number of free blacks increased sharply in Virginia between 1782 and 1810. Even though few southerners—not even Jefferson—inconvenienced themselves by freeing slaves, gradual emancipation seemed a possibility until the South discovered the cotton gin in the 1790s and consequently a new reliance on black servitude. The fact that slavery was generally unprofitable in the North facilitated emancipation there. But even when free, blacks did not secure all the rights usually assumed to accompany freedom.

Religious and educational reform also accompanied the Revolution. Since the Anglican Church was identified with Britain, those states south of Delaware, where Anglicanism was established, moved swiftly to terminate that church's privileged position. Virginia's unusual religious arrangement—virtually a congregational organization for an Anglican denomination—along with the patriotism of its Anglican clergy led to a delay in disestablishment. But finally, in 1786, Jefferson's Statute for Religious Liberty passed. The Congregational Church, entrenched in the New England states, proved less vulnerable; not until 1833 did Massachusetts move toward the separation of church and state that had been so earnestly advocated by James Madison and Thomas Jefferson. Other denominations quickly organized independently; the Methodists found their own bishop in Francis Asbury, followed by the Roman Catholics with John Carroll. But disestablishment did not necessarily mean freedom of conscience: in Massachusetts and Maryland, officeholders were required to swear an oath that they were Christians; in Pennsylvania, one had to believe in the divine inspiration of the Scriptures; in Delaware, belief in the Trinity was expected; and in New Jersey and the Carolinas, Protestantism was demanded of officeholders. In short, the Revolution advanced freedom of worship but not religious liberty.

The separation of church and state increased the number of academies and colleges throughout the nation since enthusiasm for higher education had both religious and political sources. Religious sects continued to seek the promotion of their faith and its continuity, and states assigned some undeveloped landholdings for the support of colleges and "Seminaries of Learning." The revived quest for knowledge advanced medicine, increased libraries, and gave new life to learned societies, such as the American Philosophical Society and the American Academy of Arts and Sciences.

In this difficult, unsteady process of becoming fully independent, Americans slowly discovered their new identity and revealed the character of their reluctant Revolution. There was no abrupt, sudden reversal of colonial customs and practices. But there was moderate social, political, and religious change—and answers were earnestly being sought for new questions. Some four years after the war had ended, Benjamin Rush recalled that, while the war was indeed over, the Revolution was not: "on the contrary, nothing but the first act of the great drama is closed. It remains yet to establish and perfect our new forms of government."

The Critical Period, 1783—1787

Perfecting "new forms of government" proved an extended and difficult task. The Articles of Confederation, first debated in 1776 and finally ratified in 1781, furnished as much central government as the member states were then prepared to accept. Although the Articles provided a structure adequate to the needs of waging and winning the war, they appeared inadequate to deal with national needs in the postwar years. The nineteenth-century historian John Fiske argued in *The Critical Period of American History* that the weaknesses of the Confederation threatened the very survival of the nation. Modern historians have conceded the seriousness of the problems but have found that the nation's condition was far less perilous than previously thought. In fact, Americans in that time achieved independence and made progress on a number of tasks, but some major problems could only be resolved by the creation of a vastly stronger national government.

Legislation for the national domain was the most constructive work of the Congress of the Confederation. Since disputes over western lands had delayed ratification of the Articles themselves, it was fitting that the Congress should successfully establish policy governing the future development of the West. Virginia's formal cession of western claims in 1784 permitted the Congress to proceed. With the Land Ordinance of 1785 the Congress established a pattern for orderly settlement of the land north of the Ohio River. The ordinance called for townships of six miles square, subdivided into thirty-six sections of 640 acres, each section to be sold by auction for at least one dollar an acre. The resulting revenue would help pay the vast national debt. Revenue from one section in each township was to be used to support public education.

The Congress thus acknowledged both its responsibilities and its opportunities: it sought to bring order and government to the West and at the same time to secure revenue. Well-organized speculators discovered a marvelous opportunity for quick wealth. The Ohio Company of Associates had earlier acquired some 1.5 million acres for a dollar of inflated colonial currency per acre—or about eight or nine cents an acre in hard money. Having gained legal title, speculators had to evict squatters and Indians; thus law and order was an early political concern. The Congress responded with the Northwest Ordinance in 1787, providing for the evolution of territorial government: the territory would be under federal rule until the population reached 60,000, when statehood might be granted. New states were to enter without slavery but otherwise with privileges identical to those of the original thirteen.

Congressional success in legislating for the western domain was not matched by its conduct of postwar foreign policy. The Congress had authority to negotiate but little power to hold the states to treaty obligations. The lack of power gave foreigners little reason to respect the new republic that so hopefully called itself the United States. Relations with Britain were particularly uneasy. John Adams served as minister in London, where he was usually snubbed. Britain declined to send a minister to the United States for eight years, suggesting that one man would hardly suffice when thirteen were needed.

Certainly there were enough postwar disputes to engage any number of diplomats. The British complained that American states had enacted

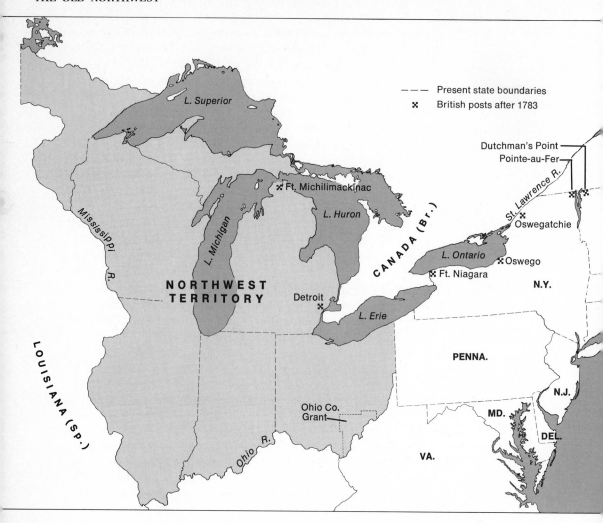

Township Survey under the Land Ordinance of 1785

A western township = 36 sq. miles
One section = 1 sq. mile (640 acres)

Half section (320 acres)

Quarter section (160 acres)

Half–quarter section (80 acres)

Quarter–quarter section (40 acres each)

6	5	4	3	2	1
7	8	9	10	11	12
18	17	16	15	14	13
19	20	21	22	23	24
30	29	28	27	26	25
31	32	33	34	35	36

Income reserved for school support → 16

1 mile

Numbering system adopted 1796

laws to obstruct collection of debts owed British merchants; they also protected continued harassment of Loyalists. On their part, Americans protested the British failure to evacuate military and trading outposts in the Northwest, as pledged in the peace treaty. These diplomatic difficulties did not disturb the flow of Anglo-American commerce, which British merchants encouraged with easy credit. With the exception of the West Indian ports, closed by Britain to American vessels, postwar trade soon took on something of its prewar pattern, including a large trade imbalance that soon drained Americans of their hard money.

Relations with Spain were complicated by Spanish resentment of the American presence in the trans-Allegheny West, by American resentment of Spanish control of the Mississippi, and by extravagant Spanish claims about the location of Florida's border. Spain's decision to close the Mississippi to American shipping in 1784 led to negotiations between John Jay and Don Diego de Gardoqui in 1785–86. Jay asked the Congress to accept a settlement whereby the United States would give up use of the Mississippi for twenty-five years in return for trading concessions from Spain. The southern states would not agree and the proposal was not ratified. As Spanish intrigue continued in the West, there was a growing suspicion among Americans on the frontier that the northern states were ready to sacrifice the West in return for trade advantages with Spain. The futility of Jay's diplomatic exercise reminded others of the inadequacy of the Congress.

France was no more a friend of the Americans than was Spain. In fact, France persisted with a policy aimed at keeping the United States weak and dependent. France limited American commerce with the French West Indies, negotiated a treaty that allowed French consuls in the United States to try certain cases involving French citizens, and complained, with reason, of America's failure to make payments on its huge debt to France. The Congress did succeed in negotiating two minor European trade treaties (with Sweden and Prussia) but met with rebuffs from other countries, which questioned the Congress's ability to enforce its agreements at home.

Lack of congressional authority also prevented the formation of a national fiscal policy. Debts not only remained unpaid but steadily increased. The inability of the Congress to levy taxes was not very serious at first: during the war there was little hard money available for taxes. Both the Congress and the states resorted to paper money to finance the war, but the depreciation of this currency—in fact a form of taxation—was so excessive that Congress abandoned its currency printing press in 1780. Instead, Congress resorted to loans, with rapidly diminishing returns at home but greater success abroad. An effort to raise revenue through a 5 percent import duty failed to secure the requisite unanimous ratification by the states. During the postwar years, the nation was in dire fiscal straits. Dutch loans and the efforts of Robert Morris, superintendent of finance from 1781 to 1784, made the nation's survival possible.

The individual states faced comparable fiscal difficulties, which contributed to the air of crisis that ultimately ended the Confederation itself. The states had also resorted to paper money to finance the war, and despite rapid depreciation many were about to issue paper currency to finance the peace as well. The trade imbalance, coinciding with a deepening postwar depression, left debtors and taxpayers alike unable to meet their obligations. Creditors did not want to be repaid in unsecured paper money worth far less than the original loan.

In a majority of the states pressure for more paper currency prevailed, but gloomy predictions of unrestrained inflation proved exaggerated. Most states controlled their currency carefully so that it gained ready acceptance although there were unfortunate and widely noted exceptions. Georgia's new currency declined in value by 75 percent within a year. Neighboring states practiced commercial warfare at New Jersey's expense by heavily discounting its well-secured paper currency. But the most alarming situation developed in Rhode Island, where a generous issue of paper money led to almost immediate depreciation. When merchants refused to accept nearly worthless paper, the legislature enacted a law forcing them to accept it. Creditors fled the state to avoid meeting their debtors. When, in December 1786, the state's supreme court decided in *Trevett* v. *Weeden* that the forcing act was unconstitutional,* the legislature roundly denounced the judges.

The paper money problem was often related to that of state indebtedness, much of which had been incurred during the Revolution. Interest on the debt alone created a heavy burden, leading some states to impose new and sometimes inequitable taxes. In Massachusetts, a conservative legislature placed the state on a hard-money base and then required redemption of outstanding debts at face value. Taxes skyrocketed, particularly for farmers, who had to pay out one-third of their income in hard money. As a consequence, by the spring of 1786 foreclosures and tax auctions became commonplace; in Worcester County 94 of 104 people in jail were debtors. The failure of the state legislature to respond to the farmers' plea for relief led directly to Shays' Rebellion.

The rebellion began in the summer of 1786, when desperate farmers started to seize courthouses in an effort to halt foreclosure proceedings. Captain Daniel Shays, a veteran of Bunker Hill, led his fellow farmers to Springfield and forced the state supreme court to adjourn. Alarmed conservatives rallied to Governor James Bowdoin's call for volunteers to suppress this threat to property and order. At Petersham in February 1787 General Benjamin Lincoln routed the rebels and Shays fled to Vermont. Shays was later pardoned, and the Massachusetts legislature modified its tax program. But the shock of the rebellion endured. More

* A Newport butcher (Weeden) refused payment in the depreciated paper. Although his case was dismissed on jurisdictional grounds, the judges established a precedent for a court test of the constitutionality of legislative action.

than any other event, Shays' Rebellion fed the growing conviction in the minds of conservatives that only a stronger central government could assure law, order, and respect for property.

The Making of the Constitution

"Something must be done or the fabric will fall," exclaimed George Washington on hearing of Shays' uprising. "We are fast verging to anarchy and confusion!" Jefferson was more sanguine—it was only "a *little* rebellion," fertilizer for the tree of liberty. But Jefferson was in France and separated from the American reality. Others had long contended that the Articles of Confederation were inadequate to the needs of the new nation; as early as 1782, New Yorkers vainly urged a national convention to propose changes. Times were more favorable in 1786, when nine states accepted James Madison's suggestion of a meeting in Annapolis to discuss interstate commercial rivalry. Representatives of only five states actually reached Annapolis, and they contented themselves with endorsing Alexander Hamilton's call for a convention to be held in Philadelphia to discuss ways in which the "federal government" might be made "adequate to the exigencies of the Union." After some indecision, Congress offered its own endorsement of the proposal and recommended a convention "for the sole and express purpose of revising the Articles of Confederation." By May 25, 1787, twenty-nine delegates were on hand from nine states; they gathered in Philadelphia State House and opened the discussions and debates that continued until September 17.

Eventually fifty-five delegates participated in the Philadelphia convention. They represented every state but Rhode Island, which refused to attend because it did not want a stronger national government at the expense of state sovereignty. With the exception of Franklin and Washington, the delegates were not heroes of the Revolution. Only eight of the delegates had signed the Declaration of Independence. Jefferson and John Adams were in Europe, and Samuel Adams, Richard Henry Lee, and Patrick Henry refused to come. But, still, it was a brilliant, relatively youthful assembly. A majority were college graduates, in an age when few had the opportunity to attend college. Most had congressional experience, and each was chosen by his state legislature. They saw themselves for what they were: practical politicians seeking realistic solutions to national problems. Most were lawyers, and many, like James Madison, had helped draft their state constitutions. Instinctively, they consulted historical precedent; theoretical abstractions were not for them. "Experience must be our only guide," warned John Dickinson. "Reason may mislead us."

Their motivations, like their purposes and achievements, have been much debated. Jefferson viewed the delegates as "demigods," while a

Philadelphia, 1787: Washington speaks for the new Constitution

later historian, Charles Beard, suggested that the Founders operated
mainly from personal economic interest. Most of the delegates were in
fact from the propertied class, and some owned securities that would
appreciate in value with a strong central government. But their political
behavior did not necessarily coincide with their economic interest. The
seven delegates who walked out of the convention or refused to approve
its result were among the heaviest security-holders present. In practice,
the delegates seem to have risen above self-interest; their common
interest was in providing a central government that could command
respect at home and abroad.

Their debates and compromises illustrate that commitment. From the
outset they thought it necessary to hold secret sessions to provide the
freest of discussions; they even kept windows closed, in spite of

Philadelphia's summer heat. Tempers rose with the temperature, sectional jealousies intruded with alarming frequency, and differences of opinion were both clear and sharp. But these disagreements have too often masked the delegates' larger measure of common purpose. No serious thought, for example, was given to merely patching up the government of the Confederation. There was general and continuing agreement that a strong national government should encompass defense, interstate commerce, taxation, law enforcement, protection of property, and the integrity of debt obligations.

The structure of the new Congress was a matter of major debate. The Virginia Plan and the New Jersey Plan assigned substantially similar authority to the new national Congress. The difference between the two drafts was one of method, not of objective: Virginia's Edmund Randolph sought a two-house national legislature with representation based on population, while New Jersey's William Paterson favored a single-house legislature in which each state would have an equal voice. The deadlock was serious; Franklin, once a religious skeptic, even went so far as to suggest prayers before each daily session. But Franklin also helped refine Roger Sherman's famed compromise, which established the bicameral system, with a Senate based on an equal voice for all states and a House of Representatives based on population.

Compromise determined the final details on most points. The electoral college and the veto power of the President appeased those fearful of too much democracy. Provisions for the President's impeachment contented those worried about potential dictators or monarchs. A compromise allowed a state to count a slave as three-fifths of a man in computing the basis for representation in the House. Another concession to the South, particularly South Carolina and Georgia, protected the slave trade at least until 1808 and prohibited taxes on exports, upon which the South depended. The senators, with their six-year terms of office, were to be elected by the state legislatures, but the members of the House were to be elected every two years by popular vote. Age requirements for federal office reflected the delegates' quest for stability: the presidency called for a person at least thirty-five years old; the Senate demanded at least thirty years; only the House would tolerate a youth of twenty-five.

By September 17, the Constitution had been drafted. The surviving delegates, thirty-nine in all, signed the engrossed copy and adjourned for self-congratulation at the nearby City Tavern. Their compromises avoided both the dangers of democracy and the hazards of despotism; they had provided a centralized national government, but one in which the states retained significant governmental authority. The conspicuous deficiencies of the Confederation were repaired: a congressional majority could now enact legislation; a federal executive replaced the impotent committees of the Confederation; the power to regulate interstate commerce, to tax, and to raise any army were fundamental advances; a federal court system provided essential legal underpinning; and it would not be unduly difficult to amend the Constitution. All that remained was to persuade the American people that it was in their interest to accept this new Constitution. That task would not be easy.

Ratification

In Philadelphia the delegates had given the process of ratification considerable thought. They recalled that unanimous consent to the Articles had emerged only after a long delay, and they were well aware of the absence of Rhode Island from their deliberations. Accordingly, they decided that approval by nine states would be sufficient for the Constitution to take effect. The delegates also decided that ratification should be by special state conventions called for that express purpose, since state legislatures were not likely to ratify a Constitution that would reduce their power; further, if state legislatures could approve a Constitution, they could later legally rescind their approval if they wished.

The delegates had calculated correctly. Only three states—Delaware, New Jersey, and Georgia—gave the Constitution their uncontested approval. Connecticut was next to ratify by a comfortable 128 to 40 vote. Elsewhere, critics of the Constitution mounted a vigorous attack. Anti-Federalists, such as Richard Henry Lee, cautioned lest "we kill ourselves for fear of dying." Patrick Henry claimed the proposed presidency "squints toward monarchy" and charged that the new Constitution would destroy the liberties secured in the Revolution. Many continued to fear that the Constitution would totally destroy the sovereignty of the states, that it would favor the propertied at the expense of the debtor class, that it was a conspiracy of the East against the aspirations of the West, that it represented a surrender to the South or, alternately, a devious victory for the mercantile North.

The best-known response to these objections came in the form of *The Federalist*, essays penned by Madison, Hamilton, and Jay between October 1787 and April 1788. In his famous tenth *Federalist* paper Madison argued that the country's vast size and conflicting interests could through checks and balances assure stability and justice. The influence of *The Federalist* was substantial. Even so, the Congress of the Confederation might not have transmitted the proposed Constitution to the states (which it did without recommendation) had it not been for the presence of ten congressmen who had recently served as delegates to the Philadelphia convention.

Federalist tactics varied from state to state. Pennsylvania, the first of the large states to ratify, did so in a questionable fashion. Federalists there rushed the call for a convention to reduce the opposition's chance to organize. Anti-Federalists boycotted the assembly so that there was no quorum for business, but the enterprising Federalists responded by forcibly dragging two Anti-Federalists into the State House. Federalists dominated the convention and on December 12, 1787, voted to ratify 46 to 23. In Massachusetts the divisions were particularly deep and the debates serious. John Hancock's final decision to support ratification proved helpful, as did the decision to recommend enactment of a federal bill of rights. The final vote was still close: 187 to 168. In Rhode Island the state legislature declined to call a convention but instead invoked a dubious referendum that resulted in overwhelming opposition to ratification. In Maryland the real debate took place during the election of convention delegates; Federalist dominance brought the 63 to 11 vote to ratify. South Carolina's Tidewater gentry were satisfied with the Constitution and by a vote of 149 to 73 made the state the eighth to enter the new union. Federalist debaters in New Hampshire proved sufficiently persuasive for many delegates to change their position and vote to ratify; the final 57 to 47 vote for ratification was cast on June 21, 1788. The delegates were unaware that theirs was the vital ninth state that would bring the new national government into existence.

The decision in New Hampshire was less conclusive than that in Virginia and New York. Virginia was the largest of the states, with one-fifth of the United States' population. A majority of Virginians probably opposed ratification at the outset, but the Federalists proved politically adroit and argued their case with skill. Washington's influence complemented the cool logic of Madison. Even so, the vote on June 26 was close: 89 to 79 for ratification and for urging a federal bill of rights. The opposition in New York was headed by Governor George Clinton and joined by upstate landowners who enjoyed low taxes thanks to the state's income from import duties. Since Anti-Federalists constituted a majority of the ratifying convention, Hamilton's task was to debate and delay. He did both. News of Virginia's decision helped his cause, as did confusion over the precise meaning of the decision finally taken by a 30 to 27 margin; some supported ratification in the belief that another constitutional convention was to take place as a condition of New York's vote. North Carolina and Rhode Island, while far from irrelevant, now seemed less important: North Carolina opposed ratification in August 1788, but reversed its position in November 1789; Rhode Island, threatened with commercial isolation, grudgingly ratified by a 34 to 32 vote in May 1790.

Obviously the new Constitution did not engender immediate reverence throughout the United States. The fight to ratify had been sometimes hard and often bitter. But it had been successful. A second, peaceful, and internal revolution had been completed; like the first revolution, it had been conducted by a dedicated and articulate leadership able to address and resolve the intellectual and constitutional issues before them and their countrymen.

Opposition to the Constitution would have been less severe had a bill

REDEUNT SATURNIA REGNA.

On the erection of the Eleventh PILLAR of the great National DOME, we beg leave most sincerely to felicitate " OUR DEAR COUNTRY."

The FEDERAL EDIFICE.

of rights been incorporated from the outset. Most delegates in Philadelphia had relied on the protection afforded by the states, but they had underestimated popular fears of the new federal power. Without a promise, tacit or explicit, that such a bill of rights would immediately follow establishment of the new government, the Constitution could not have gained approval.

Cyrus Griffin, president of the expiring Congress, formally announced ratification of the new Constitution on July 2, 1788. In August, arrangements were completed for the selection of presidential electors, and, in September, Congress designated New York the site for the new government. The following month the Congress of the Confederation concluded its business and quietly vacated the New York City Hall to permit renovation for new occupants.

The new nation could now enter into its inheritance.

Suggested Reading

John R. Alden's competence as a military historian is well demonstrated in *The American Revolution, 1775–1783** (1954); Don Higginbotham's *The War of American Independence* (1971) is both perceptive and (inevitably) more recent in scholarship. Piers Mackesy's *The War for America, 1775–1783* (1964) provides a British historian's perspective of the American Revolutionary War. Eminently readable are Marshall Smelser's *The Winning of Independence** (1972) and John Shy's *A People Numerous and Armed* (1976). The internal division within the colonies is best treated by William H. Nelson in *The American Tory** (1961) and by Wallace Brown in *The King's Friends* (1965). Social aspects of the Revolution were first reviewed by J. Franklin Jameson in *The American Revolution Considered as a Social Movement** (1926). Jackson Turner Main usefully employs statistical tools in *The Social Structure of Revolutionary America** (1965). See also Main's *The Sovereign States, 1775–1783* (1973) and H. James Henderson's *Party Politics Before the Constitution* (1973).

The creation of new state governments is thoughtfully treated by Elisha P. Douglass in *Rebels and Democrats** (1955). J. R. Pole's *Political Representation in England and the Origins of the American Republic** (1966) is a substantial study of the American indebtedness to British ideas about political representation. In *The Creation of the American Republic, 1776–1787* (1969), Gordon S. Wood examines at length the meaning of republicanism for the revolutionaries. John Fiske's *The Critical Period of American History, 1783–1789* (1888)—with which Wood is sympathetic—is still readable. In *The New Nation** (1950), Merrill Jensen is much more favorably impressed with the new republic than are Fiske and Wood, and he relates its establishment in *The Articles of Confederation** (1940). Marion L. Starkey's *A Little Rebellion** (1955) is a lively account of Shays' Rebellion.

Clinton Rossiter has provided a useful treatment of the emergence of the Constitution in *1787: The Grand Convention* (1966), as has Forrest McDonald in *E Pluribus Unum** (1965). Charles A. Beard's much criticized *An Economic Interpretation of the Constitution* (1913) deserves to be read before one turns to Robert E. Brown's intemperate *Charles Beard and the Constitution* (1956).

* Available in paperback edition

The First Century:
An Introduction

The United States proudly celebrated a century of independence with a world's fair in Philadelphia during the summer of 1876. Exhibits there properly emphasized the future more than the past, especially the new technology of the industrial future: electricity, telephones, and mass-production machinery. Innovation fascinated the visitors who crowded the Centennial Exposition, but their own lives were not altogether different from those of their American forebears in the years after the Revolution. For there was continuity in American society, as well as change—continuity that derived from the Christian ethic, the Constitution, the rhythm of agriculture, and the common desire for more of the world's goods and more of the earth's surface.

To be sure, the experience of a family in rural South Dakota in 1876 differed from that of pioneers in upstate New York a hundred years earlier. Nor were the hardships of black homesteaders in Kansas those of slaves in South Carolina. Yet farming depended on weather and sweat and soil whether the harvest was gathered with a reaper or by hand; contact with hostile Indians still marked the frontier; Protestant pulpits continued to be the fount of moral truth; communities remained small and relatively homogeneous; moving ahead, and sometimes moving on, was always the name of the game.

Fortunately for the United States, much of that first century passed without foreign interference. The nation was blessed with weak neighbors; even those with colonial ties were too distant from European empires for easy defense and became in effect hostages rather than imperial outposts. And once their former possessions achieved independence, the European powers lost interest in America and played out their strategic and colonial rivalries elsewhere. England, like the United States, had a commercial stake in preventing renewed European meddling in the Western Hemisphere. The superiority of the British fleet made the oceans an effective shield and relieved the United States of the expense of building and maintaining a large military establishment.

Conflict during the first century of independence, then, was ordinarily internal. With the major exception of the Civil War, debate took place within the political framework that the Revolutionary generation had adopted and centered on issues the Revolutionaries had discussed in their time. In particular, Americans argued about the locus of political power from the days of the Stamp Act until after the Civil War. Whatever the controversy—the authority of Parliament, the powers of Congress under the Articles of Confederation, the sovereignty and prerogatives of the states, the right to secede, the process of Reconstruction—the division of power between central and local governments was at the heart of American political discourse for more than a century.

Leaders of the American Revolution warned their contemporaries not to let political questions become sectional ones. For about half of the first century, that advice was heeded. Regional differences did not move the adversaries in early debates about money and banking, frontier settlement and public lands, tariffs, taxation, and transportation. Eventually, however, these issues and others apparently less important became pretexts for the quarrel over slavery. When slavery became an acknowledged item on the country's political agenda, sectional rivalries could no longer be obscured. And the rivalries, as the Founders had feared, could not be resolved peacefully by constitutional procedures.

The quarrel over slavery spread to the frontier, though slaves themselves rarely resided there. The right to take them to the edge of settlement seemed crucial to owners, and the matter cropped up whenever the nation secured new territory or admitted new states. Even white Americans who opposed slavery were not free of racial prejudice, which was so pervasive in the nation's first century as not to require apology. Prejudice, indeed, was one more bond that linked white Americans of various sections and generations, another thread of continuity across the change that took place during the republic's first hundred years.

Chapter 5
Parties and Policies in the Early Republic

Chronology

1789–1815 Intermittent war in Europe •

1789 Presidential election: George Washington receives one vote from every elector • Federal Judiciary Act •

1790–91 Hamilton submits financial program:
1790: Funding Act, including assumption of state debts •
1791: Bank of the United States chartered • *Report on Manufactures* •

1792 Presidential election: George Washington reelected •

1793 Washington proclaims American neutrality •

1794 Whisky Rebellion • Jay Treaty with England •

1795 Pinckney Treaty with Spain •

1796 Washington gives Farewell Address • Presidential election: John Adams (Federalist) defeats Thomas Jefferson (Democratic-Republican); Jefferson becomes Vice-President •

1797 XYZ affair •

1798 Alien and Sedition Acts; Kentucky and Virginia Resolutions •

1798–1800 Undeclared war with France •

1800 Convention of 1800 ends alliance with France • Presidential election: Thomas Jefferson and Aaron Burr tie with 73 votes; the House elects Jefferson President •

The leaders who helped to achieve independence, wrote and ratified the Constitution, established the new government, and founded political parties, deplored the public display of the political talent they so abundantly possessed. Perhaps the most creative politicians in American history, they nevertheless considered electioneering a vulgar enterprise and, hence, beneath their dignity. They condemned political parties as factions, institutional expressions of personal ambition and national division that endangered the harmony upon which survival of the republic depended. Although their own lives had been filled with political controversy—between tidewater and backcountry, between old settlers and new arrivals, between Patriots and Loyalists, between Federalists and Anti-Federalists—the Founders still believed all right-thinking Americans ought to agree.

Yet Americans obviously did not agree, as they had not agreed in the past. The Constitution did not end arguments about the relationship of local and central authority, nor about the legitimate social obligations of free individuals, nor about the practical consequence of the ideal of human equality. The Constitution merely established new rules for carrying on a long-standing dialog, a new forum for an old debate. After trying, and failing, to rout their political opposition, the nation's leaders slowly learned to live with it. The same people who had filled pamphlets with denunciations of political parties eventually realized that their writing had helped to found such parties. Slightly ahead of his contemporaries as usual, James Madison decided that he would make a virtue of what he could not prevent. Since parties seemed inevitable, Madison observed in 1792, one party should at least check the other and thereby reduce partisan damage to the republic. Madison thus conceded that opposition might be at once legitimate and a useful extra-constitutional safeguard against tyranny. The establishment and eventual acceptance of parties was the final political contribution of an extraordinary generation.

Establishing the New Government

Both in its provisions and in its omissions, the Constitution shaped the early political activity of the new nation. The men of the Philadelphia Convention had outlined broad principles and intentionally left details to the new government itself. Especially vague about the presidency, the Constitution did not specify departments or mention a cabinet, and furnished no protocol for relations between the executive and legislative branches. However imprecise the definition of the President's powers, it was clear that George Washington would exercise them. That certainty reassured most Americans, for whom Washington personified the republic. At the beginning of his administration, he was a nonpartisan focus for popular loyalty, a distinguished presence aloof from petty rivalries and arguments. Although he became increasingly identified with the Federalist faction in his second term, Washington always thought of himself as above partisanship. He conducted himself with a frosty formality that lent dignity to the presidency and helped to establish the independence of the executive branch.

Washington waited until Congress formally notified him of his election, borrowed £100 from a neighbor, and reluctantly left Mt. Vernon for his inauguration. From the Confederation, the new administration inherited a few clerks, an army of 700 men, and a staggering inventory of problems. (Washington had more employees at Mt. Vernon than were available to conduct the business of the federal government.) British troops still occupied American soil in the Northwest, and Indians and settlers menaced one another all along the frontier. The national treasury had no resources to placate importunate creditors. Paper currency was so prevalent as to be nearly worthless and specie so scarce as to be

Washington and his first cabinet

overvalued. The United States was a frail new republic with no national courts, no national taxes, and no national mail service to tie Massachusetts with Georgia.

The First Congress straggled into New York in April 1789, a month after it was supposed to assemble. This tardiness foreshadowed the nation's continuing difficulty in attracting and retaining able civil employees. Exposed to urban plagues and fevers and deprived of the amenities of home and family, the life of a federal civil servant was hardly gracious. The President's salary provided him with a degree of comfort, but other honest officials had to scrimp to stay out of debt. No salary compensated for the loss of pride and reputation occasioned by the vehement partisanship of a press unchecked by taste or responsibility. Small wonder that public men preferred to serve in state government and avoid the hazards of travel and the trials of national politics. Both Washington and Adams put up with incompetent cabinet officials rather than face the disheartening task of seeking replacements.

If tardy, the First Congress at least assembled in harmony. Many of the legislators had helped to write the Constitution or had worked to secure its ratification; only about a dozen had opposed the new system. Congress quickly exercised the power to tax with a low tariff and established Departments of State, Treasury, and War, to which Washington appointed Thomas Jefferson, Alexander Hamilton, and Henry Knox respectively as chief administrators. To enforce the nation's laws, Congress authorized appointment of an attorney general and established a federal court system. This statute, the Judiciary Act of 1789, permitted appeal to the Supreme Court of state court decisions on constitutional issues, a provision that gave substance to the "supreme law of the land" clause in the Constitution and implied judicial review. Washington appointed Edmund Randolph, a fellow Virginian, attorney general, and John Jay of New York the first chief justice. To fulfill the pledge made to Anti-Federalists during the ratification debate, Congress drafted a dozen amendments of which ten became the Bill of Rights.

Washington's conception of his office precluded personal political leadership and restricted his contacts with legislators to regular "levees," social occasions with a prescribed, starchy ritual. At first, Congressman Madison was Washington's closest adviser and provided direction to the Congress. Gradually Secretary of the Treasury Alexander Hamilton supplanted Madison as the administration's political strategist. Hamilton's political creativity became both the greatest resource of the Federalists and their major liability. He meant to nurse the returning prosperity that enhanced public support for the central government; as much as any man, Hamilton strengthened the economic bonds that tied the republic together. But his economic policies also exaggerated political divisions in the country that contributed to eventual Federalist defeat. Hamilton created a national debt and the means for paying it, a national currency and a national bank to issue it. But while his vision was in some respects national, it was in others extraordinarily narrow. His taxes fell most heavily on frontier settlers, who had the least cash. He deliberately sought the support of the "rich, the able and the well-born," and in the process alienated much of the rest of the country.

The President of the United States and M.ʳˢ Washington, request the Pleasure of Mr & Mrs Gilbert's Company to Dine on Thursday next, at 4 o'Clock. 5ᵗʰ May 1794

An answer is requested.

Hamilton's Policies

Recognition of the nation's economic difficulties in 1790 did not require unusual insight. Insufficient federal revenue and waning confidence in the government's capacity to pay its bonded debt impaired the Treasury's effort to reestablish public credit. Several unreliable currencies complicated the attempts of merchants and producers to enlarge their sales and markets. A nation of farmers slighted industrial development.

Alexander Hamilton devised a comprehensive program to correct these deficiencies and to stimulate future growth. He proposed to issue new bonds to fund at par the national debt and to meet overdue interest obligations to bondholders at home and abroad. In addition, he suggested that the central government assume state debts since, he argued, they had been contracted in pursuit of the common goal of independence. The new debt would total about $65 million. The government would raise its revenue from an excise tax on whisky, from the sale of public lands, and from a protective tariff that Hamilton asked Congress to enact in order to encourage the growth of manufacturing. He also outlined a twenty-year charter for a national bank to serve as a depository and a source of short-term credit for the government; the notes of this bank would become a national currency. Four-fifths of the capital for the Bank of the United States was to come from private investors, who would elect a proportionate share of the directors. The Treasury would provide one-fifth of the initial capital of $10 million and appoint the rest of the board.

Hamilton's program had a political as well as an economic dimension, as he himself was the first to acknowledge. Wealthy citizens received new incentives to support the central government. Funding the federal debt and assuming the state debts created speculative opportunities in a depressed bond market. The new bank and its new currency would open opportunities for investors, merchants, and entrepreneurs. Hamilton's program hurt whisky producers and those who wanted cheap public land, but these two groups often consisted of the same people—restless individual farmers, remote in the backcountry, who distilled their surplus grain to carry it more easily to market.

Hamilton's vision of an industrial America was premature, and Congress never passed his protective tariff. Otherwise, his program generally succeeded in both its economic and political dimensions. Public confidence in American securities rebounded both at home and abroad. The Bank of the United States served the government, the stockholders, and the national economy well. Wealthy, respected, and educated citizens unflinchingly supported the new Constitution. And when, in 1794, frontier farmers in Pennsylvania resisted the tax on spirits, Hamilton advised Washington to crush the Whisky Rebellion and demonstrate the central government's resolution and authority. The rebels dispersed so quickly in the face of overwhelming federal force that

Alexander Hamilton

the troops had trouble locating the rebellion. "An insurrection was announced," Jefferson remarked, "but could never be found." The President pardoned the few dissidents arrested in the operation.

Rebellion was snuffed out, but opposition to Hamilton's legislative package remained. No one objected seriously to funding the foreign debt, for the republic's international reputation was at stake. Funding the domestic debt, however, roused a good deal of antagonism. Both the Continental Congress and the state governments had used bonds to pay soldiers and suppliers, who had then sold the bonds, often at a substantial discount, when reimbursement seemed remote. But when Hamilton promised that the new government would redeem the promises of the old, speculators bought up depreciated state and federal securities with the expectation of a quick profit. Although Hamilton himself did not buy certificates, some of his associates and a good many congressmen were less scrupulous.

James Madison denounced Hamilton's proposal to fund the domestic debt at par as unjust and opposed the assumption of state debts as unnecessary. While Hamilton defended the debt as a positive economic and political benefit, Madison thought the financial burden might well be too much for the republic. Further, he charged that Hamilton's scheme would benefit profit-seekers at the expense of patriots who had helped the revolutionary cause. Simple justice, he held, demanded compensation at par for the initial holders of the bonds, while speculators should receive only their actual costs. The Treasury's policy, Madison went on, also did the entire southern section of the country an injustice. Southern bondholders owned only one-fifth of the national debt. Several southern states, including Madison's Virginia, had paid off most of their revolutionary bonds. Assumption of all state debts would force provident southern taxpayers to meet the bills of improvident ones in the North, where the debts of Massachusetts, for instance, remained largely outstanding. (So did those of South Carolina, a fact that somewhat vitiated Madison's accusation of sectional bias.)

Congress at first returned a split verdict in 1790 by affirming Hamilton's plan to pay bondholders at par but refusing to assume the debts of the states. Astute political trading, however, produced a compromise that reversed Hamilton's momentary defeat. He converted some southern congressmen to assumption by agreeing to pay debts of North Carolina and Virginia that had been omitted from the first accounting. Southern support also came as a result of an agreement to move the nation's capital to a newly established federal district on the banks of the Potomac.

The South would not barter on the national bank. With the assistance of Jefferson, whose suspicion of Hamilton's influence grew with his antagonism to Hamilton's policies, Madison rallied four-fifths of the southern representatives. But the near-unanimity of the North prevailed and the bank bill passed. When the President asked his opinion, Jefferson wrote a brief arguing that the "incorporation of a bank, and the powers assumed by the bill" had not been "delegated to the United States by the Constitution." Jefferson interpreted narrowly the elastic clause of the Constitution, which gives Congress the authority to make all laws "necessary and proper" to carry out its powers; a bank might be convenient, he declared, but it was not essential. His statement, expanded and embroidered by lesser debaters in subsequent argument, is the essence of strict construction of the Constitution.

Hamilton responded to Jefferson with the classic statement of broad construction. The Constitution not only delegated some powers expressly but it also granted others by implication. The elastic clause, Hamilton believed, gave Congress the power to select among various means to legitimate legislative ends. If the end was constitutional, the means were automatically constitutional, unless specifically forbidden. Congress clearly had the right to collect taxes, to disburse federal revenues, to borrow money, to provide for national defense, and to regulate commerce. The Bank of the United States was an entirely appropriate means to any of those ends and should be chartered even if the Constitution did not specifically give Congress the power to establish corporations. Hamilton persuaded Washington, who signed the bill. The President's support for Hamilton's fiscal program, in the face of opposition from his fellow Virginians, illustrates Washington's integrity and detachment, as well as the force of Hamilton's argument.

Madison and Jefferson did prevent action on Hamilton's *Report on Manufactures*, which requested various bounties for manufacturers, including a protective tariff. Hamilton's dream of an industrial nation generated scant political support. Instead, Jefferson's belief that "those who labor in the earth are the chosen people of God," that a nation of farmers was a virtuous nation, corresponded to Americans' image of themselves. Jefferson's interpretation of human nature and his faith in the endurance of rural virtue were happily combined in his faith in democracy, a faith Hamilton never pretended to share. Jefferson confidently looked for eventual political vindication of his beliefs; Hamilton, who thought it unlikely that anyone could be at once right and popular, soon had to rely on political manipulation because he did not have the votes.

Federalists and Republicans

Hamilton and Jefferson have come to personify the Federalist and Republican (or Jeffersonian or Democratic-Republican) parties. Neither man approved of parties, but each accepted formal political division as less dangerous for the republic than the ideas and leadership of the other. Both believed their own policies so compelling that opposition was at best stubbornly irrational and at worst unpatriotic; both believed that parties would, and should, disappear with a reaffirmation of the ideals of the American Revolution.

The trouble, of course, was that Americans did not agree on those ideals. Federalists tended to emphasize order, tradition, religion, and the stability of the community, while Republicans stressed liberty, opportunity, and the contributions of self-reliant individuals. Federalists, therefore, fretted about license and sought progress from institutions— law, government, church—while Republicans, instead, relied on the initiative of ordinary citizens and feared the restraint of institutions, especially government. Federalists, already leaders in their communities, worried about immigration, atheism, Catholicism, and the expansion of the country, all of which threatened the social homogeneity that Federalists prized; Republicans welcomed change. Neither faction could initially admit the legitimacy of the other because both postulated a unified society in which the interests of rich and poor, North and South, farmer and merchant, coincided. That assumption contributed to the initial unwillingness of political leaders to campaign, to establish political clubs and partisan newspapers, to attack those who disagreed. But since the stakes were the continued integrity of the republican ideal, the nation's first leaders soon perfected many of the techniques that have since characterized American politics.

Hamilton's program was not the only focus of political disagreement. The evolution of a foreign policy seemed for a time even more divisive. For Americans were fiercely proud of their independence and firmly resolved that the republic must endure to inspire others. Republicans at first thought the French Revolution, which broke out in 1789, followed the American example, but Federalists were more skeptical, particularly when French radicals began to confiscate property and take lives without restraint. As the struggle in Europe dragged on, so did the debate in the United States about an appropriate response.

Guarding the Republic

The new nation had slim diplomatic and military resources with which to support any foreign policy. No army, no navy, no access to the courts of Europe or to the ports of Europe's colonies—only an uneasy alliance with France and Britain's grudging diplomatic recognition buttressed American independence. A rebellious former colony could not expect a sympathetic welcome in a world dominated by empires with submissive colonies of their own. The Federalists prudently decided that neutrality would maximize the nation's economic opportunity, reduce its military risk, and thereby best serve the country. Their policy was eminently sensible, but it stirred a political uproar.

For nearly a quarter century the wars between Britain and France that began with the French Revolution upset the Western world. As governments and alliances changed, temporary truces always seemed to give way to renewed fighting until in 1812 even the United States was finally drawn in. From the initial skirmishes until the settlement in 1815, the bloody encounter commanded the attention of the American people. For in addition to the danger, the European struggle also created opportunity—the opportunity to restate the ideals of the republic and perhaps to strengthen its independence; the opportunity to discharge the debt for French assistance in the American Revolution; the opportunity to increase the export trade; the opportunity to secure additional territory; the opportunity to capitalize on momentary diplomatic success to secure political advancement of party, program, or person.

Federalists found the French Revolution distasteful. War might upset the delicate calculations upon which Hamilton's fiscal policy depended. At the very least, war with Britain would reduce imports and seriously impair the government's revenue. To Federalists, Britain represented stability and order; the British fleet was the first line of American defense. Jefferson, on the other hand, had seen the popular phase of the revolution while in Paris. Subsequently, as secretary of state, he argued that the alliance of 1778 bound the nation in honor to assist France; if Washington ignored that obligation, he should nevertheless threaten to fulfill the alliance in order to exact concessions from Great Britain. Hamilton countered that our alliance had been with the French King, whose death, in 1792, effectively released the United States from its commitment. In 1793 the President officially proclaimed American neutrality.

Neutrality rarely satisfies emotions, and the initial American response to events in France had been emotional indeed. Enthusiastic editorials and toasts welcomed Edmond Genêt, the first diplomatic representative of the revolutionary government, who took advantage of popular good will by commissioning privateers, by authorizing an "allied" army of Americans to invade Florida, Louisiana, and Canada, and by encouraging the formation of "Democratic" societies, some of which became centers of Jeffersonian political intrigue. Washington received Genêt with chilling reserve, and even Jefferson soon decided that the enthusiastic Frenchman had ventured beyond the bounds of acceptable diplomatic behavior. Washington's decision to seek Genêt's recall coincided with a change of government in France. The new government, made up of Genêt's political foes, dismissed the blundering envoy, who then sought and received political asylum in the United States.

Opportunities for friction with Britain exceeded those for disagreement with France. Neither Britain nor the United States had faithfully carried out the terms of the Treaty of Paris. Redcoats remained in forts in the Northwest Territory, and planters vainly sought compensation for slaves British troops had carried off after the Revolution. American debtors had not lived up to the spirit of the treaty, nor had Patriots returned confiscated property to Loyalists. Frontier settlers thought British garrisons supplied Indian allies and encouraged their interference with American settlement of the West. And the constant encounters of American and British ships created endless friction. The British cabinet tried to restrict American trade as if the United States were still a colony. An Order in Council in 1793, for instance, authorized seizure of neutral cargoes bound either for France or for the French colonies and resulted in the capture of more than three hundred American vessels and outcry in the United States.

Federalists suffered British interference with neutral trade more willingly than they did French interference. Republicans usually excused French action that they would have condemned if the British were responsible. In 1794 congressional opponents of the Federalists demanded an end to trade with the British Empire. From then on, economic coercion became the standard, and usually ineffective, Republican rejoinder to interference with American shipping. By the margin of the Vice-President's vote, the boycott failed in Congress, and the President decided to use negotiation instead of legislation to keep the peace.

The Jay Treaty

John Jay resigned as chief justice to undertake the thankless mission to England. Jay was to secure compensation for commercial losses and for the slaves British soldiers had taken, evacuation of forts in the Northwest, and expansion of American trading opportunities in the British Empire. But the American envoy had almost nothing to offer in return for these concessions, especially after Hamilton told the British minister that the United States would not join a coalition of European neutrals that was organizing to protect the commercial rights of nonbelligerents. James Monroe, the American minister in Paris, led British officials to suspect a continued Franco-American alliance, which complicated Jay's task. Jay could only suggest that a break in negotiation might lead to war, even though he knew his nation was unprepared for the military and economic consequences of hostility with England.

Under the circumstances, Jay did reasonably well. Lacking a compelling threat, he conciliated. Lord Grenville, the British foreign secretary, had no wish needlessly to alienate Americans, who might repudiate the large debts owed to British creditors and whose President effectively reduced French influence in the Western Hemisphere. So Grenville agreed to evacuate the posts in the Northwest, where the fur trade was declining in any case. A boundary dispute, claims resulting from commercial interference, and the unpaid debts were all referred to arbitration, with the United States agreeing to pay any reward made to British creditors. In return, Britain would permit American ships access to ports in the British Isles and, on humiliating terms, in the West Indies. The West Indian provisions were subsequently eliminated. But the United States did accept Britain's definition of neutral rights, a concession that closed French colonial ports to American vessels and added food and naval stores to the contraband list that Americans could not export to France. The treaty omitted any mention of Britain's impressment of American sailors and of its activity among the American Indians; nor, perhaps because Jay was an abolitionist, was there a reference to the slaves lost during the Revolution.

His cabinet colleagues thought Grenville too generous but defended the treaty in Parliament. Generosity was the mildest of the sins Americans attributed to Jay, however, and the Jay Treaty became a rallying point for opponents of Federalism. Frontier settlers and southern planters protested that Jay had ignored their interests in Indians and slaves to secure concessions for eastern merchants. Describing the treaty as "degradation," "submission," and "perfidy," the Republican press alleged that Britain had bought the envoy and the nation's honor as well. The accusation often went on to suggest that the Jay Treaty effectively gave back the national independence won in the Revolution.

Washington hesitated before supporting the treaty, less because of partisan hyperbole than because of continued incidents on the seas. Finally, convinced that neutrality was essential to national survival and lacking a more agreeable alternative, the President secured the Senate's consent by the closest possible two-thirds vote, 20 to 10. Republicans in the House attempted to block the appropriation that would complete congressional action on the treaty, but too many representatives from western districts wanted the concessions, however meager, that Jay had obtained. Albert Gallatin of Pennsylvania, for instance, who was emerging as a major leader of the Republican forces, advocated acceptance of the treaty in order to permit continued national expansion.

While Jay was negotiating the evacuation of British troops from the Northwest, federal forces began to drive Indians from the Ohio Valley. In 1794, General Anthony Wayne won an important victory at Fallen Timbers, and in 1795, the defeated tribes formally ceded most of Ohio to

Battle of Fallen Timbers

the United States in the Treaty of Greenville. In spite of local success against Indians, American military weakness became embarrassingly evident as the deadline for British evacuation approached. Because of the lack of ready American replacements, the United States asked the redcoats to remain at their posts temporarily to protect frontier settlers. So much for earlier spread-eagle oratory about war with England.

The Jay Treaty brought an unanticipated diplomatic bonus. Suspecting that the treaty presaged a joint Anglo-American effort to seize Spanish possessions in the Western Hemisphere, the Spanish government decided to settle several long-standing disputes with the United States. Thomas Pinckney pressed for restraints on the Indians in Spanish territory, for uninhibited American use of the Mississippi, for the right to deposit goods duty-free in Spanish New Orleans, and for the thirty-first parallel as the northern border of West Florida. Spain gave in. The delighted Senate gave the Pinckney Treaty a thumping endorsement in 1795.

French reaction to the Jay Treaty was not so useful. Within a year, privateers had captured more than three hundred American vessels. Charles Cotesworth Pinckney, the American minister to France, could not even register a formal protest because officials in Paris declined to receive him. Continued seizures of ships created one tense incident after another while channels for diplomatic discourse were closed. That situation led directly to the nation's first undeclared war, which would take place during the presidency of Washington's successor.

For in 1796 Washington insisted on retiring to Mt. Vernon. He delayed his public announcement long enough to keep Republicans off balance. In the fall, he dusted off a farewell address Madison had drafted four years before. Hamilton and the President polished the piece and released to the public the President's decision not to accept his office again. The Farewell Address became almost an unofficial supplement to the Constitution, although it was preeminently a document of its own time. Washington had, he said, observed emerging geographical and partisan rivalries. He warned "in the most solemn manner" against both. He had watched Americans become defenders of foreign causes while he himself deplored "permanent . . . antipathies against particular nations and passionate attachments for others." Even commercial relations abroad should not lead to dependence on other nations or to a political connection with them. "So far as we have already formed engagements let them be fulfilled with perfect good faith," the President remarked in an obvious reference to the alliance of 1778. But at that point, "let us stop."

The Farewell Address was a political speech, designed to lay Washington's sanctifying hand on neutrality, commercial expansion, and the rest of the Federalist program. Though he thought himself nonpartisan, Washington's words provoked Republican editors, whose criticism had grown increasingly scurrilous as he became more closely identified with the Federalists. John Adams, the heir apparent, also received his share of abuse, which Federalists returned in unrelieved criticism of Jefferson, the candidate of those who opposed Hamilton's fiscal policy, Jay's foreign policy, and Adams's politics.

Hamilton trusted Adams little more than did Republicans. Because the Vice-President was too strong to attack directly, Hamilton schemed to secure additional electoral votes for Thomas Pinckney, popularly supposed to be Adams's running mate, with the hope that Pinckney might finish first in the electoral college. To subvert Hamilton's plans, some of Adams's electors did not vote for Pinckney. When the results were tallied, Adams barely finished ahead of Jefferson, who became Vice-President, the office the Constitution prescribed for whoever finished second.

The Adams Administration

In spite of political and personal differences, John Adams and Thomas Jefferson had collaborated effectively in the cause of American independence. As the new administration opened, they sought to revive that collaboration, and the friendship strained by partisanship during Washington's second term. They agreed that peace was the first priority. Adams suggested that Jefferson might head a delegation to reopen diplomatic contact with France. When Jefferson declined, they settled on Madison. But Washington's cabinet, all of whom Adams had retained, opposed Madison's nomination on the advice of Hamilton, whom they regarded as the actual head of the government. In the end, Jefferson reported that Madison would not go to France, and Adams admitted that he could not appoint him without disrupting the executive branch.

Instead, in 1797, the President sent John Marshall, a Virginia Federalist, and Elbridge Gerry, an erratic Massachusetts politician inclined to be a Republican, to join Charles Cotesworth Pinckney, America's unrecognized minister in France. The mission's instructions ought to have signaled the difficulty of its task. The emissaries were to seek compensation for American vessels already condemned as privateers' prizes and to find an honorable way out of the alliance of 1778, which obligated the United States to defend the French West Indies. Pinckney, Marshall, and Gerry had little to provide in return for French concessions; they could only agree to commercial arrangements that did not conflict with American obligations under the Jay Treaty.

That Jay Treaty, of course, was central to the problem. Since the United States could only assist France through maritime trade that was forbidden by the Jay Treaty, the French government really had nothing to say to the American delegation. But as long as the three Americans wanted to talk, Talleyrand, the shrewd and none too scrupulous foreign minister, decided to seek a loan for his country's beleaguered treasury and a bribe for his own. The proposition itself did not shock the

John Adams

Americans. But the requirement that the funds be delivered before substantive discussion commenced seemed a dubious business arrangement. Talleyrand stalled because his informants assured him Republicans would soon force a conciliatory American policy. In the early months of 1798 Marshall and Pinckney tired of the charade and left France, while Talleyrand flattered Gerry with the idea that he alone could bring peace to the two countries.

Meanwhile, friction escalated to undeclared war. While Talleyrand was making vaguely conciliatory promises to the American mission, the rest of the French government had issued a stern new decree that led to further seizures of ships and restrictions on American commerce. The dispatches of Pinckney and Marshall, when released to the American public with "X," "Y," and "Z" substituted for the names of Talleyrand's three intermediaries who had demanded bribes, whipped up American opinion. Congress talked a good deal about war, but rather less about taxes and appropriations for defense; eventually completion of three frigates was authorized and a loan permitted to equip some militiamen. John Adams began to collect his thoughts for a message requesting a declaration of war. And near the coast French privateers continued to ply their profitable trade, quickly netting a half million dollars from operations in Delaware Bay alone.

Then, almost as if he were suspicious of mounting approval of his policies, Adams put his notes away. There would be no war message. And while he was in office, no declared war either, although the war lasted through 1798, undignified by a declaration.

When Adams's expected war message failed to arrive, Hamiltonian Federalists, now called High Federalists, discussed congressional initiative. Although they lacked the votes for war, the High Federalists did secure legislation to create and support a national army, to silence the mounting criticism of national policies, and to lengthen the probationary period and limit the activity of aliens who wished to become citizens.

None of this legislation was exactly to the President's taste. The tax on houses and slaves was politically unpopular and led to a small uprising among the conservative Pennsylvania Dutch farmers, who had previously supported the Federalists. Use of the army in 1799 to suppress this Fries Rebellion gave substance to Republican charges that Federalists had created the force to repress dissent. Adams himself thought an army less useful than a navy, but High Federalists believed the British navy made an American fleet unnecessary. Adams's misgivings increased when Washington, to whom command of the army was offered, insisted that Hamilton be given effective control of the force. But the force could never have been too effective anyhow: officers joined readily and outnumbered enlisted men roughly seven to one, an unwieldy proportion for even the most skilled general.

The Alien and Sedition Acts, Republicans charged, furnished the legal basis for repression. Passed amid feverish preparations for war in the summer of 1798, these acts sought to promote conformity to High Federalist principles. Troublesome aliens might be imprisoned or deported on the President's authority; others must demonstrate their acceptability over fourteen years residency instead of the five that had previously been required for citizenship. The Sedition Act outlawed promotion of insurrection, an offense with which both the President and the Vice-President might well have been charged two decades earlier. The statute went on to prohibit writing or speech that tended to "defame" or to "bring . . . into contempt" the President, Congress, laws, and policies of the United States. Although Adams had not asked for this legislation, he accepted it, and some Federalist officials enforced it with zeal.

Republicans, to whom the Alien and Sedition Acts were often applied, thought them unconstitutional as well as partisan. The Sedition Act, in particular, seemed designed to stifle political opposition. In making their case, Republicans relied on the First Amendment's guarantee of free speech and free press. They also argued that since the states had established the central government, the states themselves, and not the federal judiciary, should decide when that government had exceeded its legitimate authority. Jefferson secretly prepared for the Kentucky legislature a set of resolutions, based upon this compact theory, that proclaimed the right of each state to determine the constitutionality of federal action. The legislature of Virginia agreed in Madison's more moderate words. But other states did not endorse either the Virginia or the Kentucky Resolutions, and seven northern states went on record in opposition.

While High Federalists prepared for war, the President decided on another effort for peace. From his son John Quincy Adams, who represented the United States in Berlin, and from Nicholas Vans Murray, the minister to the Netherlands, the President heard that France seemed conciliatory. Elbridge Gerry reported that Talleyrand had hinted at more equitable treatment for American commerce. Early in 1799, without the consent of his cabinet, Adams nominated Murray and two other commissioners to reopen negotiations with France. Convinced that their cresting popularity depended on war with France, High Federalists, including Secretary of State Timothy Pickering, tried to obstruct the President. But Adams had made up his mind. He replaced Pickering with John Marshall, fired the other Hamiltonians in the cabinet, calmed the country, split his party, and sought peace with France. Negotiations took more than a year, but domestic hysteria dipped while they progressed toward a settlement. In effect, the United States gave up the claims of American shippers in return for an end to the alliance of 1778. This agreement, called the Convention of 1800, postponed both matters indefinitely and then specified a mutual stand for neutral rights that never seriously bound either signatory thereafter. The unofficial war was officially over.

When it ended, John Adams was on his way out of office. During the campaign of 1800, Hamilton advertised the rift among Federalists with a pamphlet criticizing Adams and advocating the election of Charles Cotesworth Pinckney, whom Federalists in Congress had designated for Vice-President. But Hamilton miscalculated even in his own New York, where Aaron Burr put together a slate of Jeffersonian electors that carried by a few hundred votes. Republicans rewarded Burr by endorsing him as Jefferson's running mate. Republican campaigners noted that government expenditure had doubled during Adams's administration and that the national debt had increased. They evoked memories of British repression with references to the Sedition Act, oppressive taxation, and a threatening and expensive standing army. Federalists answered the allegations of

Adams's tyranny with equally irresponsible charges about Jefferson's atheism. Although Adams gloomily and correctly foresaw his own defeat, his party turned out more voters than had supported him four years before. No Republican elector omitted Burr from his ballot, so Burr and Jefferson deadlocked in the electoral college.

The House, according to the Constitution, was to break the tie. Through more than thirty inconclusive ballots the rancor of the campaign persisted. Burr made no effort to discourage Federalist schemes to elect him President, although Hamilton, who knew both men well, believed Jefferson the lesser evil. Hamilton's influence among responsible Federalists had dwindled, however, and other men made the arrangement that put Jefferson in the White House and ended the Federalists' reign. Jefferson thought his election eliminated a potential despotism and reaffirmed the republican ideals he had stated in 1776. He exaggerated the danger of Federalist tyranny, but he accurately gauged the attachment of Americans to republican ideals.

The Federalists in Retrospect

In pockets of opposition that fed on their own increasing isolation, the Federalist party lingered. Though it ended in 1800 as an effective national political movement, the theories and policies of Federalism proved more hardy. A strong central government, responding to the direction of the executive branch, backed by the talent and property of influential citizens, and maintaining peace at home and overseas—this was no mean vision, nor was it the exclusive heritage of those crabbed and bitter men who claimed to keep the Federalist faith.

Another legacy of the brief Federalist era was the development of political parties and a responsible opposition. Federalists and Republicans alike accepted constitutional restraints. Both gradually discovered techniques for subordinating internal rivalries to the common pursuit of power, techniques that Republicans applied more successfully than Federalists. Both relied on journals in which partisanship had a priority higher than accuracy. Both developed constitutional interpretations to justify political programs. Both employed political organizers of elastic conscience, whom subsequent generations would call bosses. When Federalists left office, Republicans gracefully adopted portions of the Federalist creed. The tone of Republican government differed, to be sure, but much of the substance of federalism endured.

Washington, Adams, Hamilton, Jefferson, and Madison served as national rallying points for diverse local factions. But no candidate, no political issue, could for long focus the attention of most Americans on the central government. The national political climate was less important to a nation of farmers than the weather nearer home, national banks of less concern than local prices of fur, flax, and flour. National parties depended in large measure, then, on the prominence of their local adherents, for hazardous travel and unreliable communication kept national leaders and most voters apart. Local gentry benefited from "deference" voting by citizens who acknowledged their own lack of information by voting for notables who were supposed to be informed. Both parties sought the help of local opinion-makers to secure the broad support they might bring. Neither party sprang up in response to popular demand. Both, rather, were built by their leadership to demand the political program that leaders were ready to supply. The nation was fortunate that by 1800 neither choice was wrong.

Suggested Reading

Marcus Cunliffe's *The Nation Takes Shape** (1959) and John C. Miller's *The Federalist Era** (1960) are reliable, brief surveys of the Federalist period. Even briefer is Morton Borden's *Parties and Politics in the Early Republic** (1967). The policies of the Federalist Presidents are examined in *The Presidency of George Washington* (1974) by Forrest McDonald and *The Presidency of John Adams** (1957) by Stephen G. Kurtz. A more recent monograph, by Ralph A. Brown (1975) has the same title as Kurtz's book but does not replace it. Two studies by Alexander De Conde focus on the Federalists' diplomacy: *Entangling Alliance* (1958) and *The Quasi-War** (1966). James M. Smith's *Freedom's Fetters** (1956) covers the Alien and Sedition Acts and Daniel Sisson's *The American Revolution of 1800* (1974) reexamines the election that ended Federalist control of the nation.

The development of political parties is studied by Richard Hofstadter in *The Idea of a Party System** (1969), by Joseph Charles in *The Origins of the American Party System** (1956), and by William N. Chambers in *Political Parties in a New Nation** (1963). Noble Cunningham's *The Jeffersonian Republicans** (1957) describes the organization of the Republican opposition. Norman K. Risjord has edited a sample of the recent scholarship on party formation in *The Early American Party System** (1969). Although the author's major interest lies after 1800, *To the Hartford Convention* (1970) by James M. Banner, Jr., illuminates the period covered by this chapter as well.

Much of the history of the Federalist era is contained in biographies of Washington, Hamilton, Marshall, Adams, Jefferson, Madison, and a host of lesser figures, and in the collections of their correspondence and other writings. New editions of the works of all these men are in progress and provide the raw material—and much editorial guidance—for a reassessment of the period and its statesmen.

* Available in paperback edition

Chapter 6
The Virginia Dynasty

Chronology

1803 *Marbury* v. *Madison* establishes judicial review • Louisiana Purchase •

1804 Presidential election: Thomas Jefferson (Democratic-Republican) defeats Charles C. Pinckney (Federalist) •

1806 Burr conspiracy (trial, 1807) •

1807 Embargo Act •

1808 Presidential election: James Madison (Democratic-Republican) defeats Charles C. Pinckney (Federalist) and George Clinton (Democratic-Republican) •

1810 Congressional election enables War Hawks to organize House •

1812 Presidential election: James Madison (Democratic-Republican) defeats DeWitt Clinton (Federalist) •

1812 – 15 War against England (Battle of New Orleans, 1815) •

1814 Hartford Convention expresses New England's opposition to War of 1812 •

1816 Recharter of Bank of the United States • Presidential election: James Monroe (Democratic-Republican) defeats Rufus King (Federalist) •

1819 Adams-Onís (Transcontinental) Treaty negotiated (ratified 1821) • *McCulloch* v. *Maryland* upholds constitutionality of Bank of the United States •

1820 Presidential election: James Monroe (Democratic-Republican) defeats John Quincy Adams (Independent Republican) •

1820 – 21 Missouri Compromise •

1823 Monroe Doctrine announced •

Thomas Jefferson's election in 1800 broke the Federalist party's grip on the presidency and initiated a quarter century of Republican government. Three Virginia patricians—Jefferson, James Madison, and James Monroe—successively occupied the White House during those years and gave the nation dignified and occasionally distinguished direction. By the time these men had finished conducting affairs of state, more Americans were more loyal to the national government than ever before. The Federalists had won the rich, the able, and the well born to the support of the central government; the Republicans won almost everyone else. "We are all Republicans, we are all Federalists," Jefferson remarked in 1801. Before the last member of the Virginia Dynasty retired to his plantation, Jefferson's hyperbole had almost come true.

To be sure, the Republican party changed somewhat over the years from 1800 to 1825. At the outset, in 1801, the Republican creed consisted of the principles Thomas Jefferson had articulated during twenty-five years of public life. Jefferson was preeminently the spokesman for independent farmers, whom he believed to be "the chosen people of God if ever He had a chosen people." As the foremost opponent of Hamiltonian federalism, Jefferson favored a central government based on the limited powers granted by a strict interpretation of the Constitution. A corollary of this strict construction was Jefferson's advocacy of rigid governmental economy. In foreign policy, Jefferson leaned toward France and mistrusted England.

Jefferson's critics alleged that his presidency belied every one of his early policies; by 1825 the Republican party certainly had bent some of its old principles and added a few new ones. Although farmers had first claim on federal bounty, Republican policies also fostered the growth of American industry. Once Republicans took over the central government, the Constitution seemed less restrictive than it had when they were out of office, and even governmental economy became less imperative. Before the United States found itself at war with England, Jefferson himself had threatened to ally with England against France. Republican nationalism differed somewhat from the federalist variety, but it was nationalism nonetheless.

The contradiction between Jefferson's declaration of human equality and the bondage on his own estate was another of the inconsistencies in Jefferson's public career. He personified the nation's simultaneous beliefs in liberty, equality, and slavery; although he felt the tension more keenly than most, he could do no more to resolve the national dilemma than could other white Americans. He feared equally the consequences of emancipation and continued slavery. Jefferson knew at first hand the injustices and the temptations of slavery, but he could not imagine that democratic institutions would endure if blacks became free. In the last analysis, Jefferson disliked slavery, not because of what it did to slaves, but because whites had to be masters. He resented blacks because their presence made whites into tyrants, and he could think of no way out save deportation.

Deportation was never practical, although in 1805 Monroe, then governor of Virginia, asked Jefferson to set aside federal lands in Louisiana for free blacks. The following year, Virginia restricted manumission, thereby reducing the potential free black population, and required newly freed slaves to leave the state within a year. Since no area was reserved in Louisiana, and since Ohio, Delaware, Maryland, and Kentucky forbade their immigration, free blacks had few opportunities to settle elsewhere.

Yet Jefferson and his contemporaries ensured that slavery would become the peculiar institution of the South alone, even if they did not live to see abolition. Slavery gradually disappeared in New England and New York. Congress had prohibited slavery's expansion into the Northwest Territory in 1787 and outlawed the international slave trade in 1808; although the law was not fully enforced, smugglers landed fewer slaves than legitimate importers would have. Efforts to establish slavery in Indiana and Illinois failed. Whatever their motive, the nation's leaders reversed slavery's spread, isolated the South, and probably made inevitable the war that at last produced emancipation.

A New Century Begins

The remarkable political creativity of Thomas Jefferson's generation may obscure the fact that Americans lived during his presidency much as they had under King George. It was Rip Van Winkle who changed during his twenty-year nap; in Washington Irving's tale, Rip awoke to the same rural world of unfenced pigs and unaged spirits he had left.

In countless books and letters, European visitors remarked that independence had not brought civilization to the continent. Americans, these visitors reported, seemed to live on salt pork and corn; even in the best society, the conversation was as heavy as the diet. The new country had no art, no science, no church in the European sense, and no theater, which prudish Americans believed inevitably immoral. Their literature ran to sermons and to equally didactic patriotic poems. The five million Americans—of whom nearly one million were slaves—lived in isolated settlements along one edge of the continent. These settlements—and often the settlers themselves—had little contact with one another. Indeed, as Henry Adams noted, Americans had not progressed much beyond the beavers and the buffalo in the construction of roads and bridges. Jefferson had to cross eight rivers on his journey from Monticello to Washington; five of those rivers had neither bridges nor boats.

The capital city showed the pretense of the nation. The design might be grand, but in 1800 the visible result was grotesque. The President's residence stood in a field, separated by a large swamp from the domeless Capitol. A few brick houses, two buildings for federal officials, several boarding houses, the inevitable slave cabins, and some muddy streets— that was Washington when Jefferson took office. No amenities, no commerce, and when Congress recessed, no people.

And, most Americans thought, no matter. What did matter happened not in Washington but on the farms and on the docks, in the fields and in the forests. European visitors noted the Indian menace, the loneliness, and the privation of the frontier, but Americans saw opportunity. While Europeans disparaged the lack of high culture, democratic Americans boasted that they would develop a culture superior to that of decadent aristocrats. If Europeans despised the United States, Americans observed, they nevertheless continued to arrive in large numbers. European tourists described accurately enough what they saw, but optimistic natives had a vision of the future.

Jefferson: Politics and Principles

The campaign and protracted election of 1800 had been vicious, and Jefferson meant to heal old wounds in his inaugural address. He emphasized agreement as he listed the "essential principles of our

The unfinished Capitol

Government" in a series of carefully qualified statements designed to reassure Federalists as much as to remind Republicans of what they stood for: impartial "friendship with all nations, entangling alliances with none"; "support of the State governments in all their rights," coupled with "preservation of the General Government in its whole constitutional vigor"; "encouragement of agriculture, and of commerce as its handmaid." But Jefferson had begun his list with an affirmation of strict construction: "a wise and frugal government, which shall restrain men from injuring one another [and] . . . leave them otherwise free to regulate their own pursuits." That principle logically required an unconventional yardstick to measure Jefferson's administration. In his view, a law passed was a smaller triumph than a law repealed, an act to diminish the powers of the central government to be preferred to one that enhanced them.

Although Jefferson courted his opponents in his inaugural address, his hardheaded use of political patronage soon stirred Federalist resentment. By 1803 about half the principal appointive posts in the federal service had gone to Republicans. Federalist legislation, which the President believed the electorate had rejected in 1800, went the way of Federalist

Thomas Jefferson

officeholders. The Sedition Act expired in 1801 and Jefferson pardoned those who had been jailed under its provisions. Congress reduced from fourteen to five years the time an alien had to wait before becoming naturalized. Many Federalists, appointed to the judiciary in the last moments of the Adams administration, lost their positions when the Judiciary Act of 1801 was repealed. On the advice of Albert Gallatin, a worthy successor to Hamilton as secretary of the treasury, Congress removed all internal taxes, including that on whisky. Convinced that the armed forces could be drastically reduced, the administration budgeted only $1.6 million to support them; in 1799 the military budget had been $6 million.

Jefferson changed the style of government as well as its policies. Federalists, he charged, had aped the ways of monarchs; he would bring a seemly simplicity to official Washington. Working dinners for political advisers replaced presidential banquets. The President's informality scandalized foreign representatives accustomed to starchy diplomatic ritual. Jefferson even had a clerk read his annual message to Congress because he thought a personal appearance too reminiscent of the British address from the throne.

Republicans soon discovered that they could not undo all the policies of their predecessors. The charter of the Bank of the United States, for instance, had a decade to run when Jefferson took office. Nor could Gallatin and Jefferson repeal the debt Hamilton had contracted. Instead, they undertook to pay it from the revenue derived from Hamilton's tariff.

So rigorous was Republican economy that Gallatin spent more than three-fourths of the government's income to service the debt. Before the Napoleonic wars disrupted the world economy, Gallatin even managed to show a small annual surplus.

The Federalists mounted an ineffective partisan opposition to Jefferson's policies. In 1804 a few disgruntled New England Federalists went beyond partisanship and discussed with Aaron Burr a scheme to ally New York and New England in an independent northern confederation. Alexander Hamilton, true to his habitual nationalism, exposed the plot, and Burr, who was still Vice-President, killed Hamilton in a duel not long afterward. Burr then diverted his conspiratorial ambition toward the Southwest.

The Burr conspiracy—or perhaps more accurately Burr's fantasy—has never been completely untangled. Both British and Spanish diplomats in Washington heard that Burr would welcome support for some enterprise he was contemplating in Mexico and the lower Mississippi Valley. Perhaps Mexico was to have served as the center of Burr's empire; perhaps he expected to annex part of the western United States if it seceded or to conquer it if it did not. James Wilkinson, the American commander in Louisiana, whose support the plotters thought they had bought, reported the enterprise to Jefferson. The President ordered the arrest of Burr and his pathetic army of sixty men, who had begun to float down the Ohio toward their rendezvous with dishonor. Jefferson meant to have Burr's conviction for treason, but Chief Justice John Marshall insisted on the full constitutional definition of treason. The prosecution failed to produce two witnesses to the same overt act of levying war against the United States, and the jury acquitted Burr.

The Republican party prospered in spite of Burr's disgrace and the defection of other charter leaders, such as John Randolph and John Taylor of Caroline, who maintained that Jefferson had forsaken Republican principles. Replacing Burr with George Clinton, another New Yorker, as his vice-presidential running mate, Jefferson crushed the Federalists in the election of 1804. The Republican ticket lost just 14 electoral votes; Republicans took 27 of the 34 seats in the Senate and elected 119 of the 141 members of the House.

In his second term Jefferson hesitantly suggested that federal funds might be spent to improve rivers and harbors, to construct roads and canals, and to advance manufacturing and education. Although the President tactfully admitted that such appropriations might require a constitutional amendment, Congress authorized construction of the first leg of the National Road from Cumberland, Maryland, to Wheeling, Virginia. But some southern Republicans attacked Jefferson's proposal as disguised federalism, and Congress, citing the need for economy, did not appropriate money for the National Road until 1811, when Jefferson had left office. He did, however, divert some of the income from land sales to improve roads leading west.

For settlers were pouring across the Appalachians and fanning out in the eastern Mississippi Valley, even as explorers pushed on into the trans-Mississippi unknown. At the time the expedition commanded by Meriwether Lewis and William Clark began exploring the Missouri and Columbia valleys, the Ohio Valley had ceased to be frontier. Ohio became a state in 1803 and Louisiana in 1812. After 1815 the pace picked up: Indiana was admitted in 1816, Mississippi in 1817, Illinois in 1818, and Alabama in 1819.

The western migration is the stuff of legend, symbolized by coonskin caps, rough-and-tumble democracy, Indian skirmishes, high hopes, and high spirits. In reality, spirits often drooped in three-sided cabins in tiny clearings, where spindly corn grew amid the roots of trees, where pigs and a scrawny cow foraged, watched by sickly children and sallow women. Indians lurked in the forests, as did fevers and insects. The crushing isolation was broken only by occasional evangelical revivals and political rallies.

The continuing growth of the West, in spite of obstacles to settlement, gave that region the balance of political power between North and South. This political importance showed in legislation that eased the terms for purchase of federal lands. The law of 1796 had prescribed a minimum sale of 640 acres at $2.00 per acre and permitted a year's credit on half the purchase price. In 1800 Congress reduced the minimum acreage by half and permitted credit for four years. In 1804 Congress again halved the acreage requirement; now a settler could start with 160 acres and a down payment of as little as $80. Although a new law in 1820 stopped installment sale, Congress did permit purchase of units as small as 80 acres at $1.25 per acre. The open space that had inspired Jefferson's vision of "room enough for our descendants to the thousandth and thousandth generation" was fast disappearing.

Jefferson's Foreign Policy

In 1803 the nation's open space nearly doubled with the purchase of the Louisiana Territory.* Americans had hoped for years to annex this Spanish possession, but since Spain's control was tenuous and the Pinckney Treaty (1795) had granted the concessions westerners most wanted, American leaders were content to let settlement and trade gradually and peacefully bind the area to the United States. The struggle for European supremacy that developed from the French Revolution changed the timetable, and Jefferson took full advantage of new circumstances. His failure to influence the struggle in Europe was one of Jefferson's great disappointments, but the purchase of Louisiana, in large measure a result of Napoleon's preoccupation with the European war, was one of Jefferson's great triumphs.

* See map on page 142.

New Orleans, 1803

Ambitious to erect an empire in the New World to match the one he planned for the Old, Napoleon decided to acquire Louisiana to serve as a granary for the French sugar colony in Santo Domingo. In 1800 Spain ceded Louisiana to France in the secret Treaty of San Ildefonso, but continued for a time to administer the area. In October 1802 Spanish authorities notified the United States that the right to deposit goods duty-free in New Orleans had been suspended. Westerners, who were suspicious of all government and the far-off central government most of all, now made reopening the river a test case: success would secure their loyalty to the national government; failure would bring alienation and perhaps separation.

Jefferson knew the stakes. His aversion to Britain, his dedication to governmental economy, his fear of military establishments, and his strict construction of the Constitution, all were subordinated to his need to secure New Orleans. The possessor of New Orleans, he wrote, was "our natural and habitual enemy." Once France had taken possession of the city, he went on, the United States would be driven to "marry . . . the

British fleet and nation." Jefferson instructed Robert R. Livingston, the American minister in France, to negotiate for the purchase of West Florida and New Orleans. When westerners complained that Livingston's mission had had no result, Jefferson sent James Monroe, whom the West respected, to expedite negotiations in Paris. While Monroe was on his way, Napoleon decided to give up his projected New World empire and to renew the war in Europe instead. Frozen harbors in Europe that made supplying New World regiments difficult, a slave rebellion in Santo Domingo, brilliantly directed by Toussaint L'Ouverture, and the constant loss of French troops to yellow fever, convinced Napoleon that the military cost of a western empire outweighed its potential value. Two days before Monroe arrived, in April 1803, Napoleon asked if the United States would like to buy all of Louisiana.

Authorized to buy a city for $2 million, Livingston and Monroe bought an empire for $15 million. They promised the French that the United States would protect the religious freedom of the inhabitants of Louisiana and would admit them to citizenship. When asked about boundaries, the French foreign minister observed cryptically that he supposed the United States would "make the most" of its "noble bargain."

Jefferson was both pleased and dismayed. Since the Constitution did not explicitly permit the purchase of territory, Jefferson would have preferred to escape the charge of broad construction with a face-saving amendment. But, fearful that any delay would prompt Napoleon to change his mind, Jefferson sent the treaty to the Senate, remarking that "the good sense of our country will correct the evil of [broad] construction when it shall produce ill effects." The Senate sealed the bargain by a vote of 24 to 7.

Tripolitan pirates, for the moment, proved more annoying than Napoleon. For years before Jefferson took office, the United States had paid various North African chieftains for the privilege of trading in the Mediterranean. In 1801, one of these Barbary potentates chopped down the flagpole in front of the American consulate in Tripoli, and Jefferson decided that a brisk naval war would be cheaper in the long run than perpetual tribute. Without actually declaring war, he sent the navy to punish the pirates. Several years of intermittent naval skirmishes ended with a treaty in 1805, although the United States paid some tribute until 1816.

Jefferson had sufficient force to do something about Barbary pirates; he could do very little about Britain or France, which renewed the European war in 1803. The American merchant marine occasioned most of the President's trouble. As the war on the continent intensified, both Britain and France ignored the rights of neutrals. Determined to ruin the British economy, Napoleon closed the entire continent to British shipping. In the Berlin Decree (1806) and the Milan Decree (1807) he announced that France would seize British ships or ships of neutrals that complied with British trade regulations. Britain, in turn, issued a series of Orders in

Council that established a blockade of all ports under French control. Thus, any neutral ship risked confiscation, for any commerce would breach the regulations of one belligerent or the other. Still, the ship that got through returned immense profits, and many American shippers willingly incurred the risk.

While Americans protested against the seizure of goods and ships, they protested even more hotly against the British practice of impressing sailors. Many British sailors, who found sea duty disagreeable, the discipline harsh, the food unpalatable, and the pay servile, jumped ship in American ports and signed on American merchant vessels. British captains, particularly those who found themselves short-handed, resorted to impressment to keep their crews at full strength. In 1807, British naval guns killed three Americans in an attack on the *Chesapeake*, an American frigate. A British patrol then searched the *Chesapeake*, and took off four men. Firing on a naval vessel was an act of war. Had Jefferson wanted a declaration of war, Congress would probably have responded, for public feeling ran high. But Jefferson delayed, Britain eventually apologized, and the crisis evaporated.

Jefferson delayed partly because he hoped Britain might be persuaded to link a general renunciation of impressment with an apology for the *Chesapeake* incident. Since the British cabinet seemed determined to risk war rather than disavow impressment, Jefferson did not insist. Instead, he turned to Congress, which proved more responsive than British officialdom. In December 1807, at the President's urging, Congress passed the Embargo Act, which in effect made all foreign trade illegal. Jefferson believed that the loss of the American market would bring industrial distress to England, that the loss of American goods would create hardship throughout Europe, and that the absence of American shipping would disrupt all international trade and would leave several European colonies stranded. Jefferson confidently expected European distress to force changes in European policy.

Although distress at home initially exceeded distress abroad, the Embargo, in the long run, may have forced a healthy adjustment in the American economy. While some merchants lost commercial fortunes because goods piled up on the piers and ships rotted at anchor, other merchants invested in manufacturing. The Embargo and the war effectively kept European manufactured goods out of the American market, which domestic industry began to supply. Many seaport artisans remained unemployed, but some found jobs building the magnificent Federal houses that line older streets in even the smaller Atlantic ports. The Embargo unquestionably brought economic hardship, but it did not invariably bring economic ruin.

Farmers also felt the Embargo's economic jolt. As prices dropped with the loss of the export market, the farmers' frustration mounted. Tobacco, cotton, and hemp, the products of the South and the Mississippi Valley, accumulated in warehouses. Between 1805 and 1809 commodity prices in

Victims of Jefferson's Embargo had no difficulty reversing the spelling of "Ograbme"

New Orleans declined about 20 percent, and then went down still further in 1810 and 1811. The mounting hostility of farmers of the South and West focused on Great Britain, whose Orders in Council they saw as the immediate cause of their economic difficulty. In increasingly strident voices, representatives of cotton and tobacco growers demanded that the United States abandon economic coercion and declare war on Great Britain.

The Embargo had in fact failed to coerce either European belligerent. Instead Jefferson's law played into the hands of the British cabinet, which had been under pressure from mercantile interests to restrain the American merchant marine. The Embargo deprived Napoleon of his American supplies and at the same time crippled American shipping; the British found both results entirely satisfactory. The American boycott did cause British manufacturers momentary anxiety over the loss of a lucrative market, but the developing market in Latin America more than took up the slack. And Napoleon, for his part, went on confiscating whatever stray American ships reached the continent and brazenly told protesting Americans that he was only enforcing their own laws.

The Madison Administration

Domestic unhappiness with Jefferson's policy did not prevent the election of James Madison, Jefferson's chosen heir. In the election of 1808 Federalists gained support in New England and enlarged their congressional minority; but Charles Cotesworth Pinckney, their presidential candidate, ran a poor second, with only 47 electoral votes to Madison's 122. Just before Madison's inauguration, in March 1809, Jefferson reluctantly agreed to the repeal of the Embargo. Madison's diplomatic hand was no stronger than Jefferson's had been, however, and the new President also resorted to economic coercion. The Nonintercourse Act of 1809 prohibited trade with Britain and France until those nations ceased interfering with American rights, although trade with other nations was once more permitted.

After a short and unsuccessful trial, the Madison administration substituted Macon's Bill Number 2 for nonintercourse. Passed in May 1810, this measure permitted trade with both Britain and France. But the ghost of economic coercion lingered, for the law required the restoration of nonintercourse with one belligerent in the event the other agreed to respect American neutral rights. Sensing an opportunity, Napoleon promptly revoked his earlier decrees, although he added new conditions that practically reimposed them. Madison ignored the qualifications, welcomed Napoleon's deceptive offer, and once more imposed nonintercourse with Britain. Napoleon never stopped confiscating American ships, but nonintercourse did have some economic effect in Britain, which, in 1810, was in the grip of an industrial depression. Pressure in Britain rose until the cabinet suspended the Orders in Council on June 16, 1812. Unaware of this gesture, which might not have changed the course of events in any case, the United States declared war on Great Britain on June 18.

The Congress that had been elected in 1810 reflected mounting frustration, especially in the South and West, with the nation's diplomatic dilemma. Young Republicans from southern and western congressional delegations believed that negotiation and economic pressure had failed; only force would convince Europeans of the vitality, honor, and sturdy independence of the American republic. Nourished on stories of their forebears' sacrifice in the Revolution, raised in an environment that respected impetuous courage, trained to value honor above purse, these so-called War Hawks expressed the exhausted patience of their constituents. The War Hawks took control of the House, electing as Speaker Henry Clay, a Kentuckian who had forthrightly advocated war during an earlier term in the Senate. Clay appointed other War Hawks—John C. Calhoun and Langdon Cheves of South Carolina, Felix Grundy of Tennessee, Richard M. Johnson of Kentucky—to key posts in the House. The growing demand for war had found expression.

The President listed the causes of conflict in his war message: impressment, violation of the commercial rights of neutrals, and British encouragement of Indian efforts to forestall American settlement. The ensuing congressional debate revealed other reasons for war. Mixed with a genuine concern over maritime rights and the need of a new generation to dedicate itself to the cause of American honor and independence was an avowed interest in territorial expansion—at the expense of the Indians in the Northwest, the decrepit Spanish regime in Florida, and the British in Canada. All these ambitions antedated 1812; all seemed possible through war with Great Britain. To be sure, France had also violated American rights, but where could the United States attack France? Canada, as spread-eagle orators had long noted, was a hostage that the United States could seize. Henry Clay thought the conquest of Canada a small matter that might amuse the Kentucky militia for a few weeks.

Removing the British from North America, the War Hawks boasted, would also eliminate the arms that made the Indians dangerous. Settlers pushing into the valleys of the Ohio and the Mississippi were encroaching on Indian territory. In 1809 William Henry Harrison, governor of the Indiana Territory, had secured Indian assent to the Treaty of Fort Wayne, which opened most of southern Indiana to settlers. The Indians with whom Harrison dealt probably had no right to make the treaty, and the incident convinced other Indians that only war would preserve tribal territory east of the Mississippi. In 1811 two Shawnees— Tecumseh and his brother, the Prophet—put together an Indian confederation pledged to resist the white man's settlement and his corrupting bargains. British officials in Canada, dreading an American invasion, were anxious to persuade their Indian allies to conserve their strength and act in concert with the British when war came. But the Indians could not wait, nor did William Henry Harrison. In 1811, fearing a full-scale Indian war, Harrison sent a force that destroyed the Prophet's village on Tippecanoe Creek in Indiana.

The Indian menace was not the principal reason Congress voted for a declaration of war, for the western frontier had too few votes to determine a major policy. Nor was the lure of Florida or Canada the primary cause, though annexation of these areas was an important tactical objective. Rather, the basic cause of the War of 1812 lay in the fact that European belligerents, caught up in their own protracted struggle, did not treat the proud, new republic in the manner its pride and recent origin demanded. Great Britain preferred to risk war rather than give up impressment and the harassment of American shipping. The United States decided that it could not remain self-respecting and independent if it permitted either impressment or harassment to continue. So the war came.

The War of 1812

It was a war neither side was ready to fight. Subduing Napoleon was task enough for Great Britain. Madison's administration, never vigorous, was further weakened by immediate resentment of the war, particularly in the Northeast. In the election of 1812, Federalists endorsed DeWitt Clinton, the nominee of antiwar Republicans who opposed James Madison.

Madison carried the South and West and won the electoral college by a vote of 128 to 89; if Clinton had been able to add Pennsylvania to his otherwise firm support in the Northeast, he would have been elected. In Congress, the Federalists doubled their strength.

Political opposition and the failure of the Northeast to cooperate made more critical the lack of governmental competence in directing the war effort. The War Department proclaimed a need for 130,000 troops, but it never managed to put more than 30,000 in the field. Congress provided neither conscription nor revenue, for both South and West resisted internal taxation. In 1814, the secretary of the treasury openly admitted that he had no notion where he would find $50 million of his projected annual expenditure of $74 million.

Nor was the military effort better managed than the political effort. Americans failed to conquer Canada, partly because they chose to attack near Detroit instead of moving quickly to secure control of the St. Lawrence, upon which the British depended for supplies. In addition, American expeditions against Canada often fizzled out when militiamen declined to travel too far from home. The few thrusts that actually crossed the frontier ended in retreat before more determined British forces. The American navy, which faced the world's most powerful fleet, gave a better account of itself. In single-ship engagements early in the war, the *Constitution* and the *United States* defeated British vessels. Americans managed to secure naval supremacy on the Great Lakes after Captain Oliver Hazard Perry's victory at Put-in-Bay. But by 1814 the sheer number of British vessels forced American ships to stay in port. The British blockade along the Atlantic coast grew ever tighter and only the *Constitution* and a few privateers were still operating on the high seas at the end of the war.

When defeat loomed for Napoleon in 1814, Britain began to devote more attention to the American war, and the costs of sloppy American leadership rose sharply. British strategists meant to divide the United States with invasions at New Orleans, at Niagara, and along Lake Champlain. These major attacks were coupled with coastal raids, including the spectacular bombardment of Baltimore and the burning of Washington, D.C. A fierce battle at Lundy's Lane, near Niagara Falls, created a stalemate in the Northwest and ended that British thrust. The invasion along Lake Champlain stopped when the United States won naval control of the lake at the battle of Plattsburgh. And the British attempt to secure the Mississippi failed below New Orleans when southwestern militiamen commanded by Andrew Jackson gave the seasoned British regulars lessons in the uses of fortification, marksmanship, and strategic position. British casualties totaled more than two thousand; Jackson lost eight frontiersmen. This great American victory had no effect on the peace treaty, signed about two weeks before, but unknown in New Orleans.

New England had never supported the war with the patriotic fervor of

"The rockets' red glare"

the South and West. The region's lack of enthusiasm grew in some
quarters into outright hostility as the war dragged on. New England's
militia was notoriously unreliable, and enlistments in the regular forces
lagged. New England's merchants continued their international trade,
including a bustling commerce with England and Canada. New England's
banks, stronger than those in other regions, declined to provide
proportional support for the national treasury. And when the British
extended their blockade to New England, the region's dissident leaders
redoubled their angry opposition—not toward Great Britain, but toward
Washington. Timothy Pickering, the most disaffected of a group of
Federalists called the Essex Junto, had advocated secession for some
time. In December 1814 the Massachusetts legislature called a secret
meeting in Hartford, Connecticut, to assess New England's future course.

Moderates controlled the Hartford Convention. The delegates proposed to save the republic by reforming it, rather than to destroy it by leaving. They suggested several constitutional amendments, including the requirement of a two-thirds vote of Congress to declare war, to admit new states, and to enact embargoes. The doctrine of state rights had found a new and temporary home in Federalist New England. But the convention's timing could not have been worse; delegates bearing the proposals from Hartford arrived in Washington as the city was celebrating Jackson's stunning victory at New Orleans. Their suggestions disappeared in a flood of postwar nationalism.

Errors had flawed the American war effort, but the peace commissioners at Ghent made few mistakes. Negotiations had begun almost as soon as hostilities, for the British had never really meant to have a war and the Americans soon tired of it. In 1814, a talented American delegation led by Clay, Gallatin, and John Quincy Adams began serious discussions with an inferior group of British representatives. Bargaining positions changed as news arrived from the front; at one time Britain demanded the cession of an Indian buffer state and about one-third of the rest of the United States. In December 1814, following word of the American success on Lake Champlain, the negotiators agreed to stop fighting and to restore the status quo ante bellum.

It was a strange peace ending a strange war. None of the great issues that had led to war—impressment, neutral rights, traffic with the Indians, expansion—were seriously discussed, let alone settled. The Senate took twenty-four hours in February 1815 to ratify the treaty and then moved on to more congenial business. The Treaty of Ghent marked the end of an era of international tension that had kept the United States preoccupied with foreign relations; now the nation turned happily to its own affairs. The victory at New Orleans suitably climaxed the "second war for independence." Although the United States had not really won the war, it certainly had not lost it. That was not a bad record for a new nation in conflict with the world's greatest power.

American Nationalism

The United States was at peace at home as well as abroad. The war had taught Jeffersonians the wisdom of Federalist ways; at the same time it had so embarrassed Federalists that younger adherents quietly emerged as Republicans. President Madison rediscovered the nationalism he had espoused at the Constitutional Convention and joined Clay, Calhoun, and other young Republicans who made nationalism their political creed. In December 1815 Madison asked Congress to establish a uniform national currency to be issued by a revived national bank. He also suggested that newly established industries warranted the protection of a tariff. And he called congressional attention "to the great importance of establishing throughout our country the roads and canals which can best be executed under national authority." One reason the Federalist party soon disappeared was that the Republicans had stolen its program.

As recently as 1811, many Republicans had challenged the utility of Hamilton's bank and allowed it to die. Difficulty in financing the war persuaded Calhoun, backed in 1816 by Madison, to rally southern and western congressmen to the support of central banking. His bill passed over the opposition of local banking interests in New England and the Middle Atlantic states. By 1817 the second Bank of the United States was open for business in Philadelphia, with a twenty-year charter, the right to issue notes and to establish branches anywhere in the United States, and initial capital of $35 million. The government supplied one-fifth of the capital, appointed five of the twenty-five directors, and received a fee—called a bonus—of $1.5 million for the charter and for the bank's right to serve as the exclusive depository of government funds.

Calhoun had a use for that bonus. He proposed that the bonus itself, and the government's annual dividends from the bank, be spent for roads and canals—"internal improvements," in the phrase of the day—that would enhance the nation's unity, promote its commerce, and add to the comfort of its citizens. "Let us," Calhoun exhorted, "bind the republic together with a perfect system of roads and canals. Let us conquer space." But the nationalism of some Republicans did not extend so far, and the self-interest of others prevented them from following Calhoun's lead. His Bonus Bill passed the House by only two votes, and Madison vetoed it, perhaps, as the President said, because of constitutional scruples and perhaps also because it did not have truly national support.

The tariff, by contrast, did have national support. The American economy needed protection as it adjusted to a world at peace. Nascent industries could not compete with British manufacturers who hoped to bury competition under an avalanche of cheap goods. The tariff was to be moderate and temporary, and it was to protect Louisiana sugar, Kentucky hemp, Pennsylvania iron, and Ohio wool, as well as New England textiles. Actually, commercial New England, hoping to safeguard its profitable carrying trade, voted against the tariff. Nearly as many Federalists opposed protection as supported it, while Republicans overwhelmingly endorsed it. Madison certified Republican acceptance by signing the tariff of 1816.

For thirty-four years, while Presidents and Congresses came and went, Chief Justice John Marshall's nationalism never wavered. When John Adams appointed Marshall in 1801, the judiciary had neither the prestige nor the power of the other branches of government. But the Court under Marshall resisted Jefferson's attempts to reform or dominate it and continued to defend and enlarge the power of the national government long after Jefferson had gone back to Monticello. The Court was always Marshall's Court, no matter how many Republican justices Republican

Presidents sent to join him. Instead of issuing several individual opinions, the Court began to speak with one voice—more often than not that of the chief justice. Between 1805 and 1833 the Court decided 919 cases; Marshall wrote the Court's opinion 458 times and dissented on exactly 6 occasions.

Part of Marshall's genius lay in his persuasive deductions from nationalist premises. Moreover, he had a gift for stating judicial principles so that his decisions were virtually invulnerable, if not above criticism. The earliest, and for Jefferson the most frustrating, demonstration of Marshall's judicial statesmanship occurred in 1803. In *Marbury* v. *Madison,* Marshall coupled a gratuitous rebuke to the Republican administration with an assertion of the Court's power of judicial review. For the first time, the Supreme Court claimed the authority to declare federal law unconstitutional, a claim that Republicans disputed. The section of the statute in question had little significance, but Marshall's precedent had great importance, even though the Court chose not to rule against other federal legislation until 1857.

Over and over again between 1801 and 1835 Marshall cited his constitutional creed: the federal government had sovereignty independent of the states and superior to them in those respects enumerated in the Constitution. "It is true," Marshall answered proponents of state sovereignty in *McCulloch* v. *Maryland* (1819), that the people had "assembled in their several states" to ratify the Constitution. But, asked Marshall innocently, "Where else should they have assembled?" The chief justice used the *McCulloch* case to curb the states, which were hampering the Bank of the United States with taxation, and to restate and enlarge the implied powers of Congress. Marshall cribbed his argument from Alexander Hamilton's classic statement to President Washington: "Let the end be legitimate," Marshall wrote, "let it be within the scope of the Constitution, and all means which are appropriate, which are plainly adapted to that end, which are not prohibited . . . are constitutional." In 1821, in *Cohens* v. *Virginia,* Marshall lectured the Virginia judiciary on the supremacy of federal courts. In 1824, in *Gibbons* v. *Ogden,* the chief justice defined commerce so broadly that he seemed to claim federal jurisdiction over nearly all economic enterprise.

Marshall protected the rights of private property as zealously as he defended the power of the federal government. In *Fletcher* v. *Peck* (1810) he held that a legislative land grant was a contract worthy of the same protection the constitution gave other contracts. A notoriously corrupt Georgia legislature had issued a grant that a subsequent legislature had repealed. No matter how dubious the original contract, Marshall declared its repeal an unconstitutional interference with the obligation of contract. In 1819 he ruled that New Hampshire could not convert Dartmouth College into a state university. The corporate charter that had established Dartmouth, Marshall held, was a contract that could not be changed by one party without the consent of the other. Since business corporations also held charters from the states, these decisions inhibited economic regulation and may have encouraged the development of corporate enterprise.

James Monroe and the Era of Good Feelings

Swelling postwar nationalism redounded to the political credit of the Republicans. In 1817 James Monroe inherited the presidency from Madison, seemingly as a matter of right. In the election of 1816 only Massachusetts, Connecticut, and Delaware had cast electoral votes for Rufus King, the able Federalist nominee. Determined to nourish his party's dominance, Monroe undertook a presidential grand tour from Baltimore to Boston and on to Detroit. Splendid patriotic oratory and a gratifying display of political unity marked Monroe's progress. A Boston newspaper provided the new administration with a label by referring to an "Era of Good Feelings." The description was inaccurate in several respects, but it did reflect the temporary suspension of political partisanship and the equally temporary nationalism that marked the period. In the election of 1820 only one stubborn elector failed to vote for James Monroe.

Monroe named John Quincy Adams as secretary of state, the office that had become the springboard to the White House, and thereby tacitly promised to be the last of the Virginia Dynasty. Adams, like his father, the second President, was a nationalist to the core. Diplomatic nationalism meant enlarging the nation and vigorously reasserting its prestige abroad. Adams and Monroe were equal to both tasks.

More annoying than the failure to conquer Canada in the War of 1812 was the failure to conquer Florida. Although the peninsula was nominally a Spanish possession, Spain only pretended to rule it. In 1810, claiming that West Florida was part of the Louisiana Purchase, the United States had annexed the area west of the Perdido River; the seizure of Mobile during the war ended any Spanish challenge. West Florida only whetted the appetite for the rest of the territory, and Spain's failure to control the Seminole Indians and renegade slaves there provided an excuse to send in American forces. In 1818 Andrew Jackson, allegedly acting with indirect authorization from Washington, pushed into Florida with a force of frontier militiamen, burned Spanish forts at Pensacola and St. Marks, and hanged two British subjects, whom he accused of helping the Indians. Jackson's raid set off a tense debate in Monroe's cabinet; most of the members, including Calhoun, who as secretary of war was Jackson's immediate superior, wanted to disavow the impetuous general.

But John Quincy Adams, at first alone and then with Monroe's backing, defended Jackson. Already negotiating with the Spanish minister Don Luis de Onís to establish boundaries for Louisiana, Adams now added a

James Monroe

demand that Spain reimburse the United States for the expenses of Jackson's expedition. He hinted that if Spain could not keep order in Florida the United States would be forced to annex it in order to protect the residents of Georgia and Alabama from raiding Indians. Jackson's exploit had demonstrated that Spain could not hold Florida, so Onís set out to salvage what he could. In 1819 Adams and Onís agreed to a "transcontinental treaty" that ceded Florida to the United States in return for the Treasury's assumption of $5 million in American claims against Spain. The United States renounced a shadowy title to Texas by fixing the boundary of Louisiana at the Sabine River. Spain in turn renounced its claim to any territory north of the forty-second parallel, the northern boundary of California. Adams and Onís drew a line along the Arkansas and Red rivers and north to the forty-second parallel, thereby finally defining Jefferson's bargain of 1803. The Senate promptly approved the treaty, but Spain, less pleased with the outcome, delayed until 1821, when ratification became final.

Having eliminated Spain's claims to the northern Pacific coast, Adams did not propose to allow Russia to add the territory to Alaska. When the Czar barred foreign vessels from the waters off Alaska and pushed its southern limit to the fifty-first parallel, Adams protested sharply. "The American continents," he told the Czar's minister, "are no longer subjects for any new European colonial establishments." The Czar did not think the area vital to his empire, so in 1824 he revoked the maritime restriction and set Alaska's southern boundary at 54°40'.

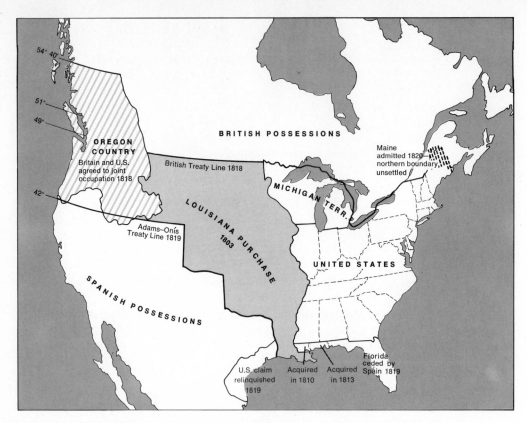

BOUNDARY SETTLEMENTS TO 1820

The principle of noncolonization that Adams tried out on the Czar was destined for a wider audience. Since the beginning of Monroe's presidency, the administration had been puzzling out a policy toward the Latin American republics that were gradually winning their independence from Spain. Although France and Russia were vaguely interested in assisting Spanish efforts to regain the empire, no European nation could intervene in the Western Hemisphere without the cooperation of the British fleet, which commanded the Atlantic. Since British merchants welcomed the Latin American independence that ended Spain's trading monopoly, the British cabinet did not encourage efforts to subdue the former Spanish colonies.

Secretary Adams too was anxious to keep European powers out of the Western Hemisphere. During 1818 and 1819 Adams had suggested that both Britain and the United States recognize the new Latin American republics. Britain was not then ready to appear to condone revolution. But in 1823 George Canning, Britain's foreign minister, proposed a joint statement opposing intervention in Latin America. Richard Rush, the American minister in London, replied that Britain ought first to extend diplomatic recognition to the new republics as the United States had done the year before. Rush then forwarded Canning's suggestion to Monroe, who liked the idea. But Secretary Adams opposed a joint declaration lest it make the United States seem the pawn of British policy—"a cockboat in the wake of the British man of war." Adams also opposed any step that might be interpreted as barring intervention by the United States in Latin America or the acquisition of territory there. Adams persuaded the President to spell out this policy, which he did in part of his State of the Union message in 1823.

The Monroe Doctrine—as it came to be called in the 1840s—began with the standard assumption that America was part of a new and better world, while Europe was different and decadent. In matters strictly European, Monroe said, "we have never taken any part, nor does it comport with our policy, so to do." So much, he implied, for those who suggested that the United States should aid the Greek revolt that was raging in the 1820s. On the other hand, the United States was, in the President's opinion, directly concerned about the Western Hemisphere, and any effort by European powers "to extend their system to any portions of this Hemisphere" would be construed as "dangerous to our peace and safety." The United States, Monroe assured his European audience, would not interfere with existing colonies. But henceforth "the American continents" were "not to be considered as subjects for future colonization by any European powers."

Even before Monroe decided to shun Canning's offer, Canning had withdrawn it. And before Monroe read his speech, the French government had assured Canning that France had no intention of repressing Latin American insurrections. Without France and Britain, Spain could not regain its colonies and Monroe's statement of policy was superfluous. Congress listened to his message politely, took no action on it, and appropriated no money for ships to enforce it. European capitals dismissed the Monroe Doctrine as Yankee bombast. But nationalistic Americans, whose only memory of the War of 1812 was the victory at New Orleans, thought the United States a good match for all continental Europe.

The End of Good Feelings

The nation stood behind the President's foreign policy, but on domestic matters unity—and good feelings—disappeared well before 1823. Prosperity was essential to harmony, and the financial panic that began in 1819 exposed rifts between sections and classes that nationalism had earlier obscured. In 1818 the price of cotton had reached 32.5 cents a pound; in 1819 the average was slightly over 14 cents. Before 1819 plantation land in Mississippi had sold at spirited auctions for as much

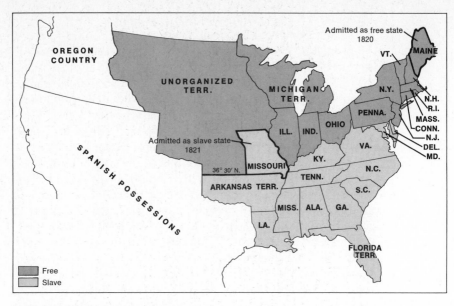

THE MISSOURI COMPROMISE, 1820

as $100 per acre; in 1819 the market was placid and the price depressed. Jefferson reported that land in Virginia could not be sold for a year's rent; rents in Baltimore dropped by half. Unemployment mounted in Philadelphia. In Pittsburgh the unemployed simply deserted the city, and the population suddenly decreased by nearly one-third.

Like all panics, that of 1819 had no single cause. In part it grew out of worldwide economic dislocation that accompanied the wars at the beginning of the century. Irresponsible American banking, from the Bank of the United States to the wildest "wildcat" bank in the West, further weakened the economy. The panic also resulted in part from the expansive postwar mood of Americans, whose optimism blinded them to economic reality. When optimism vanished, the American public tended to blame the Bank of the United States, the keystone of postwar nationalism. This popular explanation was too simple, but extensive criticism of the bank showed once more the latent fear of the power of the national government.

The concern of state-rights advocates multiplied during two years of intermittent wrangling over slavery. In 1819 Missouri applied for admission to the Union with a constitution that routinely guaranteed slavery, since 10,000 of Missouri's inhabitants were slaves. Missouri's application for statehood became anything but routine, however, when James Tallmadge, Jr., a congressman from New York, moved to prevent new slaves from entering Missouri and to emancipate gradually those already there. The Tallmadge Amendment threatened not only slavery in

Missouri but slavery everywhere, which southerners believed must either spread or die. If slavery could be ended in Missouri, where it was already established, it could be kept out of other territories and perhaps even abolished in existing states. The amendment also threatened the equality in the Senate of free and slave states, a condition that had become a tacit sectional agreement. And finally, Tallmadge's motion threatened the unity of the Republican party. Jefferson warned that Rufus King and other opportunistic Federalists thought opposition to slavery might unite Northwest and Northeast against southern Republicans.

Anxious to preserve Republican unity, Henry Clay put together the legislative package called the Missouri Compromise. Clay linked Maine's application for statehood in 1820 with that of Missouri, thereby preserving the sectional balance. He then incorporated the proposal of Illinois Senator Jesse Thomas that no other part of the Louisiana Purchase north of 36°30′ (the southern boundary of Missouri) should be open to slavery. Southern representatives supported Clay's compromise with more enthusiasm that did representatives from the free states. But unless new southern territory was added, or unless the 36°30′ line was revoked, southern equality in the Senate would be short-lived. For the compromise left only the Arkansas Territory, part of which would soon be reserved for Indians, for division into slave states, while the remaining federal territory contained a dozen potential free states.

The revised constitution Missouri submitted to Congress late in 1820 threatened to undo the compromise before it could take effect. The constitution made slavery as permanent as law could make it by requiring the consent of each slaveowner to legislative emancipation. In another section the document forbade free blacks to enter the state "under any pretext whatever." Since blacks were citizens of some northern states, this second provision violated the privileges and immunities clause of the Constitution of the United States. Those who had supported Tallmadge's amendment once more opposed statehood for Missouri. But Henry Clay borrowed from a Tennessee senator a pacifying resolution that required Missouri's promise not to construe its constitution so as to violate the privileges or immunities of citizens of other states. The promise and Clay's formula were equally worthless after Missouri was admitted in 1821, but for the moment most politicians were relieved to bury the issue.

The Virginia Dynasty occupied the political middle ground between uncompromising nationalism and state-rights Republicanism. Sensing that the nation was changing, and courageous enough to discard outworn political principles, the three Virginians at first used the powers of government on behalf of sections and classes that Federalists had overlooked. Popular confidence in the central government mounted. For a few years Republicans acted as if they were genuinely convinced that the good of the whole nation transcended personal preferment, sectional prejudices, and parochial interests. But an energetic and restless people, itching to exploit the resources of a broad continent, soon rediscovered old rivalries and then developed some new ones.

Suggested Reading

Henry Adams wrote nine volumes of *History of the United States During the Administrations of Jefferson and Madison* (1889 – 91); his study begins with an account of American society that has been published separately as *The United States in 1800** (1955). Adams's brief account of American society may be compared with Thomas Jefferson's *Notes on the State of Virginia**, written in the 1780s. Marshall Smelser has provided the most recent brief study of the Jefferson and Madison administrations, *The Democratic Republic, 1801 – 1815** (1968).

Irving Brant completed a multivolume biography of James Madison in 1961 and Dumas Malone is studying Jefferson on a comparable scale; the five volumes that have appeared carry the narrative through his second presidential term. Fawn Brodie's biography of Jefferson (1974) is concerned more with his private life than his public career. The letters and papers of both Republican Presidents are being collected and published, as are the papers of the Adams family. Samuel F. Bemis's *John Quincy Adams and the Foundation of American Foreign Policy* (1950) is excellent. Harry Ammon's *James Monroe: The Quest for National Identity* (1971) fills a gap in recent scholarship.

Several studies have focused on the War of 1812, including two detailed works of Bradford Perkins, *The First Rapprochement* (1967) and *Prologue to War** (1961), which together trace Anglo-American relations from 1795 to 1812. Julius Pratt's *Expansionists of 1812* (1925) states the case for land hunger as the cause of the war; Roger H. Brown, *The Republic in Peril: 1812* (1964), argues that national pride was more fundamental. Reginald Horsman's *The Frontier in the Formative Years* (1970) is informative. In *This Affair of Louisiana** (1976), Alexander De Conde argues that pressure from the frontier had much to do with the Louisiana Purchase.

Two accounts by George Dangerfield, *The Awakening of American Nationalism** (1965) and *The Era of Good Feelings** (1952), survey the period from 1815 to 1828. David H. Fischer, *The Revolution of American Conservatism** (1965), examines the Federalist party, while Noble Cunningham, *The Jeffersonian Republicans in Power** (1967), deals with the Federalists' successful opponents. James S. Young, *The Washington Community, 1800 – 1828* (1966), discusses the ways politicians functioned in the nation's unfinished capital city.

* Available in paperback edition

Chapter 7
The Politics of the Common Man

1824 Presidential election: The House of Representatives elects John Quincy Adams •

1828 "Tariff of abominations" • Presidential election: Andrew Jackson (Democrat) defeats John Quincy Adams (National Republican) •

1830 Senators Webster and Hayne debate principles of state sovereignty and nationalism • Indian Removal Act •

1832 Tariff of 1832 precipitates nullification crisis • Jackson vetoes renewal of charter for Bank of the United States • Presidential election: Andrew Jackson (Democrat) defeats Henry Clay (National Republican), William Wirt (Anti-Masonic Party), and John Floyd (dissident National Republican) •

1833 Compromise tariff •

1836 Specie Circular requires government land be bought with hard money • Presidential election: Martin Van Buren (Democrat) defeats William Henry Harrison, Hugh L. White, Daniel Webster, and W. P. Mangum (sectional Whig candidates) •

1837 Financial panic • *Charles River Bridge* case attacks "privileged corporations" •

1840 Independent Treasury Act (repealed in 1841) • Presidential election: William Henry Harrison (Whig) defeats Martin Van Buren (Democrat) •

1841 John Tyler succeeds Harrison •

In 1829 ordinary citizens crowded the solemn inauguration of the President of the United States. Dignity did not long endure; alcohol and popular enthusiasm for Andrew Jackson turned the ensuing reception into an uninhibited romp. As if to reassert their title, the guests milled around *their* White House, stood on *their* furniture, smashed *their* china, drank *their* punch, and exhausted *their* President with cheers and good will. The crowds, wrote a puzzled Daniel Webster, really seemed "to think that the country ha[d] been rescued from some dreadful danger."

Webster's incredulity disclosed his failure to sense the changing basis of American politics. When Webster first won national office in 1812, governing was still largely reserved to the privileged classes, as had been the case since Americans had had any voice in their own governance. Federalists and Jeffersonians alike had decried the development of political factions and parties; the harmonious, partyless, social unity of an extended "era of good feeling" was the republican ideal. An informed electorate, in this view, selected among dignified candidates, who had advanced careful arguments on the issues. But the rules changed in the 1820s and 1830s, as Webster and other politicians eventually discovered. The expanded electorate seemed to glory in partisanship and to count party loyalty more important than dignity or education or social position.

The voters responded to campaign hoopla, to candidates who identified with ordinary people, and to shared antipathy to other groups in the population, rather than to reasoned political discourse.

A rhetoric of equality, which celebrated plain folk and roused their pride in being plain, became the political style of the parties that emerged in the period. There was no shortage of consequential issues; indeed the rapidly developing economy made transportation, currency, and the tariff especially important. But it was the egalitarian style—as well as political principles—that held the interest and the loyal support of the growing electorate.

When the Constitution was adopted, many of the original states had religious qualifications for suffrage, and all either limited the vote to taxpayers or retained a property qualification. The fourteenth state, Vermont, admitted in 1791, permitted universal manhood suffrage. Upon admission to the Union, Indiana, Illinois, Alabama, Missouri, and Maine adopted white manhood suffrage. In the dozen years after 1815, state

A country inn: convivial equality

after state modified its constitution to enlarge the number of eligible voters, to establish legislative representation on the basis of population instead of tax receipts, and to increase the number of elective offices.

But if the common man voted, he did not govern. (Women, of course, did neither.) Once elected, representatives sometimes ignored their party's principles and their own promises; issues voters believed settled proved negotiable after the ballots were counted. Those who mastered the new political techniques and machinery regularly protested their humble origins—Daniel Webster thought his failure to be born in a log cabin might have kept him from the White House—but they were not ordinary folk according to the usual measures of property and prestige.

For Jacksonian society was not in fact classless, even if almost every white man could vote. Brahmins from old Protestant families dominated Boston as Main Line Quakers did Philadelphia, First Families did Virginia, and the Knickerbocker aristocracy did New York. Political democracy and legal equality did not level social and economic distinctions. John Jacob Astor was about as rich as the richest European, and some of his compatriots were not far behind. Americans simply chose not to emphasize the economic differences between rich and poor. Instead they asserted that, in their country, anyone might reasonably aspire to a Fifth Avenue mansion, a private library, and summers in Saratoga Springs. Equality of opportunity was the American way, and the individual received the reward he earned.

At least it was supposed to happen that way. More often the monetary rewards went to those who already had money. The rich enlarged their disproportionate share of the nation's wealth in the first half of the nineteenth century, and others sometimes improved their standard of living as well. Children of the rich and of old families had a head start over children of immigrants and frontier farmers. Local government, no matter how democratic, reflected the influence of wealthy taxpayers more than the demands of the poor, even after they were enfranchised.

Thus the general equality of manners, dress, and station that European visitors, including the astute Alexis de Tocqueville, invariably remarked, was not a wholly accurate reflection of American society. Still, although the United States was not precisely the classless society it seemed to contemporary observers, Americans thought it ought to be. That was the ideal that influenced their behavior, and their vote, in Jacksonian America.

The Election of John Quincy Adams

Not everyone who had the right to vote did so in the presidential election of 1824. Only about 350,000 men, perhaps one in every four eligible, bothered to cast ballots. This lack of interest did not result from a dearth of candidates, for four distinguished Americans sought the office, and a

John Quincy Adams: he lacked the common touch

fifth, John C. Calhoun, had carefully considered the race before deciding to settle for the vice-presidency, which he won easily. Henry Clay, John Quincy Adams, William Crawford, and Andrew Jackson were all nominally Jeffersonian Republicans. As long as one dignified Virginian had followed another in agreed succession, the party had remained united. Faced with a contest for the first time in 1824, the caucus of congressional Republicans failed to agree, and Jefferson's coalition broke apart.

A rump session of the caucus nominated William Crawford, the Georgian who had served Monroe as secretary of the treasury. Crawford's strict construction, his southern residence, and the source of his nomination made him appear the Jeffersonian heir. But the quasi-official status of Crawford's candidacy became a liability. For the caucus seemed an undemocratic survival from the days when gentlemen decided political matters, and its nominee, while capable, seemed uninteresting.

Nobody, on the other hand, had ever thought Andrew Jackson dull. Jackson personified the economic and social success of which all Americans dreamed; he was the poor orphan who grew up to own a prosperous plantation, to serve in both houses of Congress, and to sit as a judge. His duels, his Indian wars, and his victory at New Orleans made

Jackson the symbol of the popular preference for deeds over words. His life displayed the rugged independence, the healthy acquisitiveness, and the unpretentious good fellowship Americans admired.

Henry Clay also liked good fellowship, and perhaps no legislator before the Civil War had more close congressional friends than the magnetic Kentuckian. He had been elected Speaker at his very first appearance in the House of Representatives and, except for one year, was reelected to that position as long as he served. More clearly than any other candidate, Clay advanced a specific program, which he called "the American system." He argued that the central government should finance internal improvements with income from the sale of land at a reasonable price. And he advocated both a protective tariff and a stable national currency regulated by a national bank. Taken together, Clay held, his policies would produce a prosperous, unified nation. His genius was in transforming vaguely felt needs and aspirations into concrete legislative measures. The components of his American system were the major issues of American politics until slavery disrupted all political discourse.

John Quincy Adams, the fourth candidate in 1824, was immune to Clay's charm but agreed with his program. This son of the second President displayed both the stubborn integrity and the political ineptitude of his father. John Quincy Adams had been brought up to govern; no man who ever competed for the presidency was apparently better prepared. His brief appearance in the Senate and his distinguished diplomatic service revealed that Adams was intelligent, frank, and conscientious to a fault. Above all, he was an uncompromising nationalist.

For all his nationalism Adams had the support only of the Northeast and in both the popular and the electoral vote ran second to Jackson, whose appeal was more nearly national than that of any other candidate. "Old Hickory" won many of the southern and western states that Clay had believed were safely his. In spite of a paralytic stroke late in 1823 that left him virtually helpless, Crawford ran slightly ahead of Clay in the electoral college, where no candidate had a majority.

The Twelfth Amendment required the House of Representatives to choose among the three candidates with the largest electoral total. Henry Clay could use his immense prestige in the House only to make another man President. He really had little choice. Crawford's illness eliminated him. Although Jackson's political principles were unclear, his rivalry with Clay for political support in the West and South was evident indeed. Adams, on the other hand, shared Clay's economic nationalism and seemed to the Kentuckian a lesser political obstacle than Jackson. Both sides pressured and flattered Clay, but his decision could never have been in serious doubt. He chose Adams, who won on the first ballot in the House.

If the cooperation of Adams and Clay had stopped with the election, the Adams administration might have been less acrimonious and Clay's

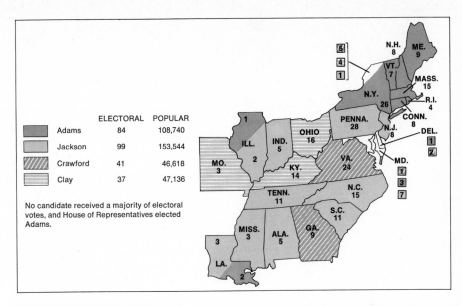

		ELECTORAL	POPULAR
▓	Adams	84	108,740
░	Jackson	99	153,544
▨	Crawford	41	46,618
▤	Clay	37	47,136

No candidate received a majority of electoral votes, and House of Representatives elected Adams.

THE ELECTION OF 1824

political future more bright. But Clay joined Adams's cabinet as secretary of state, a position that seemed to confer the right of succession to the White House. Jacksonians promptly charged that a "corrupt bargain" had mocked the people's will, and the presidential campaign of 1828 began in 1825 with Clay's appointment.

John Quincy Adams's presidency was, as one of his grandsons later wrote, a "lurid administration," illuminated by crackling political lightning. The President's proposals were plentiful and imaginative, but Congress refused to enact them. For Adams, internal improvements implied more than better roads and canals, and in 1825 he deluged Congress with suggestions for varied national projects. The powers of the federal government, Adams held, should be used for the improvement of "agriculture, commerce and manufactures, [for] the cultivation and encouragement of the mechanic and of the elegant arts, [for] the advancement of literature, and the progress of the sciences." By way of illustration, he suggested that Congress authorize geographical exploration and astronomical observation, fix a standard of weights and measures, and charter a national university.

Most congressmen, and most of Adams's contemporaries, had a more traditional and more limited view. While the President emphasized government's role in helping citizens live fuller lives, his political adversaries, claiming to stand in the true republican tradition, advocated a limited government that would permit free individuals to improve their own condition. Even if there had been no clash of principle, partisan congressmen resisted Adams's proposals simply because he made them. Any issue might serve as a pretext for bitter controversy. Adams's nomination of two delegates to discuss hemispheric cooperation at a congress in Panama provoked a filibuster that lasted most of the winter of 1825–26.

The endless talk itself was not important, but it did furnish an opportunity to broadcast the charge that Clay and Adams had corruptly secured their offices. Debate also permitted private discussions that knit several state organizations into a formidable political coalition. Martin Van Buren, an astute senator from New York, pledged his own "Albany Regency" to Jackson and undertook to secure the support of others, like Isaac Hill of New Hampshire and Thomas Ritchie of Virginia, who had been Van Buren's allies in the Crawford campaign of 1824. Calhoun also enrolled in Jackson's camp. Thomas Hart Benton in Missouri, Major William Lewis and John Eaton in Tennessee, Amos Kendall and Francis Preston Blair in Kentucky, James Buchanan in Pennsylvania—all Jacksonians with budding political machines—redoubled their efforts to discredit the President and his secretary of state. It did not matter that eventually Adams's nominees to the Panama congress were approved; one of the envoys died, and the other arrived too late to accomplish anything. The political cost of the President's seeming victory was immense. The coalition of Jacksonians, soon proudly to call itself the Democratic party, was able to limit Adams to one troubled term in the White House and to prevent Henry Clay from ever taking up residence there.

The fight over the tariff was also politically expensive. In 1827 the House heeded pleas for protection from woolen manufacturers in Massachusetts and Rhode Island. When the vote in the Senate was tied, Vice-President Calhoun killed the bill. A second bill in 1828 became the center of a thick political intrigue and eventually emerged as the "tariff of abominations." To provisions that were slightly less generous to the woolen interests than those of 1827 were added duties on iron, lead, flax, hemp, and raw wool. Jacksonians hoped to woo the middle states, whose products the tariff of 1828 protected, and simultaneously to blame Adams for the law in the South, where any tariff was an abomination. A Democratic coalition prevented any amendment, perhaps in the expectation that disgusted northern representatives would find the bill unsatisfactory and join southerners, who voted overwhelmingly against it. Although Daniel Webster and sixteen other New England congressmen grudgingly supported the measure, twenty-three New Englanders opposed it. But overwhelming support from the middle states and the Northwest was enough to put the new tariff on the President's desk. Political criticism would greet whatever action Adams took; fully aware of the hazard, he signed the bill. The intricate Jacksonian strategy was probably unnecessary, for tariff or no tariff, John Quincy Adams was already trailing in the campaign of 1828.

That campaign had begun in 1825 with doubtful accusations, boisterously stated, and then proceeded to degenerate. By election day, voters had heard that the profligate Adams had used public funds to

Jackson Forever!
The Hero of Two Wars and of Orleans!
The Man of the People!
HE WHO COULD NOT BARTER NOR BARGAIN FOR THE
PRESIDENCY!

install sinful games in the White House. While minister to Russia, the Jacksonians said, Adams had supplied a virtuous American girl for the pleasure of the debauched Russian Czar. The President's campaigners were hardly less imaginative. They exaggerated Jackson's exploits as a frontier brawler and distributed a campaign poster edged in coffins, representing the men Jackson was alleged to have murdered during the War of 1812. Jackson's opponents seized upon the fact that his wife had married him under the mistaken impression that her previous husband had secured a divorce. The charges against Old Hickory boomeranged. His duels and his military reputation were the stuff of legends and evidence of courage, decisiveness, and patriotism. And the death of his wife, the retiring Rachel, before inauguration enhanced the outrage of Jackson's partisans at the injustice of the Adams campaign.

It was the most exciting campaign in a generation, perhaps since the birth of the republic. Not issues, but furor and a developing party organization lured people to the polls. Each candidate received more votes than the total cast four years earlier; perhaps 55 percent of those eligible voted. More than 55 percent of those ballots were for Andrew Jackson, who won 178 electoral votes, while Adams won only 83. Calhoun remained as Vice-President. The electoral college, once intended to check popular enthusiasm and to keep the choice of chief magistrate from the people, had become responsive to the popular will. By 1832 only in South Carolina did the legislature choose presidential electors; elsewhere the voter had a direct choice.

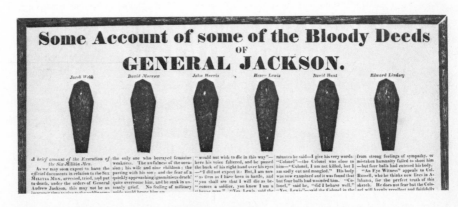

Indians and Internal Improvements

Democrats claimed the spoils of victory by displacing officeholders at all levels of the federal bureaucracy. The administration actually removed only about one out of nine federal appointees, but as other jobs fell vacant, Jacksonians filled them. The President regarded this turnover as a reform, for there had been no wholesale change since 1801, and some bureaucrats, grown musty in office, regarded their positions more as a right than a trust. Although his own appointees were predominantly well-to-do, Jackson held that offices ought to be open to every citizen; his intent to rotate positions among the party faithful was the counterpart of extended suffrage.

Like Madison and Monroe before him, Jackson questioned the federal government's right to appropriate funds for the internal improvements his western supporters demanded. In 1830 Jackson restated his constitutional qualms by vetoing a bill to subsidize a project in Kentucky called the Maysville Road. But he shrewdly conciliated the West by approving expenditures to improve rivers and harbors; indeed, during Jackson's presidency appropriations for internal improvements were considerably larger than those of the Adams administration. Only four days after vetoing the Maysville Bill, Jackson signed a measure to finance part of the National Road, which, Jackson carefully noted, was an interstate project. Perhaps only the President thought these two actions consistent. But he retained both his constitutional scruples and the loyalty of the West at the minimal cost of part of a road in Henry Clay's state.

If Jackson's policy on internal improvements seemed devious, his Indian policy was open and direct. In the end, the choice almost always was whether or not to protect the Indians' possession of tribal lands from encroachment by enterprising white hunters and settlers. Even Thomas Jefferson, who admired Indians when their land was not at stake, had connived at schemes to displace them; he authorized traders to permit tribal debts that would be paid by future land cessions. Jackson felt no need to cloak his intent to remove the Indians from Wisconsin and Georgia and elsewhere to the Indian Territory in Oklahoma. When the Sac and Fox or the Seminoles resisted, they were crushed; when the Choctaws relied on treaties, the treaties were broken; when the Cherokees won in the Supreme Court, their victory was ignored. Like most whites, Jackson thought negotiations were ceremonies in which Indians made concessions. When Chief Justice John Marshall ruled, in *Cherokee Nation* v. *Georgia* (1831) and *Worcester* v. *Georgia* (1832), that Indians were entitled to federal protection, the President is supposed to have remarked that Marshall would have to enforce his own decision. In effect, Jackson nullified the court's ruling, an action that may have encouraged southern opponents of federal legislation later to think he would accept a formal statement of nullification.

Georgia's attempt to force the Cherokees to emigrate coincided with national policy enacted in the Indian Removal Act of 1830. Passed by a small congressional majority, this law authorized exchange of tribal lands for federal territory in Oklahoma, and appropriated funds to pay for removal, to assist the tribes in their adjustment to the new area, and to compensate them for the improvements they left behind. Indeed, the first treaty with the Choctaws seemed so generous to Jackson that he refused to submit it to the Senate, thereby holding the land off the market. The delay was only temporary and removal soon began.

Privation, fraud, and occasional heroism marked the tribes' forced migration. Indians who refused to migrate were usually guaranteed the right to remain and promised title to a farm, but an unsympathetic administrator often managed to prevent them from exercising either right. Although federal officials sometimes tried to provide adequate rations and transportation, they lacked both the logistical tools and the administrative skill to do so; the country was simply not equipped to move thousands of Indians in any comfort from the Southeast to Oklahoma. Even with the best intent, federal bureaucrats could not control the weather, the diseases to which Indians had no immunity, the land-grabbers who cheated Indians of compensation for improvements, the thieves who preyed on the tribes while they were in transit, or the unscrupulous profiteers who sold them forbidden whisky and overpriced corn. Nor was Oklahoma home. The Indians called the route "the trail of tears," and Tocqueville wrote ironically of the benevolent government that took the Indians "by the hand" and transported "them to a grave far from the land of their fathers." "It is impossible," he concluded, "to destroy man with more respect for the laws of humanity."

The Tariff and Nullification

The South applauded both Jackson's Indian policy and his constitutional reservations about internal improvements. But before the end of his first term the South discovered that Old Hickory differed from many southerners in his interpretation of the rights of states, for Jackson seemed to think the Union vastly greater than the sum of its sectional parts.

The first open indication of trouble came early in 1830 during a Senate debate on a resolution that would temporarily restrict the sale of public land. Missouri's Senator Benton assailed the resolution. Southern senators, including Robert Y. Hayne of South Carolina, who may have been coached by Calhoun, supported Benton in an apparent attempt to create a political alliance between West and South. Hayne's attack on the Northeast went beyond land policy to add a denunciation of the section's broad view of federal power. In introducing constitutional interpretation,

Hayne had shifted the topic of debate, and Daniel Webster seized the opportunity.

Webster knew the peril of discussing economic and land policy, about which sections differed. Instead, he attacked southern doctrines of state sovereignty and strict construction. He appealed to the mystic bonds that knit interests and regions into one great nation, and he concluded that liberty and union were perpetual and inseparable. Some months later, in a dramatic confrontation with Calhoun, Jackson affirmed a similar nationalism in a toast to the preservation of the Union.

The rift between President and Vice-President had personal as well as political causes. Jackson discovered that in 1818 Calhoun, then Monroe's secretary of war, had supported an attempt to discipline Jackson for his conduct in Florida. Jackson demanded that the Carolinian explain his action and found Calhoun's reply unsatisfactory. Jackson was also outraged because Calhoun's wife seemed to have stirred a tempest that swept through Washington society. John Eaton, Jackson's friend and secretary of war, married saucy, attractive Peggy O'Neale, whose reputation was none too good and whom the scandalized wives of the rest of the administration shunned. Perhaps because his own wife had been slandered, Jackson defended Mrs. Eaton, as did Martin Van Buren, who used the seemingly trivial controversy in his effort to supplant Calhoun as heir apparent. By the spring of 1831 Calhoun's friends were forced from the cabinet; before the end of 1832 Calhoun resigned as Vice-President and returned to Washington as senator from South Carolina.

Even if Jackson and Calhoun had patched up their personal disagreements, the tariff would have divided them irreparably. Jackson's position on the issue before 1830 had been ambiguous, although he conceded that protective duties were constitutional. In 1831 he recommended that the "tariff of abominations" be reduced, and in 1832 Congress passed a new measure that lowered some duties while remaining basically protective.

Calhoun's native South Carolina had made the tariff a scapegoat for chronic agricultural depression. Actually, crop after crop of cotton had taken from the soil fertility that only money, fertilizer, and time could replace. But Carolinians argued that the tariff depressed the price of cotton by reducing their market abroad, and that the duty simultaneously raised the price of goods they had to buy. South Carolinians had expected Jackson to scrap the tariff of 1828; the act of 1832 suggested that ordinary political action would not provide redress.

The attack on the tariff concealed a defense of slavery. The tariff, Calhoun wrote in 1830, was only the "occasion, rather than the real cause of the present unhappy state of things." Calhoun saw protection as part of a national assault on "the peculiar domestick [sic] institutions of the Southern States," which he proposed to protect by shoring up "the reserved rights of the states." If the federal government had too much power, a condition that a protective tariff indicated, then southern states "must in the end be forced to rebel, or submit to have . . . themselves and their children reduced to wretchedness."

When politics failed to shield the South, Calhoun was ready with an ingenious substitute. In 1828 he had secretly written the *South Carolina Exposition and Protest*, which asserted state sovereignty and from that premise deduced the power of any state to nullify federal law. In 1831 Calhoun openly restated these views in the *Fort Hill Address.* Only the states, he wrote, could determine the limits of legitimate federal authority. If, after solemn consideration, a state found federal legislation oppressive and unconstitutional, the state might formally nullify the law, which would then be unenforced. The state would not abide by such a federal law until three-quarters of the states had specifically delegated to the central government the power in question. If the state still found the statute unacceptable, secession was the final recourse. The protective tariff provided an immediate test.

Calhoun's theories were a major issue in South Carolina's legislative election held in 1832. Although Unionists made up a substantial minority, most legislators favored nullification. In accordance with Calhoun's formula, the legislature called a convention that officially nullified the tariffs of 1828 and 1832, forbade collection of duties, and prohibited appeal of the issue to the federal courts. The legislature appropriated money to equip a force to resist federal coercion. South Carolina then waited for Andrew Jackson.

The President thought himself a protector of the rights of states. Like Calhoun, Jackson believed his interpretation of the Constitution was based on the Jeffersonian principles of the Kentucky and Virginia Resolutions. No one, Jackson wrote Hayne in 1831, had a "higher regard and respect than myself" for the rights of the states. Jackson acknowledged that the central government might occasionally exceed its constitutional powers but suggested that political action was the remedy for such usurpation, which, in any case, could not "be of long duration in our enlightened country where the people rule." Once the people had spoken, he warned, opposition became revolution, and all the evils of revolution "must be looked for and expected."

So Robert Hayne, governor of South Carolina in 1832, could hardly have been surprised by the vehemence of Jackson's response to nullification. The title itself—*A Proclamation to the People of South Carolina*—brushed off state sovereignty, Calhoun's basic precept. Phrase after phrase showed the President's impatience with South Carolina's constitutional pretense: nullification carried "with it internal evidence of its impractical absurdity"; South Carolina's constitutional argument was dismissed as a "strange position," or worse, as a "metaphysical subtlety." The President thought "every man of plain unsophisticated understanding" agreed that no state could disobey legitimate federal law. Plain, unsophisticated Andrew Jackson used italics to make the point: "I consider, then, the power to annul a law of the United States, assumed by one state, *incompatible with the existence of the Union, contradicted expressly by the letter of the Constitution, unauthorized by its spirit, inconsistent with every principle on which it was founded, and destructive of the great object for which it was formed."* The Union could, Jackson asserted, coerce a disobedient state. While he hinted at the horror of disunion, he emphasized the advantages of Union in the grand manner of Daniel Webster. The central government linked the states "in one bond of common interest," defended them, encouraged their flourishing literature, arts, and commerce, and conferred on their people that proud title, *"American citizen."*

Martin Van Buren, anxious to preserve a united party, worried that Old Hickory had said too much. The President's belligerent nationalism might alienate those Democrats whose devotion to state rights exceeded their devotion to Jackson. Van Buren wrote, and the New York legislature adopted, wordy resolutions that applauded Jackson's presidency but stopped short of endorsing his uncompromising affirmation of central power. Apparently Van Buren hoped to indicate agreement with Jackson's action and at the same time to reassure those, especially in the South, who were alarmed at the sweeping assertion of national authority.

Van Buren's subtlety was probably unnecessary. Northern legislatures endorsed the President's course, usually without quibble, and southern legislatures also disavowed nullification. Some self-styled defenders of the Republican tradition deserted Jackson. John Tyler, for instance, became a state-rights Whig, but neither state-righters nor Whigs were very comfortable in the alliance, as Tyler's unhappy, accidental presidency subsequently made clear. In confronting South Carolina, Jackson sought and secured national support.

Nationalism was equally visible in Congress, where legislators tried to preserve the Union. A force bill, which authorized the President to use national troops to uphold national legislation, demonstrated that the legislature's determination complemented Jackson's. Compromisers meanwhile sought a face-saving formula to make force unnecessary. Early in 1833 Henry Clay, after consulting Calhoun, proposed that the tariff be annually reduced until, in 1842, the rates reached the level of 1816. South Carolina then withdrew its nullification of the tariff, but nullified the superfluous Force Act. Both state and nation had decided, for the moment, that political action remedied hardship more safely than a stand on constitutional principle.

The controversy over nullification disclosed the President's political philosophy. Strict construction of the federal Constitution lay at the center of Jackson's creed and at the core of his party. Old Hickory had intuitively combined the Federalist-Whig vision of a strong, unified nation with Jefferson's concern that liberty might disappear if the country were too much governed. Jackson's strict construction assumed organic union of states and sections under a federal Constitution; but he believed that the Constitution restricted the government and liberated the individual.

Jackson Fights the Bank

Although South Carolinians thought Jackson a nationalist, those who sought recharter for the Bank of the United States (BUS) thought his construction of the Constitution uncommonly strict. The Constitution, as Jackson read it, required the central government to coerce a disobedient state but did not authorize establishment of a national bank. The BUS, Jackson believed, limited the opportunity for enterprising Americans to get ahead. "The monster," as Jacksonians called the bank, had too much power and was not sufficiently subject to public control.

Two incompatible groups opposed the bank on economic grounds: one faction argued that the BUS did not permit sufficient note issue by local banks, and the other opposed issuing any bank notes at all. Through its monopoly on government deposits, the BUS accumulated the notes of state banks, which it returned for regular redemption. This cycle controlled note issue, provided a more stable currency than would have resulted without central restraint, and, in a crude way, regulated the availability of credit. But in the rapidly expanding Jacksonian economy borrowers demanded more credit to finance more expansion, so the bank's caution made enemies. On the other hand, those who disliked any paper currency preferred specie, or hard money, and instinctively disliked all banks, no matter how prudently managed.

The BUS had not been prudently managed from 1816 to 1819, but had permitted a dangerous expansion of credit. Langdon Cheves, who guided the bank between 1819 and 1823, adopted the economically necessary, but politically unpopular, policy of reducing loans to produce gradual deflation. The panic of 1819, although short, brought severe economic hardship, particularly in the West and South, where land prices had soared well above land values. Criticism of the bank, never entirely stilled, grew sharper, and neither anger nor criticism subsided when John Marshall announced in *McCulloch* v. *Maryland* (1819) that the bank was not only constitutional but practically immune to state regulation.

When Nicholas Biddle succeeded Cheves in 1823, the bank was economically secure and had survived the assaults of panics and politicians. An arrogant Philadelphia aristocrat, Biddle enlarged the institution's resources and power. Bank notes circulated at a minimal discount; government deposits were secure; federal funds were efficiently transferred; and short-term loans to the Treasury were readily available. Biddle, in short, proved to be a competent banker.

But he blundered politically. In 1832, perhaps advised by Clay, who was running against Jackson, Biddle unwisely pressed for renewal of the bank's charter just as South Carolina moved toward nullification. Four years remained on the first charter, but Biddle apparently concluded that the President would not risk interference with the bank in an election year, particularly when he already had one crisis to deal with. Jackson's attitude toward the BUS had seemed ambiguous. In his first annual message, he had wondered whether the BUS was either legitimate or appropriate. Yet, Jackson had written Biddle to thank him for meeting so efficiently the fiscal needs of the government, and secretaries of state and of the treasury whom Jackson had appointed were known to favor recharter. Congress investigated Biddle's management of the BUS and then renewed the charter by relatively small margins in both houses.

Jackson interpreted Biddle's request as a personal and political challenge, and Old Hickory seldom backed away from a fight. He returned the new charter to Congress with a prompt, unwavering, and superbly political veto. He appealed to a young nation's pride by imagining the harm that foreign stockholders might do to national security through their influence on the bank. Unmoved by Marshall's decision in the *McCulloch* case, Jackson indicted the bank as unconstitutional. It was, he held, neither necessary to the financial tasks of government nor proper as an exercise of legislative power. Strict construction demanded that the central government refrain from "invasions of the rights and powers of the several states"—strange language, South Carolinians must have thought a few months later, when the thundering presidential proclamation denouncing nullification arrived. But Jackson's strict construction tried less to secure the authority of states than to secure the liberty of individuals. The President condemned the BUS as a monopoly that limited the opportunity of enterprising Americans. Further, he held, the bank was simply too powerful; a free people could not tolerate so much power in private hands.

The veto held. Enough senators resisted the persuasive arguments of Webster and the financial pressure of Biddle to sustain Jackson and send the issue into the campaign of 1832. Biddle printed and distributed 30,000 copies of Jackson's veto message. But this tactic probably backfired, for the bank had numerous enemies: those who wanted larger quantities of paper money and the inflation that would result, those who wanted no paper money at all, those who sincerely believed the establishment of such an institution invaded the rights of states, and those who owned state banks and longed both to eliminate officious regulation by the bank and to secure a share of federal deposits.

Jackson determined to distribute those deposits among deserving state bankers and deny the BUS the use of federal funds even before the charter officially expired in 1836. Following a triumphant reelection in 1832, when his electoral vote was more than three times that of Henry Clay, the President ordered Secretary of the Treasury Louis McLane to remove the government's funds from Biddle's bank. When McLane demurred, Jackson elevated him to the State Department and appointed Joseph Duane to the Treasury. When Duane also refused, Jackson fired him without ceremony and moved Attorney General Roger B. Taney to the Treasury. In spite of a resolution that Congress considered federal funds secure, Taney reduced the government's balance; new deposits were made in state banks, called "pet banks" because political favoritism influenced their selection.

Some opponents of Jackson's banking policy had a sense of humor

The federal deposits permitted state banks to lend more money and led to rapid inflation in the mid-1830s. The cost of living increased more than 60 percent in the last two years of Jackson's presidency, to the distress of urban laborers in particular. Speculation and easier credit combined to drive land sales and prices up; between 1835 and 1837 the government sold more than forty million acres, a rate of sale about twenty times greater than that of the previous decade. Foreign investment, especially in roads and canals, also stimulated economic growth.

But the speculative boom ended shortly after Jackson issued the Specie Circular in 1836, which required hard money, rather than inflated paper currency, for the purchase of government land. The demand for specie forced banks to curtail credit; before the end of 1837 more than six hundred of them had failed. Meanwhile, British demand for cotton dropped, and the sale and price of land in the new southern states dropped in response. Old Hickory retired in 1837 before the panic became a dismal depression. Martin Van Buren inherited the party, the presidency, and the political opprobrium that accompanied economic distress.

The Van Buren Administration

The nation's economic paralysis was no more acute than the political paralysis of Van Buren's administration. Martin Van Buren won an impressive victory in 1836, but he could not translate it into an impressive legislative record. Congress refused to permit a periodic gradual reduction in the price of less desirable federal land that remained unsold years after an area had been surveyed. Nor could Van Buren persuade Congress to establish permanently the system of preemption, a policy first temporarily adopted in 1830 that allowed squatters to purchase land they had improved before the area was legally opened for settlement and sale.

Like Jackson, Van Buren was an advocate of laissez faire. He believed that government must keep its fiscal affairs in order and rely on private initiative to restore public prosperity when depression struck. Van Buren's response to the financial crisis, then, was essentially negative. He would not revoke the Specie Circular, although even Democrats argued that repeal would restore public confidence and raise land values. Critical of state banks, he would not permit the Treasury's surplus to be distributed to the states, as had been done late in the Jackson administration. Instead, he asked Congress to establish an Independent Treasury system that would divorce the government from banking by establishing subtreasuries in major cities to hold federal funds. Since these subtreasuries were not to lend money, deposits would be secure at a time when bank failures were legion. But with security went deflation, for the failure to make economic use of government reserves deprived the economy of a major source of credit.

On July 4, 1840, when the Independent Treasury was enacted, Democrats hailed it as a declaration of economic independence comparable in importance to the great Declaration written sixty-four years before. Van Buren's wing of the party, which included reformers and working people, believed that the national government should keep taxes and appropriations to an absolute minimum. This coalition opposed monopoly, privilege, all banks, and paper money and held that each individual must have an equal opportunity to push aside all rivals in the race for riches. The government's responsibility was to see that the race was fair, not to enable everyone to reach the goal more quickly, as advocates of federal activity would have it, nor to encourage a favored few with such privileges as corporate charters.

Even the Supreme Court, that last bastion of federalism, succumbed to Jacksonian economic ideas. Roger B. Taney, who succeeded Marshall as chief justice in 1835, had helped write Jackson's message vetoing recharter of the BUS and then had removed the government's deposits; in 1837 he stiffened Van Buren's resolve to retain the Specie Circular. It was also in 1837 that Chief Justice Taney turned some Jacksonian economic principles into legal precedents in the *Charles River Bridge* case.

Chartered by Massachusetts in the eighteenth century, the Charles River Bridge Company collected substantial profit from the tolls on the only bridge between Boston and Charlestown. In 1828 the legislature granted another company the right to construct a second bridge not far from the first. After construction costs of the new bridge were paid, moreover, tolls would be abolished. The Charles River Bridge Company, maintaining that its franchise was exclusive, sued to prevent

Massachusetts from breaking the contract implied in its corporate charter.

Taney could find nothing in the charter making the original grant a monopoly. The company had "no exclusive privilege . . . over the waters of the Charles River," and "no right to prevent other persons" from erecting a competitive bridge from which the community would benefit. To be sure, Taney admitted, "the rights of private property are sacredly guarded," but, he added, "the community also have rights and the happiness . . . of every citizen depends on their faithful preservation." Governments did not by implication surrender these rights to "privileged corporations."

Both the attack on privilege and the finding that a popular majority could curb a corporation were sound Jacksonian doctrines. Although conservatives complained that private property was no longer safe, in fact Taney's decision unquestionably encouraged economic growth. For had the Court protected monopoly, technical innovation and economic enterprise might have been stifled.

The Whigs Organize

For two decades after James Monroe retired to Virginia, politics was the national pastime. One campaign after another kept the growing electorate in a state of excitement. Partisan editors and ambitious candidates exposed the misdeeds of their opponents. New political parties sought offices and spoils and sometimes the enactment of a program. Once a voter had identified himself with one of these parties, he tended to vote for the whole ticket, regardless of his economic or social status, his ethnic or religious affiliation, or his view of what politicians called "issues." The rank and file Democrat was more apt to be Irish or Catholic than the Whig in the street, who was more receptive to blue laws and temperance than his rival. Neither was ordinarily as well-to-do as the party leaders who sought public support; politicians, then and later, promised to do good, but meant to do well. Jackson's habit of speculating in real estate did not end when he moved to the White House; Webster's political eminence enhanced his legal fees. To be sure, the two men and the parties they led differed but not about fundamental matters like the sanctity of property, the preservation of the Union, and political democracy. Ideological differences between parties were rarely as important as personal antipathies and local disagreements over jobs, taxes, and regulations.

Opponents of the Jacksonians gradually gathered in a coherent party called Whig. In 1836 Whigs had so little resembled a national organization that different candidates, each calculated to appeal to his own section, had carried the party's hopes. Daniel Webster failed to carry the Northeast, but William Henry Harrison showed surprising strength in the Northwest, and Hugh White carried Tennessee and Georgia. Whig strategists had hoped for a scattered vote that would require the House to elect the President. But Van Buren secured a majority of both the popular vote and the electoral college.

Failure to agree on a single candidate in their first campaign was symptomatic of deep divisions among Whigs. Insofar as it had a program, the party preferred Clay's American system, but Whigs organized initially more to oppose Jacksonians than to advance a program. Adherents ranged from southern advocates of state sovereignty, who found Jackson's stand on nullification intolerable, to northern advocates of strong central authority. Whigs drew support from plantation owners like John Tyler, representatives of northern manufacturing and commercial interests like Daniel Webster, and ambitious westerners like Abraham Lincoln. Composed of diverse interests, classes, and varying political philosophies, the Whigs soon discovered that unity and victory could be achieved only by imitating the formula the Jacksonians had evolved in

Whig campaign march

1828: they emphasized what they opposed and nominated a candidate whose heroic reputation concealed uncertain political views.

The election of 1840 revealed how well Whigs had learned the techniques of mass politics. William Henry Harrison led the national ticket, which was judiciously balanced with John Tyler, a Virginian who championed state rights. The party maintained popular ignorance of Harrison's political convictions by adopting no platform at all. In lieu of issues, Whigs provided songs, slogans, symbols, fireworks, food, drink, parades, and the reiterated accusation that Van Buren had inappropriate, aristocratic taste in wine, china, and furnishings, which he indulged at public expense. Harrison, by contrast, was depicted as a simple son of the frontier, born in a log cabin, weaned on hard cider. Excitement, plus local effort by both parties, brought more people to the polls than had participated in any previous national election; nearly 80 percent of the eligible voters cast ballots. The interest of the ordinary voter turned the campaign into a contest to determine which candidate was more common. By a slim popular majority, but a wide margin in the electoral college, Harrison won.

Whigs campaigned better than they governed. Harrison named Webster secretary of state and appointed several of Clay's followers to key posts, apparently to administer the American system that was to be enacted. But a month after his inauguration Harrison died, and the new President, John Tyler, was hostile to concentrated federal power and the American system. Clay rallied the party's legislative forces and introduced a tariff, a bill to revive the BUS, and a measure to finance internal improvements from land sales. In a complex political maneuver in 1842, Clay abandoned his scheme to finance internal improvements, and Tyler accepted a tariff that restored the protective duties of 1832. Although the Independent Treasury was repealed in 1841, Tyler twice vetoed bills to charter a third national bank.

If Tyler's presidency was legislatively almost barren, it was nevertheless politically important. Following the second failure to secure Tyler's approval of a bank bill, his cabinet resigned, with the exception of Webster, who was concluding a treaty with England. The Whigs then read Tyler out of the party, whose program he had never found congenial. At the end of his term, Tyler invited Calhoun, another man without a party, to join the administration as secretary of state. Together, the two southerners secured the annexation of Texas, an action that the voters had apparently endorsed a few months earlier by electing James K. Polk, an expansionist Democrat, to succeed Tyler. Calhoun and Tyler, both of whom had left the Democratic party because of Jackson's nationalism, rejoined the Democrats after 1845. Their presence among Democrats tipped that party toward the South, while the Whigs became perceptibly less southern. And the preservation of the Union depended upon a precarious sectional equilibrium in the nation's two political parties.

Suggested Reading

A good recent survey of Jacksonian Democracy is Edward Pessen's *Jacksonian America* (revised ed., 1978), which includes an excellent bibliography. Douglas T. Miller, *The Birth of Modern America, 1820–1860* (1970), focuses on socioeconomic developments. Pessen, in *Riches, Class, and Power Before the Civil War* (1973), and Miller, in *Jacksonian Aristocracy** (1967), are responsible in part for a deemphasis on equalitarianism, which used to be the major theme of the period. Glyndon G. Van Deusen's *The Jacksonian Era** (1959) is a balanced narrative. Influential interpretations include Arthur M. Schlesinger, Jr., *The Age of Jackson** (1945), which stresses the political rivalry between classes, and Lee Benson, *The Concept of Jacksonian Democracy** (1961), which stresses the similarities between Whigs and Democrats. The perceptive account of Alexis de Tocqueville, *Democracy in America** (1855), is in a class by itself.

The crises of Jackson's first administration are analyzed in William W. Freehling, *Prelude to Civil War** (1966), which suggests that slavery as well as the tariff precipitated nullification, and in Bray Hammond, *Banks and Politics in America from the Revolution to the Civil War** (1955). Other works more favorable to Jackson's economic policies include Peter Temin's *The Jacksonian Economy** (1969) and James R. Sharp's *The Jacksonians Versus the Banks* (1970). *The Removal of the Choctaw Indians* (1970) by Arthur H. De Rosier, Jr., is more specific than Francis P. Prucha's *American Indian Policy in the Formative Years** (1962). See also *American Indian Policy in the Jacksonian Era* (1974) by Ronald N. Satz.

Jacksonian politics is the focus of Robert V. Remini's *Martin Van Buren and the Making of the Democratic Party** (1959) and of Richard P. McCormick's *The Second American Party System** (1966). Ronald Formisano's *The Birth of Mass Political Parties* (1971) concentrates on Michigan, but has a wider relevance. Marvin Meyers, in *The Jacksonian Persuasion** (1957), and John W. Ward, in *Andrew Jackson: Symbol for an Age** (1955), concentrate on the rhetoric and imagery of Jacksonian politics. Robert V. Remini has written several important books on the period, including *Andrew Jackson and the Course of American Empire* (1977), the first volume of a major biography. James C. Curtis, who has examined the presidency of Martin Van Buren in *The Fox at Bay* (1970), tries his hand at psychological interpretation in *Andrew Jackson and the Search for Vindication* (1976).

* Available in paperback edition

Chapter 8
A People in Motion

Chronology

1817—25 Construction of Erie Canal •

1819 *Savannah* becomes first steamer to complete transatlantic run •

1822 Textile factories open in Lowell, Massachusetts •

1828 Construction of Baltimore and Ohio Railroad begins •

1831 First issue of *The Liberator*, Garrison's abolitionist paper •

1838 The National Road reaches Vandalia, Illinois •

1842 Massachusetts Supreme Court permits labor organization in *Commonwealth* v. *Hunt* •

1844 Samuel F. B. Morse sends first telegraph message •

1846 Elias Howe invents sewing machine •

1847 Mormon migration to Utah begins •

1848 Women's rights convention in Seneca Falls, New York •

1851 Herman Melville's *Moby Dick* published •

1854 Clipper ship *Flying Cloud* sails from New York to San Francisco in 89 days •

In the years between the Battle of New Orleans and the shelling of Fort Sumter, a rapidly increasing population rushed to settle the expanding American nation. New Americans from Ireland, Scandinavia, and Germany poured down gangplanks and either went west to small, trim farms or stayed in the cities, where they joined established Americans who had abandoned unprofitable land nearby. All Americans grew more crops, wove more cloth, distilled more whisky, and traded with more frenzy in their headlong dash for prosperity.

Many succeeded. Optimistic Americans needed only to look about them to vindicate their faith in the perfectibility of man. While population jumped fourfold, productive capacity more than kept pace. While territory increased, canals, railroads, and telegraphs simultaneously made distances shrink. The constant ferment of democratic politics also testified to the nation's belief in the importance of the individual. Progress seemed the inevitable result of human activity and almost an additional right of American citizenship.

Yet some, who wanted to create a new heaven in the New World, were not satisfied. Visions of utopia varied. As each peddler had his own brand of snake oil, each reformer had his own panacea. New millennial sects promised salvation following an imminent day of judgement. Secular prophets preached phrenology and decried the evils of yeast with a fervor worthy of better causes. And better causes—free, universal public education, equality for women, abolition of debtors' prisons, compassionate treatment of the insane—did attract energetic reformers. Some daring souls even suggested that the black population might share the nation's progress and bounty, but the public was not yet ready to listen sympathetically to those who advocated abolition of slavery or racial equality.

Carrying the Freight

In 1816 an American importer paid about nine dollars and waited about fifty days for a ton of merchandise to cross the Atlantic; for another nine dollars, he could ship the same goods thirty miles over miserable roads into the interior, a trip that might take several days. Such expense discouraged internal trade, and each settlement consequently sought to supply most of what it consumed. Farmers produced for their table, not for market. Farmers' wives preserved food, made cloth, and bargained with itinerant vendors for needles, pans, and clocks. What manufacturing there was usually took place in the home, for factories were rare and machinery not widely available.

By 1860 an American importer paid less than five dollars to bring a ton of goods across the Atlantic in less than two weeks. He could ship these goods the 450 miles from New York to Buffalo in about the same time and at about the same expense that 30 miles had required in 1816, so internal trade flourished. American farmers in 1860 grew most of the world's cotton and had begun to export grain on a large scale. Farmers' wives bought cloth from dry goods counters; the peddler was almost a memory. Flour mills, textile mills, iron foundries, and distilleries processed the products of mine and soil. Sewing machines, reapers, and steam engines multiplied the nation's output. Some Americans, particularly on the frontier or on rural ridges in both North and South, clung to self-sufficiency; for the rest of the country, the still incomplete market economy revealed the shape of the future.

Since transportation seemed to mean prosperity, political controversy surrounded construction of roads, canals, and railroads—called internal improvements in the political vocabulary of the day. The federal government intermittently diverted to road building a fraction of the income from land sales and eventually used other federal lands to subsidize the construction of railroads. More often, states opened their treasuries and mortgaged future revenues to support local projects, especially after the spectacular success of New York's Erie Canal. The connection of the Great Lakes with the Atlantic in 1825 captured the nation's imagination, made New York the envy of every port on the coast, inspired an epidemic of canal construction, and brought prosperity and people to New York City, where the population increased more than 250 percent in the twenty years after 1820. Freight costs between New York and Buffalo dropped 95 percent between 1817 and 1857. By providing access to the eastern market, the canal permitted settlement of parts of the Northwest that could not use the Mississippi.

Philadelphia, Boston, and Baltimore also bid for the trade of the continent. Canal building did not seem formidable; amateur engineers had supervised construction of the Erie, which initially was just an overgrown ditch with only four feet of water. But the way west from these ports required more locks and such improvisations as hoists to haul canalboats over hills. Ohio, Illinois, and other western states also dug canals. But no canal could effectively compete with the railroads completed only a few years later. With the immensely important exception of the Erie and a very few other projects, canals disappointed investors. In the depression of the late 1830s, some states discovered they could not afford their canals and repudiated bonds that had financed construction, an action that outraged investors on both sides of the Atlantic.

River traffic required no bond issue and comparatively little investment. Yet the river steamer transformed American life no less than did the canalboats. Between 1815 and 1860 steamboats cut by about four-fifths both time and cost of shipment on the Mississippi River system. Between 1820 and 1850 the value of goods arriving in New Orleans from the interior increased more than thirteen times and amounted to more than $185 million. New Orleans in these years grew more rapidly than New York, and Cincinnati, St. Louis, and other river towns handled more commerce than many ocean ports. The volume of traffic on the rivers partly caused and clearly demonstrated the economic vitality of the hinterland.

By 1860 all water routes faced stiff competition from 30,000 miles of railroad track. That year rails carried as much bulk freight as did waterways, and the value of commodities carried by rail was substantially larger. The advance of the rail network was even more striking than the canal boom. In 1830 about 1,200 miles of canals, mainly in New York, Pennsylvania, and Ohio, had no competition from 73 miles of track; by 1840 canal and railroad mileages were nearly equal at 3,300 miles. While canal construction virtually ceased, railroad mileage nearly tripled before 1850 and more than tripled again before 1860. Once across the Appalachians, railroads spread rapidly through the Midwest; in 1860 Illinois contained more track than New York or Pennsylvania, and Indiana had almost twice as much as Massachusetts.

Trains cut distances and costs even more than did earlier innovations in transportation. Passengers traveled more comfortably, more cheaply, and at least twice as fast as in the best stagecoach. Steamers and canalboats could compete with railroads in cost and comfort, but they were usually much slower. Between 1816 and 1860, passenger fares dropped about 60 percent and freight rates fell more sharply. Reduced freight charges enabled midwestern farmers to supply eastern markets more cheaply than local farmers. Some of the less prosperous eastern farmers joined the urban population; a few rode the railroads to new lands in the West.

Perhaps more than any other economic change the growth of the rail network pushed the United States into the future. Railroads emancipated the nation from parochialism by fostering the growth of cities and by breaking down the isolation of outlying settlements. Rivalry among cities, states, and sections for the control and location of railroads baffled political leaders who tried in the 1850s to balance competing interests. The economic effect, even beyond the impact on freight rates, was immense. Railroads were themselves an almost insatiable market for iron, coal, and immigrant labor. Together with improved river transportation and canals, they permitted the development of a national market, without which manufacturing might have been indefinitely delayed.

Once the nation's surplus produce arrived by river or rail at New York or New Orleans, the thriving American merchant marine hauled it to markets abroad. Although the glamorous clippers were the fastest vessels afloat, most freight was carried in slower ships of greater capacity.

ROUTES TO THE WEST

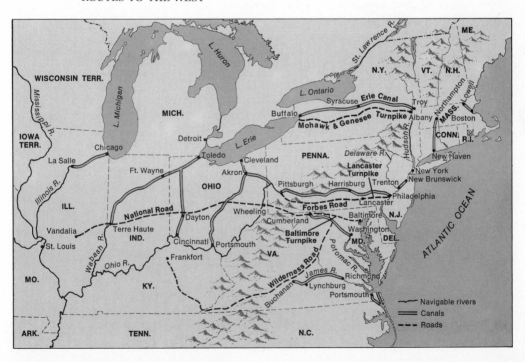

The railroad crosses the Appalachians

Clippers reduced sailing time from New York to San Francisco by nearly half; on all the world's oceans American ships and shippers set records and made money. But, perhaps dazzled by the clippers' success, Americans were slow to invest in iron vessels and steam power, and when the age of wood and sail ended, so too, for some time, did the prestige and prosperity of the American merchant marine.

Farm and Plantation

The nation's richest resource was its soil. Even in New England, the most urban part of the United States, only one-third of the population lived in towns in 1860; in the South and Midwest, more than 85 percent of the population was rural. Many of these farmers remained nearly self-sufficient, and the economy passed them by. But for the ambitious, progressive farmer in 1860, agriculture was a business; he grew a crop that he could convert to cash in the market. Cash-crop farming required a heavy investment, whether in a reaper to harvest wheat or in slaves to pick cotton. But the return was better than that of the small farmer with a patch of beans and a few hogs.

Those who remained self-sufficient did so partly because independent farming was more than a way of making ends meet; it was a way of life. These sturdy settlers—tough, thrifty, hard-working, self-reliant—raised few surplus crops. Such pioneers cut the trees of Wisconsin, broke the sod of Illinois, and planted a little cotton in the virgin soil of Alabama. Abraham Lincoln's family illustrates the pattern. Lincoln's father, a rootless farmer, migrated from Virginia to Kentucky, where Abraham was born. Before young Lincoln was twenty-one, the family had moved twice more, first to Indiana and then to southern Illinois. The hardship of Lincoln's early years is proverbial, but life for the Lincolns was no more severe than it was for thousands of other farm families. Combat with the wilderness, ague, Indians, climate, and creditors was constant; each day contained as many working hours as daylight and strength permitted. And the long working day was as common on self-sufficient farms in the hills of New Hampshire or Virginia as it was on the frontier. All these farmers, vaguely suspicious of the comfort for which they apparently toiled, itched to move on when neighbors moved too close.

Since land speculation was the national pastime, moving on was easy. In the years immediately following the War of 1812, and again just before the panic of 1837, settlers surged into new cotton lands in Alabama, Mississippi, Louisiana, Florida, and Arkansas. The same waves of migration settled grain lands in the old Northwest, Missouri, and Iowa.

The first crop in the upper Mississippi Valley was corn, which went to market in the form of hogs. Hogs could harvest the crop themselves and, if necessary, walk some distance to market. But the world preferred wheat to corn or hogs, and in the 1840s, attracted by better prices and greater profits, farmers shifted to wheat where soil permitted. In the 1850s, wheat production increased about 75 percent; widespread use of the mechanical reaper, which Cyrus McCormick began to market extensively in the 1850s, seemed to promise that farmers could harvest even greater yields.

McCormick's reaper was only one of several technological changes that permitted the rapid expansion of northern agriculture. In 1837 John Deere perfected a steel plow, which others improved in the 1850s. Deere's implement, unlike earlier ones, cut prairie sod cleanly. The revolving disc harrow, invented in 1847, and a device to knot twine, which improved harvesting machinery, further reduced time and labor required on northern fields.

But machinery and good land cost money, particularly as denser settlement drove all land prices up. And so, even before the Civil War, the Jeffersonian dream no longer corresponded to the reality of commercial

Cotton for export

farming. For the commercial farmer was as much a businessman as the owner of any store or small manufacturing establishment. He produced crops for sale, not for personal consumption—and money, as well as independence, was the object of his enterprise.

Planters, as the South called its commercial farmers, invested their capital in land and slave labor. The world price of sugar, cotton, and tobacco was as crucial to the plantation owner as the price of wheat was to the northern grain-producer. In a sense, the price of cotton affected the whole nation. Even in the 1850s, when production leveled off following a threefold increase in the preceding twenty years, cotton still made up about one-half of all American exports. The South's crop earned much of the nation's foreign exchange and provided the raw material for many of the North's mills, which, in turn, produced cheap cloth to clothe southern slaves. Northern merchants collected shipping and insurance charges, commissions on sales of cotton, and profits on consumer goods. When the planter spent his receipts, the cash barely paused on its way North, where it circulated throughout the more diversified economy, stimulating more investment and creating more capital.

Rich soil, the high price of cotton, and, while it lasted, prosperity made the South indifferent to other forms of economic activity, except for an occasional angry outburst against Yankee profiteers. When cotton prices fell, seaboard planters fared less well than those with newer, more fertile plantations in the Gulf States. South Carolina, economically pinched in the early 1830s, was quick to blame the tariff for its trouble. Although other southern states were not so vehemently opposed, the entire region eventually came to regard protective tariffs as a device to enrich northern manufacturers at the expense of southern planters.

The planters' low profits have also been attributed to slavery itself, which imposed costs and risks that those who hired workers avoided. Slave-owners had to feed, clothe, and house infants, the aged, and the sick, who were not economically productive. Both invested capital and the labor force might disappear as a consequence of an epidemic, antislavery legislation, or the lure of freedom. Yet slave-owners, who bid up the price of prime field hands from between $400 and $500 in 1800 to between $1200 and $1800 in 1860, knew that the system was ordinarily profitable, perhaps as profitable as investment in northern agriculture or industry.

Defenders of slavery, who were more prevalent and more forceful after 1830, did not rest their case on profits. Apologists cited Aristotle and the Bible to document their contention that slavery was the way of the civilized world, that the bondage of some enabled others to furnish society with direction, distinction, and progress. Few slave-owners felt a direct, personal guilt about a system they had not invented and for which they, like Thomas Jefferson and others, could imagine no acceptable substitute.

But those arguments would not have seemed so convincing to anyone had the slaves not been black, for slavery regulated race relations as well as labor. With rare exceptions, white Americans—North as well as South—believed blacks to be barbarous at worst, childlike at best, and, in any case, inferior. Slave-owners defended themselves from their antislavery critics and from their own latent misgivings by pointing to the service they performed for the entire society, including the slaves. The defense of slavery as a positive good stressed the duties of whites: a duty to provide employment and the necessities of life for those who would otherwise be helpless; a duty to discipline and govern a race that had no capacity for self-control and no acquaintance with liberty; a duty to provide the example of civilized conduct that might eventually uplift a people only recently removed from savagery. "It is the slaves who own me," remarked a planter's weary wife after a night spent attending a birth in the slave quarters.

But, of course, the slaves did not own her at law, as her husband owned the baby she had helped to deliver. Whatever mutual obligations slavery imposed, the paternalistic defense glossed over the stark fact of ownership. Whites expected labor, deference, and sometimes affection, which seemed a more than adequate recompense for the services they provided blacks. Slaves sensed that whites needed ritualistic respect to

TOTAL WHITE POPULATION AND SLAVEHOLDING IN THE SOUTH: 1860

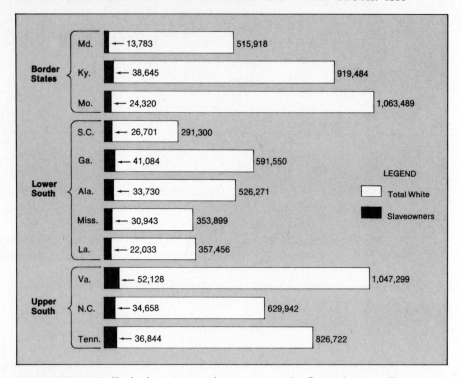

Source: Henry F. Bedford, *The Union Divides*, p. 6. Copyright © 1963 by Macmillan Publishing Co., Inc.

persuade themselves that control of their chattels rested on consent as well as on power, that they were humane individuals even if they did own slaves. Slaves occasionally withheld that respect, thereby indicating disapproval through action just short of refusing to work or running away. They could not force a "bad" owner to conform to custom, but they could, within limits, punish those who interfered with their religious observances, refused to grant holidays, whipped without cause, or disturbed family relationships.

Although the marriages of slaves had no legal standing, and although auctions did rupture families, blacks built stable relationships that extended across generations and often across miles. Owners salved their consciences, and sometimes excused their behavior, by alleging that blacks were by nature sexually promiscuous and that family ties were therefore casual and unimportant. But the innumerable examples of anguish because of families separated at auctions ought to have challenged that rationalization, and the instances of affectionate family life among slaves ought to have ended it. In so far as they could, blacks kept track of cousins and other relatives. Bonds of kinship, together with religion and the shared experience of plantation agriculture, created a

RAFFLE

DARK BAY HORSE, "STAR,"

Aged five years, square trotter and warranted sound; with a new light Trotting Buggy and Harness; also, the dark, stout

MULATTO GIRL, "SARAH,"

Aged about twenty years, general house servant, valued at *nine hundred dollars*, and guaranteed, and

Will be Raffled for

At 4 o'clock P. M., February first, at the selection hotel of the subscribers. The above is as represented, and those persons who may wish to engage in the usual practice of raffling, will, I assure them, be perfectly satisfied with their destiny in this affair.

The whole is valued at its just worth, fifteen hundred dollars; fifteen hundred

CHANCES AT ONE DOLLAR EACH.

The Raffle will be conducted by gentlemen selected by the interested subscribers present. Five nights will be allowed to complete the Raffle. BOTH OF THE ABOVE DESCRIBED CAN BE SEEN AT MY STORE, No. 78 Common St., second door from Camp, at from 9 o'clock A. M. to 2 P. M.

Highest throw to take the first choice; the lowest throw the remaining prize, and the fortunate winners will pay twenty dollars each for the refreshments furnished on the occasion.

N. B. No chances recognized unless paid for previous to the commencement.

JOSEPH JENNINGS.

black community that offered comfort and support for individuals whom the system wronged.

Abolitionists emphasized those wrongs—the individual acts of cruelty and the moral outrage of slavery itself, which no personal kindness could disguise. Some slaves were indeed badly housed, underfed, overworked, whipped, raped, bred, raised, and sold in the market like animals, as abolitionists charged. But not on every plantation, and perhaps not on most. As apologists for slavery assumed that masters everywhere treated their chattels with benign paternalism, so abolitionists postulated universal cruelty.

The contradiction stemmed not only from moral disagreement, but from the fact that slavery was an infinitely varied way of life. Some blacks never took advantage of the fact that masters needed slaves more than slaves needed masters; some blacks lacked the faith or family that sustained the determination of individuals and enabled peaceful,

THE LIFE EXPECTATION AT BIRTH FOR U.S. SLAVES AND VARIOUS FREE POPULATIONS, 1830—1920

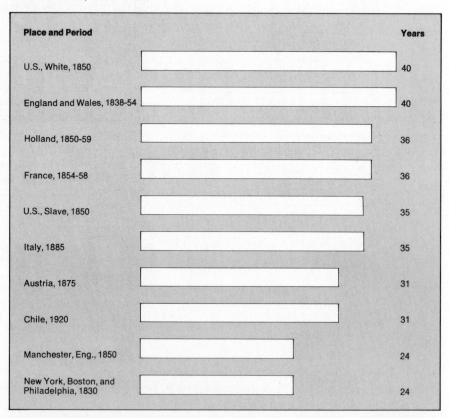

Place and Period		Years
U.S., White, 1850		40
England and Wales, 1838-54		40
Holland, 1850-59		36
France, 1854-58		36
U.S., Slave, 1850		35
Italy, 1885		35
Austria, 1875		31
Chile, 1920		31
Manchester, Eng., 1850		24
New York, Boston, and Philadelphia, 1830		24

Source: Robert W. Fogel and Stanley L. Engerman, *Time on the Cross*, p. 125. Copyright © 1974 by Little, Brown and Company. Used with permission.

collective resistance. The expectations of blacks on small farms (and the overwhelming majority of farmers owned fewer than ten slaves) differed from those on plantations or those whose labor was rented to other planters or to industries. Work norms varied with a plantation's crop and location. Slaves who were permitted to hunt, fish, and garden ate a more diverse diet than those who depended entirely on the grain their masters customarily dispensed. The religious life that gave coherence to one slave community might in another serve to abet racial control. On some plantations, house servants looked down on field hands, while on others no lines of caste divided the blacks.

As slavery differed from place to place, so also did it change from year to year. Between 1830 and 1860, for instance, the chance of securing freedom diminished and in that respect the system became more repressive. More patrols searched for runaways and more statutes prohibited manumission. Yet in the same three decades living conditions improved. Most slaves apparently had single-family dwellings roughly equal in area (though not in construction) to the tenements of urban laborers in the North, and consumed more calories (though less milk and meat) than northern workers. Health care in the slave quarters was comparable to that available in the plantation house; although infant mortality was higher among slaves than in the nation at large, the rate was about the same as for southern whites.

If slavery was not uniformly harsh, that condition bespeaks the ingenuity of blacks as well as the kindness of whites, for slave-owners were "molded by their slaves as much as their slaves [were] molded by them," the historian Eugene Genovese has observed. Yet overt uprisings did occur. In 1822, South Carolinians nipped a conspiracy led by Denmark Vesey, a free black, and Virginians put down Nat Turner's bloody insurrection in 1832. Mounted patrols and whippings and sleep made uneasy by vigilance mocked the complacent assurance that slaves welcomed their bondage, that blacks were incapable of freedom. Slave-owners heard the longing for liberty that pervaded spirituals and sermons in black congregations. But slaves ordinarily swallowed their rebellion, and masters their misgivings. Repression left psychic scars that disfigured both groups and defy the therapy of time.

Mills and Workers

Machinery made the northern mill worker more productive than the southern slave. The economic development of the North, paced by factory towns like Lowell, Massachusetts, soon outstripped the economic growth of the South. In 1815 Lowell was a sheep pasture; in the 1830s Lowell boasted nine churches, a school budget of $7,000 for about 3,000 children, a canal, the beginning of a railroad to Boston, and perhaps

15,000 inhabitants. Lowell boomed because the textile industry boomed, as revealed by the mounting number of spindles used. In 1820, the American cotton industry used 22,000 spindles. In five years, the number had nearly quadrupled, and by 1840 it had more than tripled again. In the forty years before 1860 the activity of American cotton mills increased twenty-five times, to 5,235,000 spindles. And in 1860, when 3 percent of Americans were employed in industry, 36 percent of Lowell's citizens were at work in the mills. Lowell was the prototype for other industrial cities, where mass production developed to meet the growing demand of a national market.

The Napoleonic wars interrupted commerce and stimulated domestic production of some formerly imported goods. Such manufacturing often took place in farmhouses, where families performed part of a manu-facturing operation to supplement their income and occupy their time during the winter. A middleman left raw material and collected finished produce, which then went on to another farmhouse, where another stage in the process took place. In factories, such as those established at Lowell, all these operations were performed more efficiently under one roof.

As a general principle, most Americans probably shared Thomas Jefferson's aversion to factories and his fear that the "mobs" resident in industrial cities menaced republican government. These impressions derived from descriptions of European cities where industrialization was in its grimiest, least attractive stage. The proprietors of the Lowell mills intended to make their enterprise compatible with American ideals. To avoid urban blight and a permanent factory caste, they located their factories in the country and recruited young women to work there; they expected that, after a few years, the women would leave and devote themselves to "the higher and more appropriate responsibilities of [their] sex." Employers built dormitories and monitored the conduct of their female employee-boarders, thereby avoiding the disorderly development and "anarchic" behavior associated with European cities. But Lowell and other American factory cities quickly grew beyond the control of their founders. The Irish who worked around the mills built their own "shanties" and some of the mill workers developed an independent view of appropriate "ladylike" behavior. By 1844, Sarah Bagley had organized the Lowell Female Labor Reform Association, which recruited members in other textile cities and published *Factory Tracts* to contradict the view of order and decorum that visitors like the novelist Charles Dickens and the factory owners perpetuated.

Textile factories used the labor of women and children more than other manufacturing enterprises. Although the proportion of children in the mills declined after 1820, probably about 40 percent of textile workers were women in the 1830s. Wage statistics are unreliable, and a cost-of-living index is unavailable. If estimates are accurate, however, an urban family of five needed at least $10 per week for immediate expenses;

frequently a man could not earn that much in a factory. Women and children worked, then, because their wages were essential. The conventional working day, like that on the farm, ran from sunrise into the evening, between eleven and fourteen hours.

In the usual American pattern, urban workers asked for legislation to improve their condition. They wanted education and land, two conventional nineteenth-century panaceas, and sought laws to guarantee universal, free public education as well as a Homestead Act to provide free federal land to settlers. In the 1830s a Workingman's Party championed both of these demands in New York. Workers also asked for immediate relief through legislation limiting the working day to ten hours. In 1840 President Martin Van Buren issued an executive order that limited to ten hours the workday on federal projects. State legislatures in New Hampshire, Maine, Pennsylvania, Ohio, New Jersey, and Rhode Island passed ten-hour laws by 1857. But the acts were widely violated and badly enforced.

And the organizations Sarah Bagley and others formed were not effective substitutes for the state's protection. Artisans and skilled craftsmen, such as those in the construction and shoe trades, occasionally formed local unions. But the general public was almost always hostile to a strike; those strikes that did occur were almost always futile. Textile and other industrial workers had less bargaining power than craftsmen, and unions did not ordinarily organize mass-production industries until the twentieth century. Government, furthermore, was apt to regard any labor organization as a conspiracy in restraint of trade and a violation of the common law. In 1842, in *Commonwealth* v. *Hunt*, the supreme court of Massachusetts ruled that trade unions could legitimately use strikes to back their demand for exclusive employment. In spite of this precedent unions continued to meet legal obstacles for decades afterward.

Corporations also encountered legal obstacles in state legislatures, whose approval was required early in the nineteenth century to enact corporate charters. The corporate form of business organization enabled entrepreneurs to accumulate the capital required to build factories. The syndicate that built Lowell, for instance, put $600,000 into the initial venture; by 1860, investment in Lowell's mills alone exceeded the cost of constructing the Erie Canal. However economically essential, capital on this scale roused the apprehension of egalitarian politicians, who were reluctant to support charters that sometimes implied monopoly and often appeared to protect privilege. These charters typically permitted a corporation to collect capital through a public sale of shares, which offered stockholders ownership without direct responsibility for day-to-day management. Unlike other forms of business organization, in the event the business failed, owners were liable only to the extent of their investment; other personal property could not be seized to satisfy the corporation's debts. So fast was the nation's economy expanding, and

Cincinnati, 1838: manufacturing was not a monopoly of New England

so handy was the corporate form, that many states by the 1840s had enacted standard laws of incorporation. When legislatures no longer had to enact individual charters, popular prejudice against corporate "privilege" gradually subsided.

Capital and labor combined to push goods out of the factories at an astounding rate. The value of manufactures in 1860 was twelve times the figure for 1815, whereas population had increased only four times in that period. In 1850 American industrial production topped a billion dollars and for the first time surpassed the annual total of all American agriculture, including cotton. Although by 1860 agriculture regained the lead with nearly $2 billion in crops, industrial production climbed nearly as rapidly. The Census of 1860 held bad news for those who thought cotton still king; the combined production of the iron, leather, and boot and shoe industries surpassed in value all the South's cotton.

Yet cotton was still the raw material for one of the most important industries. Manufacturers of cotton goods employed almost 115,000 workers, a number surpassed only by the total in the boot and shoe industry. Cotton manufacturing was second to no other enterprise in value added by manufacture, that is, in the difference between cost of raw material and value of finished product. Lumber, once the chief American finished product, was second in 1860, followed by boots and shoes, flour, men's clothing, iron, machinery, and woolens.

Unlike agriculture, manufacturing was not a national enterprise. More than half the mills were in New England or the middle states, where nearly three-quarters of the capital was invested and two-thirds of the total value of all manufactured goods produced. Industry was also firmly established in the Midwest. But only about one-tenth of the nation's industry was located in the slave states.

Americans invented some of the machinery that was essential to industrialization, and they applied the ideas of others as well. American inventions included the telegraph, which Samuel F. B. Morse first demonstrated in 1844; the rotary printing press, perfected by Richard Hoe in 1846; the sewing machine, invented by Elias Howe in 1846; and various adaptations of Howe's machine for use in manufacturing shoes. Equally significant were American modifications of methods and inventions borrowed from other countries. The unification of manufacturing under one roof and the use of steam power to run boats and trains as well as belts and pulleys in factories were not initially American ideas. Nor was mass production, which depends upon interchangeable parts, although Eli Whitney and other arms manufacturers were among the first to try it.

Buoyed by a swelling economy, then, the American industrial revolution had started before the Civil War began. Entrepreneurs were already combining technology, transportation, labor, capital, and raw material to produce more goods for more Americans. Government, geography, and fate also cooperated. Both land sales and the inclination of politicians kept taxes and appropriations to a minimum. Two oceans and two weak neighbors made unnecessary the expensive military establishments that might have precluded more productive uses of capital. This generation of Americans became involved in two wars, to be sure, but the Mexican War more than paid for itself in territory, and the Civil War, while tragically expensive, interrupted industrial growth only temporarily.

The Urge to Improve

Few Americans before 1860 expected the Civil War to come; such a gloomy outlook belied the spirit of the time. Most believed, rather, that voters could distinguish justice from injustice, that statesmen could balance conflicting interests, that every individual could contribute to the quality of the life of the entire nation, and that the nation must progress. Americans were habitual optimists and not at all patient with those of less faith. Embracing as ideals both individualism and equality, they sought to make society at once more responsive to individual achievement and less deferential to social distinctions. Those same ideals inspired the simultaneous efforts to enlarge economic opportunity and to secure political democracy. The age was of a piece.

There were dozens of causes and uncounted prophets. Neal Dow, Lyman Beecher, and a flock of college presidents organized temperance or prohibition societies that persuaded individuals to take the "cold water pledge" and legislatures to regulate or forbid the sale of spirits. Dorothea Dix persuaded some authorities that the insane were ill, not criminal. Elihu Burritt, called "the learned blacksmith," William Ladd, and others condemned war before, after, and during the war against Mexico. And Horace Mann persisted in his long and often lonely crusade for universal, free public education.

All the causes of the era required an act of faith, and Christianity in some form was at the root of most. Evangelists, of whom Charles Grandison Finney was perhaps the most impassioned, saved souls and stirred the spiritual energy of men and women on the frontier. In upstate New York, a region swept by religious revivals, William Miller led an excited band to witness the day of judgment in 1843. The belief of the Millerites survived one postponement, but they disbanded the next year after the faithful, garbed in white and perched in trees for a better view, miscalculated a second time.

Joseph Smith, another resident of upstate New York, founded the Church of Jesus Christ of Latter Day Saints in 1830. Assisted by an angel, Mormons believe, he discovered and translated the Book of Mormon in the 1820s. Smith and his followers moved first to Ohio and then to Missouri before settling in Nauvoo, Illinois, in 1839. The first failures were costly, but hard work, faith, and Smith's driving leadership gradually brought prosperity and influence in Illinois politics. In 1843, Smith told his followers of a divine revelation that authorized polygamy; he himself soon had twenty wives. In 1844, the righteous citizens of Illinois, aroused by denunciations of polygamy, snatched Smith from the jail where he was awaiting trial on other charges, informally condemned him to death, and carried out their own sentence. Brigham Young, one of Smith's lieutenants, led the Mormons out of Illinois and temporarily out of the United States to the Great Salt Lake, where they made the desert bloom.

Other sects sought the same kind of spiritual community the Mormons achieved. John Humphrey Noyes and his followers settled in Oneida, New York, where their unconventional habits in religion, economics, dress, and sex excited the hostility of their neighbors until the community's prosperity converted enmity to envy. A group of intellectuals established a community near Concord, Massachusetts, at Brook Farm, where many New England writers visited, and Nathaniel Hawthorne briefly lived. But the hope that common living, working, and conversing would improve the living standard and the minds of the participants was disappointed.

Socialism was a by-product of settlements at Oneida and Brook Farm, but it was the principal goal of the British industrialist Robert Owen, who established a model community at New Harmony, Indiana. Étienne Cabet, a French theorist, moved with a small band of socialists from Texas to Illinois and then to Missouri. The ideas of Charles Fourier, another French socialist, inspired some Americans to found a phalanx (as Fourierist experiments were called) at Red Bank, New Jersey. After failing as a haven for intellectuals Brook Farm also failed as a phalanx.

Occasional theoretical socialists were harmless, but abolitionist agitators in the 1830s seemed to endanger the nation's unity. Unruly Bostonians tied a rope around William Lloyd Garrison and led the strident abolitionist editor through the streets. Outraged citizens in New Hampshire and Connecticut destroyed schools that idealistic teachers had allowed blacks to enter. Elijah Lovejoy, an abolitionist printer in Illinois, replaced several presses his neighbors destroyed and died in 1838 trying to ward off yet another assault. Most Americans with a reform impulse found less dangerous outlets for their zeal.

But opponents of slavery kept trying. The most aggressive abolitionists, whose voice was Garrison's paper, *The Liberator*, insisted on immediate emancipation, without compensation to the slave-owner, and on full equality for the black. They believed that emancipation would be a sham unless based on the principle of racial equality. Moral conversion, Garrison held, must precede political action, for the nation's politics would "always be shaped by its morals, as the vane on the steeple is ever indicating in what direction the wind blows." Other abolitionists thought political action could accompany, or perhaps even cause, the nation's moral conversion. James G. Birney, an Alabama planter who had freed his own slaves, twice ran for President as the candidate of the abolitionist Liberty party. But the result was disheartening: about 7,000 votes in 1840 and 62,300—less than 3 percent of the total vote—four years later.

Two other antislavery factions lacked Garrison's interest in racial equality. The American Colonization Society, founded in 1817, wistfully hoped for the peaceful end of slavery, either through governmental purchase of slaves or through the generosity of masters, and the end of the racial dilemma through the deportation of blacks to Africa. The scheme may have owed something to plans to remove Indians, which were developed and carried out at about the same time. The society had influential sponsors, including Henry Clay, and actually did send some freed slaves to Liberia. But most free blacks preferred to remain in the United States, and the society never raised enough money to purchase and repatriate many slaves.

The Free-Soil movement, which sprang up late in the 1840s, was only incidentally concerned with slaves in the South. Free-Soilers proposed to keep slavery out of the territory Americans had secured from Britain in the Pacific Northwest and taken from Mexico in the Southwest. They opposed slavery in part because it threatened the free labor that they believed to be at the heart of the American economic and social system, and in part because they wanted to keep their section of the nation free of all blacks.

By the 1850s, the Free-Soilers had broad Northern political support — too broad, many antislavery strategists argued, to jeopardize by association with advocates of women's rights. The affinity of the two crusades was natural, and Garrison and others forthrightly argued that human rights had no restriction of race or sex. Sarah and Angelina Grimké, abolitionist daughters of a slave-owning family, presented the case to large and curious "promiscuous" (that is, composed of men and women) audiences in 1837. The Congregational clergy of Massachusetts could better tolerate abolition than lecturing women. Public activity, according to a letter of the pastoral association, threatened "the female character with widespread and permanent injury." Woman's lot was modest, inconspicuous prayer; reforming society was man's work. The ministers even chose the classic metaphor: "If the vine, whose strength and beauty is to lean upon the trellis-work, . . . thinks to assume the independence and overshadowing nature of the elm, it will not only cease to bear fruit, but fall in shame and dishonor into the dust." An abolitionist, worried that women might discredit his cause, made the same point: "I think the tom-turkeys ought to do the gobbling," wrote Elizur Wright, and "I am opposed to hens' crowing, and . . . to female-preaching."

Foreigners sometimes remarked upon the great freedom of American women, which usually meant that chaperones were less obtrusive than in Europe. American women might inherit and control property, and they often had more voice in the selection of their husband than was the case in Europe. Nevertheless, as a perceptive British visitor noted in 1837, America gave its women "indulgence . . . as a substitute for justice." They hear, Harriet Martineau wrote,

oratorical flourishes on public occasions about wives and home, and apostrophes to women: her husband's hair stands on end at the idea of her working, and he toils to indulge her with money: she has liberty to get her brain turned by religious excitements, that her attention may be diverted from morals, politics, and philosophy.

As Martineau had observed, religion became for many middle-class women a substitute for the public life society foreclosed. But Elizabeth Cady Stanton, Lucretia Mott, Susan B. Anthony, and others poured their energy into a political movement to secure women's rights. The call came in 1848 from a convention held in Seneca Falls, New York: "We hold these truths to be self-evident," the Declaration of Sentiments began, "that all men and women are created equal. . . . " The Declaration of Independence furnished the model for the rest of the document as well: "The history of mankind is a history of repeated injustices and usurpations on the part of man toward woman, having in direct object the establishment of an absolute tyranny over her." The convention insisted, in conclusion, that women receive "all the rights and privileges which belong to them as citizens of the United States." But seventy years passed before women gained the right to vote, and that was supposed to have been only the first step toward equality.

Letters, Poems, and Transcendental Thought

Even though few Americans in the second quarter of the nineteenth century had much leisure for literature, volumes of respectable literary quality began to emerge from American pens and presses. Some, like Washington Irving's *Legend of Sleepy Hollow*, derived from the American folk idiom. James Fenimore Cooper set his *Leatherstocking Tales* on the American frontier and seemed uncertain that civilization had improved the wilderness. Edgar Allen Poe, impoverished, pathetic, dissipated, and largely ignored, wrote stories and poems of macabre genius that influenced stylists on both sides of the Atlantic. William Cullen Bryant produced poetry, Jacksonian journalism, and then literature on behalf of the antislavery cause. During the early 1840s, Herman Melville went to sea, and for the next half century he used ships, sailors, and salt water as the setting for his reflections on sin and salvation, man and God. His *Moby Dick*, perhaps America's greatest novel, was published in 1851 but not widely read in Melville's own time.

A host of articulate intellectuals collected around Boston. Poets of some talent and more reputation, like Oliver Wendell Holmes, Henry Wadsworth Longfellow, James Russell Lowell, and the abolitionist John Greenleaf Whittier; essayists and slightly eccentric reformers, like Margaret Fuller and Henry David Thoreau; religious thinkers and metaphysicians, like William E. Channing, whose sermons decisively influenced Unitarianism, and Theodore Parker; historians like George Bancroft, who told the nation's story as the triumph of good over evil and served the Democratic party to make sure virtue continued victorious; novelists like Nathaniel Hawthorne, the descendant of Puritan divines, who brooded over the tension created by the materialism of his contemporaries, the abundance of his country, and the Calvinist ethic— all these and many more lived in or around Boston and sharpened their ideas in conversation with one another.

In many ways the most representative intellectual of them all was Ralph Waldo Emerson, who symbolized the vigor of American talent as his contemporary, Andrew Jackson, stood for the vigor of American democracy and economic enterprise. Emerson's family was better educated and both socially and economically a cut above Jackson's. Emerson's father, a Unitarian clergyman, died when his son was small; Jackson's father did not live to see his child. Both boys knew money was short as they grew up. Jackson matured quickly as a British prisoner during the Revolution; he knew very little about books and a great deal about making his way in the world when he arrived in frontier Tennessee. He practiced law there, speculated in land, established a handsome plantation, and became a frontier aristocrat. Emerson, on the other hand, grew up at home in Boston, studied hard, and worked his way through Harvard. He conducted a successful finishing school for young ladies and used the profits to return to divinity school at Harvard. Neither divinity school nor subsequent pastorates really satisfied Emerson, and he eventually settled down in Concord where he made thinking and writing his profession, supporting himself, eventually quite well, with lectures and essays.

Emerson wrapped optimism, nationalism, and individual independence in striking prose, and Americans avidly absorbed it. Their response was predictable, since Emerson was merely stating well the same ideals that made Andrew Jackson the political hero of the time. In 1837, Emerson asked American scholars to dare to think their own thoughts and have done with European conventions. His country, Emerson optimistically believed, would create "a new race, a new religion, a new state, a new literature." Confident individuals would bring these wonders to reality by their own efforts. In one of his most famous essays, Emerson exhorted his readers to self-reliance. "Insist on yourself," he wrote, "never imitate." Man only had strength when he stood alone, and was "weaker by every recruit to his banner." Emerson was ashamed of humanity's capacity to submerge individuality in "badges and names, . . . large societies and dead institutions." Happiness did not come to groups, but to the individual who had "put his heart into his work and done his best."

Emerson did more than make striking phrases to express his countrymen's clichés. In his religious quest and in his unorthodox answer, called transcendentalism, he reflected the interests of his time, although he differed sharply from the evangelical preachers. Emerson wrote of a mystical union between man and nature, of an impersonal, universal spirit that he called the Over-Soul. His mysticism had no place for church or clergy; the individual must discover his own unity with the infinite, must merge his own transient self with the eternal Over-Soul. In this exalted state, Emerson declared, "this world is so beautiful that I can hardly believe it exists."

And Americans, including many of Emerson's friends, tried to make that beautiful world yet better, an effort he regarded with detached good humor. "What a fertility of projects for the salvation of the world!" Emerson wrote with amusement as he catalogued the contradictory crusades for and against yeast, manure, insects, marriage, and Christianity. Yet in the 1850s Emerson also became committed to a cause: the crusade against slavery. The gallows, he remarked after John Brown's execution, had become "glorious like the cross." With that remark, Emerson ceased to be a mirror for his generation and became a somewhat tardy seer.

Suggested Reading

George R. Taylor's *The Transportation Revolution** (1951) is an indispensable beginning for the study of pre-Civil War economic history. W. W. Rostow, *The Stages of Economic Growth** (1960), argues that industrial growth became self-sustaining in the 1840s. John F. Kasson's *Civilizing the Machine** (1976) discusses the tension between industrial development and republican ideals. In *The Economic Growth of the United States** (1960), Douglass C. North interprets a great deal of economic data. In *American and British Technology in the Nineteenth Century* (1967), H. J. Habakkuk explores the interrelationship among technology, capital, and labor.

Ulrich B. Phillip's *American Negro Slavery** (1919) and Kenneth M. Stampp's *The Peculiar Institution** (1956) are two older standard accounts of slavery. Among the major works Eugene D. Genovese has written on the subject are: *The Political Economy of Slavery** (1965), *The World the Slave-owners Made** (1969), and *Roll Jordan, Roll: The World the Slaves Made** (1974). David B. Davis, *The Problem of Slavery in Western Culture** (1966), puts the subject in a broad perspective. *Time on the Cross** (1974), by Robert W. Fogel and Stanley L. Engerman, has provoked much scholarly controversy, including Herbert Gutman's *Slavery and the Numbers Game** (1975). Gutman's *The Black Family in Slavery and Freedom** (1976) presents persuasive evidence of the strength of black families. Frank L. Owsley's *Plain Folk of the Old South** (1949) shows slavery's impact on whites who were not slave-owners.

Alice F. Tyler's *Freedom's Ferment** (1944) remains a satisfactory survey of the reform movements of the 1840s; C. S. Griffen's *The Ferment of Reform** (1967) is more recent. Louis Filler's *The Crusade Against Slavery** (1960) is a sound account of the abolitionist movement; Aileen S. Kraditor emphasizes the movement's radicalism in *Means and Ends in American*

*Abolitionism** (1967). Carl Degler's *Neither Black nor White** (1971)
compares the role of mulattoes in Brazil and the United States. Alice
Rossi has edited *The Feminist Papers** (1973) and provided useful
introductions to place the documents in context, as have W. Elliot and
Mary M. Brownlee in *Women in the American Economy* (1976). Sydney E.
Ahlstrom's *A Religious History of the American People** (1972) is a work of
enormous learning, as is Henry F. May's *The Enlightenment in America*
(1976).

* Available in paperback edition

Chapter 9
The Gains and Losses
of Growth

Chronology

1836 Texas declares independence from Mexico •

1842 Webster-Ashburton Treaty •

1844 Presidential election: James K. Polk (Democrat) defeats Henry Clay (Whig) •

1845 Annexation of Texas •

1846 Oregon Treaty fixes forty-ninth parallel as boundary • Independent

Treasury reestablished • Wilmot Proviso forbids slavery in Mexican cession; not enacted •

1846—47 Mexican War •

1848 Treaty of Guadalupe-Hidalgo • Presidential election: Zachary Taylor (Whig) defeats Lewis Cass (Democrat) •

1849 California Gold Rush •

1850 Compromise of 1850 •

1851—52 *Uncle Tom's Cabin* published •

1852 Presidential election: Franklin Pierce (Democrat) defeats Winfield Scott (Whig) •

1854 Perry mission to Japan • Ostend Manifesto demands annexation of Cuba •

In February 1817 John C. Calhoun warned his fellow congressmen that the breadth of the country endangered its unity. The House, Calhoun cautioned, must "counteract every tendency to disunion," and members must not yield to "a low, sordid, selfish, and sectional spirit" that would divide the nation. Most unreflective Americans shrugged off Calhoun's warning, even when Calhoun himself later seemed to promote the "selfish and sectional spirit" he had decried. Sectional differences in the 1830s and 1840s were simply geographic facts, not portents of disaster or causes of a future civil war.

The sections, after all, had common interests and complemented one another in their diversity. The New England textile mill needed both southern cotton and customers in the West. The settler on the frontier needed credit from the East and markets in both the South and East for the surplus. The southern plantation owner was only too aware that he needed Yankee ship captains and Yankee merchants as well as Yankee mills; sometimes he also needed corn and hogs from northwestern farmers.

Since the sections were economically diverse, political questions cut across regional lines. Subsistence farmers everywhere thought taxes too high; settlers from Texas to Minnesota thought government land too expensive. The merchant in New York and the cotton planter in South Carolina both opposed protective tariffs, while the manufacturer in Massachusetts, the ironmaster in Pennsylvania, and the sugar planter in Louisiana were all protectionists. And interests everywhere changed. Daniel Webster began by opposing a protective tariff and ended as protection's most distinguished advocate. Henry Clay opposed rechartering the Bank of the United States in 1811 but in 1832 ran for President as the candidate of recharter. And John C. Calhoun, once a War Hawk and in 1817 a fervent nationalist, later forecast secession at the first sign of nationalistic legislation.

With so many imponderables, many politicians decided to transcend sectionalism, ignore economic differences, and focus on noncontroversial issues. Thus, William Henry Harrison's log-cabin simplicity in 1840. Thus, James K. Polk's expansionism in 1844. Thus, the well-advertised heroism of generals Zachary Taylor and Winfield Scott in 1848 and 1852. Thus, exaggeration of the menace of immigrants and Catholics in the American, or Know-Nothing, movement of 1856. Thus, finally, Abraham Lincoln's split rails to disguise the exclusively northern basis of his party in 1860. But economic and sectional issues refused to go away; after 1850 they were not even well hidden. In front of Harrison's log cabin ran Henry Clay's federally financed roads, and behind it lurked the rest of the American system. Before Polk's expansion was well begun, an upstart member of his own party set off a fifteen-year wrangle with the apparently innocent query "Expansion—for whom?" That simple question dominated General Taylor's brief presidency and so weakened General Scott's party that it barely survived his campaign. By the time Know-Nothings tried to distract public attention to papal plots, voters thought domestic subversion more dangerous—whether by the "slavocracy" or the abolitionists depended upon one's sectional point of view. And no number of split rails won Abe Lincoln any votes in the South.

Expansion was the most promising of these camouflaging expedients, for land speculation was the national game. But expansion only made the stakes larger and the competition more fierce.

The Canadian Frontier

The eastern end of the boundary between the United States and Canada had presumably been amicably settled in the aftermath of the War of 1812. In the Convention of 1818, American and British negotiators had left the Oregon Territory open to settlers from both nations, but had fixed the border east of the Rockies at the forty-ninth parallel. The Rush-Bagot Agreement of 1817, which provided for disarmament on the Great Lakes, was an important step toward a completely unfortified frontier.

But Americans, eager to export democracy and perhaps to add a little territory in the process, wanted every instance of friction between Canada and Great Britain to herald a revolution. Dissident Canadians counted upon American sympathy, occasional informal aid, and refuge and hospitality if a coup failed. In December 1837, the *Caroline,* a small American steamer, made three trips across the Niagara River with supplies for Canadian rebels. A detachment of Canadian militiamen crossed the river at night, killed an American while overpowering the *Caroline*'s crew, set fire to the vessel, and cut it adrift. As tension along the border mounted, President Van Buren urged Americans not to provoke British retaliation. Throughout 1838 and into 1839, Americans enlisted in secret lodges whose object was Canadian liberation, but enthusiasm evaporated in the face of evident Canadian apathy.

Meanwhile, frontier argument moved eastward. Dispute over the boundary between Maine and New Brunswick flared into the Aroostook War of 1838 − 39. In 1838 an "invasion" by Canadian lumberjacks provoked the governor of Maine to mobilize the militia. Congress appropriated $10 million and authorized a force of 30,000 men, but General Winfield Scott, Van Buren's trouble-shooter, arranged a truce in 1839 before any blood was shed. The argument was taken out of the Maine woods and referred to a diplomatic commission.

Daniel Webster headed the State Department when discussion of the Maine boundary began again in 1842. Webster and Lord Ashburton, Britain's congenial and conciliatory special envoy, met in Washington to negotiate. They drew the present northern boundary of Maine, which left 7,000 of the disputed 12,000 square miles to the United States. Britain then agreed to one minor adjustment in the frontier at the northern end of Lake Champlain and another in Minnesota that awarded the Mesabi iron deposits to the United States.

The Webster-Ashburton Treaty also resolved a potentially explosive impasse over slavery and maritime rights. In the 1830s Britain had abolished slavery throughout the empire and in the 1840s tried to stamp out the remnants of the African slave trade. Although the United States had outlawed importation of slaves in 1808, some American vessels were still engaged in the traffic. The United States refused to permit the British navy to stop and search American ships, and Webster promised that the United States would maintain its own African squadron and enforce American law on American vessels. The promise was indifferently kept.

Manifest Destiny

John L. O'Sullivan was impatient. For months the politicians had talked about treaties and titles, but what O'Sullivan wanted was land. The Oregon Territory was a long way from New York, where O'Sullivan wrote editorials, but in 1845 he wrote one that caught the spirit of many

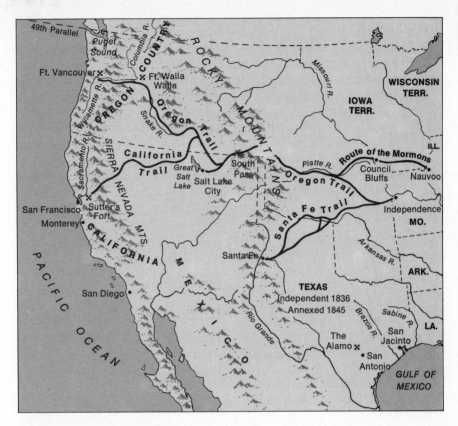

TRAILS TO THE FAR WEST

Americans. "Away, away," he wrote, "with all those cobweb tissues of rights of discovery, exploration, settlement, contiguity, etc." America's claim to additional territory was "the right of our manifest destiny to overspread and possess the whole of the continent which Providence has given us for the development of liberty and federative self-government." Britain would not settle Oregon, but in American hands "it must fast fill in with a population destined to establish . . . a noble young empire of the Pacific."

Whether applied to Oregon, Texas, New Mexico, California, Cuba, or Central America, O'Sullivan's editorial contained all the elements of the creed called manifest destiny that swept the United States in the 1840s with all the fervor of a religious revival. The West, so the faith went, was God's gift to Americans, whose responsibility was to settle it, cultivate it, and produce not only crops and cash but virtue as well. Racism, often unconscious, required no concession to Indians or Mexicans who temporarily occupied space Americans thought of as empty. The western dream combined the early Spanish explorers' visions of gold with Jefferson's picture of fertile prairies and sturdy farmers, added the greed of the land speculator, and cloaked the result in the Puritan's vocabulary of divine mission. Manifest destiny had roots deep in the American tradition: the assumption that Americans were a divinely chosen people, fit to furnish a shining example to the world; the fervent faith in self-government; the compulsion to occupy new lands.

Title mattered less than possession when in the 1820s Americans began moving into the Mexican province of Texas. The Mexican government, glad to have the thinly settled area grow, granted land to Americans and winked at their use of slaves to till it, although slavery was illegal in Mexico. But in 1830, when Americans in Texas had become annoyingly self-assertive, Mexico prohibited further American settlement and refused the Texans' subsequent demands for autonomy. In 1836 Texans declared independence and secured it when an army under Sam Houston defeated Mexican forces at San Jacinto. Before the end of the year, the Republic of Texas had a constitution and had begun to negotiate for annexation to the United States.

Neither Jackson nor Van Buren was ready to add territory that might bring war with Mexico and that surely would create political trouble within the United States. Texans then opened discussions with Britain, which was interested in a barrier to American continental growth, a source of cotton, and an unprotected market for British goods. These negotiations probably would have had no result, for Texas' ties to the United States were too close and Britain's opposition to slavery too strong. But the possibility of British influence in an area many Americans already thought of as their Southwest raised enthusiasm for annexation.

Britain was more directly concerned about American ambitions to control the harbors, trade, and territory along the Pacific shore. Merchants and ship captains from eastern ports wanted Puget Sound, San Francisco Bay, and San Diego to facilitate whaling, trade with the Orient, and the acquisition of California hides for shoe factories in New England. San Francisco and San Diego were in Mexican territory, but Americans could secure Puget Sound with the lush Oregon Territory, which merchants and missionaries advertised to restless farmers back east. By 1845 more than 5,000 Americans had followed the Oregon Trail from Missouri to the Willamette Valley. They hoped to end anomalous joint occupation and substitute exclusive American rule all the way to 54°40′, the southern boundary of Alaska.

A few hundred venturesome Americans settled in California, where the land was as fertile and vacant as Oregon and where the climate and the harbors were better. John Sutter, a German American who had acquired Mexican citizenship and an immense tract of land in the Sacramento Valley, expedited American migration. The bustling colony of Americans expected that control from Washington would soon replace the loose rein from Mexico City, but the seizure of Monterey in 1842 by a misinformed American naval officer was a few years premature and had to be disavowed.

The Alamo, 1836

Some experienced statesmen, in their concern for banks and tariffs, mistook manifest destiny for a fad. Henry Clay and Martin Van Buren, who seemed likely to be the presidential candidates in 1844, thought a debate over expansion risked reopening sectional squabbling; they decided to keep the issue out of the campaign by separately opposing immediate annexation of Texas or any other territory.

The agreement cost Van Buren the nomination. Word came that Andrew Jackson favored annexing Texas and thought Van Buren had made a mistake. The Democratic convention deadlocked when Van Buren received slightly more than a majority but less than the required two-thirds of the votes. Unable to decide among more prominent aspirants, the delegates settled on James K. Polk, an intense, humorless Tennesseean with a puritanical sense of purpose. Polk had spent fourteen years in the House, the last four as Speaker; he had twice been governor of Tennessee; he was Andrew Jackson's candidate after Van Buren fumbled the expansion issue; he was, as one of the delegates put it, "a pure, wholehogged democrat" from the Jacksonian mold. He was called "Young Hickory" and foreshadowed the arrival of a new political generation and a brief, blustering political movement called "Young America." When he defeated Henry Clay, he was at fifty the youngest President the United States had ever had.

The Democratic platform stood forthrightly for expansion. It pledged "the reannexation of Texas" and "the reoccupation of Oregon," which campaigners transformed into "Fifty-four Forty or Fight!" However dangerous Henry Clay thought the issue, large parts of the electorate—in eastern cities, on northwestern farms, and on southwestern plantations—obviously supported expansion. Clay hedged his opposition to more territory just enough to drive some voters to the abolitionist Liberty party, which polled 16,000 of its 62,300 votes in New York. If Clay had carried New York, which the Democrats won by 5,000 votes, the presidency would have been his.

The Mexican War

John Tyler sensed the popular temper before the election and ordered Secretary of State Calhoun to prepare a treaty annexing Texas. Calhoun's treaty went to the Senate just as he released a vigorous note to Great Britain defending slavery. Linking the two documents, abolitionists charged that annexation was a slave-owners' plot to extend the boundaries of bondage; Calhoun's treaty died in the Senate with only sixteen proponents. Undismayed, Tyler read the election results as a mandate for immediate annexation. Lacking the two-thirds majority for a treaty, he suggested that a joint resolution would serve as well. The Senate finally accepted the resolution by two votes three days before Tyler left the White House. Before the end of 1845 Texas was a state.

The new state brought its old boundary disputes into the Union. Texas claimed the area south to the Rio Grande, but Mexico, which hotly resented American annexation, argued that Texas had never extended south of the Nueces River. In 1845 President Polk ordered General Zachary Taylor into the disputed region; in the spring of 1846 Taylor moved to the north bank of the Rio Grande near a concentration of Mexican forces at Matamoros.

While Taylor's troops were moving south, John Slidell, a special American envoy to Mexico, tried to accomplish American aims without war. Slidell was authorized to offer Mexico as much as $30 million for the disputed part of Texas, all of California, and the intervening territory called New Mexico. While Slidell waited, one Mexican government fell and another no less stubborn replaced it. No one would officially receive the American diplomat, and no Mexican government could offend its proud citizenry by releasing so much territory. Slidell wrote Polk that only a beating would induce Mexico to discuss American propositions seriously. Foreseeing no chance of success, Slidell started home.

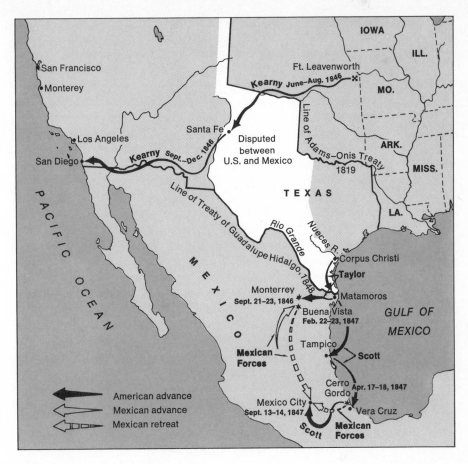

THE MEXICAN WAR, 1846 — 1848

In May 1846 Polk asked his cabinet whether the insulting treatment of
Slidell, together with other Mexican-American friction, justified war. Most
of the cabinet agreed with the President's decision to ask for a
declaration; later news that Taylor's troops had clashed with Mexican
forces at Matamoros converted the others. The foe, Polk told Congress,
had "invaded our territory and shed American blood on American soil."
Congress was aware that Polk bore some responsibility for provoking
hostilities but passed the declaration by large majorities in both houses;
measures to raise and equip troops followed.

Polk reinforced Taylor's army and ordered him to move his troops into
northern Mexico. Taylor, popularly known as "Old Rough and Ready,"
met and defeated a Mexican army at Monterrey in September. When that
victory did not induce Mexico to meet Polk's demands, he diverted part
of the army to an assault on Vera Cruz and ordered Taylor to mark time
at Monterrey. Convinced that a Democratic President was restraining him

because of his Whig politics, Taylor took the offensive again in 1847 and blundered into a far larger Mexican force at Buena Vista. The American army won a decisive victory—in spite of its disobedient commander, the President noted acidly—and Taylor's reputation at home climbed.

American settlers in California declared their independence in 1846 and mounted their own "Bear Flag Revolt" against Mexico. An American "surveying" expedition commanded by John C. Frémont joined the rebels, and an American naval squadron soon reached Monterey. By the time overland forces had arrived from Kansas by way of Santa Fe, where they had secured American control of New Mexico without a shot, Mexican rule in California was largely finished.

But Mexico seemed not to understand the war was lost. To make the point, Polk sent an expeditionary force under General Winfield Scott to Vera Cruz in March 1847. Scott secured the port and retraced the route of the Spanish conquistadors to the capital. Mexican armies contested Scott's advance, but following a decisive victory at Cerro Gordo in April, Scott moved triumphantly into Mexico City in September.

Nicholas P. Trist, the chief clerk of the American Department of State, accompanied Scott's troops and carried President Polk's conditions for peace. Trist's instructions offered Mexico virtually the same terms Slidell had presented before the war. But the Mexican government would no more deal with Trist than it had with Slidell. The disgusted President ordered Trist home just as the envoy began conversations that seemed promising. He sent Polk a patronizing note, continued the negotiations, and completed the Treaty of Guadalupe-Hidalgo in February 1848. The treaty disguised conquest as purchase, for Mexico received $15 million and the United States agreed in addition to pay claims by its citizens against Mexico. In return, Mexico ceded California, New Mexico, and the disputed portion of Texas. Although Polk was irritated with Trist, the treaty corresponded to his instructions. The President submitted the treaty to the Senate, which promptly ratified it. And the area of the United States jumped by one-fifth.

Continuing Sectional Conflict

Polk's disavowed envoy relieved the President of a war for which the nation had lost its initial enthusiasm. Bipartisan support for expansion vanished in revived sectional and partisan bickering. Even southern Whigs criticized the President for causing a "disgraceful and infamous" assault on a friendly neighbor. Thomas Corwin of Ohio, an antislavery congressman, rhetorically transformed himself into an outraged Mexican: "Have you not room in your country to bury your dead men?" Corwin shouted. "If you come into mine, we will greet you with bloody hands and welcome you to hospitable graves."

POST OFFICE, SAN FRANCISCO, CALIFORNIA.

A FAITHFUL REPRESENTATION OF THE CROWDS DAILY APPLYING AT THAT OFFICE FOR LETTERS AND NEWSPAPERS.

Some northern criticism grew out of Polk's compromise settlement of the Oregon dispute. In 1844 and 1845, Polk had pleased his northern partisans by demanding all of Oregon to the southern boundary of Alaska at 54°40'. Privately he offered to divide the territory by extending the existing boundary at the forty-ninth parallel to the Pacific. By 1846, the migration of American farmers into Oregon had reduced the profits of British fur traders, and Britain formally proposed a compromise division at 49°. Anxious to avoid simultaneous conflicts with Mexico and Britain, Polk submitted the proposal to the Senate, which ratified the treaty in spite of the protests of northwestern expansionists, who feared the party appeared more zealous in pursuit of southern than of northern territory.

More divisive than the Oregon Treaty was the argument about slavery that the Mexican War precipitated. The administration's request for $2 million to pay for negotiations with Mexico seemed a routine bill in August 1846. But when David Wilmot, a good Jacksonian Democrat from Pennsylvania, finished presenting his amendment, the bill was anything but routine. For the Wilmot Proviso made prohibition of slavery in any territory acquired from Mexico "an express and fundamental condition" of expansion. Concern for free, white labor, not disgust with slavery, probably determined Wilmot's stand. He meant to preserve, he remarked subsequently, "a fair country . . . where the sons of toil, of my own race and color, can live without the disgrace which association with negro slavery brings upon free labor." Whatever his motive, the Wilmot Proviso provided a rallying point for all who opposed the war, for all who opposed slavery or its spread, and for those northerners who soberly regretted the consequences of manifest destiny. Polk thought the proviso the device of "demagogues & ambitious politicians" who hoped "to promote their own prospects."

Polk knew the proviso would appeal to the North. Legislatures in every free state but one endorsed Wilmot's rider, and northern congressmen voted for it time after time. Although the House passed the proviso several times, the Senate always struck it out. Each debate stirred further the sectional quarrel that expansion was supposed to calm. The Wilmot Proviso made slavery an open political issue, one that would be at the core of political rivalry for the next fifteen years. In the metaphor of Missouri's Senator Benton, the proviso was one blade of a pair of shears that could sever the bonds of the Union.

Calhoun provided the other blade in four congressional resolutions asserting that Congress could not constitutionally restrict slavery at all. Congress did not vote on Calhoun's resolutions, but there was no lack of heated talk about them and about the state-rights view of union upon which they were based. The Alabama legislature wrote its own resolutions, which declared the Missouri Compromise unconstitutional, pronounced slavery guaranteed in every federal territory, and threatened secession if the Wilmot Proviso ever passed. Other southern legislatures toned down the language of the Alabama Resolves while repeating their substance.

As the hardening of sectional lines after 1846 demonstrates, expansionism was a peculiar form of nationalism that only temporarily concealed sectional ambitions. Southern zeal for expansion did not extend to annexing Oregon nor to taking all of Mexico. Calhoun, the most farsighted of southern spokesmen, did not vote for the declaration of war against Mexico and never developed any enthusiasm for Polk's expansionist schemes. Parts of the Northwest lost interest in manifest destiny when its northern limit became the forty-ninth parallel, and northeastern residents had not thought new land a primary concern for generations. Polk himself was a Jacksonian nationalist, but some other expansionists had used nationalistic rhetoric to serve sectional ends.

The domestic record of Polk's administration also demonstrates how sharply Democratic nationalism differed from the Hamilton-Marshall-Clay variety. Polk vetoed bills for internal improvements, thereby annoying Democrats of the Northwest. A Jacksonian in financial policy, Polk persuaded Congress in 1846 to reenact the Independent Treasury with legislation almost identical to that of 1840. The President cracked the whip of patronage to secure passage of the Walker Tariff in 1846, a law that reduced duties on foreign goods and consequently reduced the profits of domestic manufacturers, especially in the middle states.

Before his inauguration, Polk had promised to serve only one term. He intended to settle the Oregon boundary, to acquire California, to reestablish the Independent Treasury, to reduce the tariff, and then to retire. He accomplished those objectives and died within a year. He left his party in disarray. Van Buren's followers, still piqued by Polk's nomination in 1844, were not ready to forgive southern Democratic rivals. Other northern Democrats resented Polk's "betrayal" of northern interests in the Oregon settlement, the tariff debate, and the decision to veto bills for improved rivers and harbors. If they were to resist the growing popularity of the Wilmot Proviso, and thereby conciliate southern Democrats, northern Democrats needed more political support than Polk provided. Never really banished, slavery was right back in the middle of political discourse. Whigs had won the congressional election of 1846, and 1848 looked like another Whig year.

None of the Democratic presidential hopefuls had enthusiastic national backing. Lewis Cass, a senator from Michigan and the eventual nominee, had two different campaign biographies prepared, one to buttress the arguments of campaigners in the free states, and the other slanted to appeal to the South. However shrewd the tactic, it indicated the fragility of the Democratic coalition, which Cass sought to sustain by adopting a middle position on the expansion of slavery. Settlers themselves, Cass said, should choose whether to permit or prohibit slavery in their territory. Supporters of this plan, chiefly northwestern Democrats, called it popular sovereignty.

Shut out at the Democratic convention, Van Buren's New York followers held their own and joined Liberty party members, antislavery Whigs, and other dissidents and reformers in establishing the Free-Soil party. With the exception of a few abolitionists, Free-Soilers opposed only the expansion of slavery; they agreed on the Wilmot Proviso because it reserved the territories for white settlers and kept blacks out. The party nominated Van Buren for President and campaigned for "Free Soil, Free Speech, Free Labor, and Free Men." The former President had no following in the South, but in the North, and especially in New York where he ran ahead of Cass, Van Buren hurt the Democratic ticket.

Young, ambitious Whigs moved to snatch the opportunity. Those who had represented Whiggery for a generation, like Webster and Clay, were elbowed aside. Even before the convention met, Thurlow Weed, a New York editor whose first love was politics, William H. Seward, a former governor of New York who went to the Senate in 1848, Alexander Stephens, a staunch unionist from Georgia, Abraham Lincoln, whose single term in Congress was nearly over, and a host of Whigs from the border states, had settled on Zachary Taylor as their candidate. If Taylor had any political convictions, they were unknown, and his backers proposed to keep them that way. Taylor owned a plantation and slaves in Louisiana, yet his military service demonstrated a firm commitment to the nation. And although Old Rough and Ready had occasionally proved inept on the battlefield, he was a winner. That was not a bad qualification for a presidential nominee.

The Compromise of 1850

Whatever Taylor's program, his election gave him no mandate. He won largely because Van Buren split the northern Democratic vote. Although Democrats organized the Senate, neither party controlled the House, where Free-Soilers held the balance of power. Three weeks were consumed in just electing a Speaker. A divided Congress, an inexperienced President, two fragile parties, and several self-righteous factions were slim resources for meeting the political problems that piled up for attention. Every issue furnished an opportunity for someone to talk about slavery, which made every rift wider and every error more serious. Southerners, angry at the lack of northern cooperation in returning runaway slaves, pressed for a stiff new fugitive slave law. Northern politicians, for their part, objected to the highly visible slave trade in Washington, which Congress had the unquestioned constitutional authority to abolish.

More vexing was the need of the new territories for government. Any application for statehood—even that of Oregon where slavery had never been a serious possibility—inspired bitter debate and political posturing designed to reassure constituents at home as much as to persuade legislators in Washington. This sort of public pledge of sectional allegiance may have prolonged the careers of politicians, but it placed national political parties in peril.

After Oregon, there was California, flooded by the gold-seekers of 1849 and ready for statehood to provide law, order, and a fixed legal code to confirm land titles. President Taylor suggested that California skip territorial status, draw up a constitution, and apply for immediate admission; he hoped thereby to sidestep southern demands for protection of slavery in federal territories. But, once admitted, California would upset the sectional balance, carefully maintained in the Senate since 1820. Nor could Taylor evade the issue of slavery in the territories of Utah and New Mexico, neither of which was ready for statehood. The claim of Texas to much of eastern New Mexico and the related claim of Texas bondholders to federal redemption of their securities complicated any final arrangement in the Southwest.

The Wilmot Proviso and Calhoun's rejoinder that slavery must every-where be protected were the extremes of the debate over territorial slavery. Polk, Buchanan, and other moderate Democrats favored extend-

ing the Missouri Compromise line to the Pacific. Stephen A. Douglas, the
senator from Illinois who was emerging as the chief Democrat in the
Northwest, endorsed popular sovereignty. President Taylor and many
northern Whigs wanted to handle each region separately. California, they
held, had drafted a constitution that happened to prohibit slavery;
California met the ordinary requirements for statehood and ought to be
admitted. Other cases could be considered when they arose.

But unless statesmen could forge a legislative majority from these
disparate views, nothing would be done about anything. By common
consent, Henry Clay undertook the task with a series of resolutions he
introduced in the Senate early in 1850. The resolutions provided for
admission of California as a free state, organization of the rest of the
Mexican cession without restriction on slavery, Texas' surrender of the
disputed territory to New Mexico and federal assumption of the Texas
debt, enactment of a stringent fugitive slave law, and elimination of the

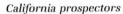

California prospectors

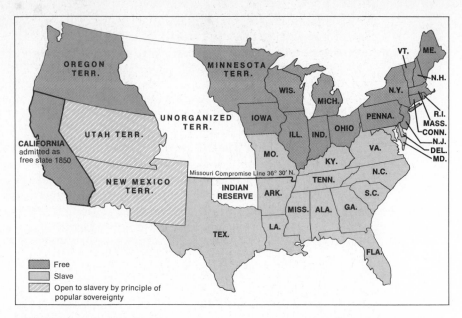

 legend:
Free
Slave
Open to slavery by principle of popular sovereignty

Map labels: OREGON TERR., MINNESOTA TERR., WIS., MICH., VT., ME., N.H., N.Y., UNORGANIZED TERR., IOWA, PENNA., R.I., MASS., CONN., UTAH TERR., ILL., IND., OHIO, N.J., CALIFORNIA admitted as free state 1850, MO., VA., DEL., MD., NEW MEXICO TERR., Missouri Compromise Line 36° 30' N., KY., N.C., INDIAN RESERVE, ARK., TENN., S.C., MISS., ALA., GA., TEX., LA., FLA.

THE COMPROMISE OF 1850

most offensive slave depots in Washington, coupled with a congressional promise not to abolish slavery there without the consent of the people of the District and of Maryland as well. Eventually Clay rolled all the resolutions into one "omnibus bill," and the prolonged debate over the Compromise of 1850 began in earnest.

It was not, on the whole, an edifying debate. Senator Calhoun, so ill that he would die before the bill came to a vote, had to have his speech read for him. Calhoun scorned compromise, ignored the specific issues under discussion, pointed out that social bonds between sections were already snapping, and demanded that Congress protect the right of southerners to take their slave property wherever they pleased. Senator Seward's Free-Soil response rested on "a higher law than the Constitution"; Seward's was a variant of manifest destiny that reserved the territories for free men.

While oratory continued on the floor, Clay encouraged the public to articulate its demand for peace through compromise. Businessmen, who blanched at the economic consequences of war, circulated petitions. Representatives of influential Texas bondholders lobbied for compromise. Stephen A. Douglas and other Democrats worked to hold their party in line. And Daniel Webster gave a courageous address that cost him the support of the growing number of Massachusetts abolitionists but inspired unionists throughout the land. Webster asserted that slavery could not survive in New Mexico's deserts, a point that Clay and other compromisers reiterated. Why, then, insist on the Wilmot Proviso merely to taunt the South? Webster condemned his own section for not returning runaways as the Constitution required. And he condemned even more sternly the ease with which both sides contemplated disunion. For Webster knew that talk of peaceful separation was drivel. The old nationalist wanted no part of war, but he wanted disunion less.

Nothing moved Old Rough and Ready. President Taylor thought the elaborate compromise unnecessary. California, he held, should be admitted and threats of southern secession faced as Andrew Jackson had faced them in 1832. Taylor's intransigence irritated unionists, who respected southern determination, and southern Whigs, who felt betrayed. But the stubborn President's opposition was almost providentially removed when he died in July of a sudden digestive disorder. Millard Fillmore, who succeeded, promptly applied the power of the executive branch to achieve compromise. Then, quite suddenly and unexpectedly, the Senate stripped the omnibus bill of all its controversial provisions and passed only a fragment organizing the Utah Territory. Weary and discouraged, Henry Clay left to repair his health and spirit at the shore. Stephen A. Douglas salvaged the Compromise of 1850.

Called the "Little Giant" because of his small stature and outsize energy, ambition, and competence, Douglas was a convinced democrat and a nationalist to the core. He knew the pressures on those with nationalist views when southern constituencies required their representatives to oppose the admission of California and when a fugitive slave law outraged the northern public. To the tiny group that would accept the entire compromise, Douglas added southern votes for northern concessions and northern support for legislation that restricted the South. One by one, Douglas delivered the components of Clay's "omnibus bill" for Fillmore's signature. So varied was the support for each bill that only twenty-eight congressmen voted for every provision of the compromise; twenty-five of those congressmen were Democrats; twenty-six were from the North.

The Compromise of 1850, then, was never based on a spirit of give and take, and never had either broad national or official bipartisan support. Several of the measures disappointed the fondest hopes of their supporters and the bleakest fears of their opponents. The New Mexico and Utah territories were organized and permitted to make their own arrangement about slavery. Texas accepted its present frontiers and federal assistance to pay off its debt. California became a free state, although state courts ruled that slavery was still legal for several years after 1850, and the state's representatives in Washington regularly voted with the South until the Civil War. The slave trade in the District of Columbia continued apace, even though the law closed down the most notorious slave pen. Most notably, the Fugitive Slave Law neither deterred slaves from flight nor secured northern cooperation in their recapture. Relieved Americans greeted the compromise with cheers and fireworks. The cheers and relief were premature; the fireworks were only beginning.

But the compromisers had their moment. Most presidential candidates for the election of 1852 supported sectional accommodation. Douglas, Cass, and Buchanan, the front-running Democrats, and Webster, Fillmore, and Winfield Scott, rivals for the Whig nomination, all professed their faith in compromise. When Democrats eventually settled on a dark horse, Franklin Pierce, he unequivocally added his endorsement. Faithful to their formula of nominating generals, the Whigs picked Winfield Scott, who was less forthright than Pierce and who southerners feared shared Seward's antislavery outlook. Only Free-Soilers outspokenly denounced the legislation of 1850, and they were seriously weakened when Van Buren's Democrats loyally supported Pierce.

The Compromise Breaks Down

Pierce's smashing victory (Scott carried only four states) seemed ultimate proof of the popularity and acceptance of compromise. But the election in fact signaled no surge of sentiment for union; rather, it marked the demise of the Whig party and a consequent growth of sectionalism. For twenty years men of all regions had come together in the Whig party. Inspired by Webster's oratorical nationalism, Whigs had consistently tried to enact Clay's nationalistic legislation. To be sure, they had sucessfully suppressed internal divisions only by nominating politically unknown generals. But in 1852 not even a politically unknown general could hold the party together. After 1852 only Democrats claimed a national constituency, and their precarious unity depended on keeping slavery out of politics.

The Fugitive Slave Law almost guaranteed that bickering would continue. For the act failed by a large margin to meet the test of northern opinion. Ralph Waldo Emerson referred to the law as a "filthy enactment" and vowed not to obey it. A Maryland planter was shot while chasing his runaways in Pennsylvania. Authorities in Detroit had to call out troops to calm a crowd enraged by the recapture of a fugitive on his way to Canada. State legislatures had earlier passed "personal liberty " laws, which had effectively prevented slave-owners from reclaiming their runaways and which had been a major reason for the southern demand for federal legislation in 1850. After the compromise, northern legislatures pounced on a southern device: in 1859 the Wisconsin legislature solemnly denounced federal enforcement of the Fugitive Slave Law as an invasion of Wisconsin's reserved rights as a state.

The provisions of the act provoked part of the furor. Appointed commissioners, sitting without juries, were not bound by the ordinary rules of judicial procedure in hearing cases. Accused blacks could not testify. The commissioner pocketed a $10 fee if he awarded the prisoner to the owner; $5 sufficed if the black were released.

For years, Harriet Beecher Stowe wrote, she had "avoided all reading

Harriet Tubman: an escaped slave who led others out of bondage

upon or allusion to the subject of slavery." In 1851, she broke her resolution with a vengeance. No Christian or humane people, she thought, had any moral duty to obey the Fugitive Slave Law. Her *Uncle Tom's Cabin* made heroes of slaves who escaped and whites who helped them. The book was not a one-dimensional abolitionist tract: Simon Legree, the villain of the piece, was a transplanted Connecticut Yankee; feckless white southerners had more compassion for blacks than did patronizing, pretentious northerners. But unsophisticated northern audiences who watched countless road companies perform dramatizations of the book, and unsophisticated northern readers who made it the first of the best-sellers, condemned the slave-owner and the Fugitive Slave Law, as they poured out their tears for Uncle Tom, Topsy, and Eliza.

Outside of fiction, fugitives were few. If official statistics are accurate, only 16 of 400,000 slaves in South Carolina escaped in 1850. Although losses in the border states were higher, perhaps 1 slave for every 5,000 who remained in bondage succeeded in escaping every year. Yet southerners, especially those in the deep South, conjured up a gigantic northern conspiracy called the underground railroad that spirited countless blacks to freedom. There *was* an underground railroad, and a few blacks did travel it, at great risk to themselves and to their courageous hosts. But it was both less successful and less ubiquitous than worried southerners fancied.

Echoes of Manifest Destiny

So the Compromise of 1850 settled few of the old arguments and created a few new ones. Franklin Pierce, a man of little imagination, had no fresh ideas as mounting sectional gales buffeted his floundering administration. For lack of creative statesmanship, some Democrats experimented again with an active foreign policy as the cure-all for domestic disharmony. President Pierce supported the mission Fillmore had authorized to open Japan to American commerce. Commodore Matthew Perry, who commanded the expedition, signed a treaty in 1854 allowing American traders to use two ports. Pierce sent Townsend Harris to exploit this initial concession; in 1858 Harris persuaded the Japanese to open other ports and to establish an embassy in Washington.

Prodded by Secretary of War Jefferson Davis, Pierce also secured about 45,000 square miles of southern New Mexico and Arizona in the Gadsden Purchase from Mexico. The most convenient route for a southern transcontinental railroad ran through the area, and Davis argued that such a prize was worth $10 million.

Cuba, sought by American expansionists from Jefferson on, was worth up to $130 million, or so William L. Marcy, Pierce's secretary of state, informed Pierre Soulé, the United States minister to Spain. In 1854 Soulé consulted at Ostend, Belgium, with John Y. Mason, the American minister to France, and James Buchanan, the minister to England. The three Americans tried to devise a strategy for prying Cuba loose from Spain without arousing the hostility of France or England. Their dispatch to Marcy, initially confidential but soon published and called the Ostend Manifesto, remarked that Spain ought for its own good to get rid of its troublesome colony. Although Cuba was a burden to Spain, they argued, paradoxically the island would be a great boon to the United States. Should Spain refuse to sell Cuba, the three ministers discovered laws both "human and divine" that authorized the United States to seize it. The Ostend Manifesto was too much for northern Democrats, who feared another debate over the expansion of slavery, and too much for the cautious Marcy, who rebuked Soulé, the manifesto's principal author.

If not in Cuba, perhaps slavery might expand in Central America. As part of the Clayton-Bulwer Treaty of 1850, Great Britain and the United States had promised not to colonize Central America nor to claim exclusive rights to any future canal, which was the major reason for interest in the area. But William Walker, an American who made manifest

A Japanese view of Perry's landing

destiny a profession, saw a different future for Nicaragua. At the head of a band of filibusters, Walker took over the country in 1856. He won the support of southern expansionists by opening the republic to slavery, but his tenuous hold on Nicaragua was soon broken and with it the slim chance for new southern territory.

American expansion in the 1850s was only a faint echo of the boisterous manifest destiny of the 1840s. Trade treaties with Japan, a slice of Mexican desert, a bombastic, disavowed demand for Cuba, and some free-enterprise filibustering in Central America aroused no enthusiasm comparable to that Americans had felt for possession of Texas, Oregon, and California. Nor could talk of renewed expansion distract Americans from the sectional rancor their earlier growth had already aggravated.

Suggested Reading

Four quite different older works are still useful. Francis Parkman's *The Oregon Trail** (1849) is the narrative of a nineteenth-century historian. Henry Nash Smith, *Virgin Land** (1950), deals with the West as a compelling symbol for Americans. Albert K. Weinberg's *Manifest Destiny** (1935) is a standard account of expansion in the 1840s. No one should study the 1850s without rereading Harriet Beecher Stowe, *Uncle Tom's Cabin** (1852).

Allan Nevins has edited *Polk: The Diary of a President** (1952) and written a distinguished study of the period, *The Ordeal of the Union* (1947). The best recent biography of Polk is the two-volume work by Charles Sellers completed in 1966. A lively account of part of the Polk administration is Bernard DeVoto's *The Year of Decision: 1846** (1943).

Norman A. Graebner's *Empire on the Pacific* (1955) emphasizes the commercial motives for expansion. David M. Pletcher's *The Diplomacy of Annexation* (1973) is an important recent study of the events surrounding the Mexican War. Ray A. Billington surveys the westward migration in *The Far Western Frontier, 1830–1860** (1956). Frederick Merk has written several books on the West including *History of the Westward Movement* (1978); on this topic, see also *The Plains Across* (1979) by Charles D. Unruh, Jr. The argument about slavery in the territories is central to Chaplain W. Morrison's *Democratic Politics and Sectionalism* (1967), Joseph G. Rayback's *Free Soil* (1970), and Kinley J. Brauer's *Cotton Versus Conscience* (1967). Holman Hamilton has written a careful study of the Compromise of 1850: *Prologue to Conflict** (1964). The early chapters of David Potter's *The Impending Crisis** (1976) add much insight to the recent scholarship that he summarizes.

*Available in paperback edition

Chapter 10
The Union Divides

Chronology

1854 Kansas-Nebraska Act •

1856 Presidential election: James Buchanan (Democrat) defeats John C. Frémont (Republican) and Millard Fillmore (American) •

1857 *Dred Scott* decision • Lecompton Constitution • Financial panic •

1858 Lincoln-Douglas debates •

1859 John Brown raids Harper's Ferry •

1860 Presidential election: Abraham Lincoln (Republican) defeats John C. Breckinridge (Southern Democrat), John Bell (Constitutional Union), and Stephen A. Douglas (Democrat) • South Carolina secedes •

1861—65 The Civil War: *1861:* Fort Sumter bombarded • *1862:* Preliminary Emancipation Proclamation, to take effect in 1863 •

1863: Battle of Gettysburg; Battle of Vicksburg • *1864:* Union Army advances across Georgia • *1864—65:* Battle of Virginia •

1862 Pacific Railway Act • Homestead Act • Morrill Land Grant Act •

1863 National Banking Act •

1864 Presidential election: Abraham Lincoln (Republican) defeats George B. McClellan (Democrat) •

As North and South lost touch during the 1850s, the nation's unity depended upon political leadership. But political parties, like Protestant churches and social institutions, gradually split along sectional lines. Whigs sought to postpone their own demise by nominating generals. The Democrats' expedient was the "doughface," a Northern candidate with Southern principles. The parties offered timid time-servers and political unknowns to fill the nation's pressing needs because strong candidates with strong convictions had too many enemies. But evasion failed: the Whig party vanished after 1852 and Democrats divided over almost every issue as the decade wore on.

The central cause of this political upheaval was the presence of black bondage in the South. The plantation, so apologists claimed, was a utopian biracial community, characterized by the paternalistic concern of whites and the affectionate gratitude of blacks. If this Southern faith rested on fallacies, most Southern whites, including those without slaves, thought it a creed worth dying for.

Northern residents, on the other hand, began to identify slavery as a threat to the free-labor system that they thought of as the American way of life. "Free labor" meant the opportunity to take up a farm on the prairie and not compete with slaves; it meant that wealth and station derived from talent and effort; it meant that the poor today might be rich tomorrow. "The man who labored for another last year," Abraham Lincoln prophesied, "this year labors for himself and next year . . . will hire others to labor for him." This view of the world accepted both human equality and the critical importance of individual differences. Traditionally, Americans had ignored the contradiction between those ideals or assumed that social mobility removed it. But Northerners became increasingly unwilling to ignore the contradiction that a slaveholding South posed to a system of free labor.

Abolitionists—a smaller band than the Free-Soilers—stood on principle: slavery, quite simply, was morally unacceptable. Bondage was wrong in the District of Columbia, wrong in the federal territories, and wrong in the Southern states. Abolitionists professed indifference, or even hostility, to political action because legislative emancipation seemed impossible. But they influenced politics profoundly in the 1850s, for they forced a dialog on the morality of slavery. When politicians talked in moral absolutes, compromise became impossible.

The Territories Again

The Compromise of 1850 produced an artificial harmony that dissipated in renewed bickering over the rights of slave-owners in the remaining federal territories. Dogmatic Southerners demanded the same right to take slaves into the federal territories that Northern farmers had to take cattle. Free-Soilers, for their part, insisted that the new lands be reserved for free—white—laborers. Those, like Webster and Clay, who had sought compromise to preserve the Union diminished in numbers and influence.

Clay and Webster died in 1852, and their passing marked the end of a political generation. Calhoun had died in 1850, the year Thomas Hart Benton lost his seat after thirty years in the Senate; after his candidacy in 1848, Martin Van Buren retired quietly to New York state. Their replacements had had a brief national apprenticeship. Sam Houston came to the Senate in 1846, Stephen A. Douglas in 1847, William H. Seward in 1848, and John C. Frémont in 1850. In 1853, the senior member of the Senate had served there for only ten years, a striking illustration of the perils of sectional politics. The ambitious politican subordinated the principles of his party, and sometimes the needs of his nation, to the demands of his fickle constituency.

Franklin Pierce manifestly had no method of counteracting these divisive forces. Sensing a lack of leadership, Stephen A. Douglas moved to provide direction. In 1854, he introduced the Kansas-Nebraska bill to establish territorial status for the region from the Indian Territory north to the Canadian border. Douglas's bill provided that settlers in the territories would themselves decide about slavery, even though the Missouri Compromise had explicitly forbidden slaves in the entire region. During the angry debate his bill provoked, Douglas accepted an amendment that explicitly repealed the compromise of 1820, and another that divided the area into two territories; this change seemed to promise that Kansas would be slave and Nebraska free, although the understanding was nowhere stated.

The Little Giant realized that his bill might reopen sectional debate, but he decided to take the risk. Once every acre of American soil had territorial government Douglas believed the question of the expansion of slavery need never again arise. Moreover, organization of the region west of Missouri and Iowa had economic advantages: territorial status would create the possibility of land grants to a transcontinental railroad running west from St. Louis or Chicago. Unless Kansas and Nebraska were formally established, a southern transcontinental route from New Orleans, which would run through territory already organized, had an advantage. The Northwest wanted a transcontinental railroad, and Douglas wanted it to reach Chicago, where he had invested in real estate. The South wanted the Missouri Compromise repealed, and Douglas believed popular sovereignty permitted this repeal without risk. He encouraged the North to believe, as he did, that migrants from the Ohio Valley would outnumber slave-owners in Kansas and Nebraska. He allowed the South to expect that repeal of the Missouri Compromise would remove the final barrier to the expansion of slavery. It was an ingenious balancing act.

But it did not work and it discredited Douglas in both sections. Northern voters heard his soft words to the South, and Southerners wanted the expansion of slavery guaranteed, not just permitted. If slavery had been an ordinary political issue, as Douglas thought it was, the Kansas-Nebraska Act might have delayed sectional conflict, enabled the construction of a transcontinental railroad, and opened the White House to the Little Giant. But, although Douglas treated the issue unemotionally, since he had no moral conviction about slavery, others could not remain dispassionate. He expected his measure to provoke a momentary crisis and the opposition of Free-Soilers and abolitionists. He did not foresee the anger of Northern Democrats, including those in his own Northwest. Four antislavery congressmen joined two senators to issue an "Appeal of the Independent Democrats" that asked for immediate, emphatic public opposition to "this enormous crime." The dazed Douglas remarked that his burning effigies lit the route from Boston to Chicago.

His bill eventually passed, but its passage was no triumph, either for Douglas or for the South. The Little Giant died almost a decade before the first transcontinental train steamed into Chicago, and the Kansas-Nebraska Act blighted, rather than fostered, his presidential aspirations. Neither Kansas nor Nebraska became a slave state, and the

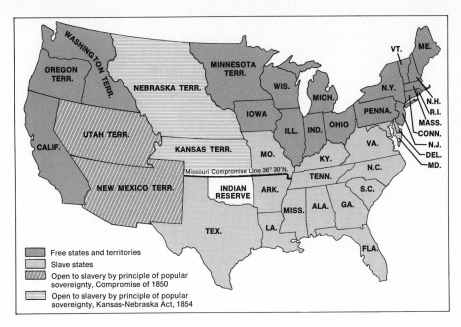

THE KANSAS-NEBRASKA ACT, 1854

Legend:
- Free states and territories
- Slave states
- Open to slavery by principle of popular sovereignty, Compromise of 1850
- Open to slavery by principle of popular sovereignty, Kansas-Nebraska Act, 1854

conflict that boiled out of Kansas had much to do with the abolition of slavery in the entire South. The legislative victory was hardly worth the cost.

Those results, of course, were not clear in 1854, as both sections undertook to fill Kansas with partisans. Massachusetts charted the New England Emigrant Aid Company to encourage and finance antislavery settlement. These settlers, like those in many western states, opposed slavery partly because they wanted to keep blacks out of the area; when they proposed a constitution for the state, these Free-Soil Kansans prohibited settlement by free blacks. "While slavery was sectional," the historian David Potter has remarked, "Negrophobia was national."

The effort to flood Kansas with Free-Soilers, and thereby to deny the South gains the section believed had been won in Congress, inspired Southern migration, especially from Missouri, where defenders of slavery organized to repel the Free-Soil challenge. "Border ruffians" from Missouri rode into Kansas to elect a proslavery legislature, which promptly produced a model slave code for the territory. Wholesale fraud marked this first Kansas election and several of those that followed. The political process broke down completely because neither faction considered binding the results of elections that its opponents won. Baffled governors sent from Washington could neither calm nor govern the quarrelsome territory.

In May 1856, "border ruffians" terrorized the Free-Soil town of

Lawrence, burned the hotel that served as the unofficial headquarters for Northern migration, and destroyed an abolitionist press. A few nights later, an antislavery group directed by a fanatic named John Brown revenged the deaths of two Lawrence residents by butchering five proslavery settlers at Pottawattomie Creek. Brown's victims had had no connection with the sack of Lawrence, but for Brown, who fancied himself God's agent appointed to destroy slavery, no connection was necessary. Sniping, arson, and guerrilla warfare persisted in Kansas through the summer of 1856.

Civil strife in Kansas rekindled the controversy over slavery in Congress. Just before the attack on Lawrence, Charles Sumner, an abolitionist senator from Massachusetts, delivered a tasteless speech denouncing "The Crime Against Kansas." In his long indictment of Southern ways, Sumner singled out Andrew P. Butler, a senator from South Carolina, for particular contempt. A few days later Preston Brooks, a South Carolina congressman and Butler's nephew, beat the Massachusetts senator senseless. Sectional rivalry had reached such a pitch that Brooks, by virtue of thrashing a defenseless man eight years his senior, became a hero in the chivalrous South, and Sumner, an irritating prig, achieved instant martyrdom in the North.

Sectional Politics

The spontaneous rage that swept the North after the passage of the Kansas-Nebraska Act confirmed the development of sectional politics. Democratic congressmen who had voted for the act felt the electorate's wrath directly; only seven of more than forty of them won reelection in 1854. Whigs, who once would have profited from Democratic disaster, were too divided and dispirited to give institutional expression to the Northern protests of 1854 and 1855. With the two familiar parties in retreat, politicians improvised local or regional coalitions as temporary replacements. The American party, for instance, mobilized voters for whom opposition to immigrants and Catholics was more appealing than opposition to slavery. Begun as a secret fraternal order, these Know-Nothings, as Horace Greeley called them, created a momentary sensation in national politics before splitting, like Whigs and Democrats, over slavery.

Thus the parties multiplied; three candidates contested the presidential election of 1856 and four that of 1860. Yet, for the individual voter, the two-party system persisted because sectional rivalry often reduced to two the number of effective choices on a ballot. Southerners, for example, would not vote for Free-Soilers; the choice in the South tended to be between a candidate who demanded "Southern rights," and an opponent who advocated giving the North one more chance to concede. The presidential contest in 1856 became, in effect, a race between Democrats and Republicans in the North and between Democrats and Americans (Know-Nothings) in the South. Moderation and compromise and union—once the elements of national political platforms—seemed to influence a smaller fraction of the electorate than did sectional loyalty in the aftermath of the Kansas-Nebraska Act.

While the American party tried to avoid a stand on slavery, the Republicans met that issue head-on, although they attracted factions on both sides of most other political controversies of the day. Conservative Whigs, who had fought the good fight with Webster and Clay, sat side by side with ambitious Democrats who found changing parties more congenial than changing constituencies. The moralists of American politics, often associated with New Englanders and their descendants elsewhere, discovered common ground with those who did not consider alcohol and slavery moral issues. Eventually Northern Know-Nothings drifted into the Republican party and thereby became political allies of midwestern German Americans. These various elements submerged their disagreements in their common enthusiasm for free soil and what they called "free labor," and in their common distaste for the expansion of slavery and the Kansas-Nebraska Act.

Republicans won control of several Northern statehouses and confidently prepared for the presidential contest of 1856. The platform affirmed the party's opposition to slavery and its extension, advocated reenactment of the Missouri Compromise, favored admission of Kansas as a free state, approved internal improvements, including a railroad to the Pacific, and hinted at the need for a tariff. John C. Frémont, the party's nominee, had no encumbering political record to alienate any voter.

Democrats found a drab, safe candidate. Since they had enacted the Kansas-Nebraska Act, they had to stand for popular sovereignty, but they wisely chose not to flaunt it. The party passed over Stephen Douglas and Franklin Pierce to pick James Buchanan, a conservative Pennsylvanian with a long political career and little political record. Legislator, secretary of state, minister to London, Buchanan was a doughface who roused little enthusiasm and had few enemies. Millard Fillmore, the candidate of the American party, campaigned in the South, where he predicted disunion if Frémont should win. Southern firebrands promised that "immediate, absolute, eternal separation" would follow a Republican victory.

Frémont did not win. Buchanan outpolled Fillmore in the South and Frémont in Pennsylvania, Illinois, and Indiana. But Republicans did carry New England, New York, Ohio, and the upper Northwest. If Frémont had won Pennsylvania and either Illinois or Indiana, his party would have carried off the prize without winning a single vote in 700 of the nation's 1000 counties. James Buchanan and the victorious, but fragile, Democratic party were the last contenders for national political support.

Democratic Unity Tested

The new President was not one to take responsibility for controversial decisions. The issue of territorial slavery had burned previous administrations. Buchanan let the Supreme Court take a turn. Through correspondence with two justices, he knew of the Court's forthcoming ruling on *Dred Scott* v. *Sanford*, which would limit congressional jurisdiction over the territories. The President promised in his inaugural address that he, "in common with all good citizens," would accept the Court's decision as a final settlement.

The facts of the case were well known. In the 1830s Dred Scott had accompanied his master from Missouri to Illinois and then to the Wisconsin Territory. Neither Illinois nor the territory permitted slavery, a technicality that both slave and master ignored. Both returned to Missouri, where Scott remained a slave until his master's death. Complicated legal maneuvering, in which Scott himself was only remotely involved, resulted in Scott's suit for freedom, first in Missouri and then in federal courts, on the ground that residence in free territory had made him a free man. Missouri's highest state court found, on the basis of Missouri law, that Scott was still a slave. A federal circuit judge ruled that no Negro was a citizen and that Scott consequently had no right to bring suit. The Supreme Court of the United States initially intended to issue a routine decision upholding the Missouri court and ignoring the divisive matters of Negro citizenship and the power of Congress to limit territorial slavery. But pressures within the Court convinced some justices to state their position fully to resolve those troublesome questions once and for all.

The *Dred Scott* decision, announced in March 1857, produced everything but the calm Buchanan expected. Each justice wrote his own opinion, and even experienced constitutional lawyers had difficulty determining precisely what a majority had decided. Chief Justice Taney wrote the official "opinion of the court," which left little doubt about the two critical questions. First, Taney held, blacks had ever been inferior to whites and, free or slave, were permanently barred from citizenship. Second, Congress had no power to prohibit slavery in any federal territory. Slaves, Taney argued, were property and were therefore protected by the due process clause of the Fifth Amendment; Congress must respect and defend the slave-owners' black property no less than any other property. The Missouri Compromise, repealed three years before, had always been unconstitutional. Five justices concurred with parts of Taney's opinion; one simply wanted to affirm the judgment of the Missouri court. Benjamin Curtis and John McLean dissented.

Curtis disagreed with both of Taney's major findings. Curtis cited evidence that blacks, including some in the South, had unquestionably exercised the rights of citizenship. And the federal Constitution, as Curtis read it, gave Congress unrestricted power over federal territories. He

Dred Scott

pointed out that several members of the Constitutional Convention, in 1820 and before, had approved legislation limiting the extension of slavery; indeed, before 1840 such congressional authority had been almost universally assumed. The Missouri Compromise was constitutional, Curtis held, and the power of Congress to permit or prohibit slavery unimpaired.

The *Dred Scott* case, which Buchanan had expected to settle everything, did not even settle the fate of Dred Scott, who was quietly emancipated. Neither decision nor dissent convinced anybody not already convinced. The ruling neither established nor protected slavery in any federal territory. Republicans conceded only the Court's ruling on the status of Scott himself; they appealed the rest of the decision to the court of Northern public opinion, where the election of 1860 overruled Taney's judgment. Republicans argued that the *Dred Scott* decision left popular sovereignty as dead as the Missouri Compromise. For if Congress itself could not keep slaves from the territories, it could not logically empower the residents to do so.

Popular sovereignty failed its practical test in Kansas too. In June 1857, convinced that the election would be unfair, Free-Soilers refused to vote for delegates to a constitutional convention. Consequently, proslavery representatives dominated the convention that assembled at Lecompton. They produced a constitution guaranteeing slave property and forbidding free blacks to settle in Kansas. The delegates evaded the spirit of popular sovereignty by asking the electorate to approve the Lecompton Constitution "with slavery" or "without slavery." Since the constitution protected slave-owners already in Kansas, Kansans could vote only to prohibit *further* slavery; they could not abolish slavery altogether. When Free-Soilers refused to vote, the version permitting future slavery carried by a large but deceptive majority.

Southern spokesmen demanded acceptance of the Lecompton Constitution, and Buchanan, who owed his election to Southern Democrats, proclaimed Kansas "as much a slave state as Georgia" and made the constitution a test of party loyalty. It was a test Northern congressmen could not take. Stephen A. Douglas, who believed popular sovereignty should rest on a full expression of the popular will, led congressional opposition. The rift between Buchanan and Douglas split the Democratic party beyond repair. The Senate accepted the Lecompton Constitution, but the House did not. After complex parliamentary maneuvering, Congress offered Kansans another opportunity to vote on the Lecompton document, with the understanding that rejection would delay statehood until the population increased substantially. In an honest election in 1858, Kansans overwhelmingly turned down the constitution and chose to wait.

The nation, and the staggering Democratic party, had taken yet another blow in 1857. A financial panic rocked the North late in the summer and continued into the early months of 1858. Railroad construction ceased, blast furnaces shut down, unemployment mounted, and ships stayed at their wharves in Boston, St. Louis, and San Francisco. Unregulated American banks and the dislocation of the world economy resulting from the Crimean War were partly responsible for the crash, but speculation in land, slaves, and corporate stocks also had severely strained the nation's credit. Distressed Northern manufacturers blamed the crash on the new low tariff passed by the Democratic Congress in 1857. No panic has ever helped a party in power, and renewed demand for a tariff, especially from Pennsylvania iron interests, increased the risks for the low-tariff Democrats.

The panic was less severe in the South. Southern banks survived while Northern banks closed; Southern businesses failed at less than half the rate of their Northern counterparts. Although declining demand sent the price of cotton down from sixteen cents in September 1857 to nine cents at the end of the year, planters simply stored their bales until prices went up in the spring. Ardent Southerners argued that their crop was the key to national recovery, that their economy was stronger than the North's, that, indeed, the South would become even more prosperous if it seceded. "Cotton is king," Senator James H. Hammond proclaimed early in 1858.

Democrats Divide

Stephen A. Douglas returned to Illinois in the summer of 1858 to run for reelection to the Senate. His opponent was an awkward, gaunt, homely man, but Abraham Lincoln was also a sharp debater with an engaging sense of humor and a growing conviction that slavery was wrong. Lincoln cast himself as the underdog David challenging the Goliath of Illinois politics. Douglas, however, was never complacent; his opponent had been among the most important Whigs in Illinois, had almost joined Douglas in the Senate in 1850, and had enough stature in Republican politics to be a serious vice-presidential contender in 1856. The two men agreed to a series of debates that raised for a national audience questions Buchanan believed dangerous to the Union, and that he had endeavored to bury throughout his presidency. To retain any support in the North, for himself or for his party, Douglas had to defend successfully a political middle ground between Southern insistence upon the expansion of slavery and the Republican demand that the blight be restricted.

Lincoln cut away the middle ground at Freeport in the second debate. Was there any way, Lincoln asked, to reconcile popular sovereignty with the *Dred Scott* decision? Could settlers in any federal territory legally exclude slaves? Residents could effectively keep slavery out of any area, Douglas explained in what became known as the Freeport Doctrine, for without local police regulations "slavery cannot exist a day or an hour anywhere." The answer made sense; no slave-owner would risk his investment without the assured cooperation of local public officials. But that answer could not possibly satisfy the South; slave-owners wanted a firm guarantee of the permanence of slavery, no matter what a territory voted. Since the fight over the Lecompton Constitution, Douglas had repeatedly refused to make that pledge. He could not do so and hold Northern voters; without it, however, neither Douglas nor the party he led would have Southern support.

Lincoln was no abolitionist. He repeatedly denied Democratic charges that he favored racial equality. But Lincoln did insist that slavery was wrong and that it must ultimately be abolished; meantime, he promised, Republicans would *make provision that it shall grow no larger.* Douglas successfully shifted the debate from moral rights and wrongs to democracy and union. He won reelection when his party narrowly secured control of the gerrymandered Illinois legislature. But Lincoln won a plurality of the vote and a national reputation as an effective opponent of the nation's most prominent Democrat.

John Brown had never had much faith in any politician. He believed events in 1859 required action, and he planned to arm the slaves to begin it. Brown proposed to capture the federal arsenal at Harper's Ferry, Virginia, and to distribute weapons to blacks who would win their own freedom. But, instead of slaves, Southern militiamen swarmed to Harper's

John Brown

Ferry, and Buchanan sent Colonel Robert E. Lee with a small detachment of federal troops as well. Brown's invasion was soon confined to a small outbuilding and then snuffed out. Virginia tried the old zealot for treason. Convicted and executed in 1859, John Brown became the first martyr of the Civil War.

The trauma of Brown's raid was more serious than the expedition itself. A wave of anxiety engulfed the South, and Southern militiamen began to drill in earnest. Southerners tied Brown and violent abolition to the Republican party, in spite of constant Republican denials. The party's platform in 1860 explicitly denounced "the lawless invasion . . . of any State or Territory, no matter under what pretext." Republicans went further and affirmed "the right of each State to order and control its own domestic institutions." While the plank looked like a bid for Southern votes, it was also a shrewd device to reassure Northern conservatives who opposed all militance and hoped that the slavery dispute would quietly go away.

The Republican platform in 1860 showed other evidence of political maturity. To the pledge to limit the expansion of slavery, Republicans added planks advocating a protective tariff, internal improvements, including a railroad to the Pacific, and a homestead law granting free federal land to western settlers. The delegates rejected as possible candidates William H. Seward, who had spoken of "a higher law than the Constitution" and of an "irrepressible conflict," and Salmon P. Chase, who had signed the flaming "Appeal of the Independent Democrats" in 1854; such men were too radical. Instead the convention settled on Abraham Lincoln, an opponent of slavery, but an economically conservative former Whig whose political hero was Henry Clay. Republicans had learned the lesson of 1856; they wrote a platform to please Pennsylvania and nominated a candidate from Illinois who had also lived in Indiana.

Democrats could not do anything right. At a first convention in Charleston the party could not agree on a platform. Douglas modified the Freeport Doctrine, but Northern Democrats refused to guarantee absolutely that slavery could spread throughout the territories. Alabama's delegates walked out, and the rest of the lower South followed. What was left of the convention wrangled through fifty-seven ballots and recessed without nominating anyone.

The respite merely made division permanent. Douglas Democrats could yield neither principle nor candidate; Southern delegates were equally adamant. When the South lost a series of procedural points at the second convention, delegates from the upper South walked out with those from the cotton states; together they formed yet another convention that nominated John C. Breckinridge, Buchanan's Vice-President. Douglas's forces finally nominated the Little Giant and wound up their forlorn business. The Democratic party, which had for years protected slavery in the area where it flourished, had come apart in a dispute over the expansion of slavery to an area where most Americans agreed it could not profitably survive.

Still seeking to achieve compromise by skirting slavery, a group of border state politicians of miscellaneous party affiliation established the Constitutional Union party. The party appealed to former Whigs and Know-Nothings and to cautious Democrats who thought both Breckinridge and Douglas too extreme. After adopting a few platitudes backing the Constitution, the Union, and the laws, the new party nominated John C. Bell, a former senator from Tennessee.

The four-man campaign devolved into three two-man races: Bell and Breckinridge competed in the South, Bell and Douglas on the border, and Lincoln and Douglas in the North. Douglas won 1,383,000 votes, only about a half million behind Lincoln and considerably ahead of Breckinridge, who polled 850,000, and Bell, who received about 600,000 votes. Douglas carried Missouri and won the votes of three New Jersey electors. Bell won Virginia, Tennessee, and Kentucky; Breckinridge held the rest of the South, though his support in Southern cities and from planters was less firm than in the rural areas and among the smaller farmers who had traditionally supported Jacksonian Democrats. Lincoln won the Northern states and the presidency. Because of the split returns, Lincoln lacked a popular majority. Yet if the votes for his opponents had been cast for a single candidate, Lincoln would have lost only California and Oregon, and their loss would have reduced only slightly his decisive majority in the electoral college.

Lincoln and the Secession Crisis

While the deep South prepared to secede, James Buchanan, an ineffective lame duck, sat in the White House, and the President-elect put together a cabinet of contentious men representing all factions of his party. Few expected the prairie lawyer to dominate Seward, designated secretary of state, or Chase, who would take over the Treasury, or Simon Cameron, the wily Pennsylvanian who was to be secretary of war. Abolitionist Republicans, even before Lincoln's inauguration, criticized his failure to

Abraham Lincoln, 1860, photo by Mathew Brady. Lincoln said that this portrait, widely circulated in campaign literature, helped make him President.

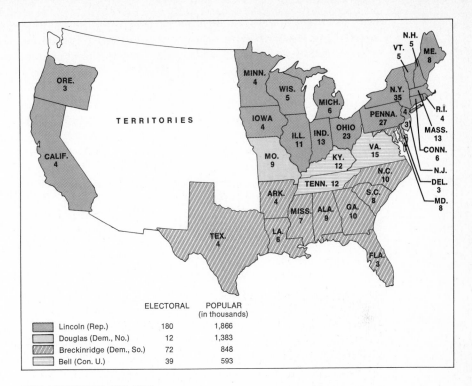

	ELECTORAL	POPULAR (in thousands)
Lincoln (Rep.)	180	1,866
Douglas (Dem., No.)	12	1,383
Breckinridge (Dem., So.)	72	848
Bell (Con. U.)	39	593

THE ELECTION OF 1860

stand for racial equality. And the criticism, from political allies as well as foes, seldom moderated. Little in Lincoln's long career promised either the personal strength or the political and administrative genius that he was to reveal at the White House. Lincoln had been a competent, shrewd, conservative politician of the second rank. The times required more than that.

South Carolina had promised secession if Lincoln won, and the legislature immediately called a convention to carry out the threat. The convention unanimously adopted an ordinance of secession on December 20, 1860. By the first of February, in spite of some support for compromise, Mississippi, Alabama, Georgia, Florida, Louisiana, and Texas had joined South Carolina. In early February delegates gathered at Montgomery, Alabama, and modified the Constitution of the United States for use by the Confederate States of America. The convention elected Jefferson Davis and Alexander H. Stephens to lead the new republic.

Buchanan pronounced secession illegal in one breath and in the next confessed his lack of power to prevent it. But even Buchanan drew a line: although Confederates took possession of federal property, including arsenals, all over the South, the President ordered the federal garrison to hold Fort Sumter in Charleston's harbor.

The upper South hesitated and conciliators in Washington frantically tried to devise in days the formula for union that had eluded them for years. Congressional compromisers, led by John J. Crittenden, a former Whig from Kentucky, suggested several constitutional changes to ease the crisis. A committee discussed amendments reviving and extending the 36°30' line of demarcation between free and slave territories, guaranteeing the domestic slave trade, and forbidding Congress to interfere with slavery in the states. Jefferson Davis indicated that such terms might be acceptable, but Abraham Lincoln, fully aware of both principle and politics, urged Republicans in the Congress to make "no compromise on the question of extending slavery." Crittenden's committee adjourned in disagreement. A peace convention sponsored by Virginia's legislature sent Congress a program that differed from Crittenden's in a few details. The lower South boycotted the assembly and some Republicans joked about its resolutions. The nation awaited Abraham Lincoln—and war.

The President-elect was forced to sneak into Washington because his advisers feared assassination. But confidence rang in Lincoln's inaugural address. He reassured Southerners that neither President nor party endangered "their property . . . their peace, and personal security." And he reassured the North as well: the Union was indissoluble; he would honor his oath to "preserve, protect, and defend" it.

Lincoln soon had a chance to prove his determination. By the beginning of April, Fort Sumter had become for both sides a symbol of federal authority. Major Robert Anderson, who commanded the fort, informed Washington that he needed supplies and reinforcements. Any expedition seemed likely to incite trigger-happy Confederates around Charleston. Most of the cabinet advised against an attempt to relieve Anderson, and Seward even suggested that perhaps the Union could be restored by provoking a quick war, preferably with France or Spain. Lincoln decided to inform authorities in South Carolina that food was on the way to Major Anderson. Following orders from President Davis, South Carolinians demanded Anderson's immediate withdrawal. When it was not forthcoming, the ceremonial first shot was fired on April 12, 1861. Forty-eight hours and 5,000 rounds of artillery fire later Anderson surrendered; no one was killed in the war's first military engagement.

Abraham Lincoln called for 75,000 militiamen to put down the rebellion and Jefferson Davis summoned 100,000 troops to secure Southern independence. The border states could no longer hesitate. Ten days before the barrage on Fort Sumter, Virginia had voted decisively against secession; two days after Lincoln called for troops, Virginia seceded, and Arkansas, Tennessee, and North Carolina soon followed. Delaware remained loyal to the Union. After a riot occurred as Union troops marched through Baltimore on their way to the front, Lincoln used the army to hold Maryland. Kentucky and Missouri had pro-Confederate governors and pro-Union legislatures, an accurate indication of divided popular sentiment. Both states contributed troops to both armies, both served as battlegrounds, and both remained in the Union. The counties of Virginia beyond the Blue Ridge, which were relatively free of slaves and intensely loyal to the Union, seceded from the Old Dominion in 1861 and, as West Virginia, became a state in 1863. Lincoln's grip on the border states was less dramatic than a victory in the field, but it was in the long run far more important than the early Confederate military success.

Early Southern victories confirmed prevailing Confederate optimism. For years the South had derided Yankees as pen-pushers and counting-house clerks; for years the South had claimed that it was more heroic to grow cotton than to weave or market it; for years the South had believed in the perfect harmony of Southern society and sneered at debilitating internal dissent in the North. So Confederates overlooked the fact that 22 million people lived in the North and only about 9 million, of whom 3.5 million were slaves, lived in the Confederate South. And eager Confederates ignored the North's overwhelming superiority in manufacturing, shipping, finance, and railroad transportation. Confident of the righteousness of their cause, Southerners went gloriously to war.

But it was not a glorious war. Dreary, tedious, terrible, trying, bitter, and unbelievably bloody—all these it was, but not glorious. To be sure, camaraderie among opposing pickets occasionally relieved the horror, and there were songs and campfires and parades and waving flags as well as bravery that passed comprehension. Yet, as "The Battle Hymn of the Republic" revealed, there was a self-righteous identification of the cause with Christ and a pitiless determination to crush the satanic foe to lifelessness. Compassion, nostalgia, and years have since sentimentalized the Civil War, and uniforms with bullet holes look more impersonal in museums than on the battlefield when mangled flesh protrudes. About 35 percent of the participants became casualties; more than a half million Americans died, and 400,000 wounded survived.

The costs were incredibly high. But the war proved, in Lincoln's words, that a "nation, conceived in liberty, and dedicated to the proposition that all men are created equal" could indeed endure. Americans in the 1860s took a bold first stride toward the ideal of human equality. They postponed too long any sequential steps, but out of their war came a new nation, tempered in tragedy, that had resolutely settled a half century of argument about the power of the central government and that had at last abolished slavery.

Civil War Begins

Few foresaw the long, agonizing struggle. Lincoln's initial call was for ninety-day volunteers; Southern cavalrymen promised to have the horses home in the fall; spectators from Washington went out in carriages to watch the rebels lose the war at the first battle of Bull Run. But Winfield Scott, Lincoln's strategist, looked toward a war of attrition, one in which

the North's superior resources, numbers, and money would eventually provide victory. Scott suggested an immediate blockade. Then he planned to use the army to cut the Confederacy into pieces, beginning along the rivers. Eventually the Union carried out Scott's "Anaconda plan," but not before a great many men had died in several futile attempts to win quickly by striking at the Confederate capital at Richmond.

Although battles between the capitals attracted the public's attention in the first years of the war, the struggle in the West was at least as important. Early in 1862, a Union army under Ulysses S. Grant moved south from Illinois and captured Fort Henry on the Tennessee River and a garrison of 12,000 Confederates at Fort Donelson on the Cumberland.

Southern forces commanded by Albert Sidney Johnston regrouped in northern Mississippi and caught Grant's army by surprise just north of the Tennessee-Mississippi line at Shiloh. Johnston died in the fierce first day's action; Northern reinforcements enabled Grant to drive off the Confederates on the second day. Casualties totaled about one-fourth of the 100,000 men involved in the gory battle.

The Union secured the lower Mississippi River in April 1862, when forces under Benjamin F. Butler occupied New Orleans after David Farragut's gunboats had bombarded the city. But Union commanders were unable to press their advantage until the spring of 1863, when Grant besieged Vicksburg, Mississippi, the most formidable Confederate base on the river. Shortly after the surrender of Vicksburg on July 4, 1863, the Union controlled the Mississippi from source to mouth. In a series of bitter battles fought around Chattanooga, Tennessee, in the fall of 1863, Union forces broke the last remaining link between Richmond and the Confederate Southwest. By the end of the year, the western wing of the Confederate army was based in Georgia.

Meanwhile, the northern wing of the Confederate army, given superb tactical leadership by Robert E. Lee and Thomas J. "Stonewall" Jackson, repulsed forays into Virginia by Northern forces. Lee and Jackson took uncanny advantage of the mistakes of the shifting Northern command. Confederates compensated for smaller numbers by concentrating their forces to attain tactical superiority at a particular point, while otherwise avoiding contact.

Following the embarrassing retreat of sadly disorganized Union troops after the first brush at Bull Run in July 1861, Lincoln put George B. McClellan in command of the Army of the Potomac. A fine administrator, McClellan drilled his troops into a disciplined army. But, his critics contended, once he had created the army, he did not want to spoil it with use, and McClellan's fumbling campaign in the peninsula of Virginia in the spring of 1862 gave substance to the charge. But Lincoln's replacements proved even worse, and he recalled McClellan to command late in 1862, when Lee began to advance into Maryland. In September McClellan caught Lee at Antietam Creek, where casualties on both sides exceeded 10,000 in the bloodiest day of the war. Perhaps a draw, perhaps a defeat for both armies, Antietam compelled Lee to abandon his invasion of the North, but so weakened McClellan that the Union was unable to pursue the retreating Confederates.

The Emancipation Proclamation

If the Battle of Antietam had no victor, it was nevertheless decisive in one respect: Antietam was the occasion for announcing the Emancipation Proclamation. Initially Lincoln had made reunion the war aim to which all others were subordinate: "If I could save the Union without freeing

The 107th U. S. Colored Infantry

any slave," the President wrote Horace Greeley in August 1862, "I would do it; and if I could save it by freeing *all* the slaves, I would do it; and if I could do it by freeing some and leaving others alone, I would also do that." Lincoln himself would have preferred gradual, compensated emancipation and voluntary colonization of the freedmen abroad. But not even the loyal border states undertook gradual emancipation, and political pressure for abolition was growing in the North as the war continued. In the summer of 1862, even before his letter to Greeley, Lincoln had drafted the Emancipation Proclamation. On Seward's advice, to avoid the appearance of desperation, Lincoln decided to await a military victory to announce the change in Union policy. Antietam, though not precisely a victory, was made to serve.

The Emancipation Proclamation, announced in 1862, was to become effective on January 1, 1863. The President's war powers served as a shaky constitutional basis for his declaration that "all persons held as slaves within any state or designated part of a state, the people whereof shall be in rebellion against the United States, shall be then, thenceforward, and forever, free." As disappointed abolitionists pointed out at the time, the proclamation freed slaves only in areas where Lincoln's decree had no effect; in the border states and in other areas under federal jurisdiction, slavery remained. But the Emancipation Proclamation unquestionably changed a war for reunion to a war for a new union without slaves. Lincoln's proclamation doomed the whole degrading, anachronistic system, though it permitted loyal Union slave-owners a reprieve.

The proclamation, and the Battle of Antietam, dashed Confederate hopes for military supplies, diplomatic recognition, and perhaps even intervention from Britain or France. For diplomatic purposes the Union had maintained that the war was just a domestic disturbance, that the Confederacy was not independent, and that the whole affair was of no interest to other countries. But Lincoln's formal announcement of a blockade early in 1861 unintentionally accorded the Confederacy status as a belligerent, and Britain's official proclamation of neutrality, to the Union's great annoyance, had the same effect. When the war did not abate in 1862, Britain and France seriously considered recognition and perhaps intervention to force a negotiated settlement. British officials connived to sell the Confederacy fast, maneuverable vessels designed to destroy Northern merchantmen. The *Florida* slipped out of England in March 1862, and the *Alabama*, the most effective Confederate raider, set out a few months later. But the Battle of Antietam and the Emancipation Proclamation changed the diplomatic situation. Antietam indicated that Lee could not win Southern independence; and Britain shelved the idea of recognition and mediation. By making abolition the Union's avowed goal, the Emancipation Proclamation helped rally British popular opinion to the Union's cause. In 1863 the British government refused to permit delivery of the "Laird rams," English-made vessels designed to smash the Union's blockade. Confederate efforts to secure foreign intervention had failed.

Gettysburg and Southern Defeat

Early in the summer of 1863, Lee decided to take the war to the North. After an impressive but costly Confederate victory at Chancellorsville, where Stonewall Jackson and more than 1,600 Southern soldiers died, Lee headed into Pennsylvania. The Union army, commanded by George G. Meade, stayed between Lee and Washington. Neither commander really chose the site, but the two armies squared off at Gettysburg on July 1. Meade held the high ground through three days of vicious fighting. More than 7,000 men died at Gettysburg, 4,000 of them Confederates, and more than 40,000 were wounded or missing. Lee retreated to Virginia, where in 1864 and 1865 he was only able to delay ultimate Confederate defeat.

To corner Lee in Virginia, Lincoln brought Grant in from the West. Grant left William T. Sherman the task of crushing the remaining Confederate army based in Georgia. Sherman and Grant, with Lincoln's full support, determined to apply relentless pressure to the Confederate army, whatever the cost, and to use Sherman's force to divide the Confederacy again. Sherman left Chattanooga in May and slowly made his way toward Atlanta, which he captured on September 1, 1864. Sherman then detached his army from any Northern base and began to live off the Georgia countryside on his march from Atlanta to Savannah, which fell before the end of the year. When Sherman turned his army north and entered South Carolina in 1865, Carolinians paid dearly for having led the South to secession.

In Virginia both armies bled. One battle blended into another as Grant pressed on regardless of losses. The armies fought in tangled swamps at the Wilderness, in trenches at Spotsylvania and Cold Harbor, and finally settled down for a long siege at Petersburg. In the spring of 1865 Grant's unwavering pressure cracked Confederate resistance. Lee abandoned

THE CIVIL WAR, 1861 – 1865

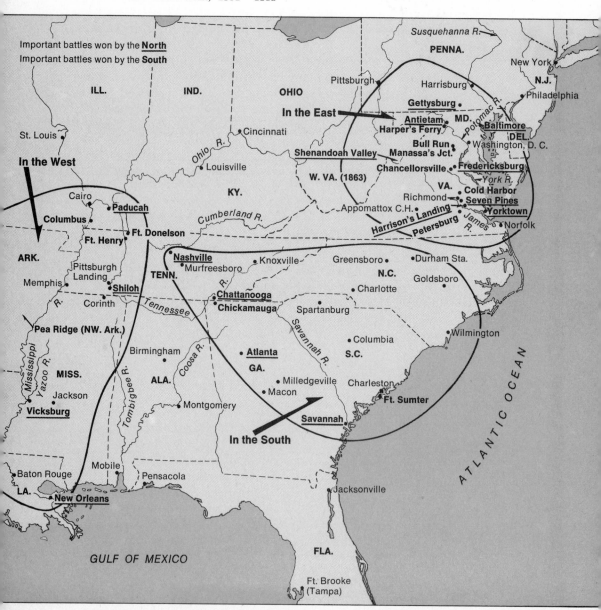

Petersburg and Richmond on April 2; one week later, at Appomattox Court House, it was all over.

No one knows what it cost. Statisticians have guessed at the extent of destruction; one estimate holds that Southern wealth dropped by 43 percent but ignores the financial loss caused by abolition. And no statistic measures suffering. Confederates were never able to breach the Northern blockade, which caused mounting distress as the war went on. In 1864, when Southern transportation had almost completely collapsed, shortages of metals, manufactured goods, clothing, and even food were felt all over the South. Nor was hardship confined to the armies or limited to the South. If destruction in the North was less widespread, Yankees too had empty sleeves, and Northern homes had empty chairs.

Behind the Lines

To launch a new nation is a formidable enterprise; to do so in the midst of a war for survival was beyond the power of Southern leaders. Some disillusioned Southerners maintained that they had the wrong leaders, that Jefferson Davis spent too much time on details, meddled unduly with Lee's military plans, quarreled unnecessarily with his administration and the governors of the states. The charges were true—and probably irrelevant. All the charm, energy, and administrative skill in the world would have availed the South nothing once the blockade took effect and Grant and Sherman took over.

The Southern economy showed the strain almost as soon as the war began. In an attempt to coerce European assistance, Davis forbade the export of cotton and thereby lost valuable foreign exchange. The Confederate congress displayed political cowardice and poor economic judgment by refusing until 1863 to enact a realistic tax program. The Union's blockade kept customs revenues to a minimum. Eventually the Confederacy taxed both property and income, but the measure was tardy and inadequate. Confederate bonds were speculative from the moment of issue and failed to raise much specie. Lacking other resources, the Confederacy had to print currency in ever larger amounts, a policy that brought serious inflation as early as 1862. Meaningless money and few goods combined to produce fantastically inflated prices and widespread discontent. Conscription, too, caused dissension, especially because slave-owners or overseers of twenty (and later fifteen) slaves were exempt. That provision further alienated the non-slave-owning population, which had never been totally committed to Southern independence.

Dissenters resorted to the traditional Southern doctrine of state rights. Governors of several Confederate states undermined Richmond's policies. A governor of Alabama directed state officials not to collect taxes levied in Richmond. Several states officially opposed conscription on constitutional grounds. State judges used state law to release prisoners held under Confederate authority. In most such confrontations the Richmond government was helpless.

Abraham Lincoln had problems as well. Slavery, economic interests, and personal rivalries kept his party on the verge of division. Democrats, buoyed by success in the off-year elections of 1862, took advantage of wartime discouragement to promote their demand for a negotiated peace. The conscription law allowed men of money to hire a substitute or purchase exemption for $300. The Union, like its foe, was thus vulnerable to the charge that it was conducting "a rich man's war and a poor man's fight." Resentment of the inequitable draft law, racism, and other, more local problems erupted in four days of serious rioting in New York City in July 1863. Lincoln's critics, like those of Davis, charged that he exceeded his constitutional authority in using martial law and military courts to silence opponents or jail "Copperheads," as Northern supporters of the Confederacy were called.

But the Northern economy, stronger and more diverse than that of the South, was able both to supply the civilian population with horseshoes and yard goods and to meet the needs of the army for cannon and uniforms. Republicans gained revenue and simultaneously fulfilled a campaign pledge by raising the tariff, first with the Morrill Tariff of 1861, and again in 1862 and 1864. A small income tax in 1861 also contributed to federal revenue. But war costs spiraled beyond tax resources, and the Union secured about ten times as much income from bond sales—about $2.6 billion—as from taxes. "Greenbacks," unsecured paper money, furnished another source of federal funds. The Treasury issued more than $400 million in greenbacks to meet wartime expenses. At its worst, the greenback dollar depreciated to about forty cents. The value revived with the success of the Union armies, and at the end of the war a greenback was worth about sixty-seven cents.

Congress also reorganized the Union's banking with the National Banking Act of 1863. To join the national system, banks had to invest one-third of their capital in federal bonds. Since these bonds paid about 7 percent interest, the investment was attractive. In addition, banks received national banknotes to 90 percent of the market value of their bonds. National banks were subject to some federal regulation, a provision that made many state institutions hold back. In 1865, however, Congress put a prohibitive 10 percent tax on the notes of state banks, and most of them became a part of the national system.

Republicans used federal lands to fulfill other campaign promises. In 1862 Congress pledged land grants and loans to finance the transcontinental railroad. In the same year Congress also passed the Homestead Act, which promised 160 acres of federal domain to a settler who lived on the land and improved it for five years. Finally, in the Morrill Act of 1862 Congress granted land to the states to endow colleges of agriculture and engineering.

Supplies ready for Grant's campaign in Virginia, 1864

While this legislation had a diverse political appeal—to manufacturing, railroad, business, and agricultural interests—the war was the overriding political issue until it ended. In 1864 Democrats nominated General McClellan on a platform that branded the war a failure and demanded a negotiated armistice. McClellan repudiated the platform but still appealed to those voters who were sick of the struggle. Although so-called Radicals in the Republican party were disgusted with Lincoln's slow acceptance of abolition and feared that he would be too lenient when the South surrendered, they could not unite on a single candidate to replace him. For a while in the summer, the President feared defeat in the election, but Sherman's success, especially at Atlanta, came opportunely; 55 percent of the electorate and a 212 to 21 margin in the electoral college returned Lincoln to office.

The meeting of Lee and Grant at Appomattox Court House was about a month away when Lincoln took the presidential oath a second time. His inaugural address sounded no note of triumph and betrayed no trace of satisfaction; he promised only continued resolution, humility, and compassion:

With malice toward none, with charity for all, with firmness in the right as God gives us to see the right, let us strive on to finish the work we are in, to bind up the nation's wounds, to care for him who shall have borne the battle and for his widow and his orphan, to do all which may achieve and cherish a just and lasting peace among ourselves and with all nations.

Suggested Reading

Thomas J. Pressly, *Americans Interpret Their Civil War** (1954), provides an introduction to the vast literature on this subject. Distinguished narratives include multivolume accounts by Allan Nevins, *The Emergence of Lincoln* (1950) and *The War for the Union* (1959–60), and by Bruce Catton, *Mr. Lincoln's Army** (1951), *Glory Road** (1952), and *A Stillness at Appomattox** (1954). A more general account is *The Civil War and Reconstruction* (1961) by James G. Randall and David Donald. David M. Potter's *The Impending Crisis** (1976) is judicious and informed through the research of a lifetime.

Lincoln's career is best traced in his writings, as edited by Roy P. Basler (nine volumes, 1953–55). Don E. Fehrenbacher's *Prelude to Greatness** (1962) illuminates Lincoln's development in the 1850s. Two brief biographies of Lincoln are *Abraham Lincoln** by Benjamin Thomas (1952) and the more recent *With Malice Toward None** (1977) by Stephen B. Oates. Robert W. Johannsen's *Stephen A. Douglas* (1973) is balanced, and David Donald's *Charles Sumner and the Coming of the Civil War* (1960) is full of insight. John Brown's complex life is explored in *To Purge This Land with Blood** (1970) by Stephen B. Oates.

Roy F. Nichols traces the disintegration of the Democratic party in *The Disruption of American Democracy** (1948). Elbert B. Smith interprets some of the same events quite differently in *The Presidency of James Buchanan* (1975). Eric Foner's *Free Soil, Free Labor, Free Men** (1970) examines the ideology of the emerging Republican party. Some of the essays by C. Vann Woodward in *American Counterpoint** (1971) and *The Burden of Southern History** (1960) are directly relevant to the coming of the Civil War. David Potter's *Lincoln and His Party in the Secession Crisis** (1942) is excellent and may be complemented by Kenneth M. Stampp's *And the War Came** (1950). James M. McPherson's *The Struggle for Equality** (1964) outlines the effort to make equality replace union or emancipation as the Union's objective. *Their Tattered Flags* (1970) by Frank E. Vandiver is a recent survey of the Confederacy.

* Available in paperback edition

Chapter 11
Reconstruction

Chronology

1864 Wade-Davis Bill, vetoed by Lincoln •

1865 Lincoln assassinated; Andrew Johnson succeeds • Thirteenth Amendment abolishes slavery • Presidential Reconstruction: Amnesties for whites and enactment of Black Codes •

1866 Civil Rights Act • Freedmen's Bureau Act •

1867 Congressional Reconstruction: Reconstruction Act creates military districts in South; Tenure of Office Act •

1868 Fourteenth Amendment ratified • Johnson impeached but not removed from office • Presidential election: Ulysses S. Grant (Republican) defeats Horatio Seymour (Democrat) •

1870 Fifteenth Amendment ratified •

1870—71 Force Acts to combat Ku Klux Klan •

1872 Presidential election: Ulysses S. Grant (Republican) defeats Horace Greeley (Liberal Republican, Democrat) •

1876 Presidential election: Rutherford B. Hayes (Republican) defeats Samuel J. Tilden (Democrat) when a special electoral commission awards Hayes all 20 disputed votes in January 1877 •

1883 Civil Rights cases •

1895 Booker T. Washington addresses Atlanta Exposition •

1896 *Plessy* v. *Ferguson* establishes doctrine of "separate but equal" •

Reconstruction, Abraham Lincoln remarked as he received the news of Appomattox, "is fraught with great difficulty." The President's victory speech soberly emphasized the uncertain future instead of the triumphant past, for he lacked specific programs to offer his shattered nation. In the dozen years after Lincoln's death the effort to reconstruct subtly changed to a search for peaceful accommodation. And the dilemmas he had foreseen endured, like the monuments both sections erected to the dead.

There are no monuments to Reconstruction, for people rarely celebrate failures. Reconstruction just ended, its promises unkept. Although the South rejoined the Democratic party and once more participated in national politics, regional peculiarities set the section off from the rest of the land for a century. Although diligent Southerners of both races slowly rebuilt their agrarian economy, industrialization rapidly transformed the rest of the country, creating problems and opportunities that much of the South did not share. Finally, although emancipation made racial equality possible, that goal has not yet been achieved.

Racial equality and the place of black Americans in white society were the central issues of the Reconstruction years. The need for a policy, which Lincoln and nearly everyone else felt, showed how the paternalism of slavery lingered. For if blacks were really free, then they were not objects to be disposed of by the law of any legislature. Free people, after all, should make their way unfettered in a free society. But most whites then, and many whites since, expected to be their black brother's keeper, sometimes to help him, and sometimes to help themselves. One of those who tired of helping the freedmen captured the history of Reconstruction in a paragraph:

Force may for awhile restrain the passions of men, [but] it is at least questionable whether the evil resulting does not overbalance the good. We never contemplated when we took the freed blacks under the protection of the North that the work was to be for an unlimited time. We hoped that if for a few years we lent them a helping hand, self interest, if not a sense of right, would prompt the Southern whites to do their duty by them. That in this we have been disappointed is partly their fault, partly ours in permitting so many disreputable men to take the office of protectors and so bring discredit on the whole system.*

Lincoln Plans for Reconstruction

Lincoln had begun to improvise a Reconstruction policy as soon as Union armies moved into the Confederacy. In 1863 the President promised amnesty to all Southerners (except a few Confederate officials) who would swear allegiance to the Constitution and the Union. When the number of oath-taking voters reached 10 percent of a state's vote in the presidential election of 1860, military authorities were to permit formation of a state government. Lincoln promised the executive recognition that signified completion of Reconstruction as soon as that state government abolished slavery.

But executive recognition, as the South was to discover repeatedly, was only one hurdle. Congress alone could permit Southern states to rejoin the national legislature. Many Republicans in Congress thought the President too lenient and his conception of Reconstruction too narrow. Political rivalries and disagreement about legislative tactics kept these legislators, imprecisely called "Radicals," divided. Individual Radicals—Thaddeus Stevens, Charles Sumner, Benjamin Wade—initiated some Reconstruction legislation and kept the principle of racial equality constantly before their less radical Republican colleagues. The legacy of the faction is the vision of these individuals, not the legislation that emerged from complex compromise within the Congress and with the President. The program for Reconstruction that was eventually called

* Francis R. Cope to Laura Towne, Nov. 19, 1877, as quoted in Willie Lee Rose, *Rehearsal for Reconstruction* (1964), pp. 403–04.

Lincoln's last portrait. Compare with the 1860 portrait (p. 228) for a visual indication of the strain of the presidency during the Civil War.

"Radical Reconstruction" was not fully faithful to the principles of the sternest Radicals, who considered it neither radical nor reconstruction.

Lincoln's critics countered his "ten-percent plan" with the Wade-Davis Bill, which Congress passed in July 1864. Whereas Lincoln had been willing to accept a promise of future loyalty from a minority, Congress demanded proof of past loyalty from a majority. Before military occupation could give way to civil government, Congress insisted, a majority of white male citizens must take an oath of past and future allegiance to the federal Constitution. No one who had supported the Confederacy could vote or participate in the formation of reconstructed state governments, which must abolish slavery, repudiate any debt incurred during the war, and deprive former Confederates of political rights.

Although Lincoln killed the Wade-Davis Bill with a pocket veto, he indicated a willingness to modify his own policy. The President did not insist on one method of reunion; if a Southern state wished to reconstruct itself as the Wade-Davis Bill prescribed, Lincoln would not object. Lincoln's pose of flexibility conceded nothing, since no Southern state would choose harsh congressional terms while the President's less demanding option was available. Sponsors of the bill responded to the veto with an indignant manifesto. The dispute over Reconstruction, which divided Congress and the President as deeply as any issue in American political history, had begun in earnest.

On the surface, the debate centered on legal and constitutional questions. Were Southern states still states with full constitutional rights? Or were they, as Thaddeus Stevens claimed, "conquered provinces," subject to the unlimited power of Congress to regulate federal territories? Was Reconstruction a presidential function—for the executive power to pardon was clearly relevant—or could Congress assume full responsibility, since it must consent before a Southern state could rejoin the national legislature?

Abraham Lincoln knew that Reconstruction was more than a constitutional nicety and dismissed the whole controversy over the legality of secession as "a merely pernicious abstraction." He thought Reconstruction might be accomplished "without deciding or even considering" whether the Confederacy had ever been outside the Union. Lincoln hoped to subordinate dispute to agreement: "We all agree that the seceded states, so called, are out of their proper practical relation with the Union; and that the sole object of the government . . . is to again get them into that proper practical relation." Perhaps Lincoln, with his political genius, could have enlisted the Radicals in his effort to rebuild the Union without bitterness. His assassin did not give him the chance.

The Radical Vision

As they thought about the relationship of free individuals in society, Republican legislators tended to divide personal rights into three categories: civil rights, political rights, and social rights. Civil rights accompanied citizenship and included equality before the law; that much, most Northerners agreed, was inherent in emancipation. Political rights included the right to vote and hold office, rights that even many Radicals were not ready to allow newly freed blacks to exercise until they had acquired property or literacy. Most Northern states did not permit blacks to vote, a prohibition that referenda in several states explicitly confirmed after the war. Social rights, according to the legal theories of the day, were beyond the law; no government could coerce citizens to accept other citizens as associates, friends, or customers.

Thaddeus Stevens thought government ought to try to do just that. The cantankerous congressman from Pennsylvania looked beyond the

South's ruined plantations to a day when economically independent farmers of both races would till their own small farms. He proposed to confiscate all Southern land except individual holdings of less than two hundred acres. He suggested that some of the land thus obtained be granted to former slaves in order to assure their economic independence. The rest of the confiscated lands, Stevens said, should be sold at auction and the proceeds put toward reducing the national debt, establishing a fund for Union soldiers or their widows and children, and replacing Northern property destroyed during the war. The South must pay for the hardship its war had brought. If the losers paid no reparation, Northern taxpayers would in effect subsidize the defeated enemy by bearing the war's indirect costs. That situation, Stevens charged, was absurd.

He may have been right; without economic security the freedom of blacks was not firmly based. Although freedmen all over the South anticipated a redistribution of land as the war ended in 1865, the radicalism of Stevens's Republican colleagues never extended to the confiscation of slaveholders' plantations. If Congress disappointed the

Lincoln's body arriving in Chicago, May 1, 1865

hopes of the freedmen for farms, it did offer them temporary support and protection in their transition to freedom.

The Freedmen's Bureau, established about a month before Lee's surrender, was to provide this support. In the confusion immediately after Appomattox the bureau fed refugees of both races and helped them to relocate. It helped freedmen secure jobs and then supervised employers to prevent the concealed reestablishment of slavery. The agency also set up and maintained public facilities, such as schools and hospitals, that had never been readily available to Southerners of either race. Finally, the Freedmen's Bureau attempted to protect the legal equality of blacks and to prevent social discrimination. To be sure, there were occasional abuses: some agents were corrupt; some abused the trust of blacks; some used the political possibilities inherent in the bureau to promote their own careers.

Indeed, no part of Radical Reconstruction was free of political overtones. Thaddeus Stevens, forthright as usual, declared that any program must "secure perpetual ascendancy to the party of the union." The Thirteenth Amendment, Stevens pointed out, abolished the former practice of counting a slave as three-fifths of a person; consequently, the South, once readmitted, would be entitled to more congressmen than had represented the section before the war. More congressmen meant more electoral votes, thus endangering Republican control of the White House, for Democrats could fuse their Northern minority with white voters of the South to create a national majority. Stevens's demand for black suffrage derived from his desire to perpetuate Republicanism through Southern support as well as from egalitarian conviction.

Stevens probably believed that the republic could not be entrusted to "whitewashed rebels" and those whom he regarded as apologists for treason. But his motive may have been less disinterested than he acknowledged, and some Republicans certainly hoped to use Reconstruction to serve themselves. Stevens, for instance, owned an iron mine in southern Pennsylvania that Confederates had damaged extensively during the war; his interest in compensating Northern property-holders for wartime destruction may have been related to his own losses. Like other owners of iron mines, Stevens was also a confirmed advocate of the protective tariff; protection seemed to depend upon continued Republican supremacy, for Democrats had traditionally opposed the policy.

As Stevens's motives were mixed, so too were those of other Republicans. Although the party represented conflicting economic interests, most Republicans believed in the comprehensive legislative program that the fortuitous secession of the South had allowed them to bring about—protective tariff, the national banking system, the Homestead Act, and federal grants to transcontinental railroads. Before the war Southern Democrats had blocked this legislation. Postwar Democrats were still hostile to some of it and were also flirting with

Freedom: Richmond, 1865

various forms of economic heresy, such as the notion that national bonds should be redeemed in the inflated greenbacks with which they had often been purchased, instead of in gold as the bond promised. Some Republican businessmen, glimpsing industrial affluence in the future, advised against such economic experimentation.

The white South was equally unready for social experimentation, and Abraham Lincoln may have agreed. Once a staunch Whig, Lincoln perhaps hoped to gain support for gradual change from the same coalition of moderates in both sections that had sustained his old party. Some Radicals so mistrusted the President that they welcomed

Vice-President Andrew Johnson's succession. For Johnson, a self-made man from Tennessee and a thoroughly Jacksonian Democrat, seemed to have nothing in common with those substantial Southerners whom Lincoln hoped might become the pillars of a Southern Republican party. But to the surprised dismay of the Radicals, Andrew Johnson, who had never acted like a Southerner during the war, seemed to join the Confederacy after Appomattox.

Presidential Reconstruction

Johnson probably intended Reconstruction to transfer control of the South from slaveholders to other whites who owned and worked their own small farms, the independent yeomen who had sustained his own political career in Tennessee. When he offered the South a general amnesty, the President excluded from it people he thought of as aristocrats—major Confederate officials and individuals with taxable property in excess of $20,000. He encouraged amnestied Southern whites to write new state constitutions and to establish state governments. Once these governments had ratified the Thirteenth Amendment, repudiated the Confederate debt, and repealed ordinances of secession, the President believed, Reconstruction would be completed.

White Southerners accepted Johnson's generous terms and even persuaded him to extend presidential pardons to some whose wealth or Confederate service made them ineligible for the general amnesty. Whatever Johnson's intent, the voters in the newly reconstructed states then chose many of the same men who had led them out of the Union to lead them back in. Mississippi and South Carolina elected governors who had been Confederate generals; Georgia chose Alexander Stephens, the Confederacy's Vice-President, for the Senate of the United States. Neither the Southern voter nor Andrew Johnson made any tactful gesture to quiet mounting Northern suspicion that a costly victory was being cheaply given away. That victory and the Civil War, after all, were the central events in the lives of millions of Yankees, whose sacrifices had to be dignified by dramatic changes in the South. Southern whites ignored this dimension of Reconstruction in an understandable attempt to salvage what they could from defeat.

While Radicals fumed because Congress was in recess until December 1865, reconstructed Southern legislatures began to adopt Black Codes to replace prewar regulations governing slaves. These laws permitted blacks to marry one another and held parents responsible for their children. The codes also spelled out freedmen's legal rights, which were more restricted than those of whites. In some states, for instance, blacks could not offer courtroom testimony against whites.

Other provisions of the codes limited the civil rights of freedmen and denied them even a small measure of equality. Apprenticeship regulations bounded the economic and social freedom of young blacks; courts had to order the apprenticeship of unemployed young freedmen and give preference to their former masters. The resulting arrangement often differed little from slavery. Vagrancy regulations and laws forbidding disorderly conduct gave enforcement officers wide discretion and restricted the social and economic life of black adults. Any Mississippi black who lacked regular employment or who could not pay the poll tax was guilty of vagrancy. Those convicted could be leased to employers who paid fines and costs; former masters again had preference and the result again might be only technically distinguishable from bondage. Even if a black obeyed all these statutes, other laws kept him out of the white community. The only black passengers permitted in first-class railroad cars in Mississippi, for instance, were maids, who were allowed to wait on their white mistresses.

The freedman's lack of land and money reinforced provisions of the Black Codes that limited his mobility. Any black without a contract certifying steady employment had to have a license. Contracts often specified annual wage payments, a practice that forced the employee into debt for expenses incurred while earning the first year's wage. And if he left his employer before the expiration of the year, he forfeited what he had earned up to that time.

Congressional Reconstruction

Radicals were positive that Johnson's program was a sham; even Republican moderates doubted that representatives of a loyal, reformed, and contrite people had approved the Black Codes. Rebels had reestablished " 'the white man's Government,' " Thaddeus Stevens charged, and Congress should resolutely prove that such governments were entirely unacceptable components of the federal republic. Demagogues, including "some high in authority," he continued, with a barbed reference to the President, had appealed to the "lowest prejudices of the ignorant" to maintain the dominance of Southern whites. Stevens held that the white race had "no exclusive right forever to rule this nation," nor could it convert "other races and nations and colors" to mere subjects. He did not shrink from the conclusion: this nation, he said, must be "the Government of all men alike."

Most Republicans stopped short of Stevens's stand. Yet if they were not ready to admit the black man to full political equality, as Stevens demanded, they did insist on more than President Johnson had required. So, in December 1865, Congress refused to let Southern legislators take

Andrew Johnson

the oath and sent them home. Congress then began work on two bills
and a proposed constitutional amendment that became the
congressional terms for reunion. The President vetoed both bills and
encouraged those who opposed the amendment. His intransigence made
more difficult the task of moderate Republicans, who sought a program
less extreme than Stevens advocated, but more equitable to blacks than
the unreconstructed white governments Johnson approved. The
President's political ineptitude and the adamant refusal of white
Southerners to concede to the blacks more than technical emancipation

eventually drove the Republican party toward radicalism and military Reconstruction.

Moderates began with a bill to prolong the life of the Freedmen's Bureau and to give it a quasi-judicial authority over disputes arising from discrimination or denial of civil rights. The bill deprived state courts of jurisdiction in such cases, and specifically contradicted Southern Black Codes by making punishable the sort of discrimination they mandated. Although the bill's sponsors thought they had secured the President's approval, Johnson vetoed the measure in February 1866. The bureau, the President held, had grown out of the war's emergency and was based on the constitutional grant of power for war, which Congress could not legitimately invoke in peace. Once ordinary institutions, including civil courts, were reestablished, the bureau should disband.

Congress could not immediately override Johnson's veto, and moderates instead began to consider the Civil Rights Bill of 1866. This bill declared blacks to be citizens of the United States, thus burying the *Dred Scott* decision, and guaranteed "the full and equal benefit of all laws . . . for the security of person or property" to black citizens. Federal courts were to have jurisdiction over cases in which citizens had been deprived of equal rights. Political rights—including suffrage—were still not part of the program, but Republicans clearly insisted on civil equality. The bill received the support of every Republican in the House and all but three in the Senate. Andrew Johnson vetoed it because it infringed the reserved powers of the states.

This time Congress overrode the veto and, for good measure, salvaged the Freedmen's Bureau Bill too. To preserve its handiwork, Congress framed the constitutional amendment that eventually became the Fourteenth, which confirmed the status of blacks as citizens and prohibited state legislation that denied equal legal protection to all citizens. Johnson could not prevent the submission of the amendment to the states, but his hostility encouraged Southern states to reject it and temporarily blocked ratification. Tennessee, the President's own state, ratified the amendment and was rewarded by full restoration to the Union. Other Southern states rejected the amendment and waited.

They waited too long, for the Congress that assembled in 1867 raised the price of readmission. In the crucial congressional election of 1866 Andrew Johnson had taken his cause to the country. His performance on the stump struck people as undignified and seemed as inept as his performance in the White House. Voters sent a new Congress to Washington with enough votes to overwhelm the President.

The legislation that emerged from this new Congress did not satisfy doctrinaire Radicals. Republican leaders, most of whom were not radical, compromised to balance the constitutional scruples of conservatives, the political interests of the party, and the ideals of the Radicals. In 1867 Congress passed a Reconstruction Act that combined ten Southern states into five military districts and subordinated state governments to military commanders. The governments and constitutions Johnson had approved in 1865 were to be discarded and new constitutions granting suffrage to blacks and guaranteeing their equality were to be established. (The Fifteenth Amendment, delayed until 1870, prohibited states from abridging the suffrage "on account of race, color, or previous condition of servitude," but did not affirmatively guarantee blacks the right to vote. Sponsors of the amendment warned feminists that adding sexual equality would jeopardize ratification; it required another half century to repair that omission.) The Reconstruction Act unquestionably mocked the traditional rights of states, as both Johnson and the South charged. The Radicals, however, had minimal interest in the political principles and the constitutional pretenses of the defeated section. They counted the doctrine of state rights an unmourned casualty of the Civil War.

Congress abridged the President's powers, as it had the rights of states. Johnson's power to direct the army was limited by a requirement that all orders be issued through the General of the Army, who could not be removed or reassigned without the Senate's consent. The Tenure of Office Act required the Senate's approval for removal of any official for whom senatorial confirmation was necessary. Congress hoped thereby to protect Secretary of War Edwin Stanton, who opposed the President's program, and whose support for military Reconstruction was crucial.

Radicals then turned to impeachment, both to remove this stubborn President and to warn future Presidents. The charge against Johnson specified eleven offenses, most of which arose from his attempt to remove Stanton from the cabinet. But, Thaddeus Stevens confessed, he did not mean to impeach the President for any particular offense or even for all of them together. Stevens meant to banish Johnson for his political mistakes, not for moral or legal lapses. Stevens wanted nothing less than to subordinate the President to Congress—to make future Presidents responsible to future Congresses—and impeachment was the means to his end.

The House debated all of Andrew Johnson's alleged crimes: his partiality toward the South, his public disrespect of Congress and its leadership, his drunken inauguration as Vice-President, his rumored complicity in Lincoln's assassination, and his deliberate violations of the Tenure of Office Act. The President was acquitted partly because the Senate found the bill of particulars too flimsy a basis for so unprecedented a step and partly because a few senators decided to support the independence of the executive branch rather than establish a precedent that might lead to a ministry responsible to the legislature, as is a parliamentary cabinet. Still, the margin in the Senate was slim; Johnson survived by one vote. Thirty-five Republicans voted to convict; twelve Democrats and seven Republicans found for the President. After the roll calls in the Senate, Washington ceased to be the main forum for debate over Reconstruction until the effort was abandoned in the compromise of 1877.

FORTIETH CONGRESS U.S. SECOND SESSION

SENATE CHAMBER.

MAY 16TH AND 26TH 1868.

The vote of the Senate, sitting as a High Court of Impeachment for the trial of ANDREW JOHNSON, President of the United States, upon the 11th, 2nd and 3rd Articles.

S. P. Chase, Chief Justice.   *J. W. Forney*, Secretary.

~ Guilty. ~

1 *B. F. Wade*	13 *Jas Harlan*	24 *Charles Sumner*
2 *H. W. Corbett*	14 *O S Ferry*	25 *Alex. G. Cattell*
3 *Cornelius Cole*	15 *Alex. Ramsey*	26 *Geo. H. Williams*
4 *L. M. Morrill*	16 *John Conness*	27 *Z. Chandler*
5 *Wm M Stewart*	17 *Geo. F. Edmunds*	28 *E. D. Morgan*
6 *J. W. Patterson*	18 *Fred. T. Frelinghuysen*	29 *John Sherman*
7 *Justin S. Morrill*	19 *H. B. Anthony*	30 *John M. Thayer*
8 *James W. Nye*	20 *J. M. Howard*	31 *Roscoe Conkling*
9 *Timo. O. Howe*	21 *S. C. Pomeroy*	32 *C. D. Drake*
10 *Henry Wilson*	22 *W. T. Willey*	33 *Simon Cameron*
11 *A. W. Cragin*	23 *Rich'd Yates*	34 *T. W. Tipton*
12 *W Sprague*		35 *O. P. Morton*

~ Not Guilty. ~

1 *T. A. Hendricks*	7 *J. B. Henderson*	14 *J. W. Grimes*
2 *C. A. Buckalew*	8 *Lyman Trumbull*	15 *David T. Patterson*
3 *D. Fenton*	9 *E. G. Ross*	16 *Willard Saulsbury*
4 *J. R. Doolittle*	10 *W. P. Fessenden*	17 *Reverdy Johnson*
5 *Tho. C. McCreery*	11 *Garrett Davis*	18 *P. G. Van Winkle*
6 *George Vickers*	12 *J. A. Bayard*	19 *James Dixon*
	13 *Jos. S. Fowler*	

Entered according to the Act of Congress in the year 1872 by JAMES D. McBRIDE, in the Clerks Office of the District Court for the District of Columbia.

Reconstruction Ends

The emotional intensity that had sustained Radical idealism gradually waned after the effort to remove President Johnson failed. Thaddeus Stevens died; in other hands the egalitarian cause became little more than election-day rhetoric calculated to remind voters of the sanctity of the Union, the martyrdom of Lincoln, and the treason of Democrats—a tactic known as "waving the bloody shirt." "We hoped," a saddened Ralph Waldo Emerson wrote, that peace would produce "true freedom in politics, in religion, in social science, in thought." But there was no "great expansion in the mind of the country" because "the energy of the nation seems to have expended itself in the war." Emerson's observation, remarked the cultural historian Lewis Mumford, was "an old story":

War does not bring the martial virtues into the subsequent peace: it merely prepares a richer soil for the civilian's vices. One might as well expect a high sense of tragedy in an undertaker, as heroism in the generation that follows a war: meeting death is one thing, and disposing of the remains is another.*

The presidential election of 1876 disposed of the remains of Reconstruction. Both Samuel J. Tilden, the conservative Democratic nominee, and Rutherford B. Hayes, an honest Republican nominated as an antidote to retiring President Ulysses S. Grant, favored removing the occupying troops from the unreconstructed states. The count clearly showed that Tilden had a popular majority and 184 electoral votes, while Hayes had only 165 for certain. Republicans claimed one disputed vote in Oregon that had been awarded to Tilden on a legal technicality, and nineteen from three states in the South. Democrats throughout the South had systematically harassed black voters to keep them from the polls; Republican officials and federal troops in Louisiana, Florida, and South Carolina had perhaps overcompensated by stuffing the ballot boxes.

If the election had been absolutely fair, black voters in these three Southern states might well have carried Hayes to victory. But instead Hayes owed his election to the partisan decision of a commission, and his claim to the presidency seemed flawed to his contemporaries and to many observers since. The commission, established by Congress to settle the matter, consisted of five members each from the House, Senate, and Supreme Court. The appearance of impartiality disappeared when the commission's one uncommitted member withdrew and was replaced by a convinced Republican. There was a good deal of bargaining, and some chicanery on both sides, before the commission awarded all twenty disputed votes, and the presidency, to Hayes.

* Lewis Mumford, *The Brown Decades* (1931), pp. 13–14.

Republicans paid a political price for the White House. Southern Democrats won assurance that federal funds would become available for construction of Southern railroads, for improvements to Southern harbors, and for projects that would make Southern rivers more navigable and less apt to flood the countryside. In addition to capital for internal improvements, white Southerners were to be given the respectability (and the salaries) of federal jobs. Hayes appointed David M. Key, a former Whig from Tennessee, as postmaster general, the traditional post for the administration's patronage broker. Finally, civil government was restored throughout the South when Hayes recalled the last of the troops.

The experiment in reconstruction was over. Although the settlement in 1877 meant different things to different people, it clearly signaled a return to sectional compromise. Republicans probably hoped that conciliation would persuade conservative Southerners to make common cause with conservatives to the north. The promised flow of federal capital seemed to Southerners to herald a "New South," where industry and transportation would complement agriculture and produce unparalleled prosperity. For blacks, however, the New South turned out to be quite like the old.

The View from the South

The prevailing Southern view after 1877 held that Radical Reconstruction was a tragic blunder. Blacks, their venal Northern allies (called "carpetbaggers"), and a few unprincipled Southern whites (known as "scalawags") had a ten-year private orgy at public expense. No matter that no Southern state had a black governor and that in only one did blacks even briefly control the legislature. No matter that many of the carpetbaggers had come to the South to teach or to farm or to make a living, not to change racial customs or to wield political power. No matter that some of the scalawags bore some of the South's oldest and most respected family names. The legend of "Black Reconstruction" holds that white conservatives rescued the region from barbarism and bankruptcy in 1877. D. W. Griffith's classic film *Birth of a Nation* (1915), for instance, depicts Southern whites as the victims of Reconstruction.

So, in fact, they were, though not in the way Griffith's film suggests. Blacks were also victims, and so was the rest of the nation. For the errors of Reconstruction lie both in what happened and in what might have happened but did not. Generations of Southerners of both races paid in poverty, in prejudice, in fear and violence, and in a thousand other ways for the failure to create equitable relations between the races. The rest of the nation has gradually begun to discover how much of that failure is shared.

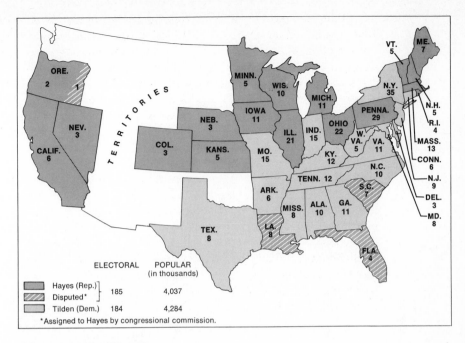

	ELECTORAL	POPULAR (in thousands)
Hayes (Rep.)	⎱ 185	4,037
Disputed*	⎰	
Tilden (Dem.)	184	4,284

*Assigned to Hayes by congressional commission.

THE ELECTION OF 1876

    Reconstruction myths, like most myths, had a basis in fact. Taxes in Southern states did rise to unprecedented levels, and the receipts were not always honestly spent. Florida paid more for printing in 1869 than for all the expenses of state government in 1860. South Carolina's debt either tripled or increased six times, depending upon which unreliable accounting was accepted; a restaurant and bar, maintained at public expense, served imported delicacies impartially to South Carolina's black and white legislators.

    But blacks neither caused nor benefited from all that legislative corruption. Much of it derived from attempts to entice factories and railroads into the South. Since individual investors lacked credit and capital to finance these ventures, states issued bonds to pay for construction. Public funds were often converted to private use, and politicians pocketed "fees" that might more candidly have been called bribes. In short, the graft that accompanied the building of the nation's railroads also occurred in the South, and Southern politicians, like their counterparts in Northern political machines, were occasionally for sale.

    Blacks received the blame for corruption, but rarely the profit. The promoters who purchased politicians were almost invariably white, and white Northern stockholders often collected the tainted dividends. Although some black officeholders accepted bribes and misused public funds, none stole so much as the white treasurer of Mississippi embezzled immediately after the state had been saved from the

An English view of the South Carolina legislature, 1876

supposedly irresponsible blacks. The corrupt nickels and dimes, no matter who took them, were not the important costs of Reconstruction anyway. Those bills are still coming due.

Poverty

The first costs were those of repair. Yankee armies and wartime neglect combined to ruin the South's prewar prosperity. General Philip Sheridan's troops had destroyed so much in the Shenandoah Valley that he boasted that even a crow would have to carry rations to survive a flight over the area. A Northern reporter described Charleston, South Carolina, as a city "of ruins . . . of vacant houses, of widowed women, of rotting wharves, of deserted warehouses, of weed-wild gardens, of miles of grass-grown streets, of acres of pitiful and voiceful barrenness." But at least the houses and warehouses still stood in Charleston. Columbia, the same reporter noted, was a "wilderness of ruins, . . . blackened chimneys and crumbling walls." In the business district "not a store, office, or shop escaped; and for a distance of three-fourths of a mile on each of twelve streets, there was not a building left."

The ruins of Charleston

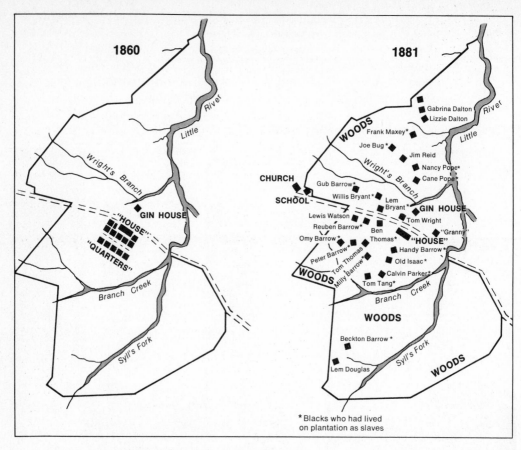

A GEORGIA PLANTATION IN 1860 AND 1881

Damage in the countryside was less immediately visible, but not less economically severe. Weeds ruined cotton fields as surely as they did Charleston's gardens. Throughout the rural South, men had to restore fertility to the soil, fences to the fields, and stock to the barns, and had to produce an initial crop for food and seed. When buildings had to be rebuilt, the hardship was compounded.

Southern wealth had traditionally taken the form of land and slaves. Since slavery had ended, land had to serve as the basis for renewing the Southern economy, and sharecropping gradually evolved as the link between land and labor. Impoverished landowners permitted impoverished tenants of both races to work the land. Owner and laborer then shared the crop according to a formula that depended partly on prevailing rates in the community and partly on whether the tenant furnished his own seed and mule. Both parties often had to survive on credit advanced at the local store, where interest charges might increase costs as much as 40 percent. Profits from farming were sometimes inadequate to carry either owner or tenant through another year, when the cycle began again.

"I was in debt," wrote John Solomon Lewis, a Louisiana sharecropper, in 1879.

. . . the man I rented land from said every year I must rent again to pay the other year, and so I rents and rents, and each year I gets deeper and deeper in debt. In a fit of madness I one day said to the man I rented from: "It's no use, I works hard and raises big crops and you sells it and keeps the money, and brings me more and more in debt, so I will go somewhere else and try to make headway like white workingmen.*

The landowner warned Lewis that "you will get your head shot away" for leaving, but the sharecropper, his wife, and their four children successfully hid in the woods until they caught a boat for Kansas.

* Quoted in Nell Irvin Painter, *The Exodusters* (1976), p. 3.

Black homesteaders on the Plains

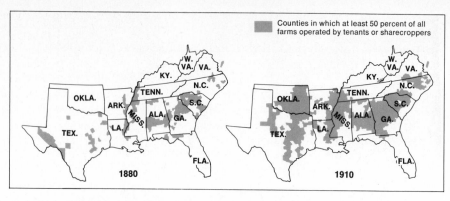

Counties in which at least 50 percent of all farms operated by tenants or sharecroppers

1880

1910

TENANCY ON SOUTHERN FARMS

As Lewis's experience demonstrates, sharecropping was no formula for prosperity. There was no capital for machinery and no margin to experiment with new crops or new methods of cultivation. Plots were smaller than prewar plantations, production less efficient, fertilizer more scarce, management less competent. While land values rose outside the South, the price of Southern farms fell so low that sometimes they could not even be mortgaged. Absentee ownership became the rule; in parts of Georgia in 1880 about 1 percent of black farmers owned land, and their share of total wealth in stock and soil was probably even smaller.

Southern cities reflected the region's rural poverty. The description of Charleston after the war retained some validity fifteen years later. Although commerce continued to flow through New Orleans, the scars of war still showed and conditions in the slums grew worse; the State Board of Health reported "472 miles of dirt streets . . . choked up with garbage, filth and mud." Southern textile workers received lower wages than their Northern counterparts, who were among the least well paid of industrial workers. Southern mills paid handsome dividends, usually to Northern owners, but male workers took home about fifty cents a day, and children, who constituted perhaps a quarter of the labor force, received about a dime. Although other industrial workers fared somewhat better than textile workers, Southern wages always lagged behind Northern wages.

Investment in Southern textile facilities increased seven times in the twenty years after 1880, a statistic that testifies to low wages and high profits. Investors also built other factories to process the region's agricultural staples and to exploit such natural resources as bauxite, sulphur, and the oil of Texas and Oklahoma. Coal and iron deposits made Birmingham a major center for the production of pig iron. The American Tobacco Company, which James Buchanan Duke organized in 1890, brought new machines and new marketing techniques to one of the South's oldest crops. But the Southern economy remained what C. Vann

Sharecroppers

Woodward has called "a colonial economy," dependent upon, and paying tribute to, other parts of the country. As late as 1919, the eleven states with the lowest per capita income were all in the South. In 1880, per capita wealth in the South was $376, almost $1,000 less than the comparable statistic for the Northeast. Blacks may have borne a disproportionate share of the South's poverty, but there was plenty to go around. Secession and civil war had impoverished an entire region. In this respect, there was no Reconstruction.

Prejudice and Violence

Reconstruction probably hardened racial prejudice. Slavery had permitted interracial contact according to a code that emancipation legally ended. But the habits of centuries do not quickly disappear, and whites were slow to discard their expectation that blacks would remain deferential. When freedmen seemed disposed to claim equality, and when Radicals seemed willing to help, white Southerners closed ranks to keep blacks in the inferior place they were assumed to deserve.

Sharecropping and poverty helped fasten inferiority on blacks; peonage differed from slavery only in degree. Where economic bonds were not sufficient, there was violence. The Ku Klux Klan and other terrorist bands avowed their intent to force blacks into renewed submission and thereby reestablish white supremacy. These groups adopted mysterious rituals and regalia, but they left no mystery about their methods—the torch, the lash, and the rope were plainly visible. A frightened Louisiana tax collector wrote a Northern senator that thirty-eight blacks in his district had recently met violent death. He asked urgently for federal intervention, a plea that Congress met with the Ku Klux Klan Acts, or the "Force Acts," of 1870 and 1871. These measures set stiff penalties for those convicted of interfering with the right of any citizen to vote and permitted the use of troops against terrorists, as if they constituted a renewed Confederate rebellion.

The Klan was no match for the army; while troops remained in the South, federal law was outwardly obeyed. But the troops did not stay, and violence never really ceased. In 1890, without counting lynchings, South Carolina reported three times as many homicides as all of New England; Mississippi had 106 murders, Georgia 92, and Tennessee 105, compared to 20 in Wisconsin, 16 in Massachusetts, and 23 in Nebraska. The auditor of Alabama reported in 1881 that the aggregate worth of weapons in the state was greater than his assessment of agricultural implements; Alabama's swords had not become plowshares. Residence in an armed camp was one price of white supremacy.

Inferior public services was another. Taxpayers always resent high taxes, but in the devastated South they came on top of the private costs of the war. Public services were associated with discredited Radical legislatures, which had for the first time established public schools, state hospitals, and public assistance for the indigent and ill. When conservative white politicians, called Redeemers, took office in the 1870s, taxes and state expenditures dropped, especially for education, which blacks regarded as a perquisite of freedom. A governor of Virginia declared public schools "a luxury . . . to be paid for . . . by the people who wish their benefits"; he ignored the warning of school officials that about half the state's schools could not open in the fall of 1878.

While children were slighted, convicts were exploited. Southern states leased prisoners to favored contractors, who used their labor and

THE TRIAL IS AT HAND!

The appointed day and hour will soon come!! Fail not—
& if thou dost— *the stars upon 7 o'clock*

At night when the clock strikes ____ be ye faithful
unto your trust—nor wind, nor hail, nor rain, nor storm,
nor conscience, nor craven fear, shall excuse.

Dost Hear! Dost Heed!

Thus now do I call, and yet ONCE AGAIN, and if ye heed
not, ... K.X.R.T.E.H.Y. ...

CYCLOPEAN. Secretary.

By order of the GRAND CYCLOPS!!

simultaneously saved the state board and room. Too frequently, the contractor also saved the services of an executioner, for mortality rates among leased prisoners sometimes exceeded 15 percent.

The Politics of Prejudice

Political democracy was yet another price of white supremacy. For beginning in the 1880s and then more insistently in the 1890s, poorer whites demanded public services that Redeemers had dispensed with.

Redeemers had accepted the Fifteenth Amendment, and exchanged promises, polite words, and a few local offices for black votes, which helped turn back the Redeemers' white challengers. As political rivalry intensified, prosperous politicians bought black votes more or less openly, and less prosperous aspirants for public office revived intimidating tactics pioneered by the Klan. A delegate to the Mississippi constitutional convention in 1890 remarked that there had "not been a full vote and a fair count in Mississippi since 1875." He ran down the list: "we have been stuffing ballot boxes, committing perjury, and . . . carrying elections by fraud and violence." When an honest count in a fair election could no longer be assured, white Southerners blamed blacks, whose support was being corruptly sought, rather than the white politicians who profited from public office. So the black man lost his right to vote in the cause of reform and honest elections; black men were disfranchised so that white men would no longer have to count one another out.

The North accepted disfranchisement with only occasional bursts of self-righteous outrage. While in the House, James A. Garfield three times introduced bills to reduce the number of congressmen from Southern states as the Fourteenth Amendment required. Garfield's bills failed to pass, and he dropped the crusade before he became President in 1881. In 1890, Henry Cabot Lodge, a young Republican congressman from Massachusetts, sponsored a bill to permit federal supervision of federal elections. Some Republicans hoped, as had their predecessors during Reconstruction, to break the Democratic hold on the South with the black vote. But the Lodge bill failed to pass, and Northern interest in helping Southern blacks vote died with it. One important Northern newspaper consoled its readers with the observation that disfranchisement by law was less wrong than disfranchisement through terror.

The threat of renewed federal supervision made the South hasten to find legal means for securing exclusive white control of the political process. Between 1890 and 1905, various methods of restricting black suffrage were proposed, refined, and adopted. Some states used property qualifications and poll taxes, but these devices also excluded many poor whites. Literacy tests or tests requiring an "understanding" of selected passages from the state or national constitution left more discretion to the local examiners who administered the test. Louisiana permitted an exemption from such tests for those entitled to vote on January 1, 1867, or for sons and grandsons of such voters. Because blacks did not vote before the Reconstruction Act of March 1867, Louisiana's "grandfather clause" exempted only whites. The president of the convention that proposed the change admitted that it seemed a bit ridiculous. But, he asked, "Doesn't it let the white man vote and doesn't it stop the negro from voting, and isn't that what we came here for?" No one could quarrel with results: the number of registered black voters in Louisiana promptly fell from over 130,000 to 5,320.

Although the Supreme Court of the United States subsequently invalidated the crude "grandfather clause" technique, other methods of disfranchisement survived the Court's scrutiny. The Court was also tolerant of the growing Southern demand for social separation of the races. In 1873, in the Slaughterhouse cases, which did not directly involve the rights of blacks, the Court held that the Fourteenth Amendment protected only those rights derived from federal citizenship. Most civil rights, the Court decided, derived from state citizenship, and a citizen must appeal to his state to protect them.

Thomas Nast foresees the return of white supremacy

THE POLITICS OF PREJUDICE

In the Civil Rights cases of 1883, the Court held that the Fourteenth Amendment only prevented the discriminatory political acts of states and did not outlaw social discrimination by individuals. Congress had exceeded its authority, then, in passing the Civil Rights Act of 1875, which required individuals to furnish equal access to such public facilities as inns, theaters, and transportation. In spite of a prescient and persuasive dissent from Justice John Marshall Harlan, the Court told blacks to appeal to state legislatures to secure equal public accommodations.

The Court's decisions permitted discrimination on racial grounds; Southern legislatures in the next two decades gradually required the practice. Separate sections of public buildings or vehicles, separate schools, churches, lodges, and jails kept the races from social contact. And in 1896 the Supreme Court, in *Plessy* v. *Ferguson*, again went along. So long as the facilities were substantially equal, even if separate, the Court said no rights were abridged. Separation did not imply inferiority, the Court held, nor could either the Constitution or legislation "eradicate racial instincts or . . . abolish distinctions based upon physical differences." Justice Harlan was still unconvinced. "Our Constitution," he wrote, "is color-blind." The pose of equal accommodations for black citizens he called a "thin disguise" that would neither "mislead any one, nor atone for the wrong this day done."

At enormous psychic and material cost, the South had established two societies, even more separate than they had been before the war. Not only were the schools and the toilets and the streetcars separate but there were separate occupations and separate businesses and a separate Christianity and even a separate vocabulary and etiquette. Blacks had once been artisans and shopkeepers and worked in factories. Gradually those became "white jobs." Black barbers cut only black hair, and the only blacks on industrial payrolls were janitors. The North at least accepted this situation, and then almost reproduced it when the Northern black population increased.

The informal code governing interracial contact in the South became as formal as the Constitution, especially where black men and white women were involved. Blacks must not look whites in the eye, must maintain a deferential bearing, must go to the back door, as well as to to the back of the bus. Whites referred to blacks by their first names or something less respectful. Blacks might occasionally be the object of white charity, but only if they accepted white values, including the central tenet of black inferiority.

Booker T. Washington did not go quite that far. But he did raise a great deal of money among white philanthropists for the Tuskegee Institute, which he directed, and in white society he was the most influential black of his day. In 1895, a cheering white nation thought Washington accepted segregation on behalf of his race. In a speech at the Atlanta Exposition, where the New South displayed its initiative and its produce, he appealed to his fellow blacks to learn trades, to become producing

Booker T. Washington

Tuskegee classroom

members of society, to earn—not demand—equality. He asked whites for help, for employment, for a chance to hew the wood and draw the water of the New South. But discussion of social equality Washington branded "the extremest folly," and he seemed to accept the Jim Crow laws that were requiring racial separation. "In all things that are purely social," said Washington with a superb metaphor, "we can be as separate as the fingers, yet one as the hand in all things essential to mutual progress."

Washington specifically did not accept disfranchisement and opposed any measure that permitted "an ignorant and poverty-stricken white man to vote" while it kept a "black man in the same condition" from the polls. But whites heard only Washington's seeming renunciation of equality. This was one time when they took the black man at his word.

Suggested Reading

In *Rehearsal for Reconstruction** (1964), Willie Lee Rose discusses Reconstruction policies tried out by Union officials on islands off South Carolina before war's end. Three brief, recent accounts of the period correct some of the old historical myths: W. R. Brock's *An American Crisis** (1963), John Hope Franklin's *Reconstruction** (1962), and Kenneth M. Stampp's *The Era of Reconstruction** (1965); a fourth, Forrest G. Wood's *The Era of Reconstruction** (1975) includes a discussion of the historical literature since the 1960s.

Howard K. Beale defends Andrew Johnson and discusses the economic motives of the Radicals in *The Critical Year* (1930). LaWanda and John H. Cox are concerned with the same period in *Politics, Principle, and Prejudice, 1865–1866** (1963). Eric L. McKitrick's *Andrew Johnson and Reconstruction** (1960) documents Johnson's political ineptitude. C. Vann Woodward's *Reunion and Reaction** (1951) covers the election of 1876, and his *Origins of the New South** (1951) carries the history of the region into the twentieth century. Woodward's *The Strange Career of Jim Crow** (1957, since revised) is an important book on segregation. Keith I. Polakoff's *The Politics of Inertia* (1973) attempts to modify Woodward's interpretation of the election of 1876, while Martin E. Mantell's *Johnson, Grant and the Politics of Reconstruction* (1973) concentrates on the election of 1868. In *A Compromise of Principle* (1974), Michael L. Benedict sorts out the various congressional factions of the Reconstruction period. Other important books on Reconstruction politics include J. M. Kousser's *The Shaping of Southern Politics* (1974) and Sheldon Hackney's *From Populism to Progressivism in Alabama* (1969). Nell Irvin Painter's *The Exodusters* (1976) deals with the migration of freed blacks to Kansas.

W. E. B. Du Bois emphasizes the positive accomplishments of Radicals of both races in *Black Reconstruction** (1935). Fawn Brodie's *Thaddeus Stevens** (1959) illuminates all of Radical Reconstruction. David

Montgomery studies the effort to extend radicalism to economic and social reforms in *Beyond Equality** (1967). Joel R. Williamson's *After Slavery** (1965) deals with the progress of the freedmen. George M. Frederickson's *Black Image in the White Mind** (1971) is an important study of racism. Booker T. Washington argues his views in *Up from Slavery** (1901). Another perspective emerges in Nate Shaw's autobiography, *All God's Dangers** (1974), edited by Theodore Rosengarten.

* Available in paperback edition

Industrial America, 1870 — 1945: An Introduction

During the colonial period and the first century of independence Americans were predominantly a farming people. Although different in detail, the pattern of their lives would have been recognizable to forebears who had migrated from Western Europe or the British Isles a century before. But as the nineteenth century closed, American farmers worried that their best days were past. Their children moved to cities and took jobs in factories. A farmer's produce and labor brought too little in a market that seemed rigged for the benefit of others. The status and influence of rural residents slipped until the stereotypical farmer seemed more often "embattled" than the personification of virtue that Thomas Jefferson had described.

By 1900 Jefferson's strictures about cities also sounded dated. The number of city-dwellers did not exceed the rural population until the Census of 1920, but the United States was unquestionably emerging as an urban society before statisticians confirmed the fact. Industrialists and financiers captured the nation's attention and imagination as had planters and preachers of an earlier time. Political controversy centered on economic power and conditions in factories, rather than on transportation and land. A cultural pluralism associated with urban diversity began to threaten the cultural homogeneity of small towns.

Economic determinists argue that social, cultural, and political change stemmed from economic development—from, in this instance, American industrialization. Whenever the industrial revolution began in the United States (most scholars fix the date before the Civil War), the process accelerated during the last three decades of the nineteenth century. This rapid industrialization not only produced more goods and an urban society, but more government as well, since political issues, as a big-city politician once remarked, often boil down to a question of who gets what. In fact, much of the legislation of the first half of the twentieth century bears on that question—especially the legislation proposed by progressives before the First World War and by New Dealers before the Second World War.

To mitigate the effect of industrialization, or to distribute the bounty more equitably, politicians devised new governmental institutions (such as regulatory agencies) and discovered new dimensions in the Constitution. Yet the rights of private property were only abridged, not abolished; laissez faire and competitive free enterprise were preserved, not abandoned; reformers remained within rather traditional limits.

American foreign policy after 1870, also in part the result of the nation's industrial development, broke with tradition more sharply than did domestic reform. The international caution associated with Washington, Jefferson, and Monroe seemed too confining when the nation's exports climbed well above imports, when overseas possessions betokened international prestige, and when America's factories altered the world's balance of power. By the end of the Second World War, power in the world had indeed shifted, and Americans, secure in the strength of their industrial economy, confident of the responsive creativity of their democratic government, and possessed of a mature faith in the fundamental justice of their urban society, surely believed they were the most fortunate people on earth.

Chapter 12
The Industrial
Transformation

Chronology

The careers of Abraham Lincoln and his son Robert illustrate the bewildering pace of change in the half century after 1860. Legend has made the President's youth a familiar tale: frontier privation, self-education, hard work, dedication to principle, and unrelenting ambition. His son Robert, by contrast, graduated from an eastern boarding school and Harvard, practiced corporate law in Chicago, was president of the Pullman Company, served as secretary of war and minister to Great Britain, entertained royalty, and belonged to the proper clubs. When Abraham Lincoln moved to Illinois, Chicago was a land speculator's idle dream; when he became President, the city boasted a population of 100,000. In 1870, when Robert Lincoln had begun his law practice, Chicago had become a major railway center and home for 300,000 people. Stockyards, manufacturing, the continued expansion of the railroads, and the arrival of thousands of immigrants drove the population to 500,000 in 1880 and past 1,000,000 in 1890, when Robert Lincoln was the nation's representative in London.

The Dimensions of Change

Tables of population growth only begin to indicate the complexity of urbanization. Between 1880 and 1890, for instance, Boston's population increased by about 24 percent from 362,839 to 448,477. But that relatively small net increase inaccurately reflected the movement of people through the city. During the decade, perhaps as many as 800,000 people had moved into Boston and more than 700,000 had moved out. However modest the change in population, then, many Bostonians in 1890 had not lived there ten years before. The assimilation of new residents on such a scale overloaded urban institutions that had evolved in simpler times.

Many of Boston's residents had only recently come to the United States. In 1890, more than one-third of the city's population had been born abroad and more than two-thirds had at least one foreign-born parent. Irish immigrants had been arriving in the city for decades, but as the century ended, more and more arrivals were so-called "new immigrants" from southern and eastern Europe. In 1890, half as many Italians lived in New York City as lived in Naples; in 1910, the Polish population of Chicago was larger than that of all but two cities in Poland. The "old" immigrants had been predominantly English-speaking, Protestant, and rural; exceptions like the Roman Catholic Irish stood out. But the "new immigrants" were all exceptions: they learned English slowly and with difficulty; they were faithful Catholics or Jews; and they settled in cities in their own distinctive districts called Little Italy or the ghetto or Chinatown.

Into the same cities, but not usually into the same neighborhoods, poured native Americans for whom the agrarian dream had become a nightmare. The number of farms declined, both from abandonment and from consolidation, not only in New England but in the Middle West as well. Forty percent of the nation's townships lost population in the 1880s, including more than half of those in Ohio, Illinois, and Iowa. A student of the Wisconsin frontier has written that the land was "filled with the . . . voices of women mourning for their children and the . . . mutterings of men asking about jobs."

Jobs in the city meant jobs in the factories, which sent all the economic indices climbing. By 1885, the market value of American manufactured goods exceeded that of any other nation, and between 1885 and 1900, the production of manufactured goods doubled. In the half century after Appomattox, the production of American factories increased twelve times. The statistics for specific industries, such as steel, were even more spectacular. In 1870, American steel production was less than 70,000 tons; two years later it exceeded 140,000 tons; by 1880, the figure was more than 1 million tons; in 1900, 3 million tons came from Andrew Carnegie's plants alone and the industry as a whole produced more than 10 million tons.

Inside The Breakers

Not everyone shared equally in that enlarged output. If some Victorian parlors were overly full, others were bare; it was an age of too little as well as too much. On the grounds of the Vanderbilts' summer estate at Newport, Rhode Island, stood a playhouse with its own setting of imported English china; in textile cities nearby, families of eight or ten people lived in quarters smaller than that playhouse, and they furnished them with less than the cost of a half dozen of the Vanderbilts' salad plates. The main Vanderbilt mansion, called The Breakers, was a triumph of Victorian architecture, complete with gargoyles, French furniture, Norman tapestries, and Italian marble. The house required a staff of thirty servants and was used by the Vanderbilt family for but a few weeks during the summer season. To house a family of five or six in a four-room tenement, an urban worker not far from Newport paid two or three dollars of his eight- or ten-dollar weekly wage.

The popular press made the gulf between rich and poor one of the clichés of the period. A stenographer, who might earn about $600 in the course of a year, or an artisan, whose wages might reach $1000, could

New York tenement: an age of too little as well as too much

contrast their incomes with that of Andrew Carnegie, which was estimated to be about $25 million. In 1914, 1 percent of the nation's families owned 80 percent of the nation's wealth. Yet the genteel American middle classes—professional people and ordinary proprietors—may never have lived so well. Servants were plentiful and cheap, and the index of wholesale prices fell from 135 in 1870 to 100 in 1880, and then to 82 in 1890. Falling prices, on the other hand, meant less income for farmers, who felt increasingly exploited with each drop in the price of wheat or cotton.

There were numerical measures of other phenomena too. Between 1840 and 1890, the amount of labor required to produce a bushel of wheat dropped from three hours to ten minutes. The number of children in schools increased five times in the twenty years after 1878, and the number of public high schools rose from less than 200 in 1870 to more than 6000 in 1900. Fewer people perished in industrial warfare than at the hands of lynch mobs; in 1892 ten strikers and three guards died in a battle at one of Carnegie's steel mills, but lynching parties condemned and executed 241 people, most of whom were black. In 1870, New York City already had about 200 miles of sewers and more than 500 miles of streets; Philadelphia in 1877 had 82,000 cesspools. New York City's William Marcy (Boss) Tweed, the most notorious of the elected looters of municipal treasuries, was indicted in 1871 on 204 separate charges of malfeasance. In the 1890s, 57 of Chicago's 68 aldermen allegedly took bribes. Infant mortality in the nation declined by almost half between 1850 and 1900, but in the textile city of Lawrence, Massachusetts, in 1900, the average age at death was fifteen.

Statistics reveal change, but they conceal the individual lives that change affects. Numbers do not describe the desperation of the unemployed and unskilled worker whose family needed coal. And tables cannot convey the anguish of Indians who longed for unfenced plains and buffalo and white men who kept promises. No graph effectively suggests the psychic dislocation that was visible in the columns of small town newspapers in the 1890s, where descriptions of epidemics and insanity and bankruptcy and arson jostled notices of prayer meetings and funerals and advertisements for patent medicines.

Opportunity

Few Americans at the time paused to wonder what miraculous social cement held their turbulent society together. They were not any more reflective than their descendants, and they had much less leisure, which they would never have squandered on such an inquiry. Most Americans probably believed they got about what they deserved in life; if their measure was short, they blamed themselves, and only rarely their employer, or the government, or a remote Protestant God. There was no lack of frustration and anger, but these emotions usually produced despair or a crippling guilt in the individual, not an organized attempt to change the system. Eventually, Americans believed, society would reward hard work, thrift, and self-reliance; the gospel according to Benjamin Franklin still prevailed in the land. Dissidents occasionally remarked that even a diligent factory worker could not be too thrifty if he lived on the edge of subsistence, and they questioned the self-reliance of railroad tycoons who had received 180 million acres of public lands. But such critics infrequently disturbed the Victorian complacency that smothered any effort to make social change keep pace with the dynamic economy.

Americans made simple moral judgments about their complex industrial economy. Henry Ward Beecher, one of the nation's most eminent preachers, asserted that every successful business had God as one of its partners. Nor did Beecher shrink from the logical consequence of the proposition: "no man suffers from poverty unless it be more than his fault—unless it be his *sin.*" Christians must distinguish, then, between the deserving poor and the slothful poor lest charity reward

The stewardship of wealth: Carnegie gives away libraries

evil. So philanthropists supported institutions that perpetuated the values of the donor, as dozens of Carnegie libraries attested.

Carnegie himself was the symbol of the age: the immigrant who became a magnate, the living demonstration of equal opportunity, the rags-to-riches dream come true. Reflecting on American society in 1889, Carnegie ruled "objections to the foundations upon which society is based" out of order. Individualism, competition, and the unfettered rights of property-owners were essential to human progress and "inevitably" gave "wealth to the few." That wealth imposed responsibility. The rich acted as society's stewards, by accumulating what capital could be spared as a trust to be returned wisely to society. "Wealth, passing through the hands of the few, can be a much more potent force for the

A banquet, served on horseback, to celebrate the completion of the host's stable. Sherry's Ballroom, New York, 1903.

elevation of our race than if it had been distributed in small sums to the people themselves," who would waste it "in the indulgence of appetite."

Carnegie practiced what he preached. He built libraries, endowed universities, and supported the search for international peace. None of these enterprises coddled any undeserving or self-indulgent paupers; his philanthropy emphasized the same self-improvement moral that his life exemplified. But there was not much compassion in this "Gospel of Wealth," nor was there much warmth in Victorian Christianity. Protestant ministers began to worry as workingmen drifted away from the church.

The rich had scientific as well as religious defenders, for the new biological theories of Charles Darwin had economic and social corollaries. Darwinism and revealed religion seemed in some respects incompatible, and clergy and scientists argued into the twentieth century about the origin of man and the creation of the earth. But Darwinism and the Gospel of Wealth complemented one another in demanding work, competition, and self-reliance. Professors taught the natural law of "the survival of the fittest," and clerics explained the divine order that placed "Godliness . . . in league with riches," as Bishop William Lawrence put it in 1901.

For William Graham Sumner, who taught at Yale, Darwinian evolution clarified and excused the temporary social dislocation of the 1880s. Economic competition, he argued, not only rewarded able individuals but also made the nation more prosperous. The rich were the agents of evolutionary progress, their riches the result of prudence and self-denial. Any attempt to interfere with the wonderful working of natural law, Sumner held, would be both foolish and futile. He captured the essence of Social Darwinism in the title of an essay published in 1894: "The Absurd Effort to Make the World Over."

But, of course, the world had been made over, in Sumner's lifetime, by precisely the sort of people he defended—those who cleared the Indians off the plains, those who pocketed the profits of railroad construction, those who cornered the market in sugar and oil and tobacco, those who owned the tenements, those who checked credit ratings and wrote contracts and kept the poor in the place God and nature had intended. It was the time of the entrepreneur, the man-on-the-make, the up-and-at-'em go-getter, and a time for sanctimonious exploitation in the name of progress, or evolution, or the good of the race. The heroes of the day were those who got there first—to the railhead with the cattle, to the six-shooter at the hip, to the city council with a bid or a bribe. Competition, after all, meant coming in first and not asking too many questions about the rules of the game.

In fact, the American public was mesmerized by a moral shell game in the latter nineteenth century. Entrepreneurial morality was not necessarily inevitable or just or natural or divinely sanctioned merely because it was so proclaimed by those who benefited from it; society had not been organized exclusively for the happiness of those who came in first. The endless killing of Indians, the crippling industrial accidents, the corruption of government, the relentless driving of defenseless employees might be explained, but could hardly be justified. Yet most Americans believed in the immorality of the untrustworthy Indians, of the lazy and careless poor, and the profligate slum-dwellers. This entrepreneurial morality never fooled the Indians. The other victims sometimes objected, but more often they appeared to accept both the values and the structure of American society.

They accepted traditional ground rules in part because they believed that every entrant had an equal competitive chance in life's race. This was, so legend had it, the promised land of opportunity, where the poor could make good. The myth of equal opportunity pervaded sermons, dime novels, small town newspapers, and the minds of ambitious Americans. Because it assumed that each individual had an equal start, the myth provided a persuasive resolution of the conflicting ideals of individualism and equality. It described the society as at once equalitarian and hierarchical; it gave hope to those who were starting and satisfaction to those at the top. And it was one of the strongest bonds that held the rapidly changing American society together.

Mobility

By themselves, the examples of Abraham Lincoln and Andrew Carnegie would not have sustained society's belief in equal opportunity. But confirming evidence appeared in the immediate neighborhood. Although few laborers rose to affluence, many achieved modest gains in income, skill, status, property, and education for their children. The savings account, the little business, the mortgaged duplex, the high-school graduation, apprenticeship to a skilled carpenter—these were the signs of opportunity, and they were common enough to keep the faith alive.

Securing accurate data about social mobility in contemporary America is difficult. Americans try not to place themselves in social strata; moreover, they do not know whether to use income, occupation, family background, or education to determine social standing. Is an educated social worker higher or lower on the scale than the prosperous proprietor of a clothing store? The difficulty is compounded when such questions are asked of past generations, who left tax assessments and census returns, but often not much else, and who moved about so much that tracing them over time is nearly impossible. Historian Stephan Thernstrom has, however, made a start on such an investigation, and his data for Boston show the substance behind the hope.

If Bostonians stayed in the city (and most did not), Thernstrom wrote, the men could, and did, move up the socioeconomic ladder. At the lower occupational levels, Thernstrom found a "strikingly fluid" society. About a quarter of those who began work as unskilled laborers seem eventually to have worn a white collar, as did an equal fraction of the semiskilled workers who began a notch higher. Nor was this upward mobility at the expense of earlier generations of achieving Bostonians. Thernstrom did not discover one Bostonian who went from riches all the way to rags, and only about 15 percent of the white-collar workers slipped into what he called the laboring class.

There was, in short, opportunity. But it was not, according to Thernstrom, equally open to all. Those who started at the top stayed there, while others had to climb. Native-born Americans had a better chance than immigrants; the native-born children of one group of immigrants started with an advantage over later arrivals. The Irish editor of Boston's Catholic newspaper remarked in 1883 that "the race is not run with an equal chance; the poor man's son carries double weight." In a sense, his observation was accurate. But American social structure combined something of both worlds: as Thernstrom concluded, it "allowed substantial privilege for the privileged and extensive opportunity for the underprivileged to coexist simultaneously." It was possible, in other words, to climb the social ladder, and it was worth the effort. The reality of opportunity and the belief that it was available to all kept the society energetically at work and relatively content.

The rate of mobility, indeed, appears to have altered the subtle social distinctions that divide a people into castes and classes. Once wealth had been the major mark of status. But when flamboyant industrial freebooters could build mansions, send their children to Yale, and endow churches, the old badges of gentility did not suffice. New institutions to define respectability multiplied, along with industrial wealth, in the 1880s. These new measures of aristocracy assumed property, manners, and education, and then added the tests of ancestry and association to them. Possession of the world's goods was no longer quite enough.

After 1887 the Social Register furnished an up-to-date list of certified aristocrats and other suitable residents that one might ask to dinner. Club memberships demonstrated social standing and, in the case of some of the patriotic societies, established a hierarchy of old families. More than half the patriotic organizations in existence in 1890 had been founded in the preceding decade; the Daughters of the American Revolution (1890) and the Society of Mayflower Descendants (1892) were still to come. In 1882, in Brookline, Massachusetts, The Country Club was founded, and imitators soon followed, especially in other suburbs where the urban rich began to create homogeneous communities so their sons and daughters would not make the wrong marriages. Summer colonies on the coast of Maine or Rhode Island reflected the same social selectivity. "You can do business with anyone," J. P. Morgan once remarked, but you "only sail with a gentleman."

The upper class, then, had devised ways to separate the aristocracy from those who were only rich. The tests could be ugly, for there was more than a trace of Protestant exclusiveness in most of those newly formed social institutions. Anti-Semitism was not always disguised, and the exclusion of blacks did not even require defense. Yet the devices of the Protestant Establishment not only kept a newcomer out; they also kept the Establishment itself so removed from the rest of American society that, a century later, the Social Register, and some of those listed in it, seemed almost irrelevant.

Economic Organization: Railroads

Americans who experienced the trauma of rapid industrialization believed their challenges were wholly new. No American before them had worked in a steel mill or supplied water to a million customers or competed with Chinese coolies or European peasants for jobs. Yet, in perspective, much of the dislocation of industrialization derives from a change in scale as well as from new circumstances. Everything was multiplied so that there was, quite simply, more of everything: more soot, more sewage, more strangers, more speed and more distance, more money for some and more deprivation for others. Rural America had run on a smaller scale—family, village, 160 acres, customers and constituents and congregations one knew by name. Gradually the personal dimension was lost: businesses used the railroads to serve a national market, employees joined national unions, investment bankers formed national corporations, and Washington, D.C., became more important than Sacramento or Springfield or City Hall. National businesses provided the example and sometimes the cause for organization on a national scale. The entrepreneur was the prophet of the new era.

The age had the stamp of those who succeeded. Like James J. Hill and Leland Stanford and several Vanderbilts, who built and ran railroads, and like Daniel Drew and Jay Gould, who invented ways to loot them. Like Andrew Carnegie and John D. Rockefeller and James B. Duke, who marketed steel and oil and tobacco across the nation and around the world. Like J. P. Morgan, who managed the nation's most important bank, financed dozens of the nation's most important businesses, and had a great deal to do with the stability of the nation's currency. They were the heroes—and the innovators—of their day, and they perfected the organizational techniques that labor and other groups later imitated. They showed Americans how to manage, how to seize the advantages of the new scale of life, how to benefit from industrialization. And they seized many of those benefits for themselves.

The railroads were the first and, in many respects, the most important of these new national industries. Railroad managers not only learned how to lay rails and manipulate securities. They also met such other managerial challenges as how to persuade legislatures to establish standard time, how to control boxcars in Abilene and Akron from executive offices in Chicago, and how competitors could be persuaded to keep the rails a uniform distance apart. Railroad officials perfected techniques of communication, accounting, and lobbying that other industrialists then adapted to their needs. These managerial contributions were perhaps as important to the development of American industry as other, specifically economic, consequences of railroad construction. For a national system of transportation required enormous quantities of coal, steel, timber, and petroleum products both in construction and operation. The railroads gave access to a national market and, for many industrial products, were themselves an immense national market as well.

The growth of the railroad network was early and spectacular. Between 1865 and 1870, the nation's rail network increased from 35,000 to 53,000 miles. In the next decade it jumped to 93,000 miles, and in the 1880s more than 70,000 additional miles were built. By 1900, 193,000 miles of track crisscrossed the United States; more than $10 billion were invested in the railroads, over $2 billion more than the total investment in manufacturing. More than a half million Americans, receiving over $500 million in annual wages, worked for the railroads in 1900, when locomotive whistles echoed in the most remote valleys of the country.

In fact, the nation had more railroad mileage in 1900 than was

Railroad construction

necessary. Railroad executives sometimes built track to blackmail competitors or simply to secure the profits of construction. A shipper in St. Louis could select from twenty-two possible routes to send his goods to Atlanta. One consequence of this kind of competition was declining freight rates: from nearly two cents per ton-mile in 1870, average rates dropped to less than one cent in 1890.

And favored shippers paid less than the average rate. Even when scrupulously managed (and scrupulous management was the exception) railroads required an immense investment. Capital costs—including interest and dividends—were inevitably high. Neither capital costs nor other expenses such as taxes, insurance, and salaries, varied significantly with the amount of freight the railroad hauled. High fixed costs and increased competition led to shady competitive practices, or "abuses," which then led to demands for governmental regulation.

Since much of the railroad's expense was fixed, almost any freight carried at almost any price was better than no freight at all. Shippers served by competitive roads often secured discounts, called "rebates," in return for guaranteed shipments that gave the road a constant income. Some customers even coerced railroads into paying rebates on the shipments of competitors. This concession, called a "drawback," gave the privileged customer a dual advantage: not only were his freight costs lower than those of his rival, but in effect he also received part of the fee his competitor paid the railroad.

Those who lacked competitive leverage because their shipments were small, or because they could ship on only one railroad, paid what the traffic would bear. Fees from large-volume shippers helped meet a railroad's fixed costs; profit came from those who paid full fare. Sometimes the fare seemed exorbitant. A farmer in Elgin, Illinois, taking advantage of competing railroads, could send a tub of butter to New York City for thirty cents; less fortunate farmers within 165 miles of New York, who were served by only one line, paid seventy-five cents for the same service. The apparent injustice of this long-haul/short-haul discrimination gave critics a weapon they lacked in attacking rates that were less obviously outrageous.

Railroads and the Government

Any demand for governmental action conflicted directly with the concept of laissez faire, one of the ideological strands of the competitive ethic. Government must not take sides on the economic questions of the day, this creed held; the competitive marketplace would reward the most efficient producer, the best product, the most diligent worker. Governmental interference would promote inefficiency, favoritism, and injustice. Government at all levels should keep order, hold taxes down, and keep official hands off the nation's economy.

Unless, of course, the important people needed help. Advocates of laissez faire rarely objected to the tariff that protected their products from foreign competition, or to direct subsidies, or to troops that broke strikes, or to courts that threw out the first inept efforts of state legislatures to prohibit industrial exploitation of women and children. Such actions did not constitute interference, but were considered legitimate governmental attempts to enforce the law, to protect the constitutional rights of influential citizens, and to secure for all the rights of private property.

The railroads furnished a rough pattern for the relationship of government and other businesses. The enormous tracts of public lands, given to railroads to finance construction, were a greater direct subsidy than most industries received from governmental contracts and tariffs. The most notorious uses of troops in labor disputes came in the railroad strikes of 1877 and 1894. And when competition threatened the survival of many railroads, the government responded with legislation that both calmed the railroads' critics and restored the opportunity for profitable operation.

The land grants began even before the Civil War, when Congress assisted construction of the Illinois Central with grants of public lands. When construction of the transcontinental lines began in earnest after the war, the practice of granting land was revived and refined. Ordinarily a railroad received alternate square miles of land to a depth of ten to twenty miles on either side of the right of way in states and to a depth of forty miles in territories. For each mile of track, then, the railroad received at least ten square miles of public domain. Nor was that the limit of the subsidy. State and local governments outbid one another to attract railways; communities used tax concessions, land grants, and governmental purchases of stock to get on the tracks that promised to be the route to prosperity.

Total public aid for railway construction can only be estimated. Apparently, total land grants approximately equaled the combined area of New York, New England, and Pennsylvania. And land was only the

FEDERAL GRANTS TO THE RAILROADS

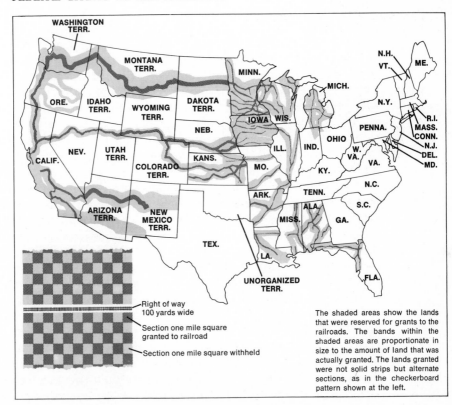

Right of way
100 yards wide

Section one mile square
granted to railroad

Section one mile square withheld

The shaded areas show the lands that were reserved for grants to the railroads. The bands within the shaded areas are proportionate in size to the amount of land that was actually granted. The lands granted were not solid strips but alternate sections, as in the checkerboard pattern shown at the left.

beginning. Both the Union Pacific and the Central Pacific, which met at Promontory Point, Utah, in 1869 to complete the first transcontinental, received federal loans for construction. The government advanced $16,000 per mile of track laid on the plains, and increased the amount to $32,000 and $48,000 per mile in more difficult terrain. The railroads eventually retired the second mortgage bonds that secured these federal loans, but less wary state and local governments occasionally lost subsidies to unscrupulous promoters who never laid a rail. Missouri, for instance, spent nearly $25 million in subsidies, of which about $19 million was wasted.

In spite of occasional corporate chicanery, land grants and subsidies made economic sense. The value of the alternate sections of land retained by the government more than doubled because of the railroad's presence. The public could give half the land away, sell the remainder at double the original price, break even on the transaction, and still have the railroad, which would not otherwise have been built. Postwar American railroads were built in the expectation of future traffic from future settlement. Unsettled public land offered no immediate market for the railroad's service, but the American people, as is their custom, were impatient. The public demanded railroads and opened public treasuries to help pay for them.

The demand for public regulation, like that for land grants, preceded the Civil War. Several states established regulatory commissions that did not seriously interfere with the railroads' independence. But state regulation in the 1870s, passed in part at the urging of rural lodges called Granges, seemed more serious. These "Granger laws" permitted state inspection of warehouses, established commissions with power to set rates for storage and transportation, and prohibited such competitive tactics as favoring a long haul over a shorter one. The Supreme Court, in *Munn* v. *Illinois* (1877), seemed to encourage state regulation. States might regulate private property, the Court held, when it was "used in a manner to make it of public consequence," and when it affected "the community at large." Although the *Munn* case derived from an Illinois statute regulating warehouses, the precedent clearly applied to railroads as well.

The prospect of a conflicting welter of state regulations, passed by legislatures subject to unpredictable regional pressures, dismayed railroad managers, many of whom preferred one set of national regulations to a host of state codes. Indeed, a railroad attorney prepared the legislative draft that emerged years later as the Interstate Commerce Act. The carriers especially wanted the government to prohibit rebates and to sanction rates at a level sufficient to justify reasonable dividends. The act, which finally passed Congress in 1887, did not specifically authorize governmental rate-setting, although it required the roads to publish and adhere to "reasonable and just" fees. The Interstate Commerce Commission (ICC), which was established to administer the act, had no effective method of checking the fairness of rates and could only enforce its orders through the courts. Between 1887 and 1905 sixteen cases contesting orders of the ICC worked their way through the courts. The railroads won fifteen. Justice John Marshall Harlan, dissenting in one of those cases, noted that the courts had left the ICC only the authority "to issue reports and make protests." Railroad officials, who had faced and solved first many of the problems of doing business across a continent, had even turned to their own advantage legislation meant to regulate them.

Economic Organization: Industry

While the railroad barons were putting together the nation's new transportation network, industrial magnates were organizing the nation's productive capacity. Textile firms had to buy wool in California and Australia; spin, weave, and dye it in Massachusetts; sell the finished fabric all over the world; and then collect the accounts. Andrew Carnegie's steel empire included everything from coal and iron deposits to factories for making finished steel products; he owned a railroad, ore boats, coking ovens, blast furnaces, and steel mills. The Carnegie Steel Company—called a vertical combination because it controlled the product from raw material to consumer—achieved internal saving by eliminating the profits of middlemen.

A ton of steel, as Carnegie described the process, required mining a ton and one-half of ore in Minnesota, which had to be loaded and unloaded several times en route to Pittsburgh. A ton and one-half of coal, converted to coke, was then consumed in smelting the ore. A ton of limestone, a small amount of manganese, and a great deal of labor went into production of the finished product, for which, Carnegie boasted, the consumer paid less than a cent per pound. That result, he said, was "little less than miraculous."

John D. Rockefeller achieved equally miraculous results through what began as a horizontal combination in the oil industry. His Standard Oil Company secured almost complete control of oil refining. Through its domination of one segment of the industry, Standard Oil gradually extended its influence into production, transportation, and marketing and eventually became, like Carnegie Steel, a vertically integrated combination as well.

Before Rockefeller's domination, the oil industry could have served as a model of free competition. The risks were great, for drillers selected sites by hunch, and the result was often an expensive dry hole. Yet the capital required to become a driller was so small that many marginal operators entered the business. With many producers, most of whom lacked the capital to provide storage facilities, both production and price fluctuated wildly. In 1859, crude oil sold for $18 a barrel; at times in 1862, the same amount of oil brought a dime. Uncontrolled production also wasted the resource, for unsold oil seeped through wooden storage tanks or spilled away at the wells. Few drillers could invest in research or technological improvements when the price of their product changed so quickly.

Oil refining was somewhat more stable than the production of crude and became even more stable as Rockefeller and his associates either bought or crushed most of their competition. Standard Oil used its competitive advantage to secure rebates from the railroads. Rockefeller's firm also cut costs, developed new marketing techniques, and sold a product that was in fact standard—a uniform product that compared favorably in quality with the output of competitors. There were, in short, legitimate economic reasons for Standard's domination of the industry.

But other reasons for Standard's success were less a result of economy than of power. Standard occasionally secured not only discounts on its own freight but drawbacks on shipments of other firms as well. The sequel to price wars that ruined independent refiners was sometimes monopolistic control of a market, with resulting price increases and mounting profits that seemed illegitimate. Like other firms in the period, Standard engaged in industrial espionage and bought political influence: one of Rockefeller's ventures, a critic remarked, had "done everything with the Pennsylvania legislature except to refine it."

Rockefeller and his associates devised new ways to control their varied enterprises. In 1882 major stockholders in the various component companies of Standard Oil gave managerial control to Rockefeller and eight other trustees in return for trust certificates. In 1892 Ohio, which had chartered Standard Oil, moved to dissolve this trust that now controlled the corporation. A decision of the state's supreme court required the trustees to disband, but centralized management was retained through an informal agreement among the major stockholders. In 1899 Standard Oil established a holding company under a New Jersey statute that permitted one corporation to own stock in another. Standard Oil of New Jersey acquired the stock of the other firms in the combination, and until 1911, when the Supreme Court ordered the holding company split into separate operating firms, the directors of the New Jersey corporation managed the whole Standard empire.

While Standard Oil was unusual in size, profits, and power, the cycle of its development occurred repeatedly in the American economy in the later nineteenth century. Free competition—unstable, chaotic, inefficient—gave way to various forms of consolidation that were usually inaccurately labeled "trusts." If the combination succeeded in imposing on an industry what businessmen called order, customers and competitors objected to the corporation's dominance. Since only the whole society seemed capable of checking the power of the largest corporations, state governments, and eventually the national government too, required the restoration of competition; presumably the cycle would then begin once more. In fact, competition did not ordinarily follow

The Senate's bosses

governmental action, but the principle that the public might control
private economic matters was asserted if not conclusively established.

In 1888 both political parties promised federal legislation to curb
monopolies. In 1890 the Sherman Antitrust Act fulfilled those promises
and declared "every contract, combination in the form of trust or
otherwise, or conspiracy, in restraint of trade or commerce . . . illegal";
those whom a monopoly had injured might bring civil suits to recover
three times the damages incurred. Although the Sherman Act seemed
unambiguous, in practice it proved ineffective, for the great age of
industrial consolidation occurred after the act had passed. The Justice
Department used the law sparingly, and the Supreme Court decided in
1895 (in *U.S.* v. *E. C. Knight Co.*) that the authority of Congress over
interstate commerce did not extend to manufacturing, and that the
Sherman Act, therefore, did not apply to manufacturers.

The rhetoric of the trust-busters once more disclosed the nation's
ambivalence about industrialization. To be sure, large enterprise had
undeniable economic advantages for the entire society. On the other
hand, most Americans believed competition an absolute moral virtue as
well as a theoretical economic one. They responded, as they had since

the days of Jefferson and Jackson, to political leaders who warned of the potential danger of concentrated economic power. Yet, most Americans also meant to emulate the rich, not to confiscate their fortunes. Industry was the current path to quick wealth, a tempting and thoroughly traditional American goal. Americans listened attentively to the trust-busters, approved the appropriate legislation, and then permitted consolidation to continue apace.

So American industrialization is not just the oft-told tale of "robber barons" and a cheated public demanding governmental protection from corporate greed. There were robber barons and cheats and bloated profits and righteous anger, and there was a great deal of greed—not all of it corporate. But it is only in retrospect that the later nineteenth century seems a time for making monopolies and fortunes. Most businesses then were small businesses; most profits were modest; most entrepreneurs felt harassed by powerful competitors, uneasy about the dizzying pace of economic change, and baffled by the barriers to industrial organization. The American economy grew, of course, but it grew in unpredictable bursts and then paused for depressions that ruined businesses and lives and caused jobs and accumulated capital to disappear.

Yet, whatever the uncertainties of the industrial future, few Americans would have exchanged them for the rural past. Although critics of milionaires abounded, envy often colored the criticism; and if Standard Oil symbolized corporate greed and power, many Americans worried more about the price of kerosene than about the company's ethics.

Economic Organization: Workers

Factory workers might well have lamented their lot, since they often spent sixty or more weekly hours in conditions that produced disease and maiming accidents, and received in return wages that barely sustained a family. Yet social critics and prophets of other economic systems evoked no broad enthusiasm; radicalism, and sometimes even reform, made little sense to American working people. Grateful for a job and lacking the bargaining power that came from a skill, factory workers were slow to organize to seek a fair share of industry's production. Joining a labor union was an admission that the individual employee was not the equal of the boss, that the worker needed help in the encounter with economic power. That power, and the hostility of employers, blocked some early attempts to organize unions. So also did the skeptical attitude of the workers themselves.

The first unions, founded before the Civil War, sought to ease labor's lot through legislation as much as through organization; they were labor parties as well as labor unions. During Reconstruction, their demands that reform extend beyond racial equality for freedmen to social justice for white workers chilled the radicalism of some Republican politicians. Many of the objectives of the National Labor Union (NLU), a loose federation of labor and reform groups founded in 1866, required legislation: restriction of immigration from China, banking reform, full equality for women. Leaders of the NLU held that the union's most important demand—a working day of eight hours—could only be achieved in the legislatures, not through strikes or other economic weapons.

Formation of the National Labor Union showed a recognition that some of labor's problems could not be solved locally. Locomotive engineers and a few groups of skilled craftsmen, such as blacksmiths, machinists, and printers, had organized nationally before 1860. The NLU hoped to combine these and other trade unions with political reformers in a powerful national coalition. But the NLU never enlisted more than 300,000 members out of a national labor force of perhaps 18 million, and it never dominated even one trade. Most of the nation's workers did not yet see the need for organization.

Membership in a cooperative enterprise might seem more attractive than membership in a labor union. William Sylvis, the ironworker who guided the NLU until his death in 1869, tried to promote cooperatives as one way of winning labor's goals. Workers, in Sylvis's vision, would pool their capital, own the factories, market the product, and pocket the profits. Laborers, in short, would become employers; the success of the union would bring its own extinction. "By cooperation," Sylvis prophesied, "we will become a nation of employers—the employers of our own labor."

Uriah Stephens, a garment worker who thought the craft union organization of the NLU too selfishly narrow, founded the Knights of Labor in 1869. His union invited all to join except bankers, lawyers, distillers, and gamblers. Rich and poor, skilled and unskilled, male and female, black and white were alike welcome in this industrial union, where no lines of craft, class, color, or sex divided the members. The initiation, the semireligious ritual, and the membership lists were secret, partly to prevent reprisals by employers and partly to enhance the organization's appeal as a fraternal lodge, although Roman Catholic suspicion of secrecy forced the Knights to drop it in 1882. By 1886 membership had reached a peak of about a million, at a time when the labor force numbered perhaps twenty-five million.

Appropriately for an organization that excluded virtually no one, the Knights preferred the boycott, which organized consumers, to the strike, which organized labor. Like the NLU, the Knights founded and mismanaged some unsuccessful cooperatives. Like the NLU also, the Knights appealed to legislatures to require the eight-hour day and to provide more currency through a reformed banking system. The Knights also asked for stricter safety regulations, the prohibition of child labor, and a graduated income tax. Arbitration, the union suggested, should settle industrial disputes.

In spite of official aversion to strikes, a local organization occasionally forced the Knights into one. In 1885 they struck Jay Gould's railway system. The strike, which the Knights had intended to avoid, was so successful that in fifteen months membership surged from 100,000 to 700,000 and the number of locals doubled. But a year later the spectacular growth turned into an equally spectacular tailspin. In Chicago a demonstration for the eight-hour day turned into a bloody melee in Haymarket Square. The Knights' reputation suffered, even though they were not responsible for the demonstration, for the strike with which it was connected, for the tension that set city, police, and workers on edge, or for the bomb that provoked the riot in which seven policemen and four workers were killed. After a farcical trial, eight anarchists were convicted of inciting the riot, although their radical views were their only crime; four were executed and one cheated the state through suicide.

Precisely as the Haymarket riot boiled to bloodshed, Jay Gould provoked another railroad strike. The year before, the Knights had caught Gould in the middle of a speculative maneuver that forced him to settle on the union's terms; much better prepared for the strike in 1886, Gould crushed the union. Most Americans shrank from class warfare and usually reacted against labor when violence flared. Unjustly blamed for the Haymarket riot and badly beaten by Jay Gould, the Knights were virtually extinct before 1900.

Neither the NLU nor the Knights could sustain an organizing drive when periodic depressions produced unemployed unskilled workers who readily served as strikebreakers. Workers—male or female—whose dependent families were at the edge of subsistence could not risk the hostility of employers determined to run their businesses without interference from unions. Labor organizations rarely secured sympathy or support from any level of government; courts, troops, and police protected the rights of property more often than the right to organize. Partly because unions could not build up the treasury necessary to sustain a strike, they resorted to politics, reform, and arbitration.

Samuel Gompers and other officials of the American Federation of Labor (AFL) set out to overcome these obstacles to organization. The AFL, established just as the Knights lost momentum in 1886, was a craft union, interested in programs that demonstrably and immediately improved the lot of the worker. Social critics, consumers, and politicians were welcome in the AFL, but they had to be skilled laborers first. "Social reformers, like bumblebees," warned the journal of one AFL union, "are biggest when they are first hatched." But, like bumblebees also, they produced more noise than honey, and lacked "all the practical . . . qualities . . . for leadership." The best labor leader, the journal continued, was unconcerned about conditions in a future utopia;

he worried about "conditions here and now." The AFL, said one of its founders, had "no ultimate ends," but worked "from day to day" for goals that could be achieved "in a few years."

The goals were simple: higher wages, shorter hours, better conditions in the shop, recognition of the union as the bargaining agent for employees. The union's muscle was the strike, to be used sparingly and only when there was a reasonable chance of success. To enable members to endure strikes and to offer disability and death benefits, most AFL unions collected high dues. Mounting bank balances made cautious union leaders more cautious. While locals, or sometimes even affiliated national unions, participated in politics or joined local reform movements, the AFL officially stayed aloof. Not until 1908 did the union formally support a presidential candidate, William Jennings Bryan, who ran on the Democratic ticket. His distant second-place finish did not encourage renewed partisanship. In 1924 the AFL endorsed Robert LaFollette, who ran on the Progressive ticket and finished a distant third. The AFL waited until 1952 before trying, and failing, again.

The AFL combined in one national organization unions of skilled craftsmen—such as carpenters, masons, iron-moulders, printers, brewers, plumbers. Such workers had more bargaining power than unskilled laborers, who were, in Gompers's view, too easily replaced. Radicals criticized Gompers for his failure to organize the unskilled, for his caution, for his refusal to support candidates of the Socialist party or other political groups of the left. But Gompers held the AFL within the ideological limits of free enterprise and private property. He led labor in a struggle to acquire property, not to abolish it; he had no grievance against industry except that workers received too little of its bounty. By 1914 his organization claimed a membership of more than two million, but since the labor force then approached forty million, the AFL could not speak decisively for American workers.

Few employers before 1900 saw the AFL as a conservative bulwark of order. Indeed, most employers jealously guarded their right to pay what they pleased to employees of their own choosing. In the depression-wracked 1890s this determination collided with the rising confidence of labor organizations. The most publicized labor disputes of the decade involved Andrew Carnegie and George Pullman, prominent industrialists who thought their labor policy enlightened but did not intend to discuss it with unions.

In July 1892, an AFL affiliate struck at the Carnegie steel mill in Homestead, Pennsylvania. Carnegie himself was in Scotland, but he fully agreed with his manager, Henry Clay Frick, who resolutely set out to break the union. Frick shut the mill down and summoned three hundred Pinkerton guards to enable him to reopen with nonunion employees. Angry strikers fired on the Pinkertons as they approached Homestead on river barges, and before the workers had driven off the subdued Pinkertons, about a dozen people were killed. Eight thousand National

Guard troops, sent by the governor of Pennsylvania, proved more efficient than the Pinkertons, and the company gradually screened out union members and broke the strike.

The Pullman strike erupted two years later. Wages were reduced at the Pullman Palace Car Company, but rents and prices in the company town George Pullman had built to house his employees did not go down at all. Pullman fired those who protested the wage cut and provoked an angry strike. The American Railway Union, to which many of the strikers belonged, was a militant independent union headed by Eugene V. Debs, a fiery idealist who had become disenchanted with the conservative railroad brotherhoods. Debs ordered his members not to handle Pullman cars. The railroad companies discharged workers who followed Debs's instructions, but whenever one worker was discharged, others walked out too. Within a few days, several thousand workers were on strike and rail traffic had virtually stopped.

Since the strike was orderly, Governor John P. Altgeld of Illinois, who sympathized with labor, refused to summon the National Guard. President Cleveland, however, alarmed at reports of interference with interstate commerce and federal mail, sent two thousand federal troops into Chicago. Meanwhile, federal attorneys secured a court order that in essence forbade Debs and other union officials to interfere with trains. In an attempt to keep the strike alive, Debs disobeyed the injunction and went to jail for contempt of court. While the union's leaders sat in jail, federal troops protected the trains and enforced the decree of a federal court that effectively broke the strike, the American Railway Union, and the morale of those laborers who wondered whom the government represented. Eugene Debs knew where he stood; in 1900, 1904, 1908, 1912, and 1920 he was the presidential candidate of the American Socialist party. But in his best year, less than 6 percent of the electorate voted for him. Even the dream of the American worker was of free enterprise—of property, profit, and personal progress.

Suggested Reading

Glenn Porter's *The Rise of Big Business** (1973) is a brief survey that discusses much of the historical literature on industrialization. *The Visible Hand* (1977), Alfred D. Chandler's study of business management, pertains in large part to the period before 1900; Chandler's *Railroads: The Nation's First Big Business** (1965) is a useful collection of sources. In *Railroads and Regulation** (1965), Gabriel Kolko argues that the railroads sought governmental regulation. See also Albro Martin, *James J. Hill and the Opening of the Northwest* (1976).

Samuel P. Hays, in *The Response to Industrialism, 1885–1914** (1957), and Robert H. Wiebe, in *The Search for Order** (1968), both see organization as society's central device for coping with industrialization. Labor organizations are covered in Philip A. Taft's *The A. F. of L. in the Time of Gompers* (1957) and Gerald N. Grob's *Workers and Utopia** (1961); Herbert G. Gutman, in *Work, Culture and Society in Industrializing America* (1976), focuses on workers rather than unions. The debate about business organization may be sampled by comparing Allan Nevins's biography of John D. Rockefeller (1940) with the acccount in Henry D. Lloyd's *Wealth Against Commonwealth** (1894). Most of Andrew Carnegie's writings, including his *Autobiography* (1920), are still interesting.

Stephan Thernstrom's work on mobility began in Newburyport, Massachusetts, with *Poverty and Progress** (1964) and moved to Boston with *The Other Bostonians* (1973). E. Digby Baltzell's *The Protestant Establishment** (1964) discusses the barriers the rich erected to preserve aristocracy.

Henry F. May outlines the religious bulwarks of laissez faire in *Protestant Churches and Industrial America* (1949), and Richard Hofstadter's *Social Darwinism in American Thought** (1959) shows the scientific ones. The businessman's point of view is variously described in Edward C. Kirkland's *Dream and Thought in the Business Community** (1956), Robert McCloskey's *American Conservatism in the Age of Enterprise** (1951), and Irvin G. Wyllie's *The Self-Made Man in America** (1954).

NOTE: See also works cited in *Suggested Reading* for Chapters 13 and 14.

* Available in paperback edition

Chapter 13
A People Adjusts

Chronology

1875 Smith, Wellesley Colleges established •

1876 Custer's "last stand" at Little Big Horn •

1882 Chinese Exclusion Act •

1887 Dawes Act gives Indians homesteads •

1889 Jane Addams establishes Hull House •

1890 Census shows end of frontier •
Chicago's population exceeds one million •

1890s "New" immigrants come from southern and eastern Europe •

1893 World's Columbian Exposition in Chicago •

1917 Literacy test restricts European immigration •

People all over America had to make a private peace with the industrial economy that boomed after the Civil War. Most Americans knew the change only as it forced them to modify habits and attitudes or shift homes and jobs. The impact of industrialization could be read in the despair of the shoemaker whose skill became irrelevant when machines manufactured shoes too efficiently. Or in the bewilderment of the sharecropper whose expenses stayed constant while the price of cotton plummeted. Or in the anguish of the Italian or Polish immigrant, uprooted from a familiar village and half-settled in a strange city where more people lived in one overflowing tenement than in a half-dozen villages in the old country. Or in the endless meetings of endless city councils where politicians alternately ignored and grappled with problems of slums and sewage and greed and garbage and parks and police and too many people in too little space.

For generations the unsettled West had provided one way out for Americans who resisted or resented change. But the new West that lay beyond the Mississippi Valley was different; it lacked trees, streams, rainfall, and the gently rolling contours of familiar eastern landscapes and midwestern prairies. Those settlers who left industrial America for the Great Plains found a new environment that tested their ability to adjust no less rigorously than did the industrial environment back east.

The Indians and Their Plains

In 1859, Horace Greeley made the arduous overland journey from New York to San Francisco. What he saw repelled him. Greeley advised young men to "Go West" only if they had no farm or shop to inherit and no family to set up a venture at home. Greeley had had a glimpse of what his contemporaries called "The Great American Desert," an area without precise boundaries that encompassed roughly the western third of the nation, omitting California and parts of Oregon. Temperatures in the region ranged from parching heat to numbing Arctic cold, and rainfall varied from ten to twenty inches—not enough for most crops. Greeley thought the area might be settled in the course of a century; his description made that prediction sound optimistic.

The flat land that Greeley found so desolate in fact supported a good deal of life. Most prominently, the plains grass supported the buffalo, which, in turn, was a walking shopping center for the Indians. At the beginning of the Civil War, perhaps twelve million buffalo roamed the grasslands; from these beasts, Sioux, Blackfeet, Pawnees, and other tribes of the plains derived their meat, their dwellings, their fuel, their clothing, and even some of their tribal ritual and religion.

As white settlers moved into the "desert," the buffalo became the first crop. Those who ran the railroads thought the animals a dangerous nuisance and hired "Buffalo Bill" Cody and other professional hunters to turn the herd into rugs and leather. The rising price of hides in the 1870s was only one of the attractions promoters used to induce settlement of the plains. Rainfall, boosters said, followed the plow, and would commence with cultivation. Wheat grew tall on the plains, it was said, and cattle fattened on unfenced range. Gold, whispered prospectors, was in the hills. Seeking a shortcut to riches in beef, mining, farming, and land speculation, migrants poured into the Great Plains. In twenty years the open spaces of the western frontier became the stuff of folklore and history.

Indians grew desperate as whites systematically eliminated the buffalo herds. Deprived of the opportunity to be independent, Indians were gradually confined to reservations and robbed of self-respect by patronizing do-gooders, of property by agents of the government sworn to protect them, and of the vindication of history by frontier clichés that are now more than a century old. However guilty white Americans feel about the nation's Indian policy, many still imagine embattled whites in

Buffalo hunting from the train

covered wagons fending off the unprovoked attacks of cruel savages. In white mythology, the Indians always were the first to take scalps, stole the horses of inoffensive farmers, and ambushed the cavalry troop. The Indians' clichés about whites, by contrast, emphasized greed and the constant violation of oaths and treaties solemnly made.

Both sets of beliefs have a basis in fact. But, in general, Indians had the better motive: they were defending their territory and their way of life. Their white antagonists only sought wealth, though they sometimes rationalized that objective as the march of democracy, or Christianity, or progress. The relationship with the Indians may be the ugliest manifestation of the competitive ethic that energized the American people. The Indians did not share the ethic and could not rely on their own technology or the conscience of their white foes for protection. The one-sided competition ultimately degraded both participants.

The Indians of the plains were no more homogeneous than the Americans of the cities. The tribes had different languages and cultures, as did urban immigrants. But Sioux and Cheyenne, Apache and Ute, Navaho and Nez Percé, all knew the buffalo herds and the prairie grass and the serpentine rivers of the area white people called the Great American Desert. Indians did not worry about frontiers: "The country was made without lines," Chief Joseph of the Nez Percé once said, "and it is no man's business to divide it." The tribes lived in harmony with their environment and, usually, with one another.

But white people did worry about boundaries and wrote them into treaties. In 1868, for instance, negotiators had agreed that whites would not settle or pass through the Black Hills without the consent of the tribes to whom the area was sacred. But there was gold in the Black Hills, and prospectors ignored the treaty. Indians frightened some, killed some, and failed to find others. General George Armstrong Custer and the Seventh Cavalry started into the area, but President Grant recalled the expedition. Custer's troops let the world know that only an Indian treaty kept lucky adventurers from golden riches. The army's subsequent effort to keep gold-seekers out of the Black Hills was halfhearted and predictably ineffective.

Failing to control the whites, the government bullied the Indians. When Sitting Bull and Crazy Horse refused to consider a cession or sale, white commissioners asked if the Indians would lease mineral rights in the area. After the gold was removed, the whites promised, the tribes could have the Black Hills back. Spotted Tail declined; would the agents lease him a mule team on similar terms, he inquired. Perhaps the tribes would trade the Black Hills for land further west, the commissioners persisted. No deal. Most of the Sioux chiefs did not bother to attend the final meetings; the Black Hills were not for sale.

The government's negotiators returned to Washington, reported their inability to secure a treaty, and recommended that Congress appropriate a fair sum and force the Indians to accept it. The War Department

Nearly 80, and finally subdued, Geronimo (in top hat) poses on the reservation

ordered all Indians herded to reservations, and set in motion the sequence of events that led Custer and the Seventh Cavalry to disaster at Little Big Horn. Since the warriors who killed Custer were beyond the government's reach, those on the reservations bore the white man's revenge. Congress declared that the Indians, by taking the warpath, had forfeited both their treaty rights and their territory. The distribution of rations on the reservation would cease, and all Indians off the reservation were to be treated as hostile (that is, shot), unless the Sioux accepted new lands along the Missouri. Without rations, without game, without arms, without ponies, and without much future, the captive Sioux chieftains agreed. Years later, a chief of the Utes remarked that an agreement between Indians and the United States "was like the agreement a buffalo makes with his hunters when pierced with arrows. All he can do is lie down and give in."

Eventually, they gave in all over the West. Sitting Bull joined Buffalo Bill Cody's Wild West Show; Geronimo, who with twenty-five braves had evaded for a time one-third of the entire United States Army, lived out his days as a prisoner of war. One by one, the tribes accepted the dole, the tedium, the whisky, and the degradation of the reservation. They had no defense against the greed of Indian agents, the most notoriously corrupt civil servants of a graft-ridden age. Reservations usually kept the Indians in, but never effectively kept white men out; when their land proved too valuable, Indians were dispossessed, as their ancestors had been before them. In 1887, Congress passed the Dawes Act to provide for the subdued remnant of a proud people. Although Plains Indians had consistently rejected the opportunity to farm like white men, the Dawes Act gave the head of each Indian family a 160-acre homestead. After twenty-five years, the family would become full citizens and receive a clear title to the land. But individual ownership and agriculture were not the Indian way, and the act undermined the tribal structure that had once sustained Indian pride. In 1934, with the Wheeler-Howard Act, Congress attempted to revive that pride by making the tribe once more the basic landowner. At that late date the policy neither made amends nor made sense.

Most white Americans saw Indians as something less than civilized because they rejected the white man's way of life. "The government feeds and clothes and educates your children now," one exasperated senator remarked to unimpressed Indians, "and desires . . . to civilize you and make you as white men." When Indians began to plow the prairie, build fences, brand cattle, attend church, and keep money in the bank, they would become good Indians. In 1879, a federal judge ruled that Indians were legal persons, entitled to the protection of the law; Standing Bear, Elmer Dundy ruled, could not arbitrarily be taken into federal custody. But since this decision endangered the principles and the profits of the reservation system, the precedent was ignored. Dundy's decision implied that Indians were human beings, even if they were not white. In the society at large, his was a dissenting opinion.

The Western Economy

Even before Indians and buffalo were expelled from the plains and mountains, the white settler moved in with prospecting kit, saddle, lariat, or plow. Western mining, ranching, and farming all went through the same economic cycle that had characterized industrial organization back east. Individual prospectors, cowboys, and homesteaders gave way to corporations, ranches, and larger farms, each of which in turn consolidated. Mining required more and more capital for expensive equipment. Ranchers, who could no longer rely on free government grazing, had to invest in their own pastures. And farmers found that small plots produced small profits.

The mining frontier moved east from California, accompanied by the techniques of the forty-niners. Word of gold strikes came from Nevada and Colorado in the 1850s, from Idaho, Montana, and Arizona in the 1860s, and from South Dakota in the 1870s. A surge of prospectors flooded towns like Deadwood, South Dakota, or Tombstone, Arizona, made them proverbial for sin, violence, and high life, and then deserted them, all within a few years. Denver and some other mining towns did survive to become cities, but their growth was to be in the future. Stability and attendant dignity then sometimes demanded that the colorful past be disowned with a change of name; Last Chance Gulch, for instance, emerged as Helena, Montana.

More permanent than the gamblers, bartenders, and whores who followed the prospectors were the mining corporations that moved in after the loose gold had been picked up. Corporations brought a more regular system of law and order than the rough justice that characterized early settlement. With hydraulic equipment and new smelting and refining techniques to recover ore from quartz, mining was only a hazardous job that paid inadequate wages rather than an independent way of life for free-lancers. Minerals came more efficiently from the earth—in twenty years Nevada's Comstock Lode poured out more than $300 million in gold and silver—and this time the riches went to stockholders with uncalloused hands.

Further east, the earth yielded a different kind of wealth. The same grass that sustained the buffalo sustained the long-horned cattle that abounded in Texas. Before the Civil War, a few visionary cattlemen had attempted to drive stock to market in Illinois, but Indians and distance made the venture unprofitable. After the war, the railroad reached the legendary "cow towns" of Dodge City and Abilene, Kansas. The steer that was worth $3 or $4 in Texas brought ten times that at the rail head. This potential profit brought about the fabled cattle drives, the cowboys who tended them, and vicarious adventure for millions of city-born Americans for generations to come.

The task was more humdrum than legend suggests. Day followed bone-wearying day of riding; restless cattle and rugged terrain were more hazardous than rustlers and revolvers; boredom was the chief occupational hazard. For twenty years cowboys pushed cattle from Texas to Kansas, until a combination of drought, terrible winters, and falling prices in 1885 and 1886 put an end to the drives.

The cattle drives would have ceased soon anyway. They had been possible only because much of the range was in the public domain. Cattle moved through open grassland on the way to market; young cattle matured on free Texas range. Because a benevolent government permitted use of the public lands, cattle barons could operate with very little capital. But by the mid-1880s, a few shrewd cattlemen began to lease range and exclude their competitors or to buy and fence water holes and streams. When ranchers purchased their pasture, cattle-raising became a settled business enterprise with heavy capital costs; cowboys were merely wage-earning employees.

Sheep were one encroachment that forced cattlemen to buy their own ranges, for cattle will not graze after sheep. More of an obstacle than sheepherders, however, were ordinary dirt farmers who demanded surveys, fences, and boundaries. The farmer brought the law of private property to the plains and ended the open range. Cattlemen occasionally cut fences, burned barns, and even murdered particularly stubborn opponents. But the ubiquitous farmers kept coming, and the rancher became a variety of farmer himself and adopted traditional American agricultural ways.

Farmers had to overcome obstacles more formidable than obstinate cattlemen. The environment was forbidding and devices to tame it at first inadequate. Matted roots of virgin grass defied the plows that broke eastern sod. Finally, in 1877, James Oliver perfected a plow that could cut a deep furrow in the plains. Trees were scarce, but farmers found that damp sod houses served until timber could be imported, and barbed wire, which was readily available in 1880, permitted them to build fences without rails. A new variety of spring wheat, which came to the plains from Russia by way of Canada, proved more adaptable to the growing season than conventional varieties brought from the east. But homesteaders had no defense against grasshoppers or blizzards, which either ate their way across the landscape or buried everything in sight.

Above all, the plains farmer needed water. Wells and windmills could supply people and livestock but were wholly inadequate for irrigating crops. Farmers developed a method of "dry farming" to conserve rainfall.

THE GREAT PLAINS

Collecting buffalo chips on the Kansas frontier

They covered a deep furrow with pulverized earth to retard evaporation and harrowed whenever there was rain. Because of the need for frequent cultivation, dry farming was expensive and, at best, unreliable. In 1877 Congress attempted to encourage irrigation with the Desert Land Act, which made up to 640 acres at twenty-five cents an acre available to farmers who would irrigate the tract within three years. After the land was irrigated, the farmer received clear title to the plot by paying an additional dollar per acre. But Congress could not create sources of water to fill irrigation ditches, and while some land was claimed under the act, there was more fraud than irrigation.

Like the farmers, Congress found the plains made past experience irrelevant. The basic land statute was the Homestead Act, which granted settlers 160 acres without charge. But while a quarter-section was an appropriate unit in Iowa or Illinois, it proved inappropriate on the plains, for no homesteader could afford to plow, irrigate, and fence so much land. Yet both grazing and commercial agriculture required much more than 160 acres to turn a profit. Congress modified the system in 1873 with the Timber Culture Act, which permitted homesteaders to claim an additional 160 acres by planting trees on 40 acres within four years. In 1878, in the Timber and Stone Act, Congress permitted the purchase at $2.50 per acre of quarter-sections whose chief resource was timber or mineral ores. Corporations, not farmers, were the chief beneficiaries of these changes in land policy. In general, settlers bought their tracts from railroads or from speculators, not from the government.

But buy land Americans did, and within twenty years after the Civil War the plains were peopled. In 1889 and 1890, Congress divided the northwestern territories into six states, and when Congress decided that polygamy had been effectively outlawed in Utah, it too was admitted in 1896. The census for 1890 omitted the usual frontier line, for, the

Superintendent of the Census announced, the line had effectively ceased to exist. The "unsettled area" had been "so broken into by isolated bodies of settlement" that the last frontier had vanished. The free land that had bolstered belief in economic opportunity had disappeared under a wave of settlers. In fact, there was still unsettled land; indeed, in the twentieth century more land has been distributed through the Homestead Act than was granted in the nineteenth. Nevertheless, the realization that they had at last settled the continent roused both pride and anxiety in Americans.

Frederick Jackson Turner, a professor of history at the University of Wisconsin, noted the conclusion of the Bureau of the Census, and went on to some conclusions of his own in "The Significance of the Frontier in American History" (1893). It was the frontier, Turner argued, that transformed Europeans into Americans; the frontier converted European institutions into American institutions; the frontier made America democratic, energetic, and enterprising. Turner did not quite suggest that the end of the frontier meant that national character would deteriorate. But he did think it would change, and there was a touch of nostalgia in his final sentence: "And now, four centuries from the discovery of America, at the end of a hundred years of life under the Constitution, the frontier has gone, and with its going has closed the first period of American history."

The World's Fair

Turner read his paper in Chicago at the World's Columbian Exposition, where the United States celebrated its own progress and (a year late) the four-hundredth anniversary of Columbus's epic voyage. The fabulous "white city" on the shore of Lake Michigan served as a showcase for the nation's artistic talent and economic enterprise, drew an audience for intellectuals and religious reformers, inspired the subsequent construction of neoclassical public buildings all over the country, and enchanted those who attended. "Sell the cookstove if necessary and come," urged Hamlin Garland, whose experience in rural America, recounted in the short stories of *Main Travelled Roads* (1891), had prepared him to migrate anyway. "You *must* see this fair."

There was a good deal to see: a swamp that Frederick Law Olmsted, the nation's foremost landscape architect, had transformed into lagoons and groves with paths, plants, and decorative bridges; buildings whose common classical style, dimension, and beauty had visitors rapt even before they saw the exhibits; technology to stimulate imagination and cupidity: electrical machines, steam engines, manufacturing processes, transportation devices; sculpture around the grounds and paintings from around the world; seminars on education, ethnology, and ethics; a midway with Polynesian huts, Egyptian dancing girls, exotic livestock, and the world's largest ferris wheel. Popular entertainment jostled fine art at the fair, and commerce was linked with culture.

Choices made by the exposition's promoters and visitors provide a glimpse of the nation's interests and aspirations in 1893, and maybe a clue to national character as well. It was somehow appropriate, for instance, that the white city was disposable—a gigantic classical facade designed to be torn off the edge of the raw new city behind it. Although Antonin Dvořák had been commissioned to compose orchestral pieces that he later integrated into the *New World* Symphony, the works were not performed at the fair, for music was among the casualties of a straitened budget. Those who selected the French paintings did not send any by Impressionists. The American exhibit, on the other hand, included not only paintings by Winslow Homer and George Inness, but also works of Mary Cassatt and other Americans greatly influenced by Impressionism. The paintings most popular with the public were those with religious subjects, and the longest and best-attended of the seminars was the one on religion, where proponents of the social gospel began to find kindred spirits. An early decision authorized a "Board of Lady Managers," which assumed responsibility for the design, construction, and contents of the Women's Building. Mrs. Potter Palmer, president of the board, claimed that "the fact that the General Government has just discovered women" was even "more important than the discovery of Columbus."

William Dean Howells, the novelist who gracefully bore his responsibilities as the "dean of American letters," asked readers of *A Traveler from Altruria* (1894) to reflect on the contrast between the beauty of the white city and the commercial bustle of the midway. He hoped the fair would dramatize the random squalor entrepreneurial energy could produce, and prove the importance of municipal controls.

The World's Fair, Chicago, 1893

Yet the people with whom Howells talked clearly divorced beauty from business. The planning that produced the fair "would never do for a business city," he was told, "where there was something going on besides the pleasure of the eyes and the edification of the mind."

City Lights

There was indeed "something going on" in American cities as Howells wrote. Most obviously, most of them seemed to be growing. Denver and Dallas quadrupled in population between 1880 and 1900; Los Angeles, Seattle, and Portland, Oregon, doubled between 1890 and 1900. Industrial cities like Akron, Youngstown, Columbus, Cincinnati, and Cleveland dotted Ohio. Of course Chicago and New York set the pace: Chicago's population increase in the 1890s was slightly less than the total population of those five Ohio cities; New York's growth surpassed that sum. People came to Chicago, wrote one scolding writer two years after the fair, "for the common avowed object of making money." The competitive ethic required everyone to cultivate "his own little bed." But, the critic wondered, who looked "after the paths between," which were fast disappearing under "the weeds of rank iniquity."

Americans had long been accustomed to thinking of cities as centers of sin; urban iniquity was nothing new. But the size of cities increased the scope of evil, and uneasy middle-class Americans worried that the customs, values, manners, and morals of a healthy rural society might succumb to urban temptations. Whether or not prostitution, poverty, crime, drunkenness, and gambling were more prevalent in cities than in rural America, they were certainly more visible. And political and social institutions that had once curbed such behavior seemed threatened by unmanageable numbers and by the unusual habits some of the immigrants brought with them.

Those who settled in urban ethnic neighborhoods had families, worshipped in churches, joined clubs, and nourished customs, just as did their WASP counterparts on the other side of town. But families living in a few tenement rooms, where the stoop or the street served as a parlor, seemed to differ from old families in single-family dwellings. And Protestants had long suspected Catholics and Jews of loyalties that transcended the competitive American creed, however competitive individual Catholics and Jews might prove to be in practice. This suspicion mounted with the proliferation of Catholic schools in the 1880s and 1890s. Ethnic associations—for fellowship, economic cooperation, community improvement, or political advantage—seemed to established Americans to challenge the established institutions they controlled. Clubs listed in the Social Register were "exclusive," but those in ethnic neighborhoods were evidence of a narrow "clannishness" and subversive of the melting-pot ideal.

Strange politics flourished in this urban environment of strange churches, strange tongues, and strange habits. Rural Americans decided that honesty had given way to corruption; graft was apparently the ordinary method of conducting a city's business. Disgruntled reformers noted that education and ability were not automatic qualifications for public office and that membership in a prominent family seemed an almost automatic disqualification. Parties stood for patronage and spurned principle; party machines and bosses dealt in contracts, franchises, jobs, and votes. Boss Tweed went to jail, but dozens of urban bosses who put city treasuries to personal political use did business in City Hall until they died.

Part of the payoff from fat contracts and municipal franchises went into partisan welfare work in an era before charity became a public responsibility. The unemployed laborer, needing a temporary job until the mill reopened, went to his precinct captain; a solicitous representative of the mayor helped the immigrant fill out the naturalization form and also showed him how to mark the ballot; attached to the basket of food that stood on the thresholds of needy families at Christmas and Easter, and sometimes in between, was the card of the local alderman, who collected his return at the polls. Bosses or their flunkeys dignified wakes and weddings, feasts and funerals, with a few moments' presence and a few trite remarks. The personal touch in an impersonal city meant more than self-righteous integrity. Bosses may not have governed cities well, but many of them governed with self-serving compassion.

The cities seemed ungovernable anyway. Municipal charters, granted by state governments, often reserved to the state authority over municipal taxes, services, and appointments. American local government had evolved to meet the needs of small communities where people knew and usually trusted one another. As cities grew larger and more anonymous, mayors and aldermen, precinct bosses and policemen lost touch with their constituents and served them less well.

Women's Work

The discovery that some preconceptions about cities had a basis in fact nurtured popular myths about a rosy rural past. Yet, especially for women, frontier life offered few amenities; the sod hut was no dream house. Even in country towns, a woman's day often included a good deal of men's work: gardening, butchering, tending chickens and pigs and cattle, chopping cotton, and becoming the extra hand at planting or at harvest or in between. When those chores were completed, there was women's work. The Bible offered consolation, and imagination provided the usual escape.

The city was a proverbially unhealthy refuge for the farmer's unskilled daughter. Urban working women were thought to be overworked, uncouth, and immoral. Aristocratic women preoccupied themselves with dinners and dances and the other trivia of a social whirl only the rich could afford. The middle-class lady—the quintessence of Victorian womanhood—kept a sober and cultured home, deferred to her husband and other men, and reared her daughters at least to appear retiring. In return for their deference, women were entitled to certain gallant courtesies—gestures of respect for their delicacy—and were usually conceded to have better artistic taste and deeper religious faith than men. A woman's home revealed her artistic talent and her attendance at church affirmed her faith. Nice women did not perform in public—on the violin, in the theater, or from the pulpit. But all those lofty Victorian ideals, Dorothy Richardson wrote, "butter no parsnips." Miss Richardson had left rural Pennsylvania for the sweatshops and box factories of New York. She knew that a girl on her own in a turn-of-the-century industrial city needed more than chivalry and prayer.

Dorothy Richardson herself survived, her virtue intact and her pride only temporarily crushed. But the life of most of the young women she encountered consisted of a dreary round of ten-hour days relieved by fantasy and dime novels, and their future promised only an early old age and a premature grave. Working married women managed to avoid boarding houses and some of the grosser propositions, but they had to contend with housework, babies, and a dominating husband instead. A working woman, Richardson wrote, needed no condescending charity. But she did need a decent boarding house and an upbringing that left her with an accurate understanding of the real world and perhaps with a trade that would enable her to avoid the oldest profession.

Every city had its red-light district, which the polite population carefully ignored, or made the object of a civic crusade, or, occasionally, patronized. For some middle-class boys, sex education was a furtive visit to a local house of prostitution; for their fathers, the same trip could be a method of keeping the family small. Urban police believed cheap prostitutes helped keep volatile male immigrants from taking the city apart. Perhaps because her editor would not publish the seamy details, Richardson did not write much about prostitutes.

But she knew it was work nobody sought. Most prostitutes, she thought, "are what they are, not because they are inherently vicious, but *because they were failures as workers and as wage earners.*" Both in her phrasing and in her emphasis, Dorothy Richardson seemed to blame the women themselves for their fate. Less emphatically, and with more justice, she also blamed the society that did not provide training and jobs, and the economic system that gave greater rewards to women who sold themselves than to those who sold their labor. A study in Pittsburgh in 1912 disclosed that most of the city's prostitutes could earn no more than $10 weekly in other jobs; $10 was a minimum weekly wage in one of the houses, where some women made $25 or more. Except for unskilled factory work, as Richardson knew, domestic service for a long time was

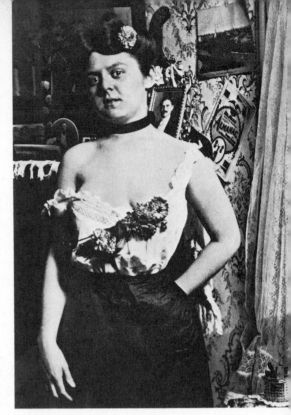

Working women: telephone operator, prostitute, housewife and maids

HOME WASHING MACHINE & WRINGER.

HOME WASHER

almost the only occupation open to women, whatever their skill or training. And marriage was the only fully acceptable career.

Gradually other—traditionally underpaid—careers opened. In the early twentieth century, women began to appear in retail shops. Indeed, a job in a department store saved Dorothy Richardson from sweatshops and laundries; she then went to night school to learn the secretarial skills that qualified her for the aristocracy of working women. More than one million women worked in offices by 1920, and another million had acquired a profession, usually nursing or teaching.

The women's colleges that appeared in the 1870s and 1880s revealed the needs and the ambitions of some women and stimulated them in others. Wellesley and Smith were founded in 1875 and Harvard began to admit women in 1879; Bryn Mawr and Barnard opened in the 1880s. Those who could not afford private eastern education began to attend state-supported universities nearer home. In 1908, women, often preparing to be schoolteachers, were attending land-grant universities in greater numbers than men in several western states, including Texas, Washington, Minnesota, and Colorado.

Jane Addams graduated from college in Illinois, traveled in Europe, established Hull House, a settlement house in Chicago, in 1889, and became the most prominent woman in America early in the twentieth century. Her contemporaries thought her the model of Victorian womanhood: a gentle reformer who radiated a compelling and contagious virtue. Although she portrayed herself in her books with a modesty Americans thought truly feminine, when she negotiated with her publisher, she was a hard-boiled entrepreneur. And if she had possessed the modesty she affected, Jane Addams would never have pushed herself to the front of organized campaigns for a half-dozen reforms, including the one to secure the vote and then full equality for women. She was an able administrator, politically shrewd, self-confident, and sometimes tough, and she needed all those qualities to satisfy both society's prescribed role for women and the one she set for herself.

The New Immigration

Among other goals, the staff at Hull House set out to help the "new" immigrants learn American ways. Although the shift in migration patterns had been discernible for some time, Jane Addams and other Americans awoke in the 1880s and 1890s to the presence of these "new" immigrants—the Italians, Poles, Greeks, Russians, and Jews who outnumbered the more traditional Irish, English, German, and Scandinavian migrants. In the 1890s, about half of the nearly four million immigrants came from southern and eastern Europe; in the first decade of the new century, the proportion of "new" immigrants rose to almost two-thirds and the total to nearly nine million. The newcomers seemed more unlike native Americans than had their predecessors. They were not what Americans of the later nineteenth century were learning to call Anglo-Saxons. Nor did they all have light complexions and Protestant faith, and few had much knowledge of, or experience with, self-government.

Once American entrepreneurs had sought migrants as the bearers of prosperity. In the years right after the Civil War, transcontinental railroads, anxious to convert western lands to cash, offered reduced fares to immigrants who purchased railroad property. Until the contract labor law was repealed in 1868, manufacturers recruited European workers, paid their passage, and secured their labor for a specified period; one-third of the labor force in American factories in 1870 had been born abroad. In the 1860s and 1870s, two-thirds of the states took active steps to attract European settlers.

Well Americans might seek immigrants, for they added much more than cultural diversity. Because they brought a bit of property, because most of them immediately became productive members of society, and because they represented an important fraction of the American market, the Treasury estimated that each immigrant was equivalent to $800 in new capital. Andrew Carnegie thought the estimate too low: $1,500 would be closer. Whatever their cash value, Americans before 1880 wanted immigrants and were confident that they could be absorbed in this broad land with its expanding economy. Surely, like their predecessors, they would be assimilated through public education, vital political democracy, and unremitting hard work.

The immigrant did indeed work, often in the least skilled, most menial trades. Immigrant women worked in textile mills or as domestics in thousands of kitchens. Immigrant men wielded picks and shovels in mines, under city streets, and across the plains where the railroad was to go. Enterprising, often unscrupulous immigrants contracted to supply employers with groups of their unskilled compatriots at substandard wages. Called the *padrone* system, this device particularly victimized unskilled Italians; in 1883 one Italian laborer in Chicago had an annual income of $270 to support his family of five. The standard of living was so meager that the family survived on less income than many other Chicago laborers spent on groceries alone.

As immigrants became more numerous and more obtrusive, some Americans worried about the apparent failure of new immigrants to assimilate. If the "melting pot" had ever existed, as Americans since colonial times had assumed, it was obviously producing a less homogeneous product in the late nineteenth century; many feared the alloy was inferior. Urban problems seemed inextricably related to unrestricted immigration. Immigrant neighborhoods often deteriorated into slums. Immigrants supported the political boss, who made a mockery of democracy and a fortune from corruption. Immigrants swelled the ranks of the poor, for whose relief the resources of private charity were hopelessly inadequate. Immigrants gambled on the one chance of a windfall that might finance escape; from the bottle flowed another kind of escape. Reformers who wanted to do something about grime and graft and poverty and despair saw no reason to admit more immigrants who would only make insoluble problems greater.

Advocates of restriction proposed to select immigrants instead of permitting immigrants to select themselves. A substantial tax would keep out the poor; an examination by American consuls abroad might screen out Europeans of undesirable character. In 1882, the same year that Congress forbade all migration from China, another act required European immigrants to be certifiably sane, capable of self-support, and free of venereal diseases. In 1896 Congress passed an act to make literacy in some language a qualification for immigration. President Cleveland's veto slowed this attempt at restriction, which by 1897 claimed such varied supporters as the AFL and Henry Cabot Lodge, the conservative Republican senator from Massachusetts. President Taft vetoed a similar bill in 1913 and President Wilson another one two years later. In 1917 Congress finally mustered enough votes to override Wilson's second veto, making the literacy test the first in a series of restrictive acts. After the First World War, Congress devised a new system of quotas based on the national origin of Americans who had already migrated. The old ideal that in the United States the poor and oppressed of Europe could be fused into a new, varied nation perished, like so many other ideals, in the slums.

Still, the immigrants arrived and survived. Dismal as their wages were, one statistician estimated that a skilled American immigrant earned about 40 percent more than his European counterpart. Some immigrants slipped through the slums and cities to the plains. The proportion of foreign-born in parts of Montana and the Dakotas was as high as in New England; Germans settled in Kansas, Nebraska, and California, and

SOURCES OF IMMIGRANTS, 1870 – 1910

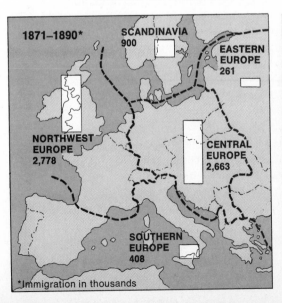

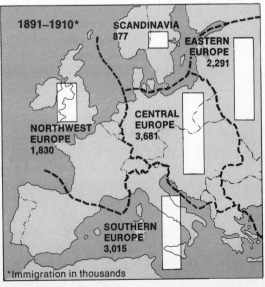

Scandinavians in Minnesota and Wisconsin. But isolation on a vast prairie could be as trying as loneliness in the frightful closeness of city quarters.

In some ways, that same isolation pervaded industrial America. The owner of a small business felt terribly alone as he faced an impersonal economic system that seemed about to dispense with his services. The anxious urban worker, trying to stretch his wage through periods of unemployment, and the frustrated farmer, who thought the whole world conspired to ruin him, also thought of themselves as isolated. Americans in an earlier, simpler age had gloried in being apart from their fellows, considered themselves self-reliant and independent, and rejoiced in their individualism. The new industrial society seemed to call for organization and groups—for corporations, unions, granges, lodges, and for responsive political parties. Once Americans discovered organization, they recovered their optimism, organized with their proverbial energy, and demanded that their new industrial plant raise their standard of living.

Suggested Reading

Helen Hunt Jackson's outrage at the nation's treatment of Indians pervades *A Century of Dishonor** (1881). Dee Brown's *Bury My Heart at Wounded Knee** (1970) makes use of the resigned eloquence of the Plains Indians themselves. Wilcomb E. Washburn's *The Indian in America** (1975) is a general account. Walter P. Webb's *The Great Plains** (1931) and Fred A. Shannon's *The Farmer's Last Frontier** (1945) are distinguished works on western farming. Some of the insights of Ole E. Rolvaag's novel *Giants in the Earth** (1927) are confirmed in Michael Lesy's *Wisconsin Death Trip** (1973), an unconventional piece of history.

William L. O'Neill has included Dorothy Richardson's autobiographical account in *Women at Work** (1972), which he edited. O'Neill has also written *Everyone Was Brave** (1969), a general account of American feminism. Allen F. Davis's *American Heroine* (1973) is a convincing study of Jane Addams. David F. Burg describes the exhibits of the World's Fair in *Chicago's White City of 1893* (1976).

Constance McL. Green's *The Rise of Urban America** (1965) and *A History of Urban America** (1967) by Charles N. Glaab and A. Theodore Brown are useful brief accounts. In *Tweed's New York** (1977), Leo Hershkowitz claims that Tweed has been maligned. Oscar Handlin's *The Uprooted** (1951) is a moving but somewhat romanticized study of the immigrant's experience in America. John Higham has probed the reaction to immigration in *Strangers in the Land** (1963).

NOTE: See also works cited in *Suggested Reading* for Chapters 12 and 14.

* Available in paperback edition

Chapter 14
Scandal, Spoils, and Silver:
Politics, 1870–1900

Chronology

1868 Presidential election: Ulysses S. Grant (Republican) defeats Horatio Seymour (Democrat) •

1872 Presidential election: Ulysses S. Grant (Republican) defeats Horace Greeley (Democrat, Liberal Republican) •

1876 Presidential election: Rutherford B. Hayes (Republican) defeats Samuel J. Tilden (Democrat) when a special electoral commission awards Hayes all 20 disputed electoral votes •

1878 Bland-Allison Act provides limited coinage of silver •

1880 Presidential election: James A. Garfield (Republican) defeats Winfield S. Hancock (Democrat); Chester A. Arthur succeeds Garfield in 1881 •

1883 Pendleton Act begins merit system in federal civil service •

1884 Presidential election: Grover Cleveland (Democrat) defeats James G. Blaine (Republican) •

1888 Presidential election: Benjamin Harrison (Republican) defeats Grover Cleveland (Democrat) •

1890 McKinley Tariff • Sherman Silver Purchase Act •

1892 Populist party enters national politics; Omaha Platform • Presidential election: Grover Cleveland (Democrat) defeats Benjamin Harrison (Republican) and James B. Weaver (Populist) •

1894 Wilson-Gorman Tariff includes income tax •

1895 *Pollock* v. *Farmers' Loan and Trust Co.* declares income tax unconstitutional •

1896 Presidential election: William McKinley (Republican) defeats William J. Bryan (Democrat) •

In the last three decades of the nineteenth century, the pageant of American politics reflected the vitality and variety of American life but had curiously little to do with it. Campaigns were earnest and exciting, but in retrospect, most of the issues seem trivial and many of the candidates interchangeable. "Garfield, Arthur, Harrison, and Hayes . . ." mused Thomas Wolfe, the twentieth-century novelist. "Which had the whiskers, which the burnsides: which was which?"

Wolfe might pardonably have lengthened his list. Although the era's leading statesmen differed, their differences were idiosyncratic, not fundamental. Some politicians were more honest than others, some more flamboyant or more stubborn or more successful. Few probed the questions that lay at the base of swirling political controversy. Would whites in any region accept blacks as unqualified equals? Did the competitive ethic encourage behavior in counting house, courthouse, and Congress that the churches condemned as immoral and the courts as unjust? Could the nation's political institutions, based on regional and local loyalties, keep pace with the evolution of a national economy? Must the government, handcuffed by laissez faire, watch impartially the unequal competition between rich and poor? Could the United States dedicate its new industrial production to the task of raising the standard of living for all, rather than for a few fabulously successful individuals?

The Politics of Deadlock

Neither political party could provide a decisive answer to any of those questions without intolerable risk. So close was the political balance that national elections usually turned on a few thousand votes in a few counties in three or four critical states. Americans displayed a loyalty to party that rivaled their devotion to church and country, but they divided their partisan allegiance almost exactly in half. Republicans usually controlled the Senate and Democrats the House. Only one presidential nominee between 1876 and 1896 won a majority of the popular vote, and he lost the election; some winners had popular margins of less than 1 percent over their rivals.

Narrow differences in the election returns reflected slight distinctions in party platforms. At the national level, both parties approved the laissez faire orthodoxy of the age; both opposed industrial regulation, and both ignored attempts to curb political corruption until an aroused public forced enactment of civil service legislation. At the local level, however, the parties divided more sharply, often along religious and ethnic lines, which seemed more relevant to politics than did lines of class or property. Working people made up the bulk of both parties, but the Democratic working people were more often Roman Catholic than were Republicans. Republicans tended to prefer a more active government, especially with respect to temperance, than did Democrats. In many communities, year in and year out, prohibition was the question that drew the electorate to the polls. Once there, voters cast ballots for national leaders as well, but before 1896, and often afterward, national politics was a secondary concern.

As the parties differed on local issues, so they differed in constituencies. A loose coalition of the solid white South and northern urban political machines formed the Democratic core. The party was slow to develop a national focus, partly because both elements cared more about local than about national policy. Neither wing of the party sought federal action, and each sometimes actively opposed it: southern Democrats wanted an end to federal intervention on behalf of blacks, and northern Democrats wanted no interference in local control of patronage and no protective tariff. Southern Democrats often called themselves Conservatives, and the term fit their northern allies as well. Most of the party's presidential nominees came from New York, where the economic ideas of Democrats differed only slightly from those of conservative Republicans. Horatio Seymour, New York's Civil War governor, lost to

Garfield, Arthur, Harrison, Hayes: "Which was which?"

Ulysses S. Grant in 1868; Horace Greeley, the quixotic editor of the New York *Tribune*, lost to Grant in 1872; another governor, Samuel J. Tilden, lost when the disputed election of 1876 was awarded to Hayes; Grover Cleveland, mayor of Buffalo in 1881 and governor in 1882, won the presidential elections of 1884 and 1892 and was narrowly defeated by Benjamin Harrison in 1888. None of these New Yorkers roused much enthusiasm on the plains, and the Democrats had little support among western farmers until William Jennings Bryan appeared from Nebraska in 1896.

Republicans counted on those midwestern farmers, on the veterans of the Grand Army of the Republic, and on the black vote in the South. The party's steadfast refusal to scale down the Union's war debt appealed to bankers, fiscal conservatives, and the numerous holders of federal bonds. Republicans made support of the protective tariff seem patriotic; their tariff policy gave the party a national dimension that Democrats, more concerned with regional issues, lacked. Republican orators lost no opportunity to remind Northern audiences that the Grand Old Party (GOP) was the party of Abraham Lincoln and union, while Democrats had attempted secession.

In the 1870s and 1880s, the GOP seemed a fragile alliance of at least three factions. "Mugwumps"—independent, idealistic, honest—tried to prevent the party of Lincoln from becoming the possession of Grant's corrupt cronies. The other two factions, the "Stalwarts" and the "Half-Breeds," divided over booty and patronage. Led by Roscoe Conkling, an accomplished spoilsman from New York, the Stalwarts openly avowed their interest in graft and the public payroll. Half-Breeds rallied around James G. Blaine, Speaker of the House, senator from Maine, twice secretary of state, and the party's presidential nominee in 1884. No important difference of principle separated Conkling's followers from Blaine's.

Gradually, national party machinery evolved to unite the party. By 1890, Republican senators had constructed an acknowledged hierarchy that had not existed twenty years earlier. The party's leadership arranged the Senate's order of business, assigned individual senators to committees, and awarded chairmanships by seniority. Decisions of the Republican caucus became difficult to disregard. And in 1896 the GOP collected enough money to finance a modern presidential campaign. Democrats copied their rivals, but lagged behind. As in other aspects of American life during industrialization, the prizes usually went to those who organized first.

Since parties differed little on principles, elections usually turned on personalities. Until Democrats divided over the currency issue in the 1890s, political discourse consisted of charges of corruption and appeals to parochial prejudices or local interests. To the major parties, in good times and hard, reform meant electing honest men to office—the safe, drawing-room sort of men who went to Protestant churches and wore whiskers and stiff collars. "Undoubtedly the tariff is an interesting and important subject," said Carl Schurz in 1884; "so is the currency; so is the bank question." But the Republican party, he asserted, must face up to an "infinitely more important" matter: "the question of honesty in government." A scrupulous Mugwump himself, Schurz tried to bring honest administration to the graft-ridden Indian Bureau. Yet he denied Indians rations and medicines in the name of governmental economy. Good government, to such reformers, was the ultimate objective; few of them meant to use government to bridge the growing gulf between rich and poor, to enable the employee to meet the employer on equal terms, or to reduce involuntary unemployment in the midst of industrial depression. Those who wanted to use government for such ends looked at politics from the outside.

Grant, Graft, and Civil Service

Ulysses S. Grant was the best-known and, in the North, the most-loved American of his day. Later generations picture the Grant of caricature—the soggy cigar, the slovenliness, the alcohol, the scandals. His contemporaries, however, thought of Vicksburg, Appomattox, and the restoration of the Union. A misfit at West Point, a failure in business, a poor judge of character of friends and family, Grant learned in the army to rely on efficient professionals and to ignore idealists and amateurs. He applied the same principle to politics.

Profiteering, dishonesty, and political corruption neither began nor ended with Ulysses S. Grant; scandal has been disturbingly constant in American political life. But during the Grant era no one seemed to mind. For a time Americans shrugged their shoulders at corruption, apparently figuring that the self-made politician compromised himself no more than the self-made industrialist, who made a fortune and became a folk hero. Even when the politician and the industrialist joined forces, the popular reaction seemed more often envy than disgust.

So a congressman from Massachusetts became the lobbyist for the Crédit Mobilier and handed out the corporation's lucrative shares to prevent a potentially embarrassing investigation of the financing of the Union Pacific. One of the members of Grant's cabinet, William W. Belknap, resigned hastily when Congress discovered that he had accepted bribes to allow a favored Indian trader to retain his profitable post at Fort Sill. The House impeached Belknap, but the Senate gave him a technical acquittal because Grant had already accepted his resignation. Grant's personal secretary, Orville E. Babcock, obstructed the investigation of the "whisky ring," a profitable enterprise that furnished distillers with cut-rate, counterfeit revenue stamps; some of the proceeds financed Republican state campaigns. By his acquaintance with Jay Gould and Jim Fisk, two notoriously unscrupulous speculators, Grant lent an air of respectability to their unsuccessful efforts to corner the gold supply in 1869, a project in which the President's brother-in-law was deeply involved.

Scandal seemed the custom, but there were honest public servants. The plans of Gould and Fisk collapsed because Secretary of the Treasury George Boutwell, with Grant's knowledge, released $4 million in gold at a strategic moment. Benjamin Bristow, another member of Grant's cabinet, uncovered the "whisky ring." President Chester A. Arthur, who had cooperated with Republican spoilsmen in New York, turned out to be conscientious in the White House. He insisted, for instance, that profiteering in the Post Office by "star route" contractors be stopped.

Arthur also signed the Pendleton Act, which inaugurated a federal civil service based on merit. Civil service reform had been long delayed, and the Pendleton Act, passed in 1883, was but a small first installment. Grant had made ineffectual gestures toward establishing a merit system during his first administration. While secretary of the interior under Hayes, Carl Schurz had adopted civil service procedures in his department. Public support for civil service reform mounted after a disgruntled office-seeker assassinated President Garfield in July 1881.

The Pendleton Act established a bipartisan Civil Service Commission to administer competitive examinations and to regulate federal employment.

Initially the act covered only about one-tenth of all federal employees, but subsequent Presidents were empowered to extend its provisions and many did so to protect their own appointees. Grover Cleveland, who succeeded Arthur, supported civil service reform in principle and allowed merit to dictate many of his early appointments; after 1885, however, he used federal offices more often for partisan purposes.

Laissez Faire in Practice

Legislation had only a slight impact on the industrial revolution of the late nineteenth century. Land grants to railroads, unrestricted immigration, a tax policy facilitating capital accumulation, and the protective tariff undeniably encouraged industrialization, but the root causes were not political. Similarly, early regulatory legislation brought little change in American industrial development. Later laws had to bolster the Interstate Commerce Act (1887) before the nation's railroads were effectively regulated. In spite of years of litigation, the Sherman Antitrust Act (1890) never became a reliable weapon against monopoly.

With the exception of those two laws, political debate about industrialization centered on the tariff and the currency, staples of American politics familiar to both politicians and public. Demands for tariff reduction came partly because the public perceived protection as an industrial subsidy and partly because the Treasury was too full. A federal surplus meant a smaller amount of currency in general circulation, a condition that tended to lower prices in a period when the nation's economy was already depressed. Instead of reducing duties, Congress preferred to eliminate the surplus by spending it for such politically inspired projects as pensions for Union veterans and "pork barrel bills" authorizing federally financed construction with attendant contracts and jobs. Cleveland vetoed pension bills about as fast as Congress passed them. He suggested the existence of a direct link between tariff and trusts and summoned his party to battle for tariff reform.

The summons generated little enthusiasm and even less reform. The Mills Bill of 1888, which was Congress's answer, was most popular in the South and roused most hostility in such areas as Indiana, which Democrats could ill afford to alienate. The bill continued protection for southern sugar and rice and for iron and coal, which were produced beyond the South. But it cut duties on wool and woolens, lumber, and various manufactured goods. Tariff reformers in the party advocated the Mills Bill with a fervor worthy of a better cause. They injected the issue into the election 1888, although Cleveland's interest in tariff reform had cooled before the campaign began.

Republicans took Benjamin Harrison's narrow victory in the election to be an endorsement of protective tariffs. In 1890 William McKinley, chairman of the House Committee on Ways and Means, reported a new tariff that raised the average duty to a new high of nearly 50 percent. The McKinley Tariff unintentionally helped eliminate the surplus in the Treasury, for the new duties reduced foreign trade and customs revenue.

The Republican Congress also mounted a direct assault on the surplus. A Dependent Pension Act granted pensions to any disabled veteran no matter how his disability had occurred. James Tanner, Harrison's commissioner of pensions and a former official of the Grand Army of the Republic, shouted "God help the surplus!" and proceeded to distribute it. The annual appropriation for veterans jumped from about $90 million to $157 million during the Harrison administration, and the number of pensioners doubled. "Pork barrel" appropriations and the Sherman Silver Purchase Act (see p. 335) further reduced the surplus. When it adjourned, the Congress had spent $1 billion for the first time in the history of the republic.

But the voters decisively rejected the "Billion-Dollar Congress" in 1890 and Harrison in 1892. Once more in the White House, President Cleveland again asked for tariff reform. In 1894 a bill making substantial reductions cleared the House, but the Senate restored many of the cuts and the disappointed President allowed the Wilson-Gorman Tariff to become law without his signature. More important than the very small reduction in duties was the income tax Congress included to replace an anticipated drop in revenue. Within a year the Supreme Court ruled in *Pollock* v. *Farmers' Loan and Trust Co.* that the income tax was an unconstitutional direct tax on personal property, not levied in proportion to population, as the Constitution required.

By 1895, neither the tariff nor the income tax stirred nearly so much public interest as did the quantity and quality of the currency. The monetary theory of conservatives had not advanced far beyond the hard-money instinct of Andrew Jackson. "Sound" currency, they held, either betokened stored gold or was coined gold itself; government ought to certify the intrinsic value of coins and hold enough gold to back anything else that passed for money. Any other action would undermine the gold standard, impair business confidence and, presumably, interfere with the natural order.

Bankers and other creditors had a special interest in the gold standard because, in their view, it guaranteed that mortgages and other debts would be repaid in dollars at least equal in purchasing power to those originally loaned. In fact, in the later nineteenth century, gold dollars—and greenbacks, silver, and national bank notes as well—increased in value, partly because the money supply grew more slowly than the expanding American economy. More and more people, harvesting more crops, building more railroads, forging more steel, needed more currency to facilitate their transactions. The nation's economic activity, advocates of inflation argued, as well as the world's gold supply, ought to affect the amount of money in circulation.

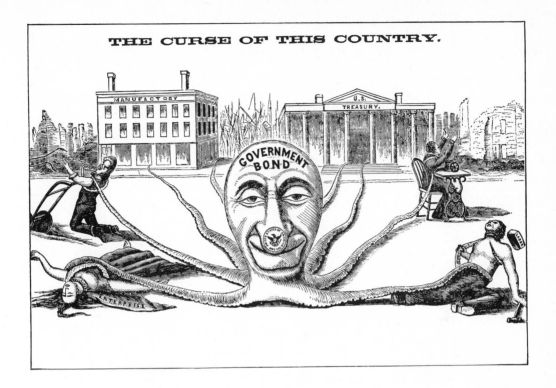

THE CURSE OF THIS COUNTRY.

Advocates of flexible currency first tried to use the greenbacks issued during the Civil War. These bills continued to circulate at a discount after the war, and could have been used instead of gold to retire the Union's debt. This scheme, called the "Ohio idea," would have substantially increased the amount of available paper currency. But in 1875, at Grant's urging, Congress passed the Specie Resumption Act, which reduced the number of greenbacks in circulation and declared the government's intention of redeeming them at par in 1879. When the Treasury in fact started to exchange greenbacks for gold, the paper note was on a par with specie.

National bank notes, like greenbacks, increased in value and diminished in quantity. Between 1880 and 1890, almost half of these notes went out of circulation. Banks had to recall their notes, which were secured by federal bonds, as the government paid off its debt. Since the government proposed to retire the debt, and since every bond a national bank sold required a proportionate reduction in national bank notes, the contraction of the currency seemed likely to continue.

When paper money became a lost cause, inflationists shifted to silver, which the federal mint had coined since the eighteenth century. But the legal ratio of sixteen ounces of silver to one ounce of gold overvalued gold after the California gold strikes of 1849 lowered its price. Since silver brought more on the open market than at the mint, the government actually coined little silver after 1850, a fact that Congress recognized in 1873 by omitting the silver dollar from the list of authorized coins. Meanwhile, the output of new silver mines in the West began to depress the price until in 1876 the official 16 to 1 ratio overvalued silver; silver dollars, then, would be inflated dollars, but the government had stopped minting them. Advocates of inflation denounced "the crime of '73" and demanded a return to "the dollar of our daddies."

In fact, Republicans responsible for dropping the silver dollar had favored a single gold standard for American currency. John Sherman, George Boutwell, and others expected silver to decline in price and acted before the event to establish a stable dollar. They had not been fully candid with the electorate or with Congress; in that sense, there was a conspiracy and a "crime of '73." And they had not foreseen the depression that began in 1873, which made inflation both politically and economically attractive. Eventually the demand for free and unlimited coinage of silver precipitated a political realignment of wheat and cotton farmers, silver miners, and advocates of positive government. Initially, however, the old party lines held: with the exception of the New Yorkers, Democrats favored inflation, and Republicans did not.

In the midst of depression, the argument for controlled inflation proved politically irresistible. In 1876 the House passed a bill providing for the free and unlimited coinage of silver at the ratio of 16 to 1, a measure that advocates claimed would produce a gentle rise in prices. The Senate, where inflation had fewer friends, amended the measure to permit the purchase and coinage of not less than $2 million and not more than $4 million worth of silver per month. Even this token appropriation offended the fiscal orthodoxy of President Hayes, but Congress overrode his veto, and the Bland-Allison Act became law in 1878. Because the Treasury purchased as little silver as possible and exchanged silver dollars for gold, scant inflation resulted.

The Populist Protest

In the three decades after the Civil War, American agriculture became more efficient and immensely more productive. Between 1866 and 1880, wheat and cotton crops nearly tripled; corn production more than doubled and tobacco almost doubled during the same period. While harvests increased, prices fell. The bushel of wheat that had brought more than two dollars in 1866 brought less than one in 1880; a pound of cotton dropped from about fifteen cents to less than ten. By 1895 wheat sold for fifty cents a bushel, corn for twenty-five or less, and cotton for six or seven cents per pound. Merely to maintain a constant income, wheat farmers would have had to double production between 1880 and 1895, and cotton farmers would have had to increase theirs by almost half. Puzzled farmers studied their increasing productivity, declining income, and rising burden of debt and decided that something was wrong with the system.

In fact, American agriculture was caught in a competitive market. Egypt, India, and other warm areas had begun to plant cotton when supplies from the South dried up during the Civil War. The Russian government encouraged the export of Ukrainian wheat in order to obtain foreign exchange. Argentina, Australia, and Canada also developed foreign markets for grain. The individual American farmer was too small to influence this world market. To sustain his purchasing power, he grew more crops, which increased world supply and thereby depressed prices further.

Outraged farmers did not embrace that dispassionate explanation of their plight. The problem, as they saw it, was not too much produce, but too little currency. Certainly they themselves had too little: entire families in the South, caught in the crop-lien system, went from year to year without seeing more than a few dollars at a time. While the per capita circulation of national bank notes in Rhode Island exceeded $77, the figure in Arkansas was thirteen cents. When more than eight hundred national banks provided credit for four northern states, just twenty-six served eight entire states in the South.

In the mid-1880s, farmers in Texas began to investigate cooperative buying and marketing as a means of breaking the chain of credit that bound them to local merchants and cotton brokers. Groups in several counties coalesced in an organization that became the Texas Farmers' Alliance, which established a cooperative warehouse and cotton exchange in Dallas. The exchange sold the cotton crop directly to northern mills and distributed fertilizer, seed, and other supplies to members. But the enterprise soon met the concerted hostility of manufacturers and even extraordinary financial support from hard pressed farmers could not save the business. A cooperative insurance company serving farmers in the Dakotas was successful, however, and the Alliance persisted in its campaign to convince farmers that ordinary people, if they banded together, could achieve and sustain economic independence from bankers and other middlemen.

Cooperation required a new point of view. The Alliance perceived farmers as workers, who had more in common with the Knights of Labor than with Jeffersonian yeomen. Members of the Texas Farmers' Alliance, for instance, jeopardized their organization by assisting striking railway workers. Cooperation also implied subordination of the individual to the group—a willingness to help market the crop of a neighbor who had once seemed a competitor.

At the heart of this heretical program was the "subtreasury system," a method of backing the currency with agricultural commodities, thereby breaking the monopoly of gold and expanding the nation's money supply. Devised in large part by C. W. Macune, a physician, lawyer, and leader of the Texas Alliance, the program called for governmental construction of warehouses and grain elevators in which farmers could store crops. This stored produce was to serve as security for a loan in legal tender notes up to 80 percent of the current price of the crop. The farmers could then sell their harvest later at peak prices, retire the loans, and pay the government a reasonable storage fee. The scheme had no safeguard against the possibility that bumper harvests or declining demand might leave the warehouses full. "Goldbugs" ridiculed the notion of "corn" and "cotton" dollars, but Alliance leaders argued that the notes would raise wages and prices, thereby assisting working people throughout the country.

Subsequent recruits to the farmers' movement, including ambitious agrarian politicians, coupled cooperation and the subtreasury with other reforms. Railroad regulation, for instance, had been a standard demand of rural political leaders for more than a decade. Since legislation had proved difficult to secure and often ineffective if passed, the Alliance soon moved beyond regulation to government ownership. A graduated income tax might shift some of the cost of government from property taxes, of which farmers believed they paid a disproportionate share. Branches of the Alliance outside the South supplemented the subtreasury with other inflationary proposals, including the unlimited coinage of silver.

Although Macune and others warned that active partisan politics would require too many compromises, alliancemen in 1890 won seats in several state legislatures, and the wheat-raising states of the Great Plains sent several angry independent representatives to Washington. In 1891 delegates from the Alliance and other agricultural groups met with social reformers and labor union officials to launch the People's party. In July 1892, the party assembled in solemn convention at Omaha to announce Populist principles and to nominate for President James B. Weaver, a dignified former Union general who had a long association with agrarian protest.

The Populist protest was more strident than dignified, and most Populists were not so reserved as was James B. Weaver. From Kansas came "Sockless" Jerry Simpson and Mary Elizabeth Lease, who was widely reported to have advised the farmers to "raise less corn and more hell." From Georgia came Thomas E. Watson, a redheaded demagogue who already held a seat in Congress. And from Minnesota came Ignatius Donnelly, who wrote a fighting preamble for the party's platform clearly indicating that Populism was no ordinary political movement. "We meet," read Donnelly's introduction, "in the midst of a nation brought to the verge of moral, political, and material ruin." He ran down the nation's problems: corruption, censorship, bribery, fraud, and a growing rift between rich and poor. "From the same prolific womb of governmental injustice," the indictment continued, "we breed the two great classes—tramps and millionaires." Other parties were no help to a

Mary Elizabeth Lease: protest from the plains

"plundered people"; they proposed to wage a "sham battle over the tariff, so that capitalists, corporations, national banks, rings, trusts, watered stock, the demonetization of silver and the oppressions of usurers may all be lost sight of. They propose to sacrifice our homes, lives, and children on the altar of mammon." Populists, Donnelly proclaimed, believed that "the powers of the government . . . should be expanded . . . as rapidly and as far as the good sense of an intelligent people and the teachings of experience shall justify, to the end that oppression, injustice, and poverty shall eventually cease in the land."

Therein lay the political innovation of the Populists. Those midwestern, southern, property-owning, Bible-quoting, old-stock farmers asked directly for the help of their government. No cant about laissez faire; no vows of rugged individualism—just a ringing statement that the government ought to help the poor and oppressed. Populism implied that economic individualism—the faith of Jefferson, Emerson, Lincoln, and Carnegie—no longer led to social improvement, however much it improved the lot of particular people. A system that provided the farmer with less income as he grew more cotton or that denied a willing worker employment, Populists held, was manifestly unjust. If the Gospel of Wealth, Social Darwinism, some other intellectual system, or even a series of laws condoned such conditions, then those creeds and codes too were unjust. The flat truism of one Populist orator wiped out much of the apology for laissez faire: "People," he said, "don't ask to be tramps."

Specifically, the Populist platform demanded that the government make land available directly to settlers instead of to railroads and speculators. The party advocated immediate expansion of the currency through the subtreasury system and the unlimited coinage of silver. Populists demonstrated their democratic faith by calling for the secret ballot, the initiative and referendum, and amendments limiting the President to one term and permitting the direct election of senators. Several resolutions revealed the interest of predominantly rural delegates in a farmer-labor alliance. They favored the eight-hour working day and the restriction of immigration, sympathized with the Knights of Labor, and despised Pinkertons. Most importantly, Populists pledged themselves to secure a graduated income tax and government ownership and operation of railroads, telephone, and telegraph. The party itself, of course, secured neither measure. But the income tax has been the most important instrument for social and economic change in the twentieth century; and in calling for government ownership, Populists challenged economic individualism head-on.

Conservatives, particularly in the East, ridiculed the parochial rhetoric of Populism and its simplistic view of agricultural distress and the measures that would relieve it. Populist campaigners were disparaged as hicks, harpies, and fanatics who dispensed rural nonsense out of a cracked pot. Lacking an urban base, the People's party was doomed, but it created a stir before subsiding. In 1892 Weaver received more than a million popular votes and carried Kansas, Colorado, Nevada, and Idaho. Ten Populist congressmen and five senators took seats in Congress, and three governors and more than a thousand state legislators proved the party's local vitality. But sturdy Grover Cleveland won the election of 1892. Although his campaigners had occasionally promised reform in his name, inflation had no sterner foe than Grover Cleveland.

The Depression of 1893

Even the cities needed inflation as Cleveland took office in 1893, for depression gripped the nation. New investments financed through stock issues dropped from $100 million to about $37 million with a resulting loss of new jobs. Nearly 500 banks failed in 1893, and another 350 went under during the rest of Cleveland's term; only about 200 had failed, by contrast, in the preceding Harrison administration. Railroads went bankrupt too, including such major lines as the Union Pacific and the Northern Pacific. President Cleveland called Congress into special session to alleviate the economic crisis.

The President believed the depression had a single cause and proposed a deceptively simple solution. He overlooked the fact that farm prices had been depressed for years; he ignored speculation, economic conditions abroad, and various other factors that together contributed to business distress. The depression, the President said, was "principally chargeable to Congressional legislation touching the purchase and coinage of silver." He asked Congress to repeal the Sherman Silver Purchase Act, and implied that prosperity would promptly ensue.

Passed in 1890 as part of a political deal to secure support for the McKinley Tariff, the Sherman Silver Purchase Act required the Treasury to make monthly purchases of 4.5 million ounces of silver, an amount roughly equivalent to the domestic output. Because the market price of silver continued to decline, the Treasury's expenditure for silver did not differ greatly from that required by the Bland-Allison Act. Since the Treasury paid for silver in legal-tender notes and then redeemed the notes in gold, the Sherman Act brought no inflation. But by 1893 the policy of paying gold for notes secured by silver brought an alarming decrease in the Treasury's gold reserve, which sank below the $100 million minimum that sound-money advocates believed essential to maintain the gold standard.

The Democratic Congress resisted Cleveland's single-minded insistence on repeal of the Sherman Act, but the President exerted every bit of executive pressure to secure repeal. Secure it he did, at the cost of a split that disabled his party and ended the effectiveness of his second administration before it had well begun. For the repeal of the Sherman Silver Purchase Act did not raise prices, restore confidence, bring prosperity, or even save the gold reserve. Cleveland had to authorize several bond issues to maintain gold stocks. One such issue, in 1895, brought J. P. Morgan and his banking syndicate a profit that, when exaggerated on the campaign trail, provided evidence for the charge of silverites that bankers and government had combined to fleece the public.

Seldom has a President been so rebuffed in an off-year election as was Cleveland in 1894. Republicans not only gained control of the House but secured a thumping margin of 140 seats. Twenty-four states sent no Democrats at all to Washington, and the party lost control of New York, Illinois, Wisconsin, and such Democratic strongholds as Maryland, Missouri, and North Carolina.

With the exception of some Republican politicians, no one could claim 1894 was a good year. Tobacco prices touched a new low for the decade, and cotton brought less than a nickel a pound. Freight loadings dropped sharply, indicating a widespread lull in economic activity. Although the number of strikes declined from earlier levels, unprecedented numbers of workers were affected. Estimates of the extent of unemployment ranged as high as one of every five urban workers.

Government at almost every level seemed content to let the depression

"General" Coxey leads the unemployed

cure itself, but in the West and South, silver orators held up the prospect of immediate inflation and instant prosperity. A little pamphlet called *Coin's Financial School* appeared in 1894 and spread the message more widely than any speaker. "You increase the value of all property by adding to the number of money units," said the imaginary Professor Coin to the imaginary students in his imaginary school. "You make it possible for the debtor to pay his debts, business to start anew, and revivify all the industries of the country, which must remain paralyzed so long as silver as well as all other property is measured by a gold standard." To fiscal conservatives, such promises were worse than misleading; they were immoral and anarchistic. But the lines gradually became firm: those who would do something about the depression favored the free and unlimited coinage of silver; those who would abide by the "immutable" principles of political economy favored unflinching support of the gold standard.

Cleveland did his part to eliminate alternatives and drive compromisers into one camp or the other. His use of troops in the Pullman Strike showed little inclination to let labor secure better wages through unions.

When "armies" of the unemployed marched on Washington to file "a petition with boots" for federal relief, the administration jailed or dispersed the petitioners. Jacob Coxey, who led one of these groups, suggested that the unemployed be put to work constructing a system of roads financed by $500 million in legal-tender notes; Coxey was arrested for walking on the grass in front of the Capitol.

The Battle of the Standards

Jails, troops, and a hard heart—such, claimed opponents in Cleveland's own party, was the President's program. Through 1895 and 1896, Democratic silverites worked to control the convention and dictate the nominee in 1896. Before Democrats assembled in Chicago, Republicans nominated William McKinley, endorsed existing fiscal policies, and incurred the wrath of a few western silverites who stalked out of the party. Democratic silverites, insisting on giving the voters a choice, wrote a platform that in effect disavowed Grover Cleveland. The platform specifically condemned the bond issues Cleveland had used to maintain the gold reserve and denounced the national banking system for good measure. The party pledged to restore the graduated income tax, to regulate railroads, and to establish more effective federal control of trusts. In the crucial plank, the platform demanded the free and unlimited coinage of silver at the ratio of 16 to 1.

Debate over the plank on money provided the party with its candidate. William Jennings Bryan, a young, handsome former congressman from Nebraska, mesmerized the convention with his speech for silver; before the spell wore off, he was the party's nominee. Bryan's economic ideas were no less primitive, however, than Cleveland's. Once "we have restored the money of the Constitution," Bryan proclaimed, "all other necessary reform will be possible; but until this is done, there is no other reform that can be accomplished." And Bryan's rhetoric showed his acceptance of the business ethic of his day:

We say to you that you have made the definition of a business man too limited in its application. The man who is employed for wages is as much a business man as his employer; the attorney in a country town is as much a business man as the corporation counsel in a great metropolis; the merchant at the cross-roads store is as much a business man as the merchant of New York; the farmer . . . is as much a business man as the man who goes upon the Board of Trade and bets upon the price of grain; the miners . . . are as much business men as the few financial magnates who . . . corner the money of the world.

Bryan spoke to and, he fervently believed, for "this broader class of business men."

Bryan's nomination surprised Populists no less than it enraged Cleveland's followers. Populists had expected to wage the campaign on the silver issue, but to do so with their own candidate risked splitting the vote. To fuse with Democrats, on the other hand, risked the loss of a separate identity and the subordination or disappearance of other political objectives. Southern Populists were especially reluctant to merge with the conservatives who dominated the Democratic party in the South; Tom Watson termed such a retreat a return of "the hog . . . to its wallow." But so important had silver become to the public and to most Populist leaders that they preferred surrender disguised as compromise to a campaign that would surely divide the silver forces. The party endorsed Bryan for President, but substituted Watson for the unsatisfactory Democratic nominee for Vice-President. Win or lose, the Populists were doomed, for a victorious Bryan would have rewarded Democrats and a defeated Bryan did in fact leave Populists divided, bickering, and leaderless. Bryan accepted Populist support, rejected his Populist running mate, and took to the stump with a vigor no previous presidential candidate had ever displayed.

William McKinley, a benign, gracious, courtly man, conducted his campaign from his front porch in Canton, Ohio. But the Republican campaign, directed by McKinley's close friend Mark Hanna, more than matched the Democrats' in energy. Political delegations arrived at Canton, conferred with McKinley, and shared his views with the press. The nominee favored a protective tariff and pointed out that as governor

William Jennings Bryan on the stump

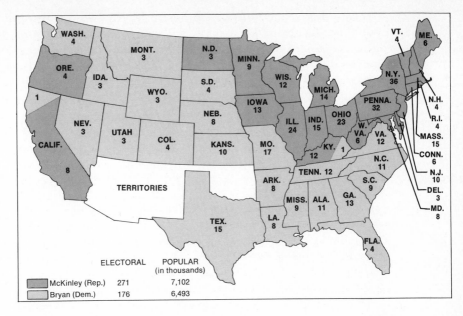

	ELECTORAL	POPULAR (in thousands)
McKinley (Rep.)	271	7,102
Bryan (Dem.)	176	6,493

THE ELECTION OF 1896

of Ohio he had enjoyed the support of many urban workingmen. McKinley reached more voters through the Republican press than Bryan did in 18,000 miles of speech-filled travel. Hanna efficiently shook down worried conservatives and amassed a campaign fund at least ten times as great as Bryan's. And in pamphlet after pamphlet, article after article, Republican publicists hammered the theme that Bryan was a dangerous lunatic, if not a communist or anarchist revolutionary. McKinley carried California and Oregon, the northern Midwest, and the industrial East, where urban working people suspected that inflation was not a fundamental answer to their problems. Bryan swept the Plains, the Rockies, and the South. But McKinley had 600,000 more votes than his opponent, and almost 100 more electors.

The "battle of the standards" was probably less important than the excited electorate believed in 1896; in the last analysis, prosperity did not depend upon silver and gold. But at least the campaign was the result of an honest effort to deal politically with economic questions—that much the Populists and Bryan had accomplished. However superficial his solution, Bryan instinctively responded to the needs and fears of simple people, and he believed the government must do so too. The "Great Commoner" never moved to the White House, but he had more impact on American politics than any President between Lincoln and Theodore Roosevelt.

Prices took a turn for the better as McKinley assumed office, partly because the world supply of gold increased with new discoveries in Alaska and South Africa. Agricultural prices climbed from the troughs of the early 1890s, and industrial productivity resumed its upward course. Republicans nurtured prosperity with time-honored legislation. In the Dingley Tariff of 1897 they restored protective duties to record levels that averaged about 50 percent. In 1900 Congress passed the Currency Act, which established a gold reserve of $150 million and officially put the country on the gold standard. Conservatives thought it was a good way to close the books on the old century.

Suggested Reading

Matthew Josephson's *The Robber Barons** (1934) and *The Politicos** (1938) typify an older view of the post-Civil War years. More recent surveys of the period include John A. Garraty, *The New Commonwealth** (1968), Ray Ginger, *The Age of Excess** (1965), and a collection of essays edited by H. Wayne Morgan, *The Gilded Age** (1963; revised in 1970). Morgan has also written a detailed political survey, *From Hayes to McKinley* (1969), which should be supplemented by two books on the Middle West—Paul Kleppner's *The Cross of Culture* (1970) and Richard Jensen's *The Winning of the Midwest* (1971)—and by one on the Northeast—Samuel P. McSeveney's *The Politics of Depression* (1972). David J. Rothman shows the emergence of modern legislative leadership in *Politics and Power** (1966).

Allen Weinstein's *Prelude to Populism* (1970) traces the silver controversy to 1878. Irwin Unger's *The Greenback Era, 1865–1879** (1964) is an excellent study of financial policy. John D. Hicks has written the lasting work on midwestern Populism in *The Populist Revolt** (1931). Norman Pollack, in *The Populist Response to Industrial America** (1962), sees the Populists as radicals, while Richard Hofstadter, in *The Age of Reform** (1955), emphasized their ties to the agrarian past. In *The Democratic Promise* (1976), Lawrence Goodwyn stresses the southern origin of Populism in the Farmers' Alliance and points up the importance of cooperation to the movement. Biographies of Populist leaders include Peter H. Argersinger's *Populism and Politics* (1974) on William A. Peffer and C. Vann Woodward's superb *Tom Watson** (1938).

Paul W. Glad's *McKinley, Bryan and the People** (1964) is one of several accounts of the election of 1896. The best recent biographies of McKinley are Margaret K. Leech's *In the Days of McKinley* (1959) and H. Wayne Morgan's *William McKinley and His America* (1963). Paolo E. Coletta has written three biographical volumes on Bryan (1964, 1969). Horace S. Merrill suggests in *Bourbon Leader** (1957) that Grover Cleveland has been overrated in some respects.

NOTE: See also works cited in *Suggested Reading* for Chapters 12 and 13.

* Available in paperback edition

Chapter 15
Extending American Influence

Chronology

1867 Archduke Maximilian shot by Mexican patriots • Alaska purchased from Russia •

1883 Construction of modern navy begins •

1895 Cleveland intervenes in boundary dispute between Venezuela and British Guiana •

1898 Spanish-American War; Philippines, Puerto Rico, Wake, Guam annexed • Hawaii annexed •

1899 Samoa annexed • First Open Door notes •

1900 Second Open Door notes •

1904 Roosevelt Corollary to the Monroe Doctrine •

1905 Treaty of Portsmouth ends Russo-Japanese War •

1906—14 Construction of the Panama Canal •

1914, 1916 Armed intervention in Mexico •

1917 Virgin Islands purchased from Denmark •

Occasionally a passing crisis or a political campaign reminded Americans in the later nineteenth century of the inhabitants of the rest of the globe. Other nations created a moment's sensation by arresting American sailors or refusing to buy American pork or ignoring the bombast of nationalistic American politicians. When the United States reacted to events abroad, the response usually depended on personality or circumstance, for the country lacked a coherent foreign policy to guide decision making. Only toward century's end did the practice of expanding American diplomatic and economic influence become a conscious policy.

In the twenty-five years after the Civil War, few Americans saw the need for an active foreign policy. Nor did Congress provide the means to implement one. The State Department in 1885 had sixty employees. Many of the nation's representatives abroad were second-rank political figures whose major qualification was partisan loyalty. The United States Navy in the 1880s was inferior not only to those of major European powers, but even, Rudyard Kipling scoffed, to the Chinese fleet, which "if properly manned could waft the entire American navy out of the water." The army in 1890 was somewhat smaller than that of Bulgaria and did not rank among the first dozen military establishments in the world. The United States, Kipling continued, was "as unprotected as a jellyfish."

In fact, the United States needed no more protection than a jellyfish. Two oceans patrolled by the British fleet guarded the country from the Bulgarians and other, larger armies, and from the Chinese, and other, more effectively commanded fleets. Such military force as the United States possessed was adequate to overawe even weaker neighbors in the Western Hemisphere. There were no colonies to protect, no alliances to uphold, no merchant marine to assist, few interests to advance.

But economic interests developed with industrialization. Although exports never constituted 8 percent of the gross national product before 1900, they grew rapidly after 1880. Americans became increasingly aware of existing markets in Europe and of potential ones in Asia. At the same time, the growing volume of imports, particularly from Latin America, raised the importance of Mexico, for instance, and Brazil, which sent more than half of their exports to the United States. Economic links—through exports to the world's major powers and through imports from areas those powers coveted—involved the United States in the international scramble for colonies late in the century.

Once involved, a swelling nationalism made it difficult to come away with empty hands. The faith that sustained expansion across the continent also encouraged expansion around the world. According to this revived view of manifest destiny, the United States should provide enlightened leadership, democratic institutions, schools, hospitals, Protestant religion, and consumer goods for less fortunate (and usually dark-skinned) people. This creed had overtones of Anglo-Saxon supremacy and was undeniably sentimental, condescending, and self-serving. Nevertheless, Americans were more tentative in their drive to annex colonies than were the greediest of the European powers, and more considerate of native peoples whose lands were absorbed. Further, though the interest in foreign markets remained intense, the urge to add colonial possessions soon passed.

The Need to Color the Map

William Henry Seward, secretary of state in the 1860s, caught imperial fever before most of his countrymen did. He proposed annexation of Santo Domingo after disease and the aroused inhabitants had combined to end Spain's attempt to repossess the island. He challenged Napoleon III, the Emperor of France who had installed a Hapsburg price on the throne of Mexico during the American Civil War. In 1867, Seward's diplomatic pressure, a lack of French reinforcements, and the resistance of Mexican insurgents ended the brief reign of Maximilian of Mexico. Seward also suggested the purchase of the Virgin Islands from Denmark

and of Alaska from Russia. Congress passed over the beckoning
Caribbean empire and almost refused Alaska as well. But Seward extolled
the untapped Alaskan mineral wealth, modestly compared his bargain
with the Louisiana Purchase, and suggested that the Aleutian chain
"extended a friendly hand to Asia" that might grasp the Oriental market.
Congress gave in and completed the purchase in 1867.

But that was all. Seward's contemporaries subordinated expansion to
their immediate concern with Reconstruction and industrialization. They
preferred to invest at home and to shoulder domestic racial problems
before undertaking new ones abroad. Yet, as the century went on, the
circumstances that stalled Seward lost force. Reconstruction ended, and
with it doctrines of racial equality that might make heavier the white
man's imperial burden. Some felt a renewed urge for free land as the
census disclosed a disappearing frontier. The national Treasury,
pledged in Seward's day to paying off the Union's war debt, brimmed
embarrassingly full two decades later. Descendants of Civil War veterans,
unlike their elders, had no haunting fear of conflict; instead they sought a
chance to revive the nation's patriotic and military spirit. Other countries,
particularly England, which had been disillusioned with empire at
midcentury, set an example of renewed acquisitiveness as the century
concluded. Capitalists and merchants needed a foreign outlet for
investment and goods when demand at home fell during the industrial
depressions that plagued the latter part of the century.

As restraints became less confining, positive support for expansion
grew. Concern about foreign markets extended throughout the economy.
Wheat farmers knew that domestic prices would sag even lower if
markets abroad were closed. Exporters ordinarily sent more than half the
tobacco and cotton crops overseas, and the fraction sometimes climbed
to four-fifths. American steel, oil, and textile companies competed with
European industries in all corners of the world. During the two decades
after 1875 imports exceeded foreign sales in only two years, and the drive
to secure yet larger foreign markets had formidable political support.

Walter Q. Gresham, a Republican who served as Cleveland's secretary
of state, believed commercial expansion essential to the nation's social
and economic tranquility. Strikes and labor violence, socialism and
income taxes, Populism and inflated currency—these and other ills,
Gresham believed, would disappear if a waiting market absorbed what a
healthy economy could produce. "Our mills and factories," Gresham
observed, "can supply the [domestic] demand by running seven or eight
months out of twelve." More foreign trade, the secretary thought, would
suffice; Americans did not need more territory. Yet not all who accepted
Gresham's diagnosis of the nation's malaise were content with his limited
prescription.

Specifically, the small sector of the American public most concerned
with foreign policy—editors, educators, merchants, missionaries, and
politicians—began to advocate expansion. Theodore Roosevelt

exemplified the ambitious young politicians who linked enlarging the nation's domain with enlarging their own reputations. Henry Cabot Lodge, the junior senator from Massachusetts, and Albert J. Beveridge, soon to become the senator from Indiana, also promoted annexations. Henry and Brooks Adams, descendants of Presidents, were not themselves politicians but advocated expansion in their writing and at the highest level of Washington society. John Hay, Abraham Lincoln's private secretary and William McKinley's secretary of state, was an ardent expansionist, a close friend of the Adamses, and a social acquaintance of most of the Republican elite.

Protestant missionaries joined an international effort to bring Christianity to the world's heathen in a single generation, an effort that political control might hasten. American missionaries called the nation's attention to Hawaii and shaped policy in Korea. They gave eager audiences in churches all over the land a first-hand account of the hardships of thousands of misgoverned, backward pagans (or Catholics) who yearned for democratic government, American textiles, and Protestant Christianity. Contributions from the faithful discharged only part of the congregation's responsibility; Christians should also support a national policy that backed the Protestant gospel with American marines. "God . . . is training the Anglo-Saxon race for an hour sure to come in the world's future," wrote Josiah Strong, a leader of the American Home Missionary Society. His *Our Country*, published in 1885, made expansion an American Christian duty.

Duty pervaded the imperial urge. Duty to the Deity dictated that His earth be efficiently used and His word be spread. Duty to humanity dictated uplifting inferior races with kerosene lamps, calico, schools, and elections. Duty to the Darwinian law of nature dictated competing with other nations to refine the American system and make it even more fit for future generations. Duty to the nation dictated raising the flag over outposts that protected our coastlines and our trade. Duty effectively concealed, sometimes from the imperialists themselves, economic, political, and strategic interests.

Protection of those interests rested primarily on the navy, which in the 1880s was notoriously unable to support aggressive policies. Captain Alfred Thayer Mahan had been lobbying for a modern navy for years before his *The Influence of Sea Power upon History* appeared in 1890. Mahan and other officers of the Naval War College told Roosevelt, Lodge, and other receptive politicians that greatness came to nations that mastered the oceans. Congress ordered four cruisers in 1883, the first American battleships in 1886, and twenty-five new vessels, including three battleships, in 1890. Because these coal-burning ships required fuel depots and naval bases, the nation's new navy not only protected colonies but also required them.

Earlier in the century a big navy and colonial expansion would have caused diplomatic friction with England, the major naval and imperial power in the world. But by 1890 English-speaking peoples had reached a tacit understanding that had survived diplomatic provocation and dozens of anti-British appeals for the Irish-American vote. Opportunities for diplomatic misunderstanding abounded: the United States resented England's failure to keep the Confederate raider *Alabama* in port during the Civil War; England resented episodic American eagerness to add Canada to the United States; American fishermen off Nova Scotia and Canadian seal-hunters off Alaska angered rivals who claimed exclusive rights in territorial waters. Yet successive British governments patiently tolerated frivolous American treatment. Changes in Europe, especially the threatening increase in German naval power, made Britain willing to overlook American diplomatic immaturity and to allow the United States to dominate areas like Central America, where American and British policies coincided. Gradually, an unspoken Anglo-American agreement joined the Monroe Doctrine as one of the guiding principles of American foreign policy. "I think," predicted Theodore Roosevelt in 1900, "the twentieth century will be the century of the men who speak English."

The Beginning of Empire

Most of William H. Seward's nineteenth-century successors in the Department of State believed, as he had, in expanding the trade and influence of the United States. Until the Spanish-American War, they ordinarily stopped short of expanding the nation's territory. "Our great demand is expansion," Secretary of State James G. Blaine proclaimed in 1890. But, he added immediately, "I mean expansion of trade with countries where we can find profitable exchanges. We are not seeking annexation of territory."

There were occasional exceptions. As Santo Domingo had tempted Seward, so it tempted President Grant, but he could not persuade either his secretary of state or the Senate to share his enthusiasm. Cuban insurrections in the 1870s seemed to expansionists an invitation to annex the island. Politicians with Irish constituencies periodically proposed to raise the flag over Canada. The navy wanted a base in Haiti. Eventually the navy did secure two magnificent harbors in the Pacific: Pago Pago, on Tutuila in the Samoan group, and Pearl Harbor, in Hawaii, to which the navy secured exclusive rights in 1887. In both cases, naval bases proved to be a step toward annexation.

Samoa also attracted British and German naval strategists, and for a dozen years the three nations tried various methods of sharing control. The United States insisted that Samoa remain at least nominally independent and refused to permit simple partition and annexation of territory. But if the United States did not absorb the entire Samoan group, neither did it permit others to do so. In 1899 the United States finally

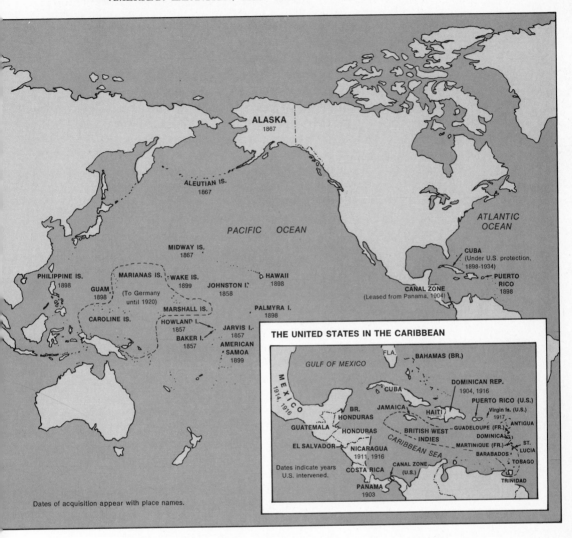

THE UNITED STATES IN THE CARIBBEAN

Dates indicate years U.S. intervened.

Dates of acquisition appear with place names.

divided the archipelago with Germany and formally added Tutuila to the Pacific empire, which by that time also included the Philippines and Hawaii.

A reciprocity treaty, negotiated in 1875, gave Hawaiian sugar planters privileged access to the American market until 1890, when the McKinley Tariff awarded domestic producers a bounty and repealed the duty on imported sugar. Annexation would make Hawaiian planters, many of whom were of American extraction, eligible for the bounty. In 1893 they overthrew the native dynasty and established a republic under the presidency of Sanford Dole. John L. Stevens, the American minister in Honolulu, recognized the new government almost immediately and secured American marines from Pearl Harbor to intimidate remaining supporters of Queen Liliuokalani. The republic quickly concluded a treaty of annexation, and the exuberant Stevens raised the American flag.

Stevens's treaty arrived in Washington in the final weeks of the Harrison administration and by common consent was held for the new Congress and the new President. Cleveland sent James Blount, a former congressman from Georgia, to Hawaii to test the sentiment of the inhabitants. Blount reported that Stevens had acted imprudently and that most islanders favored independence. But the Queen promised to behead the members of Dole's government, who naturally refused to surrender control of the state.

Cleveland decided to let the Hawaiians resolve the impasse themselves, made a few partisan observations about Stevens's action, and withdrew the treaty. Lack of a formal agreement, however, did not break America's close economic link with the islands or preclude naval control there. The President simply followed the traditional policy of seeking the economic and strategic advantages of empire without assuming the political liabilities. Formal annexation of Hawaii came in 1898 with the Spanish-American War.

Cautious and deliberate in handling Hawaiian annexation, Cleveland was hasty and bellicose in 1895 when he stepped into a long-simmering dispute about the boundary between Venezuela and British Guiana. The President may have been trying to recapture lost political initiative, though he had no personal political future in 1895. A shrewd lobbyist had convinced influential journalists and politicians that a renewed drive to enlarge the British Empire might extend to the Western Hemisphere and endanger the Monroe Doctrine; certainly Cleveland knew of this fear, and perhaps he shared it. At any rate, without consulting the Venezuelan government, he instructed Secretary of State Richard Olney to intervene on its behalf. "Today," Olney's note to London asserted, "the United States is practically sovereign on this continent." The secretary followed this tactless premise with a demand that Britain either permit arbitrators to draw a frontier line or face war with the United States. The British government delayed for some months before denying Olney's assertions, rejecting his demands, and calling the administration's bluff.

But Cleveland meant what Olney had said. In December 1895, again without informing the Venezuelan ambassador, the President announced that the United States would appoint a commission, send it to Venezuela to determine the boundary, and then enforce the decision. War with Britain was possible, Cleveland warned, but "supine submission to wrong and injustice" would be worse than war. Once he had revealed his inflexible determination, Cleveland permitted flexible diplomats to avoid the war he had invited. Partly because one war at a time seemed enough—and the Boers in South Africa were proving unexpectedly stubborn—Britain resolved that no colonial boundary was worth a war with the United States. This decision implicitly accepted the Monroe

Doctrine, confirmed the developing Anglo-American diplomatic entente, and frankly acknowledged the admission of the United States to the fraternity of world powers. As an incidental result of Britain's decision, an international tribunal awarded most of the disputed territory to British Guiana, a decision the indifferent State Department accepted in 1899.

The Spanish-American War

Although Cuba was a Spanish colony, the island's economy meshed with that of the United States. American tariffs affected the profits of Cuban sugar planters, and the changed duties of 1894 helped spark a rebellion against Spain that rocked the island in 1895. Senator Lodge predicted that an independent Cuba would become "a great market for the United States" and a great "opportunity for American capital." But other Republicans feared that American intervention would interrupt recovery from the depression of 1893 and foster instead the monetary inflation that the party had presumably put down in the presidential election of 1896. Business leaders, taxpayers, and strategists anxious to block European influence in China, opposed a Caribbean adventure that would jeopardize prosperity, cost money, and divert American forces.

Other groups were less timid. The AFL resolved in favor of intervention. Patriotic societies and veterans' organizations thought a war for Cuba would renew the nation's spirit and revive its glorious martial tradition. Republican partisans who had critized Cleveland's hesitant course were unhappy when William McKinley's seemed no different. Protestant clergymen encouraged their congregations to take up the Cuban cause against Spain. As early as 1896, 1,200 hardy St. Louis volunteers offered to serve the cause of Cuban freedom, and a ten-year-old from Newark, New Jersey, stole a pair of pistols and started to hike to Havana. A shrewd politician—which William McKinley was—could hardly miss the signs.

But McKinley was also cautious. Presidential intimates announced, for instance, that McKinley would "use his powers to stop the bloodshed insofar as he can without involving the United States in war"—whatever that meant. For more than a year adroit variations on that ambiguous theme enabled the President to keep the simultaneous support of businessmen who opposed war and Republican "jingoes" who demanded it. His negotiations with Spain never came to anything. The Spanish government talked of reform in Cuba while its generals used concentration camps to discourage civilian support of Cuban guerrillas. McKinley proposed Cuban autonomy, as Grover Cleveland had, and looked into ways of purchasing Cuban independence. One by one, McKinley exhausted the alternatives to military intervention.

Two New York newspapers did their shrill best to exaggerate, or even create, Spanish atrocities and to encourage American intervention.

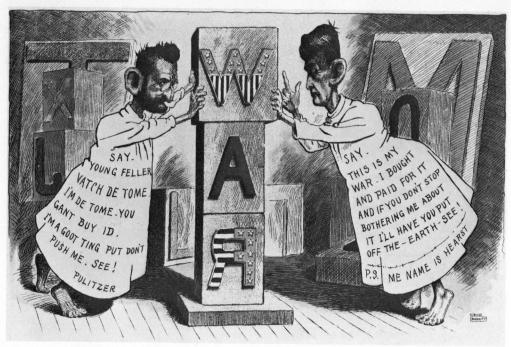

"The Yellow Kids"

William Randolph Hearst's *Journal* and Joseph Pulitzer's *World* engaged
in a circulation race that required sensational headlines whether or not
events justified them. One too scrupulous artist, sent to Cuba to cover
the insurrection, was said to have wired Hearst that there was no war.
"You furnish the pictures," was Hearst's reported response, "and I'll
furnish the war." This "yellow journalism," in New York and elsewhere,
certainly whipped up popular demand for war. But Hearst and Pulitzer
did not single-handedly manufacture that demand. The public bought
their newspapers because they contained what people wanted to read;
the "yellow" newspapers catered to popular enthusiasm as much as they
enhanced it.

Events in February 1898 furnished copy that required little journalistic
exaggeration. The Spanish ambassador, Enrique Dupuy de Lôme, belittled
President McKinley in a private letter that became public in the Hearst
press. The ambassador questioned McKinley's willingness to stand up
against popular opinion, which was about what Theodore Roosevelt was
saying at the same time. De Lôme's letter caused a momentary stir that
was soon forgotten in the excitement over the sinking of the *Maine*.

McKinley had sent the *Maine*, one of the nation's new battleships, to
Havana harbor to safeguard American lives and property. On February 15
more than 250 American sailors died when the vessel blew up. The press,

and the public, held Spain responsible for the explosion, though the most recent investigation suggests a much more prosaic explanation: an undetected fire in one of the ship's coal bunkers. Whatever the explosion's cause, the resulting hysteria in the United States made McKinley's continued restraint more difficult than ever.

Yet, until McKinley sensed a united demand from the American people for a free Cuba, his restraint persisted. Those opposed to war gradually stilled their objections; by March, William Jennings Bryan had made the demand for intervention officially bipartisan. McKinley's cables to Madrid became more firm. The Spanish government backed down until in early April all that was left to concede was Cuban independence. And that step Spain would not take. On April 19, Congress authorized McKinley to use American troops to expel Spanish forces from the island. Before the declaration passed, Congress showed the nation's unselfish zeal in the Teller Amendment, which explicitly stated that the United States would not annex Cuba. But Congress neglected to forbid other territorial additions, and the crusade against Spanish colonialism brought the United States a colonial empire.

When John Hay subsequently referred to the "splendid little war," he was not speaking for the ordinary trooper. The army launched the crusade from an unsanitary staging area near Tampa, Florida, and in June inexpertly landed an invading force in Cuba. Confused lines of command linked regular units and volunteer regiments such as the Rough Riders, which Theodore Roosevelt had recruited. Soldiers received woolen uniforms, spoiled rations, and inadequate medical support.

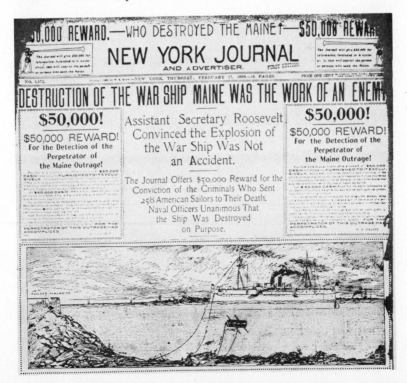

Spanish forces killed fewer Americans than did mosquitoes. The only major land engagement of the war took place at San Juan Hill near Santiago. And even that battle was probably unnecessary because the navy had already blockaded the city. The Spanish fleet, holed up in Santiago harbor, tried to salvage Spanish honor in a running battle along the Cuban coast. One American sailor died in the encounter, but the entire Spanish fleet was sunk. Six Americans were wounded in the most intense fighting on Puerto Rico, which American forces occupied in July.

Nor were casualties greater on the other side of the world, where the navy added to the American empire before the army landed in Cuba. A week after the declaration of war, Commodore George Dewey's Pacific squadron destroyed the Spanish fleet in Manila Bay without the loss of one American ship or a single American life. A naval lieutenant had written the war plan that set off this chain of events, but Theodore Roosevelt, then assistant secretary of the navy, and McKinley had both approved the orders to Dewey. The navy had intended simply to strike the Spanish fleet where it was vulnerable; the plan did not include annexation, and the army was totally unprepared when McKinley ordered troops to occupy the Philippine archipelago. Naval strategists knew that the United States could not defend the islands and that Japan and perhaps other imperial powers would be tempted to move in. Nevertheless, when the war ended a few weeks after it began, McKinley hesitated only briefly before instructing delegates to the peace conference to insist on the cession of the Philippines as well as Guam, Wake, and Puerto Rico; Cuba, of course, was to be independent. Partly because American conquest of the Philippines was not complete, and partly to disguise seizure as purchase, the United States agreed to pay Spain a face-saving $20 million.

A disgusted Andrew Carnegie offered to write the check himself. Former Presidents Harrison and Cleveland, several key senators, and influential editors joined Carnegie in opposing annexation. This aging band of anti-imperialists reminded the nation of the principles espoused in its own Declaration of Independence. The United States, they predicted, would not escape the military and diplomatic responsibilities that were the price of empire. Colonies required a standing army, alliances, and expenses that would consume the nation's resources and belie the nation's heritage. Carnegie scorned the notion that the United States should "interfere with distant races for their civilization" as the argument of "either a fool or a hypocrite." The anti-imperialists might swallow Puerto Rico, but not the Philippines.

They almost blocked McKinley's treaty in the Senate. From whatever misguided motive, Bryan, who opposed annexation, persuaded a few wavering Democrats to vote for the treaty. Lack of an attractive alternative persuaded others to accept the Philippines rather than permit them to fall to another imperialistic power. Filipinos continued against the United States the insurrection begun against Spanish control, and the insult to the flag influenced those who cherished national honor. (It took three years, 70,000 troops, and many of the same antiguerrilla methods Spain had used in Cuba to convince the Filipinos of the benefits of American civilization.) McKinley took the public pulse on a speaking tour and became satisfied that the public favored annexation. Senator Mark Hanna, the Ohio industrialist who was widely, if incorrectly, thought to be the brains behind McKinley, announced the nation's determination to secure "a large slice of the commerce of Asia." The United States had "better . . . strike for it," Hanna continued, "while the iron is hot." McKinley did just that.

The Chinese Market: A Continuing Fantasy

Hanna thought the Philippines would serve as a warehouse and thereby give American merchants an immense advantage in the markets of China. But Russia, Germany, France, and Japan also dreamed of dominating the China trade, to say nothing of Britain, which had nearly 80 percent of the market in the 1890s. All these countries were bringing diplomatic pressure on the feeble Chinese Empire to grant exclusive trading privileges. American exporters feared that these spheres of influence would block American trade. John Hay, the new secretary of state in 1898, did not know much about China, but he recognized mounting interest in enlarging America's share of the market there.

In 1899, Hay sent the first Open Door notes, which became the basic American policy for Asia. Hay asked powers with Chinese spheres of influence not to discriminate against traders from other nations. Since a sphere of influence was intended to prevent equal access to Chinese trade, Hay's notes met a cool reception in European foreign ministries. Britain conditionally agreed to the American request, and Japan, France, Italy, and Germany agreed subject to the full acceptance of all other powers. Russia's qualified refusal effectively released the other countries from their consent. But Secretary Hay, calculating correctly that none of the powers would publicly avow reservations, boldly announced that all had endorsed the Open Door.

John Hay sent his second series of Open Door notes a year later, in the aftermath of the Boxer Rebellion. In their protest against concessions to foreigners, Chinese patriots, known as Boxers, had cut off the entire diplomatic community in Peking, which had to be rescued by a multinational force. When some of the affronted powers suggested territorial reprisal, Hay broadened American policy. The United States, Hay wrote, required not only the preservation of the trading rights he had mentioned in 1899, but also the preservation of "Chinese territorial and administrative entity."

The tone of disinterested protection for other people in the Open Door

The Open Door in China

notes appealed to American idealism in much the same way as did the Monroe Doctrine. But Hay's attempt to preserve China was not simply a generous gesture toward the Chinese people. The United States preferred a weak, independent China to any other arrangement, since a change in the balance of Asian power might endanger American control of the Philippines. And, of course, the Open Door, like the Monroe Doctrine, restored to American expansion the commercial connotation it had had before 1898. The bitter debate over the Spanish treaty, the insurrection in the Philippines, and the possibility of more trade in China combined to dampen lingering American desire for more colonies. To be sure, the United States added territory after 1898, but the popular urge to color the map had gone. Although Bryan tried to make the election of 1900 a referendum on empire, the electorate had already tired of the issue. A vote for William McKinley, who dealt Bryan his second crushing presidential defeat, was a vote to keep what we had and to drop the subject.

The Open Door was more easily stated than maintained. Indeed, two months after he had sent the notes, Secretary Hay himself inquired about establishing a naval base on the Chinese mainland at Samsah Bay. The Japanese government, with a nice sense of irony, suggested that Hay's request might infringe China's "territorial and administrative entity," and Hay did not pursue the matter further. A year later, when Japan asked if the United States planned any response to expanding Russian influence in Manchuria, Hay confessed that the United States would not risk war to keep the door open. The Open Door policy expressed hope, not determination.

And the hope soon withered. American trade with China never developed, and investment opportunities went to those whose strategic control enabled them to extort concessions. At the turn of the century, China's share of American exports hovered around 1 percent; its share of American investment was about the same. At the outbreak of the First World War, the statistic had not grown. Although the American China Development Corporation secured the right to build a Chinese railroad in 1898, J. P. Morgan and the other directors decided to sell out before completing the project. Not even President Roosevelt could convince the company to change its decision. President Taft encountered chilling apathy when he tried to persuade American capitalists to construct a Manchurian railway. American businessmen realized before their Presidents did that China was a market without purchasing power and that geography gave Russia and Japan advantages that the Philippines in no way offset. By 1907 Roosevelt admitted that the Philippines were "our heel of Achilles." To protect the islands, Roosevelt went on, would require enormous fortification and "a navy second only to that of Great Britain." Lacking both, Roosevelt and his successors sought a balance of power in East Asia to discourage excessive ambition by any single nation.

Russia, Roosevelt believed, most threatened the balance of Asian power. The Czar had secured control of Port Arthur and the right to link the port with the Trans-Siberian Railway; Russian intrigue in Korea was badly disguised. Both in Manchuria and in Korea Russian plans conflicted with those of Japan. Before confronting Russia directly, Japan signed an alliance with Great Britain in 1902 and secured Roosevelt's benevolent neutrality. Then, on February 8, 1904, without a declaration of war, Japan smashed the Russian Pacific fleet at Port Arthur. "Japan," Theodore Roosevelt wrote to his son, "is playing our game."

The game threatened to go on too long. Roosevelt hoped Japan would thwart Russian expansion but stop short of establishing its own hegemony in East Asia. Japan won impressive victories, both at sea and in Manchuria, but the economic drain led the Japanese cabinet to ask Roosevelt to mediate. Even though Russian armies had been soundly defeated, and in spite of strikes and demonstrations that merged in the Revolution of 1905, Czar Nicholas II at first resisted Roosevelt's overtures. The President patiently and skillfully brought Russian and Japanese delegates together at Portsmouth, New Hampshire, and kept them there until the Treaty of Portsmouth ended the Russo-Japanese War in 1905.

For his effort, Theodore Roosevelt won the Nobel Peace Prize and the resentment of both belligerents. The settlement at Portsmouth satisfied neither Russia, which gave up territory, nor Japan, which failed to secure the indemnity to which it felt entitled. Nor did the balance of Asian power, renewed by Roosevelt's compromise, ensure American access to Asian markets. Although Roosevelt himself never thought that market vital, the country, in his administration and later, continued to pay lip service to the Open Door. Restating the policy did not make other powers respect it, however, and the open door was soon only slightly ajar.

Roosevelt ranked the diplomatic support of Japan ahead of economic opportunity in China. In the Taft-Katsura memorandum of 1905, the President recognized a Japanese protectorate in Korea that closed the Open Door there. In 1908, an exchange of notes between Secretary of State Elihu Root and Japanese Ambassador Kogoro Takahira solemnly reaffirmed both nations' support for the Open Door. This Root-Takahira agreement also pledged Japan and the United States to respect each other's Pacific possessions, a promise the United States wanted in order to protect the Philippines. Although Roosevelt warned against irritating the Japanese by seeking too aggressively to promote American investment in Manchuria, the Taft administration urged Americans to invest in railroads there. But the Manchurian portion of the Asian market vanished in 1911, when Japan and Russia divided Manchuria into a northern sphere of Russian influence and a southern sector, where Japan predominated. In 1915 Japan took advantage of the preoccupation of European powers with the First World War to make the Twenty-One Demands on China, which, if conceded, would have permitted Japanese domination of China. Bryan, then Wilson's secretary of state, protested, but Robert Lansing, who followed Bryan in the State Department, signed another executive agreement in 1917. The Lansing-Ishii agreement once more reaffirmed the Open Door and simultaneously admitted that Japan had "special interests" in China as a result of "territorial propinquity." The determination of strong rivals, particularly Japan, had forced a quiet American diplomatic retreat from East Asia. In 1909 the navy abandoned plans for a primary Pacific base near Manila and concentrated on the development of Pearl Harbor. Without the fleet, American policy could not be enforced.

As if Russia, China, Manchuria, and the Philippines did not sufficiently complicate Japanese-American relations, California added another dimension. In 1906 a decision by the San Francisco Board of Education to educate Japanese Americans in segregated schools brought outraged objection from the Japanese Foreign Ministry. While Roosevelt sympathized with Japan, the Constitution gave him little control over education in California. Eventually, the President persuaded the Californians to reverse their decision and the Japanese not to permit laborers to emigrate to the United States. But this Gentlemen's Agreement, completed in 1908, did not exclude all Japanese immigrants and did not satisfy California. In 1913 the state legislature outlawed Japanese ownership of land in spite of pleas from President Wilson and Secretary Bryan and protests from Japan.

The Western Hemisphere: Influence and Intervention

Growth of American influence in the Western Hemisphere more than balanced gradual withdrawal from East Asia. As "territorial propinquity" made Manchuria a zone of Japanese influence, so the Caribbean became an American lake. Construction of the Panama Canal increased the strategic interest of the United States in all of Central America. But American policy-makers substituted informal protectorates there for the policy of territorial expansion that had been followed in the Philippines.

Barriers that for a half century had prevented construction of a canal were gradually surmounted. Medical research controlled tropical diseases that had resisted earlier efforts. Improvements in locks enabled engineers to drop the unworkable plans of a French company for a sea-level canal. New York speculators bought control of the French company, so its exclusive Panamanian franchise would not hinder American efforts to complete a waterway. Following cordial discussions with the British ambassador, Sir Julian Pauncefote, John Hay announced in 1900 that Britain had renounced the right, guaranteed in the Clayton-Bulwer Treaty of 1850, to joint construction and control of any interoceanic canal. When in 1901 the Senate wisely refused to ratify the treaty unless it included permission to fortify the waterway, Hay and Pauncefote negotiated a second treaty, which removed that diplomatic block. In 1902 Congress authorized President Roosevelt to pay the American stockholders of the French company $40 million for its exclusive franchise. Thomás Herrán, Colombia's representative in Washington, obligingly granted the United States a ninety-nine-year lease on a canal zone in Colombia's Panama province in return for $10 million and an annual payment of $250,000.

But the Colombian legislature unexpectedly resisted Hay's financial inducement and rejected the Hay-Herrán treaty. Since the French company's rights reverted to Colombia in 1904, Colombia decided to delay a year in order to collect the company's $40 million too. Roosevelt privately raged about the "Dagoes" of Colombia who perversely halted the progress of civilization. He stationed the U.S.S. *Nashville* off Colón to protect American interests in the isthmus. In 1903, when a Panamanian rebellion broke out, the *Nashville* prevented Colombian troops from disembarking. Two days later Hay informally recognized the rebel regime. Within two weeks Hay concluded a treaty with Philippe Bunau-Varilla, a Frenchman and lobbyist for the French canal company, who coincidentally represented the new Panamanian republic in Washington. In spite of objections from Panamanian nationalists, Bunau-Varilla accepted the financial terms Colombia had rejected; the United States secured a ten-mile-wide canal zone in perpetuity as one of the provisions of the Hay-Bunau-Varilla Treaty.

With the right to build the canal, the United States also acquired the resentment of much of Latin America. If Roosevelt had waited for the Colombian "bandits," construction would not have been delayed more

ON TO PANAMA.

than eighteen months. And Roosevelt's public delight in his accomplishment showed little sensitivity to Latin American pride: "If I had followed traditional, conservative methods," Roosevelt boasted in 1911, "I would have submitted a dignified State paper . . . to Congress and the debates on it would have been going on yet; but I took the Canal Zone . . . and while the debate goes on the Canal does also." Recognizing that Roosevelt's impetuous action rankled south of the border, the Wilson administration offered to pay Colombia $25 million, but Republican partisanship blocked any compensation until 1921.

Proud Latin American neighbors also resented the Roosevelt Corollary to the Monroe Doctrine, which the President announced in 1904. Monroe's pronouncement sheltered only those nations that kept order and paid their bills, Roosevelt remarked; "chronic wrongdoing . . . may . . . ultimately require intervention by some civilized nation." For Roosevelt, the "civilized nation" in the Western Hemisphere was the United States. The Roosevelt Corollary publicly avowed the protectorate policy already practiced in Panama and in Cuba, where the Cuban constitution granted the United States the right to intervene. Within the next few years, under the guise of preventing European debt collection, Americans landed marines, took over customs houses, and reorganized the fiscal systems of the Dominican Republic, Haiti, and Nicaragua. The last of the marines returned to the United States in 1934.

Roosevelt's immediate successors did not alter his policies. Without Roosevelt's vigor and without conspicuous success, William Howard Taft tried to encourage American investment abroad. When Latin American debtors neglected their obligations, the State Department brought diplomatic pressure to secure repayment. Woodrow Wilson criticized Taft's "dollar diplomacy" and assured the world in 1913 that the United States would "never again seek one additional foot of territory by conquest." Wilson's administration kept the letter of his pledge; the Virgin Islands, added in 1917, were purchased from Denmark, not conquered. But protectorates in Haiti, the Dominican Republic, and Nicaragua, and Yankee armies in Mexico certainly seemed out of keeping with the spirit of Wilson's remarks.

Like Roosevelt, and like the progressive generation for whom both men were spokesmen, Woodrow Wilson acted on moral conviction. Wilson intensely disapproved of General Victoriano Huerta, one of a series of strong men who tried to master political and social upheaval in Mexico. Since Wilson believed diplomatic contact officially bestowed American approval on foreign governments, he refused to recognize Huerta's regime. Wilson thereby overturned a longstanding practice of exchanging representatives with whatever government was in power. The President also imposed an arms embargo in his determination to "teach the South American republics to elect good men." But every faction suspected his motives, and he twice blundered into armed intervention in Mexico.

Conflict in the first instance was relatively brief. In April 1914 Wilson abruptly ordered the bombardment and seizure of Vera Cruz to prevent delivery of German arms for Huerta's forces. The Mexican army put up stiff resistance before leaving the port to American troops. Wilson's action may have benefited Huerta's Mexican opponents, but they denounced it no less vehemently than Huerta himself. A few days after the landings, Wilson eagerly accepted arbitration from Argentina, Brazil, and Chile, which led to evacuation of American forces within six months.

Wilson's second Mexican conflict occurred because Venustiano Carranza, Huerta's chief rival and successor, could not subdue Pancho Villa, a swashbuckling political maverick. Perhaps because he thought an American invasion would discredit Carranza, Villa deliberately provoked a punitive expedition by American troops. In 1916 Villa's men abducted sixteen Americans from a Mexican train and shot them; in March Villa raided Columbus, New Mexico, and left nineteen Americans dead. With Carranza's grudging consent, General John J. Pershing led 6,000 American troops into Mexico to administer justice to Villa's raiders. The expedition never found Villa. Instead it clashed with Mexican forces and nearly set off another war with Mexico. Finally in January 1917, as American participation in a bigger war across the Atlantic became more and more imminent, Wilson ordered Pershing back to Texas. The general soon found German armies in France less elusive than Mexican outlaws.

That war in France confirmed, for those who might be unaware of what had happened in the preceding half century, that the United States had progressed from regional to world power. This change was not the result of new protectorates in the Caribbean or new possessions in the Pacific, nor even the result of dismembering the Spanish empire and sinking its sorry fleet. Events at home were more responsible than events abroad for the nation's diplomatic eminence, which far-sighted, often imperious leaders from Seward to Roosevelt had instinctively understood. The United States became a full-fledged world power when the American people realized that their industrial economy gave them diplomatic leverage in proportion to their enormous potential strength, and when they consciously decided to use that leverage.

Suggested Reading

Twentieth-Century American Foreign Policy (1971), edited by John Braeman, Robert H. Bremner, and David Brody, includes articles by Charles E. Neu and David F. Trask on the interpretive historical literature about expansion. Robert L. Beisner's *From the Old Diplomacy to the New, 1865–1900** (1975) is a good, brief survey. Walter LaFeber's *The New Empire** (1963) is a stimulating economic interpretation. The essays of John A. S. Grenville and George B. Young, *Politics, Strategy, and American Diplomacy* (1966), argue that partisanship, military considerations, and sometimes chance were as important as economic influences. Ernest R. May's *American Imperialism* (1968) documents the importance of the European example to American opinion-makers; see also his *Imperial Democracy** (1961). One opinion-maker, Alfred T. Mahan, states his case in *The Influence of Sea Power upon History** (1890). Milton Plesur covers American expansion before 1890 in *America's Outward Thrust* (1971). *The Martial Spirit** (1931), by Walter Millis, is the classic account of the coming of the Spanish-American War. Admiral H. G. Rickover includes the most recent investigation in *How the Battleship Maine Was Destroyed* (1976). Robert L. Beisner's *Twelve Against Empire** (1968) is an important study of the anti-imperialists.

The foreign policy of Theodore Roosevelt is examined in Howard K. Beale's *Theodore Roosevelt and the Rise of America to World Power** (1956), and in Raymond Esthus's *Theodore Roosevelt and Japan* (1966). Paul A. Varg's *The Making of a Myth* (1961) and Warren I. Cohen's *America's Response to China** (1971) are two of a host of books on the diplomatic contact between the United States and China; Michael H. Hunt's *Frontier Defense and the Open Door* (1973) focuses on Manchuria. Two recent studies of the Panama Canal are David McCulloch's *The Path Between the Seas* (1977) and Walter LaFeber's *The Panama Canal* (1978).

* Available in paperback edition

Chapter 16
Presidents and Progressives

Chronology

1900 Presidential election: William McKinley (Republican) defeats William Jennings Bryan (Democrat) •

1901 McKinley assassinated; Theodore Roosevelt becomes President •

1902 Roosevelt intervenes to settle coal strike •

1904 Supreme Court rules against Northern Securities Company • Lincoln Steffens's "The Shame of the Cities" published • Presidential election: Theodore Roosevelt (Republican) defeats Alton B. Parker (Democrat) •

1905 Supreme Court rules against laws regulating maximum hours in *Lochner* v. *New York,* a precedent

modified in *Muller* v. *Oregon* (1908) • Founding of Industrial Workers of the World •

1906 Hepburn Act gives ICC power to set railroad rates •

1907 Financial panic •

1908 Presidential election: William Howard Taft (Republican) defeats William Jennings Bryan (Democrat) •

1909 NAACP founded •

1912 Presidential election: Woodrow Wilson (Democrat) defeats Theodore Roosevelt (Progressive) and William Howard Taft (Republican) •

1913 Underwood-Simmons Tariff reduces duties • Federal Reserve System

established • Sixteenth Amendment (permitting income tax) ratified; Seventeenth Amendment (providing for direct election of senators) ratified •

1914 Clayton Antitrust Act and Federal Trade Commission Act complete Wilson's New Freedom program •

1916 Wilson prods Congress to enact more social legislation • Presidential election: Woodrow Wilson (Democrat) defeats Charles Evans Hughes (Republican) •

1920 Nineteenth Amendment (permitting women to vote) ratified •

The message Theodore Roosevelt sent to Congress in December 1901 began appropriately with grief for his murdered predecessor and closed with sympathy for the British people on the death of their Queen. The passing of William McKinley and Queen Victoria marked the end of the nineteenth century; the presidency of Theodore Roosevelt symbolically opened the twentieth. Much of the old endured; in many respects, Theodore Roosevelt was as Victorian as the Queen. But he foreshadowed the future as well—the fifteen years Americans have called the progressive era.

The term "progressive" lacked precision and the "progressive movement" seemed so inclusive that few Americans were left out. The label stretched to cover such disparate groups as businessmen, who sought federal regulation in order to curb unfair competitors, and industrial workers, who sought state regulation of factory conditions. Progressive ministers preached the social gospel and progressive agnostics scoffed at churches. Reformers promoted the income tax, votes for women, prohibition, and many other measures to correct what they called abuses or corruption or inefficiency. Society's evils, progressives believed, derived from the misuse of power, or from some individual failing, not from competition or democracy or the American way. The nation's institutions, as progressives saw them, needed to be tuned, not replaced.

But the multiple changes associated with rapid industrialization late in the nineteenth century did require institutional corrections in the twentieth. Industrialization had upset the social order by transferring wealth, prestige, and influence from one group to another. The customs and faiths of millions of new immigrants threatened the Protestant morality and cultural homogeneity most Americans thought central to national unity. Concentrated economic power seemed to overshadow the autonomy of individuals and the authority of the state. Society had no adequate mechanism to protect or to care for the victims of change— those who were cheated and exploited, the uneducated and the unemployed.

The programs progressives advanced to assist such people were sometimes tainted with self-interest and frequently with condescension; their reforms were *for* people as often as *of* them. It was not "the people" who demanded effective railroad regulation so much as the merchants, farmers, and manufacturers who paid freight charges. It was not "the people" who demanded an end to corrupt urban politics so much as those whose influence at City Hall had diminished and whose taxes had risen. Few reformers stopped to wonder whether honest government actually made ordinary voters happier, whether competition effectively met the economic needs of the whole population, or whether Anglo-Saxons in fact had an innate edge over everybody else. "You nivir heerd iv a man rayformin' himsilf," the humorist Finley Peter Dunne remarked through Mr. Dooley, his genial Irish saloonkeeper. But, Mr. Dooley continued, "he'll rayform other people gladly."

The order that progressives hoped to impose was typically a slight modification of the old order, where property was protected, where people behaved with middle-class decorum, and where the upright, self-reliant individual collected society's reward. Many of the reforms progressives proposed derived from their fear that change would continue, that slums would nurture the disease and dissatisfaction that might menace public health and republican government, that socialists and other labor agitators would foment a social revolution, that monopolies would crush competition. William McKinley would have approved the progressives' fiscal policy and Horatio Alger their faith in self-improvement. Actions that now seem illiberal—prohibition, the disfranchisement of southern blacks, restriction of immigration—seemed reforms to progressives anxious to forestall major modifications in the society they confidently believed to be the world's best.

A Smorgasbord of Reform

If progressives were occasionally selfish, suspicious, and intolerant, they were more characteristically confident, generous, and eager to help right

Child labor

the world's wrongs. The most obvious social evils were those nearest home—dishonest aldermen, noisome tenements, high fares on streetcars. The variety of the progressive movement, and much of its vitality as well, reflected its local roots. In thousands of communities "respectable" citizens united to do battle with the county political "ring" or with the boss who presided over a community's contracts and payroll. These local movements sought parks, schools, and public transportation; higher wages and shorter hours for municipal employees; municipal home rule and more democratic local government; municipal ownership of utilities or public regulation of their rates; more equitable taxation; faster assimilation of immigrants; and, above all, clean elections and respectable political leaders. Tammany Hall in New York, the nation learned, was only the most notorious political machine; others in Pittsburgh, St. Louis, Minneapolis, and elsewhere were only less cynically corrupt. But in Cleveland, where Mayor Tom Johnson flamboyantly fought "the interests," in Toledo under Mayor Samuel M. "Golden Rule" Jones, in Detroit, and in smaller cities across the land, progressives happily attacked dishonest representatives of the status quo.

Those representatives proved resilient and had several prepared lines of defense. As one frustrated reformer said: "When I was in the city council . . . fighting for a shorter work day, [my opponents] told me to go to the legislature; now [my fellow legislators] tell me to go to Congress for a national law. When I get there and demand it, they will tell me to go to hell." This buck-passing from one level of government to another drew progressives first into state governments, which enacted many progressive proposals, and then into national politics.

In Iowa, where Jonathan Dolliver challenged standpat Republicans, in

Georgia, where Hoke Smith challenged standpat Democrats, in California and New Hampshire, where Hiram Johnson and Robert Bass challenged railroads, and in other states, progressives gathered support. Robert F. Wagner, a German immigrant who represented part of New York City in the state senate, did not have the typical progressive's family background, but the bills he introduced made him part of the movement. He asked for the direct election of senators, direct primaries, the short ballot, and the vote for women; he proposed to regulate child labor and enact minimum wages for women; he wanted to permit the cities to own utilities and the state to conserve water resources. Robert M. LaFollette goaded Wisconsin into enacting a direct primary and regulation of railroads, banks, and lobbyists. His new tax laws, including an income tax, demanded more of corporations and railroads. Wisconsin was soon known as the "laboratory of democracy," and LaFollette's political organization inspired reformers beyond his state.

In 1906, the year that Wisconsin sent LaFollette to Washington, progressive journalists had identified the Senate as the graveyard of reform. Earlier that year, David Graham Phillips had written a trenchant article entitled "The Treason of the Senate" that gave substance to the popular belief that a clique of millionaires and corporate lawyers ran the upper chamber as a gentleman's club. Phillips's article exemplified the publishing fad President Roosevelt derisively called "muckraking," a practice, he said, that exposed sordid conditions without proposing constructive ways to correct them. Muckrakers did generally share a progressive faith that people who knew of evil would discover ways to end it. Thus a single issue of *McClure's Magazine*, the leading muckraking journal, disclosed malfeasance in government, business, and labor. One article was an installment of the influential series called "The Shame of the Cities" by Lincoln Steffens. Another was part of Ida Tarbell's critical history of the Standard Oil Company, which revealed the abuses of industrial competition and the overweening power that resulted from competitive survival. Ray Stannard Baker's article on "The Right to Work" condemned racketeering among labor union officials. S. S. McClure's editorial called attention to "the arraignment of American character" contained in the three articles and suggested that such conditions existed only on the sufferance of complacent citizens. While Steffens indicted corrupt politicians, Tarbell greedy businessmen, and Baker powerful labor barons, McClure blamed the public that permitted its own exploitation.

Other magazines—*Cosmopolitan, Munsey's, American*—copied McClure's successful formula. If the flurry of activity that greeted each new exposure was usually temporary and inconclusive, some of the literature brought results. Lincoln Steffens's assault on urban corruption stimulated reform movements in San Francisco and Kansas City, which Steffens had not even written about, as well as in Philadelphia and St. Louis, which he had. Upton Sinclair's *The Jungle,* a harrowing account of working conditions in the stockyards, and Charles Edward Russell's series of articles on the beef trust aroused popular concern that helped secure passage of the Meat Inspection Act in 1906. But the Meat Inspection Act was not exactly what either had had in mind; Sinclair thought he was making a case for socialism and Russell's concern was irresponsible economic power.

Ray Stannard Baker's *Following the Color Line* (1908) did not even produce an unintentional result. For racial equality was not a goal of white progressives. Nice people, progressives believed, helped uplift dark-skinned people in the Philippines or the Caribbean, but equality for those on the other side of town was out of the question. California progressives excluded Orientals almost as ruthlessly as southern progressives excluded blacks. The racism of northern progressives, less visible and less conscious, was nonetheless present. Theodore Roosevelt ate lunch and discussed patronage with Booker T. Washington at the White House. But Roosevelt himself squelched demands that an affirmation of racial equality be included in the Progressive party's platform in 1912, and he allowed lily white southern delegations to participate in the party's convention. Woodrow Wilson permitted southern postmasters to drop blacks from the federal payroll and allowed segregation to become the rule in government buildings and in the federal civil service. Progressives did more than accept disfranchisement and segregation; they often wrote the laws and then excused them in the name of honest elections and democracy.

A few progressives of both races established the National Association for the Advancement of Colored People (NAACP) in 1909. To edit its journal, *The Crisis*, the NAACP hired W. E. B. Du Bois, a brilliant young northern-born black with a doctorate from Harvard and several books to his credit, including the anguished autobiographical *Souls of Black Folk*. But neither *The Crisis*, nor its angry editor, nor the organization's legal efforts to secure equality ruffled the white community, which preferred to keep blacks firmly and quietly in their subordinate place.

The Vote for Women

A woman's place, of course, was in the home, even though for more and more women home was where one worked after a full day of work somewhere else. In 1890, about 4 million women had wage-earning jobs, a number that jumped to almost 7.5 million twenty years later. Many of those jobs, to be sure, were doing another woman's housework, but industrialization also broadened the economic horizon. Some employers applied new machines and processes to traditional female tasks—cooking, washing, sewing—in canneries, bakeries, laundries, and sweatshops. Working women found new tasks in retail stores, offices, schoolrooms, and hospitals.

Both the Knights of Labor and the American Federation of Labor made sporadic, halfhearted attempts to organize women in unions. The Knights had even less success with women than with men. Since many women worked at unskilled industrial jobs, the craft unions of the AFL gave little encouragement and less energy to the task. So women began to form their own unions, and in 1909 New York's garment workers demonstrated that they could sustain a long strike. That strike strengthened both the International Ladies Garment Workers Union (ILGWU) and the Women's Trade Union League, which had coordinated the moral and financial support of other women's organizations. Although the ILGWU failed to secure recognition as the exclusive bargaining agent for the strikers, the movement to organize women and the garment trades gathered momentum.

If a union could not legally represent workers, it could not compel employers to provide safe working conditions. About a year after the garment workers' strike was settled, a sudden fire erupted in the Triangle Shirtwaist Company, which occupied the three top floors of a ten-story building in lower Manhattan. The city's fire department arrived promptly, but not quickly enough for 146 employees, most of whom were young immigrant women. They had jumped out of windows and down elevator shafts; they had piled up in front of locked doors and at the bottom of collapsed stairways. They had never had a fire drill, and there was only one inadequate fire escape: the building was supposed to have been fireproof.

For years, suffragists had been saying that working women needed the ballot to protect themselves. The Triangle fire certainly belied the complacent rebuttal that protecting women had always been a man's responsibility. An officer of the National American Woman Suffrage Association (NAWSA) proclaimed her determination not "to consign unwilling women or helpless young girls to any such tender mercies" as male owners of the Triangle Shirtwaist Company had felt for their employees. "And we claim in no uncertain voice," she continued, "that women . . . should have the one efficient tool with which to make for themselves decent and safe working conditions—the ballot."

That kind of rhetoric irritated radical feminists who argued for total sexual equality. Why, they asked, should suffrage be sought to obtain special legislation protecting fragile women from industrial abuse when society ought to protect all industrial workers, male and female alike? But in *Muller* v. *Oregon* (1908) the Supreme Court accepted the contention that long hours impaired the health and reproductive capacity of working women. Louis Brandeis's brief on behalf of Oregon emphasized the physical differences between the sexes, since the Court had previously ruled against legislation limiting the hours of male workers. Middle-class suffragists, hoping for the support of women in industry, ignored the contradiction between discriminatory protection and sexual equality. Other progressive women worked for reform through settlement houses, unions, temperance societies, and school boards. But for most feminists,

as for most progressives, the right to vote was the change that made all other changes possible. The campaign for women's suffrage is sufficiently typical of the progressive impulse to reveal some of the aims and some of the faults of progressives, as well as something of their standpat opponents.

Suffragists' opponents stood squarely for Home and Motherhood. Politics, they said, was a dirty business that would debase women and distract them from tasks that God (and man) had ordained. A husband might legitimately flatter his wife, but no other man was permitted to, which ruled out her participation in political campaigns. Moreover, the peculiar spiritual and emotional traits of women prevented the practical outlook required in voting and office-holding. The Darwinist Herbert Spencer wrote that "overtaxing the brains" led to diminished reproduction, a discovery that gave a "scientific" blessing to restricting the suffrage. A judge in New York put it directly: "If some of the women who are going around advocating equal suffrage would go around and advocate women having children they would do a greater service."

Suffragists had begun with the simple appeal to equality. Some of them in 1890 were veterans of the abolitionist crusade and had swallowed their disappointment when Radical Reconstruction did not include the enfranchisement of women. Women in Wyoming had the right to vote when the state joined the union in 1890. Colorado, Idaho, and Utah soon followed. But then the procession stopped, and some suffragists decided that promises might persuade more quickly than principles. They promised support for prohibition, for compulsory education, for industrial regulation, if only male advocates of those causes would help women gain the ballot.

Nor was the appeal always to reform: suffragists pointed out that there were more native-born women than immigrant slum-dwellers of both sexes, and that white women, if permitted, could outvote all the blacks in the South. Laura Clay, daughter of a Kentucky abolitionist, gradually narrowed her conception of equality until she came to believe that any extension of the franchise must be limited to white women. Other suffragists pointed out that educated women were being governed by the votes of their uneducated gardeners and coachmen. Anna Howard Shaw, president of the NAWSA for a decade, appealed overtly in 1904 to the pride of native white men, and by implication to their concern for the purity of white women: "There is no race, there is no color, there is no nationality of men, who are not the sovereign rulers of American women." Like many male progressives, who supported or at least did not protest segregation and the restriction of immigration, suffragists betrayed the ethnic prejudices of middle-class white Americans. Which is what most of them were.

Neither suffragists nor progressives found the support they thought they deserved among groups they often called "the lower classes." But neither the suffragists nor the progressives challenged the economic order in any fundamental way. (Lucy Stone, one of the older generation of suffragists, wondered in 1892 why the Homestead strikers had not saved enough to open their own businesses.) Only the radical edge of the women's movement seemed to threaten existing social institutions, and most of these radicals also professed to be trying to strengthen, rather than destroy, such social bulwarks as marriage and the family.

By 1913 radical suffragists thought the time for petitions had passed and the time for demands had come. Influenced by the direct-action tactics of English suffragists, Alice Paul and the small Woman's Party she led called attention to the gap in Woodrow Wilson's reform program. Demonstrations by the Woman's Party at Wilson's inauguration provoked a bullying response that discredited opponents of women's suffrage. When Wilson's first term ended without a proposed constitutional amendment, the Woman's Party campaigned against Wilson and his party in the states where women could vote. When Wilson proclaimed the nation's democratic principles during the First World War, the Woman's Party provided pickets with placards mocking the President's commitment to democracy. The NAWSA thought the Woman's Party divisive, counterproductive, and unladylike, but the militants probably hastened Wilson's trip to Congress to ask for the Nineteenth Amendment. The battle was over in time for the election of 1920.

For some, the effort to secure the vote was the means to another end—better divorce laws, prohibition, improved industrial conditions, new attitudes and new legislation about birth control. But the immediate legacy of the women's movement, like that of the progressive movement itself, was greater political democracy. For a few years, legislatures proved responsive to the pleas of female lobbyists. The nonpartisan League of Women Voters attempted to sustain the reform impulse, but politicians soon discovered that middle-class women voted like middle-class men. Both marriages and political corruption survived the Nineteenth Amendment, and the babies continued to arrive; most people must have wondered in retrospect why the controversy had been so heated.

Coping with Change

Although political democracy was a goal worth achieving, it was for some progressives only a first step. They wished to use government's power for social purposes: to check selfish "interests," to curtail waste, to control economic change. These measures were not simply instances of shielding the general public from entrepreneurial greed. The public, for example, probably preferred cheap lumber and jobs to the conservation practices that bureaucrats in the forestry service outlined to protect the nation's timber supply from the inefficient harvests of lumbermen. The effort to conserve the nation's resources, so close to the heart of Theodore Roosevelt and other progressives, illustrated the elitist strain in the reform movement: in taking the long view of efficiency and in preventing the squandering of the nation's trees, governmental experts believed they were responding to demands the people would have made if they had recognized their own best interest.

Economic rationalization—the process of efficiently organizing the economy instead of trusting the random disorder of competition— appealed to many business executives as a means of controlling change. The process was by no means complete in the progressive era, but economic rationalization had begun and the prophets were persuasive. Frederick W. Taylor used time-and-motion studies to determine the most efficient use of worker, machine, and plant; his system of scientific management was widely imitated. The creation of a Graduate School of Business Administration at Harvard University testified that business had become a profession, not a competitive jungle. Smaller manufacturers banded together in the National Association of Manufacturers to promote common interests through the press and the legislatures. Other industrialists joined with conservative labor leaders in the National Civic Federation, which advocated an early form of welfare capitalism and the arbitration of industrial disputes.

Theodore Roosevelt was persuaded that business consolidation was the inevitable result of competition: "This is an age of combination," he remarked in 1905, "and any effort to prevent all combination will be not only useless, but in the end vicious." Yet the trusts must behave; they must not take advantage of their economic power to cheat the public. Roosevelt distinguished early between tolerable "good" trusts and "bad" trusts, which must be taken to court. Almost every progressive eventually made a similar judgment in order to restrict the power of business while preserving its efficiency. "I am for big business," said Woodrow Wilson, making Roosevelt's distinction in other words, "and I am against the trusts." The Supreme Court drew a similar line when it dissolved Standard Oil in 1911 with a decree that distinguished between "reasonable" and "unreasonable" restraint of trade.

The Court, like the other branches of government, found the pace of change confusing and had great difficulty separating the individual's economic rights from his social responsibilities. By the 1920s the justices had embraced laissez faire, but earlier decisions were less consistent. In 1898, for instance, in *Holden* v. *Hardy*, the Court held that Utah could legitimately set an eight-hour workday for miners and smelters. But in 1905, in *Lochner* v. *New York*, a law restricting bakers to a sixty-hour week was thrown out as an unjustifiable limitation on freedom of contract. Many legal authorities thought the *Lochner* precedent was overruled three years later in *Muller* v. *Oregon*. Yet in *Adkins* v. *Children's Hospital* (1923), the Court brushed off the *Muller* precedent and cited *Lochner* in declaring unconstitutional a federal statute limiting the working hours of women in the District of Columbia. Evidently the Court was unsure of the proper role of the state in the economy.

The Court was, however, consistently opposed to labor unions. Although suspicious of the Sherman Act when corporations were on trial, the federal courts had no difficulty applying the statute to unions. In *Loewe* v. *Lawlor* (1908), the Court forbade the secondary boycott, the device whereby one union cooperated with another in withholding patronage or respecting pickets. Samuel Gompers and the AFL asked both parties to promise legislation to upset the decision, and the union endorsed the Democrats in 1908 when they responded. But Democrats did not win in that election, and neither, in general, did unions in the progressive era.

With the reluctant help of President Roosevelt, the United Mine Workers did win a partial victory in 1902. The anthracite miners, ably led by John Mitchell, walked out in the early summer. They demanded recognition of the union, substantial wage increases, reforms in the method of measuring their output, and other changes. As summer turned to fall and coal stocks dwindled, the railroads that controlled the mines held fast to the divine right of property. But Republican congressional candidates in the chilly East demanded a quick settlement, and Roosevelt stepped in. When management proved stubborn, Roosevelt invoked J. P. Morgan's aid, and the combination of government and Wall Street induced the owners to agree to a compromise settlement by arbitration. The arbiters awarded the miners a 10 percent raise but denied recognition of their union, and the strike ended.

Regulation Under Roosevelt

Specific governmental regulation to prevent specific abuses, Theodore Roosevelt came to believe, served the public more effectively than indiscriminate competition. Since regulation reduced the number of imponderables that businessmen encountered in competitive enterprise, federal action was less abhorrent to many large businesses than the rhetoric of laissez faire suggested. And the alternative of state regulation, with dozens of different and perhaps conflicting codes, frightened any corporate executive interested in a national market. As the *Wall Street Journal* noted at the end of 1904:

As between governmental regulation by forty-five states and governmental regulation by the . . . federal government, there can be but one choice. . . . The choice must be that of a federal regulation, for that will be uniform over the whole country and of a higher and more equitable standard.

Besides, federal standards of quality or federal labor regulations might well reduce competition from marginal producers whose profit depended on selling a shoddy product or exploiting their workers. For competition remained in spite of consolidation. The share of the market held by United States Steel, for instance, dropped steadily between 1901 and 1920. Regardless of Standard Oil's market dominance, the number of major oil-refiners increased. Competition was the rule among firms in new industries, such as automobile and telephone companies at the beginning of the century. Consolidated corporations failed in attempts to monopolize copper-mining and meatpacking. Major meatpackers, indeed, apparently welcomed federal meat inspection as a way of protecting themselves from the competition of fly-by-night slaughterhouse operators.

Responsible railroad men had long understood the benefits of regulation. The Elkins Act, passed in 1903, forbade rebates as had the Interstate Commerce Act some years before. The practice was, however, more carefully defined so that the shippers who received rebates, as well as the railroads that paid them, were liable to punishment. Most railroads, no longer anxious to preserve their competitive right to give rebates, supported the bill.

The Hepburn Act, which Congress passed only after adept presidential intervention in 1906, was another matter. When a shipper complained, this law gave the Interstate Commerce Commission (ICC) the power to set rates and forced the railroad to go to court to challenge them. The ICC also received regulatory jurisdiction over pipelines, express companies, and ferries, and the authority to examine a corporation's financial records to establish equitable rates. To get the bill through, Roosevelt threatened conservatives with a reduction of the tariff and progressives with no legislation at all; he used Democrats when his own party balked. Progressives like LaFollette protested that unless the ICC had the authority to establish independently the value of a railroad's property, the right to set rates was meaningless. LaFollette's charge proved correct, and Congress soon had to remove the loophole. But Theodore Roosevelt settled for the measure that his sense of political timing told him he could get, rather than risk no legislation at all.

Roosevelt's efforts to strengthen the ICC indicated his reliance on governmental regulation to prevent the abuse of economic power. His restrained use of the Sherman Act disclosed his lack of faith in competition. Paradoxically, Roosevelt gained an undeserved reputation as a trust-buster from one important case against the Northern Securities Company, the holding company that controlled the railroads of the Northwest. Behind the Northern Securities Company were some of the most important names in American finance: J. P. Morgan and Jacob Schiff of Wall Street and railroad tycoons E. H. Harriman and James J. Hill. When in 1904 the government won the suit, the Sherman Act and the power of the public seemed enhanced; the verdict confirmed that the public, represented by its agent, the government, had property rights too. The restatement of the public's rights had immense political significance, and the decree reasserted Washington's role in economic decision-making. But dissolving the company had little direct economic

"The Lion-Tamer"

effect. The promoters of the monopoly went unpunished. Morgan and Schiff continued to cooperate with one another and even with Theodore Roosevelt, to whose presidential campaign in 1904 they contributed a total of $250,000.

Roosevelt understood politics; his knowledge of finance was rudimentary. When a sharp panic buffeted the nation's banks in 1907, he was nearly as bewildered as the general public. Lacking a program and the theoretical means of formulating one, the President relied on the advice of Wall Street financiers whom he considered trustworthy. Morgan and Judge E. H. Gary of United States Steel offered to purchase control of Tennessee Coal and Iron from a distressed firm in New York, an action they said would restore confidence and avert the failure of several important financial institutions. Roosevelt agreed not to invoke the Sherman Act, even though the acquisition of an important competitor certainly enhanced the dominance of Gary's firm in the steel industry. Subsequently the panic subsided, for reasons other than the merger, and Roosevelt's anxiety was relieved.

Economic distress meant political disaster, which Roosevelt usually avoided. He carefully distinguished himself from "professional politicians," but his control of the party was the envy of all professionals, and his contact with most of them in Congress was cordial. He easily secured his own nomination in 1904 and dictated that of William Howard Taft in 1908. With exuberant overstatement and a superb talent for public relations, the President converted modest advances into momentous triumphs, for which he claimed, and duly received, public praise. He was, as a progressive social worker observed in 1912, "America's first publicity man." Cautiously at first, but with increasing assurance after he secured his own political mandate in 1904, Roosevelt publicized what he called "reform," which he made more fashionable than did any muckraker. In the process, of course, he drew attention both to himself and to his office. Roosevelt's tenure in the White House left the public accustomed to dazzling presidential leadership. The dynamic modern presidency, in which the chief executive serves as the political representative of all the people, as the initiator of legislation, and as the defender of the interests of the inarticulate public is a legacy of the progressive years.

Taft Takes Over

Roosevelt made the White House a "bully pulpit," but his successor had no call to preach. An administrator by training and temperament, William Howard Taft had served Roosevelt loyally as secretary of war and all-purpose trouble-shooter. But Taft had no flair for politics, no aptitude for public relations, and not a fraction of Roosevelt's energy. Taft proposed to consolidate the progressive reforms his predecessor had

Theodore Roosevelt

Woodrow Wilson

CONTRASTING PRESIDENTIAL STYLES

William Howard Taft

made, to enforce effectively laws already on the books, to soothe where Roosevelt had ruffled. To a public grown accustomed to activity and change, however, mere administration seemed a static, boring substitute. Taft was consistent, while his constituency shifted; he even lost touch with Theodore Roosevelt, who had been his friend as well as his mentor. Taft's presidency turned into a prolonged political uproar that obscured an impartial consideration of what the President did.

Like Roosevelt, Taft knew that economic injustice accompanied industrial consolidation. Roosevelt had relied chiefly on administrative commissions to redress injustice, but Taft preferred to use courts and the Sherman Act, which he thought "a good law that ought to be enforced." In four years, his administration instituted twice as many antitrust proceedings as had Roosevelt in eight; in one of them, Taft asked that United States Steel be required to give up Tennessee Coal and Iron, in spite of Roosevelt's earlier assurance that the merger was legitimate. An annoyed Roosevelt responded that unregulated competition was as anachronistic as issuing flintlocks to the army. Yet the public continued to think of Roosevelt as a trust-buster and of his successor as a defender of the industrial status quo.

Nor did Taft receive much public credit for other progressive policies. The Mann-Elkins Act of 1910 complemented earlier railroad legislation and once more expanded the regulatory power of the ICC. The commission could initiate rate schedules without requiring a prior public complaint; once the rate was established, the carrier had to prove the schedule unfair. The new law, like the Hepburn Act, provided no method of impartially evaluating the railroad's capital investment, which had an immense effect on costs and therefore on rates. But the Physical Valuation Act, passed three days before Taft left office in 1913, remedied that defect. Although the President quietly encouraged Ohio, his own state, to ratify the constitutional amendment permitting a federal income tax, progressives remembered instead that he had publicly opposed a tax before there was an amendment. In 1912, when Congress sent to the states the amendment permitting direct election of senators, Taft kept a prudent silence that was promptly interpreted as hostility. He never found the middle of the political road; he alienated both progressives and their opponents, and in the process split his party.

It all began even before Taft was inaugurated. The rules of the House of Representatives permitted a Speaker to dictate the committees and nearly to shape the legislation as he chose. Joseph Cannon, usually called "Uncle Joe," a ruthless, cynical conservative from Illinois, used all the Speaker's powers. A group of Republican progressives led by George Norris of Nebraska proposed to strip the Speaker of some of his power when the new Congress opened after Taft's inauguration. Taft disliked Cannon and at first encouraged Norris's insurrection. But Roosevelt and Nelson Aldrich, who was Cannon's counterpart in the Senate, pointed out that the insurgents lacked the votes. If his administration opened with a disgruntled Speaker, Taft was told, his legislative program would be stillborn. Aldrich and Cannon promised the President their cooperation in his effort to reduce the tariff, and Taft publicly supported the Speaker's traditional powers. Two years later, when the question came up again, Taft once more backed Cannon. But this time Norris had enough support to change the rules. Cannon's defeat was also a defeat for the President.

Meanwhile, Taft had also lost the battle for a lower tariff. The Republican platform in 1908 had declared ambiguously for tariff reform, and the House reported a bill making significant reductions. But the Senate debate bogged down in questions about revenue and inheritance and income taxes. Conservatives carried most of those arguments, and the bill ultimately emerged with more than 800 amendments, almost all of which made it more satisfactory to the party's eastern industrial constituents. Although pressure from Taft improved the final Payne-Aldrich Tariff, it still outraged progressive Republicans of the Midwest. Taft's complacent remark that the law was "on the whole . . . the best tariff bill that the Republican party ever passed" did little to reconcile the insurgents.

Taft also alienated Theodore Roosevelt. Already uneasy about his successor when he retired to hunt African big game, Roosevelt came out of the bush in 1910 to find Gifford Pinchot bearing tales of Taft's betrayal. As chief forester, Pinchot had been one of Roosevelt's closest associates in the conservation effort, of which Roosevelt had been so proud. As President, he had removed land from public sale, created national forests and parks, encouraged irrigation, sponsored dams, and held off the economic interests that wanted to convert public resources to private profits. Pinchot charged that Taft, abetted by Richard A. Ballinger, his secretary of the interior, had given up the cause.

In fact, the Ballinger-Pinchot controversy was not so simple as Pinchot claimed, and neither Taft nor Ballinger was a conspiring foe of conservation. But Ballinger had made available for sale public lands that had been withdrawn in the Roosevelt administration, and Taft had dismissed Pinchot's protests. Pinchot then took his case to Congress and to the press. A congressional investigation whitewashed Ballinger, and Taft reluctantly fired Pinchot for insubordination, an action that neither Roosevelt nor conservationists forgave.

The Election of 1912

Only fifty when he retired and full of vigor, Roosevelt began to wonder whether Taft was, after all, the appropriate agent to carry out his policies. Robert LaFollette, whom Roosevelt had never liked, was planning a campaign to commit the Republican party to progressive principles and

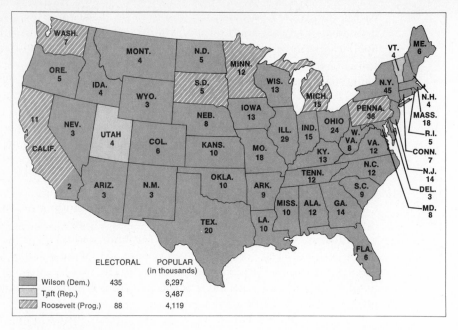

	ELECTORAL	POPULAR (in thousands)
Wilson (Dem.)	435	6,297
Taft (Rep.)	8	3,487
Roosevelt (Prog.)	88	4,119

THE ELECTION OF 1912

to wrest the presidential nomination from Taft. Other progressives hesitated, hoping Roosevelt would lead the crusade. Roosevelt began speaking on political subjects in the summer of 1910, and what he said differed profoundly from what Taft had come to stand for. Progressives united behind Roosevelt when LaFollette's health seemed to break in the midst of his exhausting campaign.

But as no one knew better than Roosevelt, an incumbent President could keep a firm grip on his party. Taft controlled the Republican convention, received the nomination, gave his acceptance speech, and lapsed into almost complete inactivity for the rest of the campaign. To the strains of "Onward Christian Soldiers," Roosevelt's followers founded the Progressive party and made the Republican schism official. Roosevelt gave the new party a symbol with the remark that he was "strong as a Bull Moose." He began with characteristic élan to carry his New Nationalism to the country.

The "New Nationalism" was only a new slogan to describe what Roosevelt had been saying for some time. Industrial regulation, which Roosevelt had advocated as President, was at the heart of the Progressive economic program, an emphasis that pleased George W. Perkins, the Morgan associate and industrialist who financed the campaign. The platform also revealed a new concern for the victims of industrial growth in a series of planks that demonstrated the mounting influence of social workers and other professional advocates of social justice. The Bull Moosers promised new legislation to reduce the hazards of factories, to end child labor, to establish minimum wages for women and workman's compensation. Under Roosevelt's direction, the federal government would improve the quality of rural life, maintain the health of all citizens, and preserve the beauty and the resources of the nation.

The Republican split cheered the Democrats, who had lost four consecutive presidential elections. In 1912 the party took forty-six ballots to find the candidate, but, in selecting Woodrow Wilson, Democrats chose well. A southerner by birth and upbringing, a northerner by education, an educator by trade, an upright Calvinist by conviction, conservative on economic matters but acceptable to Bryan and Democratic progressives, Wilson had impressive credentials. What he lacked was political experience, personal warmth, and the capacity to see the point of view of anyone else. In 1910 Woodrow Wilson had resigned from the presidency of Princeton University to run for governor of New Jersey. As governor, he survived a widely approved fight with the bosses of his party and convinced the legislature to enact controls on railroads and utilities, to institute workman's compensation, and to adopt the direct primary. In 1912 his New Freedom was the major alternative to Roosevelt's New Nationalism.

On inspection, the New Freedom looked quite like the old laissez faire. Roosevelt dismissed Wilson's program as "rural Toryism." Wilson responded that Roosevelt's notion of regulating business would end with business in control of government instead of the reverse. Only competition, secured through enforcement of the antitrust laws, Wilson argued, would preserve economic democracy. He branded Progressive demands for more government as paternalistic assaults on personal freedom. Not government but the self-reliant individual, Wilson held, created social justice.

The election of 1912 justified change, although precisely what kind of change was not clear. Taft, the most conservative man in the field, won about 3.5 million votes and carried just two states. Nearly a million voters thought progressives inadequate and voted for the Socialist candidate, Eugene V. Debs. Roosevelt won over 4 million votes and the electoral votes of six states. Woodrow Wilson won the rest—over 6 million popular votes, a landslide victory in the electoral college, and a solidly Democratic Congress.

Wilson's First Term

Like Wilson himself, many of those Democratic congressmen went to Washington because the opposition had divided. Dozens of the legislators were new to Congress, and the party's congressional leadership had little experience directing a majority. The President filled the void. He was as active a President as Roosevelt had been and more of a legislative leader.

He declared himself the people's lobbyist, and for the first time since John Adams, a President went to Congress to deliver his message in person.

He asked for a new tariff and a new banking system. In response the House produced the Underwood Bill, which lowered the general tariff level, ended protection of many items altogether, and added a small income tax to replace lost revenue. But tariff reform had come from the House before, only to die in the Senate. This time Wilson cajoled, pleaded, and invoked public support, and the Senate actually lowered the Underwood Tariff still further and raised the tax rate on larger incomes. Wilson finally signed the bill late in 1913; he had undertaken what Roosevelt had refused to undertake and succeeded where Taft and Cleveland had failed.

The panic in 1907 had shown the need for banking reform. The existing system was not sufficiently responsive to the demand for more currency and could not meet credit requirements in an expanding economy. In addition, a few Wall Street banks held the reserves of too many of the nation's smaller banks; these funds gave New York institutions great power and transmitted any tremor in the city's banking business to the rest of the country. The panic in 1907, for instance, began with a run on New York's Knickerbocker Trust.

Shortly after this panic, a commission headed by Senator Aldrich and a House committee whose chairman was Louisiana Democrat Arsène P. Pujo began investigating banking reform. The Aldrich Commission recommended establishment of a new, privately managed central bank not too different from that of Alexander Hamilton or Nicholas Biddle. The Pujo report revealed that financial power was too concentrated on Wall Street and recommended legislation to prevent further consolidation through interlocking directorates or the direct control by banks of insurance companies and industrial concerns.

The party of Andrew Jackson could not reestablish Biddle's bank, although the banking system did remain in private hands as the Aldrich Commission had recommended. The Federal Reserve Act created twelve regional Federal Reserve banks, owned by the private banks of the district. To ensure stability, private banks had to keep a percentage of their assets on deposit in the Federal Reserve. The Federal Reserve banks issued legal-tender notes, which were an obligation of the United States government but were secured partly by gold and partly by the short-term commercial and agricultural loans made by member banks. This arrangement permitted expansion of the currency as the demand for credit increased, and the regional division permitted response to local conditions. Although regional banks, especially the one in New York, continued until the 1930s to shape monetary policy, the Federal Reserve Board, appointed by the President, provided the opportunity for central direction and control. The rediscount rate—the charge made by the Federal Reserve for exchanging currency for the secured paper of member banks—was expected to help control fluctuations in the business cycle. In addition, the Federal Reserve could expand the supply of currency quickly by buying large quantities of federal bonds with Federal Reserve notes or take currency out of circulation by selling bonds and withholding the currency used to purchase them.

When the Federal Reserve Act passed in December 1913, Woodrow Wilson thought his presidential mission virtually complete, for neither the New Freedom nor its author had set the government the task of securing social justice. Wilson refused in 1914 to support a child-labor bill and opposed measures to ease agricultural credit and to eliminate the injunction in strikes, because such bills were "class legislation." He did sign the LaFollette Seaman's Act in 1915, which greatly improved working conditions for merchant sailors, but the administration merely accepted, rather than supported, the measure.

Wilson did not even have much interest in the "trusts," to which he had devoted so much campaign oratory in 1912. The administration lost enthusiasm for the Clayton Antitrust Act before it passed in 1914. The bill had been intended to strengthen the Sherman Act and at the same time exempt labor unions from antitrust prosecution. But the compromise that finally passed effectively did neither, even though Samuel Gompers chose to pretend that labor had won a political victory. The Wilson administration instituted even fewer antitrust suits than did the subsequent administrations of Presidents Harding and Coolidge, neither of whom was known as a trust-buster.

Instead, Wilson turned, as Roosevelt had, to regulation. Congress replaced Roosevelt's Bureau of Corporations with the Federal Trade Commission (FTC) in 1914. The FTC was empowered to investigate corporations and to issue "cease and desist" orders to prevent unfair competitive practices. Wilson appointed conservatives to the FTC (as he did to the Federal Reserve Board), and through consultation with concerned businessmen the commission helped provide efficiency and, in some cases, less competition among entrepreneurs. The FTC resembled the New Nationalism rather more than the New Freedom.

As the election of 1916 approached, Wilson borrowed several other items from Roosevelt's platform and appealed to former Progressives with an extraordinary year of legislative activity. In 1916, for the first time, Wilson responded to the movement for social justice. He signed the Keating-Owen Act, which outlawed interstate shipment of goods produced by children. In 1919, after the Court, in *Hammer* v. *Dagenhart*, had declared the Keating-Owen Act unconstitutional, Wilson signed another law that attempted to prevent child labor with a confiscatory tax, which the Court in turn struck down after Wilson left office. The Workman's Compensation Act (1916), for the first time insured federal employees against some of the hazards of accidents. Under the threat of a nationwide strike, Congress required the railroads to maintain wages, though the working day of employees was reduced from ten hours to eight by the Adamson Act. The President also pleased reformers by appointing Louis D. Brandeis to the Supreme Court and by withstanding the wave of conservative criticism that greeted the appointment.

Democrats also had to pacify farmers in 1916, particularly Bryan's followers, who thought the Federal Reserve Act had done them less than full justice. The Smith-Lever Act (1914) had furnished funds to provide county agents to advise farmers on new agricultural techniques. In 1916 two acts made agricultural credit more readily available. The Warehouse Act was the old Populist subtreasury scheme under another name; it permitted farmers to use deposited crops as collateral for loans. The Farm Loan Act used federal funds as initial capital for twelve regional banks that were to finance farm mortgages at reasonable rates.

Wilson's record was remarkable, and just barely good enough. He attracted some of Roosevelt's following when the Rough Rider's consuming interest in the European war led him to abandon the Progressive party. Roosevelt suggested that it nominate Henry Cabot Lodge, the thoroughly traditional senator from Massachusetts. Instead, the Progressive party collapsed. Republicans nominated Charles Evans Hughes, an associate justice of the Supreme Court who had been an able, progressive governor of New York. The raging European war haunted the campaign, and by linking the moderate Hughes with the bellicose Roosevelt, Wilson appealed to the electorate's overwhelming desire for continued neutrality. Narrow margins in Minnesota and California provided the President's small majority in the electoral college; his edge in the popular vote was about 600,000 ballots. As his first term closed, Wilson had selected well from progressive proposals for social justice; in his second term, the effort to create a better society at home yielded to an attempt to make the world safe for democracy.

Progressivism in Retrospect

Progressives did not achieve either democracy abroad or social justice at home. They did make the domestic political process more democratic, and they curbed some of the worst excesses of selfish interests. They also left economic power largely undisturbed and perhaps even accelerated consolidation. And they clung so closely to traditional American values that they rejected out-of-hand those who suggested that self-reliance, for instance, might be a self-serving doctrine of the "haves" in an industrial society, and not an eternal truth.

Lawrence, Massachusetts, in 1912 was a community in need of social justice. Most of Lawrence's nearly 90,000 inhabitants were immigrants or the children of immigrants; 30,000 of them worked in the mills of the city, and fully two-thirds of the population was directly dependent on the textile industry. The average weekly wage of a textile worker in 1912 was $8.76, an amount that the commissioner of labor declared "entirely inadequate to sustain a family." An hour's labor bought a pound of hamburger or perhaps four eggs in the city's grocery stores. The census showed that on the average seven people lived in four or five rooms in Lawrence's tenements, and many families took in boarders to help pay the three-dollar weekly rent.

Under progressive pressure, the Massachusetts legislature reduced the standard industrial work week from fifty-six hours to fifty-four. But to the surprise of progressives, when the new law took effect, Lawrence's textile workers walked out spontaneously. Although less than 10 percent of the employees belonged to unions, workers of a dozen nationalities maintained a united front for two months. Police and inexperienced militiamen patrolled the city as social tension mounted and fear became almost tangible. The Industrial Workers of the World, a radical organization whose goal was the end of capitalism, heightened fear by taking over the strike and threatening to take over the mills and perhaps take the city apart. Management eventually met almost every one of the strikers' demands, including a three-cent-an-hour increase and a bonus for overtime.

The strike in Lawrence shows progressivism in a harsh light. The reformers who legislated a reduction in hours did not believe the state had the constitutional authority to require that wages be maintained. So two hours less work brought two hours less pay, which the textile workers of Lawrence needed more than leisure. Many progressives did not know the people for whom they thought they were acting any better than the Lawrence city missionary, a Protestant who lived in a plush suburb, knew the thousands of Catholic immigrants he was supposed to serve; his reaction to social conditions in Lawrence was surprise at how well the poor managed. Progressives were sympathetic and well intentioned, but the world of the immigrant industrial worker was simply not a world they knew.

And when the people progressives wanted to help tried to help themselves or rejected ready-made programs, the sympathy of progressives grew strained. They did not much like strikes and labor unions, for instance, or neighborhoods with strange music, foreign food, and strong drink, or bloc voting for Catholics, or any suggestion of socialism. Real unity among working people in Lawrence frightened the progressives of Massachusetts more than all the corporate capital in the East. Progressives did not want to redistribute wealth except among nice, middle-class people; they wanted to lift the worthy poor into the middle class. When working people had reservations about temperance, or remained loyal to a political boss, or when they were tainted with economic radicalism, affronted progressives, as is the American way, advocated laws to curb such obstinacy. Disillusioned prewar progressives often turned into staid supporters of the postwar status quo.

Suggested Reading

John M. Blum has written two outstanding, brief, interpretive studies of progressive Presidents: *The Republican Roosevelt** (1954) and *Woodrow Wilson and the Politics of Morality** (1956). Elting E. Morison has edited eight volumes of the *Letters of Theodore Roosevelt* (1951—54); Arthur S. Link is the chief editor of a similar project to publish the Wilson papers on a more extensive scale. Link has also written five volumes of biography of Wilson (1947—65). Paolo E. Coletta's *The Presidency of William Howard Taft* (1973) confirms much of the account in Henry F. Pringle's *The Life and Times of William Howard Taft* (1939). David P. Thelen's *Robert M. LaFollette and the Insurgent Spirit** (1976) is another relevant biography.

Two complementary surveys of the progressive years are those of George E. Mowry, *The Era of Theodore Roosevelt** (1958) and Arthur S. Link, *Woodrow Wilson and the Progressive Era** (1954). Accounts of William L. O'Neill, *The Progressive Years** (1975), and Otis L. Graham, *The Great Campaigns** (1971), are briefer. Influential interpretations of the period include Richard Hofstadter, *The Age of Reform** (1955), Gabriel Kolko, *The Triumph of Conservatism** (1963), Robert H. Wiebe, *Businessmen and Reform** (1962), David P. Thelen, *The New Citizenship* (1972), and John D. Buenker, *Urban Liberalism and Progressive Reform** (1978).

Samuel P. Hays's *Conservation and the Gospel of Efficiency** (1959) illuminates many aspects of progressivism, as does Aileen S. Kraditor's *The Ideas of the Woman Suffrage Movement** (1965). Eleanor Flexner's *Century of Struggle** (1959) and William L. O'Neill's *Divorce in the Progressive Era** (1967) are two other works pertaining to women. Henry F. May's *The End of American Innocence** (1959) re-creates the intellectual climate of the period.

* Available in paperback edition

Chapter 17
The Great War and the Lost Peace

Progressives conducted foreign policy with the same moral assurance that distinguished their assault on domestic social ills. "When properly directed," Woodrow Wilson once remarked, revealing the condescension, the self-righteousness, and the optimism of progressives, "there is no people not fitted for self-government." In promoting self-government and other worthy goals, the United States used diplomatic leverage and sometimes military force. Public discussion of these policies ordinarily stressed moral principle, though critics, then and later, noted that American leaders tended to find principles that coincided with the country's economic and strategic interests. It was principle, nevertheless, nobly enunciated by Woodrow Wilson, that justified the lives and money Americans poured into the Great War; principles Americans espoused, Wilson said, would sustain a lasting peace thereafter. To be sure, Wilson promised the American people too much, for their faith in liberal institutions was not held worldwide. Disappointed Americans themselves then wearied of their effort to make the world better.

The progressive impulse would revive, but much that the Great War destroyed would not: dynasties, capital accumulated in the sweat of generations, a complacent faith in human progress, the conviction that civilization centered in Western Europe, and millions of lives. The First World War reduced Europe's economic and military edge over the rest of the world, sapped the vitality of Western democratic institutions, and snuffed out Russia's brief experiment with democracy. The war brought disillusionment that paralyzed postwar reform, economic instability that precipitated a worldwide depression, and political upheaval that resulted in modern totalitarianism in Germany and the Soviet Union. And the unsatisfactory peace made inevitable a rematch in the Second World War.

Europe's War

Europe was ready for war before it came. Two alliance systems— Germany and Austria-Hungary arrayed against England, France, and Russia—ensured that no conflict would long remain local. Opportunities to fight multiplied in the decade before 1914: Germany's drive for naval parity threatened England; British and French efforts to thwart German expansion annoyed Germany; Russia and Austria quarreled about the Balkans; every power watched for territorial opportunity in the decaying Turkish empire; trading concessions anywhere stirred jealousies throughout the continent.

In the end, an assassination that grew out of Balkan rivalries sparked the explosion. Serbian nationalists killed the heir to the Austrian throne. An Austrian ultimatum demanded concessions Serbia thought humiliating. When the Czar backed the Serbs and the Kaiser backed the Austrians, the great powers could not halt the fatal progression. Russia ordered mobilization. In response, Germany invaded France to eliminate Russia's western ally. The campaign against France began with Germany's occupation of Belgium, whose neutrality Britain had guaranteed for nearly a century. So, in August 1914, most of Europe found itself at war.

It was supposed to be brief and glorious. Few foresaw the way trenches, barbed wire, tanks, and machine guns would keep the world's most powerful armies penned in a small patch of French real estate for four bloody years. There was more motion on the Eastern Front, but the same monotonous human harvest. The war quickly became a sour stalemate from which no belligerent could retire.

Americans took sides in the struggle, even though Woodrow Wilson's initial proclamation of neutrality had asked for absolute impartiality "in thought as well as in action." Some took sides because of sentimental or family ties with the "old country"; Irish Americans, for instance, favored the Central Powers because any enemy of England was a friend of Ireland. Allied propagandists portrayed Britain and France as the defenders of humanity and civilization against German atrocities. Economic interest probably convinced some industrialists, investors, and bankers that virtue, as well as profit, was on the Allied side. Woodrow Wilson had long admired British scholarship and British parliamentary government; he personified the cultural link among English-speaking peoples. Members of the diplomatic corps understood that American security rested in large part on the British fleet. As a result, the United States had a strategic interest in maintaining the European balance of power that Germany intended to upset. In addition, the State Department had a tacit understanding with Great Britain that had grown since the Spanish-American War. German policies, on the other hand, had irritated American diplomats in discussions about Samoa, the Philippines, the Monroe Doctrine, and tariff reductions.

Whatever their prejudices and whatever their ethnic heritage, Americans vehemently opposed participation in Europe's war. They did not know that their defense budget had become one of the largest in the world, a fact that complicated neutrality by rousing the interest of every belligerent. They did not understand that submarines required a redefinition of the traditional rights of neutral nations. When they finally went to war, the American people naively assumed that their allies shared the aims and beliefs of progressive Americans: legal procedure, orderly progress, social justice, human decency. No nation ever went to war with more honorable intent; no nation ever believed it made peace more selflessly. The errors were well intentioned, but they were errors nonetheless.

America's Attempt to Stay Out

As signs of a coming conflict multiplied during the decade before the war, all the powers made gestures to strengthen the fabric of international peace. Theodore Roosevelt helped end the Russo-Japanese War in 1905 and used diplomatic pressure in 1906 to bring Germany and France to a conference at Algeciras where they resolved their conflict over Algeria. With Secretary of State Elihu Root, Roosevelt supported international conferences at The Hague, which attempted to codify neutral rights and to devise automatic procedures for referring dangerous disputes to impartial settlement. Root himself negotiated twenty-four bilateral treaties, with every major power except Russia and Germany, that referred legal disputes to arbitration.

William Jennings Bryan thought the effort insufficient. "I believe that this nation could stand before the world today," Bryan proclaimed in 1910, and declare "that it did not believe in war, . . . that it had no disputes that it was not willing to submit to the judgment of the world." Three years later, as Wilson's secretary of state, Bryan began to commit the country to that creed. He negotiated Treaties for the Advancement of Peace with thirty nations. These agreements automatically referred disputes to an investigatory commission. To permit a thorough investigation, neither party would increase armaments or resort to war for a period of twelve months. The treaties would, Bryan said, "provide a time for passion to subside, for reason to regain its throne."

In August 1914 no "cooling-off period" permitted reason to subdue passion, and Europe went to war. The initial public reaction in the United States was surprise, then panic, then a surge of Allied sympathy, and finally a fervent belief that neutrality best served American interests. Surprise came from a decade of false alarms and a rather general belief that humanity had outgrown tantrums. Panic pervaded the financial centers, for 1914 was already a bad year, and the war threatened to interrupt international commerce. Without shipping, American goods could not reach foreign markets; without imports and the duties on them, the government lost about 40 percent of its revenue in 1914 and 1915. Trade and tradition sustained sympathy for the Allies, which the German chancellor reinforced with his tactless dismissal of a broken treaty as a mere "scrap of paper." Yet neutrality was not only the safest initial policy but the most practical one as well, for the United States was not ready to dedicate its military capacity to a more resolute alternative.

Neutrality might have served in a short war. But as the war dragged on, the strategic needs of the belligerents and the economic interests of the United States combined to require constant diplomatic discussion. Traditionally, neutrals might sell, but not deliver, military equipment to belligerents; neutrals could use the sea only for commerce that did not directly contribute to the war machine of a belligerent; neutral citizens and ships had the right to a warning before attack, to legal process before confiscation, and to rescue if a vessel provoked hostility.

In practice, belligerents, not traditions, determine the rights of neutrals. A neutral nation has no appeal, short of abandoning neutrality altogether. Diplomatic initiative, then, lay in London and Berlin; Washington simply reacted. When Woodrow Wilson asked Congress to declare war in April 1917, the responsibility for the decision rested as directly on the German Kaiser and his government as it did on the President and his cabinet.

Sinkings Bring War

For more than two years before 1917, German strategists and diplomats had argued with one another and with Americans about the use of the submarine. Submarines simply could not abide by traditional rules for belligerent behavior. U-boats were too fragile to risk warning even lightly armed merchantmen and were too small to rescue survivors. Submarines could not establish blockades as surface vessels did. To be effective, undersea craft had to rely on stealth, which violated what Americans believed were their neutral rights.

Yet Germans, with considerable justification, argued that the American interpretation of neutral rights favored Great Britain. The British blockade effectively kept American goods from German markets, while the German effort to keep goods from Britain generated outraged protest in the United States. Germany charged that the British had violated American rights by confiscating products not previously defined as contraband and by interdicting the sale of food.

As the conflict became a war of attrition, Britain tightened the blockade and mined the North Sea. Neutrals could secure passage through the minefields only by opening cargoes to British inspection. British officials also examined American mail to trace German-American trade. The British government published a blacklist of American companies doing business with Germany; to boycott these firms became an Englishman's patriotic duty. This blacklist was a tactless mistake, but Britain made few others in probing the limits of American toleration. When the cabinet prohibited the shipment of cotton to Germany, for instance, Britain offered to buy the entire American crop, if necessary, to sustain the price and to retain the good will of southern members of Congress.

Eventually, Germany's dilemma was reduced to its simplest form: submarine warfare would bring American intervention. The German government decided to run the risk. In February 1915 Germany declared that submarines would sink, without warning, vessels in the waters surrounding the British Isles. The State Department protested this abridgement of American rights for which Germany would be held to "strict accountability." In April one American was killed when a British vessel went down; on May 1 an American tanker was torpedoed. That same day the German embassy placed advertisements in New York papers advising Americans of the risk of travel on belligerent vessels. American passengers boarding the British liner *Lusitania* received telegrams and subsequent oral warning of the dangers of travel in the war zone. On May 7, eighteen minutes after a torpedo had crashed into the *Lusitania*, she went to the bottom of the Irish Sea, taking 4,500 cases of ammunition and nearly 1,200 people with her, 124 of whom were Americans. It was a deed, the *Nation* charged, "for which a Hun would blush, a Turk be ashamed, and a Barbary pirate apologize." A people that condoned such warfare had become "wild beasts against whom society has to defend itself at all hazards."

Shock, horror, anger, and incredulity—these were the popular responses to the tragedy. But in spite of the first moments of rage, the demand for a revenging war never came. "We must," one Baptist editor wrote, "protect our citizens, but we must find some other way than war." Secretary Bryan thought Wilson asked Germany to concede too much and resigned rather than sign a protest he thought too forceful. James W. Gerard, the American Ambassador to Berlin, wondered whether American tourists might not as conveniently sail on neutral ships to avoid diplomatic complications.

Wilson pressed Congress to kill a resolution forbidding Americans to use belligerent ships, for he and Robert Lansing, who succeeded Bryan,

NOTICE!

TRAVELLERS intending to embark on the Atlantic voyage are reminded that a state of war exists between Germany and her allies and Great Britain and her allies; that the zone of war includes the waters adjacent to the British Isles; that, in accordance with formal notice given by the Imperial German Government, vessels flying the flag of Great Britain, or of any of her allies, are liable to destruction in those waters and that travellers sailing in the war zone on ships of Great Britain or her allies do so at their own risk.

IMPERIAL GERMAN EMBASSY

WASHINGTON, D. C., APRIL 22, 1915.

REMEMBER THE
LUSITANIA

THE JURY'S VERDICT SAYS:

"We find that the said deceased died from their prolonged immersion and exhaustion in the sea eight miles south south-west of the Old Head of Kinsale on Friday, May 7th, 1915, owing to the sinking of the R.M.S. Lusitania by a torpedo fired without warning from a German submarine.

"That this appalling crime was contrary to international law and the conventions of all civilized nations, and we therefore charge the officers of the said submarine, the Emperor and Government of Germany, under whose orders they acted, with the crime of wilful and wholesale murder before the tribunal of the civilized world"

IT IS YOUR DUTY TO TAKE UP THE SWORD OF JUSTICE TO AVENGE THIS DEVIL'S WORK.

ENLIST TO-DAY

"All the News That's Fit to Print."

The New York Times.

EXTRA
5:30 A. M.

VOL. LXIV...NO. 20,923.   NEW YORK, SATURDAY, MAY 8, 1915.—TWENTY-FOUR PAGES.   ONE CENT In Greater New York, Jersey City and Newark. | Elsewhere THREE CENTS

LUSITANIA SUNK BY A SUBMARINE, PROBABLY 1,260 DEAD;
TWICE TORPEDOED OFF IRISH COAST; SINKS IN 15 MINUTES;
CAPT. TURNER SAVED, FROHMAN AND VANDERBILT MISSING;
WASHINGTON BELIEVES THAT A GRAVE CRISIS IS AT HAND

SHOCKS THE PRESIDENT

Washington Deeply Stirred by the Loss of American Lives.

BULLETINS AT WHITE HOUSE

Wilson Reads Them Closely, but Is Silent on the Nation's Course.

HINTS OF CONGRESS CALL

Loss of Lusitania Recalls Firm Tone of Our First Warning to Germany.

CAPITAL FULL OF RUMORS

Reports That Liner Was to Be Sunk Were Heard Before Actual News Came.

Special to The New York Times.
WASHINGTON, May 7.— Never since that April day, three years ago, when word came that the Titanic had gone down, has Washington been so stirred as it is to-night over the sinking of the Lusitania. The early reports told that there had been no loss of life, but the relief that those affa tives caused gave way to consternation when the news reached the capital that the loss of American lives is likely to bring about a crisis in the international relations

The Lost Cunard Steamship Lusitania
X Where the First Torpedo Struck.   XX Where the Second Torpedo Struck.

SOME DEAD TAKEN ASHORE

Several Hundred Survivors at Queenstown and Kinsale.

STEWARD TELLS OF DISASTER

One Torpedo Crashes Into the Doomed Liner's Bow, Another Into the Engine Room.

SHIP LISTS OVER TO PORT

Makes It Impossible to Lower Many Boats, So Hundreds Must Have Gone Down.

ATTACKED IN BROAD DAY

Passengers at Luncheon—Warning Had Been Given by Germans Before the Ship Left New York.

Only 650 Were Saved, Few Cabin Passengers

QUEENSTOWN, Saturday, May 8, 4:28 A.M.— Survivors of the Lusitania who have arrived here estimate that only about 650 of those aboard the steamer were saved, and say only a small proportion of those rescued were saloon passengers.

Cunard Office Here Besieged for News; Fate of 1,918 on Lusitania Long in Doubt

List of Saved Includes Capt. Turner; Vanderbilt and Frohman Reported Lost

Saw the Submarine 100 Yards Off and Watched Torpedo as It Struck Ship

were determined to secure the full measure of neutral rights. Germany met most of Washington's demands with an apology, an indemnity, and secret instructions to submarine commanders not to attack passenger liners. In spite of this order, the British liner *Arabic* was torpedoed in August, and two American passengers died. Under diplomatic pressure from Wilson, Germany publicly promised not to sink unresisting passenger ships. In May 1916, after a torpedo crippled the French steamer *Sussex*, endangering the twenty-five Americans aboard, Wilson prodded the German government to a promise to warn merchant vessels before attack. The condition of this "*Sussex* pledge" was that the United States require Great Britain to be equally scrupulous in observing the rights of neutrals. Wilson accepted the pledge, ignored the condition, and secured a lull of several months without submarine incidents. Although the Kaiser reversed himself early in 1917, Wilson had temporarily deprived Germany of the full use of a major weapon.

Wilson's persistence in holding Germany to his interpretation of international law contrasted with his forbearance in the face of Britain's failure to observe neutral rights. Historians have blamed one-sided economic commitment, British propaganda, and the Anglophile sentiment of the President and his advisers for this apparent favoritism. In fact, trade did flow predominantly to the Allies; trade and loans to the Central Powers between 1914 and 1917 totaled less than $250 million, while the Allies received more than $10 billion in credit alone. British propaganda may have increased the enthusiasm of those who favored the Allies. Woodrow Wilson did indeed prefer the Allied side, and his administration, especially Secretary Lansing and Walter Hines Page, the ambassador to England, were hardly neutral "in thought"; Lansing believed that German domination of Europe would be a diplomatic disaster for the United States.

But Wilson's Anglophilia did not entirely determine his policy, for the negotiated "peace without victory" he hoped to secure would not have fulfilled Britain's ambitions. Moreover, Wilson did keep his nation neutral until Germany knowingly provoked intervention. Since there never was a possibility that the United States would ally with the Central Powers, Wilson's brand of neutrality was the best Germany could hope for and about as impartial a posture as the United States could assume.

Wilson attempted to keep each successive crisis from tugging his country into war, and he simultaneously launched a long-term effort to end hostilities and thereby prevent American intervention. Colonel Edward M. House, Wilson's closest adviser on foreign affairs, spent much of 1915 seeking a formula for mediation. In 1916, House and British Foreign Secretary Sir Edward Grey initialed a memorandum stating that the United States would "probably" join the Allies if Germany spurned an international peace conference, but no belligerent was ready for the balanced compromise Wilson had in mind. Germany subsequently offered peace in return for annexations along the Baltic, domination of

Poland, cessions from France and Belgium, and reparations—conditions that were entirely unacceptable to the Allies. Undaunted, Wilson tried once more to find an area of agreement to start negotiations. But at the end of January 1917, Germany renounced any restrictions on submarine warfare. Wilson's peace efforts were obviously finished, his mediation firmly rejected. The official declaration of war came in April.

Mobilization and War

The United States had learned remarkably little from the war that had raged in Europe for two years. That war clearly demanded mobilization of the whole nation, efficient use of industrial resources, psychological preparation for trench warfare, and new equipment—airplanes, gas masks, radios, tanks. Yet no fact better indicates the nation's neutrality than its lack of preparation. When informed in 1916 that the army had begun to plan for American participation, President Wilson curtly told Secretary of War Newton D. Baker, "I think you had better stop it." Partly in consequence, a month after the American declaration of war the army still had no plan for moving American units to France and no strategic concept of what to do with them when they got there.

The Army Reorganization Act of 1916 authorized a larger National Guard and a gradual increase to 200,000 men for the regular army; a year later, the army needed 200,000 *officers*, and had only about 9,000 in uniform. In 1916 the Signal Corps possessed precisely two radios and the Infantry 285,000 rifles; the army's chief of staff was an authority on the languages of American Indians. Three weeks after the declaration in 1917 only 32,000 men had enlisted, a number far short of the million the administration wanted. Wilson had decided to rely on conscription even before the first apathetic response to his call for volunteers. After the Selective Service Act passed in May, more than twenty-four million men registered, of whom about three million eventually served with nearly two million others who volunteered. Before the Armistice, more than two million Americans had landed in France.

Secretary Baker, General John J. Pershing, and General Peyton C. March successfully improvised in the absence of advance planning. Pershing, commander of the American Expeditionary Force, went to France in 1917 without strategic guidance, tactical plans, or soldiers. He insisted on intensive training of American troops before committing them to battle and on adequate numbers before replacing embattled Allied organizations with American units. His estimate of the importance of training was correct, as was his decision to hold Americans out of major engagements until he had enough force to make a significant impact, for drooping morale in some Allied battalions might have infected American replacements.

American troops in the Argonne

Early in 1918, Pershing's growing forces met the enemy in the spring campaigns north of Paris. By late in the summer, more than 250,000 Americans were engaged in an Allied counteroffensive that eliminated a threatening German salient along the Marne River. In September, Pershing took over the southern sector of the front near Verdun and began the first independent American operation of the war with an offensive in the Argonne Forest and along the Meuse River. The month-long battle caused more than 100,000 American casualties, but forced the Germans to retreat and contributed significantly to their decision to seek an armistice in November. On November 11, 1918, when the Armistice was signed, the American army had occupied its own sector for just sixty days. The American contribution to victory on the Western Front was significant, but brief.

The United States Navy, in conjunction with the British fleet, whipped the submarine menace and deposited American troops in Europe without the loss of a single doughboy. The U-boat failed in part because of the addition of American vessels to those already hunting undersea craft. Probably more important than additional ships was the convoy system that Admiral William S. Sims persuaded the British Admiralty to try. Military escorts, Sims correctly maintained, could protect merchant

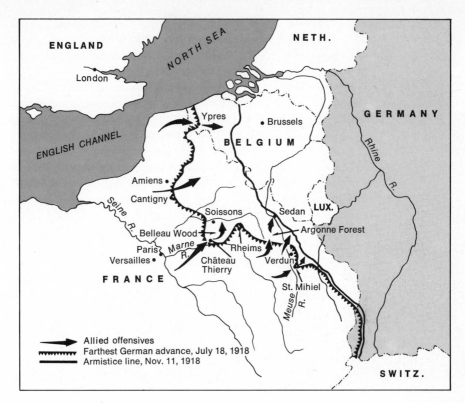

ALLIED OPERATIONS ON THE WESTERN FRONT, 1918

vessels from marauding submarines. The convoys ensured the almost uninterrupted arrival of American troops and supplies and proved the folly of Germany's expectation that submarines could win the war.

Along with the military success in France there was a triumph of organization at home. Domestic mobilization, like victory abroad, came at considerable cost and only after trial-and-error experimentation. The army's procurement system, unable to adjust leisurely habits to frantic times, bogged down in red tape. American quartermasters had no helmets; consequently British steel shielded American heads. Less than 500 of 3,500 artillery pieces in American batteries in France came from American arsenals; of the nearly nine million shells those guns fired, about 8,400 were made in the United States. The American Expeditionary Force received seven million tons of supplies from home, and purchased ten million tons in Europe, a statistic that suggests the Allies had not reached the last ditch when the United States entered the war.

Although the Armistice came before America had completed industrial mobilization, the process was well begun by 1918. The Lever Act of 1917 created federal agencies to raise production and control distribution of food and fuel. Under the direction of Harry Garfield, the son of the assassinated President, the Fuel Administration increased coal and oil supplies and incidentally encouraged the consolidation in both industries that inhibited postwar competition. The Food Administration, given imaginative leadership by Herbert Hoover, encouraged cultivation of "Victory Gardens" to give civilians a sense of patriotic participation. (President Wilson even grazed a few sheep on the White House lawn.) Hoover secured voluntary observance of wheatless Mondays and meatless Tuesdays to conserve staples. The Food Administration guaranteed the price of wheat, thereby bringing into production thousands of marginal acres that later produced unsaleable surpluses.

Industrial mobilization demanded more than voluntary measures. Late in 1917, when the nation's railroads proved unable to cope with the tremendously increased volume of freight, Wilson ordered Secretary of the Treasury William G. McAdoo to run them. Three months later Congress passed the Railroad Control Act, which authorized federal management and fixed the compensation stockholders would receive. A National War Labor Board, approved by Samuel Gompers, recognized labor's right to bargain collectively but denied the right to strike in wartime. To organize American industry, Wilson turned to a successful Wall Street operator named Bernard Baruch. Wilson delegated to Baruch's War Industries Board the extraordinary regulatory authority that Congress conferred on the President in the Overman Act of 1918. Baruch streamlined the American economy, allocated strategic materials without waste, and in the long run, reduced competition in the interest of industrial efficiency.

If the war brought regulation beyond the dreams of progressives, the contact between business and government was, on the whole, friendly. Wartime collaboration served the public interest in a way that close ties between government and business in the following decade did not, for business tended then to become the dominant partner. The war also served private interests; corporate profits tripled between 1913 and 1917, and wartime taxes did not absorb the entire increase. Steel companies, in particular, received large military orders and earned large profits. Copper producers, bankers, and, though farm prices broke soon after the war, commercial farmers also prospered. The wages of industrial workers came close to matching wartime inflation, while the purchasing power of salaried workers dropped, perhaps by a fifth. Although statistics on the distribution of income and the concentration of wealth are imprecise, the war to advance democracy abroad appears not to have enhanced economic democracy at home.

Democracy at Home

The war also brought restrictions on personal liberty. The President's warning of June 1917 was stern: "Woe to the man or group of men that seeks to stand in our way in this day of high resolution." War, as Wilson remarked on another occasion, demanded "force to the utmost, force without stint or limit." The steamroller state, with Wilson at the controls, flattened the radical, the pacifist, or the nonconformist with the same inexorable discipline and determination that General Pershing displayed in France. Unless critics were of the stature of Theodore Roosevelt, whose criticism of Wilson was shrill and unchecked, they ran afoul of the Espionage Act of 1917 and the Sedition Amendment to that act, passed a year later. State statutes also promoted loyalty, and various unofficial agencies enforced their own brand of patriotic conformity.

The federal legislation outlawed disrespectful language about the flag, the government, or the armed forces, and prohibited speech or action that interfered with the conduct of the war, conscription, or the sale of bonds. Congressional sponsors promised that these provisions would not stifle legitimate criticism, but even so enthusiastic a war hawk as Henry Cabot Lodge thought the Espionage Act unnecessary. Lodge pointed out that the statute would not trap "a single spy or a single German agent," but rather was "aimed at certain classes of [domestic] agitators." He voted against the bill, which soon became the basis for the attorney general's boast that "never in its history has this country been so thoroughly policed."

Public pressure put an end to the performance of German music, instruction in the German language, and the careers of a few people with Germanic names. Energetic policemen and prosecutors, with and without legal authority, hounded those whose patriotism seemed wanting. A New Yorker went to jail for circulating copies of the Declaration of Independence with the concluding question: "Does your government live up to these principles?" Raids in Pennsylvania, Texas, Missouri, and California harassed Jehovah's Witnesses, who refused to salute the American flag. Conscientious objectors faced military courts, military prisons, and physical abuse. A district attorney in Los Angeles suppressed a film entitled *The Spirit of '76* because it showed British atrocities during the American Revolution and thereby criticized an ally. Yellow paint—on houses, automobiles, store fronts, and people—became a standard method of identifying wartime "slackers."

Less than a week after Wilson asked for the declaration of war, the Socialist party pledged "continuous, active, and public opposition" to the struggle brought on by capitalist rivalries. Many Socialists promptly left the party. Those who remained and took their platform literally found judges ready to impose stiff sentences; whether sedition or economic radicalism provoked the penalties was never entirely clear. Eugene Debs opposed conscription, as did any number of congressmen, but a ten-year sentence in the Atlanta Penitentiary effectively removed the Socialists' best-known speaker and candidate. Without a warrant, the government seized the party's national headquarters, rifled the files, and then indicted five members of the executive committee for conspiracy, all of whom eventually received twenty-year sentences. Although the Supreme Court ordered a new trial and none of the defendants actually went to

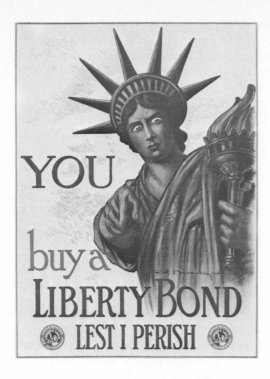

YOU
buy a
LIBERTY BOND
LEST I PERISH

jail, their conviction left the party without direction at a time when direction was sorely needed. When Milwaukee elected Socialist Victor Berger to Congress, the House refused to permit him to sit. When Socialists presented periodicals at the Post Office, federal officials declined to distribute them. When peace came, the comatose Socialist party did not revive.

In addition to making dissent dangerous through sedition legislation, the government endeavored to stir positive support for war. The Committee on Public Information (CPI) contrasted the unselfish American crusade with the German threat to Western civilization. Through the Committee's propaganda efforts, an extensive international audience read Woodrow Wilson's idealistic speeches. The CPI also furnished American journalists with guidelines that enabled them at once to promote the war and to avoid prosecution through "voluntary" censorship.

The editor of a black newspaper in Texas was not sufficiently discreet. Following a racial incident in Houston, for which military authorities hastily hanged thirteen black soldiers, the San Antonio *Inquirer* suggested that perhaps death in defense of black Texans was better than fighting in Europe "for a liberty you cannot enjoy." The judge awarded the editor two years for attempting to promote mutiny among the 360,000 blacks in the nation's service.

The migration of southern blacks to northern cities, which was to become a flood during the Second World War, began during the First.

Northern employers lured southern sharecroppers from worn-out cotton land to dreary urban slums. But blacks discovered that old prejudices persisted in new locations, and racial tension soon erupted into riots, of which the most prolonged took place in 1917 in East St. Louis, Illinois. One outraged observer reported that black citizens endured atrocities "worse than anything the Germans did in Belgium."

Racial equality had never been high on progressives' agenda, but the war did undermine other reforms that had once been important. The progressive faith in economic individualism became subordinate to the need for production and industrial efficiency. In the administration of a Jeffersonian Democrat born in Jefferson's own state, freedom of speech did not include the right to question the President's judgment. Among a tolerant people, religious toleration did not extend to those who took seriously the sixth commandment. The crusade to crush tyranny abroad evidently required tyrannical conformity at home.

The Fourteen Points

Woodrow Wilson thought the great end of the Great War worth its cost in temporary domestic repression. He asked the world to swear allegiance to the noblest elements of the Anglo-American tradition, to make a peace that secured every people an "equal right to freedom and security and self-government and to a participation upon fair terms in the economic opportunities of the world." So great was his belief in humanity that it survived successive disappointments as the French, the Italians, the Japanese, the British, and even his fellow Americans persisted in protecting their national interest instead of doing their international duty.

The President disclosed his blueprint for peace in an address in January 1918. The Fourteen Points showed that American belligerence had not ended Wilson's hope of securing a generous peace through personal mediation. Some of his propositions, such as the evacuation of Belgium and the return of Alsace-Lorraine to France, were not controversial. The re-creation of Poland and the establishment of new nations from the remnants of the Austro-Hungarian empire derived from Wilson's progressive belief in national self-determination. Tariff reduction and uninhibited commercial use of the oceans would reduce economic privilege and bind the nations together through trade. Finally, "a general association of nations" would preserve the peace Wilson's martyred generation had won.

Even as the President enumerated his fourteen idealistic points, Germany was dictating peace terms to Russia that were softened by no lingering idealistic scruple. The price of peace that Germany offered Lenin's new Russian regime was high and unnegotiable. Failure to halt the grinding war had already undermined the short-lived liberal

President Wilson's Fourteen Points

1 Open covenants openly arrived at . . . diplomacy shall proceed always frankly and in the public view.

2 Absolute freedom of navigation . . . alike in peace and in war. . . .

3 The removal . . . of all economic barriers and the establishment of an equality of trade conditions. . . .

4 Adequate guarantees . . . that national armaments will be reduced to the lowest point consistent with domestic safety.

5 A free, open-minded and absolutely impartial adjustment of all colonial claims based upon a strict observance of the principle that . . . the interests of the population concerned must have equal weight with the equitable claims of the government. . . .

6 The evacuation of all Russian territory . . . and a sincere welcome into the society of free nations under institutions of her own choosing. . . .

7 Belgium . . . must be evacuated and restored. . . .

8 All French territory should be freed and the invaded portions restored, and the wrong . . . of Alsace-Lorraine . . . should be righted. . . .

9 A readjustment of the frontiers of Italy . . . along clearly recognizable lines of nationality.

10 The peoples of Austria-Hungary . . . should be accorded the freest opportunity of autonomous development.

11 Rumania, Serbia and Montenegro should be evacuated . . . Serbia accorded free and secure access to the sea. . . .

12 The Turkish portions of the present Ottoman Empire should be assured a secure sovereignty, but the other nationalities which are not under Turkish rule should be assured . . . opportunity of autonomous development, and the Dardanelles should be permanently opened as a free passage to the ships and commerce of all nations. . . .

13 An independent Polish State should be erected . . . which should be assured a free and secure access to the sea. . . .

14 A general association of nations must be formed . . . for the purpose of affording mutual guarantees of political independence and territorial integrity to great and small States alike.

government that had succeeded the Czars in March 1917; to secure peace in March 1918, Lenin agreed to give up territory that included most of Russia's iron and coal deposits, one-third of its industry, and one-fourth of its population. The Allies, however, refused to accept either the Russian Revolution or the peace that released thousands of Germans for duty at the Western Front. When diplomatic persuasion failed to keep Russia in the war, the Allies maintained thousands of troops in the Soviet Union. These forces protected Allied war materials, secured harbor facilities, and offered comfort and occasional aid to domestic opponents of the Bolsheviks. After the Russians made peace, Wilson reluctantly agreed to small American expeditions to Murmansk and Siberia, a halfhearted and ultimately ineffective intervention that dragged on for nearly two years.

The Treaty of Versailles

The Russian Revolution was a constant reminder of the incalculable cost of military exhaustion and political default, conditions that by mid-1918 prevailed in much of Central and Eastern Europe and were not unknown in the West. In October the German High Command decided to abandon the struggle and asked Wilson for an armistice based on the Fourteen Points. The President preferred to discuss peace with a representative government, a preference that was in part responsible for the creation of the fragile new German republic that had to complete capitulation. The Armistice of November 11 was in fact a disguised German surrender, for Wilson's terms deprived Germany of the capacity to renew the war. But German civilians greeted their returning veterans as heroes because no Allied armies had sullied German soil and because the Fourteen Points guaranteed an honorable peace.

Wilson's guarantee, a postwar generation of bitter Germans argued, was a high-sounding fraud. His universal disarmament turned out to be German disarmament. National self-determination did not apply to thousands of Germans in Italy, Czechoslovakia, and Poland and precluded forever a union of Austrian Germans with their northern kin. An "equitable" adjustment of colonial claims gave Japan the German possessions in the North Pacific and divided those in the South Pacific between Australia and New Zealand. Although Wilson had promised consideration of the interests of colonial inhabitants, the interests of the great powers clearly predominated; Britain and France, for instance, received control of the oil-rich areas of the Middle East.

As angry, helpless Germans discovered, Woodrow Wilson could not prescribe the terms of the Treaty of Versailles. For the delegates raced against events, especially against the possibility that Bolshevism might spread beyond Russia: "Better a bad treaty today," ran conventional

The "Big Four": (left to right) Vittorio Orlando (Italy), David Lloyd George (Britain), Georges Clemenceau (France), and Woodrow Wilson (U.S.)

wisdom in Paris, "than a good treaty four months hence." Bolshevism was the backdrop for the peacemakers, but the need of France for guaranteed security shaped the actual negotiations. In successive generations, German troops had twice overpowered their French opponents; only an extraordinary coalition had saved Paris the second time. Georges Clemenceau, the tough septuagenarian premier of France, meant to make sure that Germany had no third opportunity. Clemenceau raised no objection to Wilson's idealism until it inhibited French supremacy on the continent; at that point, Clemenceau became unyielding.

Under the circumstances, Wilson probably did about as well as anyone could have. But to the distress of the Germans, he compromised on the Fourteen Points. To the distress of the ambitious Italians, he refused to regard as binding the Treaty of London, which had promised Italy the South Tyrol and territory at the head of the Adriatic. To the distress of the Japanese, Wilson appeared to keep a declaration of racial equality out of the treaty, although he did not vote against it himself. To the distress of the French, Wilson blocked their possession of the mines of the Saar and their permanent occupation of the strategic Rhineland. To reassure Clemenceau, Wilson and the British Prime Minister David Lloyd George promised military assistance to counter future unprovoked German aggression. Germany had to confess responsibility for the war and assume unlimited financial obligation for damages. Wilson modified national self-determination in order to give Poland access to the sea, to satisfy Japan's economic demands in China's Shantung Peninsula, and to give Czechoslovakia defensible frontiers. Nevertheless, the terms of the Treaty of Versailles, and the subsequent treaties with the other Central Powers, were less severe than the promises the Allies had made to one another in their secret wartime agreements.

Whatever his compromises, Wilson believed he had also created the agency to correct all the hasty mistakes of Versailles and of fallible statesmen to come. For the one point Wilson would not yield was the fourteenth; he wrote the Covenant of the League of Nations into the treaty, and those who would accept the peace must accept the new association of nations that, Wilson fervently hoped, would keep it. Although the League lacked its own military force, Article X, which Wilson called "the heart of the Covenant," committed members to protect other members from external aggression and to respect their political independence and territorial integrity.

The Senate Rejects the Treaty

The Armistice ended nonpartisan political support for Wilson's wartime leadership. The President stubbornly underestimated the revived opposition and naively overestimated his capacity to rally the electorate to his cause. He had compromised at Versailles, but his refusal to do so in Washington cost him his health, his party its majority, his nation the treaty, and the world, his supporters believed, an effective League of Nations and peace.

As the war neared an end and the congressional election of 1918 approached, Republicans took advantage of sectional jealousies (southern congressional Democrats had controlled the price of wheat, while uncontrolled cotton prices soared), dissatisfaction with the prospect of national prohibition (enacted in the Eighteenth Amendment partly, it was argued, to save grain), resentment of taxation (which exceeded 60 percent in some income brackets), and a pervasive war-weariness. Wilson's ill-advised, last-minute plea for Democratic candidates in effect made the contest a vote of confidence, which the President lost.

Yet, Wilson made no concession to Republicans or to the Senate in selecting American representatives to accompany him to Paris. The President himself led the delegation, an unprecedented decision that personalized the treaty. His closest diplomatic advisers, Secretary of State Lansing and Colonel House, were natural choices. General Tasker Bliss, another delegate, had combined military and diplomatic missions during the war. Only Henry White, a retired career diplomat, was nominally a Republican, and no senator was invited. A boatload of specialists was supposed to advise the delegation, but their advice was seldom asked in Paris and even more rarely taken.

Both House and Lansing counseled the President not to ignore the advice of the treaty's domestic opponents. Henry Cabot Lodge, chairman of the Senate's Committee on Foreign Relations, had once had kind words for international peace-keeping. But Wilson's treaty aroused Lodge's nationalistic instincts. The proposed League might inhibit what Lodge and Roosevelt had called a "large policy"—the ability to respond diplomatically wherever opportunity knocked and to establish, where necessary, American protectorates or possessions. No international body, warned Lodge and other opponents of the treaty, could impair the sovereignty of the United States, regulate American immigration, set American tariffs, limit American markets, send American troops into battle, or modify the Monroe Doctrine. Irish Americans denounced Wilson's failure to press for Irish independence, and Italian Americans, German Americans, and Polish Americans resented various territorial compromises. In March 1919, Senator Lodge published a "round-robin" letter in which more than one-third of the Senate declared the Covenant unacceptable. Negotiators at Versailles, at Wilson's insistence, made gestures to relieve the Senate's apprehensions about tariffs, immigrants, and the Monroe Doctrine. But to a suggestion that he permit further revision, Wilson peevishly responded that "the Senate must take its medicine."

Had the Senate acted quickly, Wilson might have had his way. Lifted by the President's rhetoric and elated by their military victory, most Americans probably approved the treaty in July 1919 when Wilson submitted it to the Senate. Lodge waited for this initial enthusiasm to subside while opponents of the treaty organized a campaign from the platform and in the press to alert the public to the need to "Americanize" (and "Republicanize") Woodrow Wilson's peace. There was no love lost between Woodrow Wilson and Henry Cabot Lodge. Personal antipathy may have strengthened the President's resolve to resist compromise and the senator's determination to amend the treaty. But politics was more important than pique in setting Lodge's course. A split in his Republican party had permitted Wilson to become President. Disagreement among Republicans over the treaty might renew that split and continue the party's exclusion from the White House. About a dozen Republicans, many of them veterans of the Progressive schism, opposed the League of Nations in any form. One of these "irreconcilables," Senator Hiram Johnson of California, was actively seeking the Republican presidential nomination; another, William E. Borah, threatened to bolt the party if Lodge did not commit the Republican majority to the defeat of the League. A dozen Republicans supported Wilson's treaty with slight modifications. And the remainder, among whom Lodge counted himself, favored attaching "strong reservations" to the treaty to limit what they called Wilson's delegation of American sovereignty. Only a few Democrats, on the other hand, thought amendments necessary. Most of Wilson's party saw things Wilson's way.

The division of the Senate lent itself to several political strategies, but the President was unyielding. Although he needed two-thirds of the Senate and his own supporters numbered less than half, he would not accept even minor explanatory reservations to the treaty, some of which he had himself prepared. Nor would he permit Democrats to support Lodge's more stringent reservations, even though that course of action would almost certainly have resulted in ratification.

Several of Lodge's reservations required no fundamental revision of the treaty. He proposed to reserve explicitly the right of Congress to declare war and to legislate about tariffs and immigration, powers that the President did not intend to delegate in any case. The most important of the reservations would have undermined Wilson's attempt to coerce future aggressors with international boycotts; Lodge's amendment would not promise automatic American support for economic sanctions.

Whatever the content, the tone of the Lodge Reservations was suspicious and grudging. Wilson believed that the American people supported the treaty wholeheartedly. True to his progressive ideals, he planned a whirlwind speaking tour to rally the nation and save the treaty from mutilation. The tour would have taxed a young and vigorous statesman. Wilson was no longer young, and eighteen months of wartime decisions, an exhausting round of negotiations in Paris, a slight stroke, and blinding headaches resulting from arteriosclerosis had all combined to deplete his vigor. His tour began without evoking much response but picked up momentum and support as he worked his way westward across the continent. And then, when he seemed on the verge of success, he collapsed in Pueblo, Colorado, and had to cancel the rest of the trip. About a week after his return to Washington, Wilson suffered a disabling stroke that precluded all activity for three weeks and left him partially paralyzed for the rest of his life. The isolation of the sickroom hardened his resolve, and he brusquely dismissed all suggestions of compromise as the treaty neared a decision in the Senate.

Wilson: before his stroke and after

In November 1919, Lodge presented the treaty with his reservations. Democrats and irreconcilables combined to defeat Lodge's motion. Subsequent parliamentary jockeying in effect provided a vote on the treaty with mild Democratic reservations, which lost when irreconcilables joined Lodge's forces. Finally, fifty-three senators voted not to consent to the treaty as negotiated, and only thirty-eight stood up for Wilson's unamended document. The treaty did not even achieve majority support, let alone the two-thirds of the Senate required by the Constitution. The first action was not conclusive, however, and the treaty came up for reconsideration in March 1920. About half the Democrats decided that a treaty with reservations was better than no treaty at all; they joined twenty-eight Republicans in support of the Lodge Reservations. The remaining Democrats dutifully followed Wilson's demand to be counted for principle; they joined the irreconcilables. The forty-nine senators who supported the amended treaty were seven votes short of the necessary two-thirds. And this time the question was closed.

The End of the Progressive Crusade

The President's progressive faith survived even the shock of the Senate's vote. The people, he believed, would overturn the verdict in the coming presidential election, a "solemn referendum" on the League. This unshaken belief that the public was always behind him had lured Wilson into serious political errors in his second term. He assumed that the rest of the world shared his view of the war, whereas other people had simply used his magnificent phrasing to avoid deciding what the war was about. He mistook the adulation of throngs in Italy and France for support of his idealistic peace; in fact, the crowds cheered in anticipation of the rewards of military triumph. Not even his own people wanted a peace without victory; their version of a settlement was one that would make the world safe for the United States, whether or not the rest of humanity approved. Wilson overestimated the sophistication of his American audience, which preferred the comforting fantasy of isolation and diplomatic independence to his harder message of the collective responsibility of all great nations to preserve the peace for all mankind.

And, like many other progressives, the President misjudged the persuasive force of causes he believed morally right. Self-righteous himself, he failed to reckon with the power of political, economic, and strategic self-interest. Entrenched political bosses, corporations, and isolationist senators had resisted the progressive assault remarkably well. The military establishments of other nations, their economic interests, and their territorial ambitions also survived Wilson's onslaught. He had summoned the world's peoples to a moral crusade; they settled for bigger boundaries, punitive reparations, and what they thought was national security.

Because the United States was unready to accept the international role that Wilson envisioned, the decision to stay out of the League probably made little long-term difference. One more grudging great power in Geneva would not have prevented the Second World War. As it turned out, Britain and France converted the League to a quasi-alliance in defense of the status quo, and American policy in the interwar years would not have markedly changed the League's direction. The League never dealt with the unfulfilled national aspirations of Japan and Italy, with the legitimate desire of Germany for relief from an absurd burden of reparations, with the tensions caused by keeping the Soviet Union an international outcast, with the economic trauma of the Great Depression, or with the diplomatic trauma of renewed aggression. In an age of rampant nationalism, Woodrow Wilson unsuccessfully preached international cooperation; in an acquisitive time, he appealed to forbearance. He would not compromise, nor did he gladly suffer fools, foes, or inferiors. Such is the stuff of prophets, but prophecy is only one element of political leadership.

Suggested Reading

Arthur S. Link's brief, interpretive *Wilson the Diplomatist** (1957) is supplemented in his multivolume biography of the wartime President. Ernest R. May studies Wilson's policies in the years of American neutrality in *The World War and American Isolation, 1914–1917** (1959), as does Daniel M. Smith in *The Great Departure** (1965). William A. Williams, in *The Tragedy of American Diplomacy** (1962), stresses the economic basis of American diplomacy.

Edward M. Coffman gives the military history of the war a personal dimension in *The War to End All Wars* (1968). In *The War Industries Board* (1973), Robert D. Cuff examines the relationship between business and government. The assault on individual liberties at home is the subject of *Opponents of War, 1917–1918** (1957) by Horace C. Peterson and Gilbert C. Fite. Two volumes by George F. Kennan, *The Decision to Intervene** (1956) and *Russia Leaves the War** (1958), discuss the impact of the Russian Revolution on American policy, as, in quite different ways, do N. Gordon Levin's *Woodrow Wilson and World Politics** (1968), and Arno J. Mayer's *Politics and Diplomacy of Peacemaking* (1967).

Thomas A. Bailey has written two studies of Wilson's diplomacy: *Woodrow Wilson and the Lost Peace** (1944), which deals with the negotiation of the treaty, and *Woodrow Wilson and the Great Betrayal** (1945), which is critical of Wilson's political tactics and judgment. John M. Keynes criticizes the treaty's economic provisions in *The Economic Consequences of the Peace** (1919). Ralph A. Stone's study, *The Irreconcilables** (1970), is dispassionate and definitive. John A. Garraty's *Henry Cabot Lodge* (1953) is the best biography of Wilson's formidable opponent.

* Available in paperback edition

Chapter 18
Cultural Collision
in the 1920s

1919 Strikes reflect postwar economic dislocation • Race riots break out •

1920 Presidential election: Warren G. Harding (Republican) defeats James M. Cox (Democrat) • Esch-Cummins Transportation Act returns railroads to private management •

1920—27 Sacco-Vanzetti trial and appeals •

1921, 1924 National Origins Act restricts immigration •

1921 Washington Naval Conference •

1923 Calvin Coolidge succeeds Harding • H. L. Mencken founds the *American Mercury* •

1924 Presidential election: Calvin Coolidge (Republican) defeats John W. Davis (Democrat) and Robert M. LaFollette (Progressive) •

1927 *The Jazz Singer*, first motion picture with sound, released •

1927, 1928 Coolidge vetoes McNary-Haugen bills to subsidize farmers •

1928 Presidential election: Herbert C. Hoover (Republican) defeats Alfred E. Smith (Democrat) • Kellogg-Briand Pact outlaws war •

There are dozens of symbols to evoke the decade between Versailles and the Crash: flappers and ticker tape, Charles A. Lindbergh and Babe Ruth, flasks and fundamentalism, provincial "boosters" and "lost" intellectuals. Yet the images do not cohere; one reason there are so many is that no one will do. The 1920s were not just a "jazz age," though the phrase captures part of the mood of the time. Nor does the conflict between an emerging urban culture and the traditional rural ethic wholly explain the period, though that conflict did take place. The 1920s were years of privation as well as prosperity, of bigotry as well as urbanity, of illusions as well as disillusionment. If the vigor of the prewar progressive spirit diminished after the Armistice, the reform impulse did not perish. The old and the new blended in a decade of transition.

As much as anyone, and on a much larger scale, Henry Ford personified the contradictions of the day. Ford was an authoritarian entrepreneur, so rigidly independent he would not share control of his business with partners or bankers or unions or government. He built a museum to preserve an idealized old-time America, staged old-time dances, and believed in old-time religion; he thought Jews, jazz, and Wall Street endangered the American way of life. He shared a narrow intolerance with contemporaries who harassed radicals, joined the Ku Klux Klan, and restricted immigration. His simple Protestant view of right and wrong sustained prohibition and property rights. Yet Ford also paid good wages, employed blacks when others did not, and served as the engineer-prophet of modern industrial technology. It was his assembly line and its product, his sales and his profits—the big business he ran and the inexpensive automobile he produced—that doomed the America Henry Ford hoped to keep. Like other Americans who wanted both the past and progress, Ford did not realize that one would preclude the other.

All That Jazz

The journalist Walter Lippmann called the battle to repeal prohibition "a test of strength between social orders." Repeal, Lippmann asserted, would mark "the emergence of the cities as the dominant force in America." In fact, "drys" were not universally set in rural ways and "wets" were not uniformly urban. But Lippmann let "urban" and "rural" stand for attitude as much as residence, and there was indeed a clash.

The struggle over prohibition colors the entire decade. Elections that ought to have settled other matters turned on whether a candidate was wet or dry. For militant drys, any wavering condoned immorality: "It is either loyalty to the country or to the outlawed traffic," observed a spokesman for the Anti-Saloon League. Wets could not seriously advance drinking as a moral duty, but they did think it a right and they caricatured the moral certainty of their opponents. Since the most open defiance of the law took place in cities, which many rural Americans believed had always tolerated sin, the argument did have overtones of cultural conflict.

Intellectuals of the "lost generation" thought of themselves as emancipated from the rural values of middle-class America. Progressive writers had used words in the cause of justice, but Ernest Hemingway and several other expatriate writers of the 1920s had tired of causes. Hemingway's *A Farewell to Arms* directly challenged the idealism of the progressive generation. The American small town, once the object of sentimental reverence, became narrow and confining in Sherwood Anderson's *Winesburg, Ohio* or in Sinclair Lewis's *Main Street.* Characters in the novels of F. Scott Fitzgerald thought the way to happiness lay through high society; not every reader perceived that Fitzgerald's characters did not always reach their destinations. T. S. Eliot made emptiness the theme of *The Waste Land,* the most admired poem of the decade.

A "ladies' magazine" looks at housework

Former certainties—small towns, friendliness, sobriety, self-denial, optimism, Protestantism, and even patriotism—came under assault, most notably by H. L. Mencken, the most quoted voice of urban sophistication. In the *Smart Set* and later in the *American Mercury*, which he edited, Mencken made fun of the "booboisie," "debunked" Puritanism and national heroes, and made religious fundamentalism a national joke. Instead of pointing new ways to familiar goals, Mencken and other intellectuals denied that any ways existed and doubted that the goals were worth achieving. Optimists, like the philosopher John Dewey, continued to preach the progressive faith, but a rootless lack of orthodoxy was more in style.

Even orthodox sexual morality was questioned. Women living a corseted life of Victorian respectability daydreamed about what they supposed the flappers did. In 1912, a Socialist newspaper began publishing a column entitled "What Every Girl Should Know." When the United States Post Office refused to accept the paper for mailing, the paper observed ironically that the government's position was that girls ought to know nothing. But women in the 1920s knew about, and many of them practiced, birth control.

Margaret Sanger, the young woman whose newspaper column had

been suppressed, would not be silenced. She joined radicals like Emma Goldman and Elizabeth Gurley Flynn, who were preaching birth control to American working-class audiences. In 1916, Mrs. Sanger set up a clinic in Brooklyn, New York, to dispense contraceptives and information about birth control; after a few days of overflow crowds, the police arrested her and closed the clinic. Her trial publicized her cause, as did her lectures, her writing, and the organizations she founded and her wealthy husband supported. During the 1920s, due in part to her efforts, birth control became a public as well as a private matter, and by 1930 it was almost old-hat. Mrs. Sanger's victory was incomplete: the Catholic Church in particular opposed birth control, and poorer families usually did not practice it. But large segments of the population had manifestly altered the Victorian sexual code and discarded, for the moment, some preconceptions about the role of women.

Yet the movement to secure equality for women lost momentum. Feminist unity did not survive the victory of the Nineteenth Amendment. Flappers, and young women generally, had other things on their minds and little interest in the women's movement. Advertisers, who had a keen sense of the public's mood, used pictures of healthy housewives to induce other ladies to purchase cosmetics or cigarettes or vacuum cleaners. More women were employed at the end of the decade than at the beginning, but the increase was almost exactly proportional to the increase in population.

Census takers in 1920 found that population divided about equally between town and country: 51 million Americans lived in rural areas and 54 million in places with more than 2500 inhabitants, a number that did not signify urban congestion, but did indicate a drift toward centers of population. The nation's popular culture, carried in magazines, movies, and radio programs, reflected this division more accurately than the work of novelists and poets, who tended to identify with cities. Producers of motion pictures, for instance, were not artists but entrepreneurs, marketing entertainment that displayed the advantages of urban life and then concluded with a moral that was welcome in the provinces. The films of the 1920s broadened vicarious experience in small towns and spread a homogeneous urban culture that reduced regional differences. But movies also skirted political, economic, and social controversy and stood squarely for the values of the middle class. Clara Bow, the "It" girl, might flirt for the first three reels, but in the end "It" was marriage and the nice boy next door. The bold adventurers Rudolph Valentino and Douglas Fairbanks, Sr., portrayed never did their sexual swashbuckling on camera. Jail, or worse, awaited cinema gangsters, however attractive life outside the law might temporarily seem. The industry accepted voluntary censorship, administered by Will Hays, whose reliability was certified by a term as chairman of the Republican National Committee.

The Hays Office kept screen morality well within middle-class limits but did not seriously inhibit the imagination of the industry's pioneers.

Buster Keaton and Charlie Chaplin, among others, explored every artistic dimension of the silent comedy, as Chaplin's *Gold Rush* (1925) attests. John Ford's *Iron Horse* (1924) helped establish the western as an artistic genre and set a standard that imitators have seldom reached. Cecil B. DeMille produced several big-budget epics, but the biggest, *Ben Hur* (1925), which cost $4 million to make, was the work of others. No one in the five decades since has excelled Walt Disney in animations or in an understanding of the mass audience; Disney's only apparent error in a long career was to name Mickey Mouse initially Mortimer.

The addition of sound in 1927 stimulated the industry's growth and brought changes in names and faces. If Keaton and Chaplin did not immediately embrace the new dimension, the Marx Brothers and Mae West and W. C. Fields did. Actors who had begun on the stage, such as James Cagney, Katherine Hepburn, and Edward G. Robinson, replaced Mary Pickford and other stars who did not adapt to the "talkies." The first "talkie," *The Jazz Singer*, foreshadowed the musicals that would become staples of Hollywood, and typified the industry's preoccupation with entertainment.

It was altogether appropriate that the first "talkie" should be about a jazz singer, for contemporaries and historians alike have sensed that music was the characteristic expression of the time. Jazz was associated, then and now, with flappers and speakeasies, with unbuttoned sex and cabaret romance, with high life and low morality. Jazz inspired dancers, *Variety* remarked, to "loosen up and go the limit in their stepping." When

The "It" girl

Harlem

the music had lyrics, its critics thought them suggestive; when there were no words, the rhythm seemed obscene.

Jazz was initially black music; Al Jolson played the jazz singer in blackface. But white musicians polished and tamed the free-wheeling music that burst out of New Orleans and black districts in Chicago, St. Louis, and Kansas City. Rudy Vallee and Paul Whiteman made jazz respectable (with white performers), and George Gershwin moved some of the musical ideas from the dance hall to the concert hall, where Whiteman's orchestra performed *Rhapsody in Blue* in 1924. Whether they acknowledged it or not, Whiteman and Gershwin and the other white jazz artists had learned from Pine Top Smith, Bessie Smith, Jelly Roll Morton, Scott Joplin, Louis Armstrong, and other black musicians who played ragtime and Dixieland, blues and boogie woogie, and other forms of jazz. The first spectacular wave of innovative energy subsided well before the stock market crashed, and many of the musicians who had begun playing jazz gradually switched to the more predictable musical formulas of swing. In Harlem, however, where Duke Ellington began to perform at the Cotton Club in 1927, the jazz idiom remained alive and well.

Indeed, it was in Harlem that most of the strands of black culture came together in the 1920s. Marcus Garvey, the founder of the Universal Negro Improvement Association (UNIA), had moved there from Jamaica in 1916. Garvey taught his followers to "buy black," to use their purchasing power to lift the whole black community. His black nationalism, in another form, ran through the writing of the talented blacks who sparked the Harlem Renaissance. "There is," wrote the editor of an anthology of these writers in 1925, "a renewed race-spirit that consciously and proudly sets itself apart. . . . Uncle Tom and Sambo have passed on." The obituary for Uncle Tom was premature, for he still lived in Harlem as well as on impoverished Southern farms, as William E. B. Du Bois knew.

Editor of the journal of the National Association for the Advancement of Colored People, Du Bois exhorted blacks to continue the fight for democracy at home after the Armistice. We fought, Du Bois wrote, for a nation that practices "lynching, disfranchisement, caste, brutality, and devilish insult." "We are," he continued, "cowards and jackasses if now that war is over, we do not marshal every ounce of our brain and brawn to fight a sterner, longer, more unbending battle against the forces of hell in our own land." Especially in northern cities, to which a half million southern blacks had moved during the war, this sort of determination encountered white resistance. Economic competition and racial tension over housing and public facilities triggered race riots in Chicago, Omaha, and Knoxville, and more than 70 lynchings in 1919 alone. The riots eventually subsided, but other manifestations of the prejudice Du Bois noted did not.

Returning to Normalcy: Wilson, Harding, Coolidge

Politicians of the decade thought to progress by going back to pre-progressive verities. Although Republicans usually claimed these policies, Woodrow Wilson set the tone for his successors. The postwar Wilson, paralyzed by his stroke and politically bankrupt after the defeat of the League, had lost his legislative mastery. He evidently had no plan for demobilization or for conversion to peacetime production. This reluctance to manage the dynamic economy was to become a matter of principle for Warren Harding and Calvin Coolidge, who followed Wilson in the White House. The economic legislation that Congress passed favored the business community, whose power Wilson had once eloquently opposed. And, with tacit presidential consent, Wilson's attorney general presided over a hysterical hunt for subversives that both outraged and intimidated the people who had once thought Wilson their prophet. His last two years in office were years of reaction.

This reaction was visible partly in legislation that awarded the spoils of peace to business groups. The Merchant Marine Act (1920) restricted foreign shippers and subsidized American companies with federal loans, profitable mail contracts, and favorable terms for purchase of the merchant fleet the government had built during the war. The Esch-Cummins Transportation Act (1920) authorized the return of the railroads to private ownership and increased the regulatory power of the ICC. But the legislation did nothing to conserve the gains in efficiency achieved during the war and, in effect, increased the competitive advantage of those systems that least needed help.

As important as what the Wilson administration accomplished was what it failed to do to ease the transition to a peacetime economy. The War Department shelved a plan to coordinate demobilization and employment and simply released men as quickly as possible. Wartime industries found their orders abruptly canceled; government construction almost stopped. The government's *monthly* expenditures in the first half of 1919, nevertheless, exceeded *annual* spending for 1915. More anxious to balance the federal budget than to curb rising unemployment, Wilson suggested that perhaps local governments might undertake public works projects.

Labor organizations tried to preserve high wartime wages in a series of strikes in 1919. At the President's orders Attorney General A. Mitchell Palmer served an injunction that sent disappointed coal miners back to the pits. Steelworkers, who struck to secure a forty-eight-hour week, found federal troops protecting strikebreakers in Illinois; the steel industry remained unorganized. So did the police in Boston, where municipal and state authorities ended the walkout on their own terms with federal approval but without federal intervention.

Alerted by Communist activity in Europe that followed the Russian Revolution of November 1917, some Americans saw the strikes of 1919 as the American proletariat's first stride toward power. In fact there were no great conspiracies and precious few Communists. Labor's demands were traditional: recognition of the union, better wages, shorter hours. But beginning in 1918 and on into 1920, the nation looked for radicals who were supposed to be plotting the nation's postwar distress.

At its worst, popular hysteria denied free speech, free press, and the protection of ordinary judicial procedure. Aroused legislatures forbade the display of red flags and made membership in radical organizations a criminal offense. These criminal syndicalism laws harassed the Industrial Workers of the World, whose suppression had started during the war. The House of Representatives and the New York state legislature refused to seat duly elected Socialist representatives. Attorney General Palmer ordered a series of raids in 1920 that took several thousand people into custody, including many who just happened to be in an area where radicals were thought to congregate. Eventually about 500 aliens were deported.

And then, before Woodrow Wilson left office, the Red Scare was over. The results of the frantic search for radicals were ludicrously out of proportion to the energy expended: an occasional IWW member, some aliens whose radicalism was nostalgic habit rather than a response to American conditions, and a few native nonconformists. Charles Evans Hughes, whose conservatism and patriotism were equally unimpeachable, denounced the New York legislature's exclusion of its Socialist members. Humorists pointed to the incongruity of a mighty nation's debilitating fear of frustrated dissenters. In New York, in December 1919, a teary would-be bride told reporters and a church full of disappointed guests that Reds must have abducted the missing groom. A day or two later, the sheepish young man surfaced, complete with a previous wife and family, and the "Red menace" was suddenly a joke.

One haunting remnant lingered. In May 1920, two Italian anarchists were arrested and charged with robbery and murder in South Braintree, Massachusetts. More than a year later, after a trial many observers thought a mockery, both defendants, Nicola Sacco and Bartolomeo Vanzetti, were sentenced to death. Critics argued that execution would make the two men martyrs for their political radicalism and their southern European origin. Others, including much of respectable America, held that the trial had been fair, and that the defendants were undesirable anyhow. Whatever the truth, the nation wrangled interminably about the case even after the two men were finally executed in 1927.

The Red Scare and the Sacco-Vanzetti case were manifestations of a provincialism that sometimes surfaces in national politics, and which may produce social violence. A suspicion that foreign influence and ethnic diversity were undermining national unity lay beneath the demand that immigration be restricted. An act in 1921 limited annual immigration to 357,000 and the total from any one nation to 3 percent of Americans of that national origin enumerated in the Census of 1910. An act in 1924 further reduced the annual quota to 150,000 (to take effect in 1929), and the quota for each nation to 2 percent of the Census of 1890. Changing the base for the quota from 1910 to 1890 effectively held back Catholic and Jewish immigrants from southern and eastern Europe.

Keeping the aliens out was only one step, in the prejudiced view of those who believed national unity required a homogeneous, white, Protestant, English-speaking population. The Ku Klux Klan revived in the 1920s and became as powerful in parts of the North as it had been in the South, where the black population remained generally cowed. As the wartime migration to the North continued during the 1920s, the Klan spread among northern whites, who for the first time encountered blacks in numbers large enough to make them more than a curiosity.

"Americanism" was the political code word for parochial patriotism,

The Klan goes to Washington, 1925

and the theme recurred throughout the decade. Americanism helped defeat Wilson's treaty and several proposals to join the World Court. In its anti-Catholic form, Americanism helped frustrate the presidential aspirations of Alfred E. Smith, the nation's most eminent Catholic politician. Warren G. Harding defined the term as precisely as anyone needed with his statement that the country required "not nostrums, but normalcy." James M. Cox, Harding's opponent in the presidential contest of 1920, had no close association with Wilson's internationalism. But neither Cox nor his attractive running mate, Franklin D. Roosevelt, could convince the electorate that Democrats were quite so "American" as Republicans. Harding won an unprecedented 60 percent of the popular vote.

Wilson had proclaimed the election a solemn referendum on the League of Nations, and in a sense it was. Harding had followed the lead of Henry Cabot Lodge while the treaty was before the Senate and during the campaign had indicated continued personal opposition. A few Republicans who favored the League argued that a vote for Harding was a vote for the League, but the argument displayed more ingenuity than accuracy, and the voter for whom the League of Nations was the primary issue probably cast his ballot for Cox. But there simply were not enough.

President Coolidge and friend

"Americanism" and "normalcy" meant a placid nationalistic foreign policy and an unruffled government at home. Warren G. Harding, whose inclination was inaction, was admirably qualified to preside over both.

The personal qualities that secured Harding's nomination ensured his failure as President. Harding became the Republican nominee because he depended upon other people for direction, because he responded enthusiastically to the call of party and personal loyalty, because he was handsome and one of the boys, and because he was ordinary. He never fully mastered his administration. His cronies abused his confidence and had virtually no program except their own advancement. Their venality overshadowed Harding's ineffective effort to bring order to the war-swollen federal bureaucracy and to return to the fiscal orthodoxy of William McKinley.

Harding's cabinet combined three eminent Republicans with others unqualified for public office and unworthy of public trust. Charles Evans Hughes was a dignified secretary of state; Herbert Hoover turned the somnolent Commerce Department into a hive of innovation; Andrew Mellon was an honest, if extremely conservative, secretary of the treasury. On the other hand, Harry Daugherty, Harding's political mentor and attorney general, Edwin M. Denby, the secretary of the navy, and Albert B. Fall, the secretary of the interior, were all implicated in the Teapot Dome scandal, which was exposed after Harding's death in 1923. Fall was convicted of taking a bribe from oilmen who wanted to tap the navy's underground reserves at Teapot Dome in Wyoming. Some of Harding's subcabinet appointees were equally unscrupulous. Charles Forbes, the chief of the Veterans Bureau, systematically enriched himself at the expense of the veterans he was supposed to serve. The President knew his friends had betrayed him, but he was incapable of any action sterner than privately deploring the situation. While Harding himself did not share the booty, the cynical air of easy morality extended to the White House, where poker, bootleg whisky, and a presidential mistress gave a dubious distinction to Harding's brief lease.

Harding died in August 1923 before the scandals of his administration were fully known. And Calvin Coolidge, who had a knack for being in the right place at the right time, took the presidential oath from his father in the candle-lit parlor of the family's farmhouse in Plymouth, Vermont. The ceremony gave Coolidge an aura of rural simplicity that he was at pains to preserve as an antidote for the easygoing good fellowship, the cards, the alcohol, and the scandals that were soon associated with Harding. Fresh from rural Vermont, radiating rural virtue, came the honest hayseed Calvin Coolidge, who never did anything that anyone could call convivial. No one could blame "Silent Cal" for Harding's scandals, and they blew over without exacting a political price from the Republicans; indeed, those who persisted in investigating Teapot Dome, like Senators LaFollette and Walsh, were sharply criticized for their pains.

Prosperity

The collapse of the stock market in October 1929, and the long depression that followed, made the 1920s seem by contrast a decade of fabulous prosperity. That fond recollection was only partly accurate, though the stock market did, of course, reach unprecedented levels and some shrewd operators made speculative fortunes. Ordinary people enjoyed a more modest prosperity—a short vacation with pay, fresh vegetables and a little life insurance, an improved standard of living.

A few months before the Crash, Henry Ford asked the Bureau of Labor Statistics to measure the standard of living of the "typical" employee of the Ford Motor Company. Although Ford's workers received wages of about $7 per day and were better paid than most industrial workers, the survey nevertheless suggests the general economic progress of which people in the 1920s were so proud. Ford's employees ate more roast beef than stew and nearly as much steak. They lived not in crowded tenements but in purchased or rented quarters large enough to provide a room for each member of the family. Closets held a good deal of wool clothing and hats for all seasons and all members of the family. Virtually all the dwellings had electrical service, which cost less than $2 per month, but only a few had telephones, which were more expensive. Four families out of five contributed to a church. One in two owned (or was purchasing on the installment plan) an electric washing machine, one in five a vacuum cleaner, one in ten an electric refrigerator, one in three a radio, and one in two a car—almost invariably a Ford, which was used for recreation. Public transportation took people to school and factory and market.

The market where Ford's workers and other plain people shopped, not the stock market, was the key to the prosperity of the decade. Eager customers spent their rising wages on the consumer goods that were the decade's new toys. Widespread use of automobiles brought a burst of highway construction, billions in new investment, and expanded output among suppliers of oil, glass, steel, and rubber. Sales of refrigerators and radios depended on wide distribution of electricity, which in turn required heavy investment in copper, rubber, and other basic industries. The movies whetted consumer appetites and prescribed fashion for Americans, who were increasingly concerned with what they wore and owned.

But this generally improving standard of living was not a universal experience in America. A brief, but severe, postwar economic crisis left nearly 5 million people unemployed and reduced the national income by 10 percent. Close to 100,000 bankruptcies and nearly a half million farmers who lost their farms testified to the breadth of the disaster. Wholesale prices and industrial production plummeted. Wheat that had brought $2.50 in 1919 sold for less than $1.00 in 1921; a bushel of corn dropped from $1.88 to $.42. Although most of the economy pulled out of the depression in 1922, many farmers struggled until the Second World War. A prudent Minnesota Swede bought a good farm in 1912, improved it, and paid off half his mortgage by 1920. In 1925 prices had fallen to the point where his net income for long days of hard work and his return on a large investment amounted to half what his eighteen-year-old daughter received for typing in a downtown office. Farmers' perception that their measure of prosperity was short exacerbated the cultural clash between town and country.

Farmers, textile workers, coal miners, and others whose industries lagged in the decade could not sustain the continued consumption upon which prosperity depended. Congressmen from rural areas were particularly sensitive to rumbling discontent. Since the Presidents took no action, legislators from farm states organized loosely in a "farm bloc" to secure redress for their constituents.

The McNary-Haugen bill, introduced in 1924, proposed to protect the domestic market for American farmers and to authorize disposing of surplus production abroad at the world price. Farmers were to make up with an "equalization fee" the difference between the depressed world price and the protected domestic price. Since the nation consumed more farm produce than was exported, the measure, the farm bloc claimed, would raise rural income. But representatives from nonfarm areas proved hard to persuade, and when the bill finally passed in 1927, President Coolidge vetoed it. The bill had so many defects, Coolidge said, that he could not "state them all without writing a book." Coolidge held the proposal unconstitutional, labeled it an unjustifiable subsidy to one segment of the population, and correctly argued that it contained no mechanism for controlling surplus production, which was at the heart of the problem. Congress modified the bill somewhat in 1928, but Coolidge vetoed it again.

The presidential veto was Coolidge's substitute for a legislative program. In 1928 he vetoed Senator George Norris's bill authorizing the government to operate the nitrate plants and electrical generating facilities constructed in the Tennessee Valley during the First World War. Coolidge suggested that the complex be sold to private investors instead. The President also vetoed a bill in 1924 to pay World War veterans a bonus, but the veterans secured enough congressional support to override that veto.

Neither Coolidge nor his predecessor furnished the initiative for administration policies. In both cases, the fiscal policy was that of Andrew Mellon, who had made his fortune in aluminum and banking, and whom his contemporaries called "the greatest Secretary of the Treasury since Alexander Hamilton." Mellon believed that high corporate and income taxes penalized resourceful businessmen and discouraged private investment. He repeatedly urged Congress to reduce wartime taxes. Congress finally responded in 1926: the surtax on large incomes dropped from 40 to 20 percent; the gift tax was repealed; the estate tax was reduced by half; a variety of excise taxes disappeared completely. Senator Norris, who opposed Mellon's program, charged that it saved Mellon himself more than "the aggregate of practically all the taxpayers in the State of Nebraska."

At the direction of Herbert Hoover, the Department of Commerce helped businesses cooperate in the interest of industrial efficiency, and sometimes at the expense of competition. Hoover encouraged the proliferation of trade associations under governmental auspices; these organizations exchanged economic information, such as prices and data on cost accounting. The Commerce Department collected statistics, subsidized technological innovation, and suggested ways to keep down costs. Later, during his presidency, Hoover was identified with the outdated economic orthodoxy of laissez faire; yet his ideas about competition and the place of government in business owed more to Henry Clay and Alexander Hamilton than to those who demanded an inactive state. Hoover's direction of the Commerce Department rested on the assumption that a benign government, without itself controlling the economy, could help business create a higher standard of living for the nation.

The Supreme Court, however, held to the rules of laissez faire. The Court used the Fourteenth Amendment, the usual judicial instrument for striking down regulatory and welfare legislation, twice as often in the 1920s as in the preceding decade. Congress could not, held the Court, use the power to tax to keep children out of the mills (*Bailey* v. *Drexel Furniture Co.*, 1922). Whatever the Clayton Act said, the justices decided in *Duplex Printing Press Co.* v. *Deering* (1921) that courts could prevent unions from using secondary boycotts; the antitrust laws hampered union activity throughout the decade. In 1923 the Court revived the *Lochner* doctrine by ruling in *Adkins* v. *Children's Hospital* that Congress could not set minimum wages for women working in the District of Columbia. In harmony with its legal constituency, with the other two branches of government, and probably with the American people as well, the Court stood squarely for unfettered private enterprise.

The Politics of an Urban Nation

Americans in the 1920s found themselves poised between an exciting, uncertain, urban future and a rural past that seemed in retrospect more secure. They associated modernity with the city—and they wanted it; they associated morality with the farm—and they wanted that too. Calvin Coolidge seemed the resolution of the paradox: he was the embodiment of rural simplicity while presiding over modern, urban America, the taciturn prophet of prosperity, the symbol of thrift in an age of installment buying, the picture of serene certainty in a frantically uncertain era.

The assault on the old certainties spread. Advertising, one of the nation's newest big businesses, assailed such frugal maxims as "use it up; make it do." Even if the old car did still run, the smart driver bought a new model now and got ahead of the Joneses. Saving was unnecessary; self-indulgence was good business.

As advertising advanced materialism, so too broad acceptance of natural and social science eroded the certainties of traditional religion. Americans continued to go to church, but they were only slightly embarrassed about skipping a service for a Sunday drive. Religious doctrine, particularly that of Protestantism, became less demanding, and many churchgoers went less to worship than because "it was the thing to do." Although fundamentalists held out, most Christians conceded that modern science made impossible a literal acceptance of the book of Genesis. The 1925 trial of John Scopes, a Tennessee schoolteacher who

It hasn't a single belt, fan
or drain pipe....

*It always works
perfectly and never
needs oiling*

Oɴᴇ of the first things that made me favor this General Electric Refrigerator was the fact that it was so unusually quiet. And I liked the idea of never having to oil it. All you have to do is plug it into an electric outlet . . . and then you can forget it. It hasn't any belts, drains, fans, or stuffing boxes.

But, of course, the thing that appeals to me most is the way it has cut my housekeeping job. I only market twice a week now, because I have plenty of space and just the right temperature to keep all sorts of foods in perfect condition.

We go away for week-ends without having to worry about ice. Everything is ready for use when we get back.

Cooking has become easier, too. Desserts, which used to be the most difficult part of the dinner to prepare, now are beautifully simple —and ever so much more attractive.

Expensive to run? Not a bit. It uses very little current to make all the ice we need and give us perfect refrigeration. And, do you know, it's quite remarkable the way the top

of this box never gets dusty. The circulation of air through those coils seems to drive the dust away.

, , , ,

For fifteen years the vast laboratories of General Electric have been busy developing a simplified refrigerator that would be about

as easy to operate as an electric fan . . . and almost as portable. Four thousand models of nineteen different types were built, field-tested and improved before this new-day refrigerator was brought to its present simplicity and efficiency.

You will want to see the models. Let us send you the address of the dealer who has them on display and booklet 11-J, which is interesting and completely descriptive.

Electric Refrigeration Department
of General Electric Company

Hanna Building   Cleveland, Ohio

GE Refrigerator

GENERAL ELECTRIC

had taught Darwinian evolution in his classes, discredited fundamentalism for much of the nation, even though Scopes lost his case. Candid discussion of sexual habits in psychological or scientific terms made sex less a matter of religious dogma than a matter of casual conversation. The abject failure of prohibition to prohibit discredited the religious leaders who had promised a dry millennium. Yet Americans clung to their religion and often preserved the shell without the substance. "I believe these things," remarked a midwesterner about Christianity, "but they don't take a big place in my life."

For all the decade's boasted sophistication, Protestants could not completely allay their suspicion of Catholics, and Americans with a rural upbringing could not completely overcome their mistrust of city people. Alfred E. Smith, the governor of New York, did not apologize for his Catholicism or his urban idiosyncrasies. Indeed, disapproving rustics thought he betrayed an unseemly pride in his church, his city, and his opposition to prohibition. Smith became the primary target of the Ku Klux Klan when he ran for the Democratic presidential nomination in 1924, and for President in 1928.

Although Smith's political record showed a genuine interest in helping working people, it did not reveal much accomplishment toward that humanitarian end. His administration in New York had been efficient, honest, and rather conservative. But the record was almost beside the point in 1924, when the urban and rural wings of the Democratic party were so split that neither Smith nor William Gibbs McAdoo, the Californian who bore the colors of Bryan's still loyal supporters, could secure the presidential nomination. In a close vote the convention defeated a resolution that specifically condemned the Klan. The weary, divided Democrats eventually awarded their nomination to John W. Davis, a conservative corporation lawyer, whom Calvin Coolidge ignored during the campaign and trounced in the election.

Robert M. LaFollette summoned progressives of all parties to support his presidential candidacy in 1924. His platform contained familiar planks: conservation, political democracy, collective bargaining, tariff reduction, subsidized agricultural credit, and that progressive staple, increased regulation of railroads. LaFollette secured the endorsement of the American Federation of Labor and the American Socialist Party, but he failed to arouse the complacent electorate; "Doing Good," Mencken remarked, "is in bad taste." The Progressive party had few local candidates, little organization, and almost no money. Organized labor soon cooled on the effort, and important union leaders, such as John L. Lewis of the United Mine Workers, supported Coolidge. Republican orators tagged LaFollette as a radical, but so uninspiring was Davis that LaFollette carried his own Wisconsin and ran second to the triumphant Coolidge in several western states, including California. If, however, an attractive candidate could unite the support for Davis with LaFollette's, as shrewd political observers noted, the new coalition might in the future mount an effective challenge to the dominant Republicans.

LaFollette listens to election returns, 1924

The vote for LaFollette may have overstated the vitality of progressivism during the 1920s. Although congressional progressives were able to block, modify, and delay pro-business legislation, they could rarely enact their own proposals. Urban liberalism, which combined an active government and new economic theory in an idealistic vision of a better, more prosperous society, replaced progressivism as the reform orthodoxy of the next decade. In advocating active government, urban liberalism showed its ancestry in progressivism. But the political base of the later movement was entirely different. Progressives relied on the genteel, Protestant, upper and middle classes; urban liberals, often under patrician leadership, rallied the swarthy, swarming, and sweaty city dwellers whom most progressives had feared.

In 1928 the Democratic party turned to the candidate of its urban constituency. Al Smith could not overcome Herbert Hoover's advantage in rural, dry, Protestant America. Hoover lost the electoral votes of only eight states, and he carried such traditional Democratic bastions as North Carolina, Florida, Texas, and Oklahoma. But in urban America, Smith ran well. He carried the nation's largest cities and established the Democratic party as the political arm of urban liberals. Smith's urban gains proved more enduring than Hoover's success in the Democratic South.

The Diplomacy of Isolation

While the First World War had not made the world safe for democracy, Americans were quite sure the world had become safe for the United States. Two oceans offered more protection than collective security; isolation seemed desirable and attainable. But isolation did not preclude traditional diplomatic activity in the Western Hemisphere, continued concern about the Open Door in Asia, or American investment in Europe. Isolation was a wistful faith that the rest of the world would understand the purity of American intent and permit the United States to do as it pleased. Like so many of the nostalgic ideals of the 1920s, isolation proved impossible to achieve.

"We seek," announced Warren G. Harding in his inaugural address, "no part in directing the destinies of the world," a remark that ended any hope for American acceptance of the League of Nations. For some months Secretary of State Hughes did not open correspondence from League functionaries for fear of implying recognition. Eventually Hughes opened his mail, and his successors even sent unofficial observers to sessions of the League in Geneva. No official relationship, however, was proposed or contemplated. In lieu of signing a treaty with the Central Powers, Congress in 1921 formally terminated the war with a joint resolution that reserved to the United States all the rights of the victorious Allies. Nothing was said about responsibilities.

One of the legacies of the war was armament, which virtually all Americans hoped to reduce in order to hold down world tension and domestic taxes. In December 1920, Senator Borah urged that an international conference consider the naval arms race. In 1921 President Harding invited diplomats to meet in Washington, where Secretary Hughes amazed them with an opening speech proposing that the principal naval powers scrap more vessels, as one observer remarked, "than all the admirals of the world had destroyed in a cycle of centuries." The United States, for instance, was to sink thirty ships of more than 845,000 tons. Hughes sought parity for the American and British fleets and a somewhat smaller navy for Japan. Negotiations less public than Hughes's first proposal resulted in the Five Power Pact, which fixed a ratio of 5:5:3:1.6:1.6 for tonnage of capital ships of the United States, Britain, Japan, France, and Italy. The diplomats could not find a formula for restricting vessels smaller than battleships and aircraft carriers. Britain, Japan, and the United States also agreed to construct no new facilities in their possessions in the western Pacific. This agreement made the Japanese fleet dominant in the area, for without fortified bases, the American and British navies could not effectively challenge Japan in its home waters.

In another treaty, Britain, Japan, France, and the United States guaranteed one another's Pacific possessions, and all four nations agreed to consult in the event of a threat to the status quo in the Pacific. This Four Power Pact formally replaced the Anglo-Japanese Alliance of 1902, which had become a source of embarrassment to Great Britain and of concern to the United States. Finally, in the Nine Power Pact, in which China, Portugal, Belgium, and the Netherlands joined the signatories of the Five Power Pact, the Open Door became a multilateral agreement. The document guaranteed the "independence and . . . territorial and administrative integrity of China," but the other agreements of the Washington Conference had eliminated the military means of holding the Chinese door open.

Subsequent attempts (in Geneva in 1927 and in London in 1930) to extend naval restrictions to submarines and other naval vessels were fruitless. Italy under Mussolini was building rather than reducing its navy. France wanted an Anglo-American guarantee of French security in return for concessions. Japan had expansive ambition and intended to preserve the naval means of gratifying it. In retrospect, the Washington Conference may seem to have conceded too much to Japan. But in 1922 Americans thought the treaties a resounding success for American diplomacy and a welcome relief for the world's taxpayers. The Senate ratified the results, specifying only that the Four Power agreement did not commit the United States to any international effort to retain the Pacific status quo.

In 1928 American diplomats went beyond disarmament and solemnly agreed in the multinational Kellogg-Briand Pact to outlaw war as an instrument of national policy. Aristide Briand, the foreign minister of France, proposed that the United States and France join in a "mutual engagement tending, as between these two countries, to outlaw war." Secretary of State Frank Kellogg, who had succeeded Hughes in 1925, suggested that all nations be invited to subscribe to Briand's proposal. In August 1928, the first fifteen nations, including the United States, formally agreed to use peaceful means to settle international disputes. The Senate consented by a vote of 85 to 1, but many senators knew the treaty was, as Virginia's respected Senator Glass said, "worthless but perfectly harmless." Enforcement of the Kellogg-Briand Pact rested on international collective action, for which the treaty itself made no provision; if automatic sanctions had been included, the Senate would doubtless have withheld its ratification. For the goal of American policy was not international cooperation to end international war; the goal was rather an end to international war so that the United States could remain safely isolated.

Yet the expanding American economy made isolation difficult. American enterprise, unimpaired by the war, dominated postwar international trade, and the nation had a vital interest in the prosperity of its primary markets. The United States had long had a favorable balance of trade; after the war, America became an international creditor as well, with extensive foreign investments. But protective tariffs kept many imports out of American markets, and thereby reduced the ability of other nations to pay for American goods and credit. American loans temporarily furnished the exchange necessary for continuing international trade. Near the end of the decade, however, when domestic speculation seemed more profitable, loans dropped, and the American tariff again complicated international trade.

The related questions of German reparations and interallied war debts also troubled international economic relations. Germany did not intend to meet the reparations payments imposed at Versailles and perhaps could not have done so. Although the United States never admitted any link between reparations and the debts owed the United States by Britain, France, and other European allies, these debtor states fully expected to pay their American bills with German cash. Indeed, the Allies thought the United States ungratefully grasping for insisting on repayment at all. Most of the borrowed money had been spent in the United States for American goods and had stimulated American industry. In addition, the Allies argued, the war effort had been a common cause; if America had lent money, they had shed blood, which ought to even the transaction. But neither the government nor the taxpayers would forgive the debts. Coolidge summed up American policy by observing simply, "They hired the money, didn't they?"

Yet the question was not simple. Early in 1923 Germany defaulted on reparations payments. Before the end of the year, inflation had ruined the German currency and threatened the French franc. An international commission headed by Charles G. Dawes, an American banker, scaled down reparations payments. The Dawes Plan provided for loans, largely from the United States, to restore a sound German currency and to revive the economic activity that had to precede reparations payments. In effect, the United States lent money to Germany, which paid reparations to the Allies, which then paid their debts to the United States. Like many another economic expedient, the Dawes Plan collapsed in the depression that closed the decade.

Isolation as a diplomatic ideal never extended to the Western Hemisphere. The 1920s opened with American marines in Nicaragua, Haiti, and the Dominican Republic and with the Roosevelt Corollary as the operative American policy. Not all the marines had come home a decade later, nor had all the American restrictions on the sovereignty of Cuba, Panama, and other Latin American republics been abrogated. But in 1930 the Roosevelt Corollary was formally renounced, and the United States was irrevocably committed to a course another Roosevelt would call "the policy of the Good Neighbor."

Mexican-American relations revealed the new direction. The social revolution that began in Mexico during the Wilson administration brought constitutional changes that vexed important groups of Americans. Mexican law decreed that subsoil rights belonged to the nation and not to the individuals who owned the earth's surface.

American oil companies refused to accept this ruling and expected diplomatic help from the State Department. The Mexican government also nationalized the property of the Roman Catholic Church, prohibited religious instruction in primary schools, and curtailed the number of priests per province. American Catholics, angry at what seemed official persecution, urged the government to intervene on behalf of religious liberty.

In retrospect, neither dispute seems crucial. Yet the combination created diplomatic friction. In 1927 Dwight Morrow, whom Coolidge appointed ambassador to Mexico, began to persuade the Mexicans rather than bully them. With tact and a keen sense of public relations, Morrow secured the confidence of the Mexican government and worked out a compromise that permitted American companies once more to pump oil and Mexican churches once more to hold mass. Morrow's solutions were not final, but his quiet method of seeking them replaced the habit of sending marines.

Before his inauguration in 1929, President-elect Hoover dramatized American interest with a tour of Latin America. To be sure, he sailed on a battleship, but while in Argentina he promised that the United States would not intervene in the internal affairs of other American republics. This pledge became official policy, apparently by inadvertence, when the Clark Memorandum was published in 1930. The memorandum pointed out that the Monroe Doctrine had initially protected Latin American republics from foreign intervention but that Theodore Roosevelt's interpretation had brought constant American intervention and outraged proud, independent peoples. The new American policy still did not permit European interference in the hemisphere, but at least American control was to be more subtle.

The activity of the State Department—negotiations, treaties, a different hemispheric policy—indicates that isolation was one of the illusions of the 1920s. Yet in another sense, isolation was a fact, for it was never a policy so much as a state of mind. And after Versailles the United States certainly intended to reject the rest of the world. The difficulty was that the nation renounced only responsibility while forcefully demanding the perquisites of power.

Suggested Reading

As the 1920s closed, Frederick Lewis Allen wrote *Only Yesterday** (1931), an account of that decade that retains its charm. William E. Leuchtenburg's *The Perils of Prosperity** (1958) has the advantage of perspective. Burl Noggle's *Into the Twenties* (1974) is useful for its emphasis on Wilson's last years in the White House. Arthur M. Schlesinger, Jr., is critical of Republicans and their policies in *The Crisis* *of the Old Order** (1957), the first volume of his study of Franklin D. Roosevelt. Robert K. Murray defends Harding in *The Harding Era* (1969) and in *The Politics of Normalcy** (1973).

George E. Mowry has edited a useful collection of sources entitled *The Twenties** (1963); another collection, *The Aspirin Age** (1949), edited by Isabel Leighton, overemphasizes the bizarre but is worthwhile. More specialized works include Alfred M. Kazin's *On Native Grounds** (1942), which deals with the literature of the "lost generation"; David M. Kennedy's *Birth Control in America** (1970), which centers on Margaret Sanger; Robert K. Murray's *Red Scare** (1955), which chronicles the harassment of radicals; and Paul Carter's *Another Part of the Twenties**(1977), which focuses on culture. Dozens of books, including Norman H. Clark's *Deliver Us from Evil* (1976), deal with prohibition. Robert S. and Helen M. Lynd's *Middletown** (1929) is instructive not only for data on Muncie, Indiana, but also for what it reveals about midwestern culture and the eastern scholars who studied that city in the 1920s.

The foreign policy of the period may be followed in two works by Robert J. Ferrell, *Peace in Their Time** (1952) and *American Diplomacy in the Great Depression** (1957), and in Elting E. Morison's *Turmoil and Tradition** (1960), an excellent biography of Henry L. Stimson, Hoover's secretary of state.

* Available in paperback edition

Chapter 19
Depression

Given a chance to go forward with the policies of the past eight years," Herbert Hoover prophesied as he accepted the presidential nomination in 1928, "we shall soon with the help of God be in sight of the day when poverty will be banished from this nation." At his inauguration the following March, President Hoover proclaimed that he had "no fears for the future of our country," which was "bright with hope." Such occasions beget exaggeration; it was Hoover's misfortune that people still remembered his hyperboles when events made them seem foolish.

In the months between his inauguration and the stock market crash in October 1929, Hoover displayed the administrative energy that had made him an effective secretary of commerce and an attractive presidential candidate. He called national conferences to mobilize public support for revisions in Indian policy and for stiffer regulations to protect the health and welfare of children. He increased federal support for black education at Howard University, ordered reform in the administration of the federal prisons, and publicly identified some of the beneficiaries of inequitable tax legislation by releasing the names of those who received refunds.

Hoover also knew that the economic policies "of the past eight years" needed modification. He supported the Federal Reserve Board's futile effort to slow speculation by raising interest rates in the summer of 1929.

Privately, he urged the stock exchange to police itself more effectively. But private admonition and tardy tinkering with interest rates did nothing to change distribution of the national income, of which 30 percent went to the most prosperous 5 percent of the nation's families. At the base of the boom celebrated in Hoover's expansive statements were the new industries that produced such consumer goods as automobiles and electrical appliances. The rich alone could not consume fast enough to sustain mass production. But Republican economic policies had done more to encourage the rich to invest than to enable the poor to consume.

Some of that investment, in fact, was speculation. Twice in the 1920s a speculative mania gripped the nation. A brisk business in Florida real estate in 1925 and 1926 served as spring training for the stock market season that opened in 1927, when stock prices began their dizzying climb toward September 3, 1929, the day that marked the apex of the great bull market. On Tuesday, October 29, a decade ended. More than 16 million shares were sold, most at immense losses. And the crash in October was only the beginning. Throughout the rest of 1929 and through 1930, 1931, and 1932, the market sagged.

A Deepening Depression

The stock market crash only wiped out speculators; most Americans were just interested bystanders. Perhaps as many as a million people were actively trading stocks in 1929, and by no means all of them became destitute overnight. *Time* suggested that the panic was a brilliant coup of shrewd market operators; no one worried aloud that economic illness might spread beyond Wall Street. But slowly the nation's business atrophied. A vital economy might have shrugged off even such a serious setback as the rout in the market. The American economy in 1929, however, was less vital than it appeared. The banking system, tied to the market through loans secured by falling stocks, reeled with other speculators. Crippled banks had to curtail loans, which in turn forced a reduction in consumer spending, especially for goods purchased on the installment plan. As sales fell, prices fell and then wages. Industrial production between 1929 and 1932 declined more than 50 percent; the average wage of factory workers went down about 60 percent. New investment slumped from $10 billion to $1 billion in the same three years, and national income from $81 billion to $41 billion. While every other index declined, unemployment mounted with the same eerie monotony that had once characterized the stock market: four million at the end of 1930; seven million in October 1931; eleven million when the nation voted a year later to replace Hoover with Roosevelt; perhaps fourteen million when Roosevelt took office in March 1933.

Behind every statistic were real people with blighted dreams, pressing needs, and choking anxieties. There was the midwestern widow who lost twenty years of savings and her husband's insurance when the local bank failed. For a few moments she screamed in front of the bank's closed doors; her screams turned to sobs and finally to mute incomprehension before neighbors took her to a mental institution. And there was the Oregon sheepherder who killed his whole flock and left 3,000 sheep to rot in a canyon because it would cost him $1.10 to ship each one to market, where it would sell for $1.00. Since he could not afford to feed the animals through the winter, he slaughtered them. There was corn to feed animals in Iowa; the surplus from earlier harvests brought about $1.40 per ton in 1933. But coal cost much more than that, so cold farmers burned corn instead.

President Hoover at first attributed the Crash to a failure of business confidence. To renew it, he reiterated at every opportunity his own confidence in an early return of prosperity. He invited businessmen to the White House, asked them to maintain wages, employment, and capital spending, and joined them in a cheery reassurance to the public that the economic condition of the country was fundamentally sound. The President thought that public-spirited business leaders, encouraged but not coerced by government, could deal more effectively with the depression than could government itself.

But the economy refused to be coaxed to prosperity. As some Americans approached a second winter without employment, as charities and states ran out of funds for relief, as newspapers reported that people were foraging in dumps and garbage heaps, and as malnutrition and exposure came to public attention, Herbert Hoover became the nation's scapegoat. His optimistic statements seemed to mock the plight of the poor. Villages of shacks, invariably called "Hoovervilles," sprouted in New York's Central Park and other, less desirable locations. Though the complacent cliché maintained that "No one has starved," a few people did in fact starve, and many went hungry.

Americans blamed themselves as well as their President. Indeed, in circumstances that seemed to urge action, they were as patient and passive as Herbert Hoover seemed himself. Public inaction derived in part from bewilderment. No one was sure what action to take, either on the national level to salvage the country's economy, or on the personal level to secure a job. But Americans also displayed a belief in individual responsibility to rival Herbert Hoover's, for they saw unemployment as a personal failure and they were ashamed to need help.

Hoover Acts

The President was sensitive to the nation's distress. When confidence showed no sign of an early return and when the economy showed no sign of improvement, Hoover's sensitivity overcame his economic scruples. By comparison with Franklin Roosevelt's New Deal, Hoover's action was tentative and grudging. But he did take steps to support agricultural prices; he provided federal credit to steady staggering banks; and in 1932 he acknowledged that the government might have to assist those at the bottom of the economy who most needed help.

Even before the Crash, Hoover had called Congress into special session to consider the chronic agricultural depression that had reduced rural America's share of the national income by almost half during the 1920s. The Agricultural Marketing Act of June 1929 applied to farming principles Hoover, as secretary of commerce, had developed for other businesses. The act encouraged farmers to regulate themselves through cooperatives, which would bring supply and demand into balance and thereby stabilize the prices of agricultural produce. Congress appropriated $500 million to help these cooperatives create orderly markets, but granted the newly established Federal Farm Board no authority to restrict production.

Still prices fell. The bushel of wheat that sold for a dollar in 1928 brought less than forty cents in 1932. Cotton and corn dropped in roughly the same proportion. Nor was the tariff, which was supposed to boost rural purchasing power, effective. Passed in 1930, the Hawley-Smoot Tariff made duties that were already protective even more so. But imports did not cause the oversupply of agricultural produce in the American market, and the new tariff provoked retaliatory legislation abroad that reduced foreign purchases of American harvests.

President Hoover later decided that the depression itself had been imported from abroad. To ease the troubled international economy, he proposed, in 1931, a one-year moratorium on payments of interallied war debts and German reparations. Delay dissipated whatever economic lift this initiative might have produced. Then a wave of European bank failures set back American recovery, Hoover thought, just as his policies had begun to work. This comforting explanation catered to the popular American belief that anything unpleasant must be foreign, and to the suspicion of Europe that prevailed after Versailles. But Hoover's interpretation was self-serving and naive. The American depression began earlier, lasted longer, and was more severe than that in any European country. And prosperity had certainly not been lurking around a nearby corner when American bankers had to call in loans and thereby weakened Europe's banks in 1931.

No other contemporary explanation of the depression was wholly satisfying either. The "Brain Trust" that Franklin Roosevelt drew together provided no coherent interpretation that led to logically consistent policies. Roosevelt himself knew only that politics and humanity alike required immediate measures to alleviate hardship. Hoover later painted Roosevelt as a socialist and himself as the prophet of laissez faire; neither portrait was a good likeness. Roosevelt's New Deal may have saved American capitalism, and Hoover's laissez faire, while pretending impartiality, permitted governmental help to beleaguered banks, insurance companies, and farmers. Guiding Hoover's policy was his fixed faith in the gold standard and the balanced budget. If action were required, he would encourage private investment and employment, rather than have citizens directly dependent on their government.

In October 1930, Hoover had promised federal leadership for a state and local campaign of voluntary self-help, apparently a euphemism for charity. In 1932, the administration blocked an appropriation of $375 million for relief, but made loans for that purpose available to local governments. Hoover asked Congress in 1931 for more funds for the Federal Land Bank, an agency for rural credit established in 1916. Congress responded with $125 million, and in July 1932 added another $125 million for homeowners threatened with foreclosure. Both measures provided immediate currency for banks whose assets were sound but not readily negotiable. Early in 1932, Congress fulfilled another of Hoover's requests by chartering the Reconstruction Finance Corporation (RFC), a federal lending agency that within six months lent over a billion dollars

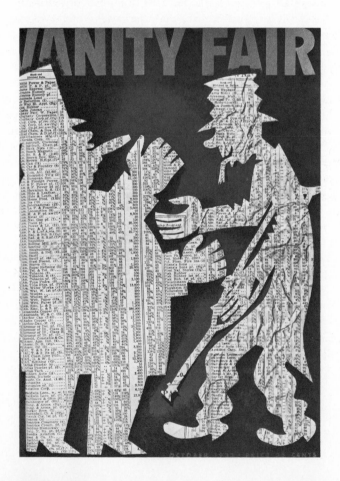

to banks and other financial institutions. Many of these loans went to the nation's financial elite, including a bank in Chicago of which former Vice-President Charles G. Dawes was an officer. A month before the loan to his bank was approved, Dawes had resigned as the president of the RFC.

The RFC was also Hoover's instrument to help ordinary people. In 1932 the agency was empowered to lend $1.5 billion to local authorities for the construction of public works, such as highways and housing, that would eventually return in tolls and rents the money advanced. And the RFC might lend $300 million to communities whose relief funds were exhausted. Neither of these authorizations was vigorously administered; the RFC had lent only about $30 million for relief—a drop in the bucket when ten million Americans were unemployed—and somewhat less for public works by the time Hoover left office.

All the indexes continued to go down while unrest mounted. A few intellectuals turned to Marx, a few farmers resorted to violence to forestall foreclosure, and a comparatively few veterans marched on Washington to lobby for immediate cash payment of the veteran's bonus that Congress had established in 1924. The Bonus Expeditionary Force (BEF) of perhaps 12,000 or 15,000 unemployed veterans camped for several days in shacks and unoccupied federal buildings on Washington's Anacostia Flats. In June 1932, the House passed a bill to pay the bonus in unbacked paper currency, but the measure died in the Senate. The disappointed veterans demonstrated their continued patriotism by singing "America" on the steps of the Capitol; about half of them accepted the government's offer to lend money for the trip home. The other half, without any reason to return or any home to return to, stayed on in the encampment, to the increasing anxiety of the administration. In late July Hoover ordered the army to disperse the BEF and clear Anacostia Flats. The chief of staff, General Douglas MacArthur, personally supervised the operation of four infantry companies and four troops of cavalry, which employed tear gas, tanks, and machine guns to rout the BEF. The veterans scattered; the shacks on Anacostia Flats burned; and the nation correctly refused to believe the administration's assertion that the ragtag BEF spearheaded a revolution.

FDR Triumphs

The nation's bankruptcy was more than economic; it was theoretical as well. Businessmen and bankers, on whose advice the nation had relied, offered homilies about thrift, hard work, and faith or, more forthrightly, they simply confessed complete bewilderment. As the election of 1932 approached, the major political parties offered little clear direction. Republicans listlessly renominated Hoover on a platform that called for a balanced budget, a protective tariff, restricted immigration, and unspecified changes in the prohibition statute. Nor did their opponents seem a sharp alternative, for the financial conservatism Democrats had displayed in the 1920s lingered in demands for reduced expenditures and a balanced budget. Although the Democrats promised new programs as well, the important contrast was in the candidates. Humorless and ponderous, Hoover plodded through defensive speeches about what ought not to be done. Roosevelt, on the other hand, hearty and confident, clearly would act, though precisely how his campaign did not disclose. In one speech, he suggested that the country had built too much productive capacity, that the government and business must plan together for a mature economy; in another he espoused the competitive creed of optimistic progressives. He opposed the expansion of bureaucracy, federal controls, and government spending, while he sketched new legislation that would expand all three. In November, 282 counties that had never before supported a Democrat voted for him. Roosevelt carried all but 6 states and swamped Hoover by more than 7 million popular votes.

It was the occasion, the tone of voice, and the mood, not the words, that made Roosevelt's inaugural address memorable. The most famous line in the speech—"the only thing we have to fear is fear itself"— echoed a platitude that provoked derision when Hoover had used it; coming from Roosevelt, the assurance seemed more authoritative. Roosevelt outlined national needs but was seldom specific in his prescription for meeting them. Yet the whole tone of his address confirmed his intention to do something. The speech bristled with allusions to war: the American people "must move as a trained and loyal army willing to sacrifice for the good of a common discipline"; Roosevelt himself "unhesitatingly" assumed "the leadership of this great army"; and he promised that if the crisis continued he would ask Congress for "broad executive power to wage war against the emergency," just as he would in the event of a foreign invasion.

Action he had pledged, and action the country got. The actions were not always coherent, and it sometimes seemed that the New Deal's left hand repaired damage done by the right. Roosevelt's critics accused him of instituting a planned economy, but the New Deal was more spontaneous than planned. Roosevelt knew better what his goals were than what his programs were. The goals were pragmatic: he wanted to restore prosperity and to reform the economic system in such a way that a similar disaster would never again overtake the American people. The President was impatient with ideologies and comprehensive schemes; all he wanted was results.

Whatever the folklore of the 1930s, the New Deal was no assault on individual wealth or on the framework of American capitalism. Those who controlled the nation's property and production in 1940 were the same people and the same corporations that had done so in 1930. Taxes

Inauguration day, 1933

imposed during the New Deal years did not significantly alter the distribution of income; indeed, the most important new tax—the social security tax—was a regressive levy that bore most heavily on the poor.

But if Roosevelt did not produce fundamental modifications in the American version of capitalism, he did foster a host of lesser ones— changes that were major for some individuals and, in the aggregate, amounted to the beginning of a welfare state. The government accepted traditional capitalism while attempting to shield Americans from the worst excesses of an unregulated industrial economy. Minimum wages, maximum hours, full employment, collective bargaining, social security, regulated competition—these were the achievements of the Roosevelt administration. Although the New Deal did not enact all the measures advocated by urban liberals, it did set the limits of political debate for the next four decades. Federal intervention became political orthodoxy; the questions were those of degree. The effort of progressives to blend individualism with equal opportunity gave way to the New Deal's effort to help those who missed their opportunity through no fault of their own. Few New Dealers shared the interest of progressives in the behavior or morality of individual citizens.

The legislation of the New Deal came in bursts, the first one in a special session called the "hundred days," from March to June 1933, and the second in 1935. Even the lulls were productive, by ordinary legislative standards, until 1938, when the New Deal as a creative force was finished. Throughout the New Deal, programs for economic recovery were mingled with more permanent programs for reform. The New Deal began as a gigantic effort to do something for everyone, but as the depression wore on, Roosevelt increased the proportion of help for the underprivileged and curtailed aid to business. In this respect, the "second New Deal" of 1935 and after showed that Roosevelt had drifted to the left. Yet the National Recovery Administration (NRA), the keystone of the first New Deal, and the Tennessee Valley Authority (TVA), created in 1933, were as abrupt departures from traditional American political and economic principles as anything that came in the second New Deal.

Outside Washington

Few local politicians shared the sense of urgency that made Congress receptive to the early legislation of the New Deal. New York, Indiana, Georgia, Minnesota, and a few other states enacted programs to complement federal ones. More characteristically, state officials assumed that the New Deal simply furnished emergency assistance that required no modification of the traditional political pattern. They welcomed federal money and expected the New Deal to go away when the money ran out. The New Deal's "imprint on the states," one historian has concluded, "was often faint and indistinct."

By some measures, the impact on the general public seemed equally fleeting. Soap operas and other radio entertainment made poverty an obstacle for individuals to overcome rather than a condition confronting the entire society. Readers borrowed Dale Carnegie's *How to Win Friends and Influence People*, a self-help manual, from the local library, not treatises on economic theory. The best-selling novel of the decade, Margaret Mitchell's *Gone with the Wind*, contained little social commentary. The film based on that novel, and other successful movies, offered escape from the depression rather than solutions for it; where economic hardship occurred in the decade's films, it tended to disappear in a happy ending. If Americans had to spend their days looking for jobs, they apparently did not spend their evenings thinking about other people's unemployment. They sought a personal accommodation with the depression, or, at most, one for a family.

In many families, a woman brought home the wage that enabled the family to survive. Working wives still risked community disapproval, especially if they seemed to deprive men of jobs and other families of livelihood. Nevertheless, the number of married women in the labor force increased by 50 percent between 1930 and 1940, a decade when labor was abundant and jobs in short supply. Some of these women, of course, were heads of households, but most were not. They worked to supplement the earnings of other members of the family, to sustain spending habits developed in better times, to maintain middle-income status, as well as to prevent deprivation.

The New Deal and the Economic Crisis

The economic crisis was acute as Roosevelt took office. On inauguration day, and for some days thereafter, not a bank in the nation opened for business. Beginning in February 1933, governors had proclaimed temporary "holidays" to prevent runs on banks. By March precautionary closings had occurred in nearly half the states, and Treasury officials urged the other half to follow suit. Roosevelt issued a proclamation making the holiday national and official and then called Congress into special session to ratify his action and provide legislation to end the emergency.

The Emergency Banking Act, passed only a few hours after Congress assembled, required most banks to have an authorization from the Treasury before reopening, permitted the RFC to make immediate loans to banks the Treasury found to be sound, and allowed the Federal Reserve system to issue notes based on the assets of strong banks. Most banks began to function again after a few days, but the Treasury refused immediate licenses to more than 1,700 shaky banks, some of which eventually consolidated their assets and reopened. On March 12, 1933, Roosevelt made his first "fireside chat," an informal radio report to the nation in which he assured Americans that the newly licensed banks were secure. Within three weeks bank deposits increased more than a billion dollars, and that crisis was over.

The Home Owners Loan Corporation (HOLC), established a few weeks later, was another device to take the pressure off both banks and their debtors. The HOLC refinanced urban mortgages, thus relieving the anxiety of those whose homes were in danger of foreclosure and at the same time providing the banks with liquid assets that were essential. Foreclosures soon declined from the rate of a thousand per day in the first months of 1933; when the HOLC wound up its affairs, it had refinanced one of every five nonfarm mortgages in the nation.

Having met the emergency, the administration moved to prevent a recurrence. The general prosperity of the 1920s had hidden the failure of nearly 7,000 banks, most of which were small ones located in areas dependent on depressed agricultural staples. The Glass-Steagall Act, passed in June 1933, required the separation of commercial and investment banking and guaranteed bank deposits up to $2,500 through the Federal Deposit Insurance Corporation (FDIC). These reforms provoked some grumbling in the financial community but were much less extensive than nationalized banking, which had been seriously proposed. Moreover, they worked: the nation had fewer bank failures between 1933 and 1940 than had occurred in any single year of the 1920s.

The Emergency Banking Act in effect took the country off the gold standard, a step that Congress confirmed officially in April 1933. For a few months in 1933 Roosevelt regularly raised the price of gold, thereby making the dollar worth less, in the vain hope that other prices would rise in response. A similar program in 1934 to buy the entire domestic output of silver at an inflated price helped the politically influential silver interests (which were economically less important than the chewing gum industry) but did not improve general price levels. Neither program generated the expected inflation, and Roosevelt turned to other methods of curing the depression.

Financial reform and inflated currency were useless without vitality in the nation's industry and agriculture, without employment, without a flow of goods in response to consumer demand. In the National Industrial Recovery Act (NIRA) of June 1933, Congress wove together several proposals designed to restore business prosperity and to permit workers to share the expected benefits.

The most orthodox provision of this act appropriated more than $3 billion for construction of roads, bridges, buildings, and other public works. Roosevelt assigned Secretary of the Interior Harold L. Ickes, a gruff, honest, former Bull Mooser, to administer the Public Works Administration (PWA). Although the need was for immediate spending, Ickes conscientiously scrutinized blueprints to make sure the public received full value, and the PWA did not inject large amounts of money into the economy until the middle of the decade.

Much less orthodox was the National Recovery Administration (NRA), which Hugh Johnson, a stormy, salty former general, ran with gusto. Under the sponsorship of the NRA, representatives of industry, labor, and government (the advocate for the consumer) assembled and drew up codes to cover a particular business. When approved by the President, these codes had the force of law and regulated production, competitive practices, and, less effectively, wages and hours. Theoretically, the codes would produce a "planned economy," whose benefits employees, producers, and the public would share. In fact, it soon became apparent that the plans were often those of the dominant firms in an industry, to which such benefits as there were accrued through price fixing. The codes suspended the antitrust laws, and the NRA tended to permit restricted production and thinly veiled price stabilization.

Franklin Roosevelt launched the NRA with the panoply of a crusade. General Johnson designed a stylized blue eagle bearing the bold legend "We Do Our Part" to symbolize the effort. The blue eagle, indeed, had to enforce the codes, for Johnson, fearing that the law might not survive a court case, could punish those who did not enlist in his crusade, or those who deserted, only by depriving them of their right to display the blue eagle. The codes, proclaimed with great enthusiasm, proved difficult to draft, more difficult to administer, and nearly impossible to enforce. Such a prominent manufacturer as Henry Ford refused to have anything to do with the NRA. Disillusion with the program was early and pervasive. And in 1935, as Johnson had feared, the Supreme Court, in *Schechter Poultry Company* v. *United States*, unanimously struck down the NRA as an unconstitutional delegation of legislative power to code-making bodies and as an unjustifiable expansion of the commerce clause to include intrastate businesses. Publicly outraged, the President was privately relieved. General Johnson had promised more than the NRA could deliver; it was a political liability and a failure as well.

By 1935 the business community had become disenchanted with FDR, and the administration proposed no comprehensive replacement for the

NRA. The Guffey Coal Act (1935) reenacted parts of the NRA code for that sick industry, but otherwise the New Deal turned from helping business to regulating it. The Public Utility Holding Company Act (1935) did not quite provide a "death sentence" for holding companies, as angry power lobbyists claimed, but it did require that holding companies demonstrate that efficiency required their continued control of operating utilities. In 1938, blaming big business for the persisting recession that had begun in 1937, Roosevelt attacked the continued economic consolidation that had brought 5 percent of the nation's corporations nearly 90 percent of the nation's corporate assets. Congress established the Temporary National Economic Committee (TNEC) to investigate concentration of economic power, and the Justice Department began to enforce the Sherman Act. So the New Deal, which began by suspending antitrust statutes, ended by reviving them.

The Program for Agriculture

The agricultural policy of the New Deal was an amalgam of proposals as old as those of the Grangers with the new notion of controlling production. Packed in one legislative bundle under the general direction of Secretary of Agriculture Henry A. Wallace, these proposals emerged in 1933 as the Agricultural Adjustment Act, to be administered by the Agricultural Adjustment Administration (AAA).

The AAA paid farmers direct subsidies in return for decreased production. The cost of the subsidy was financed by a tax on processors of agricultural produce, who passed their increased costs on to the consumer. The act carefully catered to rural sensitivity by requiring the farmers themselves to approve production agreements and by using local farmers to administer the program where possible. In order to reduce commodities in 1933, farmers had to destroy some growing cotton and slaughter five million pigs before they became marketable. No one was happy about destroying potential food and clothing when millions of people lacked both. Norman Thomas, the spokesman for America's few socialists, tartly congratulated the New Deal for removing the paradox of poverty in the midst of plenty by eliminating plenty. But the AAA appeared to work. Agricultural production declined while prices and farm income went up, sharply in the case of cotton growers. Even so, more intensive cultivation of fewer acres continued to produce more crops than forecasts called for, and the buying power of farmers did not reach the level they had enjoyed in good times.

In 1936, the Supreme Court declared the processing tax provision of the Agricultural Adjustment Act unconstitutional, thus effectively killing the AAA. The decision was strained and the dissent unusually sharp; the President was furious, partly because the election of 1936 would follow the next harvest, when prices would be still fresh in the minds of farmers. Congress put the AAA in a new wrapper by dropping the processing tax and authorizing direct payment to farmers who adopted such soil conservation practices as not planting the staple crops that were in chronic surplus. The Soil Conservation and Domestic Allotment Act was less effective in reducing production than a drought that hit the farm belt in the mid-1930s. The drought, plus strong winds and the effect of years of plowing, created the dust bowl and sent thousands of displaced "Okies" from Oklahoma, Kansas, Texas, and other parched states off to California in search of nonexistent jobs.

The pattern of American agriculture did not significantly shift during the depression, for the chief beneficiaries of the New Deal's programs, including the second AAA, which Congress enacted in 1938, were the commercial farmers. The subsistence farmer, who grew his own food and marketed his surplus locally, did not profit from efforts to support the prices of major staples. The attempt to restrict production, in fact, drove some sharecroppers from the land, since the subsidies went to landowners, not to laborers. Although the Soil Conservation Act diverted a portion of the benefit payments to tenants, poverty, pellagra, and hookworm continued to be their lot. In 1935 Roosevelt put Rexford Tugwell in charge of the Resettlement Administration (RA), which was supposed to assist both rural and urban poor to escape to new communities and presumably to new opportunities. Battered by congressional criticism, the RA actually resettled few families and was absorbed in 1937 by the Farm Security Administration (FSA), which did extend credit to agricultural laborers to enable them to purchase farms. In spite of the poverty of the borrowers, there were few defaults on these loans.

The New Deal perhaps transformed rural life most with one of the least noticed, least controversial programs. In 1935, Congress established the Rural Electrification Administration (REA) to help make power available to

Migrant workers

isolated farms. The REA encouraged the establishment of cooperatives, lent them money to build distribution facilities, and advised them about marketing power. Electricity not only eased the tasks of farming but also removed many of the differences between urban and rural life.

The Poor and the Unemployed

Probably the most comprehensive measure of the entire New Deal was the program to improve the Tennessee Valley, an area where living standards had long lagged behind those of most of the rest of the nation. The act in 1933 establishing the Tennessee Valley Authority (TVA) successfully concluded Senator George Norris's prolonged effort to have the government develop a complete plan for the valley. The three-man directorate of the TVA was to plan nothing less than a total rehabilitation of the region, to control its rivers and convert their energy to electricity, to replace eroded gullies and naked hills with productive farms and growing forests, to diversify the economy and bring prosperity to parts of seven states.

The TVA built more than twenty dams, which transformed the rampaging Tennessee River into a controlled inland waterway more than 600 miles long. The agency introduced new crops and new techniques to improve fertility and prevent erosion. And by the end of the 1930s, the TVA produced and distributed electric power, thereby providing what FDR called a "yardstick" to measure the costs of private utilities. Although competition from the TVA decreased the price of privately produced electricity by about 70 percent, utilities discovered that increased volume pushed their profits up. Nevertheless, private utilities, led by Wendell Willkie, the dynamic president of the largest holding company in the area, attacked the TVA's power operation both in court and in public. The attack in court failed, but the public attack was more successful, for Congress ignored subsequent attempts to apply TVA techniques to other river valleys. To be sure, as opponents of the TVA have argued, the taxes of the whole nation raised the economic level of one region. But the Tennessee Valley has probably repaid the nation with income taxes that would never have been paid if the area had continued to be depressed.

The Roosevelt administration also responded to distress in other parts of the country. In one of the earliest acts of the "hundred days" the need for relief was linked to the administration's interest in conservation. The Civilian Conservation Corps (CCC) employed as many as a half-million young men in reforestation, flood and erosion control, and maintenance of national parks. FDR had an almost Jeffersonian faith that fresh air and hard work would transform the temporarily unemployed into sturdy, self-reliant citizens. If the CCC did not work wonders of individual

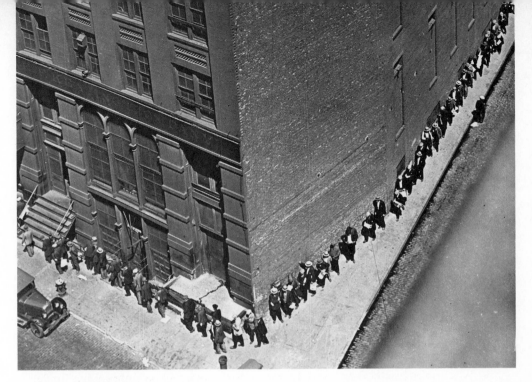

Manhattan bread line

regeneration, it did at least keep some young men off the job market and it planted more than half the trees set out by man since the nation began.

With millions of unemployed Americans requiring help in 1933, the CCC was barely a start. In May Congress established the Federal Emergency Relief Administration (FERA), and Roosevelt appointed Harry Hopkins, a young social worker, to direct the agency. Within hours after the act was passed, Hopkins had allotted several million dollars to the states for direct relief, which he disliked nearly as much as did Hoover. Hopkins preferred to provide the needy with employment, if necessary under federal sponsorship, and he persuaded FDR to his view. In November 1933, Hopkins established the Civil Works Administration (CWA) to employ about four million jobless on projects that required little equipment and much labor, such as leaf-raking and street-sweeping. The CWA enabled many families to survive the winter of 1933 before the program expired in the spring.

But unemployment did not abate. In 1935 Roosevelt made a distinction between the unemployed, for whom the federal government assumed responsibility, and the unemployable, whose welfare was left to state and local authorities or to private charity. The Works Progress Administration (WPA), of which Hopkins was the chief, employed as many as 3.5 million people on a host of projects. The WPA not only built roads, bridges, public buildings, airports, and parks, but also sponsored symphony concerts, hired artists to paint murals, established a federal theater, commissioned unemployed writers to produce a series of guidebooks to the states, and through the National Youth Administration, provided employment for college students. Hopkins believed the WPA must do more than employ people; it must also preserve their morale and their skills, which the nation would someday need again. Some of the agency's projects were not very useful—"boondoggling," the critics said—and the various arts projects were particularly vulnerable because some of them seemed to promote radicalism. But before it ended in 1943, the WPA had saved the dignity, and perhaps the lives, of millions of Americans.

The WPA was an immediate response to depression; social security was a permanent program to alleviate the curse of unemployment in an industrial society. Drafted by a group under the direction of Secretary of Labor Frances Perkins, the Social Security Act of 1935 combined unemployment insurance with a program to provide annuities for the aged or for dependent survivors of workers. Payments to the unemployed would mitigate the consequences of economic misfortune and, by making possible continued consumption, might prevent the loss of other jobs. Annuities for the aged were supposed to enable that growing segment of the population to leave the job market without burdening their families. By comparison with the politically potent appeal of Dr. Francis Townsend's scheme to grant $200 per month to every citizen over sixty-five, the New Deal's measure seemed conservative. Initially, the grants were small and many Americans were not covered, but Congresses since 1935 have expanded both benefits and coverage.

A tax on payrolls, equally borne by employers and employees, financed social security benefits. If the program was financially sound, it was fiscally regressive, for the tax was not directly tied to the taxpayer's ability to pay. The first collections under the new law took in about a billion dollars more than the agency disbursed. Combined with cuts in appropriations for the WPA and other efforts FDR made to balance the budget, this action brought a sharp recession in 1937 that undid much of the recovery the New Deal had nursed through the preceding four years.

Workers and Their Unions

Late in the depression, labor unions shook off the lethargy of the twenties and organized industries that had long resisted. The labor policy of the New Deal owed relatively little to Franklin Roosevelt and much to such congressional friends of labor as Senator Robert F. Wagner of New York. His legislation sponsored the growth of unions, which, for the first time, were able to bargain on equal terms with the nation's biggest businesses.

In Section 7(a), the National Industrial Recovery Act required all codes to guarantee the right of workers to bargain collectively and forbade employers to discriminate against union members. The NRA codes bound employers to abolish child labor and to pay a minimum wage, initially set at thirty or forty cents an hour (depending on location), for a forty-hour week. To enforce these provisions, the act created the National Labor Board (NLB), which Roosevelt appointed Senator Wagner to head. The NLB attempted to mediate industrial disputes, but it was only partially successful. Organized labor, encouraged by the law and by public opinion, which had swung decisively against business during the depression, embarked on an organizing drive that employers determined to thwart. A wave of futile strikes in 1934—in textiles, automobiles, steel, and a general strike in San Francisco—convinced Senator Wagner that new legislation was required. When the Supreme Court invalidated the NIRA in 1935, the administration no longer had a labor program, and FDR accepted the substitute Wagner had prepared.

The Wagner Act of 1935 forbade several "unfair labor practices" and created a National Labor Relations Board (NLRB) to enforce its provisions. "Unfair labor practices" included domination of company unions, discrimination against employees because of union membership or activity, and refusal to bargain collectively with any union chosen by the workers at an election. The act specifically made a union designated in this way the exclusive representative of all workers in the plant. Apparently relying on the Supreme Court to declare the legislation unconstitutional, some employers flouted it. But in 1937, in *NLRB* v. *Jones and Laughlin Steel Co.*, the Court upheld the NLRB, and employers had to learn to live with unions.

The Wagner Act contained no standard of wages and hours, which earlier NRA codes had included. Replacing these provisions was tricky, for the Supreme Court had apparently limited the power of legislatures. The Walsh-Healy Act of 1936 empowered the secretary of labor to establish minimum wage levels that all government contractors must meet, specified a forty-hour week for employees of government contractors, and prohibited child labor. Finally, in 1938, Congress passed the Fair Labor Standards Act, which, although exempting agricultural labor and several other groups, established a minimum wage of twenty-five cents per hour for workers engaged in interstate commerce. A forty-four-hour week permitted for three years was to drop to forty thereafter. Congress has subsequently raised the minimum wage and extended the number of people to whom the law applies several times.

Legislation changed the living standards of ordinary working people less than did unions, especially the Congress of Industrial Organizations (CIO). Led by John L. Lewis, David Dubinsky, and Sidney Hillman, the CIO paid no attention to the skills or crafts upon which unions in the American Federation of Labor were based. Instead, the CIO proposed to enlist all the workers in mass-production industries in one industry-wide

*Richard Frankensteen (left) and Walter Reuther (wearing dark shirt, right)
announce the campaign to organize Ford*

organization. Long unhappy at the AFL's refusal to adopt industrial organization, Lewis welcomed the Wagner Act, which he believed would provide the support necessary for a major organizational drive. Congress passed the law in the spring of 1935; Lewis left the AFL in the fall.

While the CIO continued to feud with the older union, it had energy to spare for employers. In 1936, the CIO set aside $500,000 to organize the steel industry. In March 1937, United States Steel signed a contract with the United Steelworkers without a strike. The attempt to organize smaller steel-producers resulted in pitched battles that the union lost during the summer of 1937; "little steel" was not unionized until 1941. Henry Ford used a strong-arm security force to blunt the drive of the United Auto Workers (UAW). But in 1937, after a rash of "sit-down" strikes, General Motors and Chrysler capitulated to the UAW. The sit-down strikers simply refused to leave the plants; they were orderly, but they barricaded themselves in the shop, and at least by implication, they held building, tools, and equipment hostage for a favorable settlement.

By 1939, then, labor-management relations were far different from those of a decade before. Tough unions battled employers, with the NLRB, which leaned toward the unions, as referee; many unorganized workers also had the protection of minimum wages and maximum hours. Even so, the framework remained industrial capitalism—private corporations, independent unions. The government had fostered the growth of unions, to be sure, and thereby affected the process; but the government did not write the contracts or own the industries. The result of the New Deal was about what Samuel Gompers had wanted nearly a half century before.

The Politics of the New Deal

Franklin D. Roosevelt was one of those commanding political figures to whom no one was indifferent. Those who admired him did so with a devotion that bordered on reverence; those who disliked him did so with a passion that bordered on monomania. Some thought he had delivered them and the country from destitution; others thought he had changed, and perhaps destroyed, the American way of life.

Whatever else the New Deal changed, American politics never again ran the predepression course. The central government, once committed to protecting the economic welfare of citizens, has not withdrawn. Several interest groups whose needs government previously had ignored— organized labor, for instance—won a voice in government that sometimes seemed louder than that of the business groups, which had previously been more clearly heard. Prepared for active Presidents by Theodore Roosevelt and Woodrow Wilson, the nation was accustomed to executive initiative and to presidential dominance in a more active, more powerful government in Washington. And the party of Lincoln, which had dominated national politics since 1860, gave way to the party of FDR. Between 1860 and 1933 Democrats simultaneously occupied the White House and organized both houses of Congress for only eight years; since 1933 Republicans have simultaneously organized both the executive and legislative branches for only two years. One of the changes that the depression brought was a new majority party.

For a time Democrats had to compete with several political splinter groups that advanced deceptively simple cures for the depression. Support for the Townsend Plan rolled east from California, for enactment of social security failed to dampen the zeal of Dr. Townsend's followers. From Detroit, Father Charles Coughlin, the "radio priest" who received even more mail than the President, broadcast the word that only remonetizing silver would bring inflation. If his proposals were otherwise vague, Father Coughlin's enemies were clear, including at various times bankers, Communists, Jews, "internationalists," and FDR.

Neither the physician nor the priest had the political sensitivity of the shrewd, ambitious, and formidably able senator from Louisiana, Huey P. Long. His "Share Our Wealth" program promised to make "Every Man a King" with an immediate capital grant of $5,000 and a guaranteed annual minimum income of $2,000, all of which would be obtained through a capital levy on large fortunes. Pensions, higher education, more leisure, and a variety of other fringe benefits added to the attractiveness of Long's pitch. Politics, not ideology, molded the program, for Long boasted that he never "read a line of Marx or Henry George or any of them economists."

Socialists and Communists, who did read their economists, made almost no impression on the electorate: in 1936 the Socialist presidential candidate received fewer than 200,000 votes, the Communist less than half that. The other dissidents, robbed of their most attractive candidate when Long was assassinated, rallied discordantly behind Congressman William Lemke and the Union ticket, which polled nearly 900,000 votes. Roosevelt, by contrast, had the support of almost 28 million voters.

The only important issue in 1936, Roosevelt remarked with pardonable exaggeration, was Franklin Delano Roosevelt. Republicans unwisely cooperated by attacking the President and his program from the campaign trail. Yet the Republican platform betrayed a curious ambivalence: the preamble proclaimed "America is in peril," but the promises that followed sounded suspiciously like imitations of programs the Democrats had already enacted. A similar ambivalence disarmed the Republican candidate, Governor Alfred M. Landon of Kansas, whose record had been rather progressive. Some pundits thought the election might be close, but James A. Farley, Roosevelt's postmaster general and political deputy, predicted that the President would lose only the 8 electoral votes of Maine and Vermont. In the end, FDR did in fact win the other 523 electors.

Roosevelt understandably thought his triumph a mandate. Congress, where Democratic majorities rose again, was apparently his to command. But the Supreme Court, dominated by conservative justices who seemed nearly immortal, was apparently oblivious to political majorities. The *Schechter* decision of 1935 had ended the NIRA with a decision so restricted in its interpretation of the commerce clause that Roosevelt feared any economic legislation was jeopardized. A year later Justice Owen Roberts, in an opinion for the Court in *United States* v. *Butler,* declared the Agricultural Adjustment Administration's processing tax unconstitutional because it was a device to redistribute income instead of a bona fide tax. Justice Harlan Fiske Stone filed an incisive dissent, branding the majority opinion "a tortured construction of the Constitution" and reminding his judicial brethren that "courts are not the only agency of government that must be assumed to have capacity to govern." Although the Court upheld the TVA in the *Ashwander* decision (1936), the case did not settle the agency's right to distribute power. New Deal agencies did not always meet defeat in Court, but the victories were ordinarily limited, while the defeats swept away major portions of Roosevelt's program.

Early in 1937, without consulting congressional leaders, Roosevelt sent Congress a bill to reorganize the judiciary. Seizing on the fact that several justices were over seventy years old, Roosevelt proposed that he be empowered to appoint, to a total of six, an additional justice for each superannuated one on the bench. The proposal was clearly designed to pack the Court, and opponents of the New Deal, who had been divided, united in rousing defense of the separation of powers. All of Roosevelt's prestige and political magic availed him nothing. Following a prolonged debate that split his party, the Senate killed his bill. The electorate ratified Congress's decision in 1938 by rejecting candidates whom Roosevelt had recommended in several Democratic primaries and by enlarging the Republican minority at the general election. Roosevelt survived his party's division, but the New Deal was over.

Although the flood of legislation diminished sharply, at least the Court ceased to condemn earlier New Deal measures. In 1937, during the storm over court-packing, the justices discovered flexibility in the Constitution. In *West Coast Hotel Co.* v. *Parrish*, the Court held that states could establish minimum wage laws. The narrow definition of interstate commerce in the *Schechter* decision was apparently reversed in *NLRB* v. *Jones and Laughlin Steel Co.*, in which the Court accepted the Wagner Act. In two other cases in 1937 the Court ruled that the social security program was within federal power. A year later the Court repulsed an attempt to prevent the TVA from selling electricity. The form of the Constitution, the prestige of the Court, and most of the program of the New Deal survived the contest.

The depression was a trauma in the national experience perhaps comparable only to the Civil War, and few aspects of American life escaped change. Political issues, parties, and styles of leadership were profoundly altered. The government assumed part of the regulatory role of the mythical pre-1929 "impersonal market." Yet the depression did not disappear. In 1938 almost ten million Americans lacked jobs; in 1940 the total was still seven million. The New Deal had neither spent the nation into the poorhouse, as Roosevelt's detractors charged, nor boosted it to prosperity, as some Keynesian economists had hoped. (John Maynard Keynes, the noted British economic theorist, had argued that governmental deficit spending could effectively be substituted for private investment to produce prosperity.) The depression jolted not only what had been economic orthodoxy but also such traditional American values as thrift, prudence, and hard work and such naive beliefs as the inevitability of American prosperity and the innate superiority of the nation's institutions.

Many of those values and most of the nation's institutions survived the depression. However slowly, the American political system produced reform and continued to inspire confidence and hope. However dreary the present, Americans did not reject their past; they even overlooked the follies of the 1920s and gave the decade a posthumous pizzazz. The nation that finally emerged from the depression looked like the nation that had entered it.

Suggested Reading

The Hoover Presidency (1974), edited by Martin L. Fausold and George T. Mazuzan, displays the new interest in Hoover with essays by several scholars. One of them, Joan Hoff Wilson, has completed a brief biography, *Herbert Hoover** (1975). David Burner's *Herbert Hoover: The Public Life* (1978) is more detailed. *The Great Crash** (1955), by John Kenneth Galbraith, and *The Crisis of the Old Order** (1957), by Arthur M. Schlesinger, Jr., are more critical of Hoover's policies.

David A. Shannon has edited documents in *The Great Depression** (1960) that give an individual dimension to the statistics of the period. In *Middletown in Transition** (1937), Robert S. and Helen M. Lynn complete the before-and-after picture of Muncie, Indiana. John Braeman, Robert Bremner, and David Brody have edited two volumes, *The New Deal* (1975), that summarize scholarship on the Roosevelt administration and introduce new work on the local response to depression and New Deal. Charles H. Trout's *Boston, the Great Depression, and the New Deal* (1977) is a readable local account.

The best brief survey of the New Deal is William E. Leuchtenburg's *Franklin D. Roosevelt and the New Deal** (1963). Four volumes of Frank Freidel's biography of Roosevelt (1952, 1954, 1956, 1973) carry the narrative through the "hundred days"; a fifth volume will complete the first term. Arthur M. Schlesinger, Jr., has reached 1936 in the second and third volumes of his work on the New Deal: *The Coming of the New Deal** (1959) and *The Politics of Upheaval** (1960). James M. Burns's interpretation in *The Lion and the Fox** (1956) has had wide acceptance. Otis L. Graham notes, in *An Encore for Reform** (1967), that young progressives did not always mature into New Dealers.

New Dealers themselves wrote extensively. Thurman Arnold's *The Folklore of Capitalism** (1937) is more interesting than some of the memoirs, and John M. Blum's three volumes, *From the Morgenthau Diaries* (1959–67), are more comprehensive than most of the biographies. Joseph P. Lash's *Eleanor and Franklin** (1971) is an admiring account of Mrs. Roosevelt.

* Available in paperback edition

Chapter 20
Isolation and Intervention

Chronology

1931 Japan occupies Manchuria •

1932 Stimson Doctrine announces American refusal to recognize territorial transfer through conquest •

1933 United States recognizes the Soviet Union • Montevideo Conference: United States renounces right to intervene in Latin America •

1935–39 Congress passes neutrality acts •

1935 Italy invades Ethiopia •

1936 Germany reoccupies the Rhineland •

1937 Japan invades China; bombs American gunboat *Panay* in Yangtze River •

1938 Munich Conference •

1939–45 The Second World War: *September 1939:* Germany invades Poland; Britain and France declare war • *April–June 1940:* Germany occupies Norway, Denmark, Low Countries, France • *March 1941:* Lend-Lease Act passed • *June 1941:* Germany invades Soviet Union • *August 1941:* Atlantic Conference • *December 1941:* Japanese bomb Pearl Harbor; United States enters war • *November 1942:* Allied invasion of North Africa • *September 1943:* Allied invasion of Italy • *June 1944:* Allied invasion of France • *October 1944:* American invasion of Philippines • *February 1945:* Yalta Conference • *May 1945:* Germany surrenders • *August 1945:* Japan surrenders after atom bombs destroy Hiroshima and Nagasaki •

1940 Presidential election: Franklin D. Roosevelt (Democrat) defeats Wendell L. Willkie (Republican) •

1944 Presidential election: Franklin D. Roosevelt (Democrat) defeats Thomas E. Dewey (Republican) •

1945 Harry S. Truman succeeds Roosevelt in April •

The 1930s were years of depression in the United States. Elsewhere in the world the decade was marked by renewed war, by the loss of national independence, and by the acceptance of totalitarian dictators, who promised instant national greatness, painless industrialization, or more of the earth's surface. Preoccupied with their own economic paralysis, ordinary Americans weighed events abroad more for their economic promise than for their effect on national security. Even if isolation was never achieved, it was the ideal to which Americans aspired. Until almost the end of the decade, Franklin Roosevelt worried more about his New Deal than about Adolf Hitler's New Order. Although the toll of Chinese civilians killed by Japanese bombers shocked official Washington, these numbers were, on the whole, less disturbing than unemployment statistics from Chicago.

The depression helped remove a few disputes that had plagued diplomats in the 1920s. In 1933 the lure of the Russian market made diplomatic recognition of the Soviet Union seem less dangerous than it had appeared in the previous decade. The United States had steadfastly refused to exchange ambassadors with the USSR because the Communist government had repudiated the Czarist debt, encouraged subversive propaganda, and harassed Russian Christians and Jews. After the Russians promised to curb propaganda in the United States, formal diplomatic contact was renewed. But recognition fulfilled neither the best hopes of its proponents nor the dire predictions of those who had opposed it. Propaganda did not cease, trade did not climb, and wholesale subversion did not ensue.

Economic distress also effectively ended international squabbling over war debts and reparations. Token payments unofficially prolonged until 1934 the moratorium that Herbert Hoover had officially proclaimed in 1931. As depression deepened, debtor nations, with the exception of Finland, abandoned even the pretense of payment. Congress formally ended the vexatious dispute with the Johnson Act of 1934, which forbade future loans to nonpaying nations and tacitly acknowledged default.

But the depression did nothing to reduce other international tensions and probably exacerbated some of them. The disruption of international trade was partly responsible for Japanese demands for political and economic change in East Asia. Economic dislocation in Germany enlarged the audience for Hitler's demagogic promises to redraw the map of Europe. The failure of the Italian economy to keep pace with Mussolini's grandiose vision drove him to seek colonial outlets for what he called "surplus population." Economic distress in Western Europe gave Stalin the security his diplomats had failed to provide and permitted him to turn the Soviet Union's entire national energy toward the rapid development of an industrial plant. In Geneva, the world's diplomats pretended that the League of Nations was important, until the Japanese delegation shattered the pretense by stalking out early in 1933. Within months the Germans followed. National intransigence and international depression had smashed the Versailles settlement.

Not many Americans mourned. Whatever enthusiasm there had once been for Woodrow Wilson's peace dissipated in the decade after he left the White House. Historians, journalists, and novelists spread the word that munitions merchants, bankers, propagandists, and Anglophile politicians had drawn the United States into the First World War to increase their profits and bail out their friends; idealism, these revisionists asserted, had been the sugar coating on a noxious pill. Disillusionment with the struggle rubbed off on the peace, which few Americans in 1933 defended as just. Yet any modification of that peace, Americans believed, must come in an orderly manner and must not disturb their national interest.

This unwillingness to stand firmly for the status quo, coupled with an unwillingness to permit the changes that other ambitious powers demanded, produced hesitant American policy in the 1930s. American policy-makers knew that changes in the power of Japan and Germany required a new diplomatic stance, yet they clung to the Open Door and halfheartedly opposed Hitler's demands. The American people wanted desperately to stay out of European entanglements that seemed almost certain to bring another world war. But most Americans also despised fascism, communism, and nazism, and the country needed allies in any effort to check these evils. The United States had not kept the navy up to levels permitted by the Washington Conference, and in 1933 the army ranked seventeenth on the list of the world's forces. Americans wanted international stability without being willing to pay for it; on the one hand, they sought the domestic benefits of economic nationalism, and on the other, they preached the virtues of improving international amity through international trade. These ambiguities virtually paralyzed American foreign policy, except in Latin America, where Yankee strategic and economic power still overawed potential rivals.

The Policy of the Good Neighbor

"In the field of world policy," said Franklin Roosevelt as he took office, "I would dedicate this nation to the policy of the good neighbor." The President then explained that the good neighbor kept his obligations and stayed in his own yard, a definition that effectively ruled out substantial international change. The phrase "Good Neighbor Policy" soon described only diplomatic contact in the Western Hemisphere, for some of the neighbors in Europe and Asia undertook to enlarge their share of the neighborhood.

No nation's foreign policy is entirely altruistic, and the Good Neighbor Policy was no exception. The United States appeared to give up unilateral action in the hemisphere, but renouncing Theodore Roosevelt's Corollary and making enforcement of the Monroe Doctrine a hemispheric responsibility in fact made little practical difference. Most Latin American republics were economically tied to the United States, which was the best market for their oil, sugar, coffee, copper, and bananas. Even combined, the southern republics lacked the military capacity to resist the United States, and local jealousies prevented their getting together. With more or less grace, Latin America had to follow the lead of the United States.

It was, then, tactful of American policy-makers to stop flaunting Yankee supremacy. President Hoover had begun to draw the velvet glove over the steel fist; Roosevelt and Cordell Hull, his secretary of state, completed the process. In 1933, at a Pan-American conference in Montevideo, Uruguay, Hull signed a treaty that denied the right of any state "to intervene in the internal or external affairs of another." The Montevideo agreement implied American willingness to give up the Platt Amendment, which had permitted American intervention in Cuba since 1901. In 1934 the State Department announced the formal abrogation of the amendment and in 1936 negotiated a treaty with Panama that gave up the right to intervene there too.

In return, the Latin American republics joined the United States in an attempt to seal off the Western Hemisphere from the troubled other half of the globe. In Buenos Aires in 1936, the American states promised to consult one another if an international war seemed to "menace the peace of the American hemisphere." Two years later, at Lima, Peru, the pledge to consult was strengthened by a pledge to resist "all foreign intervention." When war broke out in Europe, the Declaration of Panama of 1939 warned all belligerents to stay well outside the territorial waters of American states. In 1940 after the Nazis had overrun Western Europe, the Act of Havana proclaimed the hemisphere's unwillingness to permit the transfer of possessions from one European power to another. The Monroe Doctrine had become a hemispheric policy, not just a pronouncement of the United States.

While apparently making concessions, the United States in fact gave up nothing at all. For the Latin American republics simply joined in sponsoring a policy that the United States had previously championed. The Good Neighbor Policy was designed to ease diplomatic contact and to increase hemispheric trade, which might stimulate the depressed Yankee economy. However loose the diplomatic leash seemed to be, Latin Americans could usually be brought to heel by a tug on the economic chain. The Good Neighbor Policy was simply a benevolent new wrapping on the old policy.

Staying Neutral

The depression reinforced pervasive American disgust with world politics. Convinced that Europeans had tricked the United States into one great war, bungled the peace settlement, and then declined to pay their bills, many Americans swore off Europe along with grand international causes. After 1933 they found an outlet for their remaining idealism in the New Deal.

While the New Dealers attempted to transform America, depression and dictators were transforming Europe. Democratic institutions disappeared not only in Germany but also in Poland, Spain, and Austria. Constitutional monarchies vanished in Italy and Greece. Neither Britain nor France displayed democratic vitality at home or zeal in defense of democracy elsewhere. Nor did Americans counter dictators or their so-called ideologies. No matter how vigorously Americans disapproved of Stalin's purges, Hitler's concentration camps, or expansion by militarists from Italy or Japan, the United States' diplomatic response was ordinarily no more than a note of protest, and sometimes not even that much. Isolation, the dominant public mood, eclipsed the disapproval of dictatorship.

Since 1941, isolation has had a bad press, and even many one-time isolationists have renounced their previous faith to adopt collective security, the "internationalist" alternative. Yet, if some isolationists were naive in the 1930s, and if some were Communists or anti-Semites, most were decent Americans, as well informed and as intelligent as those with whom they disagreed. The policy they advocated had a reputable heritage from Washington and Jefferson and rested squarely on respected concepts of neutral rights and international law. Isolationists rejected the assumption that the United States had any business telling other people how to organize their lives and boasted that the United States could stand alone. Isolationists feared that traditional institutions and ancient liberties, already rocked by depression, might disappear in another war. They foresaw that such a war would require alliances and end the American habit of nonentanglement. Undoubtedly isolationists underestimated the danger to Western values that nazism and militarism posed, but they correctly predicted some of the consequences of a war to end those evils.

Isolation found legislative expression in the neutrality acts that Congress began to pass in 1935. The first neutrality act, a hasty and temporary measure, prohibited the sale of arms to belligerents upon presidential proclamation that a state of war existed. The act gave up one of the rights of a neutral nation that President Wilson had most stubbornly upheld: Congress authorized the President to prohibit Americans from traveling on belligerent ships. Subsequently, in 1936, Congress forbade loans to any belligerent, and early in 1937 Congress extended the provisions of previous neutrality acts to cover all civil wars. New legislation in May 1937 repeated all the earlier prohibitions and gave the President discretionary authority to prohibit sale of anything at all to belligerents unless the purchaser paid cash and carried the goods away in his own ships. After the European war began in September 1939, Congress permitted the sale of arms on the same "cash and carry" basis, a concession that, because of the British fleet, favored Hitler's foes.

By that time Hitler's foes needed help, for each of the neutrality acts had been a response to deteriorating conditions abroad. Late in 1935 Italy invaded Ethiopia, and Roosevelt imposed the embargo on arms sales required by the 1935 Neutrality Act. Britain and France publicly deplored Mussolini's aggression while privately informing the Fascist *Duce* that they would not interfere. With its two strongest members self-disarmed, the League imposed an ineffective embargo on arms, camels, and rubber, but not on steel, trucks, and oil. The United States continued to supply Italy with the petroleum products that eventually enabled Fascist armies to overrun Ethiopia.

While Mussolini was mopping up in Ethiopia, Hitler sent troops into the Rhineland, from which the Treaty of Versailles had barred military bases. British and French policy, in disarray after Ethiopia, could not stop Hitler; even the protests from London and Paris were muted. Later in 1936, both Hitler and Mussolini took advantage of the civil war in Spain to test their troops and equipment in support of General Francisco

Franco's fascist coup. The Spanish Republic rallied support from the Soviet Union and an extralegal "Abraham Lincoln Brigade" of American liberals. But Stalin soon turned to purging his own followers; American liberals were too few and too late; and the Spanish Republic collapsed.

In the spring of 1938, over the weak protests of the Western powers, Hitler rode in triumph to Vienna as his troops occupied Austria. Less than six months later, following some hurried negotiation at Munich, Britain and France in effect forced Czechoslovakia to cede Hitler the Sudetenland, a substantial slice of western Czechoslovakia that included a large minority of German-speaking inhabitants. In March 1939, in spite of solemn promises made at Munich that the Sudetenland had been the last demand, Hitler annexed the rest of Czechoslovakia. In August, Hitler purchased Soviet neutrality by allowing Stalin a free hand in the Baltic states and eastern Poland, a concession the Western Allies had refused. The Nazi-Soviet pact clearly signaled the end of Poland, whose independence Britain and France had sworn to support. A week after the Nazi-Soviet agreement, the German blitzkrieg began in Poland; two days later Britain and France declared war on Germany and the Second World War was formally under way.

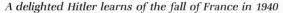

A delighted Hitler learns of the fall of France in 1940

The End of Peace in Asia

Like other industrial nations, Japan felt the impact of the depression.
Economic distress, the ambitions of military leaders, and nationalism led
to proposals that Japan should gain exclusive control of its Asian market.
Within this Greater East Asia Co-Prosperity Sphere, Japan would supply
manufactured goods in return for the raw material and agricultural
produce of other lands.

Some Asian peoples resisted Japanese mercantilism. Chinese and
Japanese economic interests clashed, most notably in Manchuria, an area
nominally under Chinese political domination, where Japan had secured
economic concessions by treaty. In September 1931, Japanese troops
used an explosion on the South Manchurian Railway as an excuse to
overrun the entire province. The Japanese garrison in Manchuria was
more belligerent than its civilian superiors in Tokyo, and the occupation
may even have been contrary to the intent of the Japanese cabinet. But
once Manchuria was secured, Japan would not budge; resolutions of the
League of Nations and Chinese protests were ignored. After threatening
sterner action, the League appointed an investigating commission, which
in 1932 reproved China for its attempt to interfere with legitimate
Japanese interests in Manchuria but more sharply condemned Japan for
the rash use of entirely too much force. Japan soon walked out of the
League and established a satellite regime in Manchuria, which was
renamed Manchukuo.

Japan paid no more attention to American protests than to those from
Geneva. The United States regarded the occupation of Manchuria as a
violation of the Kellogg-Briand Pact renouncing war and as a breach of
the Nine Power agreement to maintain the Open Door. Although Henry L.
Stimson, Hoover's secretary of state, could not formally cooperate with
the League, he favored stern international action to roll back the
Japanese advance. He got no cooperation, either in Washington or
abroad. President Hoover had too many pressing domestic problems to
undertake an active Asian policy. The American public was skeptical that
any vital national interest was at stake. Although European diplomats
agreed with Stimson in principle, they thought Manchuria too remote
and too unimportant to justify the massive effort that would apparently
be required to undo Japanese conquest. The frustrated secretary of state,
after consultation with the President, was reduced to announcing
American policy in a letter to William E. Borah, who headed the Senate
Committee on Foreign Relations. The United States, Stimson wrote, would
insist on its treaty rights in Manchuria. He hoped that other nations
would join the United States in refusing to recognize territorial
settlements imposed by force, a formula that became known as the
Stimson Doctrine.

The Stimson Doctrine, like the resolutions of the League, confessed impotence. Japan had seized Manchuria by force; short of similar force, nothing Stimson or the League could do would make Japan give up Manchuria. An embargo of strategic materials, especially oil, might have hurt Japan, but Stimson could not interest the President or any other nation in imposing such a ban. The Stimson Doctrine indicated, for those who wanted to read the moral, that appeals to conscience and reliance on international agreements would not stop any nation bent on violence.

And violence spread in Asia. In 1932 Japanese troops occupied Shanghai following the first major air assault directed against civilians. World opinion was outraged, but the Japanese withdrew a few months later for their own reasons, not from any sense of guilt. In 1937 a full-scale Japanese invasion rapidly took over much of coastal China, from which Japan did not withdraw until peace returned to the Pacific more than eight years later. President Roosevelt refused to call the struggle a war, a decision that permitted Americans to evade the neutrality legislation and lend money to China. When the United States inquired about the Open Door, Japan curtly replied that the policy was no longer relevant. When Japanese aircraft in 1937 sank the *Panay*, an American gunboat, in the Yangtze River, the State Department and the public promptly accepted Japan's apology. It would take more than a shattered gunboat to dispel American isolation.

War Ends Debate

Although Franklin Roosevelt had not objected to the neutrality acts as they passed, he discovered in 1937 and 1938 that they made him almost powerless to check Japanese aggression in China or to thwart Hitler's designs in Europe. Roosevelt tried to achieve European security and a "quarantine" of aggressors through private diplomacy and public addresses. Neither method proved successful.

In the spring of 1940, the Nazis abruptly turned west, and by the end of June they had smashed resistance in Scandinavia, the Low Countries, and France, and had the British wondering when invasion of their island would come. Hitler's rapid advance convinced isolationists that the United States should concentrate on its own defense, not dissipate its strength abroad. The America First Committee, the most active isolationist organization in the months before Pearl Harbor, stressed the dangers of diplomatic entanglement and the advantages of "fortress America"—an armed, alert nation separated from the rest of the world by two broad oceans. The America First Committee reached a national audience through an active press campaign and through the speeches of Charles A. Lindbergh, the aviator-hero of the 1920s.

But Nazi success in Europe gradually broke the isolationist spell. William Allen White, a Republican newspaper editor from Kansas, became the national chairman of the Committee to Defend America by Aiding the Allies, which countered isolationist arguments. By inclination an internationalist, Roosevelt nevertheless let White and others carry the running debate with the isolationists. The President's caution was partly political; much of the debate coincided with his campaign for reelection in 1940. But Roosevelt also hoped that events abroad would unify the country, for no responsible democratic leader wants angry domestic controversy to divide a nation at war.

The split was deep. In 1938 Congress had narrowly refused to debate the Ludlow Amendment, which would have required a national referendum to declare war. Roosevelt's successful effort to modify the neutrality acts in 1939 required all his political skill and still embittered his relationship with Congress. In August 1941, isolationists in the House came within a single vote of blocking selective-service legislation that military authorities claimed was essential to the nation's mobilization. As late as October, the United States Army was about equal to the prewar forces of Holland or Belgium, both of which the Nazis had brushed aside in a few days.

Though the debates were bitter, isolationists usually lost. The Republican National Convention of 1940 passed over well-known isolationist senators, like Robert Taft of Ohio and Arthur Vandenberg of Michigan, and selected the internationalist dark horse Wendell Willkie. Willkie's nomination took some of the partisanship out of foreign policy, for he ordinarily criticized execution of American policies rather than the policies themselves. When British Prime Minister Winston Churchill renewed his pleas for American destroyers to supplement the British navy, Roosevelt indirectly consulted Willkie before completing the "Destroyer Deal," which swapped fifty old American destroyers for ninety-nine-year leases on British bases on Newfoundland, the West Indies, and British Guiana. Although supplying warships to a belligerent obviously violated the canons of conventional neutrality, the trade strengthened American defense and thereby catered to isolationist opinion.

The Destroyer Deal illustrated Roosevelt's developing strategy. Great Britain, he believed, was the first line of American defense. Britain's survival would serve America's interests, and Britain's victory, which would require American aid, might even end the war before American troops were required. This hope, and a willingness to indulge antiwar sentiment, tempted Roosevelt into an unwise end-of-campaign pledge not to send American "boys . . . into any foreign wars."

But Roosevelt would send everything else. In the Lend-Lease Bill he sent to Congress in January 1941, Roosevelt asked for authority to buy war materials and give them to countries whose defense he thought vital to American security. He defended lend-lease with the analogy of one neighbor lending another his garden hose to fight a fire; when the fire was out, the hose was returned, and there was no need to keep books on the transaction or create debts and future disputes. Isolationists saw lend-lease somewhat differently: it was, observed Senator Burton K. Wheeler of Montana, "the New Deal's triple-A foreign policy," which would "plow under every fourth American boy." Again the debate was bitter, and again the isolationists lost; the bill and an initial appropriation of $7 billion passed in March. Shipments to Britain began at once, and after Hitler invaded the Soviet Union in June, the Red Army also received American war material.

Supply logically included safe delivery. Step by inexorable step the United States moved into the Atlantic, which German submarines in 1941 made hazardous. Hitler specifically ordered his U-boat commanders not to molest American vessels, even after they began protecting convoys halfway across the Atlantic. American occupation of Greenland and Iceland increased military traffic in the North Atlantic, and American naval forces began to cooperate with British antisubmarine units. The U.S.S. *Greer*, for instance, tracked a German submarine and radioed its position to pursuing British aircraft. The U-boat eventually fired on the American ship, to which Roosevelt responded with an order to shoot on sight any hostile submarine. The United States was informally at war in the North Atlantic several months before Pearl Harbor.

Indeed, the United States even announced its war aims before official entrance. In August 1941, Roosevelt and Churchill met at sea off Newfoundland and issued the Atlantic Charter, which was, in effect, a joint statement by a belligerent and a technically neutral power of their mutual hopes for the postwar world. The charter blended Wilson's Fourteen Points—national self-determination, freedom of the seas, and reduction of armaments—with Roosevelt's New Deal—freedom from fear, freedom from want. The document was the bland public result of the conference; privately Roosevelt and Churchill also discussed Japan's aggressive expansion in the Pacific. After France collapsed, Japan had occupied French Indochina, and in 1941 was poised to expand into Thailand, Malaya, Burma, and eventually the Dutch East Indies. Churchill pressed Roosevelt for a promise to defend Dutch and British possessions in Southeast Asia, especially the British base at Singapore. Although the President subsequently warned Japan against an attack, he gave Churchill no binding promise. Roosevelt was not ready for a final confrontation with Japan and sought peaceful means of halting Japanese aggression.

But methods short of war were running out. Early in 1940 the United States allowed a trade treaty to lapse and gradually reduced shipments of strategic goods to Japan. In September, Japan signed an alliance with Germany and Italy to secure their support against the United States. In July 1941, when Japanese troops moved into southern Indochina, Roosevelt froze Japanese assets in the United States, a step that made further commerce difficult. A few weeks later Fumimaro Konoye, the Japanese premier, proposed a meeting with Roosevelt to discuss diplomatic differences between the two nations. Although Joseph C.

Grew, the American ambassador to Tokyo, thought the proposal should be accepted, Roosevelt disagreed. In October a more aggressive Japanese cabinet, under General Hideki Tojo, took control of Japanese foreign policy. Both nations made a show of negotiating thereafter, but they were really just swapping unacceptable demands until Japanese pilots ended the charade by bombing Pearl Harbor on December 7, 1941.

Japan won an important tactical victory at Pearl Harbor. Surprise was complete; five battleships and fourteen other craft were at least temporarily put out of action; more than 2,000 Americans died. But for millions of Americans, intently listening to the incredible news on their radios that Sunday afternoon, the debate was over. The attack in Hawaii proved the foe's lack of scruples and showed that only force could stop wanton aggression. The nation united. On December 8, Congress declared war on Japan, and three days later, following declarations of war by Italy and Germany, on Japan's European allies as well.

The War Effort

The war opened with a disaster and promptly got worse. In the first months of 1942, Japanese troops swept through Southeast Asia, overran the Philippines, occupied islands in the Aleutian chain and in the Dutch East Indies, and even menaced Australia. At the same time, German submarines were sinking Allied shipping faster than it could be replaced. And across the Atlantic the advance of Germany's *Afrika Korps* threatened to turn the Mediterranean into an Axis lake, while the blitzkrieg invasion of the Soviet Union sealed off Leningrad and reached the outskirts of Moscow.

But even before 1942 was over, there were signs of Allied initiative. Although strategic planners had decided to press the European war first and to fight defensively in the Pacific, the American fleet won important engagements in the Coral Sea and near Midway Island. American marines landed on the beaches of Guadalcanal and hung on grimly, an offensive operation that marked the end of Japanese expansion. American carrier-based aircraft bombed Tokyo in April, which boosted American morale but had little significance.

Convoys, radar, covering aircraft, and improved techniques in the shipyards enabled the Allies to begin winning the battle of the Atlantic. Increased aircraft production put thousands of bombers over Europe in constant strategic missions that harassed, though they did not cripple, the German war effort. Russian troops held Moscow, won at Stalingrad, and began the counteroffensive that was to end in 1945 in the courtyard of Hitler's private bunker amid the rubble of Berlin. British troops in Egypt held the *Afrika Korps* and then began to push it back across Libya. In November, Anglo-American landings in Morocco and Algeria trapped

German forces between two Allied armies. Much destruction and many casualties lay ahead; but the tide had turned.

In part, the tide turned because the factories of the foe could not match the productivity of American industry. Massive American output was a result of careful organization as well as of fortunate location beyond the range of enemy attack. A second generation of alphabetical agencies allocated resources and manpower, controlled prices and priorities, regulated transportation, and systematically applied scientific research to military technology. The nation's hundred largest businesses, which received two-thirds of the contracts, produced every conceivable item in staggering quantity. A year after Pearl Harbor, American munitions factories were outproducing those of the enemy. Aircraft production increased twenty-fourfold between 1939 and 1942, and then doubled again before the end of the war so that nearly 100,000 new planes a year came off the assembly lines. In 1941 construction of a freighter had taken nearly a year; by the end of 1942 shipyards were launching the same ships in less than two months.

The remarkable increase in production required a remarkable increase

THE WAR IN EUROPE

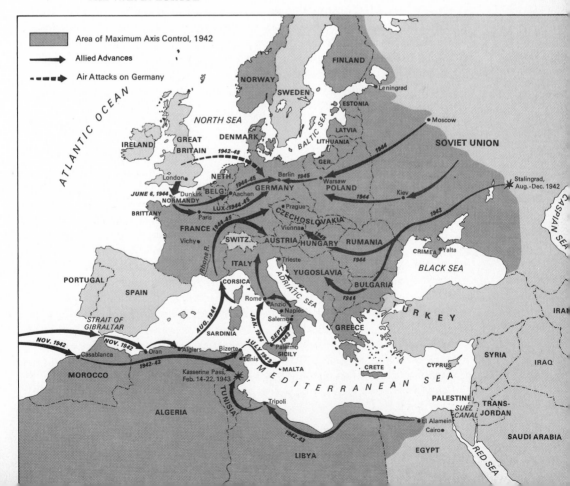

in the federal budget. In the first six months of 1942, the government awarded contracts calling for expenditures of more than $100 billion, an amount larger than the nation's gross national product in 1941. Income taxes, which rose to a maximum of 94 percent, accounted for about 40 percent of the total cost of the war and were partly responsible for a greater redistribution of the national income than had occurred during the depression. The national debt climbed from about $50 billion in 1941 to more than $250 billion in 1945. But the money was spent with little corruption. A Senate committee chaired by a peppery Missourian named Harry Truman doggedly exposed bungling, excess profits, and potentially wasteful schemes, thus reassuring most people that the government usually got its money's worth.

In addition to war production, American industry met most of the demands of civilians, who for the first time in a decade had money in their pockets. Rationing, of course, limited civilian consumption of shoes, meat, sugar, coffee, canned goods, gasoline, and tires. Other products, such as automobiles, disappeared from the market, as cuffs disappeared from men's trousers, copper from pennies, and aluminum pots from hardware stores. War-workers crammed themselves into uncomfortable temporary quarters near factories or military installations, but most were housed better than the rest of the world's population, and many improved on the way they had lived during the depression. And although they had to drink less coffee, without sugar, Americans still ate better than most other people, and many ate better than they had a few years before. Much of the prospering labor force invested part of each paycheck in war bonds, thereby building a reservoir of savings that pushed the postwar economy to the longest period of sustained prosperity and growth in history.

With American industry fully mobilized in 1943, the United States and its allies took the offensive in both theaters of war. From North Africa, Allied troops invaded Sicily, and from Sicily, Italy, where Mussolini's decrepit dictatorship fell within a week. But German troops rushed into the peninsula and slowed the Allied advance to a crawl: Rome did not fall until June 1944, only two days before the long-awaited invasion of France. On June 6 General Dwight D. Eisenhower gave the order that sent an initial wave of nearly 200,000 men to the beaches of Normandy. In August, landings in southern France threatened to envelop German forces, which withdrew in haste toward the Rhine. In the winter of 1944–45, Nazi armies mounted a last-gasp counterattack that became known as the Battle of the Bulge. But the bulge was contained, and American and British troops moved inexorably toward their rendezvous with the Russians in Berlin.

The Russian advance, by 1945, more than kept pace with that of the Anglo-American forces. In 1941 and 1942, the Russian people and the Red Army had taken the full fury of the awesome Nazi assault until it collapsed at Stalingrad. Almost without a pause, the Russians mounted

June 1944—the coast of Normandy three days after D-day

an offensive that diverted German forces from the defense of Western Europe. By 1944 the Russian offensive had become a steamroller as the Red Army moved through the Caucasus and the Ukraine into Poland, and smashed the eastern defenses of the Third Reich. His armies crushed, his capital besieged, his thousand-year Reich in ruins, Hitler took his own life on April 30, 1945. Germany surrendered on May 8.

Instead of mounting costly invasions of successive Japanese outposts, American strategists decided to take advantage of American naval control in the South Pacific and to minimize American casualties by island-hopping—bypassing some intermediate island bases on the way toward Japan. The American navy isolated these bases and prevented interference with land forces under the command of General Douglas MacArthur. In the fall of 1944, MacArthur led Americans back into the Philippines while the navy provoked an engagement at Leyte Gulf that knocked the Japanese fleet out of the war. Manila fell early in 1945, and American forces advanced, with extremely heavy losses, to Iwo Jima and Okinawa, which were to serve as bases for launching the massive air raids on Japan before the final invasion. These bases, as it turned out, were not required, for the planes carrying the atomic bombs for Hiroshima and Nagasaki took off from fields on Tinian. On August 10, 1945, four days after Hiroshima, the day after Nagasaki, and even before the quarter-million casualties of the bombings had been counted, Japan asked for peace.

The war caused American casualties too, although the losses were smaller than those of China, Germany, or the Soviet Union. Of 16 million uniformed Americans, 400,000 died and 600,000 were wounded. In a sense, Franklin Roosevelt was the nation's most prominent wartime loss. Roosevelt ran for a fourth term in 1944 almost as a matter of course; the voters elected him over Thomas E. Dewey, the smooth, young governor of New York, almost the same way. Roosevelt substituted Harry Truman, a reliable senator acceptable to the party's conservatives, for Vice-President Henry Wallace, who seemed too liberal for the times. Roosevelt and Truman carried thirty-six states and ran about 3.5 million popular votes ahead of Dewey. But the President lived only three months after his fourth inauguration. On April 12, 1945, in Warm Springs, Georgia, he died of a cerebral hemorrhage.

Diplomacy of the Grand Alliance

Franklin Roosevelt had personally directed wartime foreign policy from the time of the Atlantic Conference before Pearl Harbor through the Yalta Conference a few weeks before his death. He met frequently with Churchill, and they corresponded several times each week and often several times each day. But their relationship, though close, was not free of friction, and both disagreed frequently with Stalin. For the three major allies differed about the conduct of the war, and each had its own postwar agenda; only the Nazi menace fused their wartime foreign policies.

Desperate for relief in 1942, for instance, the Soviet Union urged an immediate Anglo-American invasion of France to draw German troops from the Eastern Front. Stalin dismissed the substitution of North Africa as a capitalist device to restore empire and influence. The United States, especially in 1943 and 1944, thought Stalin's refusal to join the war

THE WAR IN THE PACIFIC

against Japan equally self-serving. Roosevelt occasionally scoffed at Churchill's outdated imperial aspirations and expected the British Empire to shrink after the war. But other postwar changes should be relatively minor, in Roosevelt's view, and they must be acceptable to the United States. Roosevelt led the American people to expect a vaguely better world, but not one that differed markedly from the predepression world they thought they had understood. Roosevelt underestimated the needs of the world's peoples who lived outside of Western Europe, and he overestimated the ability of Western statesmen—particularly Americans—to control events in the rest of the world.

Roosevelt insisted that China be numbered among the world's great powers, as if his insistence could make up for the military futility of

Chiang Kai-shek's forces. Perhaps the President intended to build up Chinese prestige to fill the obvious power vacuum that would occur in the Pacific once Japanese might was destroyed. But China was so divided that not even the Japanese invasion could make the government of Chiang Kai-shek work with the rebelling Communists of Mao Tse-tung. American advisers, especially General Joseph W. Stilwell, pointed out that Chiang's corrupt, unpopular government could not become the peacekeeper of Asia. But Roosevelt and Churchill had to work with Chiang, and together in 1943 they defined Allied war aims for the Pacific area in the Cairo Declaration. Japan was to give up most of its outlying islands, though the fate of all of them was not specified because the United States was not sure which might be required as bases. Formosa and Manchuria were to revert to China, and Korea was to become independent "in due course."

France also pretended to world-power status. The United States maintained diplomatic relations with the remnant of France that was allowed a pretense of independence by the Nazis and that maintained a government at Vichy. In an attempt to expedite the North African landings in 1942, Roosevelt had even acknowledged the political authority of Admiral Jean Darlan, whose connection with the Nazis was embarrassingly close. Free French forces abroad disavowed Admiral Darlan, opposed Vichy's control, and looked to General Charles de Gaulle in London for leadership. De Gaulle's was only one of several governments-in-exile, usually located in London, whose paper existence offered inspiration to people in occupied Europe and sometimes created difficulty for the wartime alliance.

Poland presented the most vexing difficulty. Britain's stake in Poland was sentimental: England had promised before the war to preserve Polish independence and had gone to war to redeem that pledge. The American stake was political as well as sentimental: the Polish vote was an important ethnic bloc in politically important American states. The Soviet stake was strategic: twice in the twentieth century Poland had been the pathway for invading German troops, and Stalin did not mean to expose his country again. Stalin eventually recognized a Communist-dominated group called the Lublin government as the official voice of Poland, while London and Washington recognized the London government-in-exile. Diplomats could not resolve the impasse, but the Red Army made argument futile when it occupied the area and manifestly intended to stay.

Poland's future and other questions about the shape of the postwar world appeared on the agenda for the Yalta Conference, the first of the "Big Three" meetings devoted largely to peacemaking. The meeting early in February 1945 was badly timed for the Western Allies. The Battle of the Bulge had not been decisively won, while the Russians were rolling through Eastern Europe. American forces in the Pacific were advancing, but pessimistic planners estimated that Japanese surrender might still be

Yalta, 1945

years away. The atomic bomb was an untested hope. After twelve years in the White House and a fourth inauguration, Franklin Roosevelt was weary and suffering from hypertension. Although later charges of a sellout at Yalta were exaggerated, in fact the United States seemed to approve of arrangements that violated the spirit of the Atlantic Charter. But short of turning on the Russians, there was little that even a healthy Roosevelt could have done to deny Stalin's gains.

The expectation of victory that prevailed at Yalta made negotiation more taxing. Since the fear of Nazi Germany had held the Allies together, a crumbling Nazi Germany foreshadowed a ruptured alliance. The Polish dispute was papered over with an agreement to enlarge the Lublin faction by adding a few members from the London cabinet; "free elections" were eventually to provide a new, democratically chosen government. The homogenized cabinet proved to be a farce, and the elections were not free. The Yalta conferees awarded part of eastern Poland to the Soviet Union and appropriated part of eastern Germany to compensate Poland, which soon became a Soviet satellite.

The negotiators at Yalta carved what remained of Germany into zones of occupation and, from the British and American shares, awarded one to France. After much debate, $20 billion became the basis for future discussion of reparations, of which half would be paid to the Soviet Union. The question of access to divided Berlin, located in the Soviet zone, never arose. It was to plague postwar relations between Western occupation forces and the Soviets in eastern Germany.

Stalin repeated at Yalta his earlier pledge to enter the Pacific war, within ninety days, he said, of German capitulation. With this assurance went Soviet demands: Outer Mongolia must remain a Soviet satellite and not return to Chinese control; Russian influence in Manchuria and access to ports on the Yellow Sea must be established; Japan must cede the Kurile Islands and the southern half of Sakhalin Island to the Soviet Union. Roosevelt undertook to persuade Chiang Kai-shek to accept these arrangements, and Stalin agreed to recognize Chiang's regime, a step that implied Soviet disavowal of the Chinese Communist movement.

Finally, the "Big Three" agreed on some fundamental principles for inclusion in the charter of the United Nations. In 1943 both houses of the American Congress had indicated their willingness to commit the United States to an international organization. In 1944 delegates from the United States, Britain, China, and the Soviet Union had begun to draft a charter but left several questions unresolved. At Yalta, Roosevelt agreed that the Ukraine and Byelorussia should be represented separately in the United Nations Assembly in return for Stalin's pledge to support an American demand for three votes if Roosevelt felt them necessary. In addition, the wartime allies ensured their own postwar control of the United Nations Security Council by permitting France, China, or any of the three powers represented at Yalta to prevent action with only one dissenting vote. This veto provision meant that the United Nations would be ineffective in dealing with matters on which the great powers disagreed. Such disputes were not far in the future.

Wartime America

The Second World War lacked the romance and the innocence of earlier American wars. Bill Mauldin's magnificent Willie and Joe cartoons show tired, cynical, inventive GIs, not crusaders. Although the Third Reich was incomparably more bestial than imperial Germany had been a generation before, the German language did not disappear from academic curricula, and Germans never became "Huns" in common speech, as had happened during the First World War. Americans thought of the Second World War as a disagreeable job that had to be done. They did their share.

The worst example of wartime hysteria came early. Surprise at Pearl Harbor and the subsequent series of quick disasters in the Pacific made

Loyalty in adversity: Japanese relocation center, Wyoming

many Americans suspect a plot. In part, the fear of conspiracy rested on
a racial arrogance that could not admit defeat by Orientals; emphasis in
the press on subversion and sabotage enhanced national unease.
Americans of Japanese ancestry who lived on the Pacific coast were the
victims. To prevent imagined sabotage, the President agreed to the army's
request that Japanese Americans be moved to several "relocation
centers," which had some of the attributes of concentration camps.
Profiteers took advantage of distress sales of the property of internees as
they tried to conclude their business before relocation. In 1943 and 1944,
the Supreme Court upheld relocation as a legitimate exercise of the war
power. Yet the danger of Japanese-American subversion was a fantasy.
And in the Italian campaign, an army unit recruited in relocation centers
gave a splendid account of itself and demonstrated the continuing loyalty
of Japanese Americans in spite of their shabby treatment.

Almost a million black Americans also served loyally in armed forces that were still segregated. The war created opportunities—not only in the armed forces—and blacks, like other Americans, attempted to take advantage of the jobs the war created. Seeking a larger share of wartime prosperity, blacks moved to northern and western cities, where restricted housing and mounting population combined to produce ghettos. Although Congress passed no civil rights legislation, in 1941, when black leaders threatened a mass march on Washington to dramatize discrimination, President Roosevelt ordered defense contractors and federal agencies not to discriminate in their hiring practices. The Fair Employment Practices Commission that Roosevelt established did not, of course, bring instant economic equality, but the war itself encouraged American blacks to demand equality and perhaps increased the willingness of whites to concede it. The attempts of blacks to resist traditional forms of discrimination—unequal access to jobs and public services, mistreatment by police, segregated housing—exploded in several race riots, the most serious of which rocked Detroit in 1943. The presence of many more blacks in the North made race relations a national problem, rather than a southern peculiarity, and revealed the hollowness of the pretense of northern equality.

Another important migration occurred during the war when American housewives left their kitchens. They had been urged in the depression not to preempt jobs that men might take to support families. When men went off to war, the message was reversed; the number of women in the labor force doubled and union membership increased four times. Women threw switches on the Long Island Railroad, felled redwoods on the Pacific slopes, and operated cranes in the steel mills of Gary, Indiana. Most of these working women were mature and married, the very women whose place by tradition was in the home. Not all of them thought of their displacement as temporary.

But men, who controlled unions, corporations, and governments, often regarded working women as a wartime expedient. Unions devised seniority rules that protected the job of a draftee from the woman who filled it while he was gone. Neither industry nor government expected women to aspire to decision-making posts. Corporations located miles from shopping centers, banks, housing, and commercial transportation seemed surprised when women with families were absent more frequently than male employees. The government spent very little money very grudgingly to provide child-care facilities, which accommodated about one child in ten who needed them in 1945.

Federal authorities warned employers not to discriminate against working women after the war. But defenders of home-and-mother attributed wartime juvenile delinquency to working mothers (rather than to absent fathers) and hoped that women would graciously accept the nation's thanks for an emergency task well performed and retire. A senator from Florida suggested legislation to send "wives and mothers back to the kitchen" in order to vacate jobs for returning veterans. Women employed in defense industries did lose their jobs, but many soon found others. In 1949, the number of women employed in California, for instance, was twice the number in 1940.

There was every reason to believe the change was permanent, for women obviously did not miss their sinks. Women polled on the job in 1945, regardless of age or marital status, hoped to retain their positions. Only 4 percent of schoolgirls sampled in a national study looked to homemaking as a full-time career. Most husbands swallowed misgivings as their standard of living increased with their wife's income.

Leaving home was apparently enough. The feminist drive for equal rights, which had languished during the depression, did not revive. Working women often did not receive equal pay for equal work, nor did they have equal opportunity for promotion, equal access to professional training, or even equal credit at the bank. For nearly two decades after

the war, most women settled for jobs and children and did not worry about careers and equality.

Women's jobs contributed to the most welcome of the wartime changes: prosperity returned to the nation. Consumer goods remained scarce, and a few dour economists predicted an early return to peacetime depression. But returning veterans did not become statistics on unemployment charts, and pent-up consumer demand bought out everything from stockings and steak to station wagons and ranch houses. With full wallets, three-shift workdays, and victories on the battlefields, the national confidence, shaken by a decade of depression, returned. Americans once again decided that whatever the task, they would manage.

The Serviceman's Readjustment Act, usually called the GI Bill of Rights, provided time for the economy to absorb those released from the service and supplied funds for their education. Veterans were eligible for a year of unemployment compensation. Those who wanted education were entitled to tuition, books, and allowances for their dependents while studying, whether the course led to certification in plumbing or a doctorate in philosophy. The government guaranteed low-cost loans for those who wanted to establish small businesses or to build or purchase housing. The GI Bill was the product of the nation's earnest wish to pay the troops more than the minimal salaries they had collected while on active duty. It was the product also of congressional concern for khaki-clad voters and their dependents. And it was a hedge against recurring depression, for the various benefits kept veterans out of the job market, stimulated basic industries such as housing, and prevented economic desperation among the unemployed.

Postwar prosperity prolonged the euphoria of victory. But if the nation had subdued the Axis and the depression, other tasks loomed. The United States had yet to determine the diplomatic consequences of the destruction of Germany and Japan, and of the weakness of Britain, France, and China. The nation had yet to probe the technological and moral consequences of the use of atomic energy. Americans had yet to distribute equitably the enormous output of their economic system. Racial justice had yet to be achieved. But surviving a war and a depression had been the tasks of a generation, and survival, for the moment, seemed assured.

Suggested Reading

Selig Adler's *The Isolationist Impulse** (1957) is more extensive chronologically than Manfred Jonas's *Isolationism in America** (1966), a convincing treatment of the period after 1935. In *The Troubled Encounter*

(1975), Charles E. Neu examines American contact with Japan, as does Dorothy Borg in *The United States and the Far Eastern Crisis of 1933–1938* (1964). John Gaddis's *The United States and the Origins of the Cold War* (1972) is relevant for relations with the USSR. Two books by Robert A. Divine, *The Illusion of Neutrality** (1962) and *The Reluctant Belligerent** (1965), are reliable and brief. James M. Burns's *Roosevelt: The Soldier of Freedom** (1970) is excellent.

Two volumes by William L. Langer and S. Everett Gleason defend American policy: *The Challenge to Isolation* (1952) and *The Undeclared War* (1953). More critical of American policy, especially of relations with Germany, is Arnold Offner's *American Appeasement* (1969). Also critical are Diane S. Clemens's *Yalta** (1970) and Gabriel Kolko's important revisionist study, *The Politics of War* (1968).

Rebecca Wohlstetter's *Pearl Harbor: Warning and Decision** (1962) is the best book on that disaster. A. Russell Buchanan's *The United States and World War II** (1964) is useful, as is Gaddis Smith's brief survey, *American Diplomacy During the Second World War** (1965). Martin J. Sherwin's *A World Destroyed* (1975) focuses on atomic diplomacy.

The war of the ordinary GI is depicted in Bill Mauldin's *Up Front** (1945). Richard Polenberg has edited *America at War** (1968) and written *War and Society** (1972) about the home front, which is also examined by John M. Blum in *V Was for Victory** (1976). The war's effect on women is one of the themes of William H. Chafe's *The American Woman** (1972).

* Available in paperback edition

1945 — 1980: An Introduction

Postwar Americans had few fond recollections of the good old days before the war. Neither the depression nor the country's hesitant prewar foreign policy inspired retrospective pride. But victory permitted Americans to overlook the 1930s and to renew their faith in progress and in their own institutions. They had, after all, met the tests of depression and war.

Evidence of new assurance abounded. A soaring birthrate illustrated the collective optimism of young adults. Mortgages and installment credit demonstrated a broad popular belief that prosperity would prove to be permanent. Willingness to accept the economic and strategic consequences of international power suggested a mature confidence in the American way of life and a generous eagerness to help other people who wished to imitate it. The more Americans saw of the rest of the world, the more they congratulated themselves on free enterprise, free elections, free speech, and the other attributes of what they called their "free country."

In their celebration of prosperity and freedom, Americans sometimes forgot their own caution that "there is no such thing as a free lunch." The bills for the euphoria of the immediate postwar years gradually fell due in the decades that followed. Some of the postwar babies then grew up to be the alienated young people who troubled teachers and legislators. The social costs of rapid economic development soon became visible in the unplanned sprawl of emerging cities, the smog that plagued larger ones, and the tar and garbage on the beaches of coastal ones. The price of international influence had to be paid in the hills of Korea and the jungles of Southeast Asia. The growth of presidential power, which once seemed to buttress democratic and decisive government, would later be described by a presidential aide as "a cancer." Assertive minorities questioned the nation's integrity by demonstrating that many Americans neither believed nor practiced the egalitarian ideals the nation professed.

Those are the themes of postwar American history: the changes that the Bureau of the Census reported in the population itself—where Americans lived, what they did, how old they were; the growth, and the occasional faltering, of the economy; the Cold War and its consequences at home and abroad; the evolving rearrangement of American political institutions, with a larger role for the courts and active Presidents, and a smaller one for political parties and Congresses that initiated little; repeated challenges—by women, youth, Indians, blacks, homosexuals, convicts, and any other group with a grievance—to the values and the power of those who controlled the country. Individual Americans sensed these broad developments in various ways and felt their impact with varying intensity. But few were indifferent to these changes, and no one was unaffected.

Chapter 21
After the War

The Cold War began without public fanfare and perhaps without official realization. The Western allies and the Soviet Union had subordinated wartime differences in order to achieve a common goal; the Nazi defeat made cooperation seem less necessary. The war left the USSR and the United States alone in the ranks of world powers. Defeat removed Germany and Japan, creating a political vacuum in Central Europe and East Asia. Nominal victors, like Great Britain, France, and China, were too spent to rival their two dominant wartime allies. Demands for autonomy and independence, which spread through the British Commonwealth and other colonial empires, contributed to the shifting balance of world power and offered frequent opportunities for one great power to test the nerve of the other.

An ideological clash sharpened geopolitical rivalry. The USSR since 1917 had postulated the enmity of the surrounding world—capitalist states, according to the Leninist canon, bent on blocking the inexorable progress of communism. In fact, American policy had shown hostility toward the Soviet Union, and Americans did have an instinctive aversion to communism in any of its forms. Success of American arms and industry in the Second World War stimulated the recurring sense of national mission, which collided with an expansive Communist creed. Hindsight suggests that Soviet foreign policy derived more from Stalin's interest in establishing a zone of Russian influence in Eastern Europe than from his zeal in converting others to communism. He was happy to seize whatever opportunities for subversion or power the worldwide brotherhood of Communists provided. But probably his first concerns were the regions on his frontiers that Russians had coveted since Peter the Great founded the empire.

Americans did not always differentiate the USSR—a political entity—from communism, the ideology Soviet leaders professed. This confusion in the popular mind had political and diplomatic consequences, for Americans tended to see the evil hand of the Kremlin in the revolution of Chinese Communists, for instance, or in Arab nationalism, which had an anticapitalist bias. Similarly, the American public often explained any Soviet success as the result of a Communist plot. Cold-war stereotypes—amoral, undercover Bolsheviks and capitalist running dogs—influenced not only the rhetoric of both countries, but sometimes their perceptions and policies as well.

The Peace Chills

Accustomed for a political generation to the example of Franklin Roosevelt, Americans expected their President to personify the nation and personally to chart its course. Roosevelt had done virtually nothing to prepare his successor for these tasks, but, both by temperament and by conviction, Harry Truman was ready for the Cold War. A blunt and scrappy man, Truman believed that the United States "must stand up to" the Russians and reverse concessions that, in his view, echoed the discredited appeasement policy.

A few days after Roosevelt's death, Truman showed his determination to Foreign Minister Vyacheslav Molotov, who was on his way to San Francisco to sign the charter of the United Nations. The American people, Truman told Molotov, expected the Soviet Union to carry out the spirit of the Yalta agreement concerning Poland. The remark signaled Truman's unwillingness to concede the zone of Soviet domination that Stalin believed he had secured in Eastern Europe. Molotov replied that the USSR was abiding by the Yalta agreement, and the conversation became undiplomatically sharp. The next day, Stalin rejected Truman's protest, noting pointedly that Poland bordered the Soviet Union and was well removed from the frontiers of Great Britain and the United States. In other areas, the old Bolshevik implied, he would not dispute American influence, but Eastern Europe was his to control.

Stalin's determination did not waver at the Potsdam Conference in June 1945, when Truman and Clement Atlee, who had replaced Winston

Churchill as a result of the British election, pressed for self-government and economic autonomy for the peoples of Central and Eastern Europe. (The ideals of unencumbered world trade and national self-determination persisted among American statesmen who took up Woodrow Wilson's effort to establish permanent peace.) Partly because Stalin manifestly would not move the Red Army out of Eastern Europe, the negotiators at Potsdam moved on to other topics. They agreed that trials of Nazi war criminals should begin at Nürnberg and postponed decisions on boundaries and on the final terms of peace.

Truman may have tolerated stalemate at Potsdam because he suspected the atomic bomb would give him additional leverage. The President and James Byrnes, his secretary of state, knew that the new weapon lessened their need for Soviet participation in the Pacific war; they hoped that Stalin's desire to share in atomic secrets might induce him to adopt a more flexible posture toward Rumania, Poland, and the rest of Eastern Europe. But when the people of the region did not welcome Soviet domination or Communist principles, a series of coups and purges in the autumn of 1945 lowered what Churchill called an iron curtain from the Baltic to the Adriatic. Nor did the bomb freeze Stalin out of the Pacific war: ninety days after Germany's surrender, two days after Hiroshima, and two days before the second bomb exploded on Nagasaki, Stalin sent the Red Army into Manchuria.

No responsible American official argued that the bomb should not be used to end the war. The military staff predicted that an invasion of Japan would cause at least a million American casualties and untold Japanese lives; if these estimates were accurate, the bomb may have prevented a bigger slaughter than it caused. Yet the invasion was not scheduled for some months and Truman could have explored Japanese inquiries about a negotiated peace before ordering atomic destruction. Some scientific advisers suggested an explosive demonstration that would take no lives but would convince Japan of the futility of continued resistance. Yet Truman's reputation as a senator had rested on his investigations of wartime waste; he knew what a congressional committee might have concluded if he had tolerated heavy casualties while refusing to use a weapon developed with two billions of the taxpayers' dollars. If the first decision was not quite routine, the order to use the second bomb did not even require Truman's review.

The atomic monopoly permitted the administration to succumb to political pressure to "bring the boys home" as soon as the war ended. A year after the Japanese surrender only a small force remained abroad—too small, the experts said, to meet the responsibilities that stemmed from the nation's successful effort to disarm Axis nations, from the desire to block the territorial expansion of the USSR, and from the need to counter the spread of Communist doctrine. Containment—the usual term for postwar American foreign policy—accurately described those goals, but did not encourage distinctions among them. George

Kennan, the scholarly diplomat associated with the term, advocated a tough approach to Russian demands, not an ideological crusade against Communist ideas. But Truman obscured the difference between territorial and doctrinal aggression in March 1947, when he asked for $400 million for economic aid to Greece and Turkey. Senator Arthur Vandenburg, the Republican symbol of bipartisan foreign policy, and other associates told Truman that the appropriation depended on his ability "to scare hell out of the American people." Truman evoked the nation's reflex response to communism and played on popular sympathy for "free peoples who are resisting . . . armed minorities or outside pressures." He went beyond the immediate crisis to outline what was soon called the Truman Doctrine, which the President himself later interpreted as a pledge "to support the cause of freedom wherever it was threatened."

Greece and Turkey were only the first steps. The Western European democracies, devastated during the war, could not develop enough economic momentum to thwart the political gains of local Communists in France and Italy; economic disaster even threatened in Britain. In May 1947, Undersecretary of State Dean Acheson suggested that the United States hasten economic recovery by financing European purchases of American goods. A month later, Truman's new secretary of state, George C. Marshall, unveiled the European Recovery Program, soon known simply as the Marshall Plan.

Though designed to help European nations, the scheme was not entirely disinterested. Secretary Marshall knew that Europe's purchases, financed by American credit, would keep the American economy humming and that the commercial connection would keep the continent in economic and political orbit around the United States. Economic stability, Marshall said, would produce non-Communist political stability, which the United States obviously favored.

The European shopping list exceeded $22 billion, a massive injection of American capital that would dramatically raise production. The administration cut the request to $17 billion; the program eventually cost about $12 billion over four years. In those four years, the economic growth of participating countries climbed more than 50 percent; in West Germany, the economy grew a staggering 312 percent. Such a recovery in Germany, if unaccompanied by economic vigor elsewhere, might have caused alarm. But the general return of economic health and the multinational cooperation that the Marshall Plan required allayed some national jealousies. In that respect, the program was a magnificent success.

Like the hasty effort to shore up Greece and Turkey, the Marshall Plan relied on American dollars to restore economic vitality and political self-confidence. But the Truman administration sold both measures to a reluctant Congress and an uninformed public as ways of defeating communism. When communism did not, in fact, weaken, military aid

Marshall Plan helps Berlin to rebuild

appealed to an impatient public and an economizing Congress as a more direct method of stopping the Communist advance.

The drift toward reliance on military power began almost immediately after the Marshall Plan was enacted. Unable to reach agreement with the Soviets about German unification in March 1948, Western foreign ministers announced plans to unify at least the Western zones in the Federal Republic of Germany, which would receive aid under the Marshall Plan. The Soviet Union opposed first the creation and then any strengthening of West Germany. A dispute over new German currency served Soviet authorities as a pretext for stopping all surface traffic from West Germany to West Berlin. President Truman ordered a massive airlift that supplied the city for nearly a year until the Russians decided to call off the futile blockade. Since no agreement on access routes was reached, the first Berlin crisis ended without a long-term settlement.

During the airlift, the United States joined eleven other North Atlantic nations in a binding military alliance. The North Atlantic Treaty, of April 1949, declared that an attack on any of the signatories would "be considered an attack against them all" and established the North Atlantic Treaty Organization (NATO) to coordinate defensive efforts. Since the United States did not reinforce American garrisons in Europe, NATO's land forces remained inferior to the Red Army. Western Europe's chief military defense, then, was the same American nuclear force that had defended the continent before the alliance.

McCarthyism

For most Americans, the years after the war were a time to reestablish civilian habits—to renew marriages, eat steak, have babies, buy a car, move to a new house. But the outside world kept intruding. Maps in popular magazines seemed to show larger and larger areas colored in Communist red. Not only did Eastern Europe disappear behind an iron curtain, but in 1949 Chiang Kai-shek abandoned China to Communists led by Mao Tse-tung. Even the confidence that depended on the atomic monopoly sagged after the explosion of a Russian bomb in 1949.

Disappointed at the erosion of the nation's security, many Americans blamed the Communists. They need not always be Russian Communists; often any Communists would do. If President Truman and other political leaders often failed to separate Soviet Communists from those in Yugoslavia, Indochina, Italy, and the District of Columbia, most of the American people were not more discriminating. The discovery of Communist espionage in Canada and the revelation in 1950 that a British scientist had given classified nuclear information to the Russians located the conspiracy close to home. In fact, Whittaker Chambers told the House Committee on Un-American Activities in 1949, the espionage network had included Americans, among them Alger Hiss.

Alger Hiss had been a bright young New Dealer, had accompanied Roosevelt to Yalta, and was, in 1949, part of the nation's unofficial foreign policy elite as president of the Carnegie Foundation for International Peace. Both Dean Acheson, secretary of state in Truman's second term, and John Foster Dulles, Acheson's successor in the Eisenhower administration, were among Hiss's friends and references. But Whittaker Chambers convinced Richard Nixon, then a young California congressman, that Hiss had passed classified data to Communist agents in the 1930s. Nixon prolonged the investigation until Hiss directly contradicted Chambers, who documented his accusation with microfilm he had hidden in a hollow pumpkin. Since the statute of limitations precluded indictment for espionage, the government charged Hiss with perjury. After one case ended in a hung jury, he was convicted early in 1950.

Hiss was the least of it, bellowed a previously obscure Republican senator from Wisconsin. There were, said Joseph McCarthy, two hundred or fifty-seven or eighty-one Communists in the State Department, depending on which list he consulted at the moment. Eventually he named just one name, that of Owen Lattimore, a professor of Asian history whom the State Department had occasionally consulted, and who, McCarthy said, was the "top Soviet espionage agent" in the country, a charge for which there was no basis in fact. Indeed, a Senate committee solemnly investigated all McCarthy's statements and concluded that there was no evidence for any of them. The undaunted McCarthy

McCarthy and a visual aid

campaigned against Millard Tydings, the respected Maryland Democrat who had headed the investigation, and helped end his long political career. No reputation was immune; in 1951 McCarthy called General George C. Marshall a front man for the international Communist conspiracy.

The public responded because McCarthy offered a comprehensible explanation of the blighted American hope for a stable world. Yet his crusade was already out of date when he launched it. During the depression, Communists had, in fact, been among the most militant labor organizers and some had gained elective office in the industrial unions of the CIO. There were indeed philosophical Communists working in the mass media, particularly in the motion picture industry. A few Communist sympathizers had secured government jobs. But Stalin's terrible purges in the later 1930s disillusioned intellectuals and others who had only flirted with the doctrine. Most unions had shed their Communist leadership before the Taft-Hartley Act required them to do so in 1947. The Federal Employee Loyalty Program, which Truman had established in 1947, had scrutinized the civil service. But McCarthyism, for the moment, needed no factual basis and for a few years prospered as the "menace" receded. And Truman's unexpected reelection in 1948 gave responsible Republicans no incentive to muzzle partisan orators who blamed him for coddling Communists and thereby causing the nation's misery.

Before the spy scare ended in the Eisenhower administration, Senator McCarthy took his show on the road and sought Communists in government agencies abroad, in defense plants, in universities, and in the army. He inspired fear throughout the federal bureaucracy, uneasiness among his colleagues in the Senate, and a batch of two-bit imitators. Even President Dwight Eisenhower, who privately loathed McCarthy, avoided a collision with him until the Senate itself instituted proceedings that led to censure in 1954. For McCarthy had overreached himself when he began an investigation of the army. He had insulted the secretary of the army and a respected general, made too many of his fellow senators ashamed, and angered the President, who invoked a new doctrine of "executive privilege" when he ordered officials of the executive branch to refuse to respond to some of McCarthy's questions. Day after day a fascinated national television audience watched McCarthy employ parliamentary devices, innuendo, and an imaginary Red menace in a vain attempt to avoid the Senate's condemnation.

In four years, McCarthy had not caught a single Communist. But he blighted the careers of actors and professors, ruined the morale of the foreign service, and cost the country the service of several able diplomats and the candor of countless others. His accusations fostered a political timidity that probably inhibited new approaches to American foreign policy and new ideas about domestic programs. He made an open mind seem unpatriotic and political apathy seem prudent, for any statement might seem embarrassing when wrenched out of context. Long after his death in 1957 his influence lingered in the extent of the nation's intelligence network, and in the reflexive respect for action taken "to protect the national security."

The Postwar Economy

When the war ended, most Americans took the nation's security for granted and worried about their own. Economic planners and politicians sought a formula that would preserve full employment and national prosperity amid the dislocation of demobilization. Boosted by overtime, wartime wages had reached twice the prewar level; the gross national product had also doubled; more than $30 billion in personal savings awaited builders, manufacturers, and salesmen. Individuals with jobs, savings accounts, and growing families went on a shopping spree in 1945 that endured almost without interruption for thirty years. If every shopping cart did not contain an equal measure of the nation's goods, if the poor remained relatively poor, at least the word "depression" temporarily lost its economic connotation.

Governmental policy encouraged consumption. The Employment Act of 1946 pledged federal help for private efforts to sustain "maximum" employment, a watered-down version of the promise of full employment sponsors had wanted government to make. Although Congress took no direct action to carry out the employment act, the GI Bill and other federal programs provided subsidized mortgages that helped countless families build new homes. Tax policy, which permitted deduction of interest and local real estate taxes, encouraged ownership rather than rental. Without governmental assistance, construction might have slowed, but the basic demand for housing, long postponed, came from new families with new babies, not from legislators.

Similarly, the construction of the interstate highway system, begun following passage of the Highway Act of 1956, only encouraged, but did not cause, the nation's passion for automobiles. After 1946, eager drivers bought almost anything that moved. In 1948, dealers sold nearly four million cars; sales increased to a peak of almost eight million in 1955. By 1960, the industry regarded annual sales of six million automobiles as routine. Suburban residents depended on both cars in their two-car garages; high schools had to enlarge parking lots; developers set shopping centers amid acres of asphalt; and gasoline alleys appeared at the edge of every town as service industries proliferated to cater to the nation's automotive mania.

Those who had to travel further than from home to office took the plane. The aircraft industry, stimulated and subsidized by military procurement, continued its wartime growth. Once the leisure activity of the rich, travel became less leisurely and less costly, and spawned a host of dependent companies from travel agents to catering services. The airlines gave the traveling salesman a national territory, made rootlessness an occupational hazard for executives, put Europe within easy reach of middle-class tourists, and almost destroyed the passenger railroads.

Corporate expenditure for research and development—as much money as the nation spent for higher education at mid-century— filled stores with new products. Synthetic fibers replaced cotton and wool; detergents instead of soaps kept the nation clean; and plastics substituted for metal and glass. Transistors, aerosol valves, computers, and copying machines served as a base for hundreds of new companies and as stiff competitors for hundreds of old ones.

Along with all the goods, however, the postwar economy also produced the social problems of affluence: suburban growth and urban decay, environmental pollution, wasted resources, loss of community spirit, and the smoldering resentment of those whose measure was short. By the 1960s, when the problems became apparent and elements of the public began to doubt the joys of unbridled consumption, some of the opportunities for social planning had already passed.

The Fair Deal and the Modern Republicans

Harry Truman's domestic program, which he called the Fair Deal, built upon the programs and the political coalition of Franklin Roosevelt. But a Republican Congress, elected in 1946, was wary of Roosevelt's programs and meant to reverse at least one of them in the Taft-Hartley Act of 1947. This act required union officers to take a non-Communist oath and their organizations to allow a sixty-day "cooling-off period" before beginning a strike. In the event a labor dispute threatened national health or safety, the President might secure a court order postponing any strike for eighty days. The act outlawed the closed shop and empowered states to enact "right to work" laws to forbid contracts that made union membership a condition of employment. In his veto message, Truman charged that the law was "completely contrary to the national policy of economic freedom," but Congress, unmoved, overrode his objection.

The new labor law, passed by the only Republican Congress between 1930 and 1953, was only one indication that Harry Truman's leadership inspired little confidence. His renomination by the Democrats in 1948 caused a dual schism in his party. Dixiecrats—southern Democrats outraged by Truman's futile attempt to secure a measure of equality for blacks—nominated South Carolina's Governor Strom Thurmond for President. Another faction repudiated Truman's foreign policy as too rigidly anti-Communist and nominated Henry Wallace. Neither the

Dixiecrats nor the Progressives proved as damaging as Republicans expected when they once again nominated New York's Governor Thomas E. Dewey and teamed him with Earl Warren, the progressive governor of California.

Dewey conducted a dignified campaign, said nothing to excite or to anger, and gave the impression that he was already providing mature presidential leadership. Truman offered a clear contrast with his strident indictment of a "do-nothing Republican Congress" and his charge that the party remained dedicated to the economic policies of Herbert Hoover. Although the President often ran behind local Democrats, he won most of the black voters in crucial industrial states, unexpected support from farmers worried about Dewey's agricultural program, and—by a margin of about two million votes—the election.

But the election did not advance the Fair Deal. Truman's innovations almost invariably failed to clear Congress. Medicare, fair employment practices, federal aid to education, the Brannan Plan to support farmers' incomes instead of crop prices—these measures became the staples of subsequent Democratic platforms and the legislation of subsequent Democratic Congresses. During the Truman administration, and in the following eight years under Eisenhower, Congress expanded existing programs like social security and rural electrification, made larger appropriations for federal housing programs, and raised the minimum wage, but seldom enacted new proposals.

Eisenhower was more content with congressional inaction than was Truman. Born a few years and a few hundred miles apart, both men learned early and well the moral truths of midwestern Protestantism. Both made careers in government during the 1930s, and both had mastered the lessons about compromise and appeasement that their contemporaries drew from prewar errors at Munich. Yet the two Presidents differed profoundly in temperament, for Eisenhower radiated a benign calm and soothed the discord the combative Truman stirred. If Congress did not enact his program, Truman denounced the do-nothing Republican Congress; if critics questioned his loyalty program, they wasted the nation's time in pursuit of a red herring; if railway workers wanted to strike when he thought they should not in 1946, Truman sought authority to replace them with troops; and when a strike in the steel mills in 1952 impeded American progress in the Korean War, he simply seized the mills until the courts ordered him to give them back. Truman seemed to enjoy crises; Eisenhower faced them when he had to, but he preferred to play golf.

Eisenhower's campaign promised more change than his administration delivered. His opponent, Adlai E. Stevenson, the witty and articulate governor of Illinois, inherited the public's disenchantment with Truman. Richard Nixon, the Republican vice-presidential candidate, Senator McCarthy, and other Republican campaigners played on the public's suspicion that Democratic grafters and perhaps even Communist spies

The Republican nominees, 1952

lurked in the federal bureaucracy. But it was the nation's confidence in
the beaming Republican candidate, not innuendo or partisan sallies, that
ended the Democrats' twenty-year lease on the White House.
Eisenhower's margin enabled his party to control Congress for the first
two years of his presidency.

Dwight Eisenhower was the prophet of modern Republicanism, a creed
he vaguely defined as "dynamic conservatism." The President himself
subordinated dynamism to conservatism; on inspection, his program
resembled Herbert Hoover's wrapped in new verbiage. To free the market,
Eisenhower dropped the last wartime wage, price, and rent controls. He
signed a bill that gave jurisdiction and revenue from offshore oil deposits
to the adjacent states, a symbolic act that enhanced state rights. The
administration attempted to check the expansion of TVA, which the
President cited as an example of "creeping socialism," by contracting
with a private utility to supply power to TVA customers. But a Senate
inquiry uncovered a conflict of interest and the embarrassing contract
had to be canceled. The Revenue Act of 1954 gave more tax relief to the
wealthy than to those with lower incomes. Ezra Taft Benson, the
secretary of agriculture, wanted farmers to enjoy the benefits of free

competition, but farmers and their representatives raised such an outcry that Eisenhower proposed a "soil bank" in 1956 to pay farmers to withdraw land from cultivation in order to reduce surpluses. After the Soviet Union fired the first man-made satellite into orbit in 1957, the argument against federal aid to education abated, and Congress passed the National Defense Education Act in 1958. The act made loans available to students and funded programs to improve the teaching of mathematics, science, and foreign languages.

Although the President's personal grasp on the electorate never loosened, the voters chose a Democratic Congress after 1952. Even in 1956, when Eisenhower overwhelmed Adlai Stevenson a second time, Congress remained Democratic. While Eisenhower made most of the gestures expected of a party leader, he did so without partisan zest. He allowed other Republican officeholders to go their own way and rarely used patronage to twist congressional arms. Much of his party remained blithely untouched by the "modern" version of the Republican creed.

In the end, modern Republicanism became little more than an obsession with the balanced budget. In fact, most of Eisenhower's budgets were in the red, and the 1959 deficit of over $18 billion was at that time the largest in peacetime history. But the President kept trying to match income and expense. The administration pared research and development expenditures just as the Russian Sputnik inaugurated the space age. To the disgust of Republicans in farm states, the President defended most of Secretary Benson's attempts to hold down the government's agricultural appropriations. Dissident generals claimed that reduced conventional military forces eliminated the nation's capacity to wage small wars and gave strategists no alternative to the big bomb. Quick reduction of government spending after the Korean War unquestionably contributed to a recession in 1953 and 1954, when an alarming increase in unemployment took place. Although the economy soon bounced back, other economic slowdowns in 1957 and 1958 and again in 1960 and 1961 caused individual hardship and social uneasiness. Keynesian economists argued that government spending should be increased in times of distress, but every drop in the economic index merely made the Eisenhower administration more sure that unbalanced budgets marked the way to economic perdition.

Toward Equality for Blacks

The Second World War accelerated the migration of blacks from southern farms to cities all over the nation. In 1940, more than half the black population lived in rural areas; in 1950, nearly two-thirds of blacks lived in cities, many of which were in the North. Sharecroppers, displaced by agricultural machinery, moved to New York, Detroit, Los Angeles, and

Washington, where they took the unskilled jobs of the growing economy and crowded into segregated housing. The black birth rate, which outpaced that of the rest of the nation, made those ghettos even more crowded with every passing year.

By any standard, blacks received a small share of the nation's postwar prosperity. Per capita income, infant mortality rate, average level of education, access to goods and services—all these indices revealed the existence of two classes of American citizens. Nearly 40 percent of white wage-earners in 1950 held nonmanual jobs; the comparable statistic for blacks was less than 10 percent. About 15 percent of white laborers were skilled; the comparable statistic for blacks was less than 6 percent. Truman suggested a permanent Fair Employment Practices Commission to secure equal job opportunities, a proposal that balanced equality with competitive individualism in the traditional liberal manner.

Congress did not enact a code for fair employment. Nor did it respond to Truman's requests for a permanent commission on civil rights, for voting rights legislation, or for abolition of discrimination in interstate travel. The President used executive authority in 1948 to order integration in the military services, and he vetoed a measure that would have encouraged segregation in schools on military reservations. Military segregation did not end immediately, but by mid-1950 black and white draftees were training together on military posts across the land.

Four years later, the Supreme Court of the United States declared that black and white children should learn in the same schools. In a unanimous decision written by Chief Justice Earl Warren, whom Eisenhower had just appointed, the Court held in *Brown* v. *Board of Education of Topeka* that segregation in public schools abridged rights guaranteed by the Fourteenth Amendment. Warren's finding that separate schools could not be equal schools set aside the legal test established a half century before in *Plessy* v. *Ferguson.* The Court had led when legislatures and elected officials hesitated, and it then applied its new standard of equality to parks, swimming pools, and other public facilities.

Eisenhower had no political obligation to black voters and little personal understanding of either the depth of white racism or the rising level of black frustration. He assumed that decent people of both races would work out injustices without political intervention: "The final battle against intolerance is to be fought," Eisenhower remarked in 1956, "not in the chambers of any legislature—but in the hearts of men." In 1958, the President astounded a meeting of black leaders by advising them that they must above all have patience. He pointedly refrained from executive action to affirm the Supreme Court's rulings against segregation. This refusal may have misled White Citizens' Councils and other extremists to believe that the Court might safely be defied.

While he blinked at evasion, Eisenhower did not tolerate defiance. When the schools of Little Rock, Arkansas, opened in 1957, Governor

Sitting in

Orval Faubus used the National Guard to keep order and also to keep nine black students out of the high school where a federal court had ordered them admitted. After prolonged and inconclusive discussion with the President, Faubus withdrew the Guard, but a hysterical mob barred the blacks from the school. Eisenhower finally sent federal troops to Little Rock to enforce the Court's decree and to demonstrate to the Deep South the folly of a direct confrontation with federal authority.

Federal authority was soon to become more extensive. As the crisis in Little Rock got under way, Congress completed action on the first civil rights legislation since Reconstruction. The Civil Rights Act of 1957 created a permanent commission on civil rights to investigate discrimination and disfranchisement. Another act in 1960 authorized court-appointed officials to protect access of black voters to the polls. The President made only a nominal effort to help congressional proponents of either bill overcome entrenched southern opposition. Senator Lyndon Johnson and Speaker Sam Rayburn, the two Texans who led the Democratic majority, supported the legislation and guided it toward the White House.

Some southern blacks were well ahead of the glacial pace toward integration that the President seemed to favor. For almost a year, beginning late in 1955, Martin Luther King, Jr., led the black population of Montgomery, Alabama, in a boycott of the city's buses to force changes in the seating arrangements. King, a Montgomery clergyman, stressed black solidarity, nonviolence, and the persuasive power of demonstration. His influence grew when a federal injunction ended the boycott on the blacks' terms.

The next round of protest belonged to the young. To the black students in Greensboro, North Carolina, who politely declined to leave the lunch counter that had refused to serve them and thereby set off an epidemic of sit-ins. To the small children who walked to newly integrated schools through the invective and the spittle and the white, hate-distorted faces. To the northern students who actively supported racial equality by marching or by tutoring, either in the South or increasingly in nearby urban ghettos. Exposure to northern ghettos advanced the growing realization that racism extended throughout the nation.

But a sense of urgency was still missing. In 1957, Martin Luther King, Roy Wilkins of the NAACP, and other black leaders planned a pilgrimage to the Lincoln Memorial to direct the nation's attention to its unfinished racial business. The march drew sparse crowds and almost no attention from the nation's press. Even *Ebony*, the black magazine with the largest circulation, completely ignored the protest.

The Cold War Gets Hot: Korea

The wartime expectation that Chiang Kai-shek's China could keep the postwar peace in the Pacific was never realistic. Even before the end of 1945 Americans in China had warned the State Department that Chiang was losing popular support to the Communist faction led by Mao Tse-tung. Military observers reported that Chiang's forces were well supplied and numerically superior, but ineptly led and lacking in the will that their Communist opponents had in abundance. In 1947 General Albert Wedemeyer told Truman that military effort alone would never stamp out Chinese communism and that aid to Chiang would be nearly useless because his incompetent subordinates could not effectively manage a program like those established under the Truman Doctrine. Paradoxically, Wedemeyer then recommended increasing military assistance and sending military advisers to improve Chiang's campaign against Mao's forces. Truman's response was as confused as his advice. Although the administration believed Chiang could not win, it accepted a $500 million appropriation to help him do so.

To no avail. In 1949 Chiang and his forces left the mainland for the island of Formosa, which they converted to a fortress and which for more than two decades the United States recognized as the Republic of China. In January 1950, Secretary of State Acheson unveiled the new policy this situation seemed to require. As the State Department saw it, the great force for change in Asia was nationalism, not communism, and Acheson suggested that nationalism was anti-Soviet as well as anti-American. Military adventure, the secretary said, would not help overcome the crippling domestic difficulties most Asian states faced. But if war came to the area, the United States would defend a perimeter extending from Japan through the Philippines. The first reliance of people beyond that line, an area that included Formosa, Korea, and all of mainland Asia, must be "upon the commitments of the entire civilized world under the Charter of the United Nations." When North Koreans invaded South Korea in June 1950, the United States responded promptly to resolutions of the United Nations, just as Acheson had promised.

Neither the Communist North nor the Republic of Korea to the south regarded the thirty-eighth parallel as a permanent boundary. Both halves of the country hoped to become the dominant partner in a unified nation. The Communists jumped first, with overwhelming numbers that broke through South Korean defenses. Two days after the invasion, President Truman stationed the Pacific fleet off Formosa to isolate the conflict and to prevent either China from attacking the other. He ordered American aircraft to support South Korean forces. Then, at the request of the United Nations, he sent General Douglas MacArthur and two divisions of American troops to Korea to try to stem the Communist advance.

Although Congress never followed the President's action with a declaration of war, nothing Truman did in his second administration was so popular. The Korean War, eventually a political albatross, initially had widespread support. Prompt military action to check aggression heartened American allies and supporters of the United Nations. Shaken by Communist coups in Eastern Europe and China, many Americans were glad to strike back, to substitute the satisfaction of action for the frustration of containment. Senator Robert Taft, perhaps the most respected Republican in the nation, had been critical of Truman's foreign policy, but he reluctantly and publicly approved the Korean intervention. The American people found the minimal national sacrifice tolerable, for

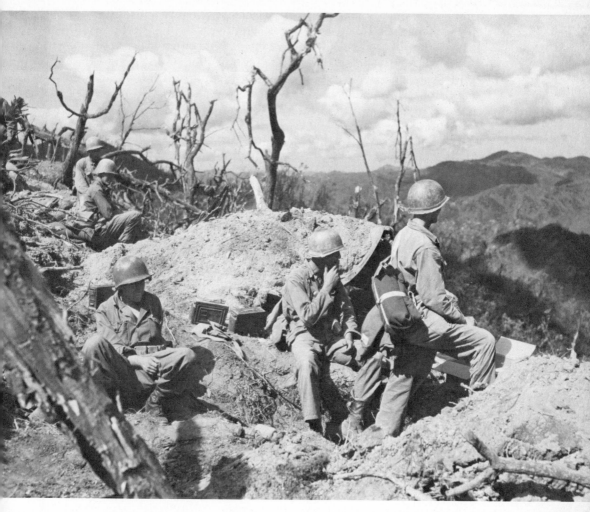

Korea, 1951

the country's astounding productivity amply supplied the troops while the domestic standard of living continued to advance.

For the first months, the war went badly. American troops retreated, along with the outnumbered forces of the Republic of Korea, to the southeastern corner of the peninsula, where they established a defensive perimeter. Then, in mid-September, MacArthur sent an amphibious expedition ashore at Inchon and nearly trapped the entire North Korean force, which fled toward the north in disorder. The United Nations hastily authorized MacArthur's troops to pursue the foe into North Korea. As the United Nations armies came within striking distance of the Yalu River, which marked the Chinese frontier, a unified, democratic Korea seemed imminent, and MacArthur said he thought American soldiers would be home for Christmas.

But they were not, nor for two Christmases thereafter. At the end of November 1950, Chinese forces, whose entry MacArthur had not expected, split the United Nations army, and another retreat to the south began. Early in 1951 the United Nations forces dug in near the thirty-eighth parallel, where for the next year and a half the war dragged on. General MacArthur had no stomach for stalemate. With the political support of administration critics, he suggested a blockade of Chinese and Manchurian ports, requested authority to bomb Chinese bases, and advocated use of the forces of Nationalist China. "In war," MacArthur said emphatically, "there is no substitute for victory."

THE KOREAN WAR

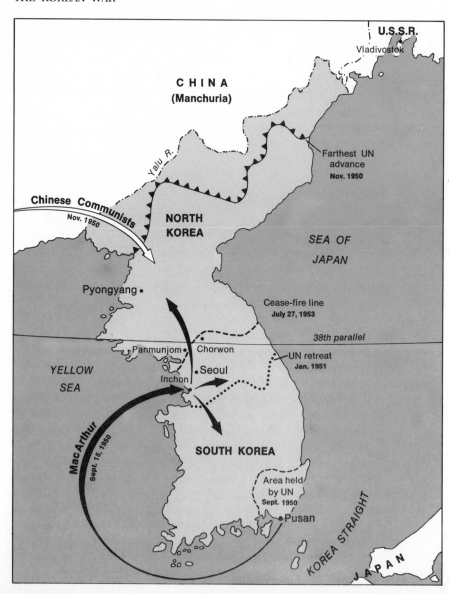

The administration saw things differently. As MacArthur used the word, "victory" was not the goal. American strategists did not intend to "defeat" Communist China, but only to hold the line in Korea. A limited objective called for a limited war, a concept that MacArthur and his supporters neither accepted nor understood. When he could not convince the administration to change, MacArthur went around it. His press releases complained of official restraints on his freedom of military action; he furnished the administration's Republican critics with material for fresh attacks. In March 1951, Truman told MacArthur he was to make no major advance into North Korea that might upset negotiations. MacArthur replied with a public demand that the foe surrender, a statement that temporarily stymied Truman's effort to open peace talks. Less than two weeks later MacArthur again called for a larger war in a letter that Joseph W. Martin, the Republican leader in the House, made public. Within the week the President dismissed the general and set the country off on an emotional binge.

For a moment, MacArthur symbolized the nation's unhappiness that the simple old rules no longer governed the complex new world. MacArthur stood for victory, service, and patriotism, against compromise, containment, and communism. A congressional inquiry probed both Asian policy and MacArthur's abrupt dismissal. One by one the Joint Chiefs of Staff testified that global strategy, especially the situation in Europe, dictated decisions about Asian policy. MacArthur's proposed war with Communist China, General Omar Bradley suggested, would have been "the wrong war, at the wrong place, at the wrong time, and with the wrong enemy."

MacArthur's successor in the field, General Matthew Ridgway, proved able to conduct the war within limits the President set. In July 1951, although fighting continued, peace talks began. When the talks dragged on into the Eisenhower administration, the new secretary of state, John Foster Dulles, threatened more force. Late in the spring of 1953, through Indian intermediaries, Dulles let China know that American restraint in the use of nuclear weapons might not endure indefinitely. Within a month negotiations gathered momentum; in July the shooting stopped. A demilitarized zone and a United Nations truce team separated the two hostile halves of the country. Frontier incidents periodically reminded Americans that the cease-fire never became a final settlement, but a fragile truce was better than none. After three years of warfare and more than 33,000 American lives, the boundary dividing the Korean peninsula stayed at the thirty-eighth parallel.

Containment Continued

The Korean truce ended only one of Asia's wars. During the negotiations, Dulles tried to barter a cease-fire in Korea for one in French Indochina, where the hit-and-run tactics of native guerrillas were exhausting

French forces. He soon abandoned his attempt to link the two wars, but the United States did help France. By 1954, when Indochinese troops surrounded the French garrison at Dien Bien Phu, the United States was paying about three-fourths of France's military expenses in Indochina. Without American military intervention at Dien Bien Phu, it was said, the investment would be lost. Eisenhower compared Southeast Asia to a row of dominoes and pointed out that if the Communists pushed over the Indochinese domino, others in the row would certainly tumble too. The secretary of state told the cabinet that, except for France, our European allies did not share his view that the United States must act: "If we take a position against a Communist faction within a foreign country, we have to act alone," Dulles reported.

The prospect of another Asian war dismayed Congress. Prime Minister Anthony Eden of Great Britain also adamantly opposed a wider war in Indochina. General Matthew Ridgway, who had returned from Korea to become the army's chief of staff, strongly advised against intervention. In the end, Eisenhower let events take their course. After Dien Bien Phu fell in May 1954, an international conference convened in Geneva to make an official end to the war. The conference divided the eastern portion of the peninsula at the seventeenth parallel and made arrangements for elections in 1956 to unite the new country, now called Vietnam. The elections were never held, and the war soon turned into a struggle between north and south.

Although Dulles had once denounced containment as "negative, futile, and immoral," he never really revised it. To prevent further expansion of Asian communism, for example, Dulles induced Britain, France, Australia, and New Zealand to join the United States, Thailand, Pakistan, and the Philippines in the Southeast Asia Treaty Organization (SEATO). The new agreement, Dulles said, in effect proclaimed any "intrusion" into Southeast Asia "dangerous to our peace and security." Modeled on NATO, SEATO did not create a comparably effective mutual defense system, in part because such Asian nations as India, Indonesia, and Burma would not participate. The signatories extended their protection to the new states of the Indochinese peninsula where nationalists perceived SEATO as a manifestation of the colonial control they were striving to end.

Dulles tried to complete a worldwide alliance system with the Baghdad Pact of 1955, which linked Turkey, Iraq, Iran, and Pakistan with Great Britain and the United States, and therefore with SEATO. Less successful even than SEATO, neither the Baghdad treaty nor the subsequent Central Treaty Organization (CENTO) provided the basis for American policy in the Middle East. Like other defensive alliances concluded in the decade after the Second World War, CENTO was supposed to thwart communism, which was less a cause of regional instability than Arab nationalism, oil, and the irreconcilable enmity of Israeli and Arab.

Gamal Abdel Nasser, Egypt's premier, was the chief Arab nationalist, the chief foe of Israel, and the focus of Soviet attempts to gain influence in the Middle East. Nasser's grand design for the modernization of Egypt required construction of a multipurpose dam on the Nile at Aswan. Both the Soviet Union and a Western consortium set up by the State Department agreed to finance the project. Meanwhile, Nasser began to purchase arms from Czechoslovakia, which alarmed American Jews, and recognized mainland China, which outraged Chiang's well-placed American supporters. In July 1956, after Dulles was advised that the Soviet Union could not finance the dam alone, he withdrew the offer of American assistance.

Within a week, Nasser nationalized the Suez Canal to provide his own capital. Since Egypt now stood squarely across the route by which most of the Middle East's oil reached Europe, Britain and France wanted to use the seizure as an excuse to overthrow Nasser. In October, when Israel invaded Egypt, British and French forces participated as well. The war caused consternation in the State Department and created an opportunity for the Soviet Union, which threatened to come to Egypt's aid with every weapon in the Russian arsenal. The United States brought great diplomatic pressure on its allies, and the war ended within a week.

Crises in the Middle East and in Southeast Asia emphasized the new complexity of the Cold War. The world no longer split neatly into partisans of the United States and satellites of the Soviet Union. A "Third World"—the emerging nations of Asia and Africa—wanted no place in either camp but hoped to borrow technical skills, industrial processes, and money from both. However annoying he was, Nasser was no Communist; nor did the leaders of India, Indonesia, or Yugoslavia fit the Cold War pattern. Although the administration perceived the change, it did little to educate either the public or the Congress.

Even in Latin America, an area that Yankees had taken for granted, the traditional policies no longer served very well. In 1954 the Central Intelligence Agency (CIA) organized a successful rebellion against a Communist-leaning government in Guatemala. But when Fidel Castro took over Cuba in 1959, he confiscated American property, sold his sugar to the Soviet Union, and proclaimed his island a Marxist state. Eisenhower protested and early in 1961 broke diplomatic relations, which hardly seemed a new hemispheric policy to meet a new situation. To cope with Castro, the CIA devised a scheme like the one that had succeeded in Guatemala. The debacle that followed waited for Eisenhower's successor.

In every upheaval, from Havana to Hanoi, the American public saw the devious hand of the Kremlin. Yet the Eisenhower administration had relatively little direct diplomatic difficulty with the Soviet Union. Disagreement about the future of Germany, particularly about the status of Berlin, furnished grounds for made-to-order crises. Otherwise, the two great powers avoided face-to-face confrontation. In October 1956, for instance, the United States did nothing to encourage rebels in Hungary, though Dulles had once welcomed such efforts by "captive peoples" in Eastern Europe. After the Soviet Union had crushed Hungarian resistance, Eisenhower said that the United States did not advocate open rebellion in the Russian satellites. With that remark, the administration tacitly accepted the division of Europe and the permanence of the iron curtain.

Direct negotiations between President Eisenhower and Soviet leaders failed to uncover a specific formula for German unity or a general plan for reducing international friction. In 1955 Nikolai Bulganin, the Soviet premier, and Nikita Khrushchev, who controlled the Communist party, met at Geneva with Eisenhower and British Prime Minister Anthony Eden. The meeting radiated good will but produced no diplomatic result. Eisenhower surprised the conference when he suggested that each bloc permit aerial inspection of its armaments and defenses. Although the West applauded this "open skies" proposal, Soviet leaders displayed a chilly lack of interest. Within a year, the United States opened Soviet skies without an agreement. In 1956 pilots employed by the CIA began regular photographic missions over Russian territory in U-2 planes, which flew above the reach of Soviet antiaircraft weapons.

One of those missions ended Eisenhower's hope for negotiated disengagement through further discussions with Khrushchev. In May 1960, as final preparations were being completed for a meeting in Paris, the Soviet Union shot down an American U-2 plane more than 1,300 miles inside the Soviet frontier. When American spokesmen lamely explained that the craft had strayed off course while seeking meteorological data, Khrushchev spiked the story with the announcement that the pilot, Francis Gary Powers, was alive and well and had admitted that his mission was photographic espionage. After further bureaucratic fumbling in Washington, Eisenhower admitted that he had authorized the flight. Khrushchev self-righteously proclaimed his refusal to sit down with an admitted spy, and although both men went to Paris, their meeting produced only recrimination. Anti-American riots in Japan, set off by the U-2 incident, forced the President to cancel a projected good-will tour. The Eisenhower administration ended, as had Truman's, in partisan criticism of American foreign policy.

Suggested Reading

Barton J. Bernstein and Allen J. Matusow have edited *The Truman Administration: A Documentary History** (1966); the counterpart on the Eisenhower years, in two volumes, was edited by Robert L. Branyan and Lawrence H. Larsen, *The Eisenhower Administration, 1953 – 1961: A Documentary History* (1971). Both Presidents wrote two-volume memoirs after leaving Washington: Truman's are entitled *Memoirs** (1955, 1956) and Eisenhower's *Mandate for Change* (1963) and *Waging Peace* (1965).

Sherman Adams's memoir, *Firsthand Report** (1961), provides an inside view of Eisenhower's presidency. Useful biographies include Robert J. Donovan's *Conflict and Crisis* (1977) on Truman's first three years in office, James T. Patterson's *Mr. Republican* (1972) on Robert A. Taft, and John B. Martin's *Adlai Stevenson of Illinois* (1976). Merle Miller's *Plain Speaking** (1974) gives a good glimpse of Truman.

No single book on the Truman administration matches the coverage of Herbert S. Parmet's *Eisenhower and the American Crusades* (1972), although Alonzo L. Hamby's *Beyond the New Deal* (1973) is a start. Barton J. Bernstein has edited a collection of critical scholarship, *Politics and Policies of the Truman Administration** (1970). R. Alton Lee's *Truman and Taft-Hartley* (1966) and Maeva Marcus's *Truman and the Steel Seizure Case* (1977) deal topically with the Truman years.

Earl Latham's *The Communist Conspiracy in Washington** (1966) is as sober as literature on McCarthy gets. Richard H. Fried argues in *Men Against McCarthy** (1976) that partisan politics had much to do with the senator's success. Allen Weinstein, the latest student of the Hiss case, concludes in *Perjury* (1978) that Hiss was guilty.

William C. Berman's *The Politics of Civil Rights in the Truman Administration* (1970) is a careful, fair treatment. Richard Kluger's *Simple Justice* (1975) is an excellent account of the *Brown* case. Martin Luther King, Jr., describes events in Montgomery in *Stride Toward Freedom** (1958). Gilbert Osofsky has collected documentary materials in *The Burden of Race** (1968).

The controversy about the origins of the Cold War may be sampled in *America and the Origins of the Cold War** (1972), edited by James V. Compton. John L. Gaddis's *The United States and the Origins of the Cold War* (1972) is balanced, and Paul Y. Hammond's *Cold War and Détente** (1975) is a satisfactory survey. Walter LaFeber's *America, Russia and the Cold War** (1976), Lloyd C. Gardner's *Architects of Illusion: Men and Ideas in American Foreign Policy* (1970), and Daniel Yergin's *Shattered Peace* (1977) are examples of moderate revisionist scholarship. Two works of Gabriel Kolko, *The Politics of War* (1968) and (with Joyce Kolko) *The Limits of Power* (1971), are critical of American policy. Gar Alperovitz's *Atomic Diplomacy: Hiroshima and Potsdam** (1965) is an early example of the revisionist critique. David Rees's *Korea: The Limited War** (1964) and John W. Spanier's *The Truman-MacArthur Controversy and the Korean War** (1959) cover the Korean conflict.

* Available in paperback edition

Chapter 22
High Hopes, Violence, and Vietnam

Chronology

1960 Presidential election: John F. Kennedy (Democrat) defeats Richard M. Nixon (Republican) •

1961 Cuban exiles defeated at Bay of Pigs • Berlin Wall divides city •

1961–1975 The war in Vietnam: *1964:* Tonkin Gulf Resolution • *1968:* North Vietnam launches Tet offensive • Paris peace talks begin • *1969:* Troop withdrawals commence • *1970:* Cambodian invasion • *1973:* Truce • *1975:* South Vietnam surrenders •

1962 Cuban missile crisis •

1963 Demonstrations in Birmingham and march on Washington lead to Civil Rights Act (1964) and Voting Rights Act (1965) •
President Kennedy assassinated in Dallas; Lyndon B. Johnson succeeds Kennedy • Test Ban Treaty •

1964 President Johnson declares war on poverty; promises Great Society •
Presidential election: Lyndon B. Johnson (Democrat) defeats Barry M. Goldwater (Republican) •

1965 American marines intervene in Dominican Republic •

1967 Urban riots •

1968 Assassinations of Martin Luther King, Jr., and Robert F. Kennedy • Presidential election: Richard M. Nixon (Republican) defeats Hubert H. Humphrey (Democrat) and George C. Wallace (American) •

1972 Nixon visits China •

1979 Recognition of China •

The bright hopes that glowed in John Kennedy's inaugural address gradually dimmed in the following decade. Then Americans soberly reconsidered the promises Kennedy and other leaders had made to "bear any burden" in freedom's cause, to conquer injustice through love and turning the other cheek, to improve for others the standard of living and the quality of life. The postwar consensus that supported containment of communism, civil rights for blacks, presidential leadership, and the socioeconomic orthodoxy of the New Deal—the consensus that Kennedy gave such eloquent expression—came under assault.

Among the most impassioned challengers were the maturing postwar babies, whose influence grew because there were so many of them. In the seventy years before 1960, the proportion of the American population between the ages of fourteen and twenty-four had increased 70 percent. In the ten years after 1960, that proportion jumped an astonishing 50 percent, a demographic shift that partly explained the youth culture of the decade and changes in American life from sexual habits to popular music. The most radical of these young people acknowledged that the cultural revolution they advocated might be violent.

There was a good deal of violence in these years—not all of which was based on principle, as the plague of murders and muggings and the looting during urban riots proved. Official violence also marred the decade: the destruction loosed by armies and police and other employees of society on those who were believed to endanger security or property or authority. The dissidence of the victims of official violence stemmed from the nation's failure to keep its promises. In particular, racial protest grew from broken pledges of equality and from the records of second-class schools, prejudiced employers, and foot-dragging legislatures. Those who opposed the nation's foreign policy evoked America's revolutionary heritage, Woodrow Wilson's international idealism, and personal moral principles to make the case against continued intervention in Vietnam.

The discrepancy between promise and practice was one form of a credibility gap that endangered public trust. Often with good reason, Americans suspected their government of telling them less than the whole truth about military operations in Southeast Asia or intelligence-gathering in Latin America. Students were skeptical of official assurances that universities had diligently recruited black students or had signed no defense contracts. Citizens doubted the personal rectitude of police, members of congress, clergy, and others who were supposed to exemplify and enforce traditional rules. Those who accepted the traditional ethic challenged claims of countercultural entrepreneurs that communes or meditation or illicit chemicals would produce instant brotherhood and lasting euphoria.

A preoccupation with what was called "style" helped to rivet the nation's attention on the appearance, rather than the substance, of things. Political candidates glossed over complex issues in thirty-second commercials designed to communicate image, not thought. Many adherents of the counterculture objected less strongly to environmental destruction and WASP domination than to ordinary standards of dress, grooming, and language. The *Pentagon Papers* suggest that domestic perceptions of foreign policy sometimes influenced planners more than circumstances abroad. A critic once dismissed John Kennedy as "an optical illusion," and the phrase could have been more broadly applied.

Indeed, for many Americans the very history of the period is an optical illusion—a series of images strung together in an impressionistic instant replay that serves as our history of the 1960s. For most of us, pictures from the latter part of the decade stand out more vividly than those from the earlier years; the violence now seems more characteristic than the hopes that went unrealized. Yet the history of the 1960s must record the dreams of Martin Luther King, Jr., as well as his assassination, the heady optimism of the war on poverty as well as the failure to win it, the romantic innocence of some of the hippies as well as the mindlessness of others, the selflessness of American willingness to help defend freedom's outposts as well as the fact that selflessness and defense alike somehow miscarried.

When Americans concluded that the more recent, more unpleasant symbols represented reality with more fidelity than earlier, sunnier ones, vague misgivings about leaders and policies swelled into a collective malaise that approached a loss of national faith. The manifest unwillingness of the white majority to move on from civil rights to racial equality was a major reason why some despaired; the multiple shocks associated with the war in Vietnam was another; the inability of the economy to sustain real growth, provide full employment, and eliminate want was a third; the misbehavior associated with Watergate was a final trauma. These failures even robbed Americans of satisfaction they might have derived from real accomplishment. The dramatic success of the space program, for instance, was often subordinated to shortcomings in statements that began "If we can send a man to the moon, we ought to be able to. . . ."

The New Frontier and the Great Society

During his presidential campaign, John Kennedy promised the adventure of a New Frontier. But the bipartisan coalition that dominated Congress was not adventuresome and Kennedy's narrow victory did not provide enough political muscle to coerce cautious legislators. Message after ringing message died in Congress without an echo. The church-state controversy snarled aid to education; the American Medical Association thwarted medical care for the aged; fiscal conservatives blocked a tax cut the President wanted to stimulate economic growth.

The social legislation that Kennedy and his successor, Lyndon Johnson, sought depended on economic growth. The government's share of the annual increase of roughly $40 billion in the gross national product (GNP) was to pay for social programs without, in effect, costing anybody anything. Stimulated by the tax cut of 1964, the economy magically fulfilled expansive presidential pledges before the additional burden of a war became too great. Until then, the GNP grew; the federal budget grew; unemployment fell to less than 4 percent of the labor force; prices remained stable; and Johnson boasted quite accurately in 1965 that Americans were "in the midst of the greatest upward surge of economic well-being in the history of any nation."

That was the sort of wave Lyndon Johnson liked to ride. With humility and dignity, he had helped the country through its grief after Kennedy's assassination in November 1963. Then the restless, ambitious Johnson put his own brand on the presidency. He prodded Congress to enact the tax cut and the civil-rights bill Kennedy had proposed. He ordered a tentative effort to ameliorate the lot of the poor blown into a "war on poverty," which he proclaimed with much fanfare in 1964. Righting economic injustice was to be a first step toward the "Great Society" in

which "the meaning of our lives," Johnson declared, would match "the
marvelous products of our labor." More and better schools, public
television, new parks, clean streams, racial justice, better highways
stripped of unsightly billboards, improved medical care in new hospitals,
and federal funds to support the arts, scientific research, poor people,
and political campaigns—Johnson's vision knew no limit.

But like his predecessor, Johnson made too many promises. Some of
them were campaign oratory that deserved to be discounted, though
probably he need not have made them since his opponent in 1964 was
never in the race. Barry Goldwater, an engaging, candid senator from
Arizona and an avowed conservative, lost the election by the largest
margin in American history and took many Republican legislators to
defeat with him. The new Democratic Congress produced the most
impressive spate of legislation since the early days of the New Deal. But
whatever Johnson said, legislation could not provide "meaning" for
people who lacked spiritual purpose. Nor did legislation redistribute the
nation's wealth: the poorer half of the population received less than a
quarter of the nation's income, about the same fraction it had received in
1950—or in 1930, for that matter. Johnson was the eventual victim of the
rage that disappointed expectations produced.

For there was no victory in the war on poverty that he had declared,
although Congress provided an Office of Economic Opportunity (OEO)

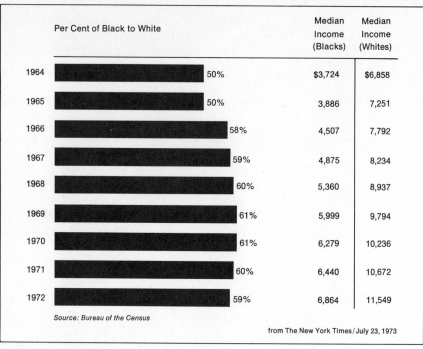

Per Cent of Black to White		Median Income (Blacks)	Median Income (Whites)
1964	50%	$3,724	$6,858
1965	50%	3,886	7,251
1966	58%	4,507	7,792
1967	59%	4,875	8,234
1968	60%	5,360	8,937
1969	61%	5,999	9,794
1970	61%	6,279	10,236
1971	60%	6,440	10,672
1972	59%	6,864	11,549

Source: Bureau of the Census

from The New York Times/July 23, 1973

THE INCOME GAP

and appropriations to assist efforts of the poor themselves to break out of "the cycle of poverty." "Head Start" programs were to help poor preschool children develop the academic skills necessary to compete in the nation's elementary schools. The Job Corps provided teenage dropouts with vocational training and an escape from cities to rural conservation projects like those undertaken during the New Deal. Better-trained young people joined VISTA (Volunteers in Service to America), which organized day-care centers, store-front schools, and other community activities. The Community Action Programs sometimes led to demonstrations by welfare mothers and to other political activity that annoyed local officials and undermined public support, even before President Nixon allowed the OEO, and much of the rest of the program, to atrophy late in the decade for lack of funds.

The Medicare Act, the Higher Education Act, and the Elementary and Secondary Education Act, all passed in 1965, combined by 1970 to create a fourfold increase in federal expenditures for social services (education, health, housing, welfare, and community development). Medicare, the largest portion of this increase, financed health care for the growing fraction of the population over age sixty-five. Johnson's reliance on payroll taxes through social security instead of on general revenue (derived largely from income taxes) placed on all employed citizens, regardless of their ability to pay, the climbing costs of hospitals and physicians for older Americans. The education measures authorized grants for college buildings, subsidized loans for students, and offered funds for curricular development, teacher training, classroom materials, and educational research.

Equality: The Wait Prolonged

However disappointed Americans were at the failure of legislation to produce either the adventure of a new frontier or the comfort of a great society, the aborting of the movement for racial justice was more central to national frustration. The promise had been so long unfulfilled, so long even since the Supreme Court in 1954 had reminded Americans of their equalitarian principles. Yet John Kennedy had skirted the issue in his campaign and, after the election, in the preparations for his administration. He established "task forces" to shape his early policies; there was none for civil rights.

Both the President and his brother, Attorney General Robert F. Kennedy, doubted that Congress would enact civil-rights statutes while the rest of the administration's legislative package gathered dust on

POPULATION, 1970

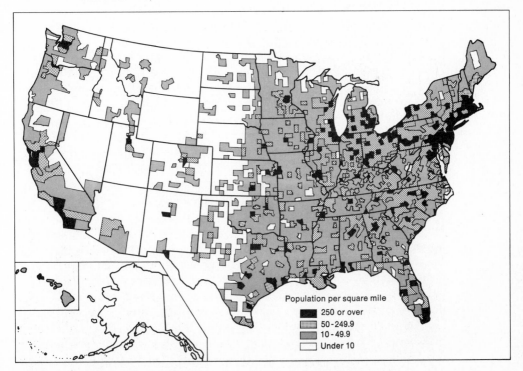

Population per square mile
■ 250 or over
▦ 50 - 249.9
▨ 10 - 49.9
□ Under 10

Capitol Hill. Where they could, without endangering Congressional support, they used executive authority to make blacks more visible in the federal civil service, for instance. Later disparaged as "tokenism," this sort of action did not indicate a vigorous commitment to racial equality.

But the administration did not control the velocity of racial change. Young blacks in Greensboro, North Carolina, inspired a host of imitators when, in 1960, they simply sat at a lunch counter awaiting service that never came. White northerners joined southern blacks in 1961 on "freedom rides" to integrate public transportation in the South. In 1961, after the widely publicized beating of "freedom riders" in Alabama, the Interstate Commerce Commission ordered an end to segregated facilities serving interstate travelers. In 1962, Kennedy had to send federal troops to enforce a court order admitting a black student to the University of Mississippi. The presence of federal troops, and the echoes of Reconstruction, had obvious political consequences and brought to a bankrupt end Kennedy's attempt to conciliate both advocates of black rights and supporters of the South's traditions.

Events a year later in Alabama banished any complacent hope that segregation would peaceably disappear. In Birmingham, the city he regarded as the citadel of segregation, Martin Luther King, Jr., determined to dramatize discrimination that kept blacks locked in routine jobs and out of public facilities. Tension built during days of marches until Chief Eugene ("Bull") Connor of the city's police ordered the use of high-pressure hoses, snarling dogs, and electric cattle prods. Connor filled the jails with black demonstrators, including King himself, whose "Letter from Birmingham Jail" eloquently stated the case for civil disobedience. "The civil rights movement," Kennedy remarked wryly, "should thank God for Bull Connor. He's helped it as much as Abraham Lincoln." Kennedy meant that Connor's actions had demonstrated the need for new federal legislation to prohibit discrimination in public accommodations—stores, hotels, theaters, restaurants. The President sent his proposal to Congress and cooperated with leaders of a massive march on Washington late in the summer of 1963. Neither the presence of 250,000 orderly demonstrators, nor King's moving "I have a dream" speech, nor the President's support hurried Congress, which did not complete the new civil rights act until after Kennedy's death.

President Johnson brought a convert's zeal and flamboyant energy to the movement. He did not conciliate blacks from Mississippi, who in 1964 attempted to subvert white supremacists in the state's Democratic party. But in 1965 he proudly signed the Voting Rights Act that became the basis for extensive participation by blacks in southern politics. The law enabled the Justice Department to intervene in the registration process in order to end discriminatory use of literacy tests and other devices that had kept blacks from the polls. The presence of significant numbers of black voters for the first time since Reconstruction worked a gradual revolution in southern politics. A dozen years after the Voting Rights Act,

Birmingham, 1963

politicians like George Wallace, who had made a career of championing segregation, were courting the black vote.

If legislation could admit blacks to restaurants and polling places, it could not immediately produce equality. Northern blacks, mired in urban ghettos, sought not civil rights, which legally they already had, but full equality. Many blacks felt entitled not only to equal access to schools, jobs, and housing, but also to equal test scores and salaries, and to luxuries many whites thought blacks ought to earn by their own efforts.

In some form, this dispute over whether blacks deserved equality of opportunity or equality of result was at the bottom of the racial violence that began with riots in Watts, a subdivision of Los Angeles, in 1965. Rioters did not seek legislation; in the sense the phrase was used in the South, they did not seek "civil rights." If the riots were more than irrational outbursts caused by summer heat and alcohol, then they were

Washington, 1967

protests against irregular, demeaning employment, inadequate public
services, bureaucratic welfare regulations, and crowded, deteriorating
living conditions.

The measure of blacks, in brief, was short, and everyone knew it. In
1965, President Johnson ticked off the statistics on adolescent alienation,
infant mortality, family income, and unemployment. He concluded that
too many blacks were "losing ground every day" in their "battle for true
equality."

Many of them were residents of northern cities, where the biblical cadences of Martin Luther King, Jr., sounded odd, and where nonviolence seemed a bad joke rather than a persuasive philosophy. Malcolm X and other Black Muslims spoke a more urban idiom when they urged blacks to nurture racial pride, to stick together, to free themselves from contaminating contact with whites. Malcolm himself perhaps softened his aversion to whites before he was shot in 1965, presumably by Muslims of a rival faction. But the Black Panthers, organized in Oakland in mid-decade by Huey Newton and Bobby Seale, and given notoriety through the harsh prose of Eldridge Cleaver, did not moderate their hostility to the white version of law and order before decade's end. The writer James Baldwin, in a prophetic novel published in 1963, promised whites *The Fire Next Time.* Stokely Carmichael, a leader of the Student Nonviolent Coordinating Committee (SNCC) popularized the slogan "Black Power!" and pushed white liberals out of the organization that had fostered sit-ins and voter registration in the South.

Martin Luther King, Jr., never shared the view that integration was a white man's trap, that it offered blacks a share in decadence that they ought to decline. Although ghetto blacks sometimes wrote him off as the white man's stooge, King continued to lead a biracial movement for reform. Indeed his concern broadened beyond civil rights and race to poverty and international policy as the decade wore on. Ironically, his assassination in Memphis in 1968 precipitated spontaneous urban riots, especially in Washington, of just the sort he had disparaged.

A year before, after the summer of riots in 1967, President Johnson appointed a commission to investigate civil disorder. Under the chairmanship of Governor Otto Kerner of Illinois, the commission produced a detailed report that documented black deprivation and blamed white racism for it. "White institutions," the commission charged, created the ghetto, "white institutions maintain it, and white society condones it." The report recommended massive expenditures to sustain blacks through make-work jobs and welfare agencies until retraining and education provided a more permanent solution. Partly because the report did not note the many programs his administration had already begun, and partly because the war in Southeast Asia absorbed more and more of the budget and his energy, Johnson put the document and its recommendations aside.

Nor did the Kerner Commission's recommendations appeal to Richard Nixon, who succeeded Johnson in 1969. Nixon's "southern strategy" rested on the votes of whites in all regions who opposed busing to achieve racially balanced schools, who thought ghettos needed more police rather than more welfare expenditure, and who believed the federal government had done enough for blacks. After narrowing late in the 1960s, due in part to large numbers of wage-earning black women, the gap between the median income of black and white families began again to widen. Exile or prison or legal proceedings muzzled many of the black-power advocates. A resigned, sullen peace replaced high aspirations in blighted black communities until, in the 1970s, residents gradually discovered that the Voting Rights Act gave them political leverage.

Vietnam: Getting In

"If only it hadn't been for . . . Vietnam," mused Averell Harriman, one of the nation's respected elder statesmen, as he reflected on Lyndon Johnson's presidency. "If only it hadn't been for Vietnam" could serve as a litany for a generation's history, for the war dragged on through a decade and a half, shaping public decisions and private plans, inflicting injury on individuals and devastation on a region, fostering inflation and doubt where there had been prosperity and confidence. The war ended the fantasy that economic growth would pay for the Great Society, because helicopters and napalm and troops had a prior claim on the government's revenue. The war also disabused some Americans of what Senator J. William Fulbright, chairman of the Foreign Relations Committee, called *The Arrogance of Power;* Americans had long understood that might was not necessarily right, but they were puzzled when it was not even power.

The decision to intervene, however misguided it eventually seemed, was intelligible at the time. Fresh from the embarrassing defeat of the Cuban invasion at the Bay of Pigs, President Kennedy needed to demonstrate to audiences at home and abroad his capacity to stop Communist advances. His administration was trying to end a rebellion of guerrillas in Laos, Vietnam's Southeast Asian neighbor, which seemed at the time the more serious threat to world peace. If Communists secured control of one state in the region, American strategists feared, other countries would topple too, like a row of dominoes in the metaphor of the day. If local Communists did not set off this chain reaction, perhaps the Chinese would. Such a loss would doubtless lead allies and foes alike to question America's willingness to carry out containment in Asia, and would precipitate a divisive and politically costly debate in the United States.

So, in 1961 when South Vietnam's President Ngo Dinh Diem asked for aid against the guerrillas of the National Liberation Front (the Vietcong), Kennedy eventually decided to provide military advisers and material. A desire to save face and the containment policy outweighed advice that the United States could not affect what was essentially a civil war, that the precedents of Munich and Korea did not obtain, that one small commitment would lead to later, larger ones, and that his temporizing policy would almost surely fail. If, before his death, Kennedy had second thoughts about the decision, he did not alert the public to his misgivings.

On the morning he was killed, he had noted with satisfaction the country's growing arsenal and the growing number of troops—about 17,000—in Vietnam.

Although Lyndon Johnson replaced Kennedy's domestic advisers rather rapidly, he retained, until he retired, most of the foreign-policy staff, which had made the crucial decisions about Vietnam. Secretary of State Dean Rusk defended intervention through news conferences and congressional inquiries. Whatever his private doubts, in 1966 and after, Robert McNamara, the secretary of defense, stayed in the cabinet until 1968. When McGeorge Bundy, Kennedy and Johnson's chief adviser on national security, left Washington in 1966, Walt Rostow, Bundy's deputy and one of Kennedy's early recruits, took over. To avoid dependence on the Pentagon for military counsel, both Kennedy and Johnson relied on Maxwell Taylor, a retired general who had had a distinguished record in Korea.

Vietnamese policy seemed exasperating to Johnson, but not complex. A brave people, bound to the United States by treaty, had asked for assistance in a struggle against internal Communist subversion and the aggression of their Communist northern neighbor. If the Communists could be kept out, Johnson believed, South Vietnam could develop an Asian version of the Great Society with abundant medicine, schools, fertilizer, electricity. "I want to leave the footprints of America in Vietnam," Johnson said in 1966. "We're going to turn the Mekong into a Tennessee Valley." He never understood those who did not share this dream, who had not learned from Munich the same lessons he had, who behaved like "nervous Nellies" when the bullets began to sing. Nor did he grasp the fact that massive aid did not shore up South Vietnam's independence, but rather made the country increasingly dependent on the United States.

Step by step that dependence grew. In the summer of 1964, Johnson interpreted a confused naval incident in the Tonkin Gulf as an unprovoked attack on American vessels by North Vietnamese torpedo boats. Johnson immediately asked Congress for a resolution, drafted even before the incident, that he interpreted as congressional permission to undertake an offensive war in Asia. Adopted with only two dissenting votes, the Tonkin Gulf Resolution became Johnson's authorization to carry out plans, already made by American strategists, for bombing military targets in South Vietnam and Laos and, by the end of the year, in North Vietnam as well.

Bombing was not enough. General William Westmoreland sent regular requests for more troops: 20,000 more, 82,000 more, 154,000 more, 200,000 more; he wanted 540,000 troops available in 1967. Their mission expanded from security around American air bases to "search and destroy" operations in the countryside. Most of those patrols consisted of shadowboxing with elusive enemies that faded invisibly into the jungle or into the civilian population. "Our brigade [was] not innately cruel," Philip

Caputo remembered after he returned. But "twenty years of terrorism and fratricide had obliterated most reference points from the country's moral map long before we arrived." We learned "rather quickly," he went on, "that Vietnam was not a place where a man could expect much mercy." Those "who do not expect . . . mercy eventually lose their inclination to grant it." Caputo was not at My Lai, and his sense of Vietnam's moral climate could not excuse the massacre there in March 1968, when American soldiers killed at least 175 unresisting Vietnamese civilians. But his recollection explains such events and documents the pervasive disillusionment that affected troops in the field as well as their relatives at home.

The war was not only inhumane and perhaps immoral; it was not even a success. While governments came and went in Saigon, the effectiveness

Vietnamese rain forest, 1972

of South Vietnamese armed forces deteriorated. Efforts to drive the Vietcong from their bases in the villages failed. Bombing left North Vietnam's determination and capacity to resist undiminished; the air war was like "trying to weed a garden with a bulldozer," one reporter remarked. American civilian observers, always more pessimistic than officials, reported that escalation had had almost no strategic effect.

The North Vietnamese confirmed that estimate in January 1968, when they opened the Tet offensive, a major effort that dramatized South Vietnamese weakness and the need for yet more American troops. Villages thought to be loyal turned out to be strongholds of the Vietcong. Guerrillas operated not only in remote hamlets but at the doors of the American embassy in Saigon. General Westmoreland asked for 200,000 more troops, but Johnson resolved instead to reconsider the American commitment. He ordered Westmoreland home and sought to negotiate an end to the war.

The road to peace had many detours. Before Tet, Johnson had tried a pause in the bombing, conversations at the United Nations, missions to Hanoi by intermediaries from other nations—all without substantial result. After Tet, Johnson restricted American bombers to targets south of the twentieth parallel, and a few weeks later North Vietnam agreed to peace talks in Paris. The talks turned into unproductive wrangling, and disappointed Americans demanded new initiatives for peace.

Vietnam: Getting Out

The demand showed in teach-ins on campuses, in speeches to the Senate, in noisy marches and silent vigils, and in the ballots of more than 40 percent of the Democratic voters of New Hampshire in 1968, where Minnesota's Senator Eugene McCarthy gave the antiwar movement enigmatic political leadership. Senator Robert Kennedy, the heir to much of his brother's political following, also decided to challenge Johnson in Democratic primaries. Late in March, after he had announced the bombing reduction, Johnson added that he would not run for another term. But neither his retirement nor the prospect of losing the White House could hold the fragmenting Democratic party together. The fissures in the party mirrored divisions in the country.

The American people saw those divisions in prime time and living color when Democrats nominated their candidate in Chicago. While delegates argued inside the hall, another confrontation took place outside. Young demonstrators, some determined to influence the political process and others determined to reveal its futility, poured into the city, disobeyed its regulations, and taunted police and the National Guard. Marches, provocation, and disobedience led to tear gas, night sticks, and brutality as jostling escalated to riot. The eventual nomination of

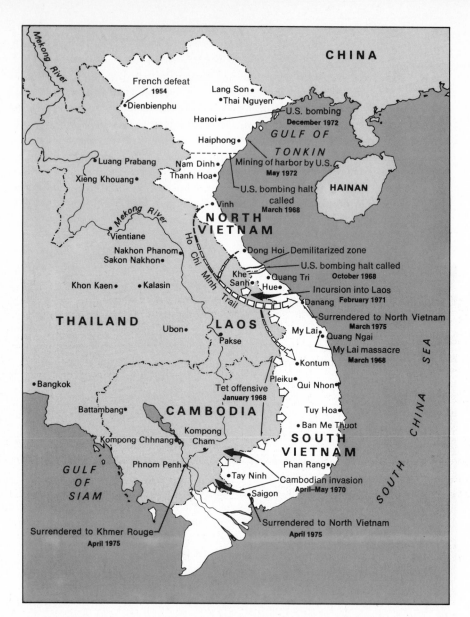

VIETNAM

Vice-President Hubert Humphrey and Senator Edmund S. Muskie seemed somehow anticlimactic, for Robert Kennedy had been assassinated in June just as his campaign had begun to build, and Senator McCarthy had given up, even if his partisans had not.

Republicans successfully masked their divisions. Richard Nixon swept triumphantly through the primaries, brushing aside the inept challenge of Michigan's Governor George Romney, the hesitant effort of New York's

Governor Nelson Rockefeller, and the last-minute blitz of California's Governor Ronald Reagan. Nixon successfully appealed to the center of his party and, in the campaign, to the center of the electorate with his pledge to extricate the United States from Vietnam without impairing national pride or national honor.

Governor George Wallace of Alabama, running on a third-party ticket, threatened briefly to win enough conservative support to throw the election into the House. At the ballot box, however, the blue-collar voter, on whom Wallace had relied, voted from Democratic habit. Wallace carried five states and won about 13 percent of the popular vote. Nixon finished with 43 percent of the electorate. In the final weeks of the contest Humphrey almost shook off the burden of his association with the Johnson administration, but he finished about 500,000 votes behind Nixon.

Kent State University, 1970

Nixon's general policy for Asia—the so-called Nixon Doctrine—called for what he termed a low profile. The United States, Nixon explained in 1970, would no longer "conceive all the plans, design all the programs, execute all the decisions and undertake all the defense of the free nations of the world." Melvin Laird, the secretary of defense, used the word "Vietnamization" to describe the application of the Nixon Doctrine to the war. Laird and Nixon gradually withdrew American troops, reducing the total by more than 500,000 before a truce was finally signed in January 1973. Instead of troops, the United States furnished weapons, strategic supplies, air power, and direction.

For a moment, Vietnamization seemed to calm the antiwar movement. Then, in the spring of 1970, following months of secret bombing, American and South Vietnamese forces invaded Cambodia. (The Pentagon later said that the neutral Cambodian government had consented to the air strikes, but official reports were falsified in order to keep knowledge of the operation from Congress and from the American people.) If the bombing was secret, the invasion was not. The invading armies failed to find the enemy force that the President said had provoked the assault, and the antiwar movement revived across the land.

Outraged students forced universities to suspend classes and cancel examinations to permit political activity and agitation to end the war. Protest ended in tragedy at Kent State University in Ohio when patrolling National Guardsmen killed four demonstrating students. A week later, Mississippi police killed two young blacks on the campus of Jackson State College. The President disdained the demonstrations, and disgusted students apparently decided that they could not make him listen.

But Congress heard and repealed the Tonkin Gulf Resolution in 1970. Antiwar senators began to use amendments to pending legislation to keep up a constant debate about the war and about Nixon's policies. More than half the Senate enlisted in a bipartisan effort to keep American forces out of Cambodia and Laos. In 1971, the Senate set a deadline for total withdrawal of nine months after the release of American prisoners. The House did not accept that deadline and often killed other antiwar amendments offered by the Senate. But in 1973, after the truce, both houses passed, over Nixon's veto, a War Powers Act designed to prevent future Presidents from waging indefinite undeclared wars. The President might, in an emergency, order American troops into battle, but the act required him to notify Congress of his action and to rescind it unless Congress confirmed his order within sixty days.

No law prevented Nixon from making an effort to end the war before the election of 1972. Although formal talks in Paris were hopelessly stalled, Nixon's foreign-policy aide, Henry Kissinger, secretly contacted North Vietnam's Le Duc Tho. Negotiations made slow progress until October, when Kissinger exulted "peace is at hand." His triumph was premature, for South Vietnam's President Nguyen Van Thieu, who had not been represented in the negotiations, objected to the settlement and forced Kissinger to resume them. Partly to placate Thieu, Nixon ordered renewed bombing of Hanoi and other targets in North Vietnam in December, offering the public explanation that the raids would force North Vietnam to reduce its demands. When the agreement was announced in January, Le Duc Tho said it was essentially the same as the draft completed before the Christmas bombing.

The truce simply confirmed territorial arrangements made initially in Geneva in 1954. The right of the people of South Vietnam to determine their own form of government was declared "sacred and inalienable." But the agreement looked toward eventual, negotiated unification of the country. The United States pledged to assist the process of reconciliation and reconstruction, and to withdraw its troops within sixty days. North Vietnam agreed to release American prisoners of war within the same period.

Statisticians began to total the costs of the nation's longest war: more than 55,000 American lives and $110 billion were two initial numbers. The indirect costs were incalculable: bitter divisions across the United States, inflation and a damaged economy that made those divisions deeper, and a loss of national confidence, especially confidence in authority. The bills for the undeclared war would be coming due for at least a generation, while the bills for destruction in Vietnam could never be paid, no matter how much aid Americans promised for reconstruction.

Those promises, in any case, were not kept, nor was the private pledge Nixon gave President Thieu that the United States would "respond with full force should the settlement be violated by North Vietnam." In the spring of 1975, after American withdrawal and Nixon's resignation, the Indochinese dominoes fell in rapid succession. Communist-led rebels took control of Cambodia and Laos. A North Vietnamese offensive swept south. President Thieu asked for the assistance Nixon had promised and Gerald Ford, Nixon's successor, tried to oblige. But Congress would not send money or supplies, to say nothing of aircraft or troops. Retreat in South Vietnam turned to panic; in six weeks it was over. Thieu left the country in April. Surrender came at the end of the month. Without enthusiasm, and often without grace, the United States accepted some responsibility for a few of the refugees displaced by more than a decade of war.

The Rest of the World

Once merely one phase of a worldwide Cold War, the struggle in Vietnam became after 1964 the focus of American foreign policy. The conflict had the first call on economic and human resources that might more effectively have been applied to problems elsewhere. Obsessed with Southeast Asia, neither policy-makers nor the American public, for instance, fully assimilated the major shift in the balance of power that took place in the fifteen years after Kennedy's inauguration. No longer could the United States and the Soviet Union expect automatic fealty from satellites in the "free world" or the "Communist bloc." American allies disagreed vehemently with American action in Asia; stress in the Communist bloc—especially friction between China and the USSR—was even more severe.

The Cold War conception of the world regarded the Third World—the countries of Africa, Asia, Latin America, and the Middle East—as pawns to be pushed about the global board by the two great powers. Even the states of Indochina—which turned out to be no one's pawns—were patronized as clients long after it ought to have been clear that roles had reversed: South Vietnam often determined American policy and North Vietnam did not docilely accept direction from either Moscow or Peking. The American public, and sometimes the Department of State as well, seemed surprised when countries that had been described as "emerging" emerged without displaying the aversion to communism that Americans thought instinctive. The facts of international life gradually forced a reappraisal of American policy for which the public was not wholly prepared.

In encouraging land reform and political democracy in Latin America through his Alliance for Progress, and perhaps in the Peace Corps as well, Kennedy may have been trying to build a new and more idealistic framework for foreign policy. But a Cold War taint clung to the Alliance,

Peace Corps instruction in Malawi

which was designed in part to forestall imitations of Castro's Cuban coup elsewhere in the hemisphere, and also to the Peace Corps, which seemed to leaders of some developing regions to be a disguised form of American colonialism. The basic American policy toward the Caribbean and the rest of Latin America was very traditional indeed.

Soon after he took office, Kennedy was briefed about plans the Eisenhower administration had developed for an invasion of Cuba. Cuban exiles, supplied and trained by the Central Intelligence Agency (CIA), were to invade the island and rally the dissident population. Wishful thinking and the potential embarrassment of canceling the expedition apparently blinded the Kennedy administration to bad tactical judgments, internal bickering, and other hints of failure. Cubans ignored their self-proclaimed liberators; Kennedy decided against the air support the invaders thought they had been promised; an impassable swamp cut off retreat to mountains where they had hoped to sustain guerrilla warfare; and Castro's army wiped them out at the Bay of Pigs.

One Castro was frustrating; two, in President Johnson's view, would be intolerable. When a rebellion broke out in the Dominican Republic in 1965, he reacted quickly to counter local Communists who, he believed, were preparing to seize power. The arrival of more than 20,000 American troops stopped both the potential Communist coup and the revolution. A year later the last of the American garrison withdrew after Dominican voters had selected a new, acceptable president. However serious the Communist threat, and most observers thought Johnson had exaggerated it, American intervention seemed a return to the gunboat diplomacy that had preceded Franklin Roosevelt's effort to turn the United States into a good neighbor.

The disaster at the Bay of Pigs may have led Soviet Premier Nikita Khrushchev to think Kennedy could be bullied. But the President's resolution did not falter in July 1961, when Khrushchev threatened to cut Berlin off from West Germany. Kennedy mobilized reserves and demonstrated the American commitment to Berlin with constant convoys that maintained access to the city. The Berlin Wall, constructed in August 1961, was a tacit East German confession that the division was permanent, that the iron curtain had a little hole at West Berlin.

More ambitious than the probe in Germany was Khrushchev's attempt to establish missile bases in Cuba during 1962. After American air reconnaissance discovered these facilities in October, Kennedy ordered a naval blockade of the island. Russian ships carrying additional missiles, already at sea when Kennedy proclaimed the blockade, turned aside at the last moment. Khrushchev offered to remove the Soviet equipment in return for an American guarantee not to invade Cuba, which Kennedy promptly gave. A month later, when Kennedy was convinced the missiles had been completely withdrawn, he lifted the blockade.

The Cuban missile crisis helped to clear the Cold War air. The United States and the USSR reflected on nuclear war and decided not to have one. Whatever face Khrushchev chose to put on his action, he had backed down, further down than Castro would have done had he controlled the response to Kennedy's blockade. Khrushchev evidently concluded that the Soviet Union had more to lose than did Cuba, and he permitted new negotiations that culminated in 1963 in a Nuclear Test Ban Treaty that ended Soviet and American nuclear explosions in the atmosphere. Kennedy's guess that the more conciliatory Soviet stance stemmed from weakness stiffened his resolve to force retreat in Indochina as well. But the President overestimated Khrushchev's ability to direct guerrillas there. By 1964, the Soviet leader was no longer even the master of his own party, which voted to replace him as premier with Aleksei Kosygin and as party secretary with Leonid Brezhnev.

By distracting the United States, the war in Vietnam gave the new Soviet leaders a respite, an opportunity to crack down on dissenters at home and, in 1968, on those in Czechoslovakia, where Russian tanks ended a brief experiment with independence. A growing dispute with China also nudged Russian officials toward a wary rapprochement with the West. A Soviet-American consular treaty, negotiated in 1964, was finally ratified in 1967. The two countries reopened consulates that had been padlocked for two decades and guaranteed one another access to nationals detained on criminal charges. In 1967, President Johnson and Premier Kosygin met in Glassboro, New Jersey, to cooperate in limiting the Arab-Israeli war. In 1968, the Soviet Union quietly returned an airplane full of troops that had strayed over Russian territory, signed an agreement to prohibit the spread of nuclear weapons, and opened discussions to curb the missile race.

Henry Kissinger, who became secretary of state in 1973, used the word "détente" to describe changing American contact with the Soviet Union. Conflict continued—over naval bases in the Indian Ocean, oil in the Middle East, the rights of Russian Jews, and the size and variety of strategic weapons. But Nixon, who had once made political capital out of a vigorous argument with Khrushchev, went back to Moscow in 1972 and 1974 in a less hostile frame of mind. The ostensible agenda for those meetings was the limitation of missiles and nuclear arms. The first trip produced a treaty restricting each country to two sites for antiballistic missiles and an executive agreement restraining production of offensive weapons. Overshadowed by the political crisis of Watergate, the second trip produced ceremonial good will.

This new relationship with the Soviet Union was both a cause and a result of modifications made by Nixon and Kissinger in American policy toward China. Their decision to end two decades of effort to isolate mainland China risked political criticism at home, outrage on Taiwan, and bewilderment in Japan and other countries that had loyally supported earlier American policy. Nevertheless, Kissinger secretly visited Peking in July 1971, and Nixon himself followed in 1972. The presidential visit had an air of ceremonial courtship, but there was a substantive result as well: in the final communiqué, Nixon and Premier Chou En-lai announced agreement on the sovereignty of China over Taiwan, and the United States promised in time to remove its forces from the island.

In that agreement, Nixon confirmed a choice between the two Chinas that he had earlier hoped to avoid. In 1971, for instance, the United States had proposed an arrangement that would admit the People's Republic to the United Nations, but retain a seat in the General Assembly for the Republic of China (Taiwan). The Communist Chinese branded the two-China policy preposterous and said that the exclusion of Taiwan was a precondition for their participation in the United Nations. The United States made an unconvincing show of salvaging a place for the Nationalists before voting to seat the People's Republic. Contact begun at the United Nations was extended in 1973, when the United States and Peking exchanged quasi-official missions. Formal diplomatic recognition followed the warm reception Americans gave Vice Premier Teng Hsiao-p'ing in 1979.†

It was Nixon's boast as he left office that he had created a "structure of peace." He had not done so alone, nor was the structure stable or the peace secure. But when Americans were in Peking and out of Vietnam, or when Richard Nixon conciliated Russians, or when the United States paid court to Arab chieftains, or when Fidel Castro celebrated his twentieth year in power, things had certainly changed since 1945. If those events did not conclusively establish the existence of a structure of peace, they surely did show a major shift in assumptions about the old Cold War.

Suggested Reading

Much of the literature of the recent past is self-serving; time has not conclusively identified the trustworthy memoirs, the useful journalism, or the competent monographs. Even the documentary collections, such as *The Pentagon Papers** (1971), which the staff of the *New York Times* has edited, have an interpretive point of view. James M. Burns has edited *To Heal and to Build* (1968), a documentary account of the Johnson administration, that contains little of the sharp criticism of *The Great Society Reader** (1967), edited by Marvin E. Gettleman and David Mermelstein.

General accounts of the decade include William L. O'Neill's *Coming Apart** (1971), Jim F. Heath's *Decade of Disillusionment* (1975), and Godfrey Hodgson, *America in Our Time** (1976). Henry Fairlie points out

---

† In March 1979, China adopted the Pinyin system of transcribing Chinese names of people and places into English. Pinyin renders Chinese words in alphabetic form instead of using apostrophes and hyphens, as did the traditional Wade-Giles system. Thus Teng Hsiao-p'ing becomes Deng Xiaoping.

Kennedy's failure to fulfill *The Kennedy Promise* (1973), but Carl Brauer argues in *John F. Kennedy and the Second Reconstruction* (1977) that JFK accomplished about as much on civil rights as could have been done. Doris Kearns's *Lyndon Johnson and the American Dream** (1976) is based on the author's extensive private conversations with LBJ. Insider memoirs of the Kennedy-Johnson years include Theodore C. Sorenson's *Kennedy* (1965), Arthur M. Schlesinger's *A Thousand Days** (1965), and Johnson's own *The Vantage Point* (1971). *RN: The Memoirs of Richard Nixon* (1978) is Nixon's account.

Frances FitzGerald's *Fire in the Lake* (1972) offers more historical perspective than David Halberstam's *The Best and the Brightest** (1972); both deal with Vietnam. Philip Caputo's *A Rumor of War** (1977) is a personal account; Michael Herr's *Dispatches** (1977) is a collection of journalism; Tim O'Brien's *Going After Cacciato* (1978) is a novelist's view of Vietnam.

The writings of Martin Luther King, Jr., carry the civil rights movement through most of the decade. *The Autobiography of Malcolm X** (1965) and Eldridge Cleaver's *Soul on Ice** (1967) offer other points of view. Howell Raines's *My Soul Is Rested* (1977) captures the early days of the movement through the recollections of participants. Peter Joseph's *Good Times** (1973) is a more general oral history of the period.

* Available in paperback edition

Chapter 23
The Third Century

Chronology

1966 National Organization for Women formed •

1969 Warren Burger appointed Chief Justice of the United States •

1971 Mandatory wage and price controls •

1972 Presidential election: Richard M. Nixon (Republican) defeats George McGovern (Democrat) •

1973 Militant Indians seize Wounded Knee, S.D. •

1973–74 Oil embargo; price of imported oil triples •

1974 Consumer price index rises 14 percent • Impeachment hearings; Nixon resigns • Gerald R. Ford becomes President •

1976 Presidential election: Jimmy Carter (Democrat) defeats Gerald R. Ford (Republican) •

1977 Department of Energy established •

1978 California voters approve Proposition 13 • *Regents of the University of California v. Allan Bakke* •

1979 Revolution in Iran; new increases in world oil prices • Nuclear "incident" at Three-Mile Island, Pennsylvania •

The buoyant national confidence that had matured after the Second World War sagged in the years following John Kennedy's assassination. In part, that change stemmed from events that shattered complacent assumptions about institutional perfection and international power. National uneasiness also grew from a reluctant realization that solutions to some of the problems on the nation's horizon might require wrenching social adjustment. In some cases, indeed, perhaps there were no solutions at all.

Headlines mocked the belief that people mastered events. Domestic violence seemed inexplicable and almost random, though discrimination and economic injustice undoubtedly precipitated some of the discontent evident in urban riots and rising crime. The so-called "counterculture" of the 1960s, whose most obvious adherents were disaffected young people, revealed that one generation of patriotic, achieving Americans had not successfully transmitted to the next the nation's cultural heritage. Political scandals, including those that led a President to resign, suggested institutional malfunctions as well as individual misconduct. On occasion, the government "of the people" failed to tell them the truth; voters manifestly mistrusted some of their most exalted public officials.

Diplomatic and military setbacks in Cuba, Africa, the Middle East, and Vietnam required reassessment of the notion that the United States could always buy or bully the rest of the world.

Some of those events exemplified long-term, often global, developments that presaged major modifications in habits, attitudes, and assumptions Americans cherished. A public vocabulary evolved to impart urgency to these trends, though ordinary people did not uniformly feel the importance of what politicians and journalists usually labeled a "crisis." At first glance, the "energy crisis" or the "urban crisis" or the "crisis in our balance of payments," or the "crisis among developing nations" seemed similar to challenges Americans had previously met with legislation, money, or military force. But the complexity and danger of many of these new conditions made the old tools seem inadequate to the tasks.

Worse yet, perhaps no tools would serve. Could the planet's resources sustain the global economic growth that seemed essential to fulfill human aspirations? Must industrialization, which in turn seemed crucial to that continuing growth, also produce the pollution that endangered the earth's oceans, atmosphere, and climate, and perhaps ultimately life itself? Could Americans tolerate the lower standard of living that a more equitable distribution of the world's shrinking resources might impose? Did the United States—to say nothing of its international rivals—possess sufficient spiritual strength and political maturity to accept, without war, compromises that a few decades before would have been unthinkable?

These questions originated in data that were well known. Census statistics showed the growth of population in developing parts of the world and the aging of people in industrialized regions. Most Americans, according to polls, simply refused to face the economic and diplomatic consequences of information on any chart of oil production and use. Tables of per capita income pointed to unrealized hopes that would continue to plague efforts to establish international political stability. Any collection of economic data showed that inflation had for a decade resisted the manipulation of monetary experts.

Doubt about the competence of particular experts threatened to become a paralyzing mistrust of all expertise. The apparent blunders of "the best and the brightest" architects of American foreign policy had important educational as well as strategic consequences. Inaccurate forecasts of the reliability of nuclear power led some Americans from a suspicion of engineers to the dubious conclusion that technological skill produced more and bigger problems instead of more and better solutions. After the government's economic experts failed to control inflation, a grass-roots movement to require a balanced budget, a measure virtually every expert opposed, gained considerable popular support. When the nation's political leaders—even when they were earnest and conscientious—could neither lead nor legislate effectively, a large percentage of the electorate lost interest in the political process.

Nor did other experts offer assured direction. A striking number of lawyers, including two of the country's attorneys general, had trouble with the law. Churches, which ought to have provided ethical and moral guidance, divided over race relations, birth control, war, and liturgy. Parents, lacking time, inclination, or experience, could not effectively counsel their children. Teachers, who were supposed to know how to educate children, reduced requirements and standards, actions that implied diminished confidence in what had been called "education." Without confident guidance from the professions, the church, school, or family, the nation seemed adrift.

The Economy: Inflation

Except in foreign policy, the nation did not need direction anyhow, Richard Nixon remarked in 1968. Certainly he did not offer the economy consistent management, partly because inflation baffled him as much as everyone else. When an aide sought to discuss foreign currency devaluation, Nixon snapped that the subject was "too complicated for me to get into." His economic policy wobbled with changing advisors and the election returns; no nostrum revived the postwar economic boom.

Nixon's frustration derived in some measure from the fact that many of the symptoms of economic distress were evident before his inauguration in 1969. American industrial productivity had for some time lagged behind similar rates in Japan and several European countries. (Labor maintained that management had not reinvested enough capital to keep pace with new, more efficient competitors; management usually blamed government regulation or restrictions imposed by unions.) The expense of war in Vietnam and of strategic commitments on other continents, together with a booming domestic demand for foreign products and a declining world market for American goods, brought a deficit in the nation's balance of payments that weakened the dollar. The federal government, meanwhile, aggravated that weakness by spending beyond its revenue, thereby contributing to serious domestic inflation.

Signs of trouble multiplied during Nixon's presidency. Unemployment and interest rates went up. The stock market and the purchasing power of the dollar fell. A group of oil-producing countries tripled the price of petroleum in 1973—74, an increase that helped push the consumer price index up 14 percent in 1974. Although Nixon had once said he did not want and would not use statutory power to control prices, in August 1971, he announced a ninety-day freeze on wages and prices. During the freeze, the administration designed a system of controlled prices that slowed inflation in 1972. But Nixon disliked this sort of governmental invervention and abandoned it during 1973. A few days before he resigned, in what he called "a major address on the economy," Nixon counseled patience and fortitude and not much else.

His successors were hardly more effective. President Gerald Ford's proposals included higher taxes, reduced spending, and restrictive monetary policy. Although the economy slowed to a recession in 1975, inflation persisted and Ford then reversed his policies and rang up large deficits. Jimmy Carter, Ford's rival in the presidential election of 1976, criticized Ford's economic policies. But Carter's substitute, offered in

Drawing by Price; © 1974, The New Yorker Magazine

THE ECONOMY: INFLATION

1978 when the annual rate of inflation once again approached 10 percent, was "voluntary" restraints on wages and prices, a practice called "jawboning" when President Kennedy had tried it fifteen years before. Meanwhile Carter accepted an inflationary increase in the minimum wage and tacitly retracted his campaign pledge to balance the budget by 1981. Regardless of administration, and almost regardless of policy, the consumer price index doubled in the ten years before 1978, and the cost of housing, gasoline, medical care, and other services climbed even more dramatically. Speaking to a convention of Democrats in 1978, Vice-President Walter Mondale warned that the party might well find inflation as politically costly as Vietnam had been.

Mondale accurately sensed the public's mood. Polls showed an increasing uneasiness about the economic future and mounting doubt that Carter could do much to improve it. Inflation undermined thrift, since saved dollars might in the future buy fewer goods than those spent immediately. Long accustomed to believing in the power of American money, Americans discovered it bought little at home and even less abroad. The strength of the Japanese yen, for instance, reflected rising productivity and competitive success; a lieutenant colonel in the American Air Force, paid in dollars while on duty in Japan, actually received less salary than a Japanese civilian, paid in yen, who guarded the gates of the American base. An anxious electronics engineer in Los Angeles, who earned about $30,000 annually, doubted that "people making my salary used to worry like we do now." Even with two incomes, a thrifty couple in Baltimore could no longer save; it was some consolation when they determined that "no one else was saving either." After years of rising expectations, Americans began to fear that the economy had run out of steam.

Energy: The Emptying Tank

Or more likely out of gas, as happened first during the energy crisis of 1973—74 and then again in 1979. In the earlier shortage the panic subsided after a few weeks, and the national sense of urgency vanished with the lines at the pumps. The ostensible cause of this crisis was the decision of Arab oil-producers to indicate through a boycott their displeasure with American diplomatic support of Israel; a revolution in Iran was blamed for the shortage in 1979. More fundamental, however, was the mounting global demand for fuel and electrical power, an increase that could not fail to affect the United States, the world's largest user of energy.

President Nixon unveiled "Project Independence," an integrated scheme that would, he predicted, eliminate the need for imported fuels by 1980. Although he often disparaged governmental programs as "throwing money at problems," he proposed to throw a great deal of money at this one by sponsoring research to develop new energy sources and to reduce dependence on imported oil. Geologists, engineers, and economists agreed that the nation could not become self-sufficient before the President's deadline, and Congress only authorized portions of the expenditure Nixon recommended.

Disagreement between a Democratic Congress and a Republican President was only one facet of the national debate over energy policy. Many Americans—a majority according to some polls—believed that the oil companies had contrived the shortage of energy to raise prices and profits. Those who believed the shortage real could not agree on even the first steps to alleviate it. Could conservation effectively reduce consumption? Would the public cooperate with mandatory rationing of gasoline? Were solar heat and wind power only the eccentricities of backyard ecologists, or did those sources of energy have general applicability? Could the nation afford not to use its coal, or were costs in air pollution, strip mining, and miners' lives too high? Were the prophets of nuclear power to be trusted more than the environmentalists and the disillusioned engineers who foresaw disaster?

None of these questions had a simple answer. All required elaborate analyses of costs and benefits, and much public discussion to create the informed public opinion that might support a national policy. President Carter doubted that the country had enough time for that process. In one of his first speeches as President, Carter called the effort to achieve a national policy "the moral equivalent of war." He tried to enlist patriotic idealism behind an effort to reduce consumption, to cut back oil imports and the consequent deficit in the national balance of payments, and to encourage the use of other fuels. His complicated plan encouraged conservation through higher prices, a portion of which would return to consumers in tax credits. Congress established a Department of Energy in 1977, but held up the rest of Carter's program with a long debate over regulation of the price of natural gas. When legislation finally emerged in 1978, most of the incentives to conserve fuel had been removed. Consumers paid higher prices anyway, but part of the increase went to oil-exporting nations, which raised charges by 15 percent early in 1979.

Not long after that increase, and yet another imposed in the wake of a revolution that interrupted oil production in Iran, the Nuclear Regulatory Commission (NRC) ordered five northeastern nuclear generating stations to stop production. For several months before that order, members of the commission had wondered in public about safety regulations applied to the construction of nuclear power plants; the five stations the NRC ordered closed were located in areas where earthquakes might release radioactivity. Since the decision in effect forced utilities to use scarce, expensive petroleum instead of atomic energy, the outcry was sharp. But those objections diminished a few days after the decision when what engineers laconically called an "incident" shut down the nuclear generating station at Three Mile Island, near Harrisburg, Pennsylvania. While experts debated techniques for averting nuclear disaster, the governor of Pennsylvania suggested that pregnant women and young children leave the area; many other residents decided not to wait for further instructions that might include them. At one time, state and federal authorities worried about ways to evacuate nearly a million people. It never came to that. Nuclear experts gradually cooled the reactor, but with it cooled much of the public's enthusiasm for building a neighborhood nuclear power plant.

Watergate

Failure to enact an effective, comprehensive energy policy was symptomatic of broader political deadlock. Most of Nixon's domestic program in the first term stalled in a Democratic Congress that reflected national divisions over the war and national concern about inflation. Nixon himself had made a campaign promise to check the initiative of the Supreme Court. Chief Justice Earl Warren's retirement provided an opportunity to inhibit the Court's activism, and the Senate quickly confirmed Warren Burger, whose strict-construction views Nixon applauded. But the Senate balked at Nixon's next two nominees to the Court, one of whom, G. Harrold Carswell, had a record that seemed racially insensitive. The Family Assistance Plan, a reform of welfare legislation that would provide poor Americans with a minimal guaranteed income, also died in Congress. The scheme was probably too innovative for Nixon's taste anyway and he did not lament its demise.

However legislatively empty Nixon's first term, his reelection seemed assured in 1972. He had staked out a popular position on most of the social issues of the day by stern opposition to "unpatriotic" demonstrations, to judicial leniency, and to "forced busing" and other steps toward desegregation. He had opened the way to renewed contact with China, outlined a more harmonious relationship with the USSR, and reduced the number of Americans fighting in Vietnam. After paralysis from a would-be assassin's bullets removed Governor George Wallace of Alabama from the campaign, Nixon had no rival for the conservative vote. And dispirited liberals had no effective candidate either.

Eventually, a disorganized Democratic convention nominated Senator George McGovern of South Dakota, a long-time critic of the war in Vietnam whose difficulty securing a running mate foreshadowed a disastrous campaign. McGovern eventually forced the withdrawal of the convention's vice-presidential nominee, Senator Thomas Eagleton, when his history of psychiatric treatment was disclosed. But McGovern failed to persuade several subsequent choices to join the ticket and eventually settled for Sargent Shriver, the former director of the Peace Corps and the

Office of Economic Opportunity. The Democratic campaign never developed any momentum.

By contrast, Nixon's campaign was professionally managed and abundantly financed. Vice-President Spiro Agnew and members of the cabinet made partisan speeches while the President himself adopted a statesmanlike stance above the battle. The Committee to Reelect the President (later dubbed CREEP) avoided identification with other Republican candidates and sought exclusively to win a majority for Nixon that might be called a mandate, even if the voters returned another Democratic Congress to Washington. To enable the administration to accomplish its objectives in spite of that Congress, Nixon expected to rely on the personal loyalty and political expertise of brisk, young aides whom he planned to place throughout the federal bureaucracy.

On election day, when Nixon received the votes of 61 percent of the people and all but 17 electors, there was only one small cloud on his expansive horizon. In June 1972, five burglars had been surprised in the headquarters of the Democratic National Committee in Washington's Watergate office building. The men carried wiretapping equipment and cash that investigators traced to CREEP. There the trail seemed to end.

It required more than two years and the combined efforts of grand juries, investigative reporters, congressional committees, and the Supreme Court of the United States to put the Watergate narrative on the public record. In the process, Americans learned that Nixon and his aides had sometimes equated political score-settling with the nation's security; that federal agencies, including the Internal Revenue Service, the FBI, and the CIA, had been sent on partisan errands; that the President had used public funds to improve his private residences; and that he had taken income-tax deductions a congressional committee concluded were not legitimate. Moreover, Nixon and the White House staff had attempted to inhibit investigation; when they could not block the inquiries, they had at least condoned, and perhaps had encouraged, perjury.

While Congress investigated the President, federal prosecutors checked allegations that Vice-President Agnew, a former governor of Maryland, had accepted money for political and personal purposes from firms doing business there. Agnew implied that the Justice Department was using him to divert the public's attention from the lack of dramatic results in the Watergate affair. While he protested his innocence, his attorneys agreed that he would resign and not contest charges that he had evaded income taxes. He was fined, sentenced to three years of unsupervised probation, and disbarred. Nixon selected Gerald R. Ford, leader of the Republican minority in the House, to replace Agnew as Vice-President.

As evidence of "White House horrors" mounted—the phrase was Attorney General John Mitchell's—several of the President's aides went to court, and some to jail. Mitchell himself was convicted of obstruction of justice along with Nixon's chief assistants, H. R. Haldeman and John

The President's men

Ehrlichman. Richard Kleindienst, who had replaced Mitchell as attorney general, received a suspended sentence for misleading testimony before a committee of the Senate. Maurice Stans, secretary of commerce in Nixon's first cabinet, pleaded guilty to five violations of campaign-fund laws. The President's personal lawyer and his official counsel both admitted participation in schemes to obstruct justice and went to prison.

Nixon disclaimed detailed knowledge of the behavior of subordinates he called overzealous and misguided. Secret tape recordings of his conversations, he said, exonerated him, but he could not release the tapes themselves without damage to the presidency. Both a special Senate committee and Archibald Cox, the special prosecutor appointed to remove the probe from direct oversight by the Justice Department, wanted several of the President's tapes. Nixon ignored subpoenas and ordered Cox fired in October 1973 when he persisted. That action, and the resignation of Attorney General Elliot Richardson in consequence, precipitated a public outcry including demands for impeachment that convinced Nixon to surrender some of the tapes and to replace Cox with Leon Jaworski. As pressure mounted during the spring of 1974, Nixon released edited transcripts of tapes sought by the Judiciary Committee, which was the agent of the House in impeachment proceedings. Other documentation before the committee indicated that Nixon had excised more than salty language.

Nixon's conversations incriminated him, in the view of several members of the Judiciary Committee. Chairman Peter Rodino carefully nursed what he hoped would be a bipartisan majority toward a report in August 1974. By a margin of 27 to 11, the committee decided that Nixon had obstructed justice in assisting his aides to cover up the Watergate scandals. He had also, the committee charged by a vote of 28 to 10, failed to execute the laws faithfully and abused his authority over several federal agencies. Every member of the committee agreed that Nixon had defied subpoenas from the House, but only a narrow majority thought his defiance cause for impeachment. The committee dismissed proposed articles of impeachment charging illegal presidential activity in connection with his personal income tax and the secret bombing of Cambodia. The earnest sincerity of the committee may have persuaded part of its television audience, and its bipartisan majority probably had persuaded the House of the President's guilt before events overtook impeachment.

While the Judiciary Committee deliberated, the Supreme Court unanimously ruled that Nixon must release sixty-four tapes to the special prosecutor for use in the coming trial of Ehrlichman, Haldeman, and Mitchell. Chief Justice Burger's decision boiled down to the proposition that no man is above the law. The President's attorney listened to the disputed tapes for the first time and knew that his client had no defense. Less than a week after the Watergate burglary, Nixon and Haldeman had discussed ways to short-circuit the investigations and to avoid identifying officials of the campaign and of the administration who were responsible. All Nixon's statements thereafter had been no more than partial truths; he knew of, and by his silence condoned, the lies of his aides. He was certain to be removed from office, for his support in the Senate had dropped below the one-third necessary to prevent conviction. He resigned within the week.

Political Paralysis

President Ford could not transform the relief that greeted Nixon's resignation into political support. Ford dissipated the good will of his first weeks in office with a comprehensive pardon for his predecessor that came before the nation was ready. By contrast, the President's offer to allow those who had evaded service in Vietnam to clear their records with another form of national service seemed less generous. Partisan carping also greeted his selection of Nelson Rockefeller as Vice-President.

Ford shifted his economic policy from monetary restraint to increased federal spending with an ease that suggested neither expedient had much basis in conviction. The Congress he faced after a Democratic landslide in the election of 1974 ignored most of his suggestions anyway and devised substitutes, which Ford in turn vetoed.

Presidential relations with Congress became more civil, but not immensely more productive, after Jimmy Carter's election in 1976. Carter had never held elective federal office before he became President, a lack of experience that both candidate and electorate seemed to count a virtue. Yet by painting himself as an outsider in campaigns against Democratic rivals and then against Ford, Carter did not build up credit within the federal establishment. His rather narrow victory—he carried only Texas in the western United States—did not command congressional deference.

What appeared to be an impasse between the legislative and executive branches of government stemmed in large part from legitimate differences over difficult issues. Public officials reflected the views of their confused constituents, for polls rarely showed decisive popular majorities on issues that were often too complex for ordinary citizens to comprehend. A few members of Congress looked at the record and doubted whether even legislators were sufficiently well informed. Much of the country, one senator remarked in 1979, wondered whether Congress did not cause at least as many problems as it solved. Further, unlike legislation of the New Deal or proposals for the Great Society, whatever Congress seemed likely to pass would anger some segment of the public. No one energy program had more support than any other; government simply could discover no way to harmonize conflicting interests and no politically safe way to choose among them. Congress will be "ineffective in dealing with real problems," mused a member of the House leadership as he looked at the agenda for 1979. "I can't think of a single positive thing that lies ahead. What good news are we going to provide the American people?"

Conditions within the Congress, as well as tough issues, contributed to a barren legislative prospect. The political upheaval precipitated by Nixon's resignation brought more than 70 new members to the House, who insisted on changes that reduced the advantages of seniority and the power of committee chairmen. These reforms made procedure more democratic but less efficient than had been the case when long-time members of Congress did the nation's legislative business. After the election of 1978, more than a third of the senators were serving their first term, a fact of enormous consequence in a body that prided itself on continuity, tradition, and expertise developed through long acquaintance. In an attempt to keep pace with constituents' demands and increasing complexity, Congress enlarged its own staff. This larger supporting organization made Congress much less dependent on information and guidance from the executive branch.

ARC DE TRIOMPHE

The refusal of Congress to respond automatically to tugs of the
presidential leash also stemmed, of course, from the reduced prestige of
the office. The "credibility gap" that had opened between President and
people in the Johnson administration became a chasm in that of Richard
Nixon. Carter's personal loyalty to his chief budgetary adviser, Bert Lance,
who resigned amid barbed questions about his banking practices, hardly
seemed in keeping with the President's professions of administrative
integrity. To be sure, Congress had its own scandals: a powerful
committee chairman who later conceded that alcohol had erased an

entire year or two from his memory; another who resigned when a secretary disclosed that her governmental salary seemed compensation for sex rather than typing; convictions for padded payrolls and expense accounts, for converting campaign funds to personal use, and for accepting illegal payments from representatives of foreign governments. Though the offenses betrayed a contempt for the public like that shown in the Watergate affair, the public weighed congressional misdeeds as peccadilloes beside Nixon's breach of trust.

Presidential disgrace and a pervasive mistrust of leadership contributed to voter apathy, to a gnawing sense that the politicians were of smaller stature than the difficult issues they faced. Polls regularly disclosed more public confidence in used-car salesmen than in Congress, a sentiment some members of Congress, in their weary moments, understood. One retiring legislator conceded that his faith in the effectiveness of good will and money had seriously eroded in fourteen years. "We have a feeling we're not as great as we thought we were," another observed. Only about a third of the constituency bothered to vote in the congressional elections of 1978. Four of ten voters did not identify with either political party, a statistic that indicated a lack of vitality in both. Parties had once been crucial to the ordinary citizen's identification with the political process, but federally financed campaigns and the tendency of candidates to play down partisanship in their pursuit of independent voters weakened party discipline and loyalty.

Yet some politicians longed for more, not less, apathetic voters. The shrinking influence of parties and diminishing concern on the part of the general electorate enhanced the influence of single-issue pressure groups. Zealots in these movements rewarded or punished elected officials for their stand on one issue; any compromise was branded a betrayal. Opponents of a treaty that gradually returned jurisdiction over the Canal Zone to Panama scorned bipartisan support for the policy and tried to defeat senators who voted for ratification. Both the fervent advocates and the most convinced opponents of the proposed Equal Rights Amendment, which would prohibit discrimination on the basis of sex, raised campaign funds, lobbied incumbents, and used sophisticated organizing techniques. Anti-abortion groups in New York promoted the Right to Life party, which achieved a place on that state's official ballot.

Single-issue politics of this sort, institutional changes in Congress, terribly difficult political questions, reduced presidential influence, and weakened political parties—all these factors combined to reward errand-running legislators. Successful ones concentrated on serving their constituents by playing intermediary with the federal bureaucracy— securing access to federal services, finding jobs or grants or facilities. Such a view of the job did not nurture much breadth of vision and was part of the reason so little innovative legislation emerged.

Nor did the Burger Court provide the legal leadership that had characterized the Warren Court in the 1960s. The new judges did not modify all the precedents the Warren Court had established, though some of the restraints earlier decisions had placed on law-enforcement officials were relaxed. But fuzzy decisions on the death penalty, abortion, women's rights, and obscenity produced legislative and judicial confusion throughout the country. The ruling that "community standards" determined what was obscene, for instance, not only seemed to reduce the First Amendment's protection of unpopular views, but doomed publishers to the caprices of hundreds of local juries. The decision in the first of what seemed likely to be many cases involving "reverse discrimination," or the legality of affirmative-action programs, rested precariously on the opinion of one judge in the case of *Regents of the University of California* v. *Allan Bakke*. In effect, the Court confessed that it found the social issues of the day as difficult and divisive as did the other branches of government.

Impatient with government that they perceived as bloated and unresponsive, some citizens turned to devices for direct democracy established by progressives more than a half-century before. Environmentalists used referenda to try to prevent construction of nuclear power plants and sale of disposable beer bottles. Critics of the size and expense of government urged voters to put a ceiling on taxes. In the summer of 1978, Californians passed Proposition 13, a referendum that in effect reduced property taxes. Similar proposals blossomed on ballots in other states. Several state legislatures, in their turn, formally requested a constitutional convention, a procedure not used since 1788, to propose an amendment requiring a balanced federal budget. These schemes indicated taxpayers' dissatisfaction both with government's failure to deliver services and with the bill for them.

Rising Consciousness

In the absence of effective national political leadership, people coalesced in other ways. Residential communities organized to keep schools open and to keep blacks out of them, to secure street lights and restrictive zoning. Homosexuals came "out of the closet" and into the streets to protest police harassment. Women raised one another's feminist consciousness and tried to counteract sexual stereotyping that, they maintained, held them in menial jobs, subordinate social status, and the homes Betty Friedan dismissed as "comfortable concentration camps." A new ethnic consciousness stimulated some to demand more representation in public hierarchies and sent others to libraries to trace their genealogical roots.

The civil rights movement provided the organizational model for many of these groups. Students who pressed in the 1960s for changes in campus regulations and curricular requirements learned tactics from participants in voter-registration drives and sit-ins. The National Organization for Women (NOW, formed in 1966) and other moderate feminist groups followed the course earlier charted by moderate blacks. The male chauvinism of the civil rights movement and of the New Left furnished much of the impetus for subsequent radical feminism. Angry urban Indians, led by the American Indian Movement (AIM), turned to violence that was sometimes counterproductive, as the violence of radical urban blacks had sometimes been. Armed seizure in 1973 of the village of Wounded Knee, South Dakota, was supposed to focus public attention on Indian demands, but instead resulted in lessened governmental effort to improve conditions on the Indian reservations.

More obviously than was the case with blacks, Hispanics were not a single, unified minority. Cubans, Mexicans, Puerto Ricans, and immigrants from South America did not automatically share more than language and a Roman Catholic heritage. Isolated in enclaves in New York, Florida, Texas, and the Southwest, Hispanics could not easily cooperate on a national scale. Some had immigrated illegally—the Immigration and Naturalization Service estimated the number at a million each year in the 1970s—and others retained a lingering identification with their native land that blocked application for citizenship and political action. Language and intermarriage preserved ethnic identity but hindered assimilation. (In contrast to the overwhelming tendency of Hispanics to marry other Hispanics, marriage among Japanese Americans, for instance, fell in the 1970s to fewer than three of five.)

Yet by 1980 the sheer size of the nation's fastest growing minority brought public recognition of Hispanic demands for bilingual education, economic opportunity, and political influence. Hispanics replaced blacks as the largest ethnic minority in Los Angeles, constituted a majority of the population of Miami, and numbered more than 2.5 million in and around New York City. Potential voters and customers in those numbers could not indefinitely be ignored. The thriving small businesses Cubans established all over southern Florida, and the appointment by the governor of California of two dozen Mexican American judges offered hints of influence to come.

Culture and Counterculture

Cultural consciousness among Hispanics, blacks, Indians, and other minorities challenged some of the nation's dominant attitudes and values. Indeed, much of what middle-class America believed in 1963 came under attack in the decade that followed. The incidence of violence, vandalism, inflation, sexual promiscuity, and drug abuse seemed to indicate declining allegiance to values like thrift and hard work, and to

FARMWORKERS BUILD THEIR UNION
SI SE PUEDE!

by the Salinas Citizens Committee
in Defense of Farmworkers

show mounting mistrust of reason and the fundamental decency of people.

Some of the manifestations of the so-called "counterculture" posed no serious threat to basic beliefs and principles. The "alternative lifestyle" was often merely fashion—a taste for rock music, miniskirts, or mandalas. More serious was the countercultural perception that ordinary Americans were spiritually unfulfilled and personally repressed, even if the solutions—marijuana, meditation, or sexual experimentation— sometimes seemed less impressive than the insight. The New Left—a phrase that should not connote ideological unity—offered a varied critique of American institutions as unresponsive, impersonal, exploitive, prejudiced, and outmoded. For politics as usual, New Leftists urged, substitute participatory democracy; for competition, community and cooperation; for social convention, "do your own thing." The thread that made the New Left a movement was a common mistrust of authority that stemmed partly from opposition to the nation's policy in Vietnam.

Perhaps the official violence in Southeast Asia—the napalm, the defoliants, the preoccupation with body-counting—induced numbness to violence at home. Or perhaps, as one militant black claimed, "violence is as American as cherry pie," and only recognition was novel in the later 1960s. In any case, the victims were no longer just the poor, the eccentric, and the black, for assassins stalked public figures and open disorder became one of the distinguishing features of the time.

Urban riots for a few years seemed as much a part of summer as baseball. These disturbances often had a racial origin and took an impersonal toll of life and property in Watts, near Los Angeles, in 1965, in Detroit in 1967, in Washington after the assassination of Martin Luther King, Jr., in 1968, and in dozens of smaller cities. Dissatisfaction with race relations or foreign policy disrupted universities, especially when officials invoked assistance from police or the National Guard. Clashes between shouting young people and armed representatives of society often brought injury, and sometimes tragedy, as at Kent State University in Ohio during protests against the Cambodian invasion in May 1970.

Almost any of those confrontations might stand as a metaphor for the social conflict of the time. Tense police and part-time soldiers saw students as the personal manifestation of a counterculture—coddled, unpatriotic, immoral, and undeserving of privilege. Students, on the other hand, jeered society's defenders as pigs, racists, and Nazis. The words changed somewhat if the scene took place at a draft-induction center, in a black neighborhood, or at a nuclear-power site. But any of those conflicts developed, at least in part, from divergent assumptions that revealed an important rift in American society.

Much of the anger went out of the conflict about the time Nixon resigned. Nixon's absence, the end of the draft and the war in Vietnam, and the need to impress conservative employers in a slowing economy helped calm many young rebels. Blacks seemed willing to try conventional politics as a means of correcting discrimination and unemployment. Academic competition, curricular requirements, and docile students reappeared on campuses; holidays once declared to permit political activity became simply holidays. But traces of countercultural protest remained in the growing tolerance of marijuana and sexual freedom; in a nagging suspicion that large size and efficiency and economic growth would not automatically benefit the entire society; in the women's movement and the absence of public racial bigotry; in a volunteer army, a preference for low-key political leaders, and an aversion to major commitments abroad.

As social divisions healed, most Americans once again counted themselves members of the middle class. The term "middle class" had neither economic nor sociological precision, for almost 90 percent of the population, with annual incomes ranging from less than $10,000 to more than $25,000, so classified themselves. If the term denoted neither income nor status, it did signify a renewed association with hard work and common sense and conventional standards. Middle-class Americans thought of themselves as economically and culturally superior to the lower class and morally superior to the "idle rich."

Many of those middle-class Americans also described themselves as religious, an assertion that belied a continuing decline in public worship. Yet the same surveys that documented diminished attendance at church paradoxically confirmed the persistence of traditional religious belief. More than half the people in 1978 who had not attended a worship service in the preceding six months nevertheless professed a belief in basic Christian tenets and claimed that religion was "very important" in their lives.

Other traditional beliefs also enjoyed a modest resurgence in the later 1970s, including the faith that self-reliant individuals solved their own problems. Books about self-improvement littered the best-seller charts. Professors remarked the renewed competitiveness (and the drooping social conscience) of students. Prosperous blacks, their black critics alleged, showed more concern for personal advancement than for the progress of other members of the race. Thomas Aquinas Murphy, chairman of General Motors, was a Carnegie-like demonstration of social mobility, for he had begun his career carrying ice in Chicago. Asked in 1976 about her success, Mary Wells Lawrence, who ran one of the nation's premier advertising agencies, had an appropriately true-blue response: "I worked hard," she said, "and so I made it."

A National Portrait

As the American people began their third century of political independence, the Bureau of the Census drew up a numerical portrait. There were, of course, more Americans than ever before to count: more than 220 million in 1980. Not until 1915, nearly a century and a half after independence, had the population reached 100 million; the second 100 million had come in a third the time. But the rate of growth dropped dramatically after 1960. For every ten Americans born in 1915, there were eight in 1960, six in 1970, and five in 1976; for every three births in 1976, there was one legal abortion. As the birth rate declined, the median age of the population resumed the climb that the postwar babies had interrupted. By 1980, one in two Americans was over 30 and one in nine was over 65.

Some of the consequences of those demographic facts could be foreseen. For example, federal budgets for national defense and for elderly Americans were roughly equal in 1978, each requiring about a quarter of federal revenues. But Secretary of Health, Education, and Welfare Joseph Califano predicted that social security benefits and other payments to older citizens, already "the largest income redistribution in the history of this country," would climb predictably higher. His projections showed a progressively smaller working force supporting a progressively larger retired population: the ratio in 1940 had been nine workers for every retired person; forty years later, the ratio had fallen to six to one. The "graying of the budget" seemed likely to enhance competition among other groups for what was left; the consequences of an aging population for employment policy, medical care, and for individuals themselves, were not discernible in 1980.

Like their younger compatriots, older Americans moved. Suburban "white flight" and the urban migration of blacks were the most widely cited illustrations of traditional American wanderlust. But native Californians joked about transplanted retired Iowans, and whole communities sprang up in Florida and Arizona to accommodate older Yankees. The center of population continued on its course to the South and West, a development that energy costs could only accelerate. The old Confederacy emerged as a booming region with economic indices that outstripped those of the Ohio Valley and the Northeast. Five of the country's ten largest cities—Los Angeles, San Diego, Houston, Dallas, and San Antonio—were in Texas and California. Arizona and Florida grew at four times the national average. The humming southern economy diversified; the payroll at one aircraft factory in Georgia equalled half the value of that state's cotton crop.

North and South, the American people were better educated than their parents had been, and better than their older brothers and sisters. More than 80 percent of whites and nearly 70 percent of blacks were finishing high school in the 1970s, a sharp increase over the previous decade. More schooling did not, however, guarantee greater proficiency, better jobs, or more personal satisfaction. One in five teen-agers seeking work could not find it; the number doubled if the applicants were male and black.

Yet women worked in unprecedented numbers and constituted almost

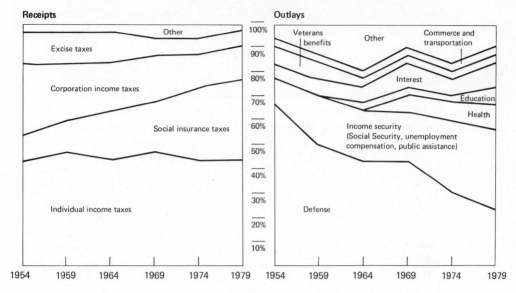

Shifting Priorities in 30 Years of Budgets

Elements of income and spending as percentages of budgets

Receipts

Other

Excise taxes

Corporation income taxes

Social insurance taxes

Individual income taxes

Outlays

100%

90%

80%

70%

60%

50%

40%

30%

20%

10%

Veterans benefits

Other

Commerce and transportation

Interest

Education

Health

Income security (Social Security, unemployment compensation, public assistance)

Defense

1954   1959   1964   1969   1974   1979

40 percent of the labor force in the 1970s. Most of those women were married and about half had husbands and children at home, but their families were smaller than families had been when the postwar babies were growing up. Projections indicated that the average family would consist of 3 persons by 1990, down from 3.7 persons in 1965 and from 3.4 in 1975. The number of single-parent families seemed certain to rise, for illegitimate births increased—to 50 percent or more of births among minorities in some urban areas—and the national divorce rate approached one for every two marriages.

Family instability was sometimes blamed on economic circumstance. Although half the labor force had white-collar jobs, about one family in nine remained at what the federal government called the poverty level, and the proportion among blacks was one in three. The Department of Commerce estimated in 1976 that if welfare and other governmental payments were excluded, one of four American families fell below the poverty line. Family income, measured in constant dollars, doubled in the thirty years after the Second World War, and most of that advance came before the inflation of the 1970s. This rising national income flowed, in almost the same proportions, to those who had always received it. In 1975, the share of the least prosperous Americans was less than one percent larger than it had been in 1950, and that of the most prosperous Americans was less than one percent smaller.

Toward a New Century

Whatever their economic circumstances, and however dismaying the problems their society faced, Americans were glad the discord and doubt of the late 1960s and early 1970s had passed. There were disturbing, occasionally lurid, reminders that the passage of time had not ended discrimination, poverty, violence, and alienation. But continuing imperfection induced a healthy humility—a realization that the United States, its government and its economy, could not instantly end every global evil. The confidence of liberals early in the 1960s had bordered on arrogance; the radical critique of liberalism late in the decade had produced self-doubt and institutional paralysis. New, and lower, expectations did not imply that Americans had abandoned their hope for a better world, but that they would go about its construction with more attention to environmental, international, social, and even personal consequences. It was as if, after almost four centuries of social evolution and two of political independence, the country had outgrown its frantic, youthful exuberance and had begun to mature.

Suggested Reading

Most of the history of contemporary America is in fact journalism and is contained in periodicals. The issue of *Daedalus* (Winter 1978) entitled "A New America" is a case in point. William P. Bundy has collected articles from *Foreign Affairs* in *The World Economic Crisis* (1975). Godfrey Hodgson's *America in Our Time** (1976), attempts to be comprehensive. William L. O'Neill emphasizes the cultural stress of the 1960s in *Coming Apart** (1971).

Memoirs and journalists' accounts of the Nixon presidency and the Watergate affair abound. John Dean's *Blind Ambition** (1976), Leon Jaworski's *The Right and the Power** (1976), and H. R. Haldeman's *The Ends of Power** (1978) are samples. Robert Woodward and Carl Bernstein's *The Final Days** (1976) is an absorbing account of the resignation. Jerald F. terHorst's *Gerald Ford and the Future of the Presidency* (1974) presents the view of Ford's first press secretary and *It Sure Looks Different from the Inside* (1978) is that of Ron Nessen, the second press secretary. Two journalists' reports of Carter's campaign are Jules Witcover, *Marathon** (1977), and James Wooten, *Dasher* (1978).

E. F. Schumacher's *Small Is Beautiful** (1973) is a provocative statement of the hazards of economic growth. Barry Commoner's *The Poverty of Power** (1976) presents the economic case against nuclear power. In *The Control of Oil* (1976), John M. Blair describes the influence of the major

international oil companies. Nathan Glazer's *Affirmative Discrimination**
(1975) analyzes the programs that the Supreme Court considered in the
Bakke case. Robert L. Heilbroner's *An Inquiry into the Human Prospect**
(1974) is a stimulating and rather bleak view of the global future.

* Available in paperback edition

Appendix

The Declaration of Independence*

The unanimous Declaration of the thirteen United States of America.

When, in the Course of human events, it becomes necessary for one people to dissolve the political bands which have connected them with another, and to assume, among the Powers of the earth, the separate and equal station to which the Laws of Nature and of Nature's God entitle them, a decent respect to the opinions of mankind requires that they should declare the causes which impel them to the separation.

We hold these truths to be self-evident, that all men are created equal, that they are endowed by their Creator with certain unalienable Rights, that among these, are Life, Liberty, and the pursuit of Happiness. That, to secure these rights, Governments are instituted among Men, deriving their just Powers from the consent of the governed. That, whenever any form of Government becomes destructive of these ends, it is the Right of the People to alter or to abolish it, and to institute new Government, laying its foundation on such Principles, and organizing its Powers in such form, as to them shall seem most likely to effect their Safety and Happiness. Prudence, indeed, will dictate that Governments long established should not be changed for light

* The original spelling, capitalization, and punctuation have been retained.

and transient causes; and, accordingly, all experience hath shewn, that mankind are more disposed to suffer, while evils are sufferable, than to right themselves by abolishing the forms to which they are accustomed. But, when a long train of abuses and usurpations, pursuing invariably the same Object, evinces a design to reduce them under absolute Despotism, it is their right, it is their duty, to throw off such Government, and to provide new Guards for their future Security. Such has been the patient sufferance of these Colonies; and such is now the necessity which constrains them to alter their former Systems of Government. The history of the present King of Great Britain is a history of repeated injuries and usurpations, all having in direct object the establishment of an absolute Tyranny over these States. To prove this, let Facts be submitted to a candid world.

He has refused his Assent to Laws the most wholesome and necessary for the public good.

He has forbidden his Governors to pass Laws of immediate and pressing importance, unless suspended in their operation till his Assent should be obtained; and when so suspended, he has utterly neglected to attend to them.

He has refused to pass other Laws for the accommodation of large districts of People, unless those people would relinquish the right of Representation in the legislature; a right inestimable to them and formidable to tyrants only.

He has called together legislative bodies at places unusual, uncomfortable, and distant from the depository of their Public Records, for the sole Purpose of fatiguing them into compliance with his measures.

He has dissolved Representative Houses repeatedly, for opposing, with manly firmness, his invasions on the rights of the People.

He has refused for a long time, after such dissolutions, to cause others to be elected; whereby the Legislative Powers, incapable of Annihilation, have returned to the People at large for their exercise; the State remaining in the mean time exposed to all the dangers of invasion from without, and convulsions within.

He has endeavoured to prevent the Population of these States; for that purpose obstructing the Laws for Naturalization of Foreigners; refusing to pass others to encourage their migrations hither, and raising the conditions of new Appropriations of Lands.

He has obstructed the Administration of Justice, by refusing his Assent to Laws for establishing Judiciary Powers.

He has made Judges dependent on his Will alone, for the tenure of their offices, and the amount and payment of their salaries.

He has erected a multitude of New Offices, and sent hither swarms of Officers to harrass our People, and eat out their substance.

He has kept among us, in times of Peace, Standing Armies, without the Consent of our legislatures.

He has affected to render the

Military independent of and superior to the Civil Power.

He has combined with others to subject us to a jurisdiction foreign to our constitution, and unacknowledged by our laws; giving his Assent to their Acts of pretended Legislation:

For quartering large bodies of armed troops among us:

For protecting them, by a mock Trial, from Punishment for any Murders which they should commit on the Inhabitants of these States:

For cutting off our Trade with all parts of the world:

For imposing Taxes on us without our Consent:

For depriving us, in many cases, of the benefits of Trial by Jury:

For transporting us beyond Seas to be tried for pretended offences:

For abolishing the free System of English Laws in a neighbouring province, establishing therein an Arbitrary government, and enlarging its Boundaries, so as to render it at once an example and fit instrument for introducing the same absolute rule into these Colonies:

For taking away our Charters, abolishing our most valuable Laws, and altering fundamentally the Forms of our Governments:

For suspending our own Legislatures, and declaring themselves invested with Power to legislate for us in all cases whatsoever.

He has abdicated Government here, by declaring us out of his protection, and waging War against us.

He has plundered our seas, ravaged our Coasts, burnt our towns, and destroyed the Lives of our People.

He is at this time transporting large Armies of foreign Mercenaries to compleat the works of death, desolation and tyranny, already begun with circumstances of Cruelty and perfidy scarcely paralleled in the most barbarous ages, and totally unworthy the Head of a civilized nation.

He has constrained our fellow Citizens, taken Captive on the high Seas, to bear Arms against their Country, to become the executioners of their friends and Brethren, or to fall themselves by their Hands.

He has excited domestic insurrections amongst us, and has endeavoured to bring on the inhabitants of our frontiers, the merciless Indian Savages, whose known rule of warfare, is an undistinguished destruction of all ages, sexes and conditions.

In every stage of these Oppressions, We have Petitioned for Redress, in the most humble terms: Our repeated Petitions, have been answered only by repeated injury. A Prince, whose character is thus marked by every act which may define a Tyrant, is unfit to be the ruler of a free People.

Nor have We been wanting in attentions to our British brethren. We have warned them from time to time of attempts by their legislature to extend an unwarrantable jurisdiction over us. We have reminded them of the circumstances of our emigration and settlement here. We have appealed to their native justice and magnanimity, and we have conjured them by the ties of our common kindred, to disavow these usurpations, which, would inevitably interrupt our connexions and correspondence. They too have been deaf to the voice of justice and consanguinity. We must, therefore, acquiesce in the necessity, which denounces our Separation, and hold them, as we hold the rest of mankind, Enemies in war, in Peace Friends.

WE, THEREFORE, the Representatives of the UNITED STATES OF AMERICA, in GENERAL CONGRESS assembled, appealing to the Supreme Judge of the World for the rectitude of our intentions, DO, in the Name, and by Authority of the good People of these Colonies, solemnly PUBLISH and DECLARE, That these United Colonies are, and of Right, ought to be FREE AND INDEPENDENT STATES; that they are Absolved from all Allegiance to the British Crown, and that all political connexion between them and the State of Great Britain, is and ought to be totally dissolved; and that, as FREE and INDEPENDENT STATES, they have full Power to levy War, conclude Peace, contract Alliances, establish Commerce, and to do all other Acts and Things which INDEPENDENT STATES may of right do. AND for the support of this Declaration, with a firm reliance on the protection of divine Providence, we mutually pledge to each other our Lives, our Fortunes, and our sacred Honour.

The Constitution of the United States of America*

We the people of the United States, in Order to form a more perfect Union, establish Justice, insure domestic Tranquility, provide for the common defence, promote the general Welfare, and secure the Blessings of Liberty to ourselves and our Posterity, do ordain and establish this Constitution for the United States of America.

ARTICLE I

Section 1. All legislative Powers herein granted shall be vested in a Congress of the United States, which shall consist of a Senate and House of Representatives.

Section 2. The House of Representatives shall be composed of Members chosen every second Year by the People of the several States, and the Electors in each State shall have the Qualifications requisite for Electors of the most numerous Branch of the State Legislature.

No Person shall be a Representative who shall not have attained to the Age of twenty-five Years, and been seven Years a Citizen of the United States, and who shall not, when elected, be an Inhabitant of that state in which he shall be chosen.

[Representatives and direct Taxes shall be apportioned among the several States which may be included within this Union, according to their respective Numbers, which shall be determined by adding to the whole Number of free Persons, including those bound to Service for a Term of Years, and excluding Indians not

* The Constitution and all amendments are shown in their original form. Parts that have been amended or superseded are bracketed and explained in the footnotes.

taxed, three fifths of all other Persons.][1] The actual Enumeration shall be made within three Years after the first Meeting of the Congress of the United States, and within every subsequent Term of ten Years, in such Manner as they shall by Law direct. The Number of Representatives shall not exceed one for every thirty Thousand, but each State shall have at Least one Representative; and until such enumeration shall be made, the State of New Hampshire shall be entitled to chuse three, Massachusetts eight, Rhode-Island and Providence Plantations one, Connecticut five, New-York six, New Jersey four, Pennsylvania eight, Delaware one, Maryland six, Virginia ten, North Carolina five, South Carolina five, and Georgia three.

When vacancies happen in the Representation from any State, the Executive Authority thereof shall issue Writs of Election to fill such Vacancies.

The House of Representatives shall chuse their Speaker and other Officers; and shall have the sole Power of Impeachment.

Section 3. The Senate of the United States shall be composed of two Senators from each State, [chosen by the Legislature thereof,][2] for six Years; and each Senator shall have one Vote.

Immediately after they shall be assembled in Consequence of the first Election, they shall be divided as equally as may be into three Classes. The Seats of the Senators of the first Class shall be vacated at the Expiration of the second Year, of the Second Class at the Expiration of the fourth Year, and of the third Class at the Expiration of the sixth Year, so that one-third may be chosen every second Year; [and if Vacancies happen by Resignation, or otherwise, during the Recess of the Legislature of any State, the Executive thereof may make temporary Appointments until the next Meeting of the Legislature, which shall then fill such Vacancies].[3]

No Person shall be a Senator who shall not have attained to the Age of thirty Years, and been nine Years a Citizen of the United States, and who shall not, when elected, be an Inhabitant of that State in which he shall be chosen.

The Vice-President of the United States shall be President of the Senate, but shall have no vote, unless they be equally divided.

The Senate shall chuse their other Officers, and also a President pro tempore, in the absence of the Vice-President, or when he shall exercise the Office of the President of the United States.

The Senate shall have the sole Power to try all Impeachments. When sitting for that purpose, they shall be on Oath or Affirmation. When the President of the United States is tried, the Chief Justice shall preside. And no person shall be convicted without the Concurrence of two thirds of the Members present.

Judgment in Cases of Impeach-

---

[1] Modified by the Fourteenth and Sixteenth amendments.
[2] Superseded by the Seventeenth Amendment.

[3] Modified by the Seventeenth Amendment.

ment shall not extend further than to removal from Office, and disqualification to hold and enjoy any Office of honor, Trust, or Profit under the United States: but the Party convicted shall nevertheless be liable and subject to Indictment, Trial, Judgment, and Punishment, according to Law.

Section 4. The Times, Places and Manner of holding Elections for Senators and Representatives, shall be prescribed in each state by the Legislature thereof; but the Congress may at any time by Law make or alter such Regulations, except as to the Places of Chusing Senators.

The Congress shall assemble at least once in every Year, and such Meeting shall [be on the first Monday in December,]⁴ unless they shall by Law appoint a different Day.

Section 5. Each House shall be the Judge of the Elections, Returns and Qualifications of its own Members, and a Majority of each shall constitute a Quorum to do Business; but a smaller number may adjourn from day to day, and may be authorized to compel the Attendance of absent Members, in such Manner, and under such Penalties, as each House may provide.

Each House may determine the Rules of its Proceedings, punish its Members for disorderly Behavior, and, with the Concurrence of two thirds, expel a Member.

Each House shall keep a Journal of its Proceedings, and from time to time publish the same, excepting such Parts as may in

⁴ Superseded by the Twentieth Amendment.

their Judgment require Secrecy; and the Yeas and Nays of the Members of either House on any question shall, at the Desire of one fifth of those Present, be entered on the Journal.

Neither House, during the Session of Congress, shall, without the Consent of the other, adjourn for more than three days, nor to any other Place than that in which the two Houses shall be sitting.

Section 6. The Senators and Representatives shall receive a Compensation for their Services, to be ascertained by Law, and paid out of the Treasury of the United States. They shall in all Cases, except Treason, Felony, and Breach of the Peace, be privileged from Arrest during their Attendance at the Session of their respective Houses, and in going to and returning from the same; and for any Speech or Debate in either House, they shall not be questioned in any other Place.

No Senator or Representative shall, during the Time for which he was elected, be appointed to any civil Office under the Authority of the United States, which shall have been created, or the Emoluments whereof shall have been increased, during such time; and no Person holding any Office under the United States shall be a Member of either House during his continuance in Office.

Section 7. All Bills for raising Revenue shall originate in the House of Representatives; but the Senate may propose or concur with Amendments as on other bills.

Every Bill which shall have

passed the House of Representatives and the Senate, shall, before it become a Law, be presented to the President of the United States; If he approve he shall sign it, but if not he shall return it, with his Objections, to that House in which it shall have originated, who shall enter the Objections at large on their Journal, and proceed to reconsider it. If after such Reconsideration two thirds of that House shall agree to pass the bill, it shall be sent, together with the Objections, to the other House, by which it shall likewise be reconsidered, and if approved by two thirds of that House, it shall become a Law. But in all such Cases the Votes of both Houses shall be determined by Yeas and Nays, and the names of the Persons voting for and against the Bill shall be entered on the Journal of each House respectively. If any Bill shall not be returned by the President within ten Days (Sundays excepted) after it shall have been presented to him, the Same shall be a Law, in like Manner as if he had signed it, unless the Congress by their Adjournment prevent its Return, in which Case it shall not be a Law.

Every Order, Resolution, or Vote to which the Concurrence of the Senate and House of Representatives may be necessary (except on a question of Adjournment) shall be presented to the President of the United States; and before the Same shall take Effect, shall be approved by him, or being disapproved by him, shall be repassed by two thirds of the Senate and House of Representatives, according to the Rules and Limitations prescribed in the Case of a Bill.

Section 8. The Congress shall have Power To Lay and collect Taxes, Duties, Imposts and Excises, to pay the Debts and provide for the common Defence and general Welfare of the United States; but all Duties, Imposts and Excises shall be uniform throughout the United States;

To borrow money on the credit of the United States;

To regulate Commerce with foreign Nations, and among the several States, and with the Indian Tribes;

To establish an uniform Rule of Naturalization, and uniform Laws on the subject of Bankruptcies throughout the United States;

To coin Money, regulate the Value thereof, and of foreign Coin, and fix the Standard of Weights and Measures;

To provide for the Punishment of counterfeiting the Securities and current Coin of the United States;

To establish Post Offices and post Roads;

To promote the Progress of Science and useful Arts, by securing for limited Times to Authors and Inventors the exclusive Right to their respective Writings and Discoveries;

To constitute Tribunals inferior to the Supreme Court;

To define and punish Piracies and Felonies committed on the high Seas, and Offenses against the Law of Nations;

To declare War, grant Letters of Marque and Reprisal, and make Rules concerning Captures on Land and Water;

To raise and support Armies, but

no Appropriation of Money to that Use shall be for a longer Term than two Years;

To provide and maintain a Navy;

To make Rules for the Government and Regulation of the land and naval forces;

To provide for calling forth the Militia to execute the Laws of the Union, suppress Insurrections and repel Invasions;

To provide for organizing, arming, and disciplining the Militia, and for governing such Part of them as may be employed in the Service of the United States, reserving to the States respectively, the Appointment of the Officers, and the Authority of training the Militia according to the discipline prescribed by Congress;

To exercise exclusive Legislation in all Cases whatsoever, over such District (not exceeding ten Miles square) as may, by Cession of particular States, and the acceptance of Congress, become the Seat of the Government of the United States, and to exercise like Authority over all Places purchased by the Consent of the Legislature of the State in which the Same shall be, for the Erection of Forts, Magazines, Arsenals, dock-Yards, and other needful Building;—And

To make all Laws which shall be necessary and proper for carrying into Execution the foregoing Powers, and all other Powers vested by this Constitution in the Government of the United States, or in any Department or Officer thereof.

Section 9. The Migration or Importation of such Persons as any of the States now existing shall think proper to admit shall not be prohibited by the Congress prior to the Year one thousand eight hundred and eight, but a tax or duty may be imposed on such Importation, not exceeding ten dollars for each Person.

The privilege of the Writ of Habeas Corpus shall not be suspended, unless when in Cases of Rebellion or Invasion the public Safety may require it.

No Bill of Attainder or ex post facto Law shall be passed.

[No capitation, or other direct, Tax shall be laid unless in Proportion to the Census or Enumeration herein before directed to be taken.]⁵

No Tax or Duty shall be laid on Articles exported from any State.

No Preference shall be given by any Regulation of Revenue to the Ports of one State over those of another: nor shall Vessels bound to, or from, one State, be obliged to enter, clear, or pay Duties in another.

No Money shall be drawn from the Treasury, but in Consequence of Appropriations made by Law; and a regular Statement and Account of the Receipts and Expenditures of all public Money shall be published from time to time.

No Title of Nobility shall be granted by the United States: And no Person holding any Office of Profit or Trust under them, shall, without the Consent of the Congress, accept of any present, Emolument, Office, or Title, of any kind whatever, from any King, Prince, or foreign State.

Section 10. No State shall enter

⁵ Modified by the Sixteenth Amendment.

into any Treaty, Alliance, or Confederation; grant Letters of Marque and Reprisal; coin Money; emit Bills of Credit; make any Thing but gold and silver Coin a Tender in Payment of Debts; pass any Bill of Attainder, ex post facto Law, or Law impairing the Obligation of Contracts, or grant any title of Nobility.

No State shall, without the Consent of the Congress, lay any Imposts or Duties on Imports or Exports, except what may be absolutely necessary for executing its inspection Laws: and the net Produce of all Duties and Imposts, laid by any State on Imports or Exports, shall be for the Use of the Treasury of the United States; and all such Laws shall be subject to the Revision and Control of the Congress.

No State shall, without the Consent of Congress, lay any duty of Tonnage, keep Troops, or Ships of War in time of Peace, enter into any Agreement or Compact with another State, or with a foreign Power, or engage in War, unless actually invaded, or in such imminent Danger as will not admit of delay.

ARTICLE II

Section 1. The executive Power shall be vested in a President of the United States of America. He shall hold his Office during the Term of four years, and, together with the Vice-President, chosen for the same Term, be elected, as follows:

Each State shall appoint, in such Manner as the Legislature thereof may direct, a Number of Electors, equal to the whole Number of Senators and Representatives to which the State may be entitled in the Congress: but no Senator or Representative, or Person holding an Office of Trust or Profit under the United States, shall be appointed an Elector.

[The Electors shall meet in their respective States, and vote by Ballot for two persons, of whom one at least shall not be an Inhabitant of the same State with themselves. And they shall make a List of all the Persons voted for, and of the Number of Votes for each; which List they shall sign and certify, and transmit sealed to the Seat of the Government of the United States, directed to the President of the Senate. The President of the Senate shall, in the Presence of the Senate and House of Representatives, open all the Certificates, and the Votes shall then be counted. The Person having the greatest Number of Votes shall be the President, if such Number be a Majority of the whole Number of Electors appointed; and if there be more than one who have such Majority, and have an equal Number of Votes, then the House of Representatives shall immediately chuse by Ballot one of them for President; and if no Person have a Majority, then from the five highest on the List the said House shall in like Manner chuse the President. But in chusing the President, the Votes shall be taken by States, the Representation from each State having one Vote; a quorum for this Purpose shall consist of a Member or Members from two thirds of the States, and a Majority of all the states shall be necessary to a Choice. In every Case, after the Choice of the President, the Person having the greatest Number of Votes of the Electors shall be the Vice-President. But if there should remain two or more who have equal votes, the Senate shall chuse from them by Ballot the Vice-President.][6]

The Congress may determine the Time of chusing the Electors, and the Day on which they shall give their Votes; which Day shall be the same throughout the United States.

No person except a natural-born Citizen, or a Citizen of the United States, at the time of the Adoption of this Constitution, shall be eligible to the Office of President; neither shall any Person be eligible to that Office who shall not have attained to the Age of thirty-five Years, and been fourteen Years a Resident within the United States.

[In Case of the Removal of the President from Office, or of his Death, Resignation, or Inability to discharge the Powers and Duties of the said Office, the same shall devolve on the Vice-President, and the Congress may by Law provide for the Case of Removal, Death, Resignation, or Inability, both of the President and Vice-President, declaring what Officer shall then act as President, and such Officer shall act accordingly, until the disability be removed, or a President shall be elected.][7]

The President shall, at stated Times, receive for his Services a Compensation, which shall neither be increased nor diminished during the Period for which he shall have been elected, and he shall not receive within that Period any other Emolument from the United States, or any of them.

Before he enter on the execution of his Office, he shall take the following Oath or Affirmation:—"I do solemnly swear (or affirm) that I will faithfully execute the Office of President of the United States, and will, to the best of my Ability, preserve, protect, and defend the Constitution of the United States."

Section 2. The President shall be Commander in Chief of the Army and Navy of the United States, and of the Militia of the several States, when called into the actual Service of the United States; he may require the Opinion, in writing, of the principal Officer in each of the executive Departments, upon any subject relating to the Duties of their respective Offices, and he shall have Power to Grant Reprieves and Pardons for Offenses against the United States, except in Cases of Impeachment.

He shall have Power, by and with the Advice and Consent of the Senate, to make Treaties, provided two thirds of the Senators present concur; and he shall nominate, and by and with the Advice and Consent of the Senate, shall appoint Ambassadors, other public Ministers and Consuls, Judges of the supreme Court, and all other Officers of the United States, whose Appointments are not herein otherwise provided for, and which shall be established by Law: but the Congress may by Law vest the Appointment of such inferior Officers, as they think proper, in

[6] Superseded by the Twelfth Amendment.
[7] Modified by the Twenty-fifth Amendment.

the President alone, in the Courts of Law, or in the Heads of Departments.

The President shall have Power to fill up all Vacancies that may happen during the Recess of the Senate, by granting Commissions which shall expire at the End of their next Session.

Section 3. He shall from time to time give to the Congress Information of the State of the Union, and recommend to their Consideration such Measures as he shall judge necessary and expedient; he may, on extraordinary occasions, convene both Houses, or either of them, and in Case of Disagreement between them, with respect to the Time of Adjournment, he may adjourn them to such Time as he shall think proper; he shall receive Ambassadors and other public Ministers; he shall take Care that the Laws be faithfully executed, and shall Commission all the Officers of the United States.

Section 4. The President, Vice-President and all civil Officers of the United States, shall be removed from Office on Impeachment for, and Conviction of, Treason, Bribery, or other high Crimes and Misdemeanors.

ARTICLE III

Section 1. The judicial Power of the United States, shall be vested in one supreme Court, and in such inferior Courts as the Congress may from time to time ordain and establish. The Judges, both of the supreme and inferior Courts, shall hold their Offices during good Behaviour, and shall, at stated Times, receive for their Services, a Compensation, which shall not be diminished during their Continuance in Office.

Section 2. The judicial Power shall extend to all Cases, in Law and Equity, arising under this Constitution, the Laws of the United States, and treaties made, or which shall be made, under their Authority;—to all Cases affecting ambassadors, other public ministers and consuls;—to all cases of admiralty and maritime Jurisdiction;—to Controversies to which the United States shall be a Party;—to Controversies between two or more States;—[between a State and Citizens of another State;][8]—between Citizens of different States,—between Citizens of the same State claiming Lands under Grants of different States, and between a State, or the Citizens thereof, and foreign States, Citizens or Subjects.

In all Cases affecting Ambassadors, other public Ministers and Consuls, and those in which a State shall be Party, the supreme Court shall have original Jurisdiction. In all the other Cases before mentioned, the supreme Court shall have appellate Jurisdiction, both as to Law and Fact, with such Exceptions, and under such Regulations as the Congress shall make.

The trial of all Crimes, except in Cases of Impeachment, shall be by Jury; and such Trial shall be held in the State where the said Crimes shall have been committed; but when not committed within any State, the Trial shall be at such

[8] Modified by the Eleventh Amendment.

Place or Places as the Congress may by Law have directed.

Section 3. Treason against the United States, shall consist only in levying War against them, or in adhering to their Enemies, giving them Aid and Comfort. No Person shall be convicted of Treason unless on the Testimony of two Witnesses to the same overt Act, or on Confession in open Court.

The Congress shall have power to declare the Punishment of Treason, but no Attainder of Treason shall work Corruption of Blood, or Forfeiture except during the Life of the Person attainted.

ARTICLE IV

Section 1. Full Faith and Credit shall be given in each State to the public Acts, Records, and judicial Proceedings of every other State. And the Congress may by general Laws prescribe the Manner in which such Acts, Records and Proceedings shall be proved, and the Effect thereof.

Section 2. The Citizens of each State shall be entitled to all Privileges and Immunities of Citizens in the several States.

A Person charged in any State with Treason, Felony, or other Crime, who shall flee from Justice, and be found in another State, shall on demand of the executive Authority of the State from which he fled, be delivered up, to be removed to the State having Jurisdiction of the crime.

[No Person held to service or Labour in one State, under the Laws thereof, escaping into another, shall, in Consequence of any Law or Regulation therein, be discharged from such Service or Labour, but shall be delivered up on Claim of the Party to whom such Service or Labour may be due.]⁹

Section 3. New States may be admitted by the Congress into this Union; but no new State shall be formed or erected within the Jurisdiction of any other State; nor any State be formed by the Junction of two or more States, or parts of States, without the Consent of the Legislatures of the States concerned as well as of the Congress.

The Congress shall have Power to dispose of and make all needful Rules and Regulations respecting the Territory or other Property belonging to the United States; and nothing in this Constitution shall be so construed as to Prejudice any Claims of the United States, or of any particular State.

Section 4. The United States shall guarantee to every State in this Union a Republican Form of Government, and shall protect each of them against Invasion; and on Application of the Legislature, or of the Executive (when the Legislature cannot be convened) against domestic Violence.

ARTICLE V

The Congress, whenever two thirds of both Houses shall deem it necessary, shall propose Amendments to this Constitution, or, on the Application of the Legislatures of two thirds of the several States, shall call a Convention for proposing

⁹ Superseded by the Thirteenth Amendment.

Amendments, which, in either Case, shall be valid to all Intents and Purposes, as part of this Constitution, when ratified by the Legislatures of three fourths of the several States, or by Conventions in three fourths thereof, as the one or the other Mode of Ratification may be proposed by the Congress; Provided that no Amendment which may be made prior to the Year One thousand eight hundred and eight shall in any Manner affect the first and fourth Clauses in the Ninth Section of the first Article; and that no State, without its Consent, shall be deprived of its equal Suffrage in the Senate.

ARTICLE VI

All Debts contracted and Engagements entered into, before the Adoption of this Constitution, shall be as valid against the United States under this Constitution as under the Confederation.

This Constitution, and the Laws of the United States which shall be made in Pursuance thereof; and all Treaties made, or which shall be made, under the Authority of the United States, shall be the supreme Law of the Land; and the Judges in every State shall be bound thereby, any Thing in the Constitution or Laws of any State to the Contrary notwithstanding.

The Senators and Representatives before mentioned, and the Members of the several State Legislatures, and all executive and judicial Officers, both of the United States and of the several States, shall be bound by Oath or Affirmation to support this Constitution; but no religious Test shall ever be required as a qualification to any Office or public Trust under the United States.

ARTICLE VII

The Ratification of the Conventions of nine States shall be sufficient for the Establishment of this Constitution between the States so ratifying the same.

Done in Convention by the Unanimous Consent of the States present the Seventeenth Day of September in the Year of our Lord one thousand seven hundred and Eighty seven, and of the Independence of the United States of America the Twelfth. In Witness whereof We have hereunto subscribed our Names.

Articles in Addition to, and Amendment of, the Constitution of the United States of America, Proposed by Congress, and Ratified by the Legislatures of the Several States, Pursuant to the Fifth Article of the Original Constitution.

AMENDMENT I[10]

Congress shall make no law respecting an establishment of religion, or prohibiting the free exercise thereof; or abridging the freedom of speech, or of the press; or the right of the people peaceably to assemble, and to petition the Government for a redress of grievances.

AMENDMENT II

A well regulated Militia, being necessary to the security of a free

[10] The first ten amendments were passed by Congress September 25, 1789. They were ratified by three-fourths of the states December 15, 1791.

State, the right of the people to keep and bear Arms shall not be infringed.

AMENDMENT III

No Soldier shall, in time of peace, be quartered in any house, without the consent of the Owner, nor in time of war, but in a manner to be prescribed by law.

AMENDMENT IV

The right of the people to be secure in their persons, houses, papers, and effects, against unreasonable searches and seizures, shall not be violated, and no Warrants shall issue, but upon probable cause, supported by Oath or affirmation, and particularly describing the place to be searched, and the persons or things to be seized.

AMENDMENT V

No person shall be held to answer for a capital or otherwise infamous crime, unless on a presentment or indictment of a Grand Jury, except in cases arising in the land or naval forces, or in the Militia, when in actual service in time of War or public danger; nor shall any person be subject for the same offence to be twice put in jeopardy of life or limb; nor shall be compelled in any criminal case to be a witness against himself, nor be deprived of life, liberty, or property, without due process of law; nor shall private property be taken for public use, without just compensation.

AMENDMENT VI

In all criminal prosecutions, the accused shall enjoy the right to a speedy and public trial, by an impartial jury of the State and district wherein the crime shall have been committed, which district shall have been previously ascertained by law, and to be informed of the nature and cause of the accusation; to be confronted with the witnesses against him; to have compulsory process for obtaining witnesses in his favor, and to have the Assistance of Counsel for his defence.

AMENDMENT VII

In suits at common law, where the value in controversy shall exceed twenty dollars, the right of trial by jury shall be preserved, and no fact tried by a jury, shall be otherwise reexamined in any Court of the United States, than according to the rules of the common law.

AMENDMENT VIII

Excessive bail shall not be required, nor excessive fines imposed, nor cruel and unusual punishments inflicted.

AMENDMENT IX

The enumeration in the Constitution, of certain rights, shall not be construed to deny or disparage others retained by the people.

AMENDMENT X

The powers not delegated to the United States by the Constitution, nor prohibited by it to the States, are reserved to the States respectively, or to the people.

AMENDMENT XI (1798)[11]

The Judicial power of the United States shall not be construed to extend to any suit in law or equity, commenced or prosecuted against one of the United States by Citizens of another State, or by Citizens or Subjects of any Foreign State.

AMENDMENT XII (1804)

The Electors shall meet in their respective States and vote by ballot for President and Vice-President, one of whom, at least, shall not be an inhabitant of the same State with themselves; they shall name in their ballots the person voted for as President, and in distinct ballots the person voted for as Vice-President, and they shall make distinct lists of all persons voted for as President, and of all persons voted for as Vice-President, and of the number of votes for each, which lists they shall sign and certify, and transmit sealed to the seat of the government of the United States, directed to the President of the Senate;—The President of the Senate shall, in the presence of the Senate and House of Representatives, open all the certificates and the votes shall then be counted;—The person having the greatest number of votes for President, shall be the President, if such number be a majority of the whole number of Electors appointed; and if no person have such majority, then from the persons having the highest numbers not exceeding three on the list of those voted for as President, the House of Representatives shall choose immediately, by ballot, the President. But in choosing the President, the votes shall be taken by states, the representation from each state having one vote; a quorum for this purpose shall consist of a member or members from two-thirds of the states, and a majority of all the states shall be necessary to a choice. [And if the House of Representatives shall not choose a President whenever the right of choice shall devolve upon them, before the fourth day of March next following, then the Vice-President shall act as President, as in the case of the death or other constitutional disability of the President.][12]—The person having the greatest number of votes as Vice-President, shall be the Vice-President, if such number be a majority of the whole number of Electors appointed, and if no person have a majority, then from the two highest numbers on the list, the Senate shall choose the Vice-President; a quorum for the purpose shall consist of two-thirds of the whole number of Senators, and a majority of the whole number shall be necessary to a choice. But no person constitutionally ineligible to the office of President shall be eligible to that of Vice-President of the United States.

AMENDMENT XIII (1865)

Section 1. Neither slavery nor involuntary servitude, except as a punishment for crime whereof the party shall have been duly

[11] Date of ratification.

[12] Superseded by the Twentieth Amendment.

convicted, shall exist within the United States, or any place subject to their jurisdiction.

Section 2. Congress shall have power to enforce this article by appropriate legislation.

AMENDMENT XIV (1868)

Section 1. All persons born or naturalized in the United States, and subject to the jurisdiction thereof, are citizens of the United States and of the State wherein they reside. No State shall make or enforce any law which shall abridge the privileges or immunities of citizens of the United States; nor shall any State deprive any person of life, liberty, or property, without due process of law; nor deny to any person within its jurisdiction the equal protection of the laws.

Section 2. Representatives shall be apportioned among the several States according to their respective numbers, counting the whole number of persons in each State, excluding Indians not taxed. But when the right to vote at any election for the choice of electors for President and Vice-President of the United States, Representatives in Congress, the Executive and Judicial officers of a State, or the members of the Legislature thereof, is denied to any of the male inhabitants of such State, being twenty-one years of age, and citizens of the United States, or in any way abridged, except for participation in rebellion, or other crime, the basis of representation therein shall be reduced in the proportion which the number of such male citizens shall bear to the whole number of male citizens

twenty-one years of age in such State.

Section 3. No person shall be a Senator or Representative in Congress, or elector of President and Vice-President, or hold any office, civil or military, under the United States, or under any State, who, having previously taken an oath, as a member of Congress, or as an officer of the United States, or as a member of any State legislature, or as an executive or judicial officer of any State, to support the Constitution of the United States, shall have engaged in insurrection or rebellion against the same, or given aid or comfort to the enemies thereof. But Congress may by a vote of two-thirds of each House, remove such disability.

Section 4. The validity of the public debt of the United States, authorized by law, including debts incurred for payment of pensions and bounties for services in suppressing insurrection or rebellion, shall not be questioned. But neither the United States nor any State shall assume or pay any debt or obligation incurred in aid of insurrection or rebellion against the United States, or any claim for the loss or emancipation of any slave; but all such debts, obligations, and claims shall be held illegal and void.

Section 5. The Congress shall have the power to enforce, by appropriate legislation, the provisions of this article.

AMENDMENT XV (1870)

Section 1. The right of citizens of the United States to vote shall not be denied or abridged by the

United States or by any State on account of race, color, or previous condition of servitude.

Section 2. The Congress shall have power to enforce this article by appropriate legislation.

AMENDMENT XVI (1913)

The Congress shall have power to lay and collect taxes on incomes, from whatever source derived, without apportionment among the several States, and without regard to any census or enumeration.

AMENDMENT XVII (1913)

The Senate of the United States shall be composed of two Senators from each State, elected by the people thereof, for six years; and each Senator shall have one vote. The electors in each State shall have the qualifications requisite for electors of the most numerous branch of the State legislatures.

When vacancies happen in the representation of any State in the Senate, the executive authority of such State shall issue writs of election to fill such vacancies: *Provided,* That the legislature of any State may empower the executive thereof to make temporary appointments until the people fill the vacancies by election as the legislature may direct.

This amendment shall not be so construed as to affect the election or term of any Senator chosen before it becomes valid as part of the Constitution.

AMENDMENT XVIII (1919)[13]

Section 1. After one year from

[13] Repealed by the Twenty-first Amendment.

the ratification of this article the manufacture, sale, or transportation of intoxicating liquors within, the importation thereof into, or the exportation thereof from the United States and all territory subject to the jurisdiction thereof for beverage purposes is hereby prohibited.

Section 2. The Congress and the several States shall have concurrent power to enforce this article by appropriate legislation.

Section 3. This article shall be inoperative unless it shall have been ratified as an amendment to the Constitution by the legislatures of the several States, as provided in the Constitution, within seven years from the date of the submission hereof to the States by the Congress.

AMENDMENT XIX (1920)

The right of citizens of the United States to vote shall not be denied or abridged by the United States or by any State on account of sex.

Congress shall have power to enforce this article by appropriate legislation.

AMENDMENT XX (1933)

Section 1. The terms of the President and Vice-President shall end at noon on the 20th day of January, and the terms of Senators and Representatives at noon on the 3d day of January, of the years in which such terms would have ended if this article had not been ratified; and the terms of their successors shall then begin.

Section 2. The Congress shall assemble at least once in every year, and such meeting shall begin at noon on the 3d day of January, unless they shall by law appoint a different day.

Section 3. If, at the time fixed for the beginning of the term of the President, the President elect shall have died, the Vice-President elect shall become President. If a President shall not have been chosen before the time fixed for the beginning of his term, or if the President elect shall have failed to qualify, then the Vice-President elect shall act as President until a President shall have qualified; and the Congress may by law provide for the case wherein neither a President elect nor a Vice-President elect shall have qualified, declaring who shall then act as President, or the manner in which one who is to act shall be selected, and such person shall act accordingly until a President or Vice-President shall have qualified.

Section 4. The Congress may by law provide for the case of the death of any of the persons from whom the House of Representatives may choose a President whenever the right of choice shall have devolved upon them, and for the case of the death of any of the persons from whom the Senate may choose a Vice-President whenever the right of choice shall have devolved upon them.

Section 5. Sections 1 and 2 shall take effect on the 15th day of October following the ratification of this article.

Section 6. This article shall be inoperative unless it shall have been ratified as an amendment to the Constitution by the legislatures of three-fourths of the several States within seven years from the date of its submission.

AMENDMENT XXI (1933)

Section 1. The eighteenth article of amendment to the Constitution of the United States is hereby repealed.

Section 2. The transportation or importation into any State, Territory, or possession of the United States for delivery or use therein of intoxicating liquors, in violation of the laws thereof, is hereby prohibited.

Section 3. This article shall be inoperative unless it shall have been ratified as an amendment to the Constitution by conventions in the several States, as provided in the Constitution, within seven years from the date of the submission hereof to the States by the Congress.

AMENDMENT XXII (1951)

No person shall be elected to the office of the President more than twice, and no person who has held the office of President, or acted as President, for more than two years of a term to which some other person was elected President shall be elected to the office of the President more than once.

But this Article shall not apply to any person holding the office of President when this Article was proposed by the Congress, and shall not prevent any person who may be holding the office of President, or acting as President, during the term within which this Article becomes operative from holding the office of President or acting as President during the remainder of such term.

AMENDMENT XXIII (1961)

Section 1. The District constituting the seat of Government of the United States shall appoint in such manner as the Congress may direct:

A number of electors of President and Vice-President equal to the whole number of Senators and Representatives in Congress to which the District would be entitled if it were a State, but in no event more than the least populous State; they shall be in addition to those appointed by the States, but they shall be considered, for the purposes of the election of President and Vice-President, to be electors appointed by the State; and they shall meet in the District and perform such duties as provided by the twelfth article of amendment.

Section 2. The Congress shall have power to enforce this article by appropriate legislation.

AMENDMENT XXIV (1964)

Section 1. The right of citizens of the United States to vote in any primary or other election for President or Vice-President, for electors for President or Vice-President, or for Senator or Representative in Congress, shall not be denied or abridged by the United States or any State by reason of failure to pay any poll tax or other tax.

Section 2. The Congress shall

have power to enforce this article by appropriate legislation.

AMENDMENT XXV (1967)

Section 1. In case of the removal of the President from office or of his death or resignation, the Vice-President shall become President.

Section 2. Whenever there is a vacancy in the office of the Vice-President, the President shall nominate a Vice-President who shall take office upon confirmation by a majority vote of both Houses of Congress.

Section 3. Whenever the President transmits to the President pro tempore of the Senate and the Speaker of the House of Representatives his written declaration that he is unable to discharge the powers and duties of his office, and until he transmits to them a written declaration to the contrary, such powers and duties shall be discharged by the Vice-President as Acting President.

Section 4. Whether the Vice-President and a majority of either the principal officers of the executive department or of such other body as Congress may by law provide, transmit to the President pro tempore of the Senate and the Speaker of the House of Representatives their written declaration that the President is unable to discharge the powers and duties of his office, the Vice-President shall immediately assume the powers and duties of the office as Acting President.

Thereafter, when the President

transmits to the President pro tempore of the Senate and the Speaker of the House of Representatives his written declaration that no inability exists, he shall resume the powers and duties of his office unless the Vice-President and a majority of either the principal officers of the executive department or of such other body as Congress may by law provide, transmit within four days to the President pro tempore of the Senate and the Speaker of the House of Representatives their written declaration that the President is unable to discharge the powers and duties of his office. Thereupon Congress shall decide the issue, assembling within forty-eight hours for that purpose if not in session. If the Congress, within twenty-one days after receipt of the latter written declaration, or, if Congress is not in session, within twenty-one days after Congress is required to assemble, determines by two-thirds vote of both Houses that the President is unable to discharge the powers and duties of his office, the Vice-President shall continue to discharge the same as Acting President; otherwise, the President shall resume the powers and duties of his office.

AMENDMENT XXVI (1971)

Section 1. The right of citizens of the United States, who are eighteen years of age or older, to vote shall not be denied or abridged by the United States or by any State on account of age.

Section 2. The Congress shall have power to enforce this article by appropriate legislation.

Presidential Elections [1789–1976]*

Year and number of states	Candidates	Parties	Popular vote	Electoral vote	Percentage of popular vote[1]
1789 (11)	George Washington	No party designations		69	
	John Adams			34	
	Minor Candidates			35	
1792 (15)	George Washington	No party designations		132	
	John Adams			77	
	George Clinton			50	
	Minor Candidates			5	
1796 (16)	John Adams	Federalist		71	
	Thomas Jefferson	Democratic-Republican		68	
	Thomas Pinckney	Federalist		59	
	Aaron Burr	Democratic-Republican		30	
	Minor Candidates			48	
1800 (16)	Thomas Jefferson	Democratic-Republican		73	
	Aaron Burr	Democratic-Republican		73	
	John Adams	Federalist		65	
	Charles C. Pinckney	Federalist		64	
	John Jay	Federalist		1	
1804 (17)	Thomas Jefferson	Democratic-Republican		162	
	Charles C. Pinckney	Federalist		14	
1808 (17)	James Madison	Democratic-Republican		122	
	Charles C. Pinckney	Federalist		47	
	George Clinton	Democratic-Republican		6	

* Before the passage of the Twelfth Amendment in 1804, the Electoral College voted for two presidential candidates; the runner-up became Vice-President. Figures are from *Historical Statistics of the United States, Colonial Times to 1957* (1961), pp. 682–83; the U.S. Department of Justice; *New York Times Encyclopedic Almanac, 1972*, p. 101; the *Associated Press Almanac, 1975*, p. 145; and *The World Almanac and Book of Facts, 1979*, p. 264.

[1] Candidates receiving less than 1 percent of the popular vote have been omitted. For that reason the percentage of popular vote given for any election year may not total 100 percent.

Presidential Elections [1789–1976] [cont.]

Year and number of states	Candidates	Parties	Popular vote	Electoral vote	Percentage of popular vote
1812	James Madison	Democratic-Republican		128	
(18)	DeWitt Clinton	Federalist		89	
1816	James Monroe	Democratic-Republican		183	
(19)	Rufus King	Federalist		34	
1820	James Monroe	Democratic-Republican		231	
(24)	John Quincy Adams	Independent Republican		1	
1824	John Quincy Adams	Democratic-Republican	108,740	84	30.5
(24)	Andrew Jackson	Democratic-Republican	153,544	99	43.1
	William H. Crawford	Democratic-Republican	46,618	41	13.1
	Henry Clay	Democratic-Republican	47,136	37	13.2
1828	Andrew Jackson	Democratic	647,286	178	56.0
(24)	John Quincy Adams	National Republican	508,064	83	44.0
1832	Andrew Jackson	Democratic	687,502	219	55.0
(24)	Henry Clay	National Republican	530,189	49	42.4
	William Wirt	Anti-Masonic	} 33,108	7	} 2.6
	John Floyd	National Republican		11	
1836	Martin Van Buren	Democratic	765,483	170	50.9
(26)	William H. Harrison	Whig	}	73	
	Hugh L. White	Whig	} 739,795	26	} 49.1
	Daniel Webster	Whig		14	
	W. P. Mangum	Whig	}	11	

Presidential Elections [1789–1976] [cont.]

Year and number of states	Candidates	Parties	Popular vote	Electoral vote	Percentage of popular vote
1840 (26)	William H. Harrison	Whig	1,274,624	234	53.1
	Martin Van Buren	Democratic	1,127,781	60	46.9
1844 (26)	James K. Polk	Democratic	1,338,464	170	49.6
	Henry Clay	Whig	1,300,097	105	48.1
	James G. Birney	Liberty	62,300		2.3
1848 (30)	Zachary Taylor	Whig	1,360,967	163	47.4
	Lewis Cass	Democratic	1,222,342	127	42.5
	Martin Van Buren	Free-Soil	291,263		10.1
1852 (31)	Franklin Pierce	Democratic	1,601,117	254	50.9
	Winfield Scott	Whig	1,385,453	42	44.1
	John P. Hale	Free-Soil	155,825		5.0
1856 (31)	James Buchanan	Democratic	1,832,955	174	45.3
	John C. Frémont	Republican	1,339,932	114	33.1
	Millard Fillmore	American	871,731	8	21.6
1860 (33)	Abraham Lincoln	Republican	1,865,593	180	39.8
	Stephen A. Douglas	Democratic	1,382,713	12	29.5
	John C. Breckinridge	Democratic	848,356	72	18.1
	John Bell	Constitutional Union	592,906	39	12.6
1864 (36)	Abraham Lincoln	Republican	2,206,938	212	55.0
	George B. McClellan	Democratic	1,803,787	21	45.0
1868 (37)	Ulysses S. Grant	Republican	3,013,421	214	52.7
	Horatio Seymour	Democratic	2,706,829	80	47.3
1872 (37)	Ulysses S. Grant	Republican	3,596,745	286	55.6
	Horace Greeley	Democratic	2,843,446	[2]	43.9
1876 (38)	Rutherford B. Hayes	Republican	4,036,572	185	48.0
	Samuel J. Tilden	Democratic	4,284,020	184	51.0
1880 (38)	James A. Garfield	Republican	4,453,295	214	48.5
	Winfield S. Hancock	Democratic	4,414,082	155	48.1
	James B. Weaver	Greenback-Labor	308,578		3.4
1884	Grover Cleveland	Democratic	4,879,507	219	48.5

[2] Greeley died shortly after the election; the electors supporting him then divided their votes among minor candidates.

Presidential Elections [1789–1976] [cont.]

Year and number of states	Candidates	Parties	Popular vote	Electoral vote	Percentage of popular vote
(38)	James G. Blaine	Republican	4,850,293	182	48.2
	Benjamin F. Butler	Greenback-Labor	175,370		1.8
	John P. St. John	Prohibition	150,369		1.5
1888	Benjamin Harrison	Republican	5,447,129	233	47.9
(38)	Grover Cleveland	Democratic	5,537,857	168	48.6
	Clinton B. Fisk	Prohibition	249,506		2.2
	Anson J. Streeter	Union Labor	146,935		1.3
1892	Grover Cleveland	Democratic	5,555,426	277	46.1
(44)	Benjamin Harrison	Republican	5,182,690	145	43.0
	James B. Weaver	Populist	1,029,846	22	8.5
	John Bidwell	Prohibition	264,133		2.2
1896	William McKinley	Republican	7,102,246	271	51.1
(45)	William J. Bryan	Democratic	6,492,559	176	47.7
1900	William McKinley	Republican	7,218,491	292	51.7
(45)	William J. Bryan	Democratic; Populist	6,356,734	155	45.5
	John C. Wooley	Prohibition	208,914		1.5
1904	Theodore Roosevelt	Republican	7,628,461	336	57.4
(45)	Alton B. Parker	Democratic	5,084,223	140	37.6
	Eugene V. Debs	Socialist	402,283		3.0
	Silas C. Swallow	Prohibition	258,536		1.9
1908	William H. Taft	Republican	7,675,320	321	51.6
(46)	William J. Bryan	Democratic	6,412,294	162	43.1
	Eugene V. Debs	Socialist	420,793		2.8
	Eugene W. Chafin	Prohibition	253,840		1.7
1912	Woodrow Wilson	Democratic	6,296,547	435	41.9
(48)	Theodore Roosevelt	Progressive	4,118,571	88	27.4
	William H. Taft	Republican	3,486,720	8	23.2
	Eugene V. Debs	Socialist	900,672		6.0
	Eugene W. Chafin	Prohibition	206,275		1.4
1916	Woodrow Wilson	Democratic	9,127,695	277	49.4
(48)	Charles E. Hughes	Republican	8,533,507	254	46.2
	A. L. Benson	Socialist	585,113		3.2
	J. Frank Hanly	Prohibition	220,506		1.2

Year and number of states	Candidates	Parties	Popular vote	Electoral vote	Percentage of popular vote
1920 (48)	Warren G. Harding	Republican	16,143,407	404	60.4
	James M. Cox	Democratic	9,130,328	127	34.2
	Eugene V. Debs	Socialist	919,799		3.4
	P. P. Christensen	Farmer-Labor	265,411		1.0
1924 (48)	Calvin Coolidge	Republican	15,718,211	382	54.0
	John W. Davis	Democratic	8,385,283	136	28.8
	Robert M. LaFollette	Progressive	4,831,289	13	16.6
1928 (48)	Herbert C. Hoover	Republican	21,391,993	444	58.2
	Alfred E. Smith	Democratic	15,016,169	87	40.9
1932 (48)	Franklin D. Roosevelt	Democratic	22,809,638	472	57.4
	Herbert C. Hoover	Republican	15,758,901	59	39.7
	Norman Thomas	Socialist	881,951		2.2
1936 (48)	Franklin D. Roosevelt	Democratic	27,752,869	523	60.8
	Alfred M. Landon	Republican	16,674,665	8	36.5
	William Lemke	Union	882,479		1.9
1940 (48)	Franklin D. Roosevelt	Democratic	27,307,819	449	54.8
	Wendell L. Willkie	Republican	22,321,018	82	44.8
1944 (48)	Franklin D. Roosevelt	Democratic	25,606,585	432	53.5
	Thomas E. Dewey	Republican	22,014,745	99	46.0
1948 (48)	Harry S. Truman	Democratic	24,105,812	303	49.5
	Thomas E. Dewey	Republican	21,970,065	189	45.1
	J. Strom Thurmond	States' Rights	1,169,063	39	2.4
	Henry A. Wallace	Progressive	1,157,172		2.4
1952 (48)	Dwight D. Eisenhower	Republican	33,936,234	442	55.1
	Adlai E. Stevenson	Democratic	27,314,992	89	44.4
1956 (48)	Dwight D. Eisenhower	Republican	35,590,472	457	57.6
	Adlai E. Stevenson	Democratic	26,022,752	73	42.1
1960 (50)	John F. Kennedy	Democratic	34,227,096	303	49.9
	Richard M. Nixon	Republican	34,108,546	219	49.6
1964 (50)	Lyndon B. Johnson	Democratic	43,126,506	486	61.1
	Barry M. Goldwater	Republican	27,176,799	52	38.5

Presidential Elections [1789–1976] [cont.]

Year and number of states	Candidates	Parties	Popular vote	Electoral vote	Percentage of popular vote
1968 (50)	Richard M. Nixon	Republican	31,785,480	301	43.4
	Hubert H. Humphrey	Democratic	31,275,165	191	42.7
	George C. Wallace	American Independent	9,906,473	46	13.5
1972 (50)	Richard M. Nixon	Republican	47,167,319	521	60.7
	George S. McGovern	Democratic	29,168,509	17	37.5
	John Schmitz	American Independent	1,080,670		1.4
1976 (50)	Jimmy Carter	Democratic	40,825,839	297	50.1
	Gerald R. Ford	Republican	39,147,770	240	48.0

Population of the United States [1790–1976]*

Year	Total population (in thousands)	Number per square mile of land area (continental United States)	Year	Total population (in thousands)	Number per square mile of land area (continental United States)
1790	3,929	4.5	1933	125,579	
1800	5,308	6.1	1934	126,374	
1810	7,239	4.3	1935	127,250	
1820	9,638	5.5	1936	128,053	
1830	12,866	7.4	1937	128,825	
1840	17,069	9.8	1938	129,825	
1850	23,191	7.9	1939	130,880	
1860	31,443	10.6	1940	132,457	44.2
1870	39,818	13.4	1941	133,669	
1880	50,155	16.9	1942	134,617	
1890	62,947	21.2	1943	135,107	
1900	76,094	25.6	1944	133,915	
1901	77,585		1945	133,434	
1902	79,160		1946	140,686	
1903	80,632		1947	144,083	
1904	82,165		1948	146,730	
1905	83,820		1949	149,304	
1906	85,437		1950	151,868	42.6
1907	87,000		1951	153,982	
1908	88,709		1952	156,393	
1909	90,492		1953	158,956	
1910	92,407	31.0	1954	161,884	
1911	93,868		1955	165,069	
1912	95,331		1956	168,088	
1913	97,227		1957	171,187	
1914	99,118		1958	174,149	
1915	100,549		1959	177,135	
1916	101,966		1960	179,979	50.5
1917	103,266		1961	182,992	
1918	103,203		1962	185,771	
1919	104,512		1963	188,483	
1920	106,466	35.6	1964	191,141	
1921	108,541		1965	193,526	
1922	110,055		1966	195,576	
1923	111,950		1967	197,457	
1924	114,113		1968	199,329	
1925	115,832		1969	201,385	
1926	117,399		1970	203,806	57.5
1927	119,038		1971	206,212	
1928	120,501		1972	208,230	
1929	121,770		1973	209,844	
1930	123,077	41.2	1974	211,400	
1931	124,040		1975	213,100	
1932	124,840		1976	214,700	

* Figures are from *Statistical Abstract of the United States: 1974, 1977*, p. 5. Figures exclude Armed Forces abroad and after 1940 include Alaska and Hawaii.

Admission of States

Order of admission	State	Date of admission
1	Delaware	December 7, 1787
2	Pennsylvania	December 12, 1787
3	New Jersey	December 18, 1787
4	Georgia	January 2, 1788
5	Connecticut	January 9, 1788
6	Massachusetts	February 6, 1788
7	Maryland	April 28, 1788
8	South Carolina	May 23, 1788
9	New Hampshire	June 21, 1788
10	Virginia	June 25, 1788
11	New York	July 26, 1788
12	North Carolina	November 21, 1789
13	Rhode Island	May 29, 1790
14	Vermont	March 4, 1791
15	Kentucky	June 1, 1792
16	Tennessee	June 1, 1796
17	Ohio	March 1, 1803
18	Louisiana	April 30, 1812
19	Indiana	December 11, 1816
20	Mississippi	December 10, 1817
21	Illinois	December 3, 1818
22	Alabama	December 14, 1819
23	Maine	March 15, 1820
24	Missouri	August 10, 1821
25	Arkansas	June 15, 1836
26	Michigan	January 26, 1837
27	Florida	March 3, 1845
28	Texas	December 29, 1845
29	Iowa	December 28, 1846
30	Wisconsin	May 29, 1848
31	California	September 9, 1850
32	Minnesota	May 11, 1858
33	Oregon	February 14, 1859
34	Kansas	January 29, 1861
35	West Virginia	June 30, 1863
36	Nevada	October 31, 1864
37	Nebraska	March 1, 1867
38	Colorado	August 1, 1876
39	North Dakota	November 2, 1889
40	South Dakota	November 2, 1889
41	Montana	November 8, 1889
42	Washington	November 11, 1889
43	Idaho	July 3, 1890
44	Wyoming	July 10, 1890
45	Utah	January 4, 1896
46	Oklahoma	November 16, 1907
47	New Mexico	January 6, 1912
48	Arizona	February 14, 1912
49	Alaska	January 3, 1959
50	Hawaii	August 21, 1959

Picture Credits

Index

Carnegie, Andrew, 318, 352; income, 279; on responsibility of wealth, 281–282; and steel empire, 284, 291, 297

Carnegie, Dale, 442

Carnegie Foundation for International Peace, 491

Carnegie Steel Corporation, 291; Homestead strike (1892), 279, 297–298, 369

Carolina Colony, 15

Carolina Regulators, 40–41

Caroline, steamer, 196

Carpetbaggers, 256

Carranza, Venustiano, 359

Carroll, John, 86

Carswell, G. Harrold, 544

Carter, Jimmy: and economic policy, 541–542; and energy crisis, 543–544; elected President, 548; and political paralysis, 548–551

Carter, Robert, 28

Carteret, George, 20

Cartier, Jacques, 9

Cass, Lewis, 205

Cassatt, Mary, 312

Castro, Fidel, 507, 534; and Bay of Pigs affair, 532–533

Casualties: Revolutionary War, 58; Civil War, 231, 233, 235; First World War, 394; Second World War, 472; Vietnam War, 530

Catherine of Aragon, queen of England, 11

Catholics and Catholic Church: pre-Columbian, 6–7; and conquistadors, 9; and colonization of Maryland, 14–15; in French settlements, 43; population in cities, late 1800s, 313; and birth control, 1920s, 413; and election of 1928, 426; church property confiscated, Mexico, 1920s, 431

Cattle and cattle drives, late 1800s, 308, 309

CCC (Civilian Conservation Corps), 448–449

Censorship of movies, 1920s, 413

Central Intelligence Agency (CIA): and Latin American policy, late twentieth century, 507; and Bay of Pigs, 532; and Watergate, 545

Central Pacific Railroad, 289

Central Treaty Organization (CENTO), 506

Cerro Gordo, Battle of, 202

Chambers, Whittaker, 491–492

Champlain, Samuel de, 42

Chancellorsville, Battle of, 235

Channing, William E., 189

Chaplin, Charlie, 414

Charles I, king of England, 32; and settlement of New England, 14–19

Charles II, king of England, 15, 19–21, 32, 33, 41

Charles River Bridge Co. case, 164–165

Charleston, S.C., Civil War destruction, 258, 259, 262

Chase, Salmon P., 227, 228

Chattanooga, Battles of, 233

Cherokee Nation v. *Georgia*, 156

Chesapeake, frigate, 131

Cheves, Langdon, 133, 161

Chiang Kai-shek, 474, 491; and fall of China, 501–502

Chicago: post-Civil War, 276; Haymarket riot (1886), 296; World's Columbian Exposition (1893), 311, 312; population, late 1800s, 313; race riot (1919), 416; demonstration (1968), 525–526

Child labor: textile factories, early 1800s, 182–183; Supreme Court rulings on, 381, 424; abolished, 451

China: immigration forbidden from, 319; Open Door in, 353–356; Japan invades (1937), 465; and diplomacy of Grand Alliance, 473–474; Communist takeover, 491, 501–502; and Korean War, 504–505; U.S. relations with, early 1970s, 533–534; admitted to UN, 534

Chou En-lai, 534

Chrysler Corp., 452

Church of England: establishment of, 11; and colonization of New England, 16–17; clergymen's salary and tobacco prices, 54; post-Revolution, 85–86

Church of Jesus Christ of Latter Day Saints, 186

Churchill, Winston: and Destroyer deal, 466; and Atlantic Charter, 467; and diplomacy of Grand Alliance, 472–476; iron curtain statement, 488

CIA. *See* Central Intelligence Agency

CIO (Congress of Industrial Organizations), 451–452

Circular Letter, 58

Cities: colonial, 38–39; in post-Civil War South, 262; immigrants, late 1800s, 277; growth of, 313–314; political machines, late 1800s, 314; women in, 315–317; political machines, early twentieth century, 364; and jazz, 415; race riots, post-First World War, 416; and election of 1928, 427; blacks in, post-Second World War, 498–499; riots, 1960s, 519–522, 554; population, 1970s, 556

Civil disobedience, and civil rights movement, 518

Civilian Conservation Corps (CCC), 448–449

Civil rights: post-Civil War cases, 267–268; post-Second World War movement, 498–501; 1960s movement, 517–522

Civil Rights Act (1875), 268

Civil Rights Act (1957), 501

Civil Rights Act (1964), 501

Civil Rights Bill (1866), 252

Civil service: and graft in Grant administration, 325–326; reform (1883), 326–327; Federal Employee Loyalty Program, 493

Civil Service Commission, 326

Civil War: begins, 230–233; casualties, 231, 233;

and Emancipation Proclamation, 233−235; Southern defeat, 235−237; economy, 237−238; conclusion, 237−240; *See also* Reconstruction

Civil Works Administration (CWA), 449

Clark, George Rogers, 79

Clark, William, 128

Clark Memorandum on Roosevelt Corollary, 431

Clay, Henry, 160, 161, 167, 188, 195; and War of 1812, 133, 134, 137; and Missouri Compromise, 145; and election of 1824, 151−152; as secretary of state, 152−154; and his "American system," 152; and election of 1844, 199−200; and Compromise of 1850, 207−209

Clay, Laura, 369

Clayton Antitrust Act (1914), 381, 424

Clayton-Bulwer Treaty (1850), 212, 357

Cleaver, Eldridge, 521

Clemenceau, Georges, 402, 403

Cleveland, Grover: and Pullman strike, 298, 336; and immigration, 319; elected President, 324; and tariff reform, 327, 328; and depression of 1893, 334−335; and election of 1896, 337; and beginnings of empire, 347−349, 352

Clinton, DeWitt, 134−135

Clinton, George, 95, 127

Clinton, Henry, 79, 81

Clipper ships, 173−174

Cody, William (Buffalo Bill), 303, 306

Cohens v. *Virginia*, 139

Coin's Financial School, 336

Cold Harbor, Battle of, 236

Cold War: beginnings, 487−491; and Korean War, 501−505; containment in Asia, 505−506; containment in Third World, 506−507; containment in Latin America, 507; and Eisenhower administration, 507−508; in 1960s, 530−534

College of William and Mary, 37

Colleges and universities: in colonies, 37−38; post-Revolution, 86; land grants to, 238; education for women in, 317; *See also* Education

Colombia, and Panama Canal, 357

Colonies: European context, 6−7; and early exploration, 7−11; in South, 12−16; in New England, 16−19; in middle Atlantic region, 19−22; economy, 26−30; commerce and manufacturing, 30−34; society in, 34−39; politics in, 38−42; French and Indian War, 42−46; and contest for empire, 42−46; in West, conflicting interests, 51−53; commerce and currency, 53−54; taxation, 54−61; and Coercive Acts, 61−63; intellectual origins of Revolution, 63−64; and first Continental Congress, 65; road to rebellion, 66−67; independence declared, 67−70

Colorado: gold discovered in, 307; suffrage for women, 1890s, 368

Columbia, S.C., Civil War destruction, 259

Columbia University, 37, 38

Columbus, Christopher, 6, 9

Combinations: vertical, in industry, 291; and Sherman Act, 293

Commerce: and colonization, 6−7; and manufacturing, colonies, 30−34; and currency, 53−54; *See also* Trade

Commerce Department, under H. Hoover, 423−424

Committee on Public Information (CPI), 398

Committees of correspondence, 60

Committee to Defend America by Aiding the Allies, 466

Committee to Reelect the President (CREEP), 545

Common Sense (Paine), 67

Commonwealthmen, 64

Commonwealth v. *Hunt* (1842), 183

Communism: and McCarthyism, 491−494; *See also* Cold War; Soviet Union

Community Action Programs, 516

Compromise of 1850, 206−210; and Fugitive Slave Law, 210−212

Comstock Lode, 308

Concord, Battle of, 66

Confederate States of America, 229; Gettysburg and road to defeat, 235−237; economy, 237; draft, 238; *See also* Civil War; Reconstruction; South

Confederation of New England, 41

Conflict: in western colonies, 51−53; sectional, 202−206; territorial, 217−220

Congregationalists, 35; and post-Revolution religious reform, 86; and women's rights, early 1800s, 188

Congress: as Constitutional Convention issue, 93; first, 104−105; prohibits slavery in territories (1787), 123; and Louisiana Purchase, 127; and Embargo Act (1807), 131; and War of 1812, 133; and Treaty of Ghent, 137; Jacksonian strategy, 1820s, 153−154; renews BUS charter, 162; Calhoun on, 194; Reconstruction plans, 250−253; Billion-Dollar, 328; Senate as graveyard of reform, early twentieth century, 365; and power of Speaker, 376−377; and Versailles Treaty (1919), 403−406; farm bloc, 1920s, 422; McCarthy censured, 493; and Truman administration, 495−496; and Eisenhower administration, 498; and Watergate, 547; and political paralysis, 1970s, 548−550

Congress of Industrial Organizations (CIO), 451−452

Congress of the Confederation, 96

Conkling, Roscoe, 325

Connecticut: settlement, 19; ratifies Constitution, 94

Connor, Eugene (Bull), 518

Conquistadors, 9

Conscription: South, Civil War, 237; North, Civil War, 238; in First World War, 393; opposition to, in First World War, 397; in Second World War, 466; in Vietnam War, 523, 554

Conservation: Ballinger-Pinchot controversy, 377; New Deal programs on, 448–449; and energy crisis, 543; environmental issues, 1970s, 551

Constitution, ship, 135

Constitution, U.S.: making of, 91–94; ratification, 94–96; text of (Appendix), A-5–A-21; *See also* Congress; Constitutional amendments; Government; States

Constitutional amendments, 137; Bill of Rights, 105; First, 118; Twelfth, 152; Thirteenth, 247; Fourteenth, 267–268, 424; Fifteenth, 253, 266; Eighteenth, 403; Nineteenth, 369, 370, 413; Equal Rights, 550; *See also* Constitution

Constitutional Convention, 91–96

Constitutional Union party, 227

Consumer price index, and inflation, 542

Containment: post-Second World War policy of, 488–489, 505–508

Continental Association, 65

Continental Congress: first, 65; second, 66–67

Convention of 1800, 118

Convention of 1818, 195

Coolidge, Calvin, 381, 416, 420; becomes President, 421; use of veto, 423; elected in 1924, 426

Cooper, James Fenimore, 189

Cooperatives, agricultural, 331–332

Cope, Francis, 243n

Copperheads, 238

Coral Sea, Battle of, 468

Cornbury, Lord, 39

Cornwallis, Lord, 79, 81

Coronado, Francisco, 9

Corporations: early 1800s, 183–184; and mining, 308; and land policy in West, 310; *See also* Business; Industrialization; Industry; Manufacturing

Corruption. *See* Graft and corruption

Cortés, Hernando, 9

Corwin, Thomas, 202

Cosmopolitan magazine, 365

Cotton: and slavery, early 1800s, 176–177; and textile industry, 182; manufacturing, 185; prices (1857), 224; foreign competition, post-Civil War, 331

Cotton Club, 416

Coughlin, Charles, 453

Council for New England, 16

Counterculture, 513; and culture, 552–555

Cox, Archibald, 546

Cox, James M., 418

Coxey, Jacob, 337

CPI (Committee on Public Information), 398

Crawford, William, 151, 152, 154

Crazy Horse, Indian chief, 305

Crédit Mobilier, 326

CREEP (Committee to Reelect the President), 545

Crèvecoeur, Hector St. John de, 34

"Crime Against Kansas, The" (Sumner), 220

Crisis, The (journal), 366

Critical Period of American History, The (Fiske), 87

Crittenden, John J., 230

Cromwell, Oliver, 32

Crusades, 7

Cuba: and expansion, mid-1800s, 212; annexation proposed, 346; and Spanish-American War, 349–352; Castro takes over, 507; and Bay of Pigs affair, 522, 532; and missile crisis, 532

Culture: of transcendental age, 189–191; late 1800s, 277–280; and Chicago World's Columbian Exposition (1893), 312; popular, 1920s, 413–416; blacks, jazz age, 416; and counterculture, 552–555; *See also* Society

Currency: colonies, 33; and commerce, 53–54; post-Revolution, 89–90; and greenbacks, Civil War, 238; flexible, 328–330; battle of standards, 337–340; and rediscount rate, 380–381

Currency Act (1764), 54

Currency Act (1900), 340

Curtis, Benjamin, 222–223

Custer, George Armstrong, 305, 306

Customs, and colonial taxation, 54–55, 57, 60

CWA (Civil Works Administration), 449

Czechoslovakia: Hitler annexes, 463; Soviets intervene, 533

D

Darlan, Jean, 474

Dartmouth College case, 139–140

Darwin, Charles, 282

Daugherty, Harry, 420

Daughters of the American Revolution, 285

Davis, Jefferson: and Gadsden Purchase, 212; as President of Confederacy, 229, 230

Davis, John V., 426

Dawes, Charles G., 430, 439

Dawes Act (1887), 307

Dawes Plan, 430

Deane, Silas, 79

Debs, Eugene V., 279, 298, 397

Fair Labor Standards Act (1938), 451

Fall, Albert, B., 421

Fallen Timbers, Battle of, 113

Families: colonial, 34–35; of slaves, 178; in 1970s, 557; *See also* Culture; Society

Family Assistance Plan, 544

Farewell to Arms, A (Hemingway), 411

Farley, James A., 454

Farm bloc, 422

Farmers' Alliance, 331, 332

Farm Loan Act (1916), 382

Farms and farmers: early 1800s, 174–176; sharecropping, post-Civil War South, 260–263; decline, late 1800s, 277; and railroad freight rates, 288; and western economy, 309–310; on Great Plains, 310–311; First World War prosperity, 396; Wilson's legislation for (1916), 382; economic crisis, 1920s, 422–423; and Eisenhower policy, 497–498; *See also* Agriculture

Farm Security Administration (FSA), 447

Farragut, David, 233

Faubus, Orval, 499–500

FDIC (Federal Deposit Insurance Corp.), 444

Federal Bureau of Investigation (FBI), and Watergate, 545

Federal Deposit Insurance Corporation (FDIC), 444

Federal Emergency Relief Administration (FERA), 449

Federal Employee Loyalty Program (1947), 493

Federal Farm Board (1929), 437

Federalism, of Hamilton, 122

Federalist, The (Hamilton, Jay, and Madison), 94

Federalists: and ratification of Constitution, 94–95; vs. Republicans, 109–110; foreign policy, 110; and election of 1796, 114–115; and Adams administration, 115–119; High, 117; and election of 1800, 118–119, 122; legacy, 119–120; and Burr conspiracy, 127; and election of 1808, 132–133; and election of 1812, 134–135; and Essex Junto, 136–137

Federal Land Bank, 438

Federal Reserve Act (1913), 380, 381, 382

Federal Reserve Board, 380–381, 434, 443

Federal Trade Commission, 381

Feminists, and suffrage for women, 367–368; *See also* Women

FERA (Federal Emergency Relief Administration), 449

Ferdinand of Aragon, king of Spain, 8

Feudalism: and colonial economy, 27–28; and post-Revolutionary reform, 84

Fields, W. C., 414

Fillmore, Millard: becomes President, 209; and election of 1856, 221

Finney, Charles Grandison, 186

Fire Next Time, The (Baldwin), 521

First World War: outbreak of, 387–388; and U.S. isolation, 388–389; submarines and U.S. entry into, 389–393; mobilization, 393–396; on home front, 396–399; and Wilson's Fourteen Points, 399–401; and Treaty of Versailles, 401–406

Fishing industry, colonies, 31

Fisk, Jim, 326

Fiske, John, 87

Fitzgerald, F. Scott, 411

Five Power Pact (1921), 428

Fletcher, Benjamin, 28

Fletcher v. *Peck*, 139

Florida: assigned to England by Spain, 46; border dispute, 1780s, 89; northern boundary established (1795), 114; plans to buy western segment, 130; western reaches annexed, 140; Jackson's raid on (1818), 140; ceded to United States (1819), 141; secedes, 229; real estate speculation in, 1920s, 435

Florida, ship, 235

Flynn, Elizabeth Gurley, 413

Following the Color Line (Baker), 366

Food Administration, 396

Forbes, Charles, 421

Forbes, John, 45

Force Act (1833), 160

Force Acts (1870, 1871), 264

Ford, Gerald: and Vietnam War, 530; economic policy, 541; named Vice-President, 545; and political paralysis, 547–548; and election of 1976, 548

Ford, Henry, 410–411, 445, 452

Ford, John, 414

Ford Motor Company, labor, 1920s, 421–422

Foreign policy: post-Revolution, 87–89, 110–112; Jay Treaty, 112–115; conflict with France, 115–118; Jefferson's, 128–132; Louisiana Purchase, 129–130; post-Civil War, 342–343; China relations, turn of century, 353–356; Western Hemisphere, early twentieth century, 357–360; dollar diplomacy of Taft, 359; and isolation, 1920s, 428–431; Good Neighbor, 430, 460–461; neutrality, Second World War, 461–463; Second World War, 472–476; Grand Alliance, 473–474; containment, post-Second World War, 488–489; non-Vietnam, late twentieth century, 530–535; *See also* Cold War; Empire; Expansion; First World War; Second World War; Vietnam War

Formosa. *See* Taiwan

Fort Donelson, Battle of, 232

Fort Duquesne, 45

Fort Henry, Battle of, 232

Fort Hill Address (Calhoun), 159

Fort Louisburg, Battle of, 44, 45

Fort Necessity, 44

Fort Oswego, 44
Fort Stanwix, 79
Fort Sumter, 229, 230
Fort Wayne, Treaty of (1809), 134
Fort William Henry, 44
Fourier, Charles, 187
Four Power Pact (1921), 429
Fourteen Points, of Wilson, 399−401, 467
Fox, George, 37
France: early U.S. exploration, 8−10; and contest for empire, 42−46; cedes Louisiana territory to Spain, 46; recognizes U.S. independence, 79; relations with, post-Revolution, 89, 110−112; seizure of ships, late 1700s, 114; conflict with, 115−118; Spain cedes Louisiana to (1800), 129; war with Britain, early 1800s, 130−131; blockade of ports, 131; and Civil War, 235; and Open Door in China, 353; and Versailles Treaty, 402, 403; Hitler invades, 465; Normandy invasion, Second World War, 470; and diplomacy of Grand Alliance, 474; Indochina conflict, 505−506; and Mideast conflict (1956), 507
Francis I, king of France, 9
Franco, Francisco, 462−463
Franklin, Benjamin: and Philadelphia Academy, 38; and French and Indian War, 46; and colonial relations with Britain, 51; and Stamp Act, 56; and Treaty of Paris, 82; and Constitutional Convention, 91, 93
Freedmen's Bureau (1865), 247, 252
Freedmen's Bureau Bill (1866), 252
Freedom of the press, in colonies, 38
Freedom rides, 518
Free French forces, 474
Freeport Doctrine (1858), 225, 227
Free-Soilers, 188; and election of 1848, 205, 206; and Kansas-Nebraska Act, 218−220
Freight rates: and canals, 172; railroads, mid-1800s, 173; railroads, late 1800s, 287−288
Frelinghuysen, Theodore, 36
Frémont, John C., 202, 221, 277
French and Indian War, 42−46
French Indochina. *See* Indochina; Vietnam War
French Revolution, 110, 111
Frick, Henry Clay, 297
Friedan, Betty, 551
Fries Rebellion (1799), 117
Frontier: and settlement of West, early 1800s, 128; Canadian, early 1800s, 195−196; end of, 310−311
FSA (Farm Security Administration), 447
Fuel Administration, 395
Fugitive Slave Law (1850), 209; and breakdown of Compromise of 1850, 210−212
Fulbright, J. William, 522

Fuller, Margaret, 189
Fundamental Orders of Connecticut, 19

G

Gadsden Purchase, 212
Gage, Thomas, 63
Gallatin, Albert, 113, 126−127, 137
Galloway, Joseph, 63, 65
Gama, Vasco da, 7
Gardoqui, Don Diego de, 89
Garfield, Harry, 395
Garfield, James A., 324, 326; and southern voting violations, 266
Garland, Hamlin, 312
Garrison, William Lloyd, 187, 188
Garvey, Marcus, 416
Gary, E. H., 374
Gaspee, revenue cutter, 60
General Motors Corp., 452
Genêt, Edmond, 111
Geneva conference on Vietnam (1954), 530
Geneva summit meeting (1955), 508
Genovese, Eugene, 181
Gentlemen's Agreement (1908), 356
George, Henry, 453
George III, king of England, 45, 51, 52, 56, 64, 81
Georgia: colonization, 15−16; colonial agriculture, 27; government established, 83; currency, post-Revolution, 90; ratifies Constitution, 94; secedes, 229; Sherman's march through, 235−236
Gerard, James W., 390
Germans, immigrants to colonies, 34
Germany: and Open Door in China, 353; peace proposal (1916), 392−393; and Versailles Treaty, 401−403; defaults on reparations payments (1923), 430; and Yalta agreement, 475−476; and Cold War, 490−491; *See also* First World War; Second World War
Geronimo, Indian chief, 306
Gerry, Elbridge, 115, 116
Gershwin, George, 415
Gettysburg, Battle of, 235
Ghent, Treaty of (1815), 137
Gibbons v. *Ogden*, 139
GI Bill of Rights (1944), 480, 494
Gilbert, Humphrey, 11
Glass, Senator, 429
Glassboro summit meeting (1967), 533
Glass-Steagall Act (1933), 444
Glorious Revolution (1688), 41
Gold: colonial currency, 33; and western economy, late 1800s, 307, 308; and flexible currency, 328, 330

Goldman, Emma, 413

Gold Rush, The (film), 414

Gold standard: and Hoover's economic policy, 438; New Deal policy on, 444

Goldwater, Barry, 515

Gompers, Samuel, 296, 297, 371, 381, 396, 453

Gone with the Wind (Mitchell), 442

Good Neighbor policy in Latin America, 430, 460–461

GOP (Grand Old Party). *See* Republican party

Gorges, Fernando, 16

Gospel of Wealth, 282

Gould, Jay, 286, 296, 326

Graft and corruption: during Reconstruction, 257–258; and growth of cities, late 1800s, 314; and civil service in Grant administration, 325–327; in Harding administration, 421

Grafton, Duke of, 57

Grain. *See* Wheat

Grand Alliance, diplomacy of, 473–476

Grandfather clause, in disfranchising blacks, 267

Grand Old Party (GOP). *See* Republican party

Grange and Granger laws, 290

Grant, Ulysses S., 305; in Civil War, 232–233, 235, 236; elected President, 324; administration, 325–326, 346

Grasse, Comte de, 79

Great Awakening, 36–37

Great Britain: Coercive Acts (1774), 61–63; relations with, post-Revolution, 110–112; Jay Treaty, 112–114; war with France, early 1800s, 130–131; and impressment, 131; industrial depression (1810), 133; and War of 1812, 133, 134–137; and Monroe's policy in Latin America, 142–143; and Webster-Ashburton Treaty (1842), 196; and Civil War, 235; and Venezuelan boundary dispute (1895), 347–349; and Open Door in China, 353; and U.S. neutrality, pre-Second World War, 466; and Mideast conflict (1956), 507; *See also* England

Great Depression: begins, 435–436; Hoover acts, 436–439; FDR takes over, 439–442; outside Washington, 442–443; *See also* Depression; Economy; New Deal; Panic

Greater East Asia Co-Prosperity Sphere, 464

Great Migration, 18

Great Plains: and Indians, 303–307; farming on, 310–311

Greece: revolt (1820), 143; and Truman Doctrine, 489

Greeley, Horace, 220, 234, 303, 324

Greenbacks. *See* Currency

Greensboro, N.C., civil rights protests, 501, 518

Greenville, Treaty of (1795), 114

Greer, ship, 467

Grenville, George, 54, 55, 56

Grenville, Lord, and Jay Treaty, 112, 113

Gresham, Walter O., 344

Grew, Joseph C., 467–468

Grey, Edward, 392

Griffin, Cyrus, 96

Griffith, D. W., 256

Grimké, Angelina, 188

Grimké, Sarah, 188

Grundy, Felix, 133

Guadalcanal, Battle of, 468

Guadeloupe, England returns island to France, 46

Guadalupe-Hidalgo, Treaty of (1848), 202

Guam, and Spanish-American War, 352

Guatemala, relations with (1954), 507

Guffey Coal Act (1935), 446

H

Hague conference, 388

Haiti, intervention in, 359

Haldeman, H. R., 545, 547

Half-Breeds, in Republican party, 325

Half-Way Covenant (1662), 35

Hamilton, Alexander: and Constitutional Convention, 91; and *Federalist* papers, 94; as secretary of Treasury, 105–109; and Federalists, 109–110; and French Revolution, 111; and foreign policy, 112; and election of 1796, 114–115; and Adams administration, 115; and election of 1800, 118–119; duel with Burr, 127

Hammer v. *Dagenhart*, 381

Hammond, James H., 224

Hancock, John, 95

Hanna, Mark, 338, 339, 353

Harding, Warren G., 381; elected President, 419; cabinet, 420–421; and diplomacy of isolation, 428

Harlan, John Marshall, 291; on segregation, 268

Harlem Renaissance, 416

Harper's Ferry, John Brown's raid at, 225–226

Harriman, Averell, on Vietnam, 522

Harriman, E. H., 373

Harris, Townsend, 212

Harrison, Benjamin, 324, 327, 328, 352

Harrison, William Henry, 134, 166, 167

Hartford Convention (1814–15), 136–137

Harvard University, 37, 317, 370

Hat Act (1732), 31

Havana, Act of (1940), 461

Hawaii: naval base at Pearl Harbor, 346, 356; annexation (1898), 347; Pearl Harbor bombed, 468

Hawley-Smoot Tariff (1930), 437

Hawthorne, Nathaniel, 187, 189

Hay, John, 345, 351, 357; and Open Door in China, 353–355

Hay-Bunau-Varilla Treaty (1903), 357

Hayes, Rutherford B.: elected President, 255–256; and silver coinage, 330

Hay-Herrán Treaty (1902), 357

Haymarket riot (1886), 296

Hayne, Robert Y., 157–158, 159

Hays, Will, 413

Hays Office, 413

Head right system, 13, 28

Head Start project, 516

Hearst, William Randolph, 351

Hemingway, Ernest, 411

Henry, Patrick, 54, 56, 66, 91, 94

Henry the Navigator, prince of Portugal, 7

Henry VII, king of England, 9

Henry VIII, king of England, 9, 11

Hepburn, Katherine, 414

Hepburn Act (1906), 372, 376

Herrán, Thomás, 357

Hessians, 77

Higher Education Act (1965), 516–517

Highway Act (1956), 494

Hill, Isaac, 154

Hill, James J., 286, 373

Hillman, Sidney, 451

Hillsborough, Lord, 58

Hiroshima, atomic bombing of, 472, 488

Hispanics, rights movement, 553

Hiss, Alger, 491–492

History of England (Rapin), 38

Hitler, Adolf: invades Rhineland, 462; occupies Austria, 463; annexes Czechoslovakia, 463; suicide, 471; *See also* Second World War

Hoe, Richard, 185

HOLC (Home Owners Loan Corp.), 443

Holden v. *Hardy*, 371

Holder, Christopher, 21

Holland. *See* Netherlands

Holmes, Oliver Wendell, 189

Home front: in Civil War, 237–240; in First World War, 396–399; in Second World War, 476–480

Home Owners Loan Corp. (HOLC, 1933), 443

Homer, Winslow, 312

Homestead Act (1862), 183, 247, 310, 311

Homestead strike (1892), 279, 297–298, 369

Homosexuals, rights movement, 551

Hooker, Thomas, 19

Hoover, Herbert, 420, 434; and Food Administration, 396; and laissez faire, 423–424; elected President, 427; economic policy, 436–439; defeated in 1932, 439–440; foreign policy, 460

Hoovervilles, 436

Hopkins, Harry, 449

House, Edward, 392, 404

House Committee on Un-American Activities, and McCarthyism, 491–492

House Judiciary Committee, and Watergate, 547

House of Burgesses, Virginia, 13

Housing: and HOLC, 1930s, 443; and tax policy, post-Second World War, 494

Houston, Sam, 198, 217

Howard University, 434

Howe, Elias, 185

Howe, William, 77

Howells, William Dean, 312, 313

How to Win Friends and Influence People (D. Carnegie), 442

Hudson, Henry, 20

Huerta, Victoriano, 359

Hughes, Charles Evans, 382, 418, 428

Huguenots, immigrants to colonies, 34

Hull, Cordell, 460

Hull House, 317

Humphrey, Hubert, 526–527

Hundred days, of FDR, 442, 448

Hungary, uprising (1956), 507–508

Hutchinson, Anne, 19

Hutchinson, Thomas, 56, 59, 61

I

ICC. *See* Interstate Commerce Commission

Ickes, Harold L., 444

Idaho: gold discovered in, 307; suffrage for women, 1890s, 368

ILGWU (International Ladies Garment Workers Union), 367

Illinois: statehood, 128, 149; and Mormons, early 1800s, 186; *See also* Chicago

Illinois Central Railroad, 259

Immigrants and immigration: to colonies, 34; late 1800s, 277, 317–320; post-First World War, 418; illegal aliens, 552

Immigration and Naturalization Service, 552

Impeachment: constitutional provision for, 93; of Andrew Johnson, 253; of Richard Nixon, 547

Imperialism. *See* Empire

Impressment of sailors, early 1800s, 112, 131

Incas, subjugation of, 9

Inchon landing, 503

Income: per capita, post-Civil War South, 263; rich vs. poor, late 1800s, 278–279; farmers, late 1800s, 330–331; national, early 1930s, 435; guaranteed annual, 1930s plans, 453–454; black-white gap, late twentieth century, 516; guaranteed, Nixon's plan, 544; late 1970s, 555

Income distribution: late 1920s, 435; and New Deal, 441

Income tax: Civil War, 238; ruled unconstitutional (1895), 328; Populists' proposal for, 332; in 1896, 337; in Wisconsin, early twentieth century, 365; of 1913, 380; in Second World War, 470; *See also* Tax and taxation

Indentured servants, 13

Independent Treasury, 164, 167, 204

Indiana, statehood, 149

Indian Bureau, 325

Indian Removal Act (1830), 157

Indians: pre-Columbian, 4—7; and Spanish conquerors, 9; French and Indian War, 42—46; conflicts in West, 1760s, 51—53; Battle of Fallen Timbers and Treaty of Greenville, 113—114; Battle of Tippecanoe and Treaty of Fort Wayne, 134; and Jackson's raid on Florida (1818), 140—141; resettlement, early 1800s, 156—157; and entrepreneurial morality, 283; and Great Plains, 303—307; rights movement, 1970s, 552

Indian Territory, 217

Indigo, colonial crop, 27

Indochina: Japan occupies, 467; conflicts, 1950s, 505—506; *See also* Vietnam War

Industrialization: early 1800s, 181—185; late 1800s, 277—280; and opportunity, 280—283; and social mobility, 284—285; railroads, 285—288; *See also* Industry; Manufacturing

Industrial revolution, early 1800s, 185

Industrial Workers of the World (IWW), 383, 417

Industry: economic organization, late 1800s, 291—294; production, First World War, 395—396; post-First World War, 417; production, Second World War, 469—470; *See also* Business; Corporations; Industrialization; Manufacturing

Inflation: mid-1830s, 163; and flexible currency, 328, 330; late twentieth century, 540—542; *See also* Depression; Economy

Influence of Sea Power upon History, The (Mahan), 345

Inness, George, 312

Institutes of the Christian Religion (Calvin), 6

Internal improvements, 138, 153, 171, 444; Jefferson and, 127; and Henry Clay's "American system," 152, 167; Jackson and, 156; canals, 170, 171—172; roads, 171, 494

Internal Revenue Service, and Watergate, 545

International Ladies Garment Workers Union (ILGWU), 367

Interstate Commerce Act (1887), 290, 327

Interstate Commerce Commission (ICC), 290—291, 372, 373, 376, 417; and desegregation, 518

Inventing America (Wills), 65

Inventions and manufacturing, early 1800s, 185

Irish: immigrants to colonies, 34; immigrants, late 1800s, 277

Irish Americans, and First World War, 387, 404

Iron Act (1750), 31

Iron curtain, 488, 491

Iron Horse, The (film), 414

Irving, Washington, 124, 189

Isabella, queen of Spain, 8

Isolation: diplomacy of, 1920s, 428—431; in 1930s, 461—463; and beginning of Second World War, 465—468

Israel, and Mideast conflict (1956), 506—507

Italy, and Open Door in China, 353; and Versailles Treaty, 403; invades Ethiopia, 462; Allies invade, Second World War, 470

Iwo Jima, Battle of, 472

IWW (Industrial Workers of the World), 383, 417

J

Jackson, Andrew (Old Hickory): at Battle of New Orleans, 135, 137; raid on Florida (1818), 140; and election of 1824, 151—152; elected President, 154—155; Indian policy, 156—157; and nullification, 157—160; vs. Bank of the United States, 161—163; compared with Emerson, 190; and election of 1844, 199

Jackson, Rachel, 155

Jackson, Thomas J. (Stonewall), 233, 235

Jackson State College, antiwar demonstration (1970), 529

Jacobs, Wilbur, 5

James, Duke of York, 20

James I, king of England, 12, 13, 17

James II, king of England, 22, 41, 42

Jamestown settlement, 12

Japan: and Perry expedition, 212, 213; and Open Door in China, 353—356; and Versailles Treaty, 403; resigns from League of Nations, 464; invades China (1937), 465; occupies French Indochina, 467; atomic bombing of, 472, 488; economy (1976), 542; *See also* Second World War

Japanese: segregation in San Francisco schools (1906), 356; internment, Second World War, 477

Jaworski, Leon, 546

Jay, John: and Treaty of Paris, 82; negotiations with Spain, 89; and *Federalist* papers, 94; as chief justice, 105; and Jay Treaty, 112—115

Jay Treaty (1794), 112—115

Jazz age, 410, 411—416

Jazz Singer, The (film), 414

Jefferson, Peter, 38

Jefferson, Thomas: book collection, 38; and rights of British America, 64; and Declaration of Independence, 68–70; and *Notes on Virginia*, 83; and land reform, 84; and Statute for Religious Liberty, 86; and Constitutional Convention, 91; as secretary of state, 105; on national bank, 108; and Republicans, 109; and French Revolution, 111; elected Vice-President, 115; elected President, 118–119, 122; policies and principles, 124–128; reelected in 1804, 127; foreign policy, 128–132

Jehovah's Witnesses, 397

Jenkins, Robert, 44

Jews, 277, 411, 453; immigrants to colonies, 34; and anti-Semitism, 285, 462; immigration quotas and, late 1800s, 418; and the USSR, 459; and Israeli-Arab conflicts, 506–507

Jim Crow laws, 270

Job Corps, 516

John I, king of Portugal, 7

Johnson, Andrew: Reconstruction plans, 249–250; and Congressional Reconstruction plans, 250–253; impeached, 253

Johnson, Hiram, 365, 405

Johnson, Hugh, 444, 445

Johnson, Lyndon B.: and Civil Rights Acts, 501; as President, 514–517; Great Society, 514–517; and civil rights, 518–522; and Vietnam War, 522–525; and foreign policy, 532

Johnson, Richard M., 133

Johnson, Tom, 364

Johnson Act (1934), 459

Johnston, Albert Sidney, 233

Joliet, Louis, 43

Jolson, Al, 415

Jones, Samuel M. (Golden Rule), 364

Joplin, Scott, 415

Joseph, Nez Percé chief, 305

Judiciary Act (1789), 105

Judiciary Act (1801), 126

Jungle, The (Sinclair), 365

Justice Department, 293, 446

K

Kansas: and Kansas-Nebraska Act (1854), 217–220; and Lecompton Constitution (1857), 223–224

Kansas-Nebraska Act (1854), 217–220

Keating-Owen Act (1916), 381

Keaton, Buster, 414

Kellogg, Frank, 429

Kellogg-Briand Pact (1928), 429, 464

Kendall, Amos, 154

Kennan, George, 488–489

Kennedy, John F.: as President, 514–517; and civil rights, 517–518; and Vietnam War, 522–523; foreign policy, 531–533

Kennedy, Robert F., 517–518, 526

Kent State University, antiwar demonstration (1970), 529, 554

Kentucky Resolutions, 118

Kerner, Otto, 521

Kerner Commission, 521

Key, David M., 256

Keynes, John Maynard, 455

Khrushchev, Nikita: and Geneva summit (1955), 508; and U-2 incident, 508; and Cold War, 1960s, 532–533

King, Martin Luther, Jr., 501, 513, 521

King, Rufus, 140, 145

King George's War, 44

King Philip's War, 36, 41

King William's War, 43

Kipling, Rudyard, 342, 343

Kissinger, Henry, 529, 533

Kleindienst, Richard, 546

Knickerbocker Trust, 380

Knights of Labor, 295–296, 331, 334, 367

Know-Nothings (American party), 195, 220, 221

Knox, Henry, 105

Konoye, Fumimaro, 467

Korea, and Open Door, 355, 356

Korean War, 501–505

Kosygin, Aleksei, 533

Ku Klux Klan: in post-Civil War South, 264–266; revival, 1920s, 418, 419; and election of 1928, 426

Ku Klux Klan Acts (1870, 1871), 264

L

Labor: Virginia, 1600s, 13; and indentured servants, 28, 30; and factory system, early 1800s, 181–184; in post-Civil War South, 262; convict, 264, 266; economic organization, late 1800s, 294–298; women in work force, 314–317; contract, and immigrants, 318; post-First World War, 417; living standards, 1920s, 421–422; and unions, 1930s, 450–453; in Second World War, 470; and Taft-Hartley Act, 495; *See also* Labor unions; Unemployment; Wages; Workday

Labor unions: early 1800s, 183; late 1800s, 294–298; women in, 367; Supreme Court rulings on, early twentieth century, 371; in 1930s, 450–453; and Taft-Hartley Act, 495; *See also* American Federation of Labor; *individual labor unions;* Labor; Strikes

Ladd, William, 186

LaFayette, Marquis de, 77

LaFollette, Robert M.: and election of 1924, 297, 426–427; progressive legislation in Wisconsin, 365; and ICC, 372–373; and election of 1912, 377–378

LaFollette Seaman's Act (1915), 381

343; intervention in, 359; diplomatic relations with, 1920s, 430–431

Merchant Marine Act (1920), 417

Middle colonies, settlement, 19–22

Middle East, 539, 542–543; Arab-Israeli conflict (1956), 506–507

Midway Island, Battle of, 468

Milan Decree (1807), 130

Miller, William, 186

Millerites, 186

Mills Bill (1888), 327

Mining, and western economy, late 1800s, 307, 308

Minorities: rising consciousness, 551–552; *See also* Blacks; Hispanics

Missionaries, and expansion, post-Civil War, 345

Mississippi: statehood, 128; secession, 229; anti-black legislation, post-Civil War, 250; voting, 266

Mississippi, University of, desegregation crisis (1962), 518

Mississippi River, 89, 114; and steamboat, 172; Union control of, 233

Missouri, statehood, 144–145, 149

Missouri Compromise (1820), 144–145, 204; and Kansas-Nebraska Act, 218

Mitchell, John (union leader), 371

Mitchell, John (attorney general), 545, 546, 547

Mitchell, Margaret, 442

Moby Dick (Melville), 189

Molasses Act (1733), 33

Molotov, Vyacheslav, 487

Mondale, Walter, 542

Monroe, James: as minister to Paris, 112; elected President, 140; and era of good feelings, 140–145

Monroe Doctrine, 143, 146, 354, 460, 461; and beginnings of empire, 347–349; and Wilson's Fourteen Points, 403; Roosevelt Corollary to, 358–359, 430–431, 460

Montana, gold discovered in, 307

Montcalm, Marquis de, 45

Monterey, California, seizure of (1842), 198

Monterrey, Mexico, Battle of, 201

Montevideo agreement (1933), 460

Morgan, Daniel, 79

Morgan, J. P., 285, 286, 335, 355, 371, 373, 374

Mormons, 186

Morrill Act (1862), 238

Morrill Tariff (1861), 238

Morris, Robert, 69, 89

Morris, Roger, 84

Morrow, Dwight, 431

Morse, Samuel F. B., 185

Morton, Jelly Roll, 415

Mott, Lucretia, 189

Movies, in 1920s, 413–414; in 1930s, 442

Muckraking, 365

Mugwumps, in Republican party, 324–325

Muller v. Oregon (1908), 367, 371

Mumford, Lewis, on war, 255

Munn v. Illinois, 290

Munsey's magazine, 365

Murphy, Thomas Aquinas, 555

Murray, Nicholas Vans, 118

Muscovy Company, 12

Muskie, Edmund, 526

Mussolini, Benito, 461, 468

My Lai massacre, 524

N

NAACP (National Association for the Advancement of Colored People), 366, 416

Nagasaki, atomic bombing of, 472, 488

Napoleon Bonaparte, 132, 134; and Louisiana Purchase, 128–130

Napoleon III, emperor of France, 343

Nashville, U.S.S., 357

Nasser, Gamal Abdel, 506–507

Nast, Thomas, 267

Nation (magazine), 390

National American Woman Suffrage Association (NAWSA), 367, 369

National Association for the Advancement of Colored People (NAACP), 366, 416

National Association of Manufacturers, 370

National bank: established, 108–109; Tyler vetoes, 167; regulation, Civil War, 238; notes, and flexible currency, 328, 329; *See also* Bank(s); Bank of the United States, First *and* Second; Federal Reserve Board

National Banking Act (1863), 238

National Civic Federation, 370

National Defense Education Act (1958), 498

National Guard: and Homestead strike, 297–298; and Pullman strike, 298; and First World War, 393; and Little Rock school desegregation, 500; and Chicago demonstration, 1960s, 525; and Kent State demonstration, 529

National Industrial Recovery Act (NIRA), 444, 451, 454

Nationalism, 407; post-War of 1812, 137–140; during First World War, 396–398; Henry Cabot Lodge and, 404; black, 416; and desire for a homogeneous society, 417–418

National Labor Board (NLB), 451

National Labor Relations Board (NLRB), 451, 452

National Labor Union (NLU), 295

National Organization for Women (NOW), 552

National Recovery Administration (NRA), and New Deal, 442–446

National Road, 127, 156

National War Labor Board, 396

National Youth Administration, 450
NATO (North Atlantic Treaty Organization), 491
Navigation Act (1660), 32
Navigation laws, 32, 41, 57
Navy: and Barbary pirates, 130; in War of 1812, 135; in 1880s, 342, 345, 346; base at Samsah Bay, 354; and submarines, First World War, 394–395
Nazis and nazism, 460, 462–463, 465–466, 468–469, 470–471, 472, 475; and concentration camps, 461; and Nürnberg trials, 488; See also Hitler, Adolf; Second World War
Nazi-Soviet pact, 463
NAWSA (National American Woman Suffrage Association), 367, 369
Nebraska, and Kansas-Nebraska Act, 217–220
Netherlands: colonization, 19–20; emigrants to colonies, 34; and War of Independence, 79; Hitler invades, 465, 466
Neutrality, and outbreak of First World War, 387, 388–389
Neutrality Acts (1930s), 462, 465, 466
New Amsterdam, 20
New Deal, 440–441; second, 442; and economic crisis, 443–446; agriculture program, 446–448; programs for poor and unemployed, 448–450; politics of, 453–455; See also Great Depression
New England: colonization, 16–19; and War of 1812, 135–137; manufacturing, early 1800s, 185
New England Company, 18
New England Confederation, 41
New England Emigrant Aid Company, 219
New England Restraining Act, 66
New France, 43, 46
New Freedom, of Wilson, 379, 381
New Frontier, of J. F. Kennedy, 514–517
New Hampshire: colonization, 16; ratifies Constitution, 95
New Harmony, Robert Owen's community at, 187
New Jersey: colonization, 20; currency, post-Revolution, 90; ratifies Constitution, 94
New Jersey Plan, 93
New Left, 552, 554
New Mexico: and Mexican War, 200, 202; U.S. conquest, 202; territory, 209; and Gadsden Purchase, 212; Pancho Villa's raid, 359
New Nationalism, of Theodore Roosevelt, 378, 379, 381
New Netherland, 20
New Orleans: settlement, 43; and Louisiana Purchase, 129, 130; Battle of (1815), 135, 137; shipping and growth, early 1800s, 172; Union occupation of, 233; post-Civil War, 262
Newport, Christopher, 13
Newport, R.I., 278
Newspapers: in colonies, 38; and Spanish-American War, 349–351; yellow journalism, 351

Newton, Huey, 521
New World Symphony (Dvořák), 312
New York Assembly, 57
New York City: as site of first national government, 96; early 1800s, 172; Civil War draft riots, 238; population, late 1800s, 313; Central Park, 436
New York Journal, 351
New York State: colonization, 20; ratifies Constitution, 95
New-York Weekly Journal, 38
New York World, 351
Nez Percé Indians, 305
Nicaragua: Walker's takeover (1856), 213; intervention in, 359
Nicholas II, czar of Russia, 355, 387
Nine Power Pact (1921), 429, 464
NIRA (National Industrial Recovery Act), 444, 451, 454
Nixon, Richard: and Hiss case, 491–492; elected Vice-President, 496, 497; and civil rights, 1960s, 521; elected President, 526–527; and Vietnam War, 528–530; foreign policy, 533–534; and economy, 1970s, 540–542; energy policies, 542–543; and Watergate, 544–546; resigns, 546–547
Nixon Doctrine, 528–529
NLB (National Labor Board), 451
NLRB (National Labor Relations Board), 451, 452
NLRB v. Jones and Laughlin Steel Co., 451, 455
Nonintercourse Act (1809), 133
Normandy, invasion of, 470
Norris, George, 376, 377, 423, 448
North, Frederick, Lord, 60, 61, 62, 66, 77, 79, 81
North Atlantic Treaty (1949), 491
North Atlantic Treaty Organization (NATO), 491
North Carolina: colonization, 15; ratifies Constitution, 95; secedes, 230
Northern Pacific Railroad, 334
Northern Securities Company case, 373
Northwest Ordinance (1787), 87
Northwest Territory, slavery prohibited in (1787), 123
Notes on Virginia (Jefferson), 83
NOW (National Organization for Women), 552
Noyes, John Humphrey, 187
NRA (National Recovery Act), 442–446
NRC (Nuclear Regulatory Commission), 543
Nuclear energy: safety issue, 543–544
Nuclear Regulatory Commission (NRC), 543
Nuclear Test Ban Treaty (1963), 533
Nullification, and tariff, 157–160

O

Office of Economic Opportunity (OEO), 515–516
Oglethorpe, James Edward, 16

Put-in-Bay, Battle of, 135
PWA (Public Works Administration), 444

Q

Quaker(s): settlements, 21–22; and slavery, 30
Quaker Anti-Slavery Society, 85
Quartering Act (1765), 57, 62
Quebec: settlement, 42; battle for, 45
Quebec Act (1774), 62–63
Queen Anne's War, 43
Quincy, Josiah, Jr., 59
Quitrent, 28, 84

R

RA (Resettlement Administration), 447
Race riots. See Riots
Racial equality: Lincoln and, 225, 230, 233–234;
   Civil War and, 242–243; T. Stevens and,
   245–247; Thirteenth Amendment and, 247; and
   the Supreme Court, 267–268; and Booker T.
   Washington, 268–270; in Progressive era, 366;
   women's suffrage and, 368–369; in 1950s,
   498–501; in early 1960s, 513, 517–522; in 1970s,
   551–552; See also Abolitionists; Blacks; Civil
   rights; Segregation
Radical Reconstruction. See Reconstruction
Radio, in 1920s, 413
Railroad Control Act (1917), 396
Railroads: early 1800s, 172–173, 174; map, 173;
   transcontinental, and Kansas-Nebraska Act, 218;
   and panic of 1857, 224; land grants, Civil War,
   238; economic organization, late 1800s, 285–288;
   and government, late 1800s, 288–291; strike
   (1885), 296; and cattle in West, 308; and contract
   labor, 318; bankruptcy (1893), 334; regulation,
   early twentieth century, 372–374; in First World
   War, 396; post-First World War, 417
Raleigh, Sir Walter, 11
Raleigh Tavern, 58
Ramsey, David, 74
Randolph, Edmund, 93, 105
Randolph, Edward, 41
Randolph, John, 127
Rationing, Second World War, 470
Rayburn, Sam, 501
REA (Rural Electrification Administration),
   447–448
Reagan, Ronald, 527
Reaper, 175
Rebellions: Leisler, 40; Shays', 90–91; Whisky,
   106–107; Fries, 117; slave, 181; Bear Flag Revolt,
   202

Recession. See Economy; Depression; Great De-
   pression; Panic
Reconstruction: Lincoln's plans for, 243–245; Radi-
   cal plans for, 245–249; Johnson's plans for,
   249–250; Congressional plans for, 250–253;
   Southern view of, 256–258; and poverty,
   258–263; prejudice and violence, 264–266; and
   politics of prejudice, 266–270; ends, 255–256
Reconstruction Act (1867), 253, 267
Reconstruction Finance Corporation (RFC),
   438–439, 443
Redeemers, 264, 266
Rediscount rate, 380–381
Red scare, post-First World War, 416–418
Reform: land, post-Revolution, 84–85; religious
   and educational, post-Revolution, 85–86; early
   1800s, 186–189; of civil service (1883), 326–327;
   and progressive movement, early twentieth century, 363–366; See also specific reforms
Regents of the University of California v. Allan
   Bakke, 551
Regulation: of interstate commerce, 290–291; railroads, early twentieth century, 372–374; of business under T. Roosevelt, 372–374; of business
   under Wilson, 381–382; See also specific legislation; Fair Deal; New Deal
Regulator movement, 40–41
Religion: pre-Columbian, 6, 11; and English colonization, 11; in Maryland settlement, 15; in colonies, 35–37; Great Awakening, 36–37; separation of church and state, post-Revolution,
   85–86; and social reform, early 1800s, 186–187;
   fundamentalists and Scopes trial, 424, 426; in
   1970s, 555
Renaissance, the, and colonization, 7
Reparations: Germany defaults on (1923), 430
Report on Manufactures (Hamilton), 109
Republican party: vs. Federalists, 109–110; and
   election of 1796, 114–115; and election of 1800,
   118–119; assessment, early Republic, 119–120;
   and election of Jefferson, 122–125; and election
   of 1804, 127; and election of 1812, 134–135; and
   nationalism, early 1800s, 137–140; and election
   of 1856, 221; and election of 1860, 226–228; and
   election of 1864, 239; Lincoln's plans for Reconstruction, 243–245; Radical plans for Reconstruction, 245–249; and Congressional plans for
   Reconstruction, 250–253; and election of 1876,
   255; late 1800s, 324–325; and election of 1932,
   439–440; National Convention (1940), 466; and
   election of 1948, 496; post-Second World War,
   495–498; and election of 1964, 515; and election
   of 1968, 526–527; and election of 1972, 544–545
Research and development, post-Second World
   War, 495